Contents

CONTENTS

THE WORLD NATURALIST

Otters

THE WORLD NATURALIST/Editor: Richard Carrington

Otters

A STUDY OF THE RECENT LUTRINAE

C. J. Harris

Come in the season of opening buds;
Come, and molest not the otter that whistles
Unlit by the moon 'mid the wet winter bristles
Of willow, half-drowned by the fattening floods.
Let him catch his cold fish without fear of a gun
And the stars shall shield him . . .

Weidenfeld and Nicolson
5 Winsley Street London W1

(297 76117x)

Made and printed in Great Britain by
William Clowes and Sons, Limited, London and Beccles

Plates

PLATES

Figures

Acknowledgements

I would like to express my grateful thanks to Mrs Medven of the Linguists' Club, and Mrs Peggy Rowley and Mr Trevor Fawcett of the University of East Anglia, for their work on Russian, German and Portuguese translations; to Mrs Joan Wedekind, for her photographs and information on African clawless otter cubs; to Miss Caroline Jarvis, Editor of the *International Zoo Yearbook*, for much general assistance and in particular for making available to me a copy of the paper by F. Jenne; to Mr Gavin Maxwell, not only for constant encouragement but especially for allowing me to see his extensive files and for lending me the paper by G. A. Pollock; to Dr Kenneth Backhouse, of the Charing Cross Hospital, for reading the typescript and for the photograph shown on plate 1; to the Hon. Miriam Rothschild, generous with both time and advice; to Miss Winwood Reade, for many detailed and helpful criticisms; to Mr L. G. Ellis, Publications Department, Zoological Society of London, who with much labour has persuaded my bibliography to conform to the standard of the 4th edition of the *World List of Scientific Periodicals*; and finally, to the Librarian and staff of the library of the Zoological Society of London, without whose patient and constant help this book could never have been written.

The plates listed below are of photographs from books in the possession of the Zoological Society of London, and are reproduced by kind permission of the Society: 2, 3, 9, 12, 40, 41, 44 and 45. All photographs were taken by the author, except where otherwise stated. The photograph on the jacket, of a Canadian otter at the Bronx Zoo, New York, is by Nicole Duplaix.

Preface

THIS book is an attempt to satisfy a number of requirements. First, there seemed to be a need for much of the material already published about otters to be collated, and for a comprehensive – though not exhaustive – list of such material to be made. For the last hundred years or more these fascinating but little-known animals have earned the attention, to an ever increasing extent, of professional zoologists, naturalists and amateurs interested generally in animals, and many of these have written about their suppositions, discoveries and experiences with otters. But there is no book in existence which gives advice and information about otters both in the wild state and in captivity, and this at a time when the keeping of 'exotic' animals as pets is becoming ever more popular, whatever one's view of such a trend may be.

Most of what has been published previously is hidden away in learned and obscure periodicals and 'proceedings' and is thus inaccessible to the general public and elusive even for the persistent searcher; much of it, too, is obscure to the layman. In addition, many of the older natural history books are rare and difficult of access. Accordingly, most of what appears here has appeared before, although not previously in a single volume, suitably arranged, edited and indexed.

Secondly, there is the problem of classification, or taxonomy. While this may not unduly confuse the professional, the unfortunate amateur is left to flounder unaided in a sea of Latin names, many outdated, many synonymous, and therefore nearly all confusing. The sections on this aspect have therefore been arranged in such a way as seems to me to stand the best chance of being clear. An extensive list of generic, specific and subspecific names has been provided, in strictly alphabetical order, each name, current or obsolete, being explained. This is apart from the list of races currently accepted as being valid, together with a separate synonymy of each. There is also a 'Key' to all the species.

Except where it has proved impossible, I have tried to avoid long technical descriptions of cranial and dental characteristics and have confined myself to external appearances. This is on the grounds that the serious student of such matters can generally find references to them while the majority of readers will have little use for page after page of figures within the text, none of which will help him to recognize or identify the live animal when he sees it.

For those who wish to investigate in greater detail any of the matters here dealt with, a full and detailed list of references is given in the numbered Bibliography, to which the numbers appearing in the margins of the text refer.

Mention must be made of the great debt owed by all who wish to learn about otters to Emil Liers and Gavin Maxwell. Liers has domesticated and bred the North American otter since 1928, and his knowledge of this species must be unequalled. Unfortunately he has published relatively little, although what has appeared is packed with information. Maxwell has been fortunate enough to live with three different species, European, African and Asian (the last named after him) and about all three he has written at length. I have quoted briefly from both of these writers in a number of places, but the full published work of each should be read in its entirety by anyone interested in this subject.

Of necessity, a great deal of detail has had to be omitted as well as much which it might have been interesting or amusing to include. The Bibliography, however, will point the way to further reading on most aspects of otters and their lives. While it has not proved possible for me to examine personally every reference listed, I have read the great majority of them and others that I have not seen have been verified from cross-references elsewhere.

In conclusion, I have attempted to communicate something of the pleasure and interest that I have myself derived from spending a number of years in the company of otters, in the hope that others may share it.

London, 1962–3   C.J.H.
Oxnead, Norfolk, 1964–7

Introduction

OTTERS are found in all parts of the world except for Australia and New Zealand, Madagascar, and the arctic and antarctic regions. They belong to a large group known to zoologists as the family of Mustelids, or Mustelidae, which includes stoats, weasels, polecats, mink, martens and tayras, all of which show a considerable family resemblance to the otter. Other members of the same family, the wolverines, skunks and badgers are superficially much less otter-like.

As might be expected of a group of animals whose habitat ranges from the Himalayas to the Amazonian jungles its members show a considerable diversity of size, ranging from the little clawless otter of the East Indies, which rarely exceeds three feet in length, to the giant Brazilian otter which may be nearly eight feet long. Similarly, the general appearance varies a good deal from one form to another and the colour of the fur ranges from an almost black-brown to a pale sandy hue.

All otters, however, share a number of common characteristics. All are amphibious to a greater or lesser extent, though the sea otter hardly ever leaves the water while the clawless African otter spends the greater part of its time on land. All have five digits on each foot, the webbing between them being variously developed amongst the different forms. The non-retractile claws are generally well developed, curved, laterally compressed and sharp, although otters which live in rocky areas will wear their claws much shorter and blunter than those which come from swampy districts. Two otters are found (one in Africa and the other in the Far East) which are generally referred to as clawless, but in fact this is a slight exaggeration as vestigial or rudimentary claws are always present on at least a few of the digits.

The otter is a thickset animal with short legs. Its neck is no smaller than its broad, slightly flattened head, and leads into a muscular body which reaches its greatest breadth at the hips, the whole being very 'streamlined'. Probably the most striking character of the adult otter (the sea otter excepted) is its long and powerful tail. This is fully haired like the body and tapers from a very broad base to a slender tip; it may account for almost

I

half the animal's total length. Except in the giant Brazilian otter, where the tail is very markedly flattened for its distal third, the tail of the otter is near-ly round in section with a varying degree of flattening from top to bottom. This strong tail is relatively flexible and serves the animal in a number of ways. Otters frequently stand up on their hind legs to see over obstructions and on such occasions the tail acts as a brace or third leg to balance them. While I have observed African clawless otters use their tails to sweep ob-jects towards them this behaviour is, I think, exceptional, the main use of the tail being in swimming.

Apart from paddling with its feet, the digits widely spread to make use of the webs, an otter propels itself in the water to a large extent by flexing its body dorso-ventrally, just as a fish flexes itself laterally. In the otter this flexing passes from the head and shoulders right down to the tip of the tail and at top speed the feet are hardly used at all except for manœuvring round obstacles. Top speed, incidentally, is not very fast, only some 6–7 m.p.h. ex-cept for fairly short distances. Underwater the ears and nostrils close, but the eyes remain open and vision is good – probably better than when above the surface. Otters cannot, of course, breathe under water and as a general rule will drown in three to four minutes if they cannot get air. A simple calculation, however, will show that an otter can easily swim a quarter of a mile underwater without surfacing. The otter's acrobatic ability in the water is amazing, and for those able to observe it provides a spectacle of endless fascination and beauty.

Though normally feeding in fairly shallow water, on occasions they dive to considerable depths. It seems almost certain that the otter's diving abil-ity is accompanied by bradycardia, that is a slowing of the pulse-rate and hence of the circulation of the blood, leading to a reduced rate of oxygen extraction from the bloodstream. The controlling mechanism of this pheno-menon is known as the caval sphincter. This is a band of contractile muscle, just above the diaphragm, which surrounds the first part of the thoracic in-ferior vena cava, innervated by the phrenic nerve, the same nerve supplying the diaphragm. (For a detailed account of this process *see* Harrison: 1955.) Despite the slowing of the heartbeat involved – in seals, for instance, from some 150 beats per minute to only 10 beats per minute – the arterial pres-sure remains unchanged and the supply of blood to the brain is undimin-ished. It is, of course, this ability of otters which makes it so difficult to anaesthetize them.

On land otters are far more mobile than might have been expected. When walking, the head and neck is held low with the hips and lumbar re-gion arched up and the tail extended straight behind just above the ground,

523

2

the feet on opposite sides moving alternately. Otters can run as fast as a man for considerable distances, and when running in this way the fore and hind feet are moved alternately in pairs, the back alternately humping and extending as the hind feet are brought forward under the body. At such times they are relatively 'heavy-footed', and a galloping otter makes a surprising amount of noise. On snow the gait changes to running and sliding alternately, the slide being initiated by a push-off with the back feet after which the front legs are folded back beside the body with the animal reclining on its stomach. Any small declivity is taken advantage of in this way, and even on a level surface otters can continue sliding for an amazing distance, apparently at will. In such circumstances some propulsion appears to be given by a lateral flexing of the body.

Otters will travel long distances over land, often 10 or 15 miles at a time, and are not infrequently surprised while lying up far from any water. The easiest passes through the hills and the quickest short-cuts between the bends of a river are clearly well known to them.

The otter's entire body is exceedingly flexible and the animal can bend itself round nose-to-tailtip in both directions, either backwards or forwards. Those parts of an otter not in active use at any given moment seem at once to be totally relaxed and this gives to the animal a peculiar appearance of bonelessness. In fact the skeleton is in no way unusual, though both the number of vertebrae and the number of ribs may vary. The vertebral column is: cervical 7, thoracic 14 to 16, lumbar 6, sacral 2 to 4, caudal 25 or 26; there may be 14 or 16 ribs.

The dental formulae of the various forms are shown on pages 131–3. All otters are alike in having a set of deciduous or milk teeth which are in due course shed and replaced by the permanent dentition. Although the teeth wear with age it is not so far possible to calculate how old an otter is from its teeth. Also, appearances may be deceptive, for wild-trapped otters frequently do terrible damage to their teeth in trying to extricate themselves and if such an animal is then kept in captivity its teeth will in time take on the appearance of being far more worn than is really the case.

Although closely related to the mink and displaying many of the same carnivorous habits, otters will not as a rule kill merely for the sake of killing. Although they will sometimes take fish larger than are necessary to satisfy their immediate needs, food studies carried out in the United States have shown that the normal size of their prey is comparatively small. Otters do not store food for future use. While fish forms the bulk of the diet of most otters, they will in fact kill and eat anything they can catch and master, as is shown in detail in the chapter on 'The Food of the Otter' (*see* page

50). In captivity they do not do well on fish, but thrive on raw meat if it is suitably fortified with various additions.

Otter fur varies in thickness and luxuriance to a certain extent depending on the latitude from which the animal comes. But it has always been much sought after for its aesthetic and hardwearing qualities and as a result of this persecution otters are everywhere shy and retiring animals, avoiding the bright light of day and preferring to confine their activities to very early morning or late evening and the night time. The fur itself consists of a very fine, dense undercoat overlaid with longer, shiny guard hairs, these latter often being removed by furriers. The guard hairs are water repellent while the underfur is so thick as to be impermeable. The otter's coat thus provides almost perfect waterproof insulation against both heat and cold.

While otters do not appear to lick their coats to any appreciable extent they spend a lot of time grooming them with a clipper-like motion of the incisor teeth, and where two otters are together a great deal of mutual grooming takes place. I suspect that this is partly a reflex action as I have been able to persuade a number of my otters to groom me by tickling them in the right place. Between the animals themselves I feel sure that such grooming is motivated more by social considerations than hygiene; external parasites are very uncommon, and although I have occasionally found burs of goosegrass (*Galium aparine*) entangled in the underfur these never seem to have attracted any particular attention.

Otters are relatively vocal animals and most species have a considerable range of noises. Once more, there is a good deal of difference between the different species, the 'language' of one not necessarily corresponding to that of another. It seems, for instance, that the European otter is the only one which uses a single-note, very high, piercing whistle as a call, generally repeated at least once and lasting about a second. This noise carries a long way on a still night and is often described as plaintive or flute-like. On the other hand, a strongly aspirated and explosive 'Hah!' is used both by this species and a large number of others when suddenly startled or alarmed. This sound is used at least by both clawed and clawless Asian otters, the clawless African, the North American otter and at least one South American form (*Lutra annectens colombiana*). Similarly, a low humming or 'growling', something similar to the noise made by a threatening domestic cat, is equally a threat or apprehension signal in widespread use by otters. A further noise common to most species and perhaps to all is the intimidating raucous scream accompanying an attack.

Mere bad temper or frustration is often voiced as a querulous moaning wail, this noise seemingly finding its most intense and nerve-racking ex-

4

pression in the clawed Indian races in whose throats it sounds like nothing so much as the tantrums of a very angry human baby. Confusingly enough, however, the clawless Africans employ a very similar sound, though perhaps a little less stridently, to indicate anguish or apprehension or even, on occasion, greeting.

What might be denoted as purely conversational noises – that is to say noises indicating emotions other than fear, anger or distress – are more varied and more difficult to describe; many are very bird-like. Bird-like, too, are the sounds made by very young cubs, a soft twittering which slowly develops into more of a chirp as the cub grows older. A number of adult Indian forms employ a brief, falling, two-note call, again almost a chirping sound, and a very similar noise is made by the African clawless otters. In the latter case, however, the notes are louder and more widely separated both in time and pitch. The European otter's chuckle, whiffle or chitter has been variously described, one author likening it to the sound of a soprano 777 motor mower. In contrast the little grunts or 'rumbling' noises of the North American otter are very low in key, although occasionally the last syllable in a group of five or six will suddenly emerge an octave higher, in a sort of questioning tone. This is a multi-purpose noise and clearly it is used to express a considerable range of emotional states; it may be emitted both above and below water. Further remarks on the voice of *L. canadensis* will be found on page 192.

The giant Brazilian otter's call-note has been compared with that of the 1233 buzzard (*Buteo*) while in captivity the call for food is similar but more extended. Once more, a growl is given as a warning and any sudden fright produces the familiar explosive 'Hah!' This genus is also described as 1189 snorting and snarling in menace; the cry of anger has been termed 'plain- 1038 tive, piercing and disagreeable'.

The voice of the sea otter is described in the chapter devoted to that genus.

The external senses of otters seem all to be well developed and that of sight has already been mentioned as better underwater than above, although individuals certainly vary. The eye is highly reflective at night, but the colour reflected may vary with the species for I have noted ruby-red, emerald-green and amber from three different forms. All otters, however, appear to have exceptionally acute hearing. The sense of smell again seems to vary with the individual animal, but is probably less used and relied on than the other senses. The face is equipped with several sets of strong, tactile vibrissae or whiskers (described in detail on page 143) which spring from large nerve-pads and are presumably very sensitive. It seems likely that prey

5

moving underwater arouse sensations in these vibrissae which are of great use to an animal hunting in muddy or discoloured water and they may also help in avoiding obstructions.

The different species vary considerably in the extent to which they make use of their hands and feet for purely manipulative purposes. The clawless otters are by far the most dexterous and will show remarkable ability in this respect. The African clawless otter relies on its hands to such an extent that almost all food is conveyed to the mouth with their aid. While some species of clawed otters are also very skilful others, such as the Canadian otter, make relatively little use of their hands except for holding food.

Apart from man, otters usually have no natural enemies and in general appear to get on well with other animals. Their food requirements are fairly small (the sea otter excepted), perhaps not exceeding some $1\frac{1}{2}$–2 lb. per day – varying, of course, seasonally and with the size of the animal. Otters do not hibernate, probably spend roughly equal periods asleep and awake, and when awake are extremely active. A healthy otter is never found lying about doing nothing. As a result a good deal of what might be termed their 'leisure' periods is occupied in play, this being true both for the immature and adult animal.

I am aware that a great deal has recently been written on the subject of what play 'really is' but there seems to be as yet no commonly accepted definition. Lorenz has remarked that despite this difficulty we are all able to recognize play when we see it, and we know quite well what we mean when we refer to a kitten or a child as playing. As he rightly says, all forms of play have the common quality that they differ fundamentally from 'earnest'.

It is necessary to examine this aspect in some detail as the otter is a particularly playful animal. Indeed, its playfulness is perhaps its most marked characteristic and has been noticed by innumerable naturalists from very early times. '*Alacris ad ludos est*' wrote Albertus in the thirteenth century. With many animals their play activities can be recognizably related to some other 'earnest' occupation, but with otters the urge to play, and the method of playing, appear in the main to be unconnected with reproductive, territorial, or prey/predator processes. Otters will play alone, with each other, with other animals, or with people. An otter alone will choose a small pebble, carry it to the water, swim out and drop it; before it can reach the bottom the otter will dive and come up underneath the stone and catch it on the flat top of its head. It will then indulge in a series of underwater acrobatics – continuing to balance the stone on its head. Otters together will wrestle, play tag and duck each other in the water, and communally form slides down steep muddy banks and spend hours sliding. An otter will happily play hide-and-seek with a dog in a pile of straw. One Indian otter I had delighted in a game with an ice cube. This was placed on the broad flat arm of a sofa, with the otter on one side of the arm and my wife or myself on the other, the object being to flick the ice with the hand past one's opponent and on to the floor (*see* plate 20). The otter was very good at this game and frequently won it; this was perhaps just as well, for if beaten too often he sulked!

Amongst the bedding of captive otters, and in the holts of wild ones, it is common to find small shells and rounded pebbles which they have carried in as playthings. I was once woken in the middle of the night by a terrific banging and thumping from the inside of one of my otter's sheds. On investigation, he proved to have taken to bed with him a large wooden ball from his pool and to be now engaged in a midnight game of 'fives'.

Otters have been little bred in captivity. This is probably mainly owing to the fact that they mature rather slowly and that their duration of life in many zoos is lamentably short owing to their being incorrectly housed and fed. In addition, they are somewhat retiring animals and require a degree of privacy frequently denied them in captivity. It seems, also, that the mere placing together of an adult male and female will not necessarily ensure offspring even in optimum conditions; the two animals must become spontaneously fond of each other for successful mating to take place.

Except in the case of the sea otter, the young are born in any conveniently isolated hideout, usually beside a stream in some excavation amongst tree-roots, often enlarged by the mother and having an underwater entrance. A nest of dry grass, moss, leaves etc. will be prepared by the mother (*see* plate 36) in a recess well above the level of floodwaters. The young are born blind and (probably) toothless, but covered with fine fur. In the European and North American species the eyes open after four to five weeks and the cubs start to leave the nest when around six weeks old. They are quite unable to swim but are taught by the mother, generally between their second and third month of life.

All observers are agreed that the females make exemplary mothers, caring for their young most assiduously and defending them against intruders with ferocious courage. As soon as the young are born the male is classed as an intruder and driven off. Opinions vary as to what extent the male later participates in helping to rear the family but he certainly does do so on occasion.

In general, it may be said that otters are not sexually mature until around two years of age, after which they may produce a litter of an average of two to three young not more than once a year, and not necessarily every year.

7

Again, the sea otter is an exception to this, very rarely having more than one pup at a time. For these reasons, and doubtless also because their diet is so varied, otters are not subject to intense or sudden population fluctuations.

Apart from the times when the family is together adult otters for the most part are not gregarious. Some races of Indian otters form groups to make cooperative fishing expeditions, the members forming a large semicircle and gradually driving the fish before them towards the shallows. The Canadian otter is found in groups at sliding parties, as mentioned above, and the giant Brazilian otter is less solitary than most; but the only one which lives in regular social herds is the sea otter.

When otters are together they will cooperate to help each other. This habit is taken advantage of by trappers who will place several traps in a group, thus hoping to add to their bag when the first otter to be caught calls others to its aid. This habit persists in less desperate situations as well. The first time one of my pairs of otters went upstairs – which otters will always do if stairs are available – the male was at first quite incapable of getting down again. He recalled the female from the bottom, who at once climbed back to him, and then led him slowly down, step by step, 'talking' to him all the way.

914

917

Otters have long memories. Pitt records an instance of a pet otter who disappeared for 12 months but greeted her old friends as familiarly as ever on returning. She mentions also a self-feeding device which had been dismantled for 26 months but was reassembled in the otter's absence; on seeing it, the animal immediately went over and pulled the appropriate string.

From my own experience they also have an excellent time sense or built-in 'clock'. The regularity with which they will start a certain activity at a given hour is remarkable, and if some external event only takes place once a week they will quickly learn to identify the correct day.

The sea otter may be subject to periodic migrations but other races do not seem to be, and if undisturbed probably spend the whole of their lives in a limited area. Little seems to be known about the extent of their territorial range, though some writers have suggested that their travels will cover a regular route some 50 miles in length before returning to its starting-point. Certainly they seem constantly to be on the move, rarely spending two consecutive nights in the same place except in the breeding season; they thus do not lend themselves readily to field study. Their route, often well trodden, will be marked at prominent points with regular sprainting-places, the same place often remaining in use for generations.

Unless discontented, otters will usually continue their tidy 'lavatory habits' when in captivity, one place or limited area in their enclosure being

8

reserved for this purpose. They are very clean animals by nature and in domestication some races seem to require no house-training at all. An otter with constant access to water has no smell perceptible to the human nose and a wet otter does not smell 'ottery' in the way that a wet dog smells 'doggy'. If deprived of bathing for two or three days a faint scent becomes discernible if one's nose is buried in the animal's fur: a delicious smell – to my mind – of honey and warm hay, with a faint muskiness. Their breath, too, is very sweet.

Like most members of the Mustelidae all otters except the sea otter are equipped with a pair of anal scent glands. These are used for territorial marking – though this is also done with urine – and perhaps for individual recognition purposes, but also certainly for defence in emergency. This defence is only rarely used but is caused by sudden fear. The pale milky liquid can be ejected several feet and in a confined space the effect is fairly displeasing; but the smell is not unbearably unpleasant and is not very persistent, disappearing even from clothes in 24 hours.

Otters can be extremely rewarding in the house (they are very much 'contact' animals) but at the same time they are expensive to keep, inquisitive, wilful, strong and not infrequently short-tempered. Although their jaws are so hinged that they have no lateral movement, the teeth are specially adapted for crushing bones and their bite is to be avoided. The teeth, incidentally, are fairly irregular. Colyer found a noticeable degree of irregularity in over 40% of the specimens he examined. 292

Otters vary greatly in their individual temperaments and again, different species react differently to domestication. The clawless otters of India and the Far East seem particularly docile, as does the North American race. The European otter also tames well. Most clawed Indian otters, however, have very quick tempers even if completely tame and they are not easy to coerce. In the case of the clawless otters of Africa there is a good deal of evidence to suggest that adults of either sex may not remain reliable. The giant Brazilian otter has been successfully domesticated on very few occasions by Europeans but the local Indians are said not infrequently to tame them. Experiments with the sea otter so far have shown considerable readiness to tame but an impractically high and rapid death rate.

These remarks must be taken only as generalizations, for otters are nothing if not individualists and two cubs from the same litter may differ markedly in personality and disposition.

There are no data on expectation of life in the wild and only limited information on otters in captivity. Longevity probably varies with the species but in captivity should be 10 to 15 years and can be over 20 years.

Part 1

Taxonomy, and the Classification of the Lutrinae

Taxonomy

Naturalists differ most widely in determining what characters are of generic value. *Darwin,* 1859.

They are forced to call everything by long names now, because they have used up all the short ones, ever since they took to making nine species out of one. *Kingsley,* 1863.

IT must be admitted that the taxonomy of otters is in a state of very considerable confusion, the great majority of the accepted forms having a number of synonymous names. This may not trouble the zoologist, who usually starts with a particular race which he knows by its correct (current) name, and then lists the synonyms to this name in chronological order. This has been done in the Systematic section.

But the uninitiated may well start, inadvertently, with one of the synonyms themselves and then find that he has no means, except an exhausting search, of discovering with what the name he has found is synonymous. It is to overcome this problem that a further synonymic list is provided (Appendix A); this shows the present status of the great majority of the names and the variations that have in the past been used throughout the literature on this subject. This list is arranged alphabetically; this may be quite foreign to the professional naturalist but should be familiar and acceptable to the layman. The list is not necessarily exhaustive, nor is it an attempt at any sort of reclassification of the Lutrinae, however much this may be needed, although it may assist subsequent research in that direction. In the first instance it was compiled merely for my own use, for without it I frequently found it impossible to decide which form, under an obsolete name, was really being discussed. After a time, however, I found myself referring to it with such frequency that it seemed to me it might well be of use to others. Indeed, the lack of such a synonymic list in the past may well have contributed of itself to the proliferation of synonyms that now confronts us, with its subsequent confusion.

13

As even the best of authorities are not *ad idem* in their application of names it has been necessary, for the sake of consistency, to decide which of them to follow in their various inclinations.

1073
366
Accordingly, I have generally adopted the terminology of Simpson (1945) rather than that of Ellerman & Morrison-Scott (1951). The only point, in fact, on which they differ seriously is in their respective treatments of *Aonyx* Lesson and *Amblonyx* Rafinesque – these being the generic names applied to the African and Asian 'clawless' otters. Ellerman & Morrison-
922
Scott treat *Amblonyx* as a subgenus of *Aonyx*. Simpson, and Pocock (1941), treat both as genera in their own right, reserving the generic use of *Aonyx*
12
exclusively for the African forms and *Amblonyx* for the Asian ones. Allen (1939) also adopted this system, and it seems to me very much to be preferred.

With regard to subgeneric names there is again some divergence of
367
views. Ellerman, Morrison-Scott & Hayman (1953) treat *Hydrictis* as a valid subgenus, although it was originally proposed with full generic status by
919, 252
Pocock (1921), and upheld by Cabrera (1929). I, too, have used it only subgenerically, as applying to the 'spotted-necked' (clawed) African otter. Similarly, I have treated *Lutrogale* as a subgenus only. This name was pro-
468
posed for generic use by Gray (1865) and is still so used by some authors including Pocock (1941) and Simpson (1945). But the majority of Gray's generic names have now lapsed (*Latax, Nutria, Barangia*, etc.) and I see no
1143
particular reason for preserving this one. Oddly enough, Thomas (1889) does not mention it at all, although he must have been familiar with it.
505
More recently, Hall & Kelson (1959) give *Lutrogale* as synonymous with
366
Lutra, while Ellerman & Morrison-Scott use the term subgenerically. It is these latter, in this case, whom I have followed. Finally, mention must be
566, 367
made of *Paraonyx*, proposed as a genus by Hinton (1921). Ellerman, Morri-
919
son-Scott & Hayman treat it as a subgenus, while once again Pocock (1921)
12, 1180
refers it to the higher group, as do Allen (1939) and Walker (1964). Once more, I have preferred the subgeneric usage.

There remain two further proposed subgenera neither of which has ever
900
subsequently found favour. Perret & Aellen (1956) use *Aonyx* as a subgeneric term as well as a generic one – and further, tentatively propose *Mi-*
30
crodon as an additional subgenus. Lastly, Allen (1922) argues at length for *Micraonyx* to be applied as a subgeneric name to the Asian 'clawless' otters to distinguish them from the African, assuming both to be placed in the genus *Aonyx*. If *Amblonyx*, however, is applied to the Asian group the need for *Micraonyx* disappears. Here I have followed the more usual custom and treat *Paraonyx* as a subgenus, and *Aonyx* as a genus (for the African

otters alone), thus avoiding, in this context, all use of *Microdon* and *Micraonyx*.

A final difficulty arises over which local forms should be included and which left out. Again, the various authorities are not in agreement; this is, no doubt, partly owing to the lack of accepted definitions of what constitutes a generic, specific, or subspecific difference. For the sake of completeness, therefore, I have included descriptions of a number of races which are not universally recognized as having separate validity. These doubtful forms are listed on pages 135–7.

Otters are for the most part shy and retiring animals, often mainly nocturnal or crepuscular and living in remote or inaccessible places. In many instances, therefore, the amount of material in the reference collections is small. Much larger series – and more up-to-date ones – are needed before many of the currently proposed forms can with authority be confirmed or suppressed. What Allen wrote in 1869 is to a large extent still true today: 15

... not a few characters once very naturally considered of great importance in a specific diagnosis are to be regarded as far from decisive, they now being known to be dependent upon either age, season, or locality, or to be mere individual variations ... Besides geographical or climatic variations, we have found by a careful comparison of scores of specimens of the *same species, collected at the same locality*, that there is a much greater range of variation between individuals of the same species – the variation extending to every part – than is commonly conceded; and also that differences depending upon season, as in the color, thickness, length, and general texture of the pelage, and others depending upon age and sex, instead of being always recognised by authors as such, have not unfrequently been taken to indicate a constant specific diversity. From this cause there has arisen, in numerous instances, an undue increase of so-called species. *Specimens* have too often been described instead of *species*.

It should perhaps also be mentioned that the appearance of preserved skins may alter over the years, and it is certainly true that some anatomical details, such as those of the feet and rhinarium, may present a very different appearance in the preserved state as compared with that of the live animal. Finally, no international colour code is used and observers' opinions of fur colouring are only subjective. Admittedly, the Americans quite often refer to Ridgway (1886 or 1912) but there is no comparable European publication in general use. 963, 964

Bearing in mind these difficulties, both subjective and objective, which beset any research into this group of animals, it will readily be appreciated that present research is unfinished, the material insufficient, and knowledge still very incomplete. In these circumstances it need hardly be added that many conclusions must remain tentative.

584   As Horsfield wrote of *Lutra* in 1824:

There is perhaps no genus among quadrupeds, in which the discrimination of species requires a greater nicety of comparison . . .

Part 2
Natural History of the Otter

Chapter 1

Breeding and Reproduction

Would not a pair of these have bred, Sir? *As You Like It*, iii.1.55

COMPARATIVELY little is known about the breeding of the otter, and it would seem that the only forms to have been bred successfully in captivity are the European *Lutra lutra*, the North American *L. canadensis* and, recently, the Indian smooth-coated otter *L. (L.) perspicillata*. The first has bred twice at the London Zoo, the births taking place in August 1846 (not 1836, as stated by Zuckerman) and August 1856. In both cases two cubs were born. [1237]

The first instance is well documented by the head keeper, Hunt: [596]

The female otter was presented ... on 4 February, 1840, being apparently at that time about 3 months old. She remained without a mate till 11 March, 1846, when a large male was presented ... About a month after his arrival there was a continual chattering between him and the female during the night, which lasted for four or five nights; but they did not appear to be quarrelling. Nothing further was observed in their manners or in the appearance of the female to make me think she was with young, until the morning of the 13th August, when the keeper that has the charge of them went to give them a fresh bed ... while in the act of pulling out the old bed he observed two young ones, apparently five or six days old, and about the size of a full grown rat: he immediately put back the bed, with the young on it, and left them. On the 21st [August] the mother removed them to the second sleeping-den at the other end of their enclosure, and several times after she was observed to remove them from one end of the house to the other, by pushing them before her on a little straw; her object in removing them appeared to be to let them have a dry bed; on the 9th September they were first seen out of the house; they did not go into the water, but crawled about, and appeared very feeble.

On the 26th September they were first seen to eat fish, and follow the mother into the water: they did not dive into the water like the mother, but went into it like a dog, with their head above water; and it was not until the middle of October that they were observed to plunge into the water like the old ones ...

This very interesting account indicates a gestation period of some $16\frac{1}{2}$ weeks, or about 115 days, from the mating in mid-April to the birth on around 7–8 August. As will be seen, the gestation period of the European otter is usually accepted as being about nine weeks; this is confirmed by the only other first-hand account, that of Cocks in 1881.

Cocks writes that from about the time that his female was fully grown she came in season nearly every month. After a mate had been procured for her (from Hamburg) when she was nearly seven years old, this male became ill with a premolar abscess and took no notice of the female's advances until early on the morning of 17 July,

... when they paired in the water, the female loudly chattering or whistling in a peculiar way all the while. They remained thus for about an hour ... swimming the whole time. [This was repeated on 12th August, from 6.30 to 8.0 am.] On October 2, the female being evidently heavy with young, I separated the animals and [about 5.45] in the afternoon of the 12th I heard the young ones squeaking; in all probability they had not been born more than an hour or two ... We constantly heard the cubs squeaking; but nothing was seen of them until the 25th [October], when I looked at them, and found them to be two in number ... about 8 inches in length including the tails which were about 2 inches, or perhaps rather more, in length, and were held curved tight round the abdomen, as in a foetus. They were completely covered with a fine silky coat, very different from the somewhat rough 'puppy-coat' they afterwards assume.

On November 17, while I was in the act of putting clean straw into the unoccupied bed-box, the otter came out of the other box with one of the cubs in her mouth, and, swimming with it across the tank, came right up to the box I was filling, as if totally unconscious of my presence. On finding that the bed was not ready, she swam back with the cub across the tank; and although I left the cage as quickly as possible, she made altogether about six journeys across the tank (which is between 13 and 14 feet long) holding the cub by the neck in her mouth, and carrying it most of the way under water. I could not be sure about its eyes, but believe it to have been still blind. [The cub would have been 37 days old by now.] It appeared to be about 15 inches long, or possibly hardly so much. On the 29th [at seven weeks] the cubs were about one foot long [305 mm.] in head and body, with tails 6 inches long [152 mm.]. Weight probably about 2 lb. [907 gms.]. Eyes open.

On the night of December 5, one of the cubs first showed itself, lying with its head hanging out of the box. On the 9th the cubs first came out of their own accord, and went into the water several times (both accidentally and purposely it was supposed) ... On the 10th I first saw the mother carry fish into the box to try to tempt the cubs to eat.

In the afternoon of the same day, the cubs were anxious to come out of the box, but the mother, hearing the gardeners at work close by, would not allow them.

Presently one of the cubs having become very refractory, the old Otter seized it by the side of the neck, carried it to the tank, and gave it a thorough ducking, and thence straight back to bed, where, after another short demonstration of independence, it subsided.

On the 12th one of the cubs when out, being frightened at an accidental noise, plunged without hesitation into the tank, and swam across nearly all the way under water.

On the morning of the 13th on my feeding the old Otter while the cubs were out with her, she took two small roach to them, and tried to make them eat, taking first one fish, then the other, then both together in her mouth, and moving them about close in front of the cubs to attract their attention, at the same time uttering a peculiar whine or growl, or something between the two, which sounded ferocious. This she has continued to do every day up to date of writing (January 15); and one cannot help thinking that her idea of teaching the cubs to eat is to encourage their natural rapacity by pretending she does not want them to have the food. On this first occasion, though they occasionally gnawed at the fish, they appeared to get nothing off.

On the 28th I turned out the cubs to exhibit; they had now become shy and bit fiercely.

On the 31st about 11.15 pm, I found the cubs out, and calling, as if hungry; so I gave them a supply of food which they appeared to appreciate. They have continued since that date to expect some food the last thing each night, in addition, since the 5th instant, to a meal about 6 pm; but they now lie up all through the day, and the mother, when fed at other times than those specified, makes no attempt to induce them to eat.

I have quoted this account at length as, taken in conjunction with that of Hunt, above, it comprises almost all the published information that there is [596] of this sort. It will be noted that the gestation period – from the date of last mating – is 61 days. Cocks later added that one of these cubs came in season [289] for the first time when 10 months old.

A similar account of a mother's early feeding of her young is given by Stephens: [1108]

More than one [fisherman] told me that they have seen the bitch land an eel and bite it in two for the cubs to have a piece each. If they do not eat it, she takes the pieces in her mouth and chews them, shaking out the chewed ends for the cubs.

Other bitches have been seen to catch and land small fish and then to put the wounded fish back in the water for the cubs to try themselves. When they come up without a catch she pushes them under again.

Muller, also, has an account of a mother otter feeding her cub on small eels. [830]

The fact that both pairs born in the London Zoo were produced in August must be considered a coincidence. (Unfortunately, there seems to be no account of the second instance.) Cocks, writing in 1877, before his own pair had bred, says:

I think a series of instances would show that there is no month in the year during which a newly-born litter could be considered extraordinary.

He mentions a male cub weighing approximately 2 lb. on 12 November, and a female cub of 2¾ lb. on 31 March. Southwell carried out much research into the birth dates of otters, and in an article of 1872–3 he lists a number of occasions when young otters were captured, and judging from their appearance estimates their probable dates of birth. Of the 14 instances he gives, he concludes that 4 were born in January, 5 in February, 1 in October, and probably 4 in December. In 1877 he added to this list, including in it the otters mentioned by Cocks earlier the same year. In all, he suggests likely dates in 13 instances spread over the year as follows: 3 in January, 2 in February, 1 in March, 1 in May, 1 in August, 1 in September, 2 in Oct-

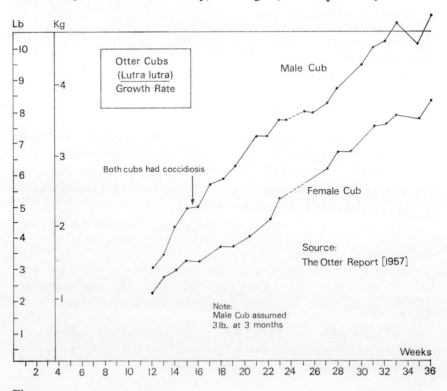

Figure 1

ober, and 2 in November. More recently, a similar survey was carried out by Stephens for the purposes of *The Otter Report* [1957] (see figure 1), of which she writes: 1108

> For the present investigation, 134 reliable instances on which cubs have been seen, together with their approximate age and size, have been collected . . . and from these it has been possible to calculate roughly their months of birth. In many cases, this has had to be very approximate owing to lack of any exact weight records, etc. However, the error should be equally distributed throughout the the year. The records cover many years and all parts of the country.

Month	Calculated number of births
January	14
February	8
March	10
April	10
May	11
June	11
July	11
August	13
September	11
October	12
November	11
December	12

If all the instances related above are set out in tabular form, a remarkable uniformity throughout the year is displayed:

January	21	July	11
February	15	August	16
March	11	September	12
April	10	October	16
May	12	November	13
June	11	December	16

Thus Cockrum's statement that the breeding season of *Lutra lutra* is con-   285
fined to the winter must be discounted, as must the opinions of many of the
earlier authorities such as Bell, who selects 'March or April' for the time of   171
birth of the young; indeed, in the table above April appears as the least
favourable month. Novikov, however, speaks of April or May as the com-   860
monest month in Russia for the appearance of the young and says that rutt-
ing is quite extended, 'usually occurring from February to April'. Provided,
however, that the gestation period is reasonably constant it is clearly

implied that in England, at least, the mating season must be similarly spread over the year.

Considering that the evidence is all against them on this point the authorities are in remarkable agreement. As long ago as 1777 Erxleben wrote that March and April were the months in which the otter bears its young, and in 1792 Kerr wrote that the otter 'procreates in February, and brings forth . . . in May'. More precisely, Cuvier (1823) selects March. Bell (1837) writes, 'The female goes with young nine weeks' and 63 days is also given as the duration of pregnancy by an anonymous writer in the *Monitore Zoologica Italiana* of 1890. More recently, Brown (1936) gives '87 days from first and 61 days from last coition'. Cantuel (1949) gives 9 weeks, Burns (1953) 55–60 days, and Morris & Jarvis (1959) 62 days; Burton (1962) says 'probably 61 days' and Cockrum (1962) gives a range of 61–63 days. Stephens gives three further references in support of a 63-day period.

Otters are not normally gregarious, at least in Europe, and adults are rarely seen together except in the mating season. They have regular sprainting places which if the animals remain undisturbed may be used by many successive generations; Elmhirst mentions one of these being in use for 30 years. Doubless these act as 'post-offices' and enable adults of the opposite sex to meet at the right time. In addition, in the words of Lloyd:

At certain seasons, when the dog feels the need for feminine companionship, he makes his presence known by scratching together heaps of grass, about 6 inches in diameter and 3 or 4 inches in height. On top of these he deposits his wedgins [spraints]. He seems to do this only once or twice in a year. In one case this occurred throughout the whole month of November and again in January . . . There were no less than ten of these soiling places in a 300 yard length of bank . . .

Grass heaps of this sort are illustrated by Hurrell, plate 41.

The North American otter seems to behave in much the same manner. Cahalane writes that:

Although rather solitary most of the time, land otters keep tabs on each other by means of scent posts. At chosen spots on the shore, almost every passing otter leaves a sign consisting of a twisted tuft of grass on which a few drops of scent from the anal glands are deposited. These scent posts are a great convenience in mating time.

With regard to the number of young normally produced by the European otter there seems little reason to disagree with Southwell's opinion that two or three appear to be about equally frequent. He adds that he had only known of a litter of four in a single instance. There are, however, a number of records of litters larger than four, an early reference to such an event

Margin reference numbers: 383, 657, 321, 171, 88a, 218, 261, 237, 825, 241, 285, 1108, 378, 713, 600, 256, 1092

being the well known passage in Walton's *Compleat Angler*, first published   1181
in 1653:

Huntsman: . . . look you . . . here's her young ones, no less than five; come let's
kill them all.
Piscator: No, I pray Sir, save me one, and I'll try if I can make her tame, as I
know an ingenious gentleman in Leicestershire, Mr. Nich. Seagrave, has done . . .

Pennant's account of the otter in his *Synopsis of Quadrupeds* (1771), which   896
repeats many of the suppositions of the earlier naturalists, says that it
'brings [forth] four or five young at a time', and this same phrase is used by
Daniel (1812), who adds '. . . about the month of June'. Bell, a more reli-   327, 171
able naturalist, writes that the otter 'produces from three to five young
ones', and Bonaparte (1839) follows the same line, saying: 196

The female comes on heat in the winter, and gives birth at the end of March to
three, four, or more rarely five young ones . . .

He is, of course, speaking of the otter in Italy.
    Mennell & Perkins (1863-4) are probably quoting Bell with their 'three   787
to five young ones in the season, about midsummer', and the earliest account I have found which might reasonably be termed factual appears
anonymously in *The Field* for 1884:   81

At the Mere, near the village of Cockshutt, in Shropshire, a litter of five young
otters has been lately discovered.

Both Ward (1919) and Stephens (1957) refer to the Report of the Lorraine   1183, 1108
Fishery Association which records a litter of six young, found on the banks
of the Moselle on 26 July 1911, but Stephens sounds a note of caution
where this report is concerned, saying:

These may not have been authentic otters however, as six 'otter cubs', found
drowning in a flooded Sussex river and sent to the Zoological Society of London
recently, turned out to be very young fox cubs!

There is, however, an account by Witchell & Strugnell of 1892 which reads   1215
as follows:

Mr. King, grocer, of Cheltenham, formerly of Chepstow, relates that at Chepstow he, in company with others, tracked an otter carrying a fish to a cavity in the
rocks, when, with the aid of dogs, they captured the male and female and four
out of the six cubs.

Would that Mr King, grocer, had stuck to his last!
    Finally, Hainard (1948) refers to Neusel – a reference I have been unable   501, 852
to examine – seeing six young on one occasion.

582   Turning now to the North American *Lutra canadensis*, Hooper & Ostenson record an undoubted occurrence of six young in one litter in Alabama, and it seems not unlikely that the European should, on rare occasions, have produced an equal number, although it must be admitted that the evidence at present available is not wholly conclusive. It would perhaps be unwise to try and draw too close a parallel between the European and North American forms, for with all their points of similarity there are many very striking differences between them, of which their respective habits of reproduction are a prime example.

    Both the American badger (*Taxidea taxus*) and the European badger (*M. meles*) appear to be subject to delayed implantation, but this state of affairs apparently does not apply to both forms of otter. For while *L. lutra*, as has been shown, is generally accorded a gestation period of nine weeks, that of *L. canadensis* is apparently some nine months or more.

1088   A brief account, by Matthews, of this process of delayed implantation may be found in Southern (1964):

> In the seals, the Roe Deer and many of the mustelids such as the Badger and Stoat (but not the Weasel) the embryo formed after fertilization in the uterine tube does not become implanted in the lining of the uterus on entering that organ. The *blastocyst*, as it is called at this stage, remains loose and unattached in the cavity of the uterus and development is halted. It is not until many weeks or months later, when activity and growth are resumed, that the blastocyst becomes embedded in the lining of the uterus. This *delayed implantation* gives an apparent gestation period longer than the period necessary for foetal growth . . . Delayed implantation . . . must presumably have some selective advantage for the species in making a compromise between the most convenient season for the sexes to meet and the most propitious season for rearing the young.

513   A full physiological account of the process of delayed implantation in mammals, although not with reference to otters, is given by Hamlett (1935).

    The precise cause of the resumption of this activity and growth, after the intervening 'dormant' period, is still in dispute, but one theory sees as a possible trigger the lengthening daylight which comes with the springtime. Experiments on these lines have been carried out on a number of mustelids

890 by Pearson & Enders, who published their results in 1944; unfortunately, the otter was not included. While not all their results appear very conclusive, in the case of the marten (*Martes americana*) a significant reduction in the gestation period was accomplished, while in the mink (*Mustela vison*) the reduction was of the order of about three days compared to a normal mean length of about 51 days. Experiments to lengthen gestation by artificially shortening the length of day were inconclusive.

26

An important paper on reproduction in *L. canadensis* in the state of New York appeared recently (1964). Hamilton & Eadie's study was conducted over a period of some 10 years and involved 93 male and 74 female specimens. From this it became clear that females mate for the first time in March or April when two years old, and that males produce mature sperm cells at the same age. Free blastocysts were recovered from November and December females, while implanted embryos were found in February, March and April. Further studies indicated that adult females mate not long after parturition; that implantation is delayed for eight or more months, and that a total 'gestation period' of approximately 12 months results. 512

Two foetuses were taken from a female collected in the first week of April which

may be described as approximating closely the condition of the newborn. One of the two fetuses measured 275, 64 and 28 mm. [10·8, 2·5 and 1·1 inches] for total length, tail and hind foot, and weighed 132 g. [4¼ oz.]. The other fetus was about the same size. These specimens were fully furred with hair 6 to 7 mm. long on the dorsum and somewhat shorter on the venter. Mystacial vibrissae were plainly evident and about 5 mm. long . . . no erupted teeth were present.

A total length of 10·8 in., or a crown-to-rump measurement of nearly 8½ in., seems extraordinarily large for an embryonic otter; indeed, a misprint would be suspected were this figure not repeated. Certainly Hooper & Ostenson's estimate of a head and body length at term of some 4·3 in. accords more closely with my own observations of a pair of cubs examined within a maximum of 48 hours of birth, and almost certainly within 24 hours. These, tails excluded, cannot have exceeded 4 in. in length. 582

Sex was established in 167 cases in Hamilton & Eadie's study. Of these 93 were males and 74 females (55·9% males). In the case of animals taken during the winter (late October to late February) the sex ratio was equal; for those taken in March and April the ratio was 151 males:100 females (75·5% males). The authors conclude that the winter figures present the true picture, those for the spring being distorted by 'a difference in activity of the sexes in the whelping and mating season'. 512

Emil Liers, who has kept and bred the North American otter for many years, writes that in the northern states the young are born in February, March and April, and, in another article: 704 703

Females in my care have been in heat in the period December to early April . . . The period that ensues between the time [of mating] and the time that the young are brought forth varies from 9 mos. 18 days to 12 mos. 15 days. This variation has been observed in one female . . .

27

Liers gives a table recording the gestation period in seven instances, in which the average period is 11 months $8\frac{1}{2}$ days.

706
In his experience females do not breed until they are two years old; he records, however, one exception to this where a female born on 30 December 1954 mated on 6, 8 and 10 April 1956, producing four cubs, three male and one female, on 24 January 1957; this represents a pregnancy of 9 months 18 days from the first recorded mating. As an instance of 'the usual case of a two-year-old first mating' he writes of a female first mated on 12 March 1957 who subsequently gave birth to quintuplets on 22 January 1958. In this case the gestation was 315 days.

707

238
Writing of conditions in Michigan, Burt says:

... one to three, usually two, blind young are born in late April or early May. The young otter is dark brown. The gestation period is believed to be about ten months ...

486
Gunderson & Beer speak of the young being born 'early in the spring' in Minnesota, 'after a gestation period of about ten months'. De Kay, for New York State, writes of the young there as being born 'about the middle or latter end of March'. Hooper & Ostenson record the breeding activities at Potter Park Zoo, Lansing, Michigan, as follows:

340

582

Adult otters were observed to mate on January 11th ... In February the female became irritable and would not permit familiarity on the part of the male. From March to early September their life was again serene, and mating was observed several times. In October the female again became quarrelsome and in November was observed to have gained weight. She fought the male at all times in December, and on January 22 gave birth to a single young.

The authors consider that

the whelping season in Michigan extends from January to May, with the peak of the season in March or April.

482
Grinnell, Dixon & Linsdale write:

Among all the otters which the trappers of California have caught in the trapping season, which closes March 1, only one female of those examined has been reported as pregnant by that date ... Most of our young otters appear to be born about the first of April ... [but] a trapper on whose word we rely says that he has seen a mother otter abroad with its brood of small young in June ... one of our most dependable observers believes that the breeding season of otters in the Delta region must extend throughout the spring and summer and even into the fall of the year, because in late December small otters are frequently caught which weigh only 6 or 7 lb. In February 1920 [he] trapped a small female otter that weighed only 6 lb. when caught.

Bailey, writing in 1936 about Oregon, the state adjoining California to the   145
north, says:

> In the far north the young are born in April but the time is much earlier in
> southern latitudes ... The *Oregon Sportsman*, 1917, p. 15 says that otters have
> two to four young in May.

Utah lies on the same latitude as California, some 400 miles inland, and
here Barnes records that the mating season occurs towards the end of Feb-   159
ruary, with the young born in mid-April. This does not accord with the idea
of a long gestation period. (Crandall, however, notes isolated cases of mat-   313
ing behaviour that do not conform to the normal pattern, and my own Canadian male appears to experience what might be termed a period of 'false
rut' early in November of each year, with copulation sometimes occurring.)
   Further north still, Macfarlane (1905) writes of otters in the northern   743
Mackenzie River district:

> By widely separated hunters, this animal is said to mate during the months of
> March, April and May. The offspring are from three to five in number ...

If this is correct, and a gestation period of 10–11 months is assumed, the
young would presumably be born in January–March.
   Maynard speaks of the Florida subspecies *L. c. vaga* dropping its young   780
in February in its native habitat. Crandall records a pair of these otters in   313
the New York Zoo, however, as producing young on 14 January 1953, 12
January 1954, and on 5 January 1956. Crandall further notes births to otters
at the National Zoological Park, Washington, D.C., as taking place on 15
December 1913, 5 January 1915, and 1 February 1922. Hamilton, writing   510
of the eastern states generally, says that the young are usually born from
mid-April to early May, while in Virginia, according to Bailey, the young   137
are born in April or May.
   Audubon & Bachman were clear that latitude was the vital factor: 133

> The American otter has one litter annually, and the young, usually two and
> occasionally three in number, are brought forth about the middle of April, ac-
> cording to Dr. Richardson, in high northern latitudes. In the Middle and South-
> ern States they are about a month earlier, and probably litter in Texas and
> Mexico about the end of February.

Seton writes: 1060

> The young are born in mid-April, or sometimes as late as May 1st. They
> usually number 1 to 3 ... W.R.Hine, of Winnipeg [Manitoba], assures me that
> in a female taken at Brokenhead, he found 5 well-developed young. These were

29

the size of a small Striped Ground-squirrel, and must have been near full time, as it was late in April . . .

If the information quoted above is set out geographically it will be seen that the correlation between date and latitude is far from exact.

Place	Approx. lat. (N.)	Date
Florida	26–30°	February
Texas	28–34°	End February
California	34–42°	March/April
Virginia	37–39°	April/May
Utah	37–41°	Mid-April
Kansas City, Mo.	39°	Feb./March
Washington, DC	39°	December/February
New York City	41°	January
New York State	41–45°	Mid-/End March
Oregon	42–46°	April/May
Lansing, Mich.	43°	End January
Michigan	42–46°	Peak March/April
Winona, Minn. (Liers)	44°	End January
Minnesota	44°	'early spring'
Manitoba	50°	Late April
N. Mackenzie	62–67°	? January/March

Wayre (*in litt.*) succeeded in breeding *L. canadensis* for the first time in England in 1965, three young being born on 28 March.

[1060] [241] With regard to Seton's striped ground-squirrel I take it that he is referring to *Citellus tridecemlineatus* which, according to Burton, has a total length of 12 in., of which 5 in. is tail. This sounds too large for newly born [582] otters, and it may be noticed that Hooper & Ostenson considered that foetuses at term would have a head and body length of about 4·3 in. (110 mm.). They give the total length of a cub estimated to be 15 days old as about 9½ [704] in. (240 mm.). Liers writes that one cub of about a week or 10 days old weight 6 oz. (187 gm.) and had increased to 16 oz. (454 gm.) 10 days later. [703] His is also the only account of the birth process and the female's subsequent behaviour.

The process of birth lasts from 3 to 8 hours, depending in part on the number of young. The mothers that I have watched stood on all four feet when bringing forth the cubs. One cub after another would be dropped until the entire litter was produced. My otters produce their young in straw nests in wooden kennels. The outside temperature is sometimes 15 to 30°F. below zero [−26 to −34°C.]. The female curls tightly around the cubs in such a way that they are almost completely shut off from the cold air.

(And from another article, of the same date):

When the babies are small, the mother curls her body into a perfect 'dough-nut', enclosing the little ones so that they are protected from the cold and can nurse. If mild danger threatens, mother otter places her head over the hole in the doughnut in which the babies are lying, thus completely hiding and protecting them. The newborn babies do not open their eyes until the 25th to 35th day . . .

(Again, from Liers' original article):

The cubs are toothless and blind at birth, and are quite helpless for 5 or 6 weeks. The mother licks them and cleans all feces from the cubs until they are about seven weeks old, when they go to one corner of the kennel for their toilet. Cubs thrive better on otter's milk than on cow's milk. [*See* page 111 for milk analysis.] . . . The eyes open when the young are about 35 days old. When the cubs are 5 to 6 weeks old they begin to play with one another and with their mother, and when 10 to 12 weeks old the mother first permits them to exercise and play outside of the nest.

Liers adds that the female normally weans the cubs at about five months.

In the case of Wayre's cubs, mentioned above, the eyes first started to open on the twenty-first day and all the cubs had them fully opened by the thirty-second day. All were swimming by the forty-eighth day, and had started to eat solids by the ninth week although they were still nursing in the thirteenth. These cubs were picked up when 14 days old and it was found that their defensive anal scent glands already worked most efficiently!

Two litters of Canadian otter cubs reared by me showed a number of disparities. Both were dropped in March 1966. The mother of the first had been purchased, together with her mate, from the Norfolk Wildlife Park the previous December and must have been pregnant on arrival. Both otters were fully adult, the male probably being quite old and the female possibly having cubbed previously while still in America. Both had been wild-trapped and although very good-tempered were extremely shy and had never been handled.

The arrival of the cubs was a complete surprise as no mating activity had ever been observed and the female showed no signs of pregnancy; on the contrary, she seemed rather thin. She did not appear for food on either 25 or 26 March and consequently her sleeping box was opened that evening. She was lying on her stomach, apparently asleep, and was still wet from swimming. Beside her were two cubs about $3\frac{1}{2}$ in. long and very dark mouse-grey in colour. The box was at once closed without the mother seeming to wake, and food was put ready outside it.

The other female had been purchased together with her mate from

Arthur Hoffmann in June 1962, and on arrival they were a little under three months old. Both had been born in captivity. They soon became completely tame and reliable and were frequently loose in the house, being exceptionally gentle and good-natured. After the animals were two years old mating took place annually between mid-February and mid-April, and during these periods the male became extremely aggressive and could not safely be handled. In 1965, exceptionally, mating was also noticed on an isolated occasion on 10 November.

The female was first noted to be apparently pregnant exactly three weeks before giving birth; four abdominal nipples started to appear and she put on a good deal of weight. Towards the end of March quarrelling was occasionally heard and the pair were separated on the evening of the 30th. The female's temperament remained quite placid and friendly when her bedding was changed that evening.

The following morning the cubs could be clearly heard, and a special meal of raw meat, liver, milk and egg was put beside the nesting-box in her enclosure. By mid-morning she was out and attempting to attack her mate in the adjacent pen, screaming at him whenever he approached. (The other female also attacked her mate, and he had to be removed for his own safety.)

After a few days it became apparent that this very tame otter had suddenly become savagely protective and was likely to attack seriously any person entering her enclosure, even if they moved away from the nest area. Similarly, anyone incautious enough to put a finger through the wire was at once bitten. In contrast, the other female remained quite unaggressive and paid little if any attention to people in her pen. After about three weeks her cubs were inspected regularly, and occasionally touched, but even then she showed only mild alarm.

All four nipples were clearly in use with both mothers and for some time it was impossible to tell how many cubs the protective mother had. From time to time she was seen to carry one of the cubs in her mouth by the scruff of its neck either to or from an artificial holt near her pool. On 24 May she appeared at the doorway of the nesting-box and threw out one of the cubs. After a few moments she hauled it back again and shortly afterwards repeated the process, either with the same or a different cub. From now on she was observed to do this fairly frequently, and subsequent behaviour made it clear that she was then starting to 'house-train' them.

One of the litter of two cubs first came out of the nest (so far as is known) on the fifty-ninth day, but only four days later both cubs were playing in shallow water on a ramp leading into their pool. Both were swimming quite well by the sixty-ninth day.

The other litter were not observed out until the first time the mother took them swimming, on the evening of their sixty-seventh day. It was then seen that there were five of them. Their pool had no ramp leading into it, but a series of rough rockwork steps. The mother went first into the pool and floated with her head against the top step, facing the cubs which were gathered on the edge, and calling to them. When they refused the step she caught each one in turn by the scruff of the neck and pulled it into the pool. The cubs proved extremely buoyant, but rather like swimmers in the Dead Sea they seemed unable to keep an even keel, their legs on one side or the other constantly rising above the surface. Once in, they showed no fear or hesitation. Those which could not get out alone the mother grasped by the scruff and lifted.

The smaller litter were first seen to eat solid food on their sixty-ninth day, the other larger litter on their seventy-sixth. One of these five cubs, a female, was discovered apparently abandoned on the seventy-eighth day and efforts to revive it failed. A post-mortem revealed the lungs to be full of water and death to be due, in effect, to drowning; presumably it had tired in the pool and the mother had not rescued it until it was exhausted.

The great discrepancy in the size of the cubs, compared litter to litter, must be mentioned. At four months old the small litter (both males) were nearly double the size of those in the other litter (two males, three females), and this difference was still largely apparent at six months. In view of this it seems that the age of cubs cannot be guessed with any accuracy from their size alone, unless the number in the litter is known and due allowance made for this.

Turning from North to South America, it is perhaps not surprising that little is known about the reproductive habits of the giant Brazilian *Pteronura*. Rengger writes of his subspecies (*paranensis*) from the Paraguay and 956 Parana rivers that mating takes place in July and August, the female producing two or three young ones in the early part of the year. He denies, however, Azara's assertion that several nesting pairs inhabit the same 136 burrow, writing that

... up to the time when the young litter is fully grown, they live in pairs and in a restricted territory. A steep slope of the river or lake which is their home is sought out, and a hole four or five feet deep is excavated, with an entrance of one and a half to two feet in diameter ... here the female gives birth to two or three young in the spring; both otters help to rear the cubs on fish.

Warden (1819), presumably writing of the typical form of *P. brasiliensis*, 1184 says:

The female brings forth in the month of March, and has three or four at a time.

³⁴⁵
¹²³³
Desmarest speaks of them as being fiercer in April, when they have their young with them, than at any other time. Zeller, however, writing of the captive female at the Cologne Zoo, says:

During the fourteen-day period of heat which, according to our observations at Cologne, occurs in the months of January and April, the behaviour of the otter is considerably changed. The call for her [human] companion is neither made nor replied to. Similarly, people are growled at even from a distance, and attempts to touch her are met with bites. Less food is taken and there is no desire to play. The otter rolls on the ground in a cat-like manner when on heat.

¹²³
⁹³⁶
Information on African otters is extremely scanty. The spotted-necked otter *L. (H.) maculicollis* is said by Ansell to bear its young in November or December in Northern Rhodesia. In Tanganyika, however, according to Procter (1963),

The breeding cycle may be somewhat as follows:

July: Mating. Old otters not greatly in evidence after breakup of family parties when young otters congregate in schools.
September: Birth of young, allowing a gestation period of a little over two months, and no delayed implantation.
November: Young being taught to fish and swim in secluded places.
January: Family parties moving about, also schools of previous year's young [mostly in groups of four to six].

In his view migration is unlikely, and he considers

the conspicuous movements of schools or packs of otters are [probably] merely local movements of non-breeding males.

¹²³
The young of the clawless *Aonyx* usually seem to appear about May, according to some accounts, though Ansell suggests they are born in July or August. (For the growth rate of *Aonyx* cubs see pages 113–4.)

²⁸⁰
To revert to the European otter, Clapham mentions one cub taken from its holt at an estimated age of 14 days, the eyes of which opened 16 days later. At the end of this 30 days it weighed 14 oz. (435 gm.), and after 66 days from its presumed date of birth its weight was just under 2 lb. (900 gm.).

^{860, 864}
Novikov's statement – probably copied from Ognev – that the eyes of the European otter cub 'open on the 9th or 10th day' does not seem to accord
^{501, 288}
with the facts, although Hainard also gives nine days. Cocks describes the
²⁸⁰
blind eyes of his fortnight-old cubs as 'very prominent' and Clapham notes

34

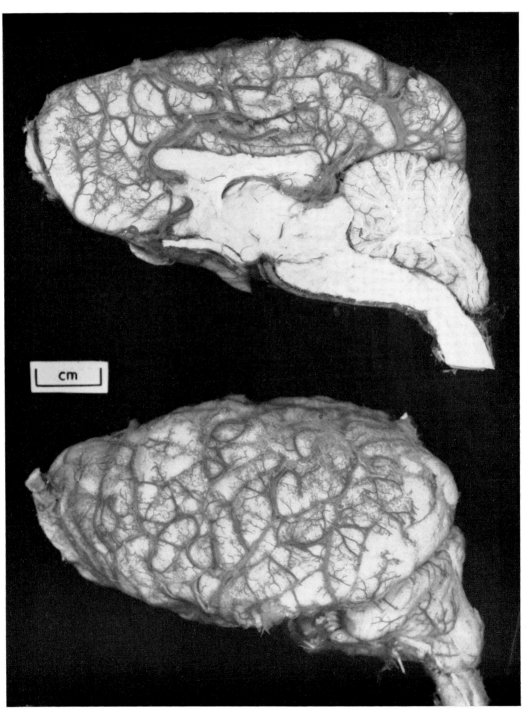

1. Brain of *Amblonyx cinerea*. Photo: Charing Cross Hospital,
Department of Medical Photography.

2. European Otter. Gesner, *Historiae Animalium*, 1551.

3. European Otter. Aldrovandi, *De Quadruped' Digitatis Oviparis*, 1645.

4 (*above*). European Otter.
Photo: P.L. Errington. American
Museum of Natural History.

5. European Otter. Photo: A.W.
Engman/Photo Researchers.

6. European Otter, ? ♀. Photo: Frances Pitt.

7. European Otter cub, about a fortnight old, ♀. Photo: Sheila Andrewes.

8. European Otter. Photo: Jane Burton/Photo Researchers.

9. *Lutra sumatrana.* Anderson, *Anatomical & Zoological Researches . . .*, 1878.

10. *Lutra sumatrana*, subadult ♀. New York Zoological Society Photo.

11. *Lutra sumatrana*, subadult ♀. New York Zoological Society Photo.

12. *L. (Lutrogale) perspicillata*. From a watercolour by B.H. Hodgson. [Hodgson MS in the possession of the Zoological Society of London.]

13. *L.* (*Lutrogale*) *perspicillata*, adult ♀.

14. *L. (Lutrogale) perspicillata maxwelli*, adult ♂. Photo: Gavin Maxwell.

additionally that the eyes of the cubs are at first much lighter than those of the parents, 'not unlike the eyes of a young fox cub' (*V. vulpes*). A young Indian otter in my possession had a bright blue ring surrounding the iris (*see* plate 19) which faded to a much paler blue as he grew older.

Very young otters have a coat which is quite different to that of the adult animal. Stephens writes: 1108

> At birth the cubs are covered with a fine, dark, silky coat which roughens and gets lighter in colour as the hair grows longer.

Andrewes (*in litt.*) described her very small *L. l. lutra* as

> ... greyish brown in colour with hair that looked harsh, but which was quite soft and which if stroked the wrong way showed a cream coloured undercoat. Round the nose and mouth there was a white patch [see plate 7] and her ears, which were rather large, had white edges.

Pocock remarks that newly born English otter cubs which he had seen 922 were the same colour as their parents. Liers describes four-day-old *L. canad-* 705 *ensis* as having fur 'downy soft and mouse-gray in color', while Cahalane 256 says they are 'very dark, almost black'.

Phillips describes a very young example of the Indian *L. l. nair* from 903 Ceylon as being

> ... a uniform silvery-grey colour all over, with the exception of the sides of the head, the chin and the throat, which were dirty white. As it grew older the general hue of its coat rapidly became darker.

Liers states that *L. canadensis* has only four nipples, and instances a case 707 of five young ones where one cub was going unfed. Not all writers are in agreement on this point; although Bailey confirms four Burt, for instance, 145 says that there are six. 238, 227

The same state of affairs applies to the European otter. Buffon remarks that the mammae are difficult to see and that he had 'found only four of them'. Johnston writes that there is 'only one pair'. Southwell, however, 635, 1090 says:

> I had the opportunity of examining the fresh skin of a female otter, killed, with its single young one, two days previously ... The skin had been roughly re-moved, and the mammary glands were left attached; those nearest the tail were distended and full of milk. The posterior pair of nipples, which were evidently those used by the young one, were about three inches from the root of the tail, the second pair, three inches from these; the latter contained a small quantity of watery fluid, but presented no appearance of having been sucked. We could find no trace of a third pair of nipples, although we removed the fur from one side for that purpose.

4—O.

1092　But Southwell was not satisfied and four years later he writes recording the capture, in early January, of

> ... an old female and three young ones. The female was still giving suck (three teats on each side all in use) ... in my [previous] article I was unable to say with certainty the number of teats found in the female otter. I have now on several occasions found it to be six.

It is not quite clear from this whether Southwell means that on the several occasions when he had been able to examine female otters they always had six teats, or alternatively that some of the females he examined had six teats and some only four. On this point Matthews says:

772

> ... the female has six teats, though only four of them may be functional.

136　　It seems worth recording that Azara mentions his tame *Pteronura* as hav-
234　ing only two nipples, 'situated far back on each side', while Burmeister's *Lutra paranensis* (= *L. platensis* Waterhouse) had four, 'two on the sides of the stomach and the other two on the upper lateral region of the abdomen
848　next below the lowest ribs'. Nehring's *Pteronura*, unlike Azara's, possessed four.

In confirmation of the fact that the number of mammae in the female
188　otter appears to be variable, here is a quotation from Blyth (1842):

> Among the recent specimens procured is a fine large female otter which appears to be the *L. tarayensis* of Hodgson [= *L.* (*L.*) *perspicillata*] ... this animal had *five* large abdominal teats, and not the slightest trace (internally or externally) of a third anterior on the left side ... the lactiferous vessels were fully distended.

Maxwell (*in litt.*) informs me that his female Cape clawless otter is similarly possessed of five teats.

While the female European otter appears to come in season 'nearly every
288　month' (Cocks: 1881), the same does not seem to apply to the North Ameri-
703　can otter. Liers writes:

> Females in my care have been in heat in the period December to early April. The testicles of males begin descending in November. The period of heat of females lasts from 42 to 46 days, unless mating takes place. A female is not equally receptive during the entire period of heat. Days of maximum receptivity within the period are about six days apart, between which the female is only mildly receptive or will completely reject the male. At the peak points the female will search out the male and give him every assistance ... In my experience, few males have the ability to mate [successfully] with a female at any time during her period of heat. I have had only two males in about seventy with this ability. I have

had forty-six males that were never able to breed a female . . . In general, a male cannot be counted on as a successful breeder until it is five to seven years of age. For some reason younger males are usually unsuccessful. An otter is not sexually mature until two years old.

As mentioned above, Liers experienced one exception to this, with a 16-month-old female mating successfully. Thus Bourlière's statement that the American otter is sexually mature at a year seems inaccurate. [707] [204]

With the European otter opinions, as usual, vary. Griffith (1827) writes that at 'about two years of age they are adult'. Ferrant (not dated) says, 'At the age of three years they are adult and able to reproduce'. Mitchell speaks of otters as being 'adult in about ten months', whereas Stephens quotes Brehm (1893) in expressing the view that 'they become sexually adult in their third year'. Pitt, however, writes: [475] [392] [813] [1108] [917]

They attain their maximum size and weight at about two years old, although for practical purposes they are mature at 12 months.

Regarding the holt that an otter will choose in which to rear her young, Stephens writes: [1108]

The bitch generally chooses her nest up a small side-stream and away from the main river and floods, and rarely are two families found nearer than about five miles apart. Alternatively the nest may be out in woodland or in a pile of sticks or brushwood, or high up in a hill tarn or reservoir. In parts of Scotland otters are often said to travel miles over land to a remote highland loch to breed. One occasionally hears tales of such lochs being ruined by a family of otters learning to fish there. In Norfolk the nests may be situated out on the reed-beds and in parts of Cornwall, besides Scotland, it is quite common for cubs to be born in caves around the coast or on islands in the salt marshes. In every case there is sure to be an abundant food supply near at hand, so that the bitch can feed and rear her cubs without exposing herself to too much danger.

Ognev writes as follows concerning the otters of eastern Europe: [864]

The otter builds its permanent burrow (e.g. during the summer) on the very shore of the body of water. The principal passage opens deep under water, slanting upward into the living chamber, which is built in such a manner as to remain permanently above water level no matter how high the water rises. A side burrow extends from the living chamber to the surface, but it is very narrow and constructed not for passage but to ventilate the subterranean habitation.

The subject of this air-hole communicating with the surface is one which clearly fascinated many of the earlier authors; Pennant, for instance, writes of the otter that it [897]

... burrows, forming the entrance of its hole beneath the water; works upwards towards the surface of the earth, and makes a small orifice, or air-hole, in the midst of some bush ...

It is almost true to say that it is impossible to find a nineteenth-century 'popular' account of the otter which does not repeat Pennant's statement, but Bell deals firmly with this conceit, saying:

171

> This statement is wholly incorrect. The otter avails itself of any convenient excavation ...

676   and while this is normally true, Lancum reports having once found a holt with cubs 'six feet up inside a hollow pollard willow'.

1090   Sometimes the otter's nest is quite an elaborate affair. Southwell describes

> ... a form of nest which is not unusual in Norfolk ... in the reed-beds where these nests are found shelter is perfect, but any depression in the ground would instantly be filled with water ... The nest referred to was found in a reed bed near Dilham in February; the man who found it describes it as a 'hillock of rushes and all manner of weeds' as much as would fill a cart. 'It had three or four side entrances and one on top.'

Another nest is also described.

> It was placed in an impenetrable morass on the top of what we call a 'gnat-hill' or 'tussock,' and was composed of little more than the rough herbage of the gnat-hill itself.

A third

> ... was carefully constructed of reeds, and lined with reed tops and 'champed' stems.

244   Buxton describes a rather similar construction, also in Norfolk:

> [During] the hard frost of 1940 ... I tracked otters, first straight across the Mere [at Horsey], then through a long reed bed on its margin to what was described as the otter's 'house.' It *was* a house with roof and portico, comfortably hollowed out of a large heap of sedge and other rubbish left on the edge of the water by a specially high tide.

This habit of nest-making is not confined to the otters of Norfolk, as is pointed out by Chapman:

273

> When observing birds in certain marshes in West Jutland ... I came across 'lairs' or 'nests' of otters, formed in reed- or cane-brakes, precisely similar to those described by Mr. Southwell [see above] ... These nests did, in fact, much resemble those of coots [*Fulica atra*], except that they were much larger, and, if memory serves me correctly, I believe I saw similar 'Otter nests' in the Outer Hebrides, in certain islets in the lochs ...

38

Seton quotes Moore-Wilson on similar activities as practised by *L. c. vaga*   1060, **822**
among the low-lying marshes of Florida.

> Here the female builds her nest, so cunningly devised that an old trapper might
> pass it by many times without any suspicion of its location. A hunter who cap-
> tured a nest of three young Otters describes it as being built in the shape of an
> Indian shack made of tall marsh lilies, and so dextrously woven and closed at the
> top as completely to conceal the occupants within. The inside of the nest was
> lined with reeds and grasses . . .

Cahalane records like constructions on the part of otters in California: 256

> In the flat marshes and the 'tules' of California . . . the mother makes a wig-
> wam. Bending tall marsh plants together at the top, she encloses a small circular
> room.

Quelch reports 'little houses or nests constructed of grass or soft leaves   937
beaten down on the banks of streams' in British Guiana, presumably by
L. enudris, as the other otter found there, the giant *Pteronura*, seems almost
invariably to live in holes in the ground, as already mentioned.

The European otter has been known to nest in unlikely places. *The Field*   74a
in 1874 records that

> In the centre of Bradford on Avon . . . an otter has formed a holt and brought
> forth her young in a drain . . . that leads from the river to a cloth manufactory . . .
> the young otters are . . . under a part of the mill where the machinery is at full
> work.

Clapham quotes the following from *The Field* of 29 October 1921:   280

> He and a clergyman were sitting quietly at dinner, when they were surprised by
> an extraordinary noise beneath the dining-table for which they could not ac-
> count, and at length they were so much annoyed by it that they sent for a work-
> man to take up the floor, when to their great astonishment they found that an
> otter which had inhabited the moat had established her nest beneath the boards
> of the floor, and had there deposited her litter of young ones, by whose uncouth
> cries it was that the dinner-party had been disturbed.

Bruce tells of a nursing otter caught in a rabbit trap set in a sewer under a   221
road with considerable traffic on it, and within a few yards of the public
slaughterhouse. Stephens notes a number of comparable instances,   1108
including one in 1952, when

> . . . a bitch otter was found in an outdoor lavatory near the village of Llanrhystyd,
> Cardiganshire. She could easily have escaped, but kept returning to the spot until
> a frightened villager unfortunately shot her. Later, two small cubs were discov-
> ered on a ledge beneath the seat, and doubtless she had returned and risked her
> own life to protect them.

692   Lee writes of an incident when a party were out with ferrets and

a young otter bolted from a hole and almost before the shooters knew what it was the little thing was unfortunately killed. Shortly after the old otter came out, and another cub, which were, of course, allowed to escape. Although the party were shooting round about the place the remainder of the day, the dam of the poor dead cub never left the neighbourhood, re-entering the burrow and continually calling in the peculiar whistling tones common to the otter when it has lost its mate or its young . . .

85   There are a number of accounts of otters defending their young at risk to themselves, and the following (anonymous) one may be taken as not untypical:

A farm labourer with a gun and dog was walking on the shore of the lake, when an otter rushed out from under a rock and attacked the dog, on which he fired at and wounded it, when the otter screamed or whistled, whereupon another and much larger otter rushed from under this same rock and both set upon the dog which they would have killed but that he struck at them with the gun. I suspect they had young ones . . .

46   Another anonymous account reads:

I learn from a person who has taken the young, that on one occasion he was at-tacked by an otter with great spirit, and wounded so severely in the leg that he suffered for months from the effects.

280   Clapham also mentions the fact that

the bitch otter shows great affection for her young, and will hang about in their vicinity in the face of hounds or human intruders.

1163   An unusual incident of this sort is recorded by Tregarthen.

One of the labourers here [at Trelowarren, in Cornwall] on his way to work . . . soon after five o'clock in the morning, saw a number of animals coming along the road towards him and stood very quietly by the hedge till they came broadside of him. He then perceived they were otters, four old ones and the rest young ones . . . as quickly as he could he got a stick out of the hedge and struck one of the young ones and ultimately killed it. The moment the young one began to squeak, all four old ones came back and stood 'grizzling' . . . against him, till all the young ones had escaped through the hedge and then went quietly off themselves, he being afraid to attack them.

Although allegedly ceremonial gatherings of animals are not uncommon in folk-lore, accounts of large numbers of the European otter being seen to-
811   gether are rare. One such instance is provided by Mitchell, who writes:

A Mull lobster fisherman told me he once saw a dozen dog otters on a small rock island at an otter 'wedding'.

40

There is a further, anonymous account, relating to the River Shannon,   66
which reads:

> The extraordinary number of twenty otters, young and old, were last evening
> seen to emerge from one drain or gullet, a short distance down the river . . . This
> account is authentic . . .

Can this have been an Irish 'wedding'?
Buckland writes of some Cornish fishermen who one day   226

> saw two young otters taking their morning bath in a quiet inlet . . . one of the
> men landed, got hold of them and brought them into the boat, and tied them fast
> with a strong cord . . . The men were about to resume their work, when, more
> than 150 yards away along the coast, they saw the dam making directly for them,
> and lay on their oars to notice the effects of the screams of the young on the parent
> otter, expecting the mother to show the white feather. She swam, however, bold-
> ly up to the boat, and tried to climb into it, but its height out of the water pre-
> vented her from doing so. Three times the otter made the attempt to mount the
> sides of the boat, and each time failed. The affectionate and plucky mother was
> eventually killed . . .

Apart from otters defending their cubs, they will also on occasion defend
themselves with great spirit. (One is reminded of the apophthegm 'Cet animal est très méchant. Quand on l'attaque il se défend'.) Thus, Nelson relates   850
the following incident:

> A hunter went out to inspect his fish traps, and, failing to return in the course
> of a day or two, his friends began to look for him. He was found lying dead by the
> side of a small lake with his throat torn open and the tail of a dead otter firmly
> grasped in both hands. One of the otter's feet was fast in a steel fox-trap, and it
> was supposed that . . . being a powerful young man he tried to swing the otter
> over his head and kill it by dashing it against the ground, but when in mid-air it
> turned suddenly and caught him by the throat . . .

Harper writes of a man being chased round a tree by an otter which he had   520
shot at and wounded, and Francis describes an otter struck by a gardener,   422
which

> attacked the man fiercely, uttering a loud cry as it did so. The cry brought two
> other otters . . . to its assistance, and the three otters attacked the gardener simul-
> taneously, compelling him to make a precipitate retreat . . .

This last incident may well have been caused by the first otter calling its
parents to its assistance.

To what extent the male participates in the upbringing of the cubs seems to be uncertain, and Stephens says:

> In odd instances where the whole family are seen out hunting and playing together, it is probable that the dog is living in a separate holt nearby and keeping a watchful eye on his family from a distance.

She quotes Batten (1953) as suggesting that some male otters pay more attention to their families than do others. Grinnell, Dixon & Linsdale relate an instance (in California) of the male taking over a brood of four half-grown young whose mother had been trapped:

> Three days later . . . the male had taken charge of the young otters. Tracks . . . showed that the male parent (positively identified by a peculiarity in his track) had in some way become aware of the location of the steel traps that had been skilfully concealed in the otter's well-worn path, and had carefully led the young ones around the traps, going through the thick tules instead of traveling the accustomed way. The male continued to lead the family about, avoiding traps, until the young were grown.

It is Lloyd's view that with the European otter, at any rate, the part normally played by the male is minor, for he writes:

> I wish that my own observations confirmed the belief of some writers that the dog and bitch pair for a long period and that the dog helps to rear and protect the cubs. I think that the dog does nothing of the kind and that he is, in fact, not greatly worried about either the bitch or the offspring after mating has taken place . . . although otters have the reputation of being great travellers, I think the habit is confined to the bitch, which travels on, leaving the dog in his own favourite hunting grounds . . .

While this may well be true of the European otter, the reverse seems to apply to the North American form, and in two senses. For the urge to travel appears both before and during the mating season and, in my own (very limited) experience, is felt far most strongly by the male. My own male *L. canadensis* becomes extremely bad-tempered and emotionally upset in the mating season, this period of unreliability lasting roughly from mid-January to early April, with a peak from mid-February to mid-March. During this time he is not invariably aggressive, but on 'bad' days will rush at the wire screaming if any person appears too close, and generally behaves in a very distraught manner. At this time also he frequently utters a sort of high-pitched hoot, quite unlike his normal deep grunting sound. If the female tries to approach any visitor he turns on her and nips her, immediately afterwards turning on the visitor whom he would undoubtedly attack were he able to do so. In these weeks also his normally tidy spraiting habits are lost, and spraint is scattered indiscriminately throughout the enclosure.

A further behavioural peculiarity is shown by the male in dragging his back legs and stomach on the ground and scratching at the grass. This is done in a very purposeful way, quite different to the casual rolling and drying on the grass of other times of the year, the animal actually moving at quite a speed over the ground, propelling himself solely with his front legs. Whether this acts as a sexual stimulus or is part of a territorial scent-depositing process, or both, I do not know, but on a few occasions at other times of the year (outside the normal mating season) a brief return to this form of movement has been immediately followed by unmistakably aggressive behaviour. Probably it would be wise always to consider such a display as threatening in intention, even in the tamest of animals.

Liers writes of his captive otters: [703]

In the breeding season the urge to travel seems to be particularly strong. This seems to be nature's way for distributing the animals over the countryside and insuring mating . . . There are exceptions to this rule however. Some males and females apparently are content to remain at home in the breeding season, and some females, after mating, remain thereafter with the male of their choice.

Liers notes the violent change in the disposition of the males at this time, saying:

Some males go berserk when they sense interference. They will charge anyone near, whether that individual be man or beast. Other males and females remain docile. They permit me to carry them to a pen or pool immediately before and after they copulate. One wild-trapped male, about 12 years old . . . if I had a female in heat in my arms, would . . . take the cuff of my trousers in his mouth and shake it, coaxing me to put the female down.

Successful copulation can take place either in the water or on the land. In wild otters it probably occurs exclusively in the water. The male approaches the female from the rear, holds the female by the scruff of the neck with his teeth, and bends the posterior part of his body around and below the broad tail of the female. Breeding [i.e. mating] is very vigorous when contact is made. The vigorous periods are interspersed with periods of rest. In two that I timed the copulatory process lasted 16 and 24 minutes, respectively. The female caterwauls when breeding.

This account may be compared with that of Crandall: [313]

Copulation sometimes took place several times daily, the male holding the female's neck with his teeth, 10–15 minutes being required for completion of the act. Mating was seen only during the day and always in the water but of course, may have taken place unobserved at night. On December 1, while the animals were out of the pool, the male was seen to seize the female's neck several times in succession and to attempt to mount, but when she refused to accept service by simply moving sideways away from him, he relinquished his grip on her neck.

With regard to the behaviour of the mother after the young are born, 703 Liers writes:

The mother usually will not allow the father or anyone else to come near the cubs until they are at least six months old. Males as well as females are usually kind to the young. When I acquire young orphan otters, males will sometimes adopt the cubs and catch food for them. In my experience, it is the young female which is more often unkind to these strange cubs. However, by far the majority of the older otters are kind and gentle with cubs. When permitted, the male will assist in the care of them. He is patient even in their most vigorous play, when they tweak his whiskers and in general make a nuisance of themselves.

704 In another article he adds:

I do not believe that the male ever lives in the den with the mother and young, but he is near by most of the time. When the young ones come out of the nest, father often joins the family party, romping and playing with the babies and helping to teach them to swim.

120 An anonymous article on the breeding of *L. c. vaga* in captivity reads:

The four Florida otters born on January 5 [1956] have begun to make daily excursions out of the den . . . in company with their mother. On their first emergence some weeks ago, the male showed immediate interest but was chased away by the outraged female. He has since taken shelter in a small box we provided some thirty feet from the den, and when the babies come out for their daily airing he looks around the corner of the box but does not attempt to join his offspring.

313 Crandall gives a rather more detailed account of this event, as well as providing the interesting information that the first cub to emerge from the nest did so when 38 days old, and that the cubs were first seen to take solid food on the sixty-third day. They started swimming at a few days over three months of age. Crandall writes that the

first notice of the birth was the ejection of the male from the shelter by the female. During the first day he was seen to re-enter several times but always emerged, hurriedly, after a brief period of excited squealing . . . A set ritual soon developed: when the female was about, the male remained hidden and only came out when she was tending her cubs. If he happened to be outside or even in the pool, the slightest sound from the nursery sent him scuttling for shelter. Later, when the mother began coming down to the pool to bathe, she did not disturb the male as long as he kept to his box but drove him to it furiously if she chanced to find him outside it. Obviously, he should have been removed entirely, had other quarters been available.

It was a full six months before he was fully accepted back into the family group.

Some foreign otters are said to be less well disposed towards their young. According to Bonhote, the Malayans believe that the old male, being poly-   199
gamous, 'always endeavoured to destroy the male pups'; and Schomburgk   1038
reports the Abbé Ricardo to have written of a South American form
[? *Pteronura*] that 'while the parent otters are in existence, they do not suffer the young to propagate their species . . .'

The vigilance of the mother over her babies is well described by Liers: 704

Even when the babies are older, the tamest mother otters I have will not per- mit me to play with their children. They growl at me, and if I disregard the hint and put my hand near the young, mother grabs me gently but firmly and forces my hand away. If I still don't take the hint, she bites hard and is ready to fight. If the children are away from her and approach me, or if I try to coax them to me, she calls and talks to them, plainly warning them to stay away from me. If they disobey and approach me or allow me to approach them, she punishes them when she gets to them by shaking and scolding them.

Liers writes that his mother otters start teaching their young to swim when they are about 14 weeks old.

She tries to coax them into the water; and if they do not go in, she catches them by the back of the neck and drags them. After a few such introductions, they become enthusiastic swimmers and make short dives.

In another article he adds: 703

On their first attempts at swimming they seem to be head-heavy; the head con- tinually tips down underneath the surface, but after much struggling and sputtering they learn to swim.

Few observers have been lucky enough to watch a wild otter teaching her young. Ward writes that   1183

. . . the mother tries to persuade them to follow her into the water, but persuasion seldom succeeds, and she has either to carry or push them into the stream. At times she enters the water with the youngsters on her back, and then sinks down so that they are left to swim. The mother, however, is not far off, and at the first sign of distress comes up below them and again lifts them onto her back.

291 It is obvious that this sort of behaviour can easily turn into play, as must have been the case in an incident observed by Collier.

> I saw two fair-sized otter cubs quickly swimming round and round in circles, as though looking for something, and at the same moment there rose about five yards above them a full grown otter ... On reaching its side they were fondly caressed, and then ... first one cub would creep onto the parent's back, only, however, to be pushed off by its mate, and *vice versa* – the large otter now and again, when the game got too troublesome, sinking slowly under water, submerging the whole of the players.

93 Possibly this method is also regularly employed by the female if she wishes to move her young any distance. An anonymous account of 1898 tells of a mother otter with two young ones pursued by a dog:

> The cubs were so young that they could not swim any distance, and the mother stopped every now and then to allow them to climb on her back ...

6 Perhaps it was such an incident as this which prompted Aldrovandi, in 1645, to write that when the otter is alerted by danger she collects her young on her back and speedily makes off ('*Supra dorsum catulos collocans . . . confestim aufugit*').

626 Sometimes, however, the young are taught the hard way, as Jennison records:

> ... a bitch otter appeared with two cubs on the shingle. There they played for a time until the mother, manoeuvring one of the cubs to the brink, put her nose under it and threw it far into the water; she then dived in and guided it safely across. She returned for the other, and after an interval of play treated it in the same manner.

280 Similarly, Clapham writes that the bitch otter will take her cubs to a rock in midstream and then either push them in, or maroon them there 'until they are at last tempted to enter the water and follow her'.

298 Coote gives a most interesting account of a female otter assisting her inexperienced cubs in the Tees floodwaters.

> [I saw a] big otter followed by three cubs all making their way upstream towards me. It was obvious the current was too strong and the water too broken for the cubs to swim up the middle of the stream. They were about the size of rabbits ... Once one cub was left behind, having 'funked' the strong stream after diving in, and made back to his starting point. On coming out of the water at the next landing place the mother otter distinctly counted her party – found one missing – led the others to a safe little cove, and set off back downstream to look for the laggard ... [Having found him] she dived in, and taking him by the scruff in

46

her mouth, exactly as a kitten is held, she swam with him to safety . . . About fifteen yards above where I was sitting on the opposite bank was a precipitous place where the full force of the current swept close along under the rock . . . Plunging off a rock some three feet above the water, she turned and watched all three cubs take their 'headers' in good style, and then at once turned with them and faced the stream at the corner . . . it was easy to see that she herself could have made the passage, but the cubs could make no headway against the flood, although they could remain stationary for a time, holding their own against the current. Seeing their predicament, the mother turned and let herself go with the stream, being swept past the struggling cubs to a point some five yards below them, where she turned and 'held on' . . . The cubs went on nobly swimming upstream, making no headway at all, until one by one they tired and were swept away in the flood. The first one to go under was 'fielded' unerringly by the mother, seized in her mouth and brought to shore. Before she could get out again the second one came past. He was completely 'done', as he was rolled over and over, and I remember seeing only his little tail showing above the waters for some distance. The pace with which, aided by the current, the mother overtook him was little short of miraculous. How she caught him exactly it was difficult to see in the tumbling waters . . . but as they came to the shore together the cub appeared to be either upon her back or swimming by her side, clinging to her coat with his mouth . . . The third cub when swept down cleverly rescued himself, and swam partly down and partly across the stream, and thus brought himself to land . . . After an appreciable interval she put them all at the dangerous corner once more, but soon saw that it was hopeless, and brought them down again before they became exhausted. She then gave it up, and took them all off downstream . . .

It seems possible that the scent normally left by a female otter becomes much diminished during the breeding season. Stephens writes: 1108

Hunters claim that pregnant and suckling bitches have little or no scent [and] they quote instances of bitches carrying their cubs within a few yards of hounds without being noticed . . .

and Clapham, himself a hunter, writes that 280

A bitch otter in cub, or one with a young family, appears to give off little or no scent . . .

Collier is even more dogmatic, saying that while the bitch suckles her cubs 291

. . . they render her powerless to leave any scent by which hound or dog may trace her to her lair.

There being no close season for otter-hunting in England these assertions, when made by otter hunters, may be considered biased.

Townshend writes in a similar manner but I find myself doubting the 1159
accuracy of a number of her observations. In an earlier article, for instance, 1065

47

she writes that 'all food is probably partially digested and then disgorged by the dam' before being fed to the cubs; that cubs will attempt to bury surplus food; and that when drinking their method is 'more akin to the method of a horse than to the lapping of a dog or cat'. I see no basis in fact for any of these suggestions. Her remarks about the cubs' teeth, also, are not quite in accord with what is found elsewhere:

> The cubs are equipped at birth with a set of exceedingly sharp teeth, those at the back being far more developed than those at the front until about eight weeks old, when all the teeth develop and thicken to a very marked extent ... [They] begin to exchange their milk teeth for a permanent set when they are from three to four months old ... [and] do not lose any of their first teeth until the complete set of second teeth has grown through to replace them, giving the jaws a crowded and most irregular appearance during the transition period.
> The definite thickening of the teeth at eight weeks would seem to indicate that the dam suckles her cubs until that age ...

703 Liers states that the North American otter is toothless at birth. Precise information on its European equivalent is scanty, although Andrewes (*in litt.*) describes her very young cub – 5 in. long overall – as having 'very sharp little white teeth'; this cub was probably 12 or 14 days old at the time.

1108, 241 Stephens, however, states that cubs are toothless at birth, as does Burton,
923 but neither gives an authority for this. Pohle, however, illustrates (page 176, figure 14, a, b, c) the skull of a new-born European otter and states that 'the teeth have not yet broken through'. It seems likely that the teeth are acquired at a very early age, otherwise the lack of them would have been mentioned more often.

287 Cocks mentions a male cub of approximately 2 lb. weight (about 900 gm.) as having milk canines and molars but no incisors cut; the first of these can-
288 ines was not lost for a further 10 weeks. He also notes a female cub of 2¾ lb.
845 (1247 gm.) with the permanent incisors just cut, and Neal illustrates (page 23, lower) the 'lower jaws of an eight-weeks-old cub [which] show the milk
1092 teeth with the permanent dentition just erupting in places'. Southwell notes that young otters 35 in. long (890 mm.) still retained their milk canines although the permanent canines were well grown and much larger than the
1093 deciduous ones. He also writes of a young otter 11½ in. long (295 mm.) weighing 9½ oz. (295 gm.) and says:

> Its closed eyes and *toothless gums* showed that it was not many days, probably not many hours, old. (My italics.)

It is puzzling that Southwell should have considered a cub (relatively) so
288 large to be so young, especially when it is remembered that Cocks' cubs

48

were about 8 in. (204 mm.) long at 13 days; but when Southwell was writing Cocks' article had not been published. In this connection it is worth recalling that Hooper & Ostenson judged foetal specimens from Michigan to be at term which had a crown to rump length of more than $4\frac{1}{3}$ in. (110 mm.). Unfortunately, they do not mention the presence or otherwise of teeth, and Southwell's large toothless example remains something of an enigma.

582

Chapter 2

The Food of the Otter

Seeking the food he eats
And pleased with what he gets.
As You Like It, ii.5.42

710 WHILE it is true, as noted by Linnaeus, that the otter happily eats fish, frogs and crabs, the full range of its natural diet is an extremely wide one, approaching almost to the omnivorous.

Many of the earlier naturalists accuse the otter of attacks on sheep and poultry, at least during periods when there is a shortage of fish, and
895 Pennant writes that:

> In very hard weather, when its natural sort of food fails, it will kill lambs and poultry.

This statement is slavishly repeated by a large number of subsequent writers, but at least with regard to sheep, while it seems probable that they have on occasion been attacked by otters, such occurrences can only be described as very rare. Accounts of otters killing sheep or lambs are difficult
491 to find and when found are often circumstantial. For instance, Gurney (1869–70) writes:

> During a hard winter many years since, a large male otter attacked and killed a sheep in a field at a considerable distance from any stream, at Briston, in Norfolk; and a man who brought some turnips to the flock, found the otter regaling itself on its victim, and killed it with the tail-board of the tumbril . . .

1090 This account is repeated a few years later by Southwell, and in 1881
492 Gurney republished it, adding that 'if I remember rightly' the sheep had
80 been killed by a bite in the neck. But an anonymous account in *The Field* of 1884 is more damning; on this occasion

> . . . a shepherd lost two young lambs . . . he searched in the sedges, where he found the [otter's] nest, with lamb's wool near it and in the excrement.

50

Harting, commenting in 1894 on Carew's *Survey of Cornwall* (1602) which   531
says that otters

... make bold now and then to visit the land, and to breake their fast upon the
good man's lambs, or on the good wives pultrie ...

writes in a footnote:

We have never known an instance in which a lamb was proved to have been
killed by an Otter, and suspect that in any such reported case a Fox must have
been to blame ...

There is a more recent account, written by Harvey in 1953, purporting to   532
show that otters kill lambs:

During the recent lambing season 44 lambs were destroyed in the space of
three days on a stretch of land approximately five miles in length adjoining the
River Dovey, from Llanymawddwy to a point just above Dinas Mawddwy. All
the carcases bore tooth marks in the back of the neck, and all had been mutilated
by having the heart and liver torn out, these latter being eaten. The same thing
has occurred during three previous lambing seasons, although on a smaller scale.
The attacks were attributed to otters, and in fact, ceased abruptly when a pair of
otters were hunted and killed.

Stephens refers to this account, and comments: 1108

As far as I know it was never confirmed that otters were the culprits, however,
and many people doubted it.

But she adds:

Three other records of lambs being taken have been received from Wales, two
of which were probably genuine. Both were in exceptional circumstances however, one during heavy snow and the other during a flood, when the lamb was
marooned on a small island.

Lancum provides one further example, saying: 676

In half a century of nature study in the field, the writer can vouch for only one
instance of an otter killing a lamb ... Not one farmer in a thousand will ever
have cause to complain of the otter ...

With regard to otters taking chickens, I have found only one factual
account relating to the European otter, that of Shepheard in 1937:   1065

A few years ago a confirmed poultry-killer was shot and it was found that a
trap polished by constant dragging over shingle was firmly attached to his hind
leg.

498 The clawless South African *Aonyx*, however, seems worse behaved in this respect. Haagner writes:

> We have known of instances where they have ravished poultry runs, devouring the eggs, and killing fowls and ducks.

1071 Similarly, Shortridge says: 'When opportunity offers they will sometimes raid poultry yards.' As will be seen, the *Aonyx* is hardly a fish-eater at all and is also considered to be more terrestrial than other forms of otter, these two facts possibly inclining it more towards poultry in its tastes.

Ducks are frequently taken by otters, and there are good grounds for thinking that waterfowl in general form a useful proportion of their diet.

984 Rodd, who was troubled by otters taking his ducks, writes:

> The otters did not appear to eat the ducks, but gave them a mortal bite from underneath as they were swimming ... A preference seemed to be shown for ducks with white underparts.

92 Conversely, an anonymous account of a few years later states that the otter on that occasion favoured especially the black Cayuga ducks.

244 Buxton tells of an otter in Wanstead Park, London, which 'fattened him-
242, 244 self for months on tame ducks', and also writes of two instances of otters taking duck he had shot, one of these being at Horsey, where

> ... some at least of these animals seem to have realised not merely that we are harmless, but that the sound of a shot at dawn may mean a cheap and appetising breakfast. One morning I was alone in a boat on the edge of the reeds, from which I shot eight mallard [*Anas platyrhynchos*]. In the middle of the shooting two otters were heard splashing and diving, and presently one of the two discovered a dead duck lying in thick covert not five yards behind my boat and began noisily scrunching up the bird. Its companion found a second duck in front of me and after eating it whistled and joined the one behind the boat. They then continued their search together and carried off a third duck ...

1065 Shepheard writes of an unfortunate occurrence in 1937:

> At a duck farm recently established in Shropshire ... the owners constructed an otterproof fence. The fence was well made, but ... it happened to confine an otter, and there were no fish in the lakes. The otter is said by the proprietors to have eaten about £600 worth of duck before it was caught.

814 The otter's taste in birds is a wide and varied one. Moffat tells in 1927 of the depredations of otters on moorland lochs in the Northumberland border country, where the owner

> ... at first suspected pike to be the destroyers, [but] he ultimately found that the work of extermination had been wholly carried out by his hill-side otters. Visiting

the 'dining-tables' of some of these animals during the summer months, he found them littered with the remains of butchered coots [*Fulica atra*], waterhens [*Gallinula chloropus*], tufted ducks [*Aythya fuligula*], pochard [*Aythya ferina*], widgeon [*Anas penelope*], shoveler-duck [*Anas clypeata*], goldeneye [*Bucephala clangula*], lapwing [*V. vanellus*], golden plover [*Charadrius apricarius*], sandpiper [*Tringa hypoleucos*], starling [*Sturnus vulgaris*], black-headed gull [*Larus ridibundus*], and (in smaller numbers) mallard [*Anas platyrhynchos*], teal [*Anas crecca*], curlew [*Numenius arquata*], and heron [*Ardea cinerea*], with one supposed black-necked grebe [*Podiceps nigricollis*] . . .

Moffat mentions another instance, in Co. Wexford, of the remains of a full-grown heron being found at an otter's feeding-place. 814

Cahn has a most interesting account of a North American otter attempting to catch a coot in open water. 258

On Mackenzie Lake [Ontario] I once watched, spellbound, while an otter stalked a coot (*Fulica americana*) that was swimming about over deep water. The otter swam across the lake, approaching the coot. Every now and again it rose to an almost perpendicular position and looked round. When about 100 yards from the bird the otter saw it. For a few seconds it watched the bird intently, apparently fixing the location in its mind. Then the otter dived . . . The coot saw the otter during this brief period of observation, and as the seconds passed while the otter was underwater, the coot seemed to become increasingly uneasy, swimming about in a zigzag course, its head bobbing from side to side. Finally the strain appeared to be too great for it, and it flapped away. Five seconds later the otter came to the surface within two feet of where the bird had been. It looked about for a moment before swimming slowly to the shore and disappearing.

It seems likely that the otter can swim submerged considerably further than 100 yards if it wishes to. Preble writes that it will swim under water 'for a distance of 200 yards or more' if hard pressed, and Lett (quoting Merriam, *Mammals of the Adirondacks*, 1882) says: 933 697 789

It can remain underwater almost as long as a loon [*Colymbus*], and I have known one to swim nearly a quarter of a mile without showing its head above the surface . . .

This same distance is given by Hamilton. 510

Hainard quotes Guenaux as saying that they can stay submerged for seven to eight minutes but this is probably an over-statement, Seton's estimate of three to four minutes being more likely. Although Maxwell (page 127) timed his otter remaining under water almost six minutes and thought this could be exceeded, an anonymous account of 1884 reports a trapped otter drowning in three-and-a-half minutes. This unfortunate 501 1060 773 82 animal, however, was presumably taken by surprise. The otter's intake of breath before diving is clearly audible, as is its exhalation on surfacing, and presumably the longer the intended dive the deeper the breath taken. The chain of bubbles rising to the surface behind a submerged otter is only partly due to the escape of air trapped in its fur, for when it has been beneath the surface for some little time it starts slowly to exhale, the air bubbles appearing in a regular slow stream from the corners of the mouth.

Such diving abilities must greatly assist the otter in its pursuit of wildfowl and doubtless most wild duck taken by otters are caught in this way. 1003 St Quintin says:

> From what I have noticed, the otter generally seizes the bird from below, diving under it, and giving it one terrible grip with his powerful jaws, and often leaving it without further injury.

This writer adds:

> On May 15th last [in 1923], a bitch otter (14 lb.) somehow got in amongst my birds, and killed a Lesser White-fronted Goose [*Anser erythropus*], and a Japanese Teal, besides destroying several clutches of eggs. My keeper pegged down the remains of the goose, and the otter was trapped. In the autumn of 1919 otters got in twice, and killed a Ross's Snow Goose [*Anser caerulescens*], and a Brent Goose [*Branta bernicla*], besides a tame Curlew [*Numenius arquata*] and nine ducks . . . I can recall six other instances of ducks being killed here by otters . . .

1108 Stephens also notes an instance of an otter taking a goose, the animal being trapped near where the bird had disappeared and having in its stomach red flesh and an unmistakable goose feather.

The otter can move very quickly on land if it feels so inclined (*see* page 59) and will not disdain any bird unwary enough to get within its reach. An 54 anonymous account of 1861 tells how a gamekeeper

> . . . saw the otter cautiously creeping down the side of a hillock till he reached the bank of a burn, where he made an eager spring, and snapped a moorcock [? *Lyrurus tetrix*], and slipped into the gully of the burn, where he sat down to dine on his victim.

531 Harting has a similar account, set in Perthshire in 1885, where a gamekeeper

> . . . came upon the track of an Otter in the newly fallen snow by the side of a mountain stream . . . After proceeding a short distance, the tracks left the waterside, and showed where the animal had made a bound and caught an old cock Grouse [probably *Lagopus scoticus*]. Returning to the stream, it had crossed onto a rock in the centre of the water, where it deposited its [half-eaten] prey.

Welch notes an instance on the bank of the Wye in Herefordshire where   1003

... an adult otter emerged from the water, and after a few seconds it made a sudden rush at a sparrow [*Passer domesticus*] about eight feet away, grabbing with its mouth – after which it returned at once into the water.

Cushny observed a similar occurrence at the London Zoo: 320

There were several sparrows inside the cage ... Suddenly one of the otters dived into the pond, swam straight across to the far side, and, springing upwards ... caught a luckless sparrow, killing it on the spot, afterwards eating it.

Novikov writes that otters will catch snipe [*G. gallinago*], and pheasants   860
[*Phasianus* sp.] are added to the list of their prey by Buxton. Although   244
Pitt believes that they take cygnets, I have seen no record of the European   918
otter doing so. Banko, however, provides good evidence of *L. canadensis*   151
taking the young of Trumpeter Swans [*Olor buccinator*], and Shortridge   1071
claims that the large African *Aonyx* sometimes kills swans,

... these being either pounced upon among the reeds or seized by the feet in open water and pulled under.

Weldon was fortunate enough to observe an otter catch a cormorant   1197
[*Phalacrocorax carbo*], this event taking place off Achill Island, Co. Mayo.

[The cormorant] had just come up from a dive, when my attention was drawn to something moving swiftly through the water. It proved to be an otter, which went along till he came under the cormorant and seized it by the leg. The otter then swam on the top of the water, and brought the cormorant to the shore. I had to go a long way round before I came to the place where he was, but when I did get there the otter bolted, and left the cormorant, having eaten its head ...

Aplin writes of the Uruguayan *L. platensis* behaving in much the same   128
manner:

I had shot ... and only wounded a Cormorant ... the wounded bird flapped away down the laguna, which curved rather sharply ... I therefore lost sight of the bird for a minute, and when I came in sight of it again I saw a great commotion going on in the water. Hurrying up I saw the smooth sleek head of an Otter, which had the Cormorant (still flapping its wings) in its mouth. As I ran up the Otter dived out of sight with the bird, and although I waited a long time I saw neither again.

Macintyre, remarking that 'Otters catch and "peel" lobsters often enough',   747
adds an interesting eye-witness account of a gannet (*Sula bassana*) being taken:

One day I saw a white object making rapid progress towards the rocks. It turned out to be a gannet which a big otter was retrieving, and as the bird was warm when I recovered it, it was clear that the otter had killed it.

55

264

As well as birds, both young and adult, some otters seem to have acquired a taste for eggs. Carter, for instance, writes of many pheasant eggs being taken by them. This habit, however, seems to be more prevalent among the African forms. Thus Sandberg, writing of the spotted-necked otter *L. (H.) maculicollis*, says:

1007

> Its food consists chiefly of fish, but natives say that it loots birds' nests, taking the eggs and young birds.

827

A captive specimen of this race is noted by Mortimer (1963) to have foraged for herself in the garden, and to have selected carrots, beans, potatoes and peas.

566

Hinton, when establishing *Paraonyx*, believed this form to be still more terrestrial than *Aonyx* and judged from the nature of its teeth that its

> ... staple diet will be found to consist of soft substances like small terrestrial vertebrates and eggs.

912

Pitman also remarks that *Paraonyx* is not chiefly a fish-eater, and writes that it lives on 'frogs, crustaceans, molluscs, eggs and young birds'; and Lönnberg, quoting Sandberg on *A. capensis*, while agreeing with other writers that its food consists chiefly of crabs, says:

720

> I have found eggshells and remains of young birds, ducklings etc. in its stomach during the season for the propagation of the birds.

He adds that no traces of fish remains were found by him in any of the clawless otters which he shot.

1108
918

Stephens remarks that she has heard of gulls' nests being robbed of eggs by otters on their journeys over the Scottish hills, but an account by Pitt tends to confirm that the English otter may be less partial to eggs than are some of its foreign relatives. She followed the track of an otter on Scolt Head Island, Norfolk, across and through the ternery there, and concludes:

> I saw no sign of the animal's having interfered with eggs or nests ... It amazed me that he had passed so many nests of common, Sandwich and little terns [*Sterna hirundo*, *S. sandvicensis* and *S. albifrons*] without interfering with them ...

1222

A rather different account is given by Wright of the behaviour of an otter in the Yellowstone Park, Wyoming.

> A black object loomed by the swan nest [*C. cygnus*]. With field glasses glued to our eyes, we saw that it was an otter stretching its full length upward to peer down into the nest. From one side it reached out toward the centre and pushed aside the material covering the eggs. Then the commotion started. With rapt interest,

the otter rooted around in the dry nest material, heaving up here and digging in there, until it was more haystack than nest. Then the otter started to roll, around and around, over and over. This went on for a number of minutes. At frequent intervals its long neck was craned upward, and the serpent-like head rotated around to discover (we supposed) if the swans were returning. At last the otter seemed to weary of this play. It climbed from the nest to the outer edge, then slid off into the water. Swimming off along the edge of the marsh grass, it was the undulating silver demon of the water world . . . we stripped off our clothes and waded out across the shallows. We were amazed to find all five eggs intact. There they were, all together, rolled to one side but perfectly whole . . .

Shortridge includes crocodile eggs as an item in the diet of the *Aonyx*, and in places where both are found this seems a likely addition. Incidentally, the crocodile can, on occasion, be one of the otter's few natural enemies. In India, for instance, McMaster makes it clear that the otter is fully aware of the danger of this creature. Quoting an account first published in *The Field* 'about the end of 1868', and relating to the Bowanee River, he says: 1071 752

One day, when sitting on the bank among the jungle, I saw a number of Otters fishing . . . About a hundred yards below where the Otters were so busily at work I suddenly saw the snout and eyes of a crocodile steal above the water for a moment and then sink back. This occurred again, and so much nearer to the fishing party that it was evident he was stalking them . . . After a short interval the crocodile rose again, about thirty yards from the Otter; but no sooner was the water broken by the hideous head of the reptile than an Otter, which evidently was stationed on the opposite bank as a sentinel, sounded the alarm by a whistling sort of sound. In an instant those in the water rushed to the bank and disappeared among the jungle . . . It was curious how instantly they seemed to know the form of danger by which they were menaced, and they evidently did so from their leaving the water, which was the very last thing they would have done had I suddenly shown myself.

Turning to Africa, Shortridge comments on *Aonyx* in the Okavango river: 1071

Once I watched an individual splashing about within a few feet of a sandbank on which five crocodiles were lying stretched out in the sun. In spite of their alertness, it is astonishing that otters manage to hold their own in crocodile-infested waters.

That they can only do so if not incapacitated in any way is shown by Stevenson-Hamilton.   1111

A hunter fired at and wounded an otter, which he saw fishing in a deep pool of the Olifants River. Although up to that moment there had not been a sign of a crocodile, almost immediately afterwards the pool became alive with the reptiles, and the otter was quickly pulled down.

1013 A strange anecdote concerning an Indian smooth-coated otter, L. (L.) *per-spicillata*, which escaped from the Calcutta Zoo, is provided by Sányál:

> Having gained its freedom it took to amusing itself in the water, and baffled all attempts of the keepers to recapture it, a large island overgrown with shrubs and undergrowth giving it a great advantage ... Next morning the animal was seen disporting itself close to the island, but on the approach of the men it disappeared until, after considerable search, it was found hidden inside a burrow. Its bewildered appearance betrayed something unusual ... [and] it was discovered that all the time it had been keeping company with a crocodile in its hiding place. That it ever escaped being devoured was a wonder.

936 It should be noted that Procter lists crocodiles, leopards and pythons as constant occasional predators of African otters, but it may be that the tables
185 are sometimes turned, for Blanford writes:

> I once came upon a party [of Indian otters] that were pulling about a small crocodile, but I cannot say whether they had killed it.

473 Although Greer (1955) found no remains of western painted turtles (*Chrysemys picta*) in the course of his extensive analyses of otter spraints,
505 Hall & Kelson include turtles among the food items taken by otters, and
1115 Stophlett has an account of Florida otters (*L. c. vaga*), in Orange County, confirming this:

> An otter was noticed dragging a large terrapin (at least fifteen inches in length) by one of its hind legs ... to the bank at the edge of the marsh; immediately, another came out of the marsh and the two of them began eating it. Shortly after, however, another appeared and still another, until there were four of them feeding on the terrapin.
>
> They soon made short work of the reptile; the legs and head were first torn out and eaten and then the viscera. An amusing incident occurred when one of the otters lay on his back with his eyes closed and ate a chunk of meat by holding it in his paws, apparently in perfect contentment.

1071 Shortridge, also, mentions 'mud-tortoises' as forming part of the diet of the African *Aonyx*.

So far as the smaller mammals are concerned, otters will probably eat
860 anything they can catch. Novikov mentions field voles [? *Microtus*], white hares [*Lepus* sp.] and shrews [*Sorex* sp.], and rather surprisingly adds that
1108 'The otter vigorously hunts minks' [*Lutreola vison*]. Stephens confirms that hares are taken in hard weather, and herself found evidence of a young leveret as prey. Prior to the myxomatosis outbreaks it is probable that rabbits [*Oryctolagus cuniculus*] were not uncommonly eaten. Thus Gates
430 writes in 1898:

58

One of my men moved a rabbit, which ran to . . . the side of the river, when it began to cry as if fixed by a stoat [*Mustela ermina*], but on the man going to the spot a large otter left it and plunged into the water. On picking the rabbit up he found it bitten through the back and almost dead.

Similarly, Harting (1894) records an instance of rabbits trapped beside a 531 small brook being regularly taken from the trap, presumably by an otter, for one was itself shortly trapped there. There are, too, numerous accounts, such as that of Robinson in 1904, of otters being bolted from rabbit bur- 979 rows by ferrets, but whether the otters so disturbed were hunting rabbits or merely lying up is difficult to say.

The otter has quite a good turn of speed on land, and Liers states that it 703 can run as fast as a man. Severinghaus & Tanck had a remarkable opportun- 1061 ity for verifying this when in March 1947 they were travelling on a snow-mobile – a motorised toboggan – across an impounded stretch of water some half a mile wide and four and a half miles long, in Hamilton County, New York, where they came across an otter.

Patches of wind-packed snow covered about half of the ice surface . . . the snow was solid enough to allow a man to walk without snowshoes. The otter [was] an adult of average size . . . During the next ten minutes we chased it north, then south, then north, and finally south again . . . During all this time the otter was travelling about 15 to 18 m.p.h. . . . on each leg of the chase we were travelling most of the distance abreast of the otter and no more than three or four feet from it. The chase was sufficiently fast and long that the otter's mouth was open and its tongue could be seen. But . . . there was no slackening of its pace as long as we observed it.

It would jump forward just three times, no more or less, and then glide. The glide would extend about 20 to 25 feet over the ice, but over the wind-packed snow the distance was somewhat shorter. Its jumping and gliding were so timed that no appreciable loss of speed was noticed.[1]

While such agility on dry land (or snow) must enable the otter to catch many small mammals, larger ones are sometimes eaten. One (*L. l. nair*?) trapped by McCann on the Pamber River in southern India came to a bait 736 of civet (*Paradoxurus jerdoni*), and an anonymous account of 1904 tells of a 101 drowned deer being 'broken into' by European otters. Stephens refers to 1108 Muller (1945) for evidence that carrion sometimes forms a large part of their diet, and instances otters being seen eating dead crows (*Corvus corone*) and a dead rat. It is implied by Waters, in Cambridgeshire at any rate, that 1188

[1] This is a good deal faster than a female individual of the African spotted-necked species 827 timed by Mortimer. Her top speeds were found to be 3·7 ft./sec. [5·4 m.p.h.] swimming, 4·8 ft./sec. [7 m.p.h.] running, and 6·6 ft./sec. [9·6 m.p.h.] galloping.

531 water-rats (presumably *Arvicola amphibius*) form a staple part of the otter's diet, and Harting quotes Salvin as saying he believed they killed 'a considerable number' of water-rats.

336
918 Day once offered his otters an ordinary rat, 'but although they ran up to it, they did not attempt to do it any injury'. Pitt, however, tells how one of her otters caught a farmyard rat and immediately devoured it.

327
1090
77 Some of the earlier naturalists, such as Daniel (1812), assert that sucking pigs are sometimes attacked. Southwell says 'it has been known to kill and partly devour a young pig', and an anonymous account in *The Field* of 1881 reads as follows:

> Some years ago the bailiff at a gentleman's house in this neighbourhood [Merioneth] told me that he lost during a week five young pigs. A large drain ran up to the house, and at last the culprit was caught in the shape of a fine otter. His tracks had been discovered previously, and the trap was set close to the entrance of the pigstye, leaving little doubt about the robber.

472, 473
1060, 516 In North America, muskrat – or musquash – remains (*Ondatra zibethicus*) were detected in otter spraints both by Green (1932) and by Greer (1955). Seton quotes Manley Hardy as saying that in winter he had known otters to depopulate entirely the houses of a large colony of muskrats.

160 To what extent the otter is a predator of the beaver (*Castor canadensis*) is more arguable. In 1863 Barnston attempted to found his '*Lutra destructor*' partly on its propensity for attacking beavers, and it may be noted that he strongly contrasted this presumed activity with the more usual habits of the typical *L. canadensis*. His account of a visit to a beaver-lodge will not, however, bear scrutiny.

> In 1823 I accompanied a few Churchill Crees, in order to be present at the taking of a beaver-lodge ... [The lodge was broken open and found to be empty.] Being scarcely acquainted with the Cree language at that period, I could not interrogate the hunters closely; but after they had surveyed the surrounding locality, and examined the lodge, they gave it as their opinion that an otter had been there to spoil their sport and destroy the beaver.

It will be noticed that this account was written 40 years after the event, and that Barnston could not at that time speak Cree; moreover, the full text states that inside the beaver-lodge there were no dead beavers, no signs of a struggle, no otter tracks and no spraint. Barnston's opinions, however, were reinforced by another Indian on the Albany River, 'an elderly man, not one of the best of characters ... deemed a conjuror by his tribe'. Barnston says:

I was told by him that it was the small otter [i.e. *L. destructor*] that killed the beavers, by breaking down their dams and getting into their houses; or so disturbing them as to take them at disadvantage abroad, devouring the young and all he could succeed in mastering ... I shall only add that [this] has been confirmed by many hunters on the shores of Lake Superior ...

Audubon, in his journals (vol. II, page 54), writing of the country near Fort Union, says 134

The Otters and Musk-rats of this part of the country are smaller than in the States; the first is the worst enemy the beaver has,

and on page 161 he adds that trapped beavers 'are often attacked by the Otter'. In his *Arctic Zoology* Pennant states that otters will 'attack and devour the beaver', giving as a reference for this 'Dobbs, 40' which I have not traced. Reeks writes that the otter has 'been known to enter a beaver's house and kill the young' and, more recently, Anthony includes 'young beaver' in his list of the otter's food. 898 950 127

Green published in 1932 a long article entitled, 'Observations on the Occurrence of the Otter in Manitoba in Relation to Beaver life', part of which reads as follows: 472

As a keen observer for the past 25 years of all western and sub-arctic forms of mammalian life there is no doubt in my mind from the strong circumstantial evidence presented that the otters ... deliberately breached the beaver dam ... for the purpose of gaining access to the [frozen] pond and creating an air space to enable them to remain therein for some appreciable time [this was in February] ...

Two dumps of fresh otter excrement were observed close by. Both contained masses of fine felted hair which later proved to be muskrat fur.

Towards evening [in June] I found the partially decomposed carcase of an adult beaver in the tall grass bordering the north shore of the pond ... There were still unmistakable lesions of deep festered sores behind the shoulders and on the right flank which only rending teeth could have inflicted.

That otter will molest beaver is, I think, proved by the obvious fear of the inhabitants ... during the period the otters inhabited their pond. [The beavers usually came when called, but refused to do so at this time.] That they will kill them may be thoughtfully inferred from the circumstantial evidence gathered from the examination of the beaver carcase found ... To support the latter belief several of my Indian friends, including 'Gray Owl', have informed me on different occasions that two or more otters will 'gang' and kill an adult beaver in water if found alone. They tell me, too, that otter will kill and eat beaver 'kittens' at every favourable opportunity.

1060 Against this view, or at least tending in that direction, is an account by Seton, quoting Mills.

> One morning I had glimpses of a battle in a Beaver pond between a large invading Otter and numerous home-defense Beavers. Most of the fighting was under water, but the pond was roiled and agitated over a long stretch . . . Several times, during this struggle, the contestants came up where they could breathe. Twice when the Otter appeared he was at it with one large Beaver; another time he was surrounded by several, one or more of which had their teeth in him. When he broke away, he was being vigorously mauled by a single Beaver . . .

204 It may be remarked that according to Bourlière the American beaver can remain submerged for up to 15 minutes – far longer than any otter, and a large one will weigh 'up to a normal maximum of 70 pounds' (31·8 kg.),
256 according to Cahalane, a good deal more than a large otter. In this context
482 the remarks of Grinnell, Dixon & Linsdale are relevant:

> Beavers and otters are said to be persistent mutual enemies, but no observation of ours substantiates this statement . . . One of us . . . examined carefully the wounds of certain beavers said to have been killed by otters and found, from the depth and size of the wounds, that these had been inflicted by other beavers and not by otters at all . . .

943 It may also be remarked that Rand gives instances of otters and beavers living in very close proximity, in one case an otter sharing the same house
473 with adult and kit beavers, without animosity. In 1955, however, Greer found – in a very few instances – definite traces of beaver fur in otter spraints, as is shown later.

To judge from the early authors it seems that the otter and the European
438 beaver (*Castor fiber*) tolerate each other, and Gesner (1551) quotes Albertus Magnus (? 1206–80) to the effect that the beaver is stronger than the otter and has very sharp teeth, on account of which it neither drives the otter away nor kills it; but it is not true, he adds, that in winter the beaver compels the otter to agitate the water around the beaver's tail so that it may not be frozen to the ice! (This 'occupational hazard' may not be quite so far-
716 fetched as it sounds; Lloyd (1879) writes:

> A farmer, residing near the River Irfon . . . observed a great commotion in the water close to the edge of some thick ice; on going nearer he found it was caused by an otter, which . . . was firmly frozen by its tail to the ice. Probably the otter had been for some time sitting on the edge of the ice in wait for a passing fish . . . The poor beast's nails were quite worn to the flesh by scratching against a rock, and its teeth broken by biting the ice . . . the otter was secured and taken home by the farmer, and I am sorry to say, died the same night.)

62

Mussels are much relished by otters although there is some difference of opinion as to the method employed to open or crack the shell. Harting writes that 526

> numbers of these shells have been found in an otter's haunt, with the ends bitten off, and evident marks of teeth upon the broken fragments, the position of the shells indicating that the otter, after having crunched off one end, had sucked or scooped out the mollusc in much the same way as those who are partial to shrimps dispose of that esculent crustacean.

This method finds confirmation in a note by Jeffery: 623

> Near Petworth, in Sussex . . . on the banks of a stream frequented by the otter, I found quantities of shells of fresh-water mussels (*Anodon cygneus* and *Unio pictorum*), the first-named being the most numerous. These shells were mostly in pairs still united, but in every case either one shell or both were chipped at one end . . .

An account by Roebuck disagrees with this, however, for the shells which 985 in his view had been opened by otters were bitten 'all round the outer edges', and he ascribed to rats such shells as had been bitten open at one end. Yet another view is taken by Coward & Oldham, one of whom heard 311 otters gnawing the shells of Anodonta early one April; they write that

> the ligament which holds the valves together is bitten away in every case, as is the posterior margin of the shell; out of scores of the shells which we examined not one had been bitten along the anterior margin.

Millais quotes a correspondent from Cheshire as saying that 798

> on a quiet night it is often possible to hear the otter crunching the hard shells. All these shells [*Anodon*] are nibbled at one end only and in quite a different way from those gnawed by rats.

Stephens gave her two young captive otters large (6 oz.) freshwater mussels 1108 which 'caused endless amusement', but the shells had to be broken for them before the contents could be eaten, and the same has happened when I have given either fresh-water or sea mussels to my own otters. Barnston's 160 pet Canadian otter was frequently taken to the river

> where it would commence diving, bringing generally from the bottom some species of small mollusc. These it would crunch and eat . . . as a hearty breakfast of fish had been had beforehand on shore, the entertainment no doubt was equivalent to a dessert and a bath.

Otters are not wholly carnivorous. Buffon mentions that they eat the 227 'bark of aquatic trees', and the otter mentioned above as trapped by

63

736 McCann had as the main contents of its stomach crabs, decayed wood, and a quantity of unidentified green leaves. He remarks that this animal was 487 none the less in very good condition. Gunn writes in 1866:

> I have been informed, on two or three occasions ... that when deprived of sustenance from their usual element, they will turn their attention to the land, root up vegetables and partly devour some of the leaves as well as the roots.

599 Hurley mentions an otter which destroyed the garden if let into it, and what 1075 must be a very unusual incident was observed by Smith (1951):

> Recently we were destroying rabbits along a river bank when my partner noticed a large thistle fall over. He drew my attention to it, and while we were talking ... another fell ... We went to investigate and ... a large otter darted back into the river. The otter had eaten the crowns out of the roots of the plants, and when we looked about we found it had eaten quite a lot.

1206 Williamson's (fictional) otter 'Tarka', or other otters in the same book – which is based on actual events – eat amongst other things: trout, peal, rabbit, eel, frog, short eared owl [*Asio flammeus*], mullet, tadpole, bull frog, drake, salmon, pollock, lamprey, pheasant, cuckoo egg [*Cuculus canorus*], moorhen egg [*Gallinula chloropus*], moorhen, vole, dab [*Pleuronectes limanda*], plaice [*P. platessa*], crab, rainbow trout, fluke, prawn, mussel, seaweed, 'shellfish', winkle [*Littorina* sp.], swan, 'firecrested wren' [? *Regulus* 913 *ignicapillus*], dace, and grass. Pitt's otters both avidly hunted small garden slugs, although they would not touch the large black meadow-slugs.

301 Copley writes that where the marshes have been drained the African *Aonyx* 'now raids the maize fields and eats the young cobs' (*Zea* sp.), but in common with other writers he agrees that their main food is the freshwater crab. It is thought that this is the most terrestrial of all forms of otter, 828 and Moseley goes so far as to say of it that 'It appears to be an otter bent on 1007 returning to land habits'. Sandberg remarks that 'it is more often found among reeds than in the water' and from an examination of stomach con-223 tents concludes that its food consists of crabs and water-snails. Bryant was told that *Aonyx* in Kenya did not touch trout and lived mainly on crabs, 566, 720 and Hinton writes of this form as 'not often able to procure fish'. Lönnberg quotes Sandberg as saying:

> ... it is only in the dry season when the fishes get confined to small pools that it succeeds in its fishing.

1119 Equally, Sweeney says of *Aonyx* that it is 'Primarily a crab-eater and found 123 chiefly in marshy areas', and Ansell confirms the preference for crabs of Northern Rhodesian examples.

It is probable that crabs will be taken by any otter living in an area where they are available. Certainly crabs and other small crustaceans form a major part of the food of Scottish coastal otters, as may easily be confirmed by a glance at the spraints in such places. Elmhirst found the remains of *Orchestia littorea*, *Porcellio scaber* and *Ligia oceanica*, as well as *Idotea granulosa* and *Gammarus duebeni* in the spraints of such otters. He found three species of crab represented, *Carcinas moenas* (shore crab), *Cancer pagurus* (edible crab), and *Portunus puber* (velvet swimmer crab) in that order of comparative frequency which, he notes, agreed with that of their occurrence on the shore. Darwin (*in* Waterhouse: 1838 [1839]) observed that

378

1187

> ... a red coloured crab (belonging to the family Macrouri) of the size of a prawn ...

was the chief food of the South American *L. felina* in the Chonos Archipelago (although cuttlefish was also eaten), and Coppinger writes of the same otter a little further south that

302

> its 'runs' are generally strewn with the shells of a large spiny crab (the *Lithodes antarctica*) which appears to form its principal food. I have seen an otter rise to the surface with one of these hideous crabs in its mouth ...

Indeed, Linnaeus included crabs as one of the three components of the otter's diet, as was seen at the beginning of this chapter, and it may be that their fondness for them accounts for otters not infrequently being found drowned in crab pots, although in one case recorded by Scheffer the bait itself seems to have been the attraction:

710

1029

> ... Mr. Fox took two otters at the same time and in the same pot. 'He figures the depth of the pots at about 10 fathoms (18.5 m.) ... The tunnel eyes on the pots are 3½ by 8 inches so the otters must have really wanted to get in. We bait with clams, and there were no crabs in the pots ...

Lobster pots also take their toll. Hackett (1873) records a lobster and an otter taken together off the Irish coast, and Cox (1947) notes three similar instances in Devon.

499
312

The detailed food analyses discussed later show that insects and 'bugs' of various sorts are commonly eaten. An anonymous account of 1863 refers to

59

> ... an otter rising to the surface of the water, and skimming it with the ostensible object of seizing the flies that were on the river at the time

427 and Frohawk refers to tame otters that

> ... were particularly fond of large beetles, especially the common dung beetles (*Geotrupes stercorarius* and *G. mutator*) which they greedily devoured; also the large water beetle (*Dysticus marginalis*) whose voracious larvae are so destructive to young fry.

> My own otters will go to great lengths to catch any moth that may happen to fly into the room in the evening, as well as pursuing bluebottles and mosquitoes.

In these circumstances it is not surprising that otters are sometimes hooked by fishermen whose bait they presumably mistake either for small fish or perhaps aquatic insects. Among a number of typical instances may 267 be mentioned that recorded by Carter (1879) and an anonymous account of 76 1878.

1130 Tate (1931) refers to otters eating large catfish in South America and they 385 are also eaten in Europe, occasionally with fatal results. Estanove, writing in 1952, attributes the diminution of otters in France partly at least to the spread of the catfish (*Ameiurus nebulosus*), at any rate in the area around Toulouse and in the Garonne, Ariège and Hers rivers. A number of dead otters examined by him were found to have perforated stomachs and viscera, or to have been suffocated by the spines of the fish lodging in the palate and lower jaw, thus preventing the fish being swallowed. As will be seen however, these fish seem sometimes to be eaten with impunity in the States; 413 and Fitter (1964) writes that the otter in France is in danger of extinction mainly owing to water pollution.

But perhaps more important than some of these rather miscellaneous items in the otter's diet is the question of to what extent the otter is a serious predator of salmon and trout. They do, of course, take both, but an anony- 115 mous comment which appeared a few years ago in *The Field* is worth quoting:

> I should not like to say how many times I have been told that a salmon has been killed by an otter ... almost invariably the fish proved to have died from natural causes and part of it had been eaten after death by rats or picked by carrion birds ... In not far short of 40 years salmon fishing ... I could count on the fingers of one hand the number of salmon which had, without doubt, been killed by otters ... I can only recall two.

531 Harting quotes a graphic account by Sobieski & Stuart from *Lays of the Deer Forest* (1848) where the authors watched two otters floating downstream almost motionless with the current until they came to a pool in which three salmon were lying.

66

The Otters were steering down the pool, bobbing and flirting the water with their snouts, and now and then ducking their heads till they came [over the salmon]. In an instant, like a flash of light, the fish were gone, and where the Otters had just floated there was nothing but two undulating rings upon the glossy surface. In the next instant there was a rush and swirl in the deep . . . and a long shooting line going down to the rapid, like the ridge which appears above the back fin of a fish in motion. Near the tail of the pool there was another rush and turn, and two long lines of bubbles showed that the Otters were returning. Immediately afterwards the large salmon came out of the water with a spring of more than two yards, and just as he returned, the Otter struck him behind the gills and they disappeared together, leaving a star of bright scales upon the surface . . .

When Ogilby attempted to separate the otter of the north-east coast of Ireland as *L. roensis* he remarked of it that

863

it feeds chiefly on the salmon, and as it is consequently injurious to the fishery, a premium is paid for its destruction.

In western Ireland, near Foxford on the Ballina, Hearns once witnessed an otter engaging itself with two salmon.

540

The first he seized hold of, but after a severe struggle, lasting several minutes, it got away; he went in pursuit of the fish again, and met a second salmon, which after some hard work in a rapid stream he succeeded in mastering, and carried to the weirs, where he left it on a wall. He then immediately returned to the spot where he had lost the first . . . and as it was not able this time to make any fight owing to its previous injuries, the otter carried him off to where he had the other . . .

An account in *The Field* for 1886 mentions an otter apparently swimming across the Menai Straits and seen to have a salmon in its mouth.

83

Apart from countless assertions that otters are great predators of salmon the only other direct reference of this sort I have found is an anonymous one of 1862, where the head keeper at Invercauld

56

hooked a fine salmon [and] was much puzzled to account for the most extraordinary movements of the fish while playing him. At last an otter showed his head above water, and bolted off with the fish.

A rather similar account of an otter taking a hooked trout appears in *The Field* for 1869, and there is another in an issue of 1899; Doveton provides a like example, and it may be supposed that in each case the otter detected that the fish was not its usual lively self and attacked it accordingly. Cocks kept both tame and wild otters for over 21 years, and must have known a considerable amount about their habits. In 1890 he writes:

68

229, 356

290

The few instances where a trout has been found partly eaten by an Otter have been so continually talked of that every one has come unconsciously to consider it as almost a common occurrence . . . Probably very few . . . readers are aware how prevalent the salmon-disease (*Saprolegnia ferax*) is in the Thames . . . I can think of no means so effectual for checking the spread of this most fatal fungus as to encourage, by every possible means, the few otters remaining along the river side, who unquestionably remove a large number of these diseased (and highly contagious) fish from the river on account of their being so easy of capture . . . I may mention that I have never found an Otter make any objection to eating a fish affected with the disease, nor any the worse for doing so.

That otters do take trout cannot be denied, and there is a strange example 357 on record where Dunscombe mentions an otter capturing one while being hunted. On occasion, too, a 'rogue' otter will take to raiding fish stews, 1183 generally causing very great damage. Ward, for instance, mentions a case of three otters visiting some yearling fish ponds and killing 2000 fish in one 748 night; another such is noted by Mackenzie (1950), who adds that this latter otter 'had to cross a mill stream abounding with eels and coarse fish' in order to get to the stews.

In 1880 there broke out one of those interminable and uninformed correspondences where each side gets more and more angry and less and less persuasive on the subject of the damage done by otters to fishing interests. On page 734 of *The Field* for that year appears a long article extolling first, the pleasure of killing otters and secondly, stressing the damage they do. 1229 This called forth an interesting answer by Yates, which reads as follows:

I think most of your readers who know anything about the otter will bear me out when I say he chiefly lives on eels and coarse fish, thereby rather benefiting a trout stream. I myself have fished all my life in streams where otters are preserved, and have never seen the remains of a trout, or have heard of any 'mangled victims' being found by the keepers – and this class of men are not slow to make much of such a find, especially if the fishermen they happen to meet on the river have had a bad day's sport.

1108 On this subject, Stephens writes that

keepers and water bailiffs say that otters are sometimes blamed for the work of herons and other predators, including human poachers.

Many authorities assert that the chief enemies of game fish are frogs, eels and pike, and I have never seen this denied – except by those who seek to include the otter in this category. There are many accounts testifying to the 291 otter's preference for these predators. Thus Collier writes:

There are no creatures of which otters are fonder than Frogs . . . [which] will devour more fish in the ova stage in a few moments than an otter would kill in a year . . .

68

Collier watched an otter

travelling up on the bottom of the river ... which instead of tackling several trout which lay lazily in its path ... contented itself with turning up stone after stone with its snout in search of food of some kind ... all at once I saw it catch an eel ... about a foot long, and with this it seemed content.

An anonymous correspondent to *The Field* in 1950 writes that 'Eels are 115 without any doubt the worst of all enemies of game fish', and goes on to describe a scene on the Tavy, where

... an angler and the water-bailiff were sitting at the tail of a long shallow pool, which held several salmon and scores of sea trout. About 4 p.m. an otter appeared and began to hunt the pool. It paid no attention at all to the game fish, but four times in less than half an hour it came up with an eel in its mouth.

Their fondness for eels sometimes leads to disaster. An anonymous 67 account of 1868 records an otter found dead, choked by an eel half-way down its throat, and there are several cases on record of otters being found drowned in eel bucks, such as the anonymous one which appeared in *The* 78 *Field* in 1881.

Millais says that eels 'seem to be its favourite prey in all waters' and also 798 mentions the otter's fondness for crayfish (*Astacus*) – another predator of fish. In this connection Stephens mentions that 1108

in parts of southern England otters are said to do considerable damage to water-cress beds [*Nasturtium officinale*] by turning over the cress in search of crustaceans.

Harting confirms that 'Otters are particularly fond of frogs' and also refers 531 to eels as being especially liked. He agreed with Isaac Walton in thinking that the otter can scent them under water, and quotes Salvin at some length in support of this view. Salvin himself had affirmed this earlier, in 1859, 425 although Ward (1919) does not believe there is any truth in the assertion. 1183

A long letter appears in an issue of *The Field* of 1861 recording the dis- 50 section of nine otters from a trout stream, all of which were full of eels. The writer adds that at another trout stream which was close to a canal the otters frequented the latter in preference, catching roach (*R. rutilus*) and other coarse fish. Hamilton reports similar findings from the dissection of 508 45 hunted otters.

Coastal otters will even tackle conger eels. Tregarthen writes in 1929 of 1163 otters engaged with a conger estimated to weigh 20 lb., and Macintyre also 747 mentions the conger eel as prey.

Lake Bunyonyi in Uganda has a very large frog population, according to Carpenter in 1925, and used to have a corresponding abundance of otters. 262

It will be recollected that one of the plagues visited upon the Egyptians was the plague of frogs (*Exodus*, 8, 1–7), and it is interesting to learn from Jennison that the Persians still hold that the death of otters brings frogs to life, and that the penalties for killing an otter are 50 in number.

626

Apparently the presence of otters in trout streams does not unduly disturb the fish, contrary to what might have been thought. Wright, for instance, says:

1221

> The best basket of trout I ever had was one night at the Mount Annan island stream, where two otters kept fishing for eels all the time, crossing and recrossing where I was casting my flies, and my catch was more than my creel could conveniently hold.

752 McMaster quotes a letter concerning trout fishing in India, saying

> ... the presence of otters seemed so little to disturb them, that I have taken fish from a pool through which a pack of otters had just passed.

There are several accounts of otters mastering very large pike (*Esox lucius*) such as that of Rees which refers to an incident on the Dee.

951

> Attention was directed to a plunging and plashing in a deep pool a little above Meloch Mill ... he saw a huge pike throw itself nearly out of the water, dragging with it the head and shoulders of a young otter, who had seized the pike by the tail. They then disappeared, but shortly the otter appeared in very shallow water, dragging the fish, who he had now seized under the throat gills, with him.

The observer then showed himself and the otter made off, leaving the pike which weighed 20 lb. (9 kg.). *The Field* of 1887 refers to a pike of 'close upon 23 lb.' being taken by an otter, and the same periodical in 1917 mentions a Swedish account of an otter landing a pike of 25 lb. (11·3 kg.). Gudger quotes an incident related by Salvin of such a contest between a trained Indian otter and a very large pike, which took place near Guildford (*see also* Harting, 1894).

84
102
484

531

> The otter entered the pond, a small but deepish one, and immediately dived. In a short time there was no doubt as to 'a find', as the rough and troubled state of the surface too plainly indicated, for it was like two express trains in full chase of each other. All this lasted but a short time, say about half a minute, and the exertion and coldness of the water, etc., seemed to take a good deal out of the animal, for he not only came up to breathe, but landed, and after rolling himself ... in he went again ... Many rounds like this took place ... until it was varied by the capture of a carp, the head of which he was allowed to eat. His appetite seemed whetted by this, for he became very eager, and whenever he came across the pike a great struggle took place ... Each round told in favour of the otter, and finally the fish [was] towed to land by its tail ... The fish, which proved to be a

female, weighed 20 lbs. 11 ozs. [9.35 kg.], and the weight of the otter is only 18 lbs. Thus ended as well-contested a battle as I ever witnessed, and a sight I would have gone any distance to have seen.

Almost no systematic research seems to have been carried out on the feeding habits of the British otter, and the main source of information remains that published by Stephens in 1957. In the United States, however, rather more work has been done on this subject, and it is to be hoped that more will follow.

1108

Before examining in detail the results of this research it may be useful to mention a few of the difficulties inherent in work of this kind, together with a comment on the relative values of stomach, intestinal and spraint analyses. Lagler & Ostenson (1942) write:

674

> Since fishes and amphibians have relatively large proportions of soft parts, they will become less and less significant in bulk as they pass through the alimentary canal, in spite of some accumulation. Crayfishes and insects have proportionately more indigestible hard parts, and these arthropods come to make up more and more of the volume of food remains as they travel the same course . . .
>
> From the volumetric point of view it is concluded that the findings for the stomachs disclose far better the relative importance of the various food items than do those for intestines . . . Scat [spraint] analyses are least valid in this respect because digestible materials have mostly been absorbed and undigestible remains are accumulated.

Regarding Stephens' own work, she remarks that 'another source of error arises from the specimens examined not being a random sample'. Contributory factors to 'unrandomness' in her case were the irregularity of the supply of spraints and the varying degrees of cooperation met with in different areas (e.g. large numbers of samples from Lancashire and Yorkshire; none from Cheshire and Sussex). Furthermore,

1108

> there has been a bias towards valuable streams and hatcheries, as contacts there have more personal interest in the depredations of otters and such places are better keepered. This bias should also be taken into account.

A further difficulty, and possible source of error, arises in the identification of fish, etc., remains in the spraints. In Stephens' case it did not prove possible to estimate reliably the number of individual fish eaten and therefore different species could only be noted as present or absent; nor was it possible to establish any very informative seasonal trends in feeding habits.

An otter's gullet is extremely small and accordingly its food is very thoroughly chewed up before being swallowed. Buckland examined a very large otter ($32\frac{1}{2}$ lb. – 14·75 kg.) taken at Yarmouth in 1887, and found

226

The oesophagus was 19 inches long, and ... was a very small tube, the size of a ½ inch gas pipe, hardly big enough to admit one's little finger, and only 1¾ inches round.

He also measured the capacity of the stomach, and found it would hold 'rather over three pints of fluid' (say, 1¾ litres).

In order to know on what an otter will feed and the choice it will exercise, it is necessary to know what food is available to it and in what proportions. Unfortunately, this information is often not easy to come by, and in Stephens' case additions to the assumed local fauna were sometimes made as a result of unexpected findings in the spraint analyses. This is not as surprising as might at first appear for an otter may easily travel several miles, from one habitat to an entirely different one, between one meal and the next. Stephens' Table 5, page 83, gives 'A Comparison of Fish Eaten with those Occurring in the Area', but as no indication of relative abundance is given I have not reproduced it. Her own conclusion from this table is that 'otters do not appear to be highly selective feeders'. Similarly, her Table 6 shows the 'Seasonal Distribution of Prey', but the figures appear to me to be largely meaningless, for as Stephens says herself:

1108

Crayfish, for instance, appeared most often in June, but this was because the spraints collected during June came from a stream where crayfish abound.

It is greatly to be hoped that the next writer in this country who proposes to carry out research of this nature will seek statistical guidance both in the method and presentation.

Despite these numerous reservations quite a good picture is built up of the variety and scope of a wild otter's food. The table below

summarises the proportions of the main food types present in spraints and bodies collected from rivers other than the two experimental stretches [referred to later], and excluding fish hatcheries and reservoirs.

I have altered somewhat the original presentation of these figures in this and in subsequent tables, in the interests of clarity.

If the percentage frequencies in the table below are grouped, it will be seen that fish occupy 50·2% (with Salmonidae less than half), crayfish, eels and frogs 29·2%, birds 11·0%, and mammals 9·6%.

Stephens selected two streams for individual attention, the Camlad and the Clettwr, the former in Shropshire and the latter a tributary of the Teifi in Cardiganshire. In each case the spraints were grouped into 'samples' according to dates of collection, although there seems no especial reason for this unusual procedure to have been adopted. This resulted in 30 samples for the Camlad and 22 for the Clettwr, although the former river provided 41 spraints and the latter 132. The figures in her Tables 7 and 8 are, therefore, somewhat distorted and would not be directly comparable with those of the preceding table, even had they been presented in the same form.

Food items	Percentage frequency	Number of occurrences
Salmonidae (salmon fam.)	21·1	62
Esocidae (pike fam.)	0·35	1
Cyprinidae (carp fam.)	11·2	33
Percidae (perch fam.)	3·05	9
Gasterosteidae (stickleback fam.)	7·1	21
Unidentified fish	7·4	22
Astacus pallipes (crayfish)	3·05	9
Anguillidae (eel fam.)	18·35	54
Rana temporaria (frog)	7·8	23
Motacilla cinerea (wagtail)	0·35	1
Turdus merula (blackbird)	0·35	1
C. cinclus (dipper)	0·35	1
Anser sp. (goose)	0·35	1
Anas sp. (duck)	2·4	7
Gallinula chloropus (moorhen)	2·7	8
Podiceps ruficollis (grebe)	0·35	1
Galliformes (game birds)	0·35	1
Unidentified bird	3·8	11
Talpa europaea (mole)	0·35	1
Sorex araneus (shrew)	0·35	1
Oryctolagus cuniculus (rabbit)	3·05	9
Lepus europaeus (hare)	0·35	1
Clethrionomys glareolus (bank vole)	0·7	2
Arvicola amphibius (water vole)	1·4	4
Microtus agrestis (field vole)	2·7	8
Unidentified mammal	0·7	2
	100·0	294

It is necessary to mention that the Camlad was considered by the Fisheries Officer to hold mainly trout, chub, eels, roach and dace, while the Clettwr is mainly a trout stream holding only brown trout, sewin and perhaps a few eels. In these circumstances it is hardly surprising that Stephens found Salmonidae to figure in some 95% of her 'samples' from the Clettwr. She states that most of the bones came from very small fish.

Food-items	Camlad		Clettwr	
	Percentage of samples	Number of occurrences	Percentage of samples	Number of occurrences
Salmonidae	23	7	95·5	21
Cyprinidae	30	9	–	–
Gasterosteidae	40	12	–	–
Unidentified fish	17	5	9·1	2
Astacus	60	18	–	–
Anguillidae	37	11	27·3	6
Rana	17	5	–	–
Anas	17	5	–	–
Gallinula	13	4	–	–
Fulica (coot)	3	1	–	–
Podiceps	3	1	–	–
Unidentified bird	33	10	18·2	4
Oryctolagus	10	3	–	–
Clethrionomys	3	1	–	–
Unidentified vole	–	–	4·5	1
Beetles	10	3	40·9	9
Snails, etc.	7	2	9·1	2
Larvae, etc.	7	2	22·7	5
Small crustacea	–	–	4·5	1

Apart from these food items some miscellaneous matter was also recovered. These are recorded as follows, together with the percentage of samples in which they occurred:

River Camlad	%
Stones and/or earth (including worm casts)	27
Small twigs or pieces of wood	13
Weed, grass, leaf etc.	10
Otter fur	10

River Clettwr	
Stones	77
Earth	23
Twigs or bits of wood	32
Straw	18
Worm casts	9
Grass	54·5
Weed or moss	27
Leaf or buds	4·5
Otter fur	18

Again, for some reason, Stephens presents these two sets of results in different forms.

Of the American accounts, the first is Lagler & Ostenson's publication of 1942, *Early Spring Food of the Otter in Michigan*. For 15 years prior to 1940 the otter (*L. c. canadensis*) had enjoyed year-round protection, but a season was opened on otters in both 1940 and 1941. In the Upper Peninsula the season ran from 1–15 April inclusive in both years; in the Lower Peninsula it extended from 20 March–10 April inclusive in 1940, and from 20 March–3 April inclusive in 1941. In all, 439 otters were trapped, 266 in the first year and 173 in the second. Of these 376 became available for this study, and the stomach and intestine contents were analysed. The following table is based on the contents of 173 stomachs and 220 intestines from both trout waters (187 specimens), and non-trout waters (105), as well as 'those lacking sufficient locality data to permit placement in either of the two previous categories (64)'.

The headings of the columns signify as follows: Stomachs: *s1* number of individuals of each item eaten; *s2* percentage of total volume of food; *s3* percentage frequency of occurrence. Intestines: *i1* number of individuals of each item taken; *i2* average estimated percentage of food by bulk; *i3* percentage frequency of occurrence.

	s1	*s2*	*s3*	*i1*	*i2*	*i3*
GAME AND PAN FISHES						
Trout (*Salvelinus* and *Salmo*)	20			52		
Bullheads (*Ameiurus*)	8			18		
Pike (*Esox lucius*)	8			10		
Perch (*Perca flavescens*)	15			35		
Bass and Sunfish						
(*Ambloplites* and *Lepomis*)	83			166		
TOTALS	134	32·0	29·5	281	15·9	47·3
FORAGE FISHES						
Suckers (*Moxostoma* and						
Catostomus)	21			55		
Minnows (Cyprinidae)	104			214		
Mudminnows (*Umbra limi*)	151			193		
Muddlers (Cottidae)	90			137		
Miscellaneous	70			73		
TOTALS	436	17·6	56·6	672	22·7	76·1

75

	$s1$	$s2$	$s3$	$i1$	$i2$	$i3$
Fish remains		3·0	37·6		13·8	53·2
Frogs (Ranidae)	32			53		
Mudpuppies						
(*Necturus maculosus*)	5			2		
TOTALS	37	16·1	16·2	55	7·5	25·4
Other vertebrates	7	25·8	4·1	1	0·9	1·0
Insects (*Coleoptera* and						
Hemiptera, etc.)	25	0·8	13·3	81	4·2	31·8
Crayfish (*Cambarus*)	64	4·7	35·3	165	35·0	59·2

The considerable proportion of the total volume of stomach contents represented by vertebrates other than fishes and amphibians is due mostly to much of a snowshoe hare (*Lepus americanus*) in one stomach, of a red-shouldered hawk (*Buteo l. lineatus*) in another, and of a goldeneye duck (*Bucephala clangula americana*) in a third. The authors add that these items obviously are not staples in the food of the otter and may or may not have been carrion. They continue:

From the volumetric point of view it is concluded that the findings for the stomachs disclose far better the relative importance of the various food items than do those for intestines (barring the atypical occurrence of bulky flesh noted above).

The following sizes of the prey eaten are given:

Trout – 2¾–9 in.; average 4½ in.
Bullheads average about 5 in.
Pike average about 10 in.
Perch estimated as under 5 in. long.
Bass and sunfishes 2–4 in.
Suckers one estimated at 16 in., remainder averaging about 5 in.
Minnows commonly 1½–5 in.
Mudminnows average a little less than 3 in.
Muddlers about 2½ in.

As mentioned above, the first table combines the results obtained from both trout and non-trout waters. From the first of these categories 95 stomachs and 133 intestines were made available for analysis, the results of which are shown below:

	s1	*s2*	*s3*	*i1*	*i2*	*i3*
GAME AND PAN FISHES		22·7	27·4		16·3	45·9
Trout	19			45		
Bullheads	5			9		
Northern pike	2			7		
Perch	4			26		
Bass and sunfish	17			36		
FORAGE FISHES		35·9	63·2		21·1	69·2
Suckers	16			40		
Minnows	51			158		
Madtoms				1		
Mudminnows	81			72		
Darters	22			5		
Muddlers	69			99		
Sticklebacks	25			41		
Fish remains		3·9	34·7		14·0	49·6
Amphibians	23	25·2	21·1	32	6·4	21·8
Other vertebrates	3	4·5	3·2	1	0·7	0·8
Insects	16	0·4	10·5	61	3·7	26·3
Crayfish	48	7·4	42·1	132	37·8	54·9
Snails				2	trace	0·8

Similarly, the results from non-trout waters were based on the contents of 40 stomachs and 51 intestines, as follows:

	s1	*s2*	*s3*	*i1*	*i2*	*i3*
GAME AND PAN FISHES		65·3	40·0		21·0	41·2
Bullheads	3			5		
Northern pike	4			2		
Perch	7			5		
Bass and sunfish	60			121		
FORAGE FISHES		11·2	45·0		22·2	66·7
Suckers	12			10		
Minnows	38			28		
Mudminnows	20			76		
Darters	2			1		
Muddlers	4			8		
Sticklebacks	8			6		

	s1	s2	s3	i1	i2	i3
Fish remains		2·0	40·0		11·8	47·1
Amphibians		14·4	10·0		8·7	21·6
Frogs	4			10		
Mudpuppies	5			2		
Other vertebrates	2	0·5	5·0			
Insects	16	2·9	25·0	129	7·0	35·3
Crayfish	10	3·7	25·0	37	29·3	51·0

The following systematic names are given for the various food items.

SALMONIDAE

Brook trout	*Salvelinus f. fontinalis*
Brown trout	*Salmo trutta fario*
Coast rainbow trout	*Salmo gairdnerii irideus*

OTHER GAME AND PAN FISHES

Bullheads	*Ameiurus* spp.
Brown bullhead	*A. n. nebulosus*
Northern pike	*Esox lucius*
Yellow perch	*Perca flavescens*

BASS AND SUNFISHES

Pumpkin seeds	*Lepomis gibbosus*
Blue gills	*L. m. macrochirus*
Gt Lakes longear sunfish	*L. megalotis peltastes*
Rock bass	*Ambloplites r. rupestris*

FORAGE FISHES

Suckers	*Moxostoma* and *Catostomus*
Common sucker	*Catostomus c. commersonnii*
Minnows	*Cyprinidae*
Western blacknose dace	*Rhinichthys atratulus meleagris*
Gt Lakes longnose dace	*R. cataractae*
Northern creek chub	*Semotilus a. atromaculatus*
Northern red-belly dace	*Chrosomus eos*
Western gold shiner	*Notemigonus crysoleucas auratus.*
Blackchin shiner	*Notropis heterodon*

FORAGE FISHES

Common shiner	*N. cornutus*
Bluntnose minnow	*Hyborhynchus notatus*
Madtom	*Schilbeodes* sp.
Mudminnow	*Umbra limi*
Darters	Etheostomatinae
Johnny darter	*Boleostoma nigrum*
Barred fantail	*Catonotus f. flabellaris*
Iowa darter	*Poecilichthys exilis*
Muddlers – Cottidae	*Cottus b. bairdii*
Brook stickleback	*Eucalia inconstans*

FISH REMAINS

? pike	*Esox lucius*
? mud pickerel	*E. vermiculatus*
Frogs	Ranidae
Bullfrog	*Rana catesbeiana*
Mudpuppy	*Necturus maculosus*
Crayfish	*Cambarus* spp.

Those specifically determined were mostly *C. virilis* and *C. propinquus*; noted once each were *C. diogenes* and *C. immunis*.

INSECTS

Large beetles (Coleoptera) of the families Dystiscidae, Haliplidae and Gyrinidae, and sizable water bugs (Hemiptera) of the family Belostomatidae (often *Lethocerus*) were found. A few aquatic insect larvae apparently eaten directly were also found and identified as Sialidae and Corydalinae (Neuroptera) and Tipulidae and Leptidae (Diptera).

It is exceedingly difficult to draw many significant conclusions from these three tables. As the authors themselves say:

Our efforts to learn the frequency of feeding and the daily food needs of the otter were unsuccessful. Such information is needed to interpret critically, for management implications, the kinds, relative amounts, numbers, sizes, and frequency of items found in the food.

Certain observations, however, can usefully be made, particularly on the table relating to otters taken from trout waters. The English term 'coarse fish' has no strict parallel in the States, and it is a pity that the figures are not broken down to show the trout content separately in columns *s2, s3, i2* and *i3*. But even when 'game and pan fishes' is taken to include many fish other than trout it will be seen that the percentage volume of food which this heading as a whole provides is still relatively low, being under one-third of the total food residue (and, presumably, intake). For technical reasons explained in the original text the figures appearing in columns *s2* and *i2* are not strictly comparable, that in *s2* being more 'true'. None the less, a good guide is given to the relative extent which different foods 'show up' in the stomach, as opposed to the intestine. The authors make the general comment that

> Forage fishes apparently constitute effective buffers against otter predation for the game and pan species in trout waters, since they are eaten frequently (in 63·2 per cent of the stomachs) in goodly numbers, and in significant bulk.

1209   The above study was followed by Wilson in 1954, whose investigation took place in north-east North Carolina, and was directed towards determining to what extent otters and mink prey on muskrats (*Ondatra zibethicus macrodon*). The otter material examined consisted of 54 digestive tracts, of which 24 contained food, and 61 spraints. It is interesting to note that Wilson observed the food in otter stomachs to be chewed into smaller pieces than food eaten by mink.

The percentage frequency of occurrence of the various classes of prey was found to be as follows: fish 91%; crustaceans (crayfish and blue crab) 39%; insects (water beetles) 6%; birds – one king rail (*Rallus e. elegans*) and two unidentified – 3%; muskrat 1%; clam (Pelecypoda) 1%; bait (from the traps) 1%. The fish, in this case including eels, were divided into 'Forage fishes' and 'Game and pan fishes', and the number of occurrences and the percentage frequency of occurrence of each type were found to be as shown below (based on 10 digestive tracts and 20 spraints):

	Times occurring	%
GAME AND PAN FISHES		
Sunfish	7	15
Catfish	5	11
White perch	3	7
Pickerel (*Esox*)	3	7
Yellow perch	1	1·5
Large mouth bass	1	1·5
FORAGE FISHES		
Carp	5	11
Suckers	5	11
Killifish (Cyprinodontidae)	4	9
Minnows	3	7
Eels (*Anguilla bostoniensis*)	3	7
Shiners	2	4
Mosquito fish (*Gambusia*)	2	4
Bowfin	2	4

Forage fish thus occurred 26 times (57%) and game and pan fishes 20 times (43%). Wilson adds that the digestive tracts of 30 otters (56%) 'contained small quantities of masticated grass and woody vegetation, apparently ingested while the animals were in the traps'. He also makes an observation important to remember when trying to analyse figures of this sort, that

... the exoskeletal remains of a couple of one-ounce crayfish would approach or exceed the residue from a one-pound bass.

It is pointed out that since the primary object of this study was to determine the extent of otter (and mink) predation on muskrats no attempt was made to identify all the fish species. While the majority of the material studied came from Currituck County, the contents of 11 spraints from Pamlico County were principally flounder (Pleuronectidae) and crustaceans.

Wilson's figures, whilst showing the expected variety, are perhaps a little surprising in having such a high percentage frequency of fish as compared to other dietary items, but without figures for the comparative volumes no real conclusion can be drawn from this fact.

The following year saw two further publications on this subject, that by Ryder being an extension of the study by Lagler & Ostenson referred to previously. In this case the material came solely from the Lower Peninsula of Michigan, and was obtained during the 1942–3 trapping season. Seventy-five stomach contents were analysed, of which 54 'contained at least a trace of food'. Of these, 25 were from non-trout waters and 21 from trout waters, the remaining eight being unclassified. In this case Ryder provides the trout content of the 'Game and pan fish' item, saying that [1001, 67] [1001]

trout were found in only 13 per cent of all the stomachs and in only one-third of the stomachs from trout waters. None of the trout were estimated to be of legal length (7 inches) or greater.

The author's tabulated findings are as follows:

	Number of Individuals	Percentage Frequency
Game and pan fishes	38	40·7
Other fishes	203	55·5
Fish remains	–	27·8
Amphibians	16	16·7
Crayfish	13	22·2
Insects	11	13·0

The systematic results, with the numbers of individuals taken, appears below.

GAME AND PAN FISHES

Salmonidae 8
Ameiurus sp. 7
Perca flavescens 4
Lepomis gibbosus 1
L. macrochirus 3
Centrarchidae 14

OTHER FISHES

Petromyzontidae 3
Amia calva 1
Catostomus commersoni 1
Catostomidae 7
Pimephales notatus 1
Notemigonus crysoleucas 3
Campostoma anomalum 1
Chrosomus eos 13
Notropis heterodon 1
N. heterolepis 1
Semotilus atromaculatus 1
Cyprinidae 10
Umbra limi 64
Etheostoma exile 6
Etheostomatinae 2
Cottus sp. 2
Eucalia inconstans 19

AMPHIBIANS

Rana clamitans 1
Rana pipiens 1
Rana sp. 6
Anura 1

CRAYFISH

Orconectes virilis 1
Cambarinae 12
Amphipoda 1

INSECTS

Dystiscidae 1
Coleoptera 9
Ephemeroptera 3
Belostoma sp. 1
Lethocerus sp. 1
L. americanus 2
Notonecta sp. 1
Corixidae 3
Hemiptera 1
Trichoptera 1
Sialis sp. 1
Tabanidae 1
Tipulidae 4
Tendipedidae 1

SPIDERS

Arachnida 3

MOLLUSCS

Pelecypoda 1

Ryder draws a number of general conclusions from his analysis, taken in conjunction with the findings of Lagler & Ostenson (above). 1001
674

1. Apparently the otter captures fish, at least to a certain extent, in proportion to their abundance in the waters. Thus, the relatively numerous forage fishes bear the brunt of the attack, whereas the normally less abundant fishes are not taken so frequently.

2. Fishes are probably captured by the otter in inverse proportion to their swimming ability. Hence the slower swimming mudminnows [*Umbra limi*] and sticklebacks [*Eucalia inconstans*] are captured more frequently than the faster swimming trout.

3. The predatory habits of the otter may actually benefit trout by removing the less desirable (and usually slower moving) competitive and 'noxious' fishes from trout waters.

4. On any but the smallest of streams or trout ponds, the depredations of the otter seem to be insignificant even when a maximum population density of otter is attained.

In 1926 Seton considered Ontario to be 'the best Otter country left in America', and estimated from trapping returns that there might be a maximum of five otters per 40 square miles. An estimate by Bailey at about the same date of the otter population in the National Forests of Oregon and Washington, which is 'considered good Otter country', gave only one otter to 70 square miles, averaging the figures over the whole area.

A further analysis of this sort, published in 1955 by Greer, is by far the most searching and extensive. Greer's study took place in the Thompson Lakes region in north-western Montana, and included Gary's Lake, about 20 miles due north of the Thompson Lakes area 'because it is somewhat isolated ands upports a greater concentration of fur bearers'. Greer estimated that six to eight otters were present in the study area.

In this instance the method used was that of spraint analysis, and a total of 2209 spraints were collected. Of these, the date of deposition was determined for 1374 specimens, and these formed the basis of the investigation. Data were transferred to punched card for sorting and cumulating, the monthly periods being separately grouped into four seasons, as follows: Winter – January, February, March; Spring – April, May, June; Summer – July, August, September; Fall – October, November, December. The data were evaluated by the occurrence of species only; that is to say, the remains of six sunfish in one spraint were recorded as one occurrence.

In the following table the first figure is the number of spraints found to contain the food item in question, while the second (bracketed) figure is the percentage of spraints which contained this item. As the spraints usually contained more than one food item the percentage figures do not total 100.

Number of Spraints

	Winter 99	Spring 596	Summer 604	Fall 75	Total 1374
INVERTEBRATES	26(26·3)	248(41·6)	267(44·2)	25(33·3)	566(41·2)
Aquatic insects	5(5·1)	117(19·6)	116(19·2)	8(10·7)	241(17·5)
Water bug	3(3·0)	2(0·3)	6(1·0)	1(1·3)	12(0·9)
Aquatic beetle	5(5·1)	71(11·9)	52(8·6)	9(12·0)	137(10·0)
Stone-fly nymphs (Plecoptera)	6(6·1)	27(4·5)	14(2·3)	3(4·0)	50(3·6)
Dragon fly	–	8(1·3)	10(1·7)	–	18(1·3)
Dragon-fly nymphs (Odonata)	8(8·1)	47(7·9)	52(8·6)	5(6·7)	112(8·2)
Fresh-water shrimp (*Gammarus*)	4(4·0)	85(14·3)	54(8·9)	8(10·7)	151(11·0)
Millipede	–	6(1·0)	3(0·5)	–	9(0·7)

	Winter	Spring	Summer	Fall	Total
FISHES	99(100)	545(91·4)	561(92·9)	75(100)	1280(93·2)
Trout	29(29·3)	141(23·7)	59(9·8)	25(33·3)	254(18·5)
Sculpin	25(25·3)	122(20·5)	126(20·9)	16(21·3)	289(21·0)
Squawfish	6(6·1)	48(8·1)	53(8·8)	1(1·3)	108(7·9)
Columbia R. chub	21(21·3)	48(8·1)	3(0·5)	5(6·7)	77(5·6)
Sunfish	33(33·3)	281(47·1)	440(72·8)	45(60·0)	799(58·2)
Sucker	59(59·6)	237(39·8)	127(21·0)	34(45·3)	457(33·3)
Whitefish	10(10·1)	27(4·5)	4(0·6)	11(14·7)	51(3·8)
Bass	4(4·0)	30(5·0)	35(5·8)	–	69(5·0)
Perch	7(7·1)	36(6·0)	28(4·6)	4(5·3)	75(5·5)
Shiner	14(14·1)	75(12·6)	14(2·3)	13(17·3)	116(8·4)
AMPHIBIANS	9(9·1)	117(19·6)	118(19·5)	9(12·0)	253(18·4)
Frog	9(9·1)	117(19·6)	116(19·2)	8(10·7)	250(18·2)
Salamander	–	2(0·3)	4(0·7)	1(1·3)	7(0·5)
REPTILES	–	1(0·2)	4(0·7)	–	5(0·4)
Snake	–	1(0·2)	4(0·7)	–	5(0·4)
BIRDS	5(5·1)	40(6·7)	25(4·1)	1(1·3)	71(5·2)
Unknown	1(1·0)	19(3·2)	9(1·5)	–	29(2·1)
Duck	4(4·0)	13(2·2)	14(2·3)	1(1·3)	32(2·3)
Grebe	–	8(1·3)	2(0·2)	–	10(0·7)
MAMMALS	2(2·0)	48(8·1)	32(5·3)	2(2·7)	84(6·1)
Unknown	1(1·0)	3(0·5)	3(0·5)	–	7(0·5)
Otter (trace)	6(6·1)	42(7·0)	72(11·9)	10(13·3)	130(9·5)
Beaver	1(1·0)	7(1·2)	1(0·2)	1(1·3)	10(0·7)
Muskrat	–	33(5·5)	27(4·5)	1(1·3)	61(4·4)
Meadow mouse	–	2(0·3)	–	–	2(0·1)
Shrew	–	1(0·2)	–	–	1(0·1)
Mink	–	1(0·2)	1(0·2)	–	2(0·1)
Ground squirrel	–	1(0·2)	–	–	1(0·1)

The author adds that although Western painted turtles (*Chrysemys picta*) were abundant in the area no trace of any was found in the spraints. A certain incidence of tapeworm was noted, proglottids of *Ligula intestinalis* being recorded from 80 spraints (5·8%), all taken during April to August inclusive; they ranged in size from ⅛ to 1½ in. To a varying extent these were also identified in squawfish (*Ptychocheilus oregonensis*), shiner and perch. Greer found evidence that 14-in. trout were not uncommonly taken,

674
1001 considerably larger than those recorded by Lagler & Ostenson ($4\frac{1}{2}$ in.) or by Ryder (less than 7 in.).

An attempt was made to relate the prey identified to the comparative availability of the food, but for the most part the results of this were inconclusive, probably because

the limited sampling of fish populations by gill netting, electric shocking, and fishing did not necessarily indicate the relative abundance of vulnerable populations.

Despite this, however, the author considers availability to be the prime factor in determining food selection.

With regard to the spraints themselves, Greer writes:

Otter scats [spraints] are readily recognized with experience. The average is approximately $\frac{3}{4}$ inch in diameter and characteristically in 2, 3, or 4 curved segments each about $1\frac{1}{2}$–3 inches long making a total length of 4–7 inches. It is not unusual for droppings to vary in size from above average to a remnant. Fresh droppings were black with a strong characteristic odor ... Heavy mucous was mixed throughout ...

473 (Illustrated by Greer, page 302, figure 2.)

1209 Similarly, Wilson noted that

Otter intestines [are] lined with about one-fourth inch of mucous for protection from fish spines and other sharp-edged foods ...

674 Lagler & Ostenson remark on the difficulty of separating 'this gelatinous, flocculent matter' from food particles, and describe their efforts to dissolve such mucosa as 'futile'.

The results of analysis of the contents of the stomach and intestines of
511 141 otters from the Adirondack region of New York were published by Hamilton in 1961. The general findings are shown in the table below:

	Number of occurrences	Percentage frequency
FISH	99	70·2
Cyprinidae (minnows)	52	35·5
Centrarchidae (bass, sunfish)	17	12·1
Percidae (perch)	13	9·3
Catostomidae (suckers)	9	6·4
Salmonidae (trout, etc.)	7	5·0
Ameiuridae (catfish)	3	2·1
Cottidae (sculpins, muddlers)	3	2·1
Umbridae (mudminnows)	2	1·4
Esocidae (pike, pickerel)	1	0·7
Undetermined fish	19	12·8

	Number of occurrences	Percentage frequency
Crayfish	49	34·7
Amphibia	35	24·8
Insects	19	13·5
Mammals	6	4·3
Birds	1	0·7

The author comments that frogs, chiefly *Rana clamitans*, occurred in 27 otters, while tadpoles had been eaten by six. A very large number of aquatic insects were found and these were not thought to have been taken originally by fish. The majority were recovered in midwinter and included large stonefly nymphs (*Perla*), tipulid larvae, dystiscid beetles, larvae of the sialid *Chauliodes*, and caddis worms. Muskrat remains were found in two cases while those of a smoky shrew (*Sorex fumeus*), a field mouse (*Microtus pennsylvanicus*), a red-backed mouse (*Clethrionomys gapperi*), and a mink (*Mustela vison*) were each found once. Crow feathers in one instance may have been carrion, but evidence of an otter preying on a partridge is given. No predation on beavers was noted although many of the otters taken had come from inhabited beaver ponds.

The most recent food study is that published by Sheldon & Toll in 1964. 1064 This involved the analysis of 517 spraints taken from the shores and islands of the Quabbin Reservoir in central Massachusetts from 1955 to 1957. It was estimated that a minimum of 12 otters was resident in the reservoir which covered 25,000 acres.

The fish population was sampled both by rotenone poisoning and fyke netting, but the authors state:

Because rotenone sampling occurred for only 2 or 3 hours a summer in any one cove, and fyke nets were set particularly for the salmonoids, the figures [below] cannot be considered valid indicators of relative abundance of the different species.

Species	Fyke net captures		Cove poisoning	
	Number of fish	Total weight in lb.	Number of fish	Total weight in lb.
Yellow perch	439	84·1	1178	57·9
Pumpkinseed	27	2·8	1629	46·5
Largemouth bass	21	6·1	5048	35·3
Bluegill	4	1·1	1712	31·3

| | Fyke net captures | | Cove poisoning | |
Species	Number of fish	Total weight in lb.	Number of fish	Total weight in lb.
Brown bullhead	4	1·4	555	29·8
Pickerel	46	38·9	1133	29·5
Golden shiner	31	6·5	558	26·6
White sucker	31	39·1	80	14·8
Spottail shiner	–	–	650	7·1
Brook trout	–	–	19	4·2
Redbreast sunfish	16	1·6	178	6·0
White perch	323	114·1	37	2·6
Banded killifish	–	–	418	2·0
Bridled shiner	–	–	639	1·2
Brown trout	11	41·2	4	0·8
Rock bass	1	0·5	4	0·7
Johnny darter	–	–	56	0·6
Lake trout	12	22·3	–	–
Fallfish	38	18·1	–	–
Walleye	3	3·3	–	–

The following scientific names are given: brook trout *Salvelinus fontinalis*; brown trout *Salmo trutta*; lake trout *Salvelinus namaycush*; yellow perch *Perca flavescens*; white perch *Roccus americanus*; white sucker *Catastomus commersoni*; golden shiner *Notemigonus crysoleucas*; chain pickerel *Esox niger*.

The table on page 89 shows the frequency of occurrence of food items to the nearest per cent, in the 517 spraints analysed.

It is pointed out that the relatively small showing of bullheads (*Ictalurus nebulosus*) in this table may not be representative owing to their lack of scales and hence the absence of these in the spraints. The otters' fondness for blueberries [*Vaccinium corymbosum*] may also be noted.

The authors remark:

It is of interest that no remains of salmonoids were found in the otter scats, suggesting that otters do not prey on trout when other warm water fishes are more readily available.

1001

The conclusions here are much the same as those of Ryder (above): that fishes preyed on by otters are in direct proportion to their abundance and in inverse proportion to the fishes' swimming ability.

None of the aforementioned authors mentions the size of the stomach or

the length of the intestine. Regarding the first, Buckland has already been 226
quoted as giving the capacity as 'rather over 3 pints of fluid'. Harting gives 531
the length of the intestine in the European race as 10 ft., 10 in. (330 cm.) in
an example examined by MacGillivray; Cantor (1846) gives 9 ft., 1 in. (277 260
cm.) for *L. sumatrana*, and Weber (1890–91) 6 ft. 5 in. (196 cm.) for the 1194
small clawless '*Lutra leptonyx*' – i.e. *Amblonyx cinerea*; for this same genus
Macalister gives 9 ft. 8 in. (294 cm.). 735

Even with all the studies that are now available, it is impossible to be
dogmatic about 'the food of the otter'. Otters are undoubtedly more omnivorous than was thought to be the case not so many years ago, and while

Number of Spraints

Season	Winter	Spring	Summer	Fall	Total
	102	73	226	116	517

FOOD ITEMS

Fishes	99	90	87	97	92
Invertebrates	34	55	68	53	56
Vegetation	–	–	28	2	13
Mammals*	3	4	4	–	3
Birds*	1	1	1	–	1
Centrarchids	74	26	39	84	54
Yellow perch	48	64	62	30	53
White sucker	17	8	4	15	10
Golden shiner	17	–	2	–	4
Chain pickerel	8	1	3	5	4
White perch	2	4	3	3	3
Brown bullhead	1	4	3	2	3
Banded killifish	4	–	3	–	2
Johnny darter	2	–	1	–	1
Crayfish	32	53	48	48	46
Wasp	–	–	24	1	11
Insects*	4	4	10	5	7
Clam or snail	2	–	3	1	2
Blueberry	–	–	28	–	12

* Unidentified.

individual animals probably acquire and develop personal preferences,
some of which are most likely to be seasonal, relative availability (and vul-
nerability) of suitable prey can almost certainly be selected as the chief
factor determining the choice of food. For instance, it may be noticed in the

last table that the frequency with which mammals are taken is highest in spring and summer, when presumably the young of the various species are at their most defenceless.

To what extent may a valid claim be made that otters ('rogues' excepted) are of more benefit than harm to the fisherman? An anonymous letter to *The Field* of 1861 points out that the diminution in the number of otters in the streams of the North Riding of Yorkshire had resulted in fewer trout and more eels and coarse fish. Hamilton (1890) writes:

51

508

> Mr. Collier, a Master of Otter Hounds, states that the otter is in reality the trout-angler's friend, from being the deadliest foe to the eel, which is in turn the deadliest enemy of the trout-angler, as eels will prove more harmful to a trout-stream by destroying the spawn than the otters will do by killing the fish.

72 A correspondent to *The Field* of 1873 writes:

> Some years ago a fishing club took a length of river. They 'put on' keepers who killed the otters ... In four years the river was full of pike and shoals of coarse fish might be seen on the gravel beds, feeding voraciously on the trout spawn.

1173 More recently, Vesey-Fitzgerald notes of the otter in his *British Game* (1946):

> Is not the menace on a salmon river that it used to be thought. Kills a great many eels, and certainly does more good than harm. Does not merit the serious consideration of the game preserver.

1174 Later still (1964) he says:

> The notion that an otter in a trout stream will wreck the fishery is absolute nonsense ... I am quite sure that an otter in the course of a year disturbs a fishery less than does a pack of otter hounds in one afternoon.

1108 Stephens is interesting on this subject, writing that an increasing number of people, including otter-hunters and Scottish keepers, are coming to believe that 'within reasonable limits' the good an otter does outweighs the harm. She goes on to mention experiments both in Sweden and on Lake Windermere in Westmorland which suggest 'that in many cases the fish population benefits from a reduction in numbers', and also states that experiments in America (D.H.Thompson, 1941, *The Fish Production of Inland Streams and Lakes* – not seen by me) showed that

> in Illinois waters hatcheries had a negligible effect on fish yield (by weight), and instead the introduction of predators to overstocked areas was recommended.

Stephens publishes figures for rod-caught salmon on the Towy (South Wales) Fishery District where otters have been protected 'for the past 25 years' – this being written in 1957:

Average number	1926–30	152
	1931–5	279
	1936–40	378
	1941–5	485
	1946–9	602
	1950	920
	1951	1290

Brief, unrelated statistics of this sort are naturally not conclusive, but at least they seem to point in the right direction. The nineteenth-century classification of everything that was not 'game' as 'vermin' is still not quite dead, although it may be hoped that it is fast dying as more knowledge becomes available and the public outlook becomes more enlightened. Lancum   676
(1951), writing for the Ministry of Agriculture and Fisheries considers that 'it is doubtful whether, taking the country as a whole, the otter does very much harm to fisheries'. Fitter (1964) writes: 413a

In Poland, as elsewhere in Europe, otters were regarded as the angler's enemies until they were exterminated. Then the fish began to decrease in numbers. Scientists found that the otters had been taking mostly sick fish; when the otters had gone, disease spread rapidly among the fish population and numbers went down. Profiting from the experience of the Poles, the Swiss have removed the otter from the list of so-called harmful animals, and given it federal protection.

Harting's observation of 1894 is still very relevant today: 531

We hear too much of the destruction of Otters. 'Capture of a large Otter' is the heading of a paragraph which appears constantly in the columns of country newspapers; and *cui bono*? Do we hear or read of any corresponding increase of fish? Not at all. If otters were as destructive to fish as some people would have us believe, their unlimited numbers before the invention of shot-guns or steel-traps ought to have resulted in the destruction of all the fish in our rivers. But all reflective persons know nothing of the sort has happened.

As Sir Harry Johnston wrote: 635

Fish are so common and otters are so rare . . .

Chapter 3

The Otter in Captivity

I have kept of them tame, and know their natures. All's Well, ii.5.50

WE passed, to my surprise, a row of no less than nine or ten large and very beautiful otters . . . tethered with straw collars and long strings to bamboo stakes on the banks . . . Some were swimming about at the full extent of their strings, or lying half in and half out of the water; others were rolling themselves in the sun on the sandy bank, uttering a shrill whistling noise as if in play. I was told that most of the fishermen in this neighbourhood kept one or more of these animals, who were almost as tame as Dogs, and of great use in fishing; sometimes driving the shoals into the nets, sometimes bringing out the large fish with their teeth. I was much pleased and interested with the sight. It has always been a fancy of mine that the poor creatures whom we waste and persecute to death, for no cause but the gratification of our cruelty, might by reasonable treatment be made the sources of abundant amusement and advantage to us . . . the simple Hindoo shows here a better taste and judgment than half the Otter hunting . . . gentry of England.

[541] So wrote Bishop Heber in the early days of the nineteenth century, and there is no doubt that many people, both before and after the good Bishop, have considered that to keep an otter might be of 'amusement and advantage'.

[134] The great Audubon, writing 'three miles from Liverpool' in 1826, described his picture of an otter in a trap as his favourite subject, but in later years one likes to think that he became less partial to it – quite apart from the fact that the teeth are drawn most inaccurately – having by then, as he [133] tells us, domesticated the otter on two occasions.

Otters when caught young are easily tamed, [he tells us], and although their gait is ungainly, will follow their owners about, and at times are quite playful . . . The individuals had been captured when quite young, and in the space of two or three days became as tame and gentle as the young of the domestic dog . . . They became so attached to us, that at the moment of their entrance into our study they commenced crawling into our lap – mounting our table, romping among the

92

books and writing materials, and not unfrequently upsetting our inkstand, and deranging our papers.

The French naturalist Buffon was not so successful; but then he does not seem to have been very partial to otters, for he says: [227]

As a rule young animals are attractive, but young otters are uglier than grown up ones. Their heads are badly made with the ears placed low down, their eyes are too small, they have a gloomy expression and are awkward of movement; their appearance is mean, their cry mechanical and continual . . . Those which I wished to tame tried to bite me, even when still only taking milk and not yet strong enough to chew fish; after a few days they became more tractable, perhaps only because they were ill and feeble; far from being easily domesticated, all those I tried to bring up died at an early age . . .

Millais also kept an otter, but his seems to have been more boisterous, for it [798]

. . . had by the following morning explored every nook and cranny in the whole room. It had even surveyed the mantlepiece and knocked a lot of bottles off the upper shelves of the room. In fact it visited parts of the room which none but an animal possessed of great leaping powers and agility could have reached.

Maxwell has well described the otter's almost uncanny ability in this respect: [777]

She . . . began to explore, briskly and impatiently . . . Having exhausted the possibilities of floor level she moved upwards, displaying a degree of acrobatic power that appeared hardly credible. In the same way that water finds its way downward between and around all obstacles by force of gravity, so she appeared to be borne upward by some like but contrary force concealed within her. High on the shelves she stepped daintily and gracefully amongst the bottles and tins and groceries; finding little to her liking, she returned to the floor with the same sinuously effortless movements . . .

Heinemann speaks of his pet otter being [544]

most mischievous and playful in the house, tearing and shaking rugs and curtains, and delighting to get in behind the books in my bookcase and turn them all out on the floor.

My own otters have all had this passion for disarranging books (see plate 13) and there is no doubt that otters and libraries do not go well together. In many ways it might seem preferable to keep one's otters strictly out of doors, but provided that at least one room is suitably adapted for their use and entertainment they need not, and should not, be excluded from the house. Such an adaptation would include providing furnishing materials which can stand up to a great deal of water and a fair degree of rough usage;

electric flexes which are encased in thick plastic hosepipe; a door adapted like that of a stable, with the upper half capable of being opened while the lower remains closed; an inaccessible telephone; a secure grille across the fireplace, not so much to prevent the otters burning themselves as to discourage them from drying themselves in the ash if the fire is not lit; and a complete absence of breakable ornaments. If it can so be arranged that the top surface of all furniture is some five feet above floor level, and that anything normally moveable is made immoveable in advance, then so much the better.

697
1060
516

It is difficult to overestimate the strength of an otter. Lett described it as 'perhaps the strongest and most muscular animal of its size living'. Seton, quoting Hardy, writes that

... no one who has not seen it would believe how an otter can twist the links of a chain which has no swivel in it. I have seen a chain which seemed strong enough to hold a Horse, broken by an otter.

777

Maxwell mentions his Scottish otters moving rocks which weighed some 60 or 70 lb., and I have watched my own Canadian pair shoulder aside a massive mahogany desk without apparent effort. Similarly, out of doors they will put their noses beneath vast logs and shift them about their enclosure; this method, when applied to the heaviest logs, induces sneezing.

Bearing in mind the relatively small size of both the European and the North American otter, one wonders what would be the strength of the Giant Brazilian otter, should it choose to exert itself. Although they are now very scarce, having been ruthlessly hunted for their fur, domesticated

1038

examples used not to be uncommon in South America, and Schomburgk mentions that as long ago as the middle of the eighteenth century Abbé Ricardo, 'in order to study their manners the more effectively, caused a large cage pond to be erected in Caraccas'. He adds that

the Indians know ... how to surprise the young ones, who are then taken home alive, and become in a short time so tractable that they follow their masters like dogs. I have seen them frequently in the Indian cabins, where they were fed on fish, meat, and fruits. In two different instances I possessed one myself, and they both met with an untimely death ...

597

Azara, in Hunter's translation, gives quite a long account of the smaller form of the South American giant otter (*P. b. paranensis*), saying that a neighbour of his

... purchased a young whelp, which, when six months old, was 34 inches in length, and was allowed to run about loose in the house, being fed on fish, flesh, bread, mandioca [manioc, or cassava], and other articles, which it eat [*sic*] without repugnance, although it preferred fish: it used to stroll into the street, and return; it recognized the persons living in the house, and accompanied them like a dog, although it was almost immediately wearied, owing to the shortness of its legs; it understood, and approached when called by name; it amused itself with dogs and cats, as well as with their masters, although caution was necessary, for it bit intolerably; it never attacked the poultry, nor any other animal except sucking pigs . . . I have possessed eight of these animals.

It is perhaps worth pointing out that the French translation of 1801 – which appears to antedate the original Spanish edition of 1802 – suggests that this otter was rather more unapproachable than Hunter makes out, for Moreau-Saint-Méry writes that she   824

jouoit avec les chiens et les chats; mais que, comme elle mordoit d'une manière insupportable, personne ne la prenoit sur soi, et que, pour la même raison, ses maîtres ne badinoient point avec elle . . .

Azara's original text reads: 136

. . . jugaba con los Perros y Gatos, y tambien con sus dueños, aunque rara vez, porque mordia mas que sufriblemente . . .

Rengger also had a young otter of this subspecies, a male, which he ob-   956
tained at two months old.

The first two weeks in captivity it was refractory and bit when anyone tried to handle it; however, this did not stop it eating in the presence of a human being. I reared it on fish, raw meat, milk and water. It gradually became so tame that after a period of two months I was able to let it run about freely outside without its seeking to escape. It played with its keeper and with cats and dogs, obeyed the keeper's call and followed him about in the house. It did not harm the poultry nor other domestic animals. As soon as it was let out, it usually visited the water-tank sunk in one corner of the courtyard and bathed there for some time. If a live fish was then thrown into the tank, it would catch it in a flash and leave the water in order to eat its prey on dry land. I often took the fish it had caught from its mouth without fuss and threw it back into the water, whereupon the otter would retrieve it instantly . . .

I have been unsuccessful in tracing any details of the Abbé's 'large cage pond' and do not know how large it was. Ashbrook, who attempted to farm   131
North American otters for their fur, suggests that a pen from 40 to 60 ft. square is ample for a pair, and recommends that such an enclosure be built in a timbered area with a stream running through it, adding that if pools 6 to 8 ft. deep and about 15 to 25 ft. across do not already exist, then these will have to be made. He further stipulates heavy woven wire being erected to a height 4 ft. above the average snowfall level (the Detroit Zoo allows for   618

2 ft. of snow and has a 7 ft. wall) with a 16 in. galvanized overhang at the top; the bottom of the fence is buried in the ground to a depth of 1 ft.

142 (Bailey also mentions the fur-farming of otters, but owing to their relatively slow rate of reproduction – especially in North America – and the complications of their diet, I am not aware that this activity has ever been practised successfully, at least for any length of time.)

318   Curtis illustrates an excellent design for an otter enclosure, as used at the Fort Worth Zoological Park, which incorporates a glass-sided tank for underwater viewing, but one wishes it could all have been somewhat

1074 larger. A rather similar arrangement is used at the Toledo Zoo, Ohio.

The most usual mistake is to provide too small an area of *land*. Otters are amphibious rather than aquatic and spend a great deal of time on land drying and grooming themselves, playing and exploring. I have observed that captive otters with sores or cracks in the skin of their feet and tails have nearly all been kept in an enclosure with insufficient dry land.

From the point of view of zoological gardens otters are undoubtedly best kept at least in pairs, although several females can be housed successfully with one male. Unless a pair or more is kept, otters in zoos very frequently become bored and listless. In any event, positive steps should be taken to provide an enclosure with as much variety as possible in the form of branches, hollow logs, rocks, sand and above all constantly running water over a small waterfall. Even a steady jet of water from a pipe goes a long way to prevent boredom, and a happy otter's antics as it plays in and out of the water are a pleasure to watch.

The North American otter is noted for its enjoyment of sliding, and the provision of a slide in the otter's enclosure may well be rewarding. The

446 most celebrated account of this recreation in the wild is that of Godman (1826):

Their favourite sport is *sliding*, and for this purpose in winter the highest ridge of snow is selected, to the top of which the otters scramble, where, lying on the belly, with the forefeet bent backwards, they give themselves an impulse with their hind legs, and swiftly glide head-foremost down the declivity, sometimes for the distance of twenty yards. This sport they continue, apparently with the keenest enjoyment, until fatigue or hunger induces them to desist.

In the summer this amusement is obtained by selecting a spot where the river bank is sloping, has a clayey soil, and the water at its base is of a considerable depth. The otters then remove from the surface, for the breadth of several feet, the sticks, roots, stones and other obstructions, and render the surface as level as possible. They climb up the bank at a less precipitous spot, and starting from the top slip with velocity over the inclining ground, and plump into the water to a depth proportioned to their weight and rapidity of motion. After a few slides and plunges the surface of the clay becomes very smooth and slippery, and the rapid succession of the sliders show [*sic*] how much these animals are delighted by the game . . .

Audubon & Bachman record similar activities; on one occasion the authors watched a pair of otters each 'making twenty-two slides before we disturbed their sportive occupation'. Grinnell, Dixon & Linsdale write that in California such slides [133] [482]

are usually about 8 to 12 inches wide and vary in length from 6 to 25 feet. They are sometimes visible after several months of disuse . . .

Such activities on the part of the European otter seem less frequent, but Pitt records one such sliding party: [914]

With an excited cry of anticipation, a wet, slippery figure made a sudden dash for a cleft in the bank . . . the rest of the party following close upon his heels. Up the bank they scrambled pell-mell, with a chorus of hysterical noises, shoving each other like children in their anxiety to reach the summit first. Father won by a good length, and, folding back his fore-paws, threw himself flat on his chest, and down he went head first with a smooth clean slide into the water. His mate followed suit, and then came the children, patting and scratching each other like kittens in their eagerness to take off first . . . [then] the whole family turned, and with one accord dashed up the bank again. And again – and then again – and yet again was that ridiculous performance repeated . . .

Although Crandall remarks that he has 'never seen [an otter] make proper use of the artificial chutes customarily provided', this may be because their construction was in some way not what the otters required. Best, of the Vancouver Zoo, considers that the angle of the sloping surface should not exceed 45°. My own otters' slide is inclined at approximately 37° and they make constant, though irregular, use of it. It may be, however, that even this angle is too steep, as they invariably slide with their forelegs extended in front of them and not trailing, as is their habit in the snow. [313] [177]

Apart from slides, toys must be provided in the form of floating logs, balls, etc. Such objects will probably be destroyed fairly rapidly and need constant replacement; a small amount of rubber or plastic in the diet appears to do no harm. Otters tend to tire of toys which they are unable, in time, to eat or pull to bits, and a new toy is always played with eagerly.

Pregnant females should be given a choice of two sleeping boxes. One will be preferred for the birth of the cubs, after which both will probably be used alternately. This arrangement enables bedding to be replaced in the empty nest without disturbing the cubs. As soon as the cubs become active it is important that some 'refuge' be provided for the mother where she can get away from them if she wants to, such as a ledge or resting place high enough to be out of the cubs' reach. Failing this they worry her continually and she gets no peace from their demands.

The problem of boredom for captive (single) animals is particularly acute with those which have been household pets and whose owners, possibly no longer able to lead the kind of life which an otter demands, mistakenly give them to zoos. Deprived of the company to which it has become accustomed, such an animal is highly likely to mope to a greater or lesser extent, and after some weeks of fruitless searching amongst the onlookers for the face and voice it knows, may well relapse into almost complete passivity.

773   Maxwell gives a vivid account of what happened when he was forced, for the first time, to leave his otter for a few days and arranged for it to be boarded at the London Zoo:

> I left him in a grim cage . . . and when the door was closed on him and he found himself alone his wails went to my heart . . . On the evening of the next day I telephoned from the north to enquire if he had settled down. Too much, I was told; in fact he had insulated himself from the world by the same deep coma into which he had sunk when shut into a box on the air journey. He had refused all food, and after digging at the iron and cement that enclosed him until his feet bled he had curled up in my sheepskin coat and refused to be roused.

Maxwell at once returned to London, and found

> . . . a lot of dead fish lying about untouched . . . there was water everywhere; the sheepskin jacket was lying in a huddle in the middle of this, and there was no movement anywhere. I came in through the steel-barred door and called his name, but nothing stirred . . . Only when I thrust my hand in beside him until I could touch his face did he begin to awaken, with a slow dazed air as if he were emerging from a trance . . .

A pair of otters give each other comfort and company, but the introduction of a new otter into an existing otter's cage is always a matter of some difficulty. Otters have a highly developed sense of territory and generally
1013   resent very strongly the advent of any stranger. Sányál, writing of his experiences with otters at the Calcutta Zoo, says:

> Otters, unknown to each other, should never be placed together . . . When one is allowed to remain for some time by itself, it becomes very exclusive in its ideas, and strongly objects to the intrusion of strangers.

39   Possibly he had in mind Anderson's experience at the same zoo some few years earlier, who recounts it as follows:

98

Only one otter is exhibited . . . It was intended that a number of otters should have been kept in this place, and two were introduced to it originally, but the enclosure not being quite completed one escaped, and the female that remains has now become so combative and jealous, that it has not been possible to allow any other otter to remain with her. After various efforts had been made to accustom her to a companion, but without success, it was thought that if one were introduced in a cage it would be protected, and she would get accustomed to its presence. So jealous and fierce, however, did she prove, that she at once dragged the cage into the water and held it down as if intending to drown the animal. Otherwise, she is perfectly gentle . . .

The same may happen even if the newcomer is a female and the resident a male. The Battersea Zoo recently tried such an introduction, and only the rapid intervention of the new female's owner – who bravely entered the pool and separated the combatants – prevented the male from drowning his new rival. Even the young are not immune to attack in such circumstances. Harvie-Brown relates how a new young otter soon died from 'the ill-treatment of its older relation', and even Pitt, with her great knowledge of animals, had a similar experience: ^{533} ^{914}

Tom was only a small cub when I got him, quite helpless and unable to defend himself; Moses was two years old, very tame and devoted to me, and of so amiable a disposition that I never thought she could be really nasty to the cub. Yet the first time she saw him, when I was holding him in my arms, she gave a furious growl, sprang up, and tried to seize him . . . there was no doubt she would have killed him if she could have got hold of him . . . it was many weeks before she was reconciled to him . . .

Probably the only way to effect such a reconciliation is to run the two otters in adjacent cages for a considerable period. Cocks used this method with outstanding success, for although he had had his female for six years before he got her a mate, by introducing them 'to each other through the bars of adjoining cages for some weeks' he subsequently persuaded them to breed – the only private individual, so far as I know, to have accomplished the breeding in captivity of the European otter. ^{288}

For the person trying to decide whether to keep one, or more otters the choice – expense apart – may be difficult. One otter tames far more quickly and easily than two and often becomes very devoted, but it is far more demanding of time and attention. Two otters are more than twice as much trouble as one when they are misbehaving, but they do keep each other occupied when they have to be left alone and are a delight to watch playing together. Apart from the comparative slowness of taming a pair (for they keep startling each other and encouraging mutual irrational fears) it is a much more painful business. They play with each other in the roughest possible way and the owner is treated likewise despite their needle-sharp teeth; a singleton can be taught to be gentle quite quickly. (Otters soon learn to react to a sharp 'No!', and may be encouraged to do so with a rolled-up newspaper.) In my view gloves should never be worn when handling otters intended for domestication. The bare hand makes a more immediate 'contact' between owner and animal, and if gloves are worn it will never learn to become gentle. Moreover, with an adult otter no gloves offer any worthwhile protection if it does really bite. An otter bite is always painful, even quite small abrasions tending to smart and ache in a way wholly disproportionate to their size, and a really angry otter can inflict 773 severe damage. On one occasion Maxwell wished to take from his otter an eel which the animal had taken into his (Maxwell's) bed, and put on three pairs of gloves for the purpose,

the outermost being a pair of heavily-padded flying gauntlets . . . He bit just once and let go; the canines of his upper and lower jaws passed through the three layers of glove, through the skin, through muscle and bone, and met in the middle of my hand with an audible crunch . . .

777 Writing three years after this incident Maxwell also tells how one of his Cape clawless otters attacked her keeper and removed the top joints from one finger on each of his hands.

By these accounts I do not necessarily mean to imply that anyone keeping otters will certainly be badly bitten, but they must at least recognize the possibility of this happening and accordingly anticipate the pain and con-1157 siderable swelling that always follows. As Topsel remarked in 1658, 'Otters are most accomplished biters'.

While a single otter generally soon gets greatly attached to its owner I think a pair, however affectionate and trusting, will always prefer each 14 other – which is, after all, as it should be. Pitt writes thus of one of her pet otters whose companion had died:

[She] fretted most pitiably and inconsolably for her sister, and often, to try to comfort her, I have taken her up in my arms and nursed her. Sitting with her thus one day, the otter dropped off asleep, only, as it was plain, to dream of her loss, for as she lay with closed eyes in my arms she sobbed in her sleep, a plaintive little sound, half sob half squeak, and her limbs twitched as if she was running.

1060, 822 Seton, quoting Moore-Wilson writing about her Florida otters, gives a vivid example of this affection:

. . . their devotion to each other was indeed touching. When the one received a whipping for some offense, the mate sat by, crying pitifully, apparently much more affected than the culprit who was receiving the punishment . . . A night came, however, when the gentler one took sick and died. The living one soon realised that something wrong had happened, and tried to arouse the mate by caressing and licking the body. Finding this of no avail, he left the bed, and no amount of coaxing would induce him to return to it. All day long . . . the male called and cried; and when night came his sorrow grew intense . . . the pathos in that 'chirp, chirp' as he hunted for the mate that would never answer, was an exquisite pain to the bystanders . . . Standing erect, with his fore paws holding on to the netting, he would peer out into the night, startled at every quiver of a leaf. Moving a few steps, as if bewildered, he would seek the open space in the yard; and rising on his hind legs, listen with a passionate earnestness, and with an expression so like humanity on his face, that to those who watched, the moment was one of intense grief . . . Every effort was made to interest the sad little creature, but for days he seemed to have only one absorbing thought. The other pair would come to him, and caress him, as was their usual fashion . . . He would turn his little black eyes from one to the other, with a pitiful look of anguish, and quietly walk away. He did not repel; he simply refused to be comforted. When exhausted, he sought some secluded spot, refusing to sleep with his playfellows, as had been his custom . . . Being approached, as he crouched in some corner, he would raise his head, and with a pitying cry, like some human creature, seemed to plead to be let alone with his sorrow. Around his little eyes, and running down his face were tears – the tears of a dumb creature for his mate.

Perhaps Seton is right to accept Manly Hardy's statement: 1060, 516

> When otters are caught in log slide-traps, or kill-heags, other otters quite often cover them up nicely with moss or leaves.

In contrast to this, Pitt has written of her two European otters which   914
were normally very fond of each other but on this occasion had quarrelled:

> When the two otters . . . fell out and fought, it was over twenty-four hours before they quite recovered from the effects of their rage. The trouble was over an eel . . . I found the eel partly eaten and two thoroughly upset otters – upset, that is, as regards their tempers . . . On opening the door . . . out darted Moses; but what a Moses she was! She appeared like a very much drowned rat. She was wet and dirty, and looked as if she had been dragged through a bush backwards. She ran to me, rolled on her back between my feet, and squeaked most piteously . . . I sat down on the grass, and the poor thing came to me, crept under my petticoats, and cried more piteously than ever . . . Aaron, too, looked somewhat dishevelled, but she did not whimper like Moses, yet there was something wrong with her. She did not come near me, but kept at a little distance, circling round in a doubtful manner, but whenever Moses caught a glimpse of her she rolled on her back again, crying . . . Then it dawned on me what the real trouble was – they had quarrelled! They had fallen out over the eel, and had had a real sisterly

scrap . . . At last I shut Aaron up and took Moses for a long walk, keeping her out for an hour or more. On returning Aaron was released, whereupon the two otters lay down upon the grass and faced one another, both giving little sobbing squeaks. For two or three moments they lay thus regarding each other, then simultaneously jumped up and moved a pace nearer, paused and eyed each other doubtfully, and then rushed together, put their paws round each other's neck and rolled hugging on the ground. But even as they rolled together one or the other gave a little sob . . . it was two days before the affair was absolutely forgotten . . .

703   That otters are very affectionate has been shown, and Liers even tells of his Canadian otters defending him:

On one occasion when I was walking with some of my otters through a field, a farmer's dog ran out to attack my Airedale that was also along with us. The otters immediately jumped into the fight and drove the stranger howling from the scene. On another occasion a strange dog attacked me . . . the otters that were loose . . . came charging to my assistance and drove the dog off of the premises.

697   As a rule, otters and dogs get on extremely well, and Lett accounts for this in an unusual way. He writes:

Tame otters are remarkably fond of dogs of every kind. They seem also to possess the power of exercising a strange fascination over the whole canine race . . . When a tame otter meets with a strange dog it advances quietly and insinuatingly towards it with a singular serpent-like motion of the head and neck. When close enough the otter endeavours to smell the nose of the stranger. If the dog undergoes this operation quietly for half a minute it is conquered and immediately transformed into a friend, no matter how hostile or uncertain its first intentions may have been . . .

While I have not observed this reptilian approach to be used by my own otters, there is no doubt that they seem to like dogs and are anxious to be friendly. Certainly they show no signs of fear at the sight of a strange dog, 704   nor any other animal for that matter, and Liers remarks that his otters have tried to make friends not only of dogs, cats and minks, but even bears.

It may be noted here that otters seem to be very susceptible to canine distemper and should accordingly be suitably immunized, using a 'dead' vaccine. They can also catch jaundice and hepatitis from their human companions, and it has been suggested to me that they are not safe from feline panleucopenia. Of 29 otters (of various species) which died in the London Zoo the cause in the case of 13 was ascribed to pneumonia. Abscesses, and perforated ulcers, are not unknown, while a double malignant tumour 1054   of the thyroid and parathyroid is described (and illustrated) by Scott.

I have often been asked how one 'tames' an otter. It seems to me that otters are much less 'wild' than most other wild animals and taming as such is hardly necessary. In the wild state the otter has no natural enemies except man (with a few special exceptions, as will be seen elsewhere) and therefore all that is needed is to secure the animal's confidence and trust, and to teach it to be gentle. Affection will then follow naturally, owing to their remarkably friendly disposition.

After the first day or two, when the animal has settled down after its arrival, as much time as possible should be spent with it. Initially I advise merely sitting – on the ground – in its enclosure, well away from where it sleeps, for prolonged periods, talking to the otter in a reassuring tone of voice. It will very quickly learn individual voices and respond to them. Before long the creature's great natural curiosity will have overcome its timidity. It will then start to explore both its new environment and anyone present, the latter being tested with sharp nips to see what it is made of and how it reacts. It is important at this stage not to frighten the animal by sudden movements, loud noises, or the arrival of strangers. A single young otter will respond to this treatment very quickly, especially if one is always present when it is eating and frequently offers it food by hand. A pocket full of small pieces of raw meat is the easiest way to manage this.

If a direct way from the outdoor enclosure into the house can be arranged, and this access left open whenever one is indoors, then curiosity will again compel the otter to explore and once inside, surrounded by the voices and smells of its new friends, the battle is as good as won. The whole process can be amazingly quick. My wife and I recently took from a dealer a three-to-four-month-old Indian otter which had never been handled, and it was sleeping on her lap (by choice) at the end of the third day after its arrival.

In England, European otter cubs hardly if ever get into the hands of dealers, and virtually all those offered for sale belong to one of the races found in India or adjacent countries. As a rule such an animal has had a long and exhausting journey, been badly housed by the dealer – who has no facilities for otters – and been improperly fed. The same frequently applies to a greater or less extent to those unfortunate cubs found 'abandoned' by their mother or dug out of their holts, which then get handed around from place to place for several days before a suitable home can be found for them.

I know of no published specification for a satisfactory travelling crate for otters, but undoubtedly its overall size should be tailored to the size of the animal or animals fated to occupy it. Too large a crate can be almost as harmful as one which is too small, as the otter gets thrown about inside it during the journey. Probably the best design would be one basically divided into two parts, one-third (provided with suitable bedding) being dark and draught-proof except for its entrance hole, and the other two-thirds open to the air on three sides but with a solid roof and floor. A stout container for water should be secured in the open part of the crate, and if a 2-in.-diameter pipe leads into this from above and protrudes slightly through a hole in the roof, the airline or individual transporting the animal can be instructed to fill the container and the pipe with crushed ice or ice cubes. This will ensure a constant replenishment of clean water for a considerable period. A notice should be prominently attached to the crate regarding this, as well as saying IF DELAYED IN TRANSIT – FEED ONLY RAW HAMBURGER.

Fortunately this product is now fairly easily obtained throughout the world. Otters *en route* should be protected from rain, wind and direct sun. 177 Best remarks that they

have a limited heat tolerance and die immediately if they become over-heated. The exact temperature which is fatal is not known nor is it possible to predict exactly the point at which an otter may be in danger, as it depends on the temperature, the airlessness of the crate, and the degree of distress of each individual animal being shipped.

Crates are best constructed of fairly fine mesh welded wire, with secure fastenings. The enormous strength of an otter, especially if frantic, must not be forgotten. My own experience with a variety of 'tranquillizers' has been wholly unfavourable where otters are concerned.

Before unboxing an otter at its final destination I have ready and laid out in the enclosure as large a variety of food as possible: milk, broken raw eggs, minced raw beef and horsemeat, chopped liver, heart, whiting, mackerel, herrings, sprats and eels. Most of this will probably be wasted, but it helps to persuade a frightened and undernourished creature that life may at last be taking a turn for the better. Having opened the box, one should then immediately *go away* and leave the animal completely undisturbed until it has slept sufficiently to recover from its recent unnatural conditions. Such a sleep may last, on and off, for two or three days, the animal only appearing briefly and at long intervals for further food or water. (For some time 521 after her arrival my first Indian otter would periodically relapse almost into a coma, a sleep so profound that it was possible to handle her without her waking – a liberty she would certainly never have allowed if awake.)

It goes without saying that a suitable sleeping-box should also have been prepared in advance. This should be stoutly built, preferably of 'tongued-and-grooved' wood to keep out draughts, and should have only a small entrance hole, not more than 5 or 6 in. square. This may, of course, have to be enlarged slightly later on when the animal grows. The box should have a hinged lid to facilitate changing the bedding, and a means of keeping this lid shut. It should be propped off the ground on bricks or logs, and put in the shadiest part of the enclosure with its entrance facing away from any prevailing wind. Straw bedding on top of a layer of dry powdered peat serves very well, although fine hay may be preferred to straw if the otter is very small. It is a useful trick to put a piece of worn – unwashed – clothing amongst the bedding to accustom the animal quickly to the smell of its new owner.

If it arrives in a very damp and filthy condition it will soon dry and clean itself in a box of sawdust, and an area of sharp sand in the enclosure, for the same purpose, should always be provided. The water pool should be full, so that the animal can drink and also so that if it falls in, as it almost certainly will, it does not damage itself on the concrete and can get out again. It should be mentioned, however, that Crandall reports the case of a 313 pair of young cubs, which had been born at the Detroit Zoological Park, drowning by accidentally falling into their pool. Accordingly, this Zoo now reduces the water depth to only an inch or two until the young leave the nest, gradually increasing this after they have begun to play in the water, 'usually at about the age of three months'.

My own practice is to house the sleeping-box in a small shed, say 6 ft. by 4 ft., and high enough to stand up in comfortably. The floor of the shed around the box is then covered with a layer of granulated peat, or straw, the reason for this arrangement being that in wet weather the otter has alternative drying material to its own bedding. With young oriental or neotropical otters some heat at night in very cold weather is probably advisable, and a thermostatically controlled infra-red lamp hung some 5 ft. above the floor of the shed will both warm the sleeping-box and ensure a constant supply of dry material on which the otter can rub itself. The lamp should therefore be directed not at the box itself but onto the floor area in front of its entrance. Depending on the weather and how much time the animal spends swimming, the bedding will probably need replacing every three or four days. Usually the otter will itself throw out any bedding that becomes too damp for its liking, but this should not be necessary.

The importance of a dry bed, weatherproof and sheltered from draughts, cannot be over-stressed.

Young otters do not start to swim until they have grown their adult waterproof coat and are some two to three months old. The first pair born at the London Zoo first followed their mother into the water when about eight weeks old, but it was some three months after this that Hunt records 596 his pleasant account of their mother rescuing them:

... the animals were shut up in their sleeping den, but they let themselves out when the pond was but half full of water, and the young ones got into it and were not able to get out without assistance. After they had been in the water some minutes the mother appeared very anxious to get them out and made several attempts to reach them from the side of the pond where she was standing; but this she was not able to do ... After making several attempts ... without success, she plunged into the water to them, and began to play with one of them for a short time, and put her head close to its ears, as if she were making it understand what she meant; the next moment she made a spring out of the pond, with the young one holding on by the fur at the root of the tail with its teeth; having safely landed it, she got the other one out in the same manner. This she did several times during a quarter of an hour, as the young ones kept going into the water as fast as she got them out. Sometimes the young held on by the fur at the sides, at others by that at the tail. As soon as there was sufficient water for her to reach them from the side of the pond, she took hold of them by the ears with her mouth and drew them out ... and led them round the pond close to the fence, and kept chattering to them, as if she was telling them not to go into the pond again.

In order to avoid having to play the mother otter's part myself on this sort of occasion, I have a sloping ramp from a little above water level across and down into the pool for a depth of some six or eight inches, and below this lower end there are concrete steps down to the bottom.

Many writers state that young otters are frightened of the water, but this is not so. They are frightened of swimming, certainly, but love to play in water within their depth; food will frequently be taken onto the sort of ramp just described, and eaten half in, half out of the water. Constant playing on such a ramp soon leads to swimming once the otter is old enough, my first Canadian pair achieving this at three months old. In fact the female was three days ahead of the male in this respect but she was always the undoubted leader of the pair, being bolder, more inquisitive and more intelligent. This pair also had a small waterfall and would spend hours playing in and around it, both before and after they learned to swim.

It is a great mistake to try to force the young otter to swim before it is ready to do so of its own accord. Fatio subjected three young ones in his care to this sort of treatment which they much resented, for he writes:

They were enormously frightened of the water and if, despite their cries, one plunged them into a basin, they emerged very quickly completely soaked ... and in such a temper that they indiscriminately went for any spectators of this forcible bath, man or beast.

I have only come across one account of an otter that appeared genuinely to hate water – possibly because she had been caught before she learnt to

391

swim and was never given the opportunity thereafter until she came into Ward's possession at about two years old. He writes that

1183

> ... on her arrival ... she was savage and frightened, and for two days took no food ... For a week it was impossible to induce her to leave the kennel; then it occurred to my man to pour water on her out of a watering can. The animal so much objected to this procedure that at once she shot out of the kennel and retired to a hole among the rocks on the bank. Here she would lie all day, and only creep out at dusk.
>
> In the pond were brown trout ... from a quarter to half a pound in weight. For three days the otter was given no food, with the idea of seeing whether she would fish for herself ... The pond was then lowered so that there was a small pool with only a foot of water over the fish ... in the end I had to feed her to prevent her from starving ... I then arranged a gradually sloping bank of shingle from the edge of the pond into two feet of water. Dead fish were first placed at the water's edge, then under the surface at increasing depths ... Still the otter made no attempt to swim out to them, but walked along the bottom until she reached the fish ... Now, when alarmed, she did not hide on land, but went into the shallow water under a rock, where she would crouch with only her nostrils above the surface. A month passed, and yet the otter showed no signs of swimming. I then pushed her into three feet of water, and she splashed and scrambled across to the other side of the pond. A day or two after this a friend and I surprised her in the evening; alarmed at the sudden appearance of a stranger, she plunged into the water with a tremendous splash and swam away under the surface ...

One hopes that after this incident her owner's evident frustration was appeased.

I have had a similar experience with an adult Indian otter who resolutely refused to swim; she only did so for the first time when suddenly surprised by a swan which walked up to the side of her enclosure and hissed at her. In my experience, otters that have learnt to swim at the appropriate age will none the less refuse to do so if they are not happy, and the happier they are the more they will swim.

In passing, Maxwell also has noted the otter's curious ability to walk on the bottom under water, remarking that his otter 'was able, as are all otters and seals, to walk on the bottom without buoyancy ...'

773

The pool provided for a tame otter should be as large as possible, and if a natural area of water can be securely fenced this would be ideal. If it is necessary to make an artificial pool this should be constructed in such a way that it can be both emptied and filled without the necessity of entering the enclosure. Apart from the natural debris that accumulates in any outdoor pool, the otters themselves will do all in their power to block up the drain outlet, both with sand and mud carried in inadvertently but also with fish-heads and eel-skins, to say nothing of stones and any toys which are small enough to be wedged tightly into the drainpipe. Such a drain should there-fore have at least a 2 in. diameter, its entrance being protected by a large solid grating properly secured in place. (The sea otter's well known tool-using ability caused Kenyon a lot of trouble in this respect; she kept removing the mesh strainer over the drain in her pool and when it was re-secured with a band of iron and a bolt, 'undaunted, the sea otter pounded the bolt with a rock until she succeeded'.)

652

It should perhaps be added that the drain and its stopcock and that part of the pipe immediately preceding it need to be accessible, so that they can be thawed with a blowlamp if they become frozen.

The enclosure itself should have a double gate, with the two gates wide enough and with sufficient distance between them so that a wheelbarrow may be taken through without difficulty. The gates should not fit too closely either to the ground or to their uprights, or at some juncture the otter's tail or fingers are bound to get caught as a gate is being closed. These gates should have strong bolts top and bottom, workable from either side of the gate.

All these precautions are not so much to prevent the otter escaping as to prevent harm coming to it should it stray unaccompanied. After a little while, when it has become accustomed to its home, it is most unlikely to go far even if it does get out.

630

Jerdon's troubles in this respect with his tame Indian otter were rather the reverse of what might have been expected.

'This otter would follow me in my walks like a dog', he writes,

and amuse itself by a few gambols in the water when it had the opportunity . . . As it grew older it took to going about by itself, and one day found its way to the bazaar, and seized a large fish from a moplah. When resisted, it showed such fight that the rightful owner was fain to drop it. Afterwards it took regularly to this highway style of living, and I had on several occasions to pay for my pet's dinner more than was necessary, so I resolved to get rid of it. I put it in a closed box, and having kept it without food for some time, I conveyed it myself in a boat some 7 or 8 miles off, up some of the numerous backwaters on this coast. I then liber-ated it, and when it had wandered out of sight among some inundated paddy-fields, I returned by boat by a different route. That same evening, about 9 p.m., whilst in the town, about $1\frac{1}{2}$ miles from my house . . . the otter entered the tem-porary shed [where I was], walked across the floor, and came and lay down at my feet!

1124

Swinhoe, who had tame otters on at least two occasions, remarks that one he had in 1867 'was very tame, and followed its keeper about like a dog'. One of my own, indeed, when taken for walks would stay far closer at hand than most dogs and would never let us out of sight for a moment. Salvin reports much the same sort of behaviour with a European otter, while Blanford also confirms the attachment of Indian otters to their masters. Liers, who has probably had more experience with tame North American otters than anyone else, writes that

1005

185

704

... after a short time [they] became so attached to their human friends and their new home that they make no attempt to leave, even when the gates to their pens are left open ... Occasionally one strays away, and they have been gone for as long as eleven days. However, they seem to be very glad to rejoin me, and all I usually have to do is to keep searching or waiting in the vicinity of the streams and ponds, and sooner or later we meet ... usually they make such a display of affection that I know they are glad to be back.

In another article, however, Liers rightly points out the great exception to this rule, which is that 'in the breeding season the urge to travel seems to be particularly strong'. From my own very limited experience it is the male who seems the most strongly affected in this way (*see* page 42). In the case of one pair of mine who escaped during the mating season the female returned of her own accord within 24 hours, and the male attempted to return the following day. Finding the gate shut, however, he returned to the river near by and remained there for a further week. Apparently quite incapable of catching any food for himself – he had been born in captivity – we called him up out of the river every day to be fed, and finally took to feeding him inside a coypu trap. At the end of the eighth day we closed this with him in the middle of his supper, and carried him home.

703

One of the major problems with domesticated otters in the past has been that of proper feeding, but now, thanks again to Liers, we have a diet that works most satisfactorily and to which I shall refer in more detail later. Previously, the feeding of otters in captivity seems to have been rather a hit-or-miss affair.

Riviere raised two young European otter cubs successfully on a diet of soaked dog biscuit and milk, fresh fish, and raw rabbit. A very young (five to six weeks old) North American otter was fed on 'about $1\frac{1}{2}$ quarts of bread pudding' each day, and lived to be over 14 years old. Day writes of a Mr Thomas who 'had some otters (*Lutra nair*) of various sizes, which he raised from babyhood ... When very young each consumed about one hundred frogs (*Rana cyanophlyctis*) daily'. Day remarks that when the otters were about two-thirds grown, and these small frogs were difficult to procure,

968

1030

336

'they were having six to eight large bull-frogs (*Rana tigrina*) daily'. He also tried feeding them a live rat, but 'although they ran up to it, they did not

1060 attempt to do it any injury'. Seton, however, reports that 'after frequent trials, I could never induce either of my pet otters to eat a frog', although 'they were always ready for fish, fresh or salt, of any kind, raw or cooked . . . When fish was not available, both of them were satisfied with bread and

133 milk, meat or potatoes'. Audubon's otters, to which I have already referred, preferred boiled corn-meal when they were young and boiled beef when older. A tame otter that once belonged to the lay sisters of the Abbey of

626 St Jean le Grand was reared

> on soup, vegetables, and kitchen scraps of all sorts; it would not touch cooked fish, or raw, if not freshly caught. It slept on their beds at night and by day in a chair. There was a bowl of water for its especial use, wherein it would dabble its head and shoulders . . .

475 Griffith relates that F. Cuvier had several otters – 'which were very familiar' – and were kept on bread and milk; indeed, bread and milk seems to have been the recognized food for domestic otters in the last century,

178 sometimes varied by 'hasty-pudding', as related by Bewick.

531 A Scottish otter in Wigtonshire 'evinced a great fondness for goose-
549 berries'; two young clawless Indian otters were weaned on to mincemeat
1108 and guppies; according to Stephens, eight tame otters once kept at Clitheroe
918 preferred roast beef above all else. Pitt's otters were given half a rabbit each a day, complete with fur, bones, and 'innards'; Hoffman has told me (*in*
1124 *litt.*) of zoo otters which died of a surfeit of peanuts; and Swinhoe remarked of one of his otters that 'it would eat almost anything in the way of food'.

704 Liers writes that his otters are partial to snakes, and adds:

> When they find a big snake, they chatter, call for help, and circle warily until the snake strikes several times. Then they kill it by biting the head. If hungry, they eat many of the snakes they kill.

91 Similarly, an anonymous writer in *The Field* had a half-grown otter whose

> . . . greatest delight was to catch a [water] snake, which it seized close behind the head, and brought out onto the bank. As soon as the snake was killed he began to eat it at once, and would finish it off. Often the snake was much longer than the otter. When he had a snake he was very savage, growled, and hissed, and would not let me touch him till it was quite finished. When eating a fish it was not nearly so savage in any way . . . it seemed far to prefer a snake to a fish.

Elsewhere the otter's natural food is examined in some detail, and its range is indeed a very wide one. In captivity, however, when all the choice bits and pieces which an otter might pick up on its travels are no longer available to it, a nutritious and balanced diet is essential.

Very young otter cubs are notoriously difficult to hand-rear successfully, but in my view the majority of failures have probably been caused by giving them cow's milk. It is true that this has sometimes been successful, as in the case of Heinemann, who fed a mixture of lukewarm milk and water, one part of milk to three of water. Cerva, too, raised three otter cubs, which he had acquired when they were still half blind, on undiluted cow's milk, supplementing this with weak milky coffee to which meal flour or white bread was added, when they were five to six weeks old. ⁵⁴⁴ ²⁷⁰

If possible, a foster-mother is much to be preferred. There are a number of instances on record of dogs acting in this capacity, and the two clawless Indian otter cubs already mentioned were initially reared in this way. An anonymous account of a baby otter caught in the Pyrenees was similarly successful and Bewick relates a further case, as does Gurney – although in this last instance the otter died on weaning. Hurley, who had much experience of otters, once fostered a pair of very young ones with a cat which was rearing kittens at the time, and an anonymous account in *The Field* also mentions three cubs, 'not more than a few days old', being successfully reared by a cat. ⁵⁴⁹ ⁹⁶ ^{178, 491} ⁵⁹⁸ ⁹⁹

Liers has remarked that otter milk contains 41% butter fat, and Miller-Ben-Shaul has published the following analysis: ⁷⁰⁷ ⁸⁰⁷

Water	Fat	Protein	Carbohydrates	Ash
62·0	24·0	11·0	0·1	0·75

She also remarks that with all animals which spend a high proportion of their time in cold water, or where the young are frequently made wet by the mother returning from the water, the milk is very concentrated and has an extremely high fat content.

For comparison's sake I show below an analysis of various other forms of milk, taken from Maynard: ⁷⁸¹

	Water	Fat	Protein	Ash	Lactose	Calcium	Phosphorus	Calories
(1)	87·2	3·7	3·5	0·72	4·9	0·121	0·095	74
(2)	82·7	6·4	5·5	0·92	4·7	0·201	0·168	109
(3)	86·5	4·0	3·6	0·81	5·1	0·131	0·104	79
(4)	89·0	1·6	2·7	0·51	6·1	–	–	54
(5)	82·0	6·8	6·2	0·96	–	0·252	0·151	113
(6)	87·5	4·4	1·0	0·21	7·0	0·035	0·013	70
(7)	75·4	9·6	11·2	0·73	3·1	–	–	163

These figures relate respectively to: (1) Cow; (2) Sheep; (3) Goat; (4) Mare; (5) Sow; (6) Woman; (7) Bitch. The marked difference of these from the otter milk analysis will be readily apparent.

Failing a foster-mother being available, a number of successful bottle-feeding formulae have now been worked out.

522

With his North American otters, Hoffman (*in litt.*) used 'Carnation' or homogenized milk as a base, and to each 8 oz. (249 gm.) of this added one drop of 'Tri-vi-sol', the yolk of one raw egg, and one teaspoonful of lime water. Shavings of lean, raw horse-meat are also offered right from the start, these being prepared by scraping the edge of a sharp knife across a joint of horse and wiping the blade on a finger. The mix is fed every four hours at blood heat from six weeks old (the age at which Hoffman takes from the parent those cubs he wishes to rear by hand), and then on demand. Hoffman assured me that when cubs reared in this way are later reunited with their naturally reared litter-mates there is no difference in size, weight or condition.

280

Clapham mentions a cub believed to be a fortnight old when first taken, which grew very thin on milk and water and was accordingly put onto 'Mellins' as mixed for a new-born child. It grew from 14 oz. (435 gm.) at about a month old to just under 2 lb. (900 gm.) at a little over two months.

Andrewes (*in litt.*) successfully reared a very small English otter cub, only 5 in. (127 mm.) in overall length on arrival (see plate 7), beginning with glucose and boiled water every 2 hours for 16 hours, plus one drop of cod-liver oil. This was followed for the next 36 hours by 'Lactol' made up as for small puppies, one-half of a fluid ounce (14·2 c.c.) being given every two hours. After this, the 'Lactol' was given on demand, up to the time that the cub's eyes started to open. Then 'Ostermilk' was substituted for 'Lactol', being made up as for human babies, with glucose and a drop of halibut-liver oil added. Weaning finally took place onto finely minced beef, chopped raw fish, brown bread, 'Ostermilk' and halibut-liver oil, at six to eight weeks of age.

An African clawless otter raised by the Macdonalds (*in litt.*), about four weeks old on arrival, was reared on a mixture of one part canned evaporated milk to two parts boiled water; this was given two-hourly, or on demand during the night, at a little above body heat (a European otter's body temperature is around 102°F. or 38·9°C. at about six months of age). The proportion of water in the above mix was increased if diarrhoea occurred. This female was weaned at about three months onto live fish, butter, eggs and fresh liver.

1108

Wedekind (*in litt.*) raised three very small cubs of *Aonyx* and kept careful records of their progress; it is from her notes that the following information is taken. Figures 2 and 3 show the rate of growth, from approximately two weeks old up to some four months, to be about 2 oz. (62 gm.) per day. All three cubs came from the Kafue River in Zambia (Northern Rhodesia) and were all born in May. The cubs were still toothless when first taken.

The first cub was raised on 'Cowlac' at half baby strength, with the addition of two drops of cod-liver oil. This was given two-hourly, 1½ oz. at a time, for the first few days. During this time 14–16 oz. were taken every 24 hours. At about three weeks of age the cub was taking up to 22 oz. daily,

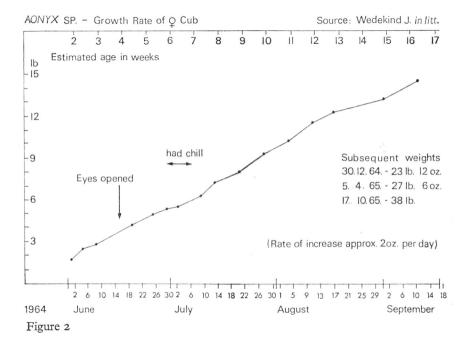

AONYX SP. – Growth Rate of ♀ Cub   Source: Wedekind J. *in litt.*

Figure 2

and from this time onwards the strength and quantity of the milk was slowly increased and both glucose and vitamins A and D were added. By six weeks old the number of feeds was reduced to seven or eight a day and the total quantity of milk consumed had risen to about 50 oz. daily. The first solid food was eaten at about seven weeks. Initially young pike (*Hepsetus odoe*) were preferred on account of their small, soft scales, but later *Mormyrus lacerda* and *Labeo* spp. were chosen while *Tilapia* and *Serranochromis* spp. were acceptable. *Clarias* later became a favourite with one female. Contrary to what might have been expected, eggs were disliked and milk was at once refused if it had the slightest amount of egg beaten into it.

The cubs' eyes opened when they weighed about 4 lb. (1800 gm.), at – apparently – just under four weeks of age. Effective eyesight was two to three weeks developing. Similarly, there was little or no reaction to extraneous noises in the early stages and the first positive sign of this appeared at about six weeks.

The permanent dentition started to appear in the ninth or tenth week, these new teeth erupting behind and between the deciduous ones. These latter were all shed by the end of the eighteenth week.

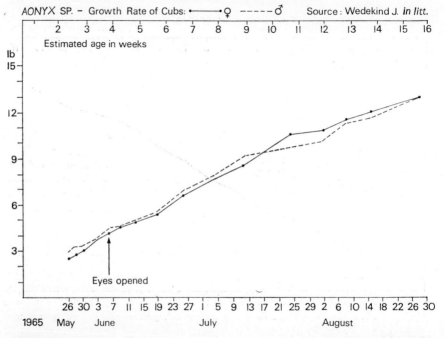

Figure 3

The moult of the baby coat seems to have been a prolonged process. Before the eyes opened the pale smoky-grey fur developed a slight flakiness, akin to dandruff, and shortly after this soft grey guard hairs started to appear. These were twice the length of the original coat and gave the cubs a rather fluffy look. In a fortnight this new fur had darkened considerably but was still very uneven, and it soon became somewhat mottled. These hairs clogged into muddy lumps which were slowly shed, and the final dark adult coat was only attained at about ten months.

671   At the Mysore Zoo, India, Krishna Gowda raises otters on the following diet. Up to one month old: 1 oz. of buffalo milk, 1 oz. of distilled water, one

15. *L. (Lutrogale) perspicillata* ♂ and Indian *Lutra lutra* subspp. ♀, at Mole Hall, Widdington, Essex.

16. *L. (Lutrogale) perspicillata* ♂ and Indian *Lutra lutra* subspp. ♀, at the London Zoo.

17. *L. l. nair* ♂, about four months old.

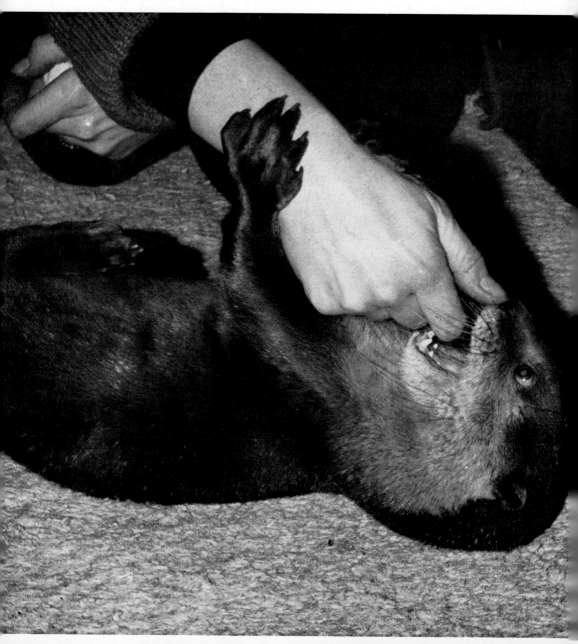

18. *L. l. nair*, adult ♂.

19. *L. l. nair*, adult ♂.

20. *L. l. nair*, adult ♂.

21 (a). *Amblonyx c. cinerea*, from southern Siam. (Photographer unknown.)

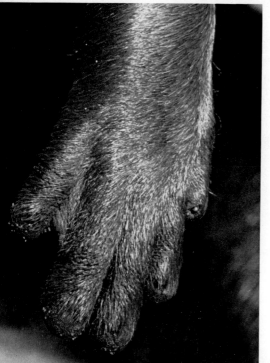

21 (b). Right fore foot of same.

22. *Amblonyx cinerea concolor*, adult ♀.

23. *Amblonyx cinerea concolor*, adult ♀. Note 'girth-marks' behind shoulders caused by fishing harness.

teaspoonful glucose, four times a day; one teaspoonful shark-liver oil, one yeast tablet, once a day. From one to two months old: $1\frac{1}{2}$ oz. (42·6 c.c.) buffalo milk, $1\frac{1}{2}$ oz. distilled water, four times per day; shark-liver oil and yeast as before. From two to three months old: 10 small live fish per day, in addition to the above diet. At three months: $1\frac{1}{2}$ oz. buffalo milk, $1\frac{1}{2}$ oz. distilled water, twice a day; shark-liver oil and yeast as before; a quarter of a kilogram (about $\frac{1}{2}$ lb.) of small live fish per day.

Nair, at the Trivandrum Zoo, raised two cubs, caught when one to two months old, on an interesting variant of the preceding diets. He made a form of 'soup' from 2 oz. of liquid made from boiling mackerel in water, mixed with 1 oz. of boiled milk. This was fed to the cubs when they were hungry, but not less often than five times a day. In this instance bottle feeding continued for four months, and the cubs only began eating small raw fish when they were six months old. [843]

These bottle-feeds are best accomplished with a doll's plastic feeding-bottle, the hole in the teat being enlarged, or with the rubber bulb of an eye-dropper with a hole bored in it, attached to a small medicine bottle. The hole may be made with a red-hot needle.

Baby otters *must* be kept warm, dry and out of draughts. It is most important that after each feed the stomach, abdomen and anus be massaged with a damp finger to assist the bowel movements, this taking the place of the licking a mother would normally give her cub.

Liers gives his mother otters special treatment. [704]

Females that have just given birth are fed abundantly every three hours. For the first feeding I put more whole milk in the mash [recipe below] and add 10% Pablum. Three hours later, I give the animal four ounces [124 gm.] of calf or beef liver. Then comes a feeding of bread and milk; and in another three hours, raw meat. Next, I give the otter a tidbit, like frogs or crayfish. Later, as a nightcap around 9 p.m. comes a regular heavy mixture with Pablum and milk and 2% bone meal.

After weaning, Liers' diet or mash, referred to above, has proved thoroughly effective. This consists of: 74% ground raw horse meat, $\frac{1}{2}$% ground raw liver, 2% bone meal, 8% bran, $\frac{1}{2}$% grated carrots, tomatoes, or lemon or orange juice, 10% raw rolled oats and 5% commercial mink meal. To this is added one teaspoonful of cod-liver oil per day per otter, 1 oz. of brewers' yeast per day per 10 otters, and one raw egg a day for each two otters. This confection is mixed with enough whole liquid milk to make a soft mash. Liers adds that when available 'such tidbits as frogs and crayfish are fed as an enjoyable entree'. [703]

1108   Stephens states that when this diet was tried on the otters at the Berlin Zoo it proved so successful that it was subsequently given to all their fish-eating animals. It is interesting to note, however, that as recently as 1960

1233   the Cologne Zoo did not use this diet for their giant Brazilian otter. Zeller writes that she eats about two kilos (4½ lb.) of food a day, and that

> her favourite foods, in order of preference, are: brightly shining fish; other, less shining fish; heart; horse or beef flesh; poultry; herring; white bread pulped with milk and egg; horse neck fat (only in small quantities). The otter is also given vitamin capsules, mineral salt mixtures and yeast preparations without difficulty, by placing these additives inside the de-gutted fish being offered as food.

He adds that the entrails, especially of the larger fishes, are not eaten.

When she is really hungry, the otter welcomes her food with loud cries. The food is frequently taken to the water pool and is there thrown into the air repeatedly before eventually being eaten to the accompaniment of much growling. Sometimes the otter will circle round and round, crying out, with the fish between her jaws, at the same time hitting the ground with her tail. The growls during eating are similar to the warning call. When the latter is heard, the otter is angry and it is best to keep one's hands out of reach of her jaws.

313   Crandall reports that otters at the New York Zoological Park are fed a daily allowance of 2 lb. butterfish (*Poronotus*), ¼ lb. smelts, ½ lb. whole raw meat, and ½ lb. of a mixture of chopped raw meat, dog meal, bone meal and cod-liver oil.

I have not myself been wholly successful with Liers' diet, probably chiefly because I was unable to obtain in England a mink meal that the otters would readily eat; I also found that both the bran and the cod-liver oil tended to cause diarrhoea. I did, however, try importing from America Kellogg's '1003 Mink Conditioner', which Hoffman used with great success. Although relatively inexpensive at source, the effective price delivered in this country was so prohibitive (over $1.00 per pound weight) that I abandoned it; in addition, the otters did not seem to care for it.

For some years now, therefore, I have been feeding an adaptation of Liers' diet, made as follows: I give two or three meals a day, depending on the animals' appetites, and each consists basically of raw, lean, minced horse meat. Each day to one of these meals is added: eight drops of halibut-liver oil; one half tablet, finely powdered, of 'Osto-Calcium'; two teaspoonfuls of 'Bemax' and one of bonemeal; one adult-sized measure (0·6 ml.) of liquid 'Abidec'; one teaspoonful seaweed powder; and one raw egg. All the above quantities are as for *two* adult otters. If the resulting mixture appears too dry a little fresh milk is added.

The easiest way to prepare this concoction is first to mix the seaweed, calcium, 'Bemax' and bonemeal into the ground meat; then to beat the raw egg and add the halibut-liver oil and 'Abidec' to it, subsequently beating again and then mixing the resulting liquid into the meat.

For variety, two meals in the week are of raw fish, usually herring or mackerel – the former much preferred – or such other coarse fish as can be caught locally and fed live. (Herrings and sprats, which contain thiaminase, are never fed for two consecutive meals.) Finally, and in my view most important of all, during the season when they can be obtained each otter has one or two live eels each day, in addition to the above.

I make no claim that this diet is in any sense a scientific one, but it appears to work very well and the otters like it. An adult North American otter will, at times, eat some 3 lb. of meat a day – although rarely more than 1 lb. at any one meal – and I have calculated that it is impossible to feed one properly for less than about £75 a year (say, $180.00 at $2.40 to £1). The cost can in fact be considerably higher, depending on the varying prices of horse meat and live eels. As an alternative to horse, raw minced beef is very acceptable, although more expensive, but lamb or mutton should never be given to otters as they have a most upsetting effect on the stomach. Additional variety can, however, be provided by mixing in chopped liver or heart and this is useful if an animal suddenly becomes bored with its food and wants a change, as happens from time to time. Otters' appetites are extremely variable, for no apparent reason, although Beecham (*in litt.*) has told me that they seem to be particularly hungry when moulting; my own experience in this country has been that the main periods of acute hunger are those just preceding the moult.

Live eels I consider to play a very important part in a captive otter's well-being. Apart from the fact that they are one of the favourite items of a wild otter's diet, as will be seen elsewhere, I have on many occasions fed a larger quantity of eels than usual to an otter which for some reason seemed a little 'off colour', and the response and improvement has been remarkable in nearly every case. Also worth noting is the fact that live eels help to satisfy an otter's natural instinct to pursue and catch its prey; so do live fish, and any other live food which can conveniently be fed is always acceptable. Young otters have considerable difficulty with the tough skin of eels, and for animals less than about three months old the eels are best decapitated and then skinned before being given to them.

It is important to ensure that the eels have been taken in nets or traps and not on hooks. As it is almost impossible to unhook an eel caught on a line, the line is in consequence simply cut, the hook remaining inside. (Finding

and removing hooks even from dead eels is extremely difficult.) While eel-
hooks are generally large and the otter's gullet small, there is at least one
recorded case of an otter suffering from an *'embarras gastrique'* in the form
of a fish-hook which was swallowed and caused its death.

Otters should be fed at regular hours, as this helps to provide a routine
which may otherwise be lacking in the unnatural circumstances of captivity. Their digestion is extremely fast, and Liers has noted that crayfish are
digested and eliminated in about an hour. It is for this reason that three
meals a day may be necessary; indeed, in the longest summer days I often
give them a fourth 'snack' late in the evening if they seem at all hungry.
(Pitt remarks that 'most of the otters kept in Zoological Gardens are half-
starved'.)

The routine mentioned above will need to be slightly elastic, the animals'
periods of sleeping and waking varying considerably both with the seasons
and sometimes from day to day. Certainly in the winter months they are
less active and in consequence generally, but not always, less hungry. None
the less, each otter should invariably have a bowl of food for itself and not
be forced to share. It is also useful to remember, as Freeman & Salvin found,
that 'Otters are particularly playful after feeding'.

If cared for properly otters have a considerable life span, and although
there are only records for a limited number of species, as Flower remarks 'it
is probable that the life-span is fairly equal in the different forms comprising the genus [*Lutra*]'. The North American otter fed on bread pudding
when young has already been mentioned; this animal was sent when three
years old to the Seattle Zoo, his owner having died, and lived there for a
further $11\frac{1}{2}$ years; 15 to 20 years would seem to be the normal expectation
of life, according to Hooper & Ostenson, but Liers (*in litt.*) records one
female attaining the age of 23.

Burton gives the longevity of the European otter as 15 years, and Flower
provides some detailed records; he also quotes Sitwell (1906), who gives
5 years 3 months as a good life for a British otter, and Cocks (1906) who
mentions 10 years 10 months. Flower records that Frankfurt Zoo kept one
for almost $8\frac{1}{2}$ years; the Jardin des Plantes, Paris, had another for just over
$9\frac{1}{2}$ years; and Basle achieved 11 years, 2 months and 23 days. So far as I am
aware, none of these animals was born in captivity and all must therefore
have been at least slightly older than the ages shown.

Flower also mentions a female Florida otter (*L. c. vaga*) which was in the
National Zoological Park, Washington, D C, for 12 years, 8 months. Despite their reputed delicacy it may be that the Florida race is a long-lived
one, for Crandall records two otters, one of which lived for 17 years, 10

96

704

913

425

419

1030

582

241, 419

313

months 10 days, and the other for 'approximately 19 years'. Both these were in the National Zoological Park. This same zoo maintained an Indian clawless otter (*Amblonyx*) for a little over 10 years, as did also the New York Zoological Park.

Concerning Indian otters, Flower records that a smooth-coated otter *L.* *(L.) perspicillata* lived 11 years 4 months in the Calcutta Zoo and that another of the same species is still alive in the Trivandrum Zoo at almost 15½. Phillips records this same zoo having kept several specimens of *L. l.* *nair* for over 12½ years, and Simon notes a *Lutra lutra* sp. still alive after 22 years there.

In some ways it seems surprising that so many of these otters lived as long as they did, for it seems likely that their feeding was somewhat unscientific. Cunningham writes in 1903:

> Those which were kept in the Zoological Gardens at Alipur were regularly and abundantly supplied with stores of fish, but in spite of this, they always seemed to be in a perfect frenzy of starvation, and ravenously devoured all the very miscellaneous food that was offered by compassionate visitors in the vain attempt to still their clamour.

Writing in 1931, Flower points out that the majority of otters do not thrive well at the London Zoo, saying that

in only about seven instances can it be found that an individual has lived there for over five years . . . the maximum record for London is of a male otter . . . 6y. 9m. 12d.

This is borne out by an earlier set of figures, published by Mitchell in 1911, showing that the average life of 36 European otters in the London Zoo was only 40 months, the maximum being 87 months. The only North American otter this zoo had died after 38 days.

More recent figures are still more depressing. Jarvis & Morris publish figures taken from the records of the London Zoological Society for the years 1930 to 1960. These show that of 19 European otters, 79% died in less than a year; of those that lived for more than a year, the average life span was 24 months; and the maximum individual life span was only 28 months. For species other than the European – although admittedly the numbers are much smaller – the results are little better, the longest lived being an *Amblonyx* which survived five years.

Happy, well-cared-for otters, suitably shown, can be one of the major attractions of any zoological garden, but until the Society in London learns to house (and exhibit) their otters better, and decides to feed them properly, this waste of the members' money and the animals' lives will continue.

The 'simple Hindoo', mentioned earlier, has employed his otters to fish for him for many centuries, and one is tempted to trace the origin of this practice, like that of so many others, to the Chinese.

484 Gudger has published a long and scholarly article on this use of the otter in different parts of the world, and has explored the literature dealing with this subject very thoroughly. He finds the earliest printed account to be that of Sir John Mandeville:

in this land [that part of China south of the Hoang-ho River] thai take a beste that es called Loyres, and thai teche him to ga in to waters and riuers, and alssone he brings oute grete fishchez, als many and as oft as thai will.

Gudger notes that this account is lifted from the travels of Friar Odoric of Pordenone, who was in China about 1323–8. Ramusio's Italian version of Odoric's book, translated by Yule (1913), is quoted by Gudger as follows:

Mine host . . . took us to where . . . we found many boats, and there was one of them employed in fishing by aid of a certain fish [*sic*] called *marigione*. The host had another such, and this he took and kept it by a cord attached to a fine collar. And this indeed is a creature that we have seen in our own seas, where many call it a *sea-calf*. It had the muzzle and neck like a fox's, and the forepaws like a dog's, but the toes longer, and the hind feet like a duck's [i.e. webbed], and the tail with the rest of the body like a fish's. Mine host made him go in the water, and he began to catch quantities of fish with his mouth, always depositing them in the boat, and I swear that in less than two hours he had filled more than 2 big baskets.

484 To quote Gudger himself:

There are many older accounts of otters being so used in S. China. Chang Tsu, a writer of the Tang dynasty (606–916) states that there are many otters living by the river side, each reared by its own master. The tail feathers of a pheasant when placed in front of its den keep the otter inside; when the feathers are removed the otter leaves its den and ascends the river bank in order to fish. The men capture a large portion of the fishes and then allow the otters to satisfy their appetite.

The Yu yang tsa tsu, written about 860 by Twan Cheng-hi, contains this notice: 'At the end of the period (807–821) there lived in the district a man seventy years old who raised ten otters for the purpose of catching fish' and there are other early references up to the end of the 16th century. There then appears to be a gap of about 270 years to 1870. This may perhaps be explained by the fact that most early travellers rarely saw any parts of the Celestial Empire save the coastal cities and the regions round about, where cormorant fishing was and is especially practised, whereas otter fishing seems to be largely confined to the upper and mountainous parts of the Yangtze and its tributaries.

Gudger next mentions a curious booklet, 'purporting', he says 'to be a translation from the *Nouvelliste*, entitled *Natural History of North China* by

Père Armand David'. Like Gudger, I have searched, to no avail, through David's work to try and trace the origin of this booklet. The full title appears to be: *Natural History of North China with notices of that of the* 74 *South, West and North-East, and of Mongolia and Thibet compiled chiefly from the travels of Père Armand David*. Reprinted from the *Shanghai Evening Courier* and *Shanghai Budget*, and translated from the *Shanghai Nouvelliste*. This work was printed by Da Costa and Co., in Shanghai in 1873, and on page 36 is found:

But the Chinese are inexhaustible in invention, when it is a question of reaping advantage from animals. During the voyage across Kiangsi, Hoopeh and Szechuen, Father David observed with admiration otters quite as dextrous and quite as tame as the cormorants. At the command of the fisherman, these animals throw themselves into the water and bring back fish to the master's bark [barque].

Gudger also mentions that there seem to be several different methods of 484 employing otters for fishing.

Percival in *The Land of the Dragons*, 1889, found the fishermen on the upper region of the Yangtze (near Ichang) using huge dip nets. A trained otter wearing a muzzle is put overboard. 'The otter runs about the bottom, swims around, and drives all the fish he can into the net. After a lapse of time the net is hoisted and the otter comes up with it.' These beasts [he says] are very tame, they come when called, and are handled and cared for by their masters with perfect safety. A well-trained one commands a high price.

Alexander Hosie, in *Three Years in Western China*, 1897, gives a slightly different account, the otter working not outside the net, but inside. 'The net was circular and fringed with sinkers . . . the net having been cast, the fisherman holds onto a rope attached to the centre of the net, where there was a small circular opening. Drawing the rope gently until the centre of the net appeared above the surface, he seized the otter, which was chained to the boat, and dropped it into the opening. After allowing the otter a short time to rout out the fish from the bottom and drive them upwards, net, fish and otter were all drawn up together into the boat.'

Navarra (*China und die Chinesen*, Bremen, 1901, vol. II, page 612) says that a cord is tied round the otter's neck to prevent his feeding, and that he is then let down inside the net.

There are many instances of Ichang being mentioned in this connection, and Pratt writes that a small village on the bank opposite is known to Euro- 931 peans as the 'Otter Village' and that 'otters may be seen any day tied up in the bows of the sampans, and appear to be quite tame'. Similarly, Sarton 1014 quotes Howlett's *Forty Years in China* where, on page 78 the author refers to Ichang and his having watched otters there being 'let down into a net in the water through a hole in the top' and always returning with fish.

484 Gudger gives further instances, including one where the otter wears a collar and has a light line attached to it, the animal of its own accord indicating to the fishermen if there were no fish in the area where they were trying.

260 Cantor mentions that the Malays use the Sumatran hairy-nosed otter (*L. sumatrana*), as well as '*L. nair*' – presumably *L. (L.) perspicillata* – and 658 also the clawless *Amblonyx* in their fishing, and J. L. Kipling states that otters are employed in a similar way in Cochin (S. India), although not in Hindustan, Central India nor the Punjab. He writes:

All that we see of the otter in Britain is a poor little beast desperately fighting for its life against murderous crowds of dogs and men; but in reality there are few animals of more amiability, talent, and docility . . . They are effectually tamed in India, which is an easy matter, and they practise for the benefit of the fisherman the art to which they are ordained by nature . . . It is certainly interesting to see . . the otters tethered to stakes near [the fishermen's house-boats] playing with the no less amphibious children and behaving like the playful and intelligent water-cats they are . . .

Although Kipling states that this sight is a most uncommon one, being seen 580 only in Cochin, part of Bengal and on the Indus, Hooker, writing a little earlier (1855) says

We did not see a village or house in the heart of the Sunderbunds (though such do occur), but we saw canoes, with fishermen, who use the tame otter in fishing.

Ross (quoted by Gudger) in *The Land of the Five Rivers and Sindh*, London, 1883, page 45, also testifies to the abundance of otters on the Indus, saying that they

. . . may be seen near the fishermen's boats in 20's and 30's, tied round the waist and secured to stakes, playing in and out of the water with children and dogs.

484 As Gudger relates, Europe has also made considerable use of the otter in this way, the first reference he found being in Vincent de Beauvais' *Speculum Naturale*, published at Strasburg in about 1480, and continuing through Albertus Magnus (1495), Olaus Magnus (1555) and many others, until as late as 1856 (C. Knight, in his *Pictorial Museum of Animated Nature*, vol. II, page 219.) Gudger quotes Olaus Magnus, in the English version of 1658.

But in Sweden with some great men they (otters) are made so tame, that when the cock [*sic*] gives them the sign, they will hop into the fishpond, and bring forth a fish of that bignesse he commands them; and then another, and a third, until he hath done enough as he was bid.

Topsel, also in 1658, after noting that the otter is 'a very crafty and subtil   1157
Beast', writes that it is sometimes tamed and used for fishing, 'especially in
Scandinavia'.

Poland, Switzerland, France and Germany all provide instances, but in
England the earliest reference, according to Gudger, is in 1618 and con-   484
cerns a payment of £66 13s. 4d. to Robert Wood, 'Keeper of His Majesty's
[James I's] cormorants, ospreys and otters'.

Bewick records a number of tame otters which fished for their masters,   178
including one near Inverness which

> was frequently employed in catching fish, and would sometimes take eight or ten
> salmon in a day . . . When tired, it would refuse to fish any longer; and was then
> rewarded with as much fish as it could devour. Being satisfied with eating, it
> curled itself round and fell asleep; in which state it was generally carried home.

Many further instances of a like nature could be cited, but few authors
give any guidance on how to train an otter to behave in so useful a manner.
Freeman & Salvin touch lightly on this problem, but they suggest a method   425
which I would not personally care to try.

> As the otter cannot eat a fish of any size when swimming, it *must* come to land
> to do so; its master must then approach it quietly, and taking hold of its long and
> strong tail . . . hold him with one hand, whilst he takes the fish from him with the
> other, immediately rewarding him with small pieces of fish, after which he will
> again take the water in search of more . . .

These authors are the only ones who mention that the fishermen on the
Indus strap leather cups over the canines of their fishing otters to prevent
them from spoiling the fish.

So far as training is concerned Gudger is, as usual, the best informant   484
and quotes an anonymous German writer of 1908 whose opinion was that
the best age for training otters was three to four months, adding that if well
cared for they would be 'available for use' for 15 or 16 years. A milk or
cereal diet, with fresh vegetables and fruits and finally cooked meat, is
recommended, all at the temperature at which they come to the master's
table; raw meat or fish, and blood, is especially advised against. The German's method of training is not perhaps a very pleasant one.

> . . . one first lets it fast for one or two days until it gets very hungry, and then
> places a freshly cooked hot fish before it. The hungry animal will at once sink its
> fangs in the fish and will get burned. If this is repeated a few times, it will forever
> afterward have a proper awe of biting into scaly creatures . . . [The otter is then

123

trained to fetch and carry like a dog, first with an imitation leather or oakum fish, then with dead and next with live fish, on land; after this, first dead then live fish are retrieved from the water.] If he cuts his burden, then one repeats the manoeuver with the hot cooked fish, or punishes the otter in which, most remarkably, beating is much less effective than sousing with water. As much as the otter loves water, he has a peculiar dread of being sprinkled or having it poured on him. [I have not myself found this to be true, my otters positively delighting in being wetted with a watering can or hose.] Before one takes the otter along for real fishing, one lets him get hungry, gives him a fine meal and only then takes him to practical work. If the animal is really well filled, it naturally follows that he will not be so apt to bite the fish he catches.

Accounts of how to train otters for fishing are given, amongst others, by Goldsmith, who wrote that this was 'the account given us of this animal by Mr. Lots, of the Academy of Stockholm'; by Bell, who is surely quoting Goldsmith, though where Goldsmith remarked that this training 'requires not only assiduity, but patience' Bell more firmly says 'the process is somewhat tedious'; by Coues, who quotes Bell; and by Desmarest, who also refers to 'un académicien de Stockholm'. Presumably, therefore, Gudger is correct in assuming that all English accounts (and clearly some French ones as well) date back to one common source, viz. Johannes Low, in the publications of the Swedish Academy. The article in question apparently appears in vol. 13 of 1752, pages 139–149, and Gudger quotes it as follows:

454
171

306, 345

725

484

When one succeeds in taking a young living otter . . . it must immediately be put under guard. For a few days it should be given fish to eat and water to drink, after which the water should be diluted more and more with milk, broth, cabbages or peas. As soon as the otter will eat these things undiluted, fish must be given to it very infrequently, bread being substituted. Finally the otter must never get a whole fish, or the viscera of a fish . . . only the head. While the otter is being taken care of in this way (which should be done in a room where there is a number of people) one must try to make it as tame as possible. This will be practicable in a short time. Next one makes an apparatus out of straw, bound with sail twine or leather . . . and of a thickness to enable the otter to close its jaws over it. On either end two short rods are placed crosswise [see fig. 4a]. Next one takes a thin band on which four or five balls the size of nuts have been fastened. In each ball four spikes are set at intervals [see fig. 4b]. This band is put around the otter's neck and fastened at the nape. Bound to this knot is a thong. After all this has been done as directed, one must train the otter so that she obeys willingly; so that when a certain command is given, for example 'Come here', and when at the same time the thong is given a strong pull, she comes quickly and obediently. Then one takes hold of the otter, puts a hand in the band at the nape of the neck and twists it until she opens her jaws. As soon as this happens one puts in front of her the apparatus and cries suddenly 'Lay hold'. As often as the otter lets go, one must twist the band until she holds the apparatus fast. Then one must call 'Let go' and twist until she does so. Thus one proceeds until the otter lays hold and lets go on command. Thereupon one lays the straw implement on the ground, where there must be no sand; pulls the otter to the apparatus with one hand, and holds this with the other. At first, one pulls the apparatus away from the otter, finally, however, bringing it to her so that upon the outcry 'Lay hold' she holds it fast. One proceeds in this manner until the otter takes hold of the implement on a very slight pull on the long cord; so that one first shouts 'Come here' and pulls the apparatus gently to the otter, and then 'Let go' and gently takes it from her. When one has finally accomplished this, and the otter goes quickly after the

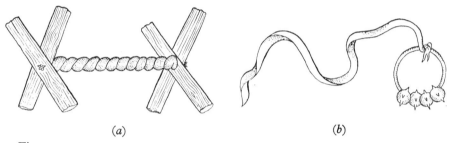

(a)   (b)

Figure 4.

apparatus when it is thrown, then one can throw, instead, a handkerchief or a glove. At last, when the otter is willing to fetch anything without being called or compelled, one can then throw it something that it likes to eat. It must, however, be forced, by the use of the cord, to bring this object back again. The thing should not be heavy . . . After the otter brings back everything that it can lift, and everything that it has been sent after, then one should take it to a clear and not too deep body of water, carrying with one a small, dead fish, and a rather large live one. One first throws the dead one in, for the otter will without doubt take this willingly. As soon as this happens, however, one should make the otter give up the fish. Finally the live fish is thrown into the water and the otter holds fast to it without difficulty. As soon as the otter brings the fish out of the water, one gives it the head to eat.

Although I have never myself attempted this method of training, I have found that until they get bored with doing so most otters will willingly retrieve, both on land and in the water. I feel sure that the procedure suggested above would involve the trainer in some nasty bites, for otters are not only extremely difficult to coerce but have very quick tempers, especially where food is concerned, even when otherwise completely tame and trust worthy.

697   Lett tells a pleasant story of an untrained (Canadian) otter getting fish for his master:

About thirty yards from the shore a fisherman came along with a canoe load of fine pickerel . . . I requested him to sell me a string of fish. He agreed to do so if I went to the market the next day. In the meantime [the otter] had . . . winded his game. He then quietly disappeared under water, and came up on the outside of the canoe, into which he climbed; and having secured one of the best strings of pickerel without having been noticed by the owner, he dropped into the water, and with his plunder, soon made his appearance at my feet . . .

Lett adds that this otter

had a nose as keen as that of a highly bred hound or pointer . . . I have seen him running on hare-tracks with the spirit and vivacity of a beagle or a harrier . . . When wanted, a call or two would bring him out instantly, and no matter how winding or circling my track might be . . . he followed it with the precision of a bloodhound, whistling almost at every jump to let me know that he was coming.

     With this account in mind – and it is only one of several similar – it is perhaps not surprising that apart from their use in retrieving fish there are
704   a number of recorded instances of otters retrieving on land. Liers writes that some of his otters 'like to go hunting [i.e. shooting], so that they can
531   retrieve ducks or pheasants on either land or water', and Harting, quoting a communication from S. J. Hurley, writes:

One day, in winter, we were going after Snipe [*G. gallinago*] in the marsh . . . my favourite Irish water spaniel being laid up at home at the time . . . I took [the otter] to the marsh, and no spaniel in the world could have performed better. She put up the snipe splendidly, and retrieved any birds that fell into the big pools or bog-holes.

     With their high intelligence and readiness to tame easily it may be wondered that otters have not more often been made use of in various ways.
220   Sir Thomas Browne provides the curious information, not found elsewhere, that otters 'are to bee made very tame and in some howses haue serued for turnespitts'; but surely the strangest – and most macabre – use for an otter is found in the story of one who lived with a pack of hounds and
531   learnt to hunt his own kind. His fate, too, was a strange one. Harting writes that one day he took out his otter-hounds, and

'Sandy,' the tame otter, would go, and into the Coquet they soon got on the lair of an Otter. They swam him through a deep pool, when he took to the bushes. Soon I saw 'Sandy' side by side with 'Rufus,' close to the wild otter . . . I thought

'Rufus' had him, but on coming in sight, to my astonishment, 'Sandy' had him fast by the neck, and held him till the dogs came up. From that time he was the leader in all our hunts, and was in at the death of nearly twenty otters. But alas! Poor 'Sandy' soon came to his end. Love of broth led him into the larder of the Star Inn. The cook, finding him wallowing in the broth, struck him with a wooden ladle – more to frighten than to hurt him; but his skull was fractured, and, after lingering for some days, he died, to the inexpressible regret of all who knew him.

It is pleasant to be able to record that Bewick writes of   178

another person, who kept a tame otter, [and] suffered it to follow him with his dogs. It was very useful to him in fishing, by going into the water, and driving trouts and other fish towards the net. – It was remarkable, that the Dogs, though accustomed to the sport [of otter-hunting], were so far from giving it the smallest molestation, that they would not even hunt an Otter whilst it remained with them; on which account the owner was under the necessity of disposing of it.

The same story is repeated both by Johnson and by Daniel, and the latter,   634, 327
in a subsequent work, having referred to otters fishing for their masters,   328
adds what may be an appropriate last word on this aspect:

Could an animal be thus tutored for use on the Sea coast, in addition to the Amusement, it would save many Qualms to the Summer Excursionist.

But apart from this utilitarian side there is also the aesthetic delight to be got from the company of otters and Seton, who knew so many animals so   1060
well, has perhaps summed this up best.

On watching a gambolling fox cub, a fawn, an ocelot, a marten, or even a well-furred pet skunk, one is apt to be carried away and declare each in turn the most beautiful and graceful creature ever seen. But when all are gone from view, when nothing but the dim impression remains, it is the Otter that stands out pre-eminently as the most beautiful and engaging of all elegant pets.

Part 3

Systematic Account
of the Otters of
the World

The whole appearance of the otter is something terrible.
PENNANT, *The British Zoology* (1768)

Key to Species and List of Accepted and Doubtful Forms of the Lutrinae

IT may occur to readers of this final section that there are far too many sub-species and this point of view is one with which the author sympathizes. At the same time, no arbitrary rule can be applied to include some and exclude others, even though a number of those included apparently rests on but slight foundations. Some, however, have expressly been arraigned as doubtful by leading authorities and these are indicated as such; others will doubtless attract the same treatment when authority gets round to them.

In many cases the reader can form his own conclusions, basing these on the amount of available material from which a type specimen has been selected, its apparent degree of divergence from neighbouring races, and the number of references to it in the literature.

Some confusion may seem to arise over the use of such subjective terms as pale brown, brown, buff, drab, etc., on the one hand; and grizzled, frosted, stippled, etc., on the other. In all cases where such descriptive words are used they are taken direct from the original author's account or from the account of a leading authority on the form in question. 'Proper names' of colours such as Prout's brown, mars brown, Mikardo brown, wood brown, etc., much used by American authors, may be presumed to be references to the colour charts published by Ridgway in 1886 and 1912. [963, 964]

Key to the species of the Lutrinae

1 Dentition 3/3, 1/1, 4/3, 1/2=36.
   2 Claws more or less strongly developed.
      3 Rhinarium naked, septum unhaired.
         4 Upper border of rhinarium more or less W-shaped. (N. Africa and Palaearctica.) . . . . . . *Lutra lutra*, p. 138
         4′ Upper border of rhinarium ∧ or 人-shaped.

5 The hind feet with four small circular rugosities on the pad near the heel. (N. America.) . . *Lutra canadensis*, p. 188

5' The hind feet without rugosities.

 6 Ventral and dorsal surfaces strongly contrasted in colour. (Chile, Patagonia.) . . *Lutra provocax*, p. 219

 6' Ventral and dorsal surfaces not strongly contrasted. (Central America, northern S. America.) . . Typical *Lutra annectens*, *L. a. colombiana*, *L. a. repanda* and *L. a. parilina*, p. 211*

4" Upper border of rhinarium almost straight ⌐, or a flattened semicircle.

 7 Tail normal, a flattened oval in section.

  8 Fur smooth. (Central America.)

   L. a. latidens, p. 213*

  8' Fur semi-erect. (West coast of S. America.)

   Lutra felina, p. 216

 7' Tail normal in section, but with a fringe of hair 'against the grain' on each lateral margin. (South Brazil, Uruguay, North Argentina.) . . . . *Lutra platensis*, p. 218

 7" Tail very markedly flattened on ventral surface, almost triangular in section. (Asia.) . *Lutra (L.) perspicillata*, p. 168

4''' Upper border of rhinarium Y-shaped.

 9 Throat spotted. (Africa, south of the Sahara.)

  Lutra (H.) maculicollis, p. 175

 9' Throat not spotted.

  10 Fore-nails rudimentary. (Costa Rica.)

   Lutra mesopetes, p. 218

  10' Nails normally developed. (Peru.)

   Lutra incarum, p. 217

3' Rhinarium haired, septum hairy (though possibly worn in old examples).

 11 Old World form. (South-east Asia.)

  Lutra sumatrana, p. 168

11' New World form.

 12 50 in. or less overall. (North-east S. America.)

  Lutra enudris, p. 214

 12' 60 in. or more overall; tail in the shape of a fer-de-lance, greatly flattened. (Central and eastern S. America.)

  Pteronura brasiliensis, p. 220

2' Claws rudimentary or partly absent; a large form, 50 in. or more overall.

---

* The fact that the shape of the rhinarium in the *annectens* 'group' appears to vary raises the question of whether they should be grouped in this way; the correct classification of *latidens* is still something of a problem.

13 Superciliary and upper genal vibrissae present; fur not frosted. (Africa, south of the Sahara.)   .   . *Aonyx capensis*, p. 179

13′ Superciliary and upper genal vibrissae absent; dorsal surface of head and neck extensively frosted.

    14 Teeth typical; fur coarse. (Central and West Africa.)

                    Aonyx (P.) congica, p. 185

    14′ Teeth typical; fur fine. (Uganda area.)

                    Aonyx (P.) philippsi, p. 186

      15 Teeth very small; skull delicate. (Cameroons.)

                    Aonyx (P.) microdon, p. 186

1′ Dentition (usually) 3/3, 1/1, 3/3, 1/2 = 34. A small form, 36 in. or less overall; claws rudimentary. (Asia.)   .   .   . *Amblonyx cinerea*, p. 171†

1″ Dentition 3/2, 1/1, 3/3, 1/2 = 32. Many unique features; exclusively maritime. (Kuriles, Aleutians, north-west coast of N. America.)

                    Enhydra lutris, p. 235

---

† Although the first upper premolar is not invariably absent in *Amblonyx* this Asian form may readily be distinguished from the African 'clawless' *Aonyx* by its very much smaller size, coupled with the fact that the fore feet of *Aonyx* are almost without webs, these extending only to the third phalange, whereas in the case of *Amblonyx* they extend to the second phalange.

Figure 5

Right fore foot of *Lutra lutra*

Figure 6

Right hind foot of *Lutra lutra*

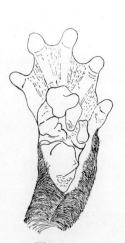

Figure 7

Right fore foot of *Amblonyx cinerea*

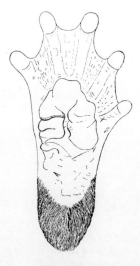

Figure 8

Right hind foot of *Amblonyx cinerea*

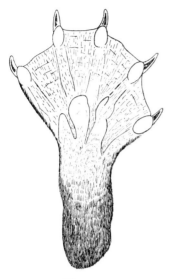

Figure 9
Right fore foot of *Lutra (H.) maculicollis*

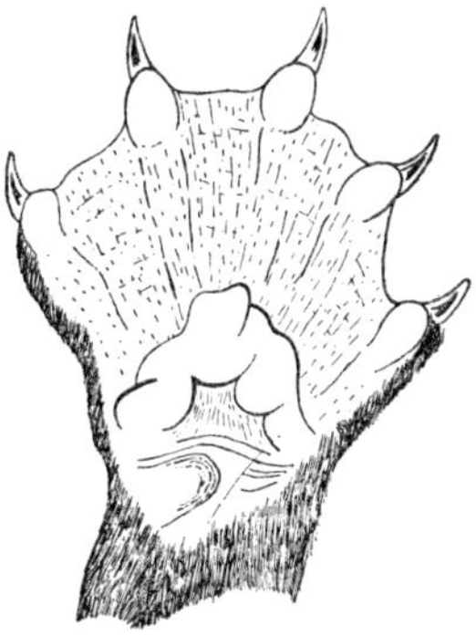

Figure 10
Right hind foot of *Lutra (H.) maculicollis*

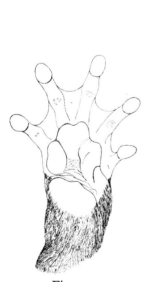

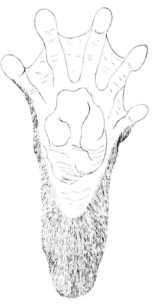

Figure 11
Right fore foot of *Aonyx capensis*

Figure 12
Right hind foot of *Aonyx capensis*

The preceding figures 5–12 are *after* Pocock: 1921 (about ¾ life size)

List of Accepted and Doubtful Forms

	Accepted forms	Doubtful forms
1 Palaearctic (those partly oriental are marked *)	*Lutra lutra lutra* L. l. aurobrunnea *L. l. barang *L. l. chinensis L. l. kutab L. l. meridionalis L. l. monticola L. l. seistanica *L. (Lutrogale) p. perspicillata L. (L.) perspicillata maxwelli L. (L.) p. sindica Amblonyx cinerea concolor	L. l. angustifrons L. l. roensis L. l. splendida L. stejnegeri
2 Oriental	L. l. nair L. sumatrana Amblonyx c. cinerea A. c. nirnai	A. c. fulvus
3 African	Aonyx capensis A. (Paraonyx) congica A. (P.) microdon A. (P.) philippsi L. (Hydrictis) m. maculicollis L. (H.) maculicollis chobiensis L. (H.) m. kivuana L. (H.) m. matschiei L. (H.) m. nilotica L. (H.) m. tenuis	A. capensis angolae A. c. coombsi A. c. helios A. c. hindei A. c. meneleki
4 North American (Nearctic)	L. c. canadensis L. canadensis brevipilosus L. c. chimo L. c. degener L. c. evexa L. c. extera L. c. interior L. c. kodiacensis L. c. lataxina	

	Accepted forms	Doubtful forms
	L. c. mira	
	L. c. nexa	
	L. c. optiva	
	L. c. pacifica	
	L. c. periclyzomae	
	L. c. preblei	
	L. c. sonora	
	L. c. texensis	
	L. c. vaga	
	L. c. vancouverensis	
	L. c. yukonensis	
5 Central and South American (neotropical)	*Lutra a. annectens*	
	L. annectens colombiana	
	L. a. latidens	
	L. a. parilina	
	L. a. repanda	
	L. e. enudris	
	L. enudris insularis	
	L. e. mitis	
	L. felina	
	L. incarum	
	L. mesopetes	
	L. platensis	
	L. provocax	
	Pteronura b. brasiliensis	
	P. brasiliensis paranensis	
6 Palaearctic/Nearctic	*Enhydra l. lutris*	
	E. lutris nereis	

Chapter 1

The European Otter

LUTRA Brisson, 1762.

Mustela lutra Linnaeus, 1758.
Lustra Erxleben, 1777.
Mustela Molina, 1782; Kerr, 1792; Desmarest, 1803.
Lutris Deméril, 1806.
Lutrix Rafinesque, 1815.
Lataxina Gray, 1843.
Lataxia Gervais, 1855.
Loutra Gervais, 1855.
Barangia Gray, 1865.
Hydrogale Gray, 1865.
Latax Gray, 1865.
Lontra Gray, 1865; Cabrera, 1924; Flower, 1929.
Lutrogale Gray, 1865.
Nutria Gray, 1865.
Suricoria Gray, 1865.
Lutronectes Gray, 1867.
Leutronectes Gray, 1869.
Hydrictis Pocock, 1921; Perret & Aellen, 1956.

Essential characters:

Of the *genus* –
Dentition 3/3, 1/1, 4/3, 1/2 = 36; claws more or less strongly developed, fingers and toes webbed; head wide, flat; tail tapering evenly, somewhat flattened.

Of the species LUTRA LUTRA Linnaeus, 1758 –
Upper borner of rhinarium more or less W-shaped, the lower border formed of two concave lines with a descending central point.
Colour: Variable; from very dark, blackish-brown through shades of chestnut to pale greyish; albinism not unknown, melanistic examples unverified.

138

Size: Average; from about 36 to about 48 in. (915–1220 mm.) overall, much larger examples occasionally recorded; weight of males from 9 to 25 lb. (4·1–11·4 kg.), much heavier examples known.

Range: Palaearctic area, into Indo-Malayan regions. Type locality – Sweden.

LUTRA LUTRA LUTRA Linnaeus, 1758 – The Common (European) Otter.

Mustela lutra Linnaeus, 1758; G. Cuvier, 1817 and 1829.
Lustra vulgaris Erxleben, 1777.
Lutra vulgaris Erxleben, 1777; and many later authors.
Mustela lutra piscatoria Kerr, 1792.
Viverra lutra Pallas, 1811.
Lutra fluviatilis Leach, ? 1816.
Lutra vulgaris var. *marinus* Billberg, 1827.
Lutra nudipes Melchior, 1834.
Lutra var. *variegata* Lesson, 1842.
Lutra ? *aterrima* Schrenk, 1859.
Lutronectes whiteleyi Gray, 1867.
Leutronectes whiteleyi Gray, 1869.
Lutra lutra var. *japonica* Nehring, 1887.
Lutra vulgaris var. *amurensis* Dybowski, 1922.
Lutra vulgaris var. *baicalensis* Dybowski, 1922.
Lutra lutra whiteleyi Pohle, 1920; Ognev, 1931.
Lutra whiteleyi Goldman, 1936; Pocock, 1941.
Lutra lutra japonensis Jarvis & Morris, 1962 (1963).

[Doubtful forms which may in time prove distinct:]

Lutra roensis Ogilby, 1834. (North-east Ireland)
Lutra lutra angustifrons Lataste, 1885. (Algeria)
Lutra lutra splendida Cabrera, 1906. (Morocco)
Lutra stejnegeri Goldman, 1936. (Kamchatka)

Linnaeus' description of the otter is quite brief: 710

With naked palmate feet, tail half the length of the body. Lives in Europe in fresh water, in rivers, pools and fish-ponds. Eats fish, frogs and crabs.

Two years earlier, in 1756, Brisson had described the otter rather more   214
fully, noting as its essential characteristics that it has six incisors in each jaw; five toes on each foot, all with nails; and that the feet were webbed. This would, of course, fit the mink equally well, and indeed for many years the mink was included in the same genus as the otter, generally under the

name 'Lutra lutreola', and was known as the Lesser Otter. Brisson, however, gives the size of his otter as 49 in. (1245 mm.). Regarding its colour, he says:

All the upper part of the body, the tail and the legs are chestnut-coloured, and moderately dark. The throat, stomach and belly are grey-white.

He describes the eyes as being very small, and the ears as small, round, and placed lower on the head than are the eyes.

383   Erxleben is, I think, the first to specify the otter as *Lutra vulgaris*, the name by which it was to be commonly known at least until the end of the last century. He gives a very long list of older references to the otter, as well as a moderately detailed account of it:

The head is broad and flat, the nose blunt and thick with crescent-shaped nostrils. The eyes are small and close to the nose. The ears are very short, and round, the lips thick, the moustachial bristles large . . . The body is elongated, with short thick legs, each palmated [foot] having five digits. There are four small nipples on the belly. The tail is broad at the base and continuously flattened towards the tip. There are two small white spots, [one] on each side of the nose, and another beneath the chin. The throat, chest and belly are whitish grey . . .

Erxleben, also, states that the otter is only found in fresh water, and never in the sea. Many early naturalists held this view, the origin of which is prob-

640
1153   ably to be traced back to Pliny (who classed the otter as a member of the beaver family) or even to Aristotle, who wrote that the seal was the only 'wild quadruped' to feed in the sea.

657
383   The size of the otter as given by Kerr (1792) agrees quite well with that of Erxleben, but Kerr also gives the weight, saying that the male weighs from 18 to 26 lb. (8·1–11·8 kg.) and the female from 13 to 22 lb. (5·8–10·0

897
895   kg.). This information is probably taken from Pennant's *History of Quadrupeds*, 1781; the same author's British *Zoology*, 1768, gives no weights. Otherwise, Kerr's description parallels that of Erxleben very closely. Kerr calls the common otter *M[ustela] Lutra piscatoria*, the first use of this term.

321   There are, of course, a very large number of early descriptions of the European otter, the majority little more than repetitions of each other and thus of no particular interest. Cuvier seems to have been one of the first authors to break away from the accounts of the eighteenth century and earlier. His 1823 description of the otter in general and the European form in particular is very detailed, and ranges more widely than was usual with

227   his predecessors, Buffon perhaps excepted. Cuvier, for instance, writes:

The senses, except for that of scent, appear not to be well developed, judging at least from external evidence. The eye is small, and the round pupil readily contracted. The external eyelids are thin and without lashes; the internal one is strong and sufficiently well developed to protect the cornea completely . . . The guard hairs are fairly long, shaggy, strong and shining, in shape like a *fer-de-lance*, that is to say, thicker at the apex than at the base.

Cuvier writes that the European otter 321

. . . has a dark brown pelage, blackish, slightly greyer on the under side; the area around the lips, the chin, and the throat are a pale reddish grey, and the tip of the ear is grey. The guard hair is a dark grey-brown on the body and whitish grey on the throat, and the underfur, which is very soft and luxuriant, is a grey-brown.

Jenyns (1835) also gives a good description: 629

. . . hair on the body of two kinds; the finer sort greyish-white; the longer and coarser greyish-white at the roots, deep brown at the extremity, the latter colour alone appearing externally: sides of the head, throat, undersurface of the neck, and breast, cinereous: hair on the feet short, brown with a reddish tinge: tail dusky brown . . .

Bell's account of 1837 gives a similar picture: 171

The fur consists of two distinct and very different kinds of hair; the shorter being extremely fine and soft, of a whitish grey colour, and brown at the tips; the longer hair stiffer and thicker, very shining, greyish at the base, bright rich brown at the points, especially on the upper parts and the outer surface of the legs: the throat, the cheeks, the breast, belly and inner parts of the legs, brownish grey throughout.

The dental formula given by Bell of I 6/6, C 2/2, FM [i.e. PM] 6/6, M 4/4 is now usually changed to I 6/6, C 2/2, PM 8/6, M 2/4 (see, for instance, Taylor: 1914). 1132

Gray seems to have been the first to note the characteristic shape of the 468 upper outline of the naked nose-pad, and describes it in 1865 as 'rather produced and angular, nearly as high as broad in the middle'. Baird, who a few 146 years before had described the rhinarium of *L. canadensis* in minute detail, compares this form with the European one and finds many salient differences. Amongst other points he notes that

the most striking peculiarity of external form in the European species is the small size of the naked muffle . . . This, in a nearly grown skin, is only about four-tenths of an inch wide, and about as long.

He also finds the guard hairs to be more sparse and scattered than is the case with the North American species, and the colour 'has in it much more of chestnut brown'.

803

Turning to more recent authorities Miller, in his *Catalogue* of 1912, gives the external characters of European *L. lutra* as follows:

Fur very dense and waterproof, alike in texture throughout the body and tail, the hairs of underfur 10–15 mm. in length, the longer overlying hairs, which almost completely conceal the underfur, about 25 mm. in length . . .

964

Colour: Winter pelage: upper parts, legs, feet and tail a rich dark brown (about the prout-brown of Ridgway or somewhat darker) with a drabby cast more evident in some lights than in others, the hairs with a conspicuous metallic gloss; underfur light grey, the extreme tips of its hairs changing abruptly to prout-brown; on underparts the drab becomes more conspicuous as well as paler, usually assuming a tinge of cream-buff, the throat and cheeks fading to buffy white; interramial region and upper lip with irregular white mottlings, the hairs of which are white to base; whiskers and claws light horn-colour. The exact colour is subject to considerable variation, but the material examined is not sufficient to show whether such differences as occur are correlated with locality or season. Sometimes the brown is darker and richer than usual, or the drab may be especially pronounced. Occasionally the long hairs of the back are a light dull buff, imparting to the animal a peculiar faded appearance.

864

It is interesting to compare this description, taken from the *Mammals of Western Europe*, with that of Ognev in the *Mammals of Eastern Europe* (1931, translated 1962):

General tone of back (in winter pelage) dark glossy brown (near warm sepia and Mars brown). Head usually somewhat darker than back, with slight mixture of rust (Verona brown). Transition of color of back to flanks very gradual and slightly marked. Underparts lighter than flanks. Somewhat yellowish tones appear here. Slight lightening and glossy silvery-yellow apparent on head and upper parts of chest. Paws dull, dark brown (tone intermediate between warm sepia and Verona brown). Tail uniformly dark brown. Claws yellowish-white, with slightly brown tinge at very base. Vibrissae glossy yellowish white, some with cinnamon brown overtones.

. . . underfur brownish-gray-white on lower two-thirds, upper parts dark brown (warm sepia) with slight violet tinge. Long guard hairs glossy, dark brown (Mars brown in centre of back and Verona brown on sides.) The general impression is of a uniformly dark color . . .

The fur of Siberian otters . . . is somewhat richer and denser than in the western forms.

864

Ognev notes that the structure of the naked part of the nose is typical, and describes it as 'an aliform figure with two tips, a small upper and a still

321

smaller lower one'. He differs from Cuvier in his assessment of the otter's external senses, saying:

It sees excellently by day and by night, can hear the slightest sound, and by its sense of smell becomes aware of the presence of prey or approaching danger. Its intelligence is highly developed.

Unfortunately Ognev gives no information about the eye itself whereby the question might be resolved as to whether the otter possesses a nictitating eyelid. Several of the earlier naturalists state that it has. Thus Bonaparte (1839) says 'the eyes are furnished with a nictitating membrane'; Griffith (1827) echoes Cuvier and speaks simply of 'a third lid, which appears entirely to cover the cornea'; while Carpenter (1857) writes that 'the eyes are provided with a *nictitating membrane* ... as a defense to their surface'. However, Rochon-Duvigneaud (1943) makes no mention of it although he examines the structure of the eye itself in considerable technical detail. He describes the otter as slightly brachyophthalmic (short-sighted), but describes its powerful intraocular musculature as resembling that of the cormorant (*Phalacrocorax carbo*) in the degree of compensation it provides against the effect of water on the cornea. He concludes that the otter's sight is far better in water than out of it. Certainly the eye seems to be furnished with a protective membrane of some sort (although I have never observed it to nictitate), for I have often seen bits of straw or grains of sand adhering to the eyeball and apparently causing the animal no discomfort whatever.

While the eyes are of course kept open under water both the ears and the nostrils are valvular and close as soon as the animal puts its head beneath the surface; the gullet similarly closes. I have noticed that in the case of some Indian otters the external ear flicks backwards very slightly just as the head submerges and then 'pricks up' again at once on surfacing; this is presumably caused by the inner ear opening and shutting.

In water that is not clear, or in muddy conditions, it is probable that the otter relies far more on its vibrissae than on eyesight. As Matthews (p. 217) writes:

... as in the seals, the facial vibrissae or whiskers of the otter are long and stout, forming a conspicuous moustache. They are, further, set in well-developed pads on the sides of the snout above the lips and their inner ends are rooted in large hair-bulbs, the nerves connected to which are proportionately large. The whole apparatus forms a very sensitive tactile organ which, by responding to small turbulences and differences in pressure, almost certainly enables the animal to be aware of moving prey at a distance without actually touching it.

In addition to the vibrissae of the upper lip the otter is provided with further 'pads' from which stout whiskers spring, one centrally under and just behind the chin, and a further pair one on each side of the upper neck a little behind the angle of the mouth. Additional smaller groups are found above and behind the eyes, and all these doubtless serve the same function as the labial ones. (Some Indian otters have, in addition, one or two thick, stiff bristles just protruding through the fur on each 'elbow'.) The skin of an adult male from Norfolk, which I have before me, shows three or four long but slender bristles on the outer point of each 'wrist'.

772

The underfur is so dense that it is virtually impossible to see the actual skin of the animal even when the hairs are carefully parted. As Matthews points out:

> . . . the very dense under-fur carries a layer of air trapped among the hairs which are so closely set and soft that the water cannot penetrate between them. The skin of the animal thus never becomes wet at all, nor does the animal become chilled by the water however cold it may be, for there is an insulating layer of air at least a quarter of an inch thick all over its body. As soon as an otter climbs out on the bank the water runs off the guard-hairs and causes them to become aggregated together into small bunches so that they no longer form a smooth close coat; each bunch tapers towards its tip, giving the animal a very peculiar spiky appearance.

There appears to be a fair amount of natural oil in the guard hairs for on emerging from swimming the water can be seen running off in a 'duck's back' effect. If chemicals known as wetting agents pollute the water and break down its surface tension, however, a degree of penetration of the animal's fur is quickly achieved, with consequent chilling and distress. Despite Matthews' assertion to the contrary, an otter forcibly restrained from landing and confined to cold water for any length of time will become noticeably chilled, and may shiver violently for some while after emerging. This may happen in the natural course of events if the animal hides under water, as it is often in the habit of doing, remaining quite motionless and only occasionally protruding its nostrils to breathe.

772

Matthews describes the colour of the European otter as

> a rich brown above shading into light brown, buffish, or silvery off-white below; the intensity of the brown on the back is variable but may be seasonal, the darkest colour generally being found in winter.

1088

In Southern's opinion the richest and darkest pelage is achieved in winter after the moult. There is unfortunately very little information on this

860

aspect, but Novikov writes that 'Molt lasts a long time and proceeds almost

772

imperceptibly'. Matthews says:

> There is probably a change of coat in the autumn but there appears to be no observation recorded on any coat-change in the spring; the winter coat may be moulted or may simply wear thin, and further investigation is needed.

144

Melanism is rare in Mustelids and there seems to be no report of a truly black otter which can be accepted without hesitation. The glossy fur is a good reflector of adjacent colours, even when wet, and the wetness itself gives the coat a darker colour. These two facts probably account for the occasional tale of a black otter. The most celebrated of these reports, and one often referred to, is mentioned by Harting, who writes: 531

> We have heard of a black Otter, but never seen one. A correspondent of the 'Fishing Gazette' reported (October 3, 1891) that a fine specimen of the black Otter had been caught at Burnhervie, Aberdeen . . .

Unfortunately, I have not seen the original text of this reference.

Conversely, albinism in the European otter seems not to be too uncommon and there are a number of accounts of white or cream-coloured otters to be found in the literature, as well as records of animals spotted with white, to a greater or lesser extent. Millais remarks that 'Albinoes, cream-   798
coloured and spotted varieties of the Otter are not very rare'.

According to Hurley, the *Fishing Gazette* for 1893 records white otters   599
being seen in Ireland in the River Shannon, and Hurley himself writes that two further examples had been seen in the same place towards the end of 1896. It is probably these reports that Scharff had in mind when he wrote,   1023
'I find that perfectly white otters have been observed in the River Shannon . . .' An anonymous correspondent to *The Field* of 1862 records two   55
cream-coloured otters being killed in the River Aln, Northumberland, 'a few years ago', and Daniel (1813) states that Dr Johnson mentions white   328
otters sometimes being seen, presumably during his tour of the Hebrides.

The west coast of Scotland provides several examples although it is not easy to decide just how many owing to the number of repetitions of the various instances, and the fact that most of them have consistently occurred in the neighbourhood of Mull, Islay and Jura. Legge writes in 1898:   693

> Some few years after I went up to Islay in 1859 I remember a white otter was got up the Sound of Islay, and between 1880 and 1890 a keeper . . . got another [in the same place].

These two may be the ones referred to by Harting, one noted as 'killed at   531
Jura' and the other as 'preserved at Kildalton House, Islay'. Both these examples are also mentioned by Harvie-Brown & Buckley. This white   534
strain appears to have been a very local one, for in 1903 Kirk writes that in   659
March that year

> there was captured at Kildalton, Islay . . . a cream coloured otter. The specimen was a male and weighed 17¾ lbs.

145

Another, 'a lovely white dog otter with pink eyes' was trapped on the north-east coast of Islay, as mentioned by an anonymous writer in 1898. What appears to be yet a further example is mentioned by Russell in 1910 as preserved at Islay House, being 'got from an animal killed a short time ago'. Nor does this seem to be the last of the strain, for in 1935 Seth-Smith exhibited a mounted specimen of an albino, 'of a delicate cream-colour, with pink eyes', to the Zoological Society of London, this animal having been taken at Torosay Castle, Isle of Mull, in March of that year. Thirty years later there is evidence that white otters still persisted in the area, for Fletcher writes in 1956:

> In June 1954 while approaching an uninhabited island off the west coast of Argyll, I saw an all-white otter. As it was close inshore to the island and lay almost direct in our path, a good view was obtained at fairly close quarters. On landing on the island I followed the otter for about ¼ mile . . . It was full grown, and, being white, was easily followed even deep into the sea. The boatman could recall having seen a white otter as a cub two years previously at the same spot. Its coat in appearance was like that of a polar bear. Local inquiries revealed that a white otter was at one time known in Loch Fyne, appropriately enough in the vicinity of Otter Ferry.

Mr Gavin Maxwell has kindly shown me a letter from Mr H. L. Cockrell of the Solway Fishery, Dumfries, recording the sighting by a number of the Tongland Dam staff of a white otter in November 1963.

In 1812 Daniel wrote that

> in Scotland, the vulgar have an opinion, that the Otter has its *King* or *leader*; they describe it as being of a larger size, and varied with white; they believe it is never killed, without the sudden death of a Man, or some other Animal at the same instant; that its Skin is endowed with great virtues; is an antidote against all infection; a preservative to the *Warrior* from wounds, and ensures the *Mariner* from all disasters upon the Seas.

Be that as it may, examples of spotted otters seem rather rarer than white ones, although again there are a number of repetitions of the same account. Alston (1872) records an otter 'with an irregular white collar round its neck', and Gunn (1869) notes an old female captured near Yarmouth which 'was slightly piebald, having a few small patches of white on the crown of its head and neck'. An anonymous correspondent to *The Field* of 1862 mentions having seen at Newcastle-on-Tyne 'a stuffed specimen of a female, spotted all over the body with white ticks, precisely similar to some pointer dogs . . .' This anonymity presumably cloaks the identity of one, Mr Gallon, who is quoted by Mennell & Perkins (1864) as using these same words. They are further repeated by Harting (1894).

146

Demarest, in his *Nouveau Dictionnaire* of 1817, especially mentions an   345
example in the Natural History Museum in Paris, saying of it:

> ... what makes this animal so remarkable is that the brown areas of the body,
> and especially the flanks are sprinkled with an infinite number of little white
> spots, round in shape and most irregularly distributed. Furthermore the flanks
> are adorned with white hairs, of which the number increases towards the sides of
> the belly, in such a way that they alone form the colour of this area.

This unusual otter was killed at the Ile-Adam, and was further described by
Cuvier in 1823. He writes that these spots, of a shining white, were confined   321
solely to the underfur, the guard hairs being unaffected.

A large otter 'dotted over with yellow spots' is recorded anonymously in   53
1861.

According to Scharff in 1909 about 1% of Irish otters show some such   1023
spotting of the underfur, but he mentions (and illustrates, facing page 141)
a specimen where the guard hairs are similarly affected. Six years later he
writes to announce the discovery of a very similar skin, this latter taken   1024
from Kilcolgan, Co. Galway.

It appears from an anonymous account of 1862 that mounted or pre-   57
served skins of apparently aberrant coloration should be viewed with some
suspicion:

> First catch an umber-brown otter ... stuff him, set him in a shop window,
> where the scorching rays of the sun will bleach him white in the course of 3 or 4
> years (sousing him occasionally in his native element will cause him to bleach
> sooner and come out pure white); shorter time makes him cream colour. If he is
> to be ticked like a pointer, keep him from the sun, wrapped in paper, and cut a
> few holes in the paper; apply nitric or other acid to turn his hair white – any
> chemist can do this. If he is to be zebraised, wind round him some lead foil in
> stripes, or hoop him up with old crinoline, before he undergoes bleaching ...

In 1834 Ogilby sought to establish the otter of the north-east coast of   863
Ireland as a separate species, *Lutra roensis*,

> On account of the intensity of its colouring, which approaches nearly to black
> both on the upper and under surface; of the less extent of the pale colour beneath
> the throat as compared with the *common Otter*, *Lutra vulgaris* Linn., as it exists in
> England; and of some difference in the size of the ears and in the proportions of
> other parts; Mr. Ogilby has long considered the *Irish Otter* as constituting a
> distinct species ...

Mr Ogilby seems to have been the first, but not the last person to hold this
opinion, although it has not found favour with the great majority of zoologists. Thompson, in his *Natural History of Ireland* (1856), quotes a Dr Ball   1154

who examined Ogilby's type specimen in 1836. The doctor's opinion is somewhat cryptic:

> I have never seen an Irish otter that was not like, nor did I ever see one like the specimen placed beside it and marked as the common otter, so that I am inclined to think that we have not the variety . . . common in England, and perhaps they have not ours.

1050   Similarly, Blanford wrote of two living examples from Co. Down:

> . . . it must be allowed that the Irish Otters which we now have seem to be rather different from the ordinary form, having the tail more flattened, a longer head, a more distinctly white under-lip, and a generally darker colour of the fur.

565   A plea for the retention of this form is made by Hinton in 1920.

> The type of *L. Roensis* . . . passed into the British Museum where it is now preserved. The nearly black colour, described by Ogilby has become, from exposure, a nearly uniform deep reddish brown.
>
> The Museum has just received three female otters from Co. Galway, caught during the last winter. These, as regards colour, accord perfectly with Ogilby's description; they are much darker (practically black above) than any English specimens examined by me. In my opinion therefore, the Irish otter should be regarded as a distinct subspecies, for which the name *L. l. roensis* is available. Such a variation characterized by colour-saturation is, of course, exactly what is to be expected in the more humid climate of Ireland.

1139   An article by Tetley, unfortunately incomplete owing to the death of the author, but published in 1945, seeks tentatively to distinguish Scottish sea-going otters. The line of argument is neither forceful nor conclusive, but suggests that as Scottish marine otters are darker, and as *L. l. roensis* is both darker and marine, hence *roensis* is only a variant of the Scottish otter.

In this connection, it seems possible that otters do occasionally cross be-
747   tween Scotland and Ireland, for Macintyre (1950) records a large otter shot in Kintyre and found to have an Irish spearhead embedded in his flesh. The distance involved is some 14 miles.

The same form extends into North Africa, and an attempt to classify the Algerian otters as a separate race under the name of *L. l. angustifrons* was
682   made by Lataste in 1885. The main differences to the nominate subspecies which Lataste sought to establish were alleged to be that the skull was much narrower between the fontal and cerebral areas, and that the tail – as compared to the body – was relatively longer. The otters described had origina-
718   ted in various parts of Algeria, in the neighbourhood of La Calle, in Lake Fetzara, and near Constantine in the River Rummel. In 1840–2 Loche had reported examining a small number of Algerian otters, some from Lake

148

Fetzara and others from Harrach, Masafran and Sig, which appeared to him indistinguishable from the European race. Similarly, Gervais had noted otters in the Rummel and in Lake Fetzara in 1855, and had examined skins at Bone; he failed, however, to obtain a skull and accordingly left open the question of whether they were a separable form. He had first mentioned these otters in a brief article in 1848. [437] [436]

Lataste himself found difficulty in separating his proposed form from the common otter of Italy as described by Bonaparte (1834), and after further comparison of cranial material from Italy, France and Denmark he abandoned *angustifrons*, finding no real differences from the common form except that the former appeared to show a larger area of yellowish white on the throat. [682] [196] [683]

Allen (1939) retains *angustifrons* as valid, while Ellerman & Morrison-Scott treat it as 'doubtful'. Both show *L. l. splendida*, published by Cabrera in 1906, as synonymous to it. Cabrera's description of his type reads: [12, 366] [247]

General characters as those of *L. lutra* of Europe; but the tail is longer, and the skull is flatter and much narrower in the post-orbital region. The pelage of the upper parts is a beautiful cinnamon colour, somewhat reddish and very lustrous, most intense on the back of the neck and darkest on the tail. The lips, throat and upper part of the chest are entirely white; the remainder of the underparts is the colour of milky coffee, very light, and there are some little spots of this same colour, very diffused, on the white area of the chest. The white whiskers spring from a grey ground. The under- or woolly-fur is a darker coffee colour, dirty white at the base.

The skull, in comparison with the typical form, is much narrower, with larger and higher zygomatic arches. The interorbital width is the same in both forms, but behind the postorbital apophysis the skull of *L. l. splendida* gradually narrows . . .

The head and body length of the male type specimen was 635 mm. (25 in.), and the tail 420 mm. (16½ in.). Lataste's *angustifrons* had a head and body length of 590 mm. (23¼ in.), with a tail of 370 mm. (14½ in.). [682]

It is Pohle's view that the intertemporal constriction narrows with age, but in his opinion the greater proportional tail length and the large area of white on the throat are constants, and as such validate the subspecies. He agrees with the other authorities quoted in regarding *splendida* as a synonym to *angustifrons*, having examined examples from Morocco and Tangier. (Cabrera's type came from Mogador, Morocco.) Pohle describes *angustifrons* as follows: [923] [247]

Skin: upper side light brown, deer brown ['*rehbraun*'] to reddish brown, very shiny, the neck lighter and the tail somewhat darker. The lips, throat and front part of the neck are pure white or yellowish white, with scattered brownish spots which may merge into a larger spot on the lips, amongst other places. The remainder of the lower side is usually lighter than in the European form, being the colour of milk coffee (this is so in the case of the specimens from Mogador, Morocco, Constantine and one of the Tangier examples; the other one from Tangier, however, has the lower side almost the same as the upper). On the front part of the nose the brown of the upper side merges into the white of the lips. In this area the whiskers are white or yellow; the underfur is whitish brown at the base and darkens towards the tip until it becomes a deep coffee colour.

The skull is hardly to be distinguished from that of the main species, but is perhaps a little flatter . . .

One further attempted subspeciation has been made in the Palaearctic area: this is Gray's separation of the Japanese otter as *Lutronectes whiteleyi* in 1867. The generic separation never found favour and in common with all Gray's other genera (except *Pteronura*) has been abandoned. Modern writers who retain *L. l. whiteleyi* as valid are Pohle, Goldman, Pocock and Ognev; Ognev and Pohle also retain *angustifrons*.

Gray based this form on two immature specimens with damaged skulls, from Hakodadi, and described it as follows:

The muzzle bald, oblong, transverse, with a straight upper and lower edge; the upper edge of the nostril bald. Ears oblong, hairy. Feet rather large; toes strong, webbed, covered with hair above, and bald beneath; toes and palm pads well developed, those of the palm separated from the toes by a broad bald space; claws strong, acute. Tail conical, covered with hair. The toes in this genus [*Lutronectes*] are strong, thick and well webbed, rather larger than in the typical Otters.[1]

Gray expanded his description in the *Catalogue* of 1869 to include a number of cranial characters. He mentions that this race is 'Dark brown; cheeks, lips, chin, and throat greyish white' and adds that it closely resembles the European otter.

Pohle assigns a number of specimens in the Berlin Zoological Museum to *whiteleyi*. He describes the skin as

brown above, greyish brown below. The throat, the sides and under side of the neck, the lower jaw and the lips are grey. On the upper lip there is a yellowish spot on each side. The upper border line of the rhinarium does not protrude as much as in our otter.

He remarks that the skull is almost completely similar to that of the European otter. Pohle gives a head and body length of 70–75 cm. (27½–29½ in.),

[1] It may be noted in this connection that Pohle describes *L. l. lutra* as having the front feet completely bare below, whereas in the case of the hind feet the distal two-thirds is bare.

and a tail length of 45–50 cm. (17¾–19¾ in.); Swinhoe had mentioned in   1125
1870 (page 626) that *whiteleyi* was 'a long-tailed species'.

It is perhaps worth adding that in his *Fauna Japonica* of 1847 Temminck   1137
shows no doubt about the identity of the Japanese otter, for he writes:

> The numerous skins received from Japan serve to confirm the identity of that
> country's species with our own European otter; a comparison of the skeletons and
> their component parts gives absolutely the same results; this goes to prove that
> our otter inhabits equally a large part of Asia, reaching even as far as the Kurile
> Islands.

Temminck notes that those skins originating from the northern provinces
and from the Kuriles are the largest and carry the finest fur, and in the esti-
mation of the Russians are much preferable to those coming from Central
Europe.

It was also Nehring's opinion that the Japanese otter was 'in no signific-   847
ant feature distinguishable from' the European otter.

Size and weight:

A number of authors suggest that young European otters weigh 3 lb.
(1·36 kg.) at three months of age and then increase by 1 lb. per month up to
the age of a year. (One anonymous writer records a cub of 2 lb. increasing   691
to 14 lb. 12 months later.) Otters which start life in captivity in poor condition may show very rapid increases in weight – sometimes as much as 1 lb.
a week in the early stages of being properly cared for. After the first year of
life there seems to be little if any correlation between weight and total
length. Males rarely exceed 50 in. (1200 mm.) and females 44 in. (1120
mm.); respective weights probably average about 24 lb. and 15 lb. (10·9
and 6·8 kg.). The following are the *normal* weights and sizes as given by the
authorities referred to:

Head and body 23 in. (584 mm.), tail 16 in. (406 mm.), total 39 in. (992
mm.). Pennant, 1768.   895

Head and body 23 in. (584 mm.), tail 15 in. (381 mm.), total 38 in. (966
mm.). Pennant, 1771.   896

Males: 18–26 lb. (8·1–11·8 kg.); females 13–22 lb. (5·9–10·0 kg.). Daniel,
1812.   327

Males: 20–24 lb. (9·1–10·9 kg.); females: 16–20 lb. (7·2–9·1 kg.). Bell,   171
1837.

Males: 44–46 in. (1120–1170 mm.), weight 24–25 lb. (10·9–11·4 kg.);
females: 17–18 lb. (7·7–8·1 kg.). Mennell & Perkins, 1863–4.   787

Weight '18 to 28 or even 30 lb.' (8·1–13·6 kg.); length 44–48 in. (1120–
1220 mm.). Southwell, 1871.   1089

1090   Weight '14 to 30 lb., or more.' (5·3–13·6 kg.). Southwell, 1872–3.

508   Length 36–42 in. (914–1067 mm.). Hamilton, 1890.

Males: 41–50 in. (1040–1270 mm.), weight 20–25 lb. (9·1–11·4 kg.);
798   females: 15–18 lb. (6·8–8·1 kg.). Millais, 1905.

Average length 44 in. (1120 mm.); males: 20–24 lb. (9·1–10·9 kg.),
975   females: 14–16½ lb. (5·3–7·4 kg.). Robinson, 1909.

Head and body 29½–33½ in. (750–850 mm.), tail 15¾–17¾ in. (400–450
923   mm.), total 45¼–51¼ in. (1150–1300 mm.). Pohle, 1920.

1155   Full grown male: 42–48 in. (1067–1220 mm.). Thorburn, 1920.

Normal range of males: head and body 27½–29½ in. (700–750 mm.), total
approximately 47¼ in. (1200 mm.); weight of males 15·4–22 lb. (7·0–10·0
864   kg.), females approximately 11 lb. (5·0 kg.). Ognev, 1931.

Length 40–54 in. (1020–1370 mm.); males 20–26 lb. (9·1–11·8 kg.),
1173   females 16–20 lb. (7·2–9·1 kg.). Vesey-Fitzgerald, 1946.

The following presumably relate specifically to French otters:

Head and body 31 in. (787 mm.), tail 18 in. (458 mm.), total 49 in. (1245
214   mm.). Brisson, 1756.

Head and body 25 in. (635 mm.), tail 13¾ in. (349 mm.), total 38 in. (965
227   mm.). Buffon, 1758.

Head and body 25½ in. (650 mm.), tail 13¾ in. (350 mm.), total 39¼ in.
437   (1000 mm.). Gervais, 1855.

Head and body 27½ in. (700 mm.), tail 15¾ in. (400 mm.), total 43¼ in.
718   (1100 mm.). Loche, 1867.

There are a number of instances recorded of very much larger otters, both in length and weight. Below, apart from two quite exceptional females, is a list of males of 30 lb. (13·6 kg.) or over, or 50 in. (1270 mm.) or more. Their places of origin are shown where these are known. It is possible that some repetition occurs despite efforts to avoid it.

Female: 27¾ lb. (12·6 kg.), length 54 in. (1370 mm.), weighed dry and
976   not carrying cubs (Westmorland). Robinson, 1917.

1108   Female: 27 lb. (12·3 kg.) (Gt Ouse, Cambridgeshire). Stephens, 1957.

Presumed males:

1090   23 lb. (10·4 kg.), 50 in. (1270 mm.) (Norfolk). Southwell, 1872–3.

27 lb. (12·3 kg.), 50 in. (1270 mm.); 27 lb. (12·3 kg.), 53 in. (1346 mm.);
28 lb. (12·7 kg.), 50½ in. (1280 mm.); 30 lb. (13·6 kg.), 53½ in. (1360 mm.)
in very poor condition; 37 lb. (16·8 kg.), 48 in. (1220 mm.) (all from
1095   Norfolk). Southwell, 1895.[1]

531   [1] The 53½ in. specimen is also referred to by Harting (1894) who gives its length as 50½
1089   in. (1280 mm.); this animal was killed at Ranworth in January 1871, and was mentioned by Southwell in that year; at that time he wrote that it 'is said to have weighed 30 lb. and measured 4 ft. 9 in. in length'.

152

28 lb. (12·7 kg.), 60 in. (1520 mm.) (Inverpolly, Ross). Lawson, 1919.   687

30 lb. (13·6 kg.) without its head. Pitt, 1938.   917

31 lb. (14 kg.) (Eden R., Cumberland). Macpherson, 1892.   753

32 lb. (14·5 kg.) (? Durham). Mennell & Perkins, 1863–4.   787

32½ lb. (14·7 kg.), head and body 36 in. (916 mm.), tail 15 in. (381 mm.), total 51 in. (1297 mm.) (Yarmouth, Norfolk). Buckland, 1887.   226

32 lb. (14·5 kg.), 48¾ in. (1239 mm.) (R. Rother, nr. Midhurst, Sussex); 32 lb. (14·5 kg.) (Munden, Herts.); 33 lb. (14·9 kg.) (Rydal Water, Westmorland); 34 lb. (15·4 kg.) (? Essex); ? 34 lb. (15·4 kg.) (Trafford Bridge); 35 lb. (15·9 kg.) (Harray, Orkney); 35 lb. (15·9 kg.), 48 in. (1220 mm.) (R. Stour, Kent); 'just under 60 inches' (1520 mm.) (R. Tyne, E. Lothian). Robinson, 1909.   974

34 lb. (15·4 kg.), 50 in. (1270 mm.) (R. Yar, Isle of Wight). Hadfield, 1874.   500

34½ lb. (15·7 kg.) (nr. Leominster in 1804). Anon., 1855.   46

34 lb. and 35 lb. (15·4 and 15·9 kg.) (both near Marlesham, Suffolk). Anon., 1922.   104

35 lb. (15·9 kg.), just over 52 in. (1320 mm.), not in good condition (R. Ouse, Cambridge). Wheeler, 1877.   1198

'Turned the scales at thirty-five pounds' (15·9 kg.). Kelway, 1944.   649

'Over 35 lb.' (15·9 kg.), 61 in. (1550 mm.) (R. Shannon, Eire). Anon., 1870.   70

40 lb. (18·1 kg.) (River Lea). Pike, 1950.   907

40–42 lb. (18·1–19 kg.). Stephens, 1957.   1108

61¼ in. (1561 mm.) 'after tanning'. Anon., 1898.   92a

'53 lbs. and a few odd ounces' (23 kg.), 'just under 48 inches' (1220 mm.) (R. Avon, nr. Ringwood, Hants.). Corbin, 1873.   304

Weight 45 lb. (20·4 kg.), length 66 in. (1676 mm.). Anon., 1867.   65

50 lb. (22·7 kg.), 66 in. (1676 mm.). Harting, 1894.[1]   531

'6 feet [1829 mm.] in length, "dealer's measure" (i.e. exclusive of 2/3 of the tail)' (Shetland Isles). Saxby, 1864.   1018

'Fully six feet' (1829 mm.) (Inverness). Anon., 1867.   64

'One drowned by being entangled in a Fisherman's Net near Bath, in 1805, measured upwards of *six feet*.' (1829 mm.). Daniel, 1812.   327

'Almost 60 lb.' (27·2 kg.) (Caithness). Stephens, 1953.   1106

Can such accounts of very large otters be substantiated? The British otter is, in general, roughly comparable with the North American in size,

---

[1] This animal is mentioned by a number of authors; it was killed by the Carmarthen otter hounds, 'at the Cowen'; the original reference is to be found in *Land and Water*, vol. II, page 51 (not seen by me).

²³⁹
⁴⁹ the hind foot of which, as illustrated by Burt (1952), measures 2·75 in. (7 cm.) across. An anonymous writer to *The Field* in 1860 records:

> On several occasions I have met with the seal [foot-print] of an otter of giant dimensions near the mouth of the Perry, a mile below Mumfordbridge. Without any exaggeration, the seal of that otter is the size of the top of an ordinary break-fast cup. The monster always appears to be accompanied by another otter, whose seal is of ordinary dimensions, that is, of the size of the top of a good sized wine glass . . .

Distribution:

Throughout Europe and Asia as far north approximately as the Arctic Circle; in Europe, south to Morocco and Algeria; absent from the Mediterranean islands except perhaps for Sicily and Corfu, where it may have been introduced (*see* Trouessart: 1910, and Cabrera: 1914); in Asia, westwards through Siberia, Manchuria, the Kuriles and Japan, but the southern limit is ill-defined, typical *L. l. lutra* possibly intergrading with *monticola* in northern India and Tibet, and with *chinensis* in northern China.

Status:

No reliable information on the present status of the otter seems to exist. In the more remote parts of its range where conditions are suitable it seems likely that it will continue to hold its own. In the British Isles, however, there is no doubt that as river boards clean up the banks and urban districts spread, so the natural habitat of the otter is year by year reduced. Water pollution can, of course, be a decisive factor. Otters will readily travel long distances and changes in the local population can be quickly accomplished. In 1957 Stephens estimated otters to be 'very numerous' in the East Suffolk and Norfolk river board area. The *Norfolk Mammal Report* for 1963 states:

> Ten years ago otters were relatively common; now they are relatively rare.

At the same time it is noted that their status in Norfolk recently had improved.

Stephens estimated the comparative frequency of otters in England and Wales, dividing the country for this purpose into appropriate River Board Areas of which she gives a map on page 22. Her findings were as follows:

'Very numerous': Yorks. Ouse; E. Suffolk and Norfolk; Devon; Cornwall; Severn; Wye; Usk; SW. Wales; NW. Wales or Gwynedd; Cumberland.

'Numerous': Northumberland and Tyneside; Trent; Lincs. Welland; Nene; Gt Ouse; Essex; Thames, including London area; Avon and Dorset; Somerset; Dee and Clwyd; Lancs.

'Fairly small population': Wear and Tees; ? Hull and E. Yorks.; Lee; Kent; E. Sussex; W. Sussex; Hants.; Glamorgan; Cheshire.

'Scarce': Bristol Avon; Mersey.

She shows that the number of otters killed by hunts for the years 1949–53 inclusive averaged just over 200 per annum.

With regard to Scotland, Stephens says that 'it can be assumed that they are numerous everywhere'. Concerning Ireland, she writes that although once plentiful throughout the country their numbers have been drastically reduced owing to the demand for pelts. Fitter (1964), under the heading 'Irish Otters and Deer in Danger', writes that   412

Irish naturalists have called on the Minister of Local Government to use his powers ... to protect the otter on a county basis.

With an animal that matures late, reproduces relatively slowly, and may breed at any time of the year, it can safely be assumed that unless an arbitrary 'close season' is instituted for at least a part of the year the otter in England will soon be limited to a very few places. Small, local populations, however, will probably continue to manage, and in the British Isles as a whole it seems in no danger of complete extinction while its strongholds in Wales and North-west Scotland remain available.

Principal illustrations:

Gesner, 1551, page 776. Woodcut. (*See* plate 2.)   438
Aldrovandi, 1645, page 295. Woodcut. (*See* plate 3.)   6
Buffon, 1758, vol. VII, plate xi. Two engravings.   227
    plates xii–xvi. Anatomical engravings.
    plate xvii. Engraving of skeleton.
Schreber, 1776, plate CXXVI A. Engraving.   1042
Bonaparte, 1839, vol. I [4th] plate. Lithograph.   196
Fitzinger, 1860 (Atlas), Figure 71. Coloured lithograph.   414
Coues, 1877, plate xviii. Drawing of skull.   306
Windle, 1897, page 374. Face muscles.   1211
    page 384. Pectoral muscles and panniculus.
    1898, page 174. Muscles of sole of foot.   1212
Nopcsa, 1905, vol. II, page 292. Diagram of os penis.   859
Pohle, 1920, page 54, figure 6. Photograph of skull from above.   923
    plate IV, figure 1. Photograph of under side of skull.
        figure 2. Photograph of lower jaw.
        figure 3. Photograph of profile of skull.
Thorburn, 1920, vol. I, facing page 65. Fine coloured plate.   1155

919   Pocock, 1921,
           page 536,
               figure 19 H. Drawing of rhinarium from front.
                       I. Drawing of rhinarium from side.
                       K. Drawing of ear.
               figure 20 A. Drawing of sole of right fore foot.
                       B. Drawing of sole of right hind foot.
922   1941, page 268. Drawing of head in profile.
649   Kelway, 1944. A number of photographs.
772   Matthews, 1952, page 235, figure 67c. Drawing of upper and lower jaws.
           page 250, figure 69. Drawings of right fore and hind feet.
           plate xxxiii. Otter swimming under water.
382   Errington, 1962, pages 12–13. Fine photograph.
845   Neal, 1962. A number of photographs, and drawing of skeleton. *See also*
       plates 2–8.

Young otters:
1108   Stephens [1957], plate 4. Two cubs in open nest.
844   Neal, 1961. A number of photographs.
777   Maxwell, 1963. A number of photographs.

Chapter 2

Middle Eastern and Asian Otters

IN the following sections the measurements given are those of adult males so far as is known or unless otherwise stated. Inches have been converted to millimetres to the nearest millimetre, and millimetres to inches to the nearest quarter-inch.

The geographical names are those used by the original authors. Neither these names, nor the sketch maps, have any political significance.

It has not seemed practicable to treat every form in the same way. Where a species (or subspecies) is well established or based on the subsequent experience of a large number of specimens certain generalizations can safely be made about its size, appearance or definitive characteristics. But in others the background material, so to speak, is less profusely authenticated, either owing to a paucity of the material itself or to the relative newness of the form described. In these cases a more detailed treatment has been preferred. Similarly, where the only diagnostic evidence for valid separation is based on cranial details, these have been given.

Without access to comparative material several of the Asian subspecies are exceedingly difficult to classify 'in the flesh' with no skull available for measurement. In many cases only knowledge of the animal's place of origin can resolve the problem with certainty.

LUTRA LUTRA AUROBRUNNEA
Hodgson, 1839.

Lutra auro-brunneus Hodgson, 1839.
Lutra aurobrunnea Hodgson, 1841.
Aonyx aurobrunnea Gray, 1843a.
? *Lutra auriventer* Blyth, 1863.
Barangia nepalensis Gray, 1865.
Barangia nipalensis Jerdon, 1874.
Lutra aurobruunea Anderson, 1878.
Lutra aureobrunnea Blanford, 1888; Fulton, 1903.
Lutra vulgaris: Thomas, 1889 [in part]; Blanford, 1891.

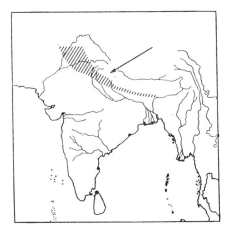

572

157

Lutra nepalensis Thomas, 1889.
? *Lutrogale barang aurobrunnea* Pohle, 1920.

Essential characters: Tail less than two-thirds body length; fur longish and rough, at any rate in winter.

Colour: Rich chestnut or light brown above, darkest on the head; more muddy coloured below, with the chest, extremities, inguinal area, and lower side of the tail golden red; all vibrissae dark brown.

Size: Small; head and body 20–22 in. (508–558 mm.), tail 12–13 in. (305–330 mm.), total 32–35 in. (813–888 mm.); weight 9–11 lb. (4·1–5·0 kg.). For skull measurements *see* page 313.

Range: Type locality – Nepal. Lower and central hilly region of Nepal; Garhwal; ? Chitral; ? Kashmir; ? eastern Kumaon.

569 *Illustration:* Hodgson, MS. [undated].

321

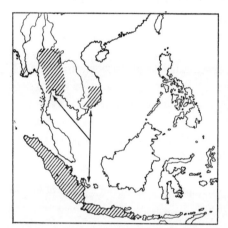

LUTRA LUTRA BARANG Cuvier, 1823.

'Simung' Raffles, 1822.
Lutra barang Cuvier, 1823.
Lutra simung Horsfield, 1851.
Lutra vulgaris barang Robinson & Kloss, 1918.
Lutra intermedia Pohle, 1920.

Essential characters: Fur rough and erect; very similar in general appearance to *L. l. lutra*.

Colour: Greyish earth-brown, occasionally darker; paler below, sometimes with a pale grizzling of the hair tips.

Size: Rather small; head and body 23–25 in. (585–640 mm.), tail 12¼–16 in. (310–406 mm.), total 37¼–44·8 in. (950–1128 mm.). For skull measurements *see* page 313.

Range: Type locality – Sumatra (?). Sumatra; Siam; Annam; ? Java.

767 *Illustration* (?): Marsden, 1811, plate XI.

462 LUTRA LUTRA CHINENSIS Gray, 1837
Lutra chinensis Gray, 1837.
Lutra indica Gray, 1843b.
Lutra sinensis Hodgson, 1855; Trouessart, 1897.
Lutra nair: Swinhoe, 1861 and 1862.

158

Lutra vulgaris: Buechner, 1892.
Lutra hanensis Matschie, 1907.

Essential characters: Pelage rather long; in general, very similar to *L. l. barang.*

Colour: Paler or darker brown above, below paler and yellower. An albino is recorded.

Size: Rather small; head and body 25–27½ in. (636–690 mm.), tail 15¾–16½ in. (400–419 mm.), total 41½–43 in. (1055–1090 mm.). For skull measurements *see* page 313.

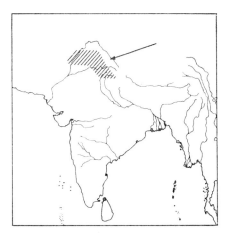

Range: Type locality – Canton. Annam; China; Hainan; Formosa.

Illustration: Pohle, 1920, page 179. Drawings of juvenile skull.   923

LUTRA LUTRA KUTAB Schinz, 1844.   1035

Lutra kutab Schinz, 1844.
Lutra katab Gray, 1865.
Lutra vulgaris: Scully, 1881.
? *Lutra lutra nair:* Ward, 1929.

Essential characters: Pelage 'stippled with white' under reflected light.

Colour: Deep brown to reddish-brown above, lower parts whitish.

Size: Average; head and body 24–30 in. (610–762 mm.), tail 15–18 in. (381–457 mm.), total 39–46 in. (991–1168 mm.); weight about 16 lb. (7·2 kg.). For skull measurements *see* page 314.

Range: Type locality – Kashmir. Upper Indus River and vicinity in Kashmir, into Tibet up to 13,500 ft. (4120 m.); ? northern Punjab.

Illustration: Ward, 1929, facing page 68. Three good photographs.   1182

864

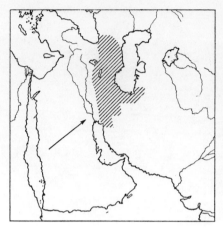

LUTRA LUTRA MERIDIONALIS Ognev, 1931.

Essential characters: Dorsal guard hairs have intense brown roots, broad white pre-terminal bands and brownish tips; an impression of faint ripples and diversity of colour is given.

Colour: Dorsally light brown with glossy straw shade; flanks and belly light straw-brown.

Size: For skull measurements *see* page 315.

Range: Type locality – vicinity of Teheran, northern Persia. From Georgia through Armenia and Persia to the Persian Gulf.

Status: Not rare in the Elbourz mountains (1959).

572 **LUTRA LUTRA MONTICOLA Hodgson, 1839.**

Lutra monticolus Hodgson, 1839.
Lutra monticola Hodgson, 1841.
? *Lutra simul* Gray, 1869.
Lutra vulgaris: Anderson, 1878;
 Blanford, 1888 [in part]; Thomas,
 1889 [in part].
Lutra lutra nair: Pohle, 1920.

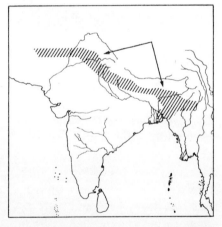

Essential characters: Fur long, rough, somewhat erect, but shorter and thinner in winter than *L. l. lutra*; guard hairs of belly extensively whitened.

Colour: Much seasonal variation; the new coat dorsally bright or rufous to deep, dull chocolate-brown; much paler below, the throat sometimes white throughout.

Size: Average; head and body 30–32 in. (762–813 mm.), tail 20 in. (508 mm.), total 50–52 in. (1270–1321 mm.); weight 24 lb. (10·9 kg.). For skull measurements *see* page 315.

Range: Type locality – Nepal. Punjab; Kumaon; Nepal; Sikkim; Assam; up to 5350 ft. (1630 m.).

569 *Illustration:* Hodgson, MS. May/[18]37. Drawing.

LUTRA LUTRA NAIR Cuvier, 1823.

321

Lutra nair Cuvier, 1823.
Lutra indica Gray, 1837.
Lutra nais Gerrard, 1862.
Lutra vulgaris Blanford, 1888 [in part].
Lutra lutra ceylonica Pohle, 1920.

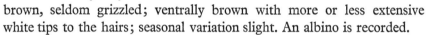

Essential characters: Fur short and soft; coat loose and somewhat up-standing, about 15–20 mm. long; chin and fore-throat commonly quite white.

Colour: Dorsally very dark lustrous brown, seldom grizzled; ventrally brown with more or less extensive white tips to the hairs; seasonal variation slight. An albino is recorded.

Size: Average; head and body 24–28 in. (610–712 mm.), tail $14\frac{1}{4}$–20 in. (362–508 mm.), total 40–48 in. (1015–1220 mm.); weight $10\frac{3}{4}$–$11\frac{3}{4}$ lb. (4·9–5·3 kg.). For skull measurements *see* page 315.

Range: Type locality – Pondicherry. Ceylon and southern India, up to 7000 ft. (2133 m.).

Status: Not uncommon in the hills of Ceylon (1939).

Illustration: Pocock, 1941, pages 275 and 304. Drawings of skull and tail.   922

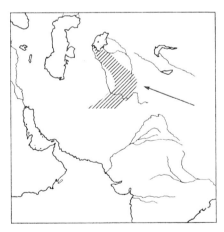

LUTRA LUTRA SEISTANICA Birula, 1912.

Lutra lutra oxiana Birula, 1915.

Birula based this form on three skins, without skulls, two in perfect condition and the third badly damaged. The original description is published in Russian, and so far as I am aware, no English translation has appeared previously. Birula writes: 181

Owing to the absence of the skulls it is not possible to determine their origin with the accuracy desirable; however, the size, the claws present on all four feet, and the general colour characteristics indicate that we have to deal here with otters of the type of *Lutra lutra* L. [Birula then discusses, in a passage of rather confused and slightly inaccurate synonymy, whether this form is more closely related to *Lutra lutra* or *Lutra (Lutrogale)*, and concludes] . . . the *Lutra seistanica* must be related to the former, because the lower edge of its nose is not straight, whereas the straight edge is a characteristic of *L. ellioti* [= *Lutra (Lutrogale)*]; but here it is in the shape of an obtuse angle turned downwards, as in the European otter. However, when comparing the skin of the *Lutra seistanica* with those of Northern European otters – although it does not distinguish itself very much from those of the Siberian form – we notice a remarkable difference in the general colouring of the fur which, in the *Lutra seistanica*, is considerably lighter; moreover, in all Seistanic skins the tail is considerably longer. Details of the difference between the colouring of the *Lutra seistanica* and the typical Northern European otter can be seen from the following comparison; for this purpose I take the Seistanic skin from the river Gilmend [Helmand] (no. 8363) and the skin of a typical otter from European Russia (Northern Livonia) [Latvia]:

Lutra seistanica:	Northern Russian Otter:
1. Upper side of head, back and tail much lighter, greyish-brown underfur with almost white base, guard hair with light brown tips of a completely different shade, much darker on upper part of back.	Upper side of head, back and tail dark brown (chestnut), underfur with light brown, greyish base, brown colour of guard hair almost the same as that of underfur.
2 Under side of whole body and tail brownish off-white, due to the rich, off-white guard hair almost completely covering the underfur, which is light brown with a yellowish-white base.	Under side of whole body and tail only a little lighter, due to rather rich light brown guard hair almost completely covering underfur, which is dark brown, with an off-white base.
3 Large white spot on throat, with yellowish-white underfur, also spreading to chin.	Normally no white spot on throat, but some specimens have a white chin.
4 Front and hind legs lighter than back, from yellowish-brown to brownish-grey.	Front and hind legs almost of the same colour as back, i.e. dark brown.
5 Tail two coloured; on upper side same colour as on back, i.e. greyish-brown; on underside off-white, becoming darker at tip.	Tail of almost uniform colour throughout, so that underside only a shade lighter than upper side, but hardly any difference. Tail does not become darker at tip.
6 Tail very long; bent backwards its tip touches the withers or even the nape of the neck.	Tail comparatively short; bent backwards its tip touches the centre of the back, or a spot slightly above it.

The relative length of the tail of the *Lutra seistanica* can be seen from the following comparative table of measurements:

	Length of body from tip of nose to base of tail	Length of tail from base to tip
Seistan no. 8364	90 cm. [35½ in.]	67 cm. [26½ in.]
Seistan no. 8363	104 cm. [41 in.]	66 cm. [26 in.]
Palestine	87 cm. [34¼ in.]	53 cm. [20¾ in.]
Livonia	102 cm. [40 in.]	40 cm. [15¾ in.]
Siberia	98 cm. [38½ in.]	45 cm. [17¾ in.]
Anadyr R. [Siberia]	92 cm. [36¼ in.]	54 cm. [21¼ in.]

From this table it can be seen that the tail length of the Northern otter varies, but it is always considerably shorter than that of the *Lutra seistanica*. Between these two, with regard to length of tail as well as colour – which is much darker than that of *Lutra seistanica* but much lighter than that of the Northern otter – is a summer skin from Palestine (Lower Jordan, no. 3249) now in the possession of the Zoological Museum.

Unfortunately I have no opportunity of making a comparison with a typical skin of *L. l. nair* F. Cuvier which has been described as originating from Southern India (Pondicherry, Coromandel Coast), but from the detailed description given by Blanford in *Fauna of British India* (p. 182) [actually a description of *L. (L.) perspicillata*] it can be seen that *Lutra seistanica* has preserved the majority of the colour peculiarities of the Indian otter; however, I cannot discern in the skin of *Lutra seistanica* ' a more or less rufous tinge' on the upper side of the body; as a characteristic of the Indian otter the same author mentions 'a grizzled appearance' of the back which mainly distinguishes the *Lutra seistanica* from the Northern otter. This grizzled appearance is particularly distinct in skin no. 8365; here the back is somewhat darker than in the skins described above, and therefore the light tips of the guard hair stand out more clearly. Skin no. 8364 has almost the same appearance as no. 8363, but it is slightly rust-coloured; this may be the 'rufous tinge' of the Indian otter mentioned by Blanford.

All further descriptions of skins were obtained by N.A. Zarudny in Seistan (Eastern Persia), in the region of vast rivers, among them mainly the rivers Chamun [Hamun] and Gilmend [Hilmand], and the famous river Neisar [Naizar] (Nei=Persian for 'Reed') – according to travellers a continuous 'sea' of profusely growing reed, swarming with all sorts of animals. ([footnote] N. Zarudny, Excursion to North-East Persia; published by the Academy of Sciences (8th series) X, no. 1, 1900, pp. 40–42.) Thus we find, not surprisingly, in the immense water flows of Persia and the neighbouring parts of Afghanistan a type of otter whose morphology – due to the isolated position of the water reservoir – is slightly different. According to information compiled by N.A. Zarudny the otter occupies an

185

important position in the trade of the Seistanic population, and 'the skin of this animal is so highly priced that in our money we have to pay 10 roubles or more for a good specimen' . . .

923 Pohle examined three Palestinian skins as well as one from the Khabur River and came to the conclusion that they, also, were *seistanica*. But before examining Pohle's views it may be as well to consider Birula's *Lutra lutra* 366, 864 *oxiana*, treated by Ellerman & Morrison-Scott, and also by Ognev, as a synonym of *seistanica*.

182 Birula published his account of this latter form in 1915, in a parallel Russian/Latin text. Freely translated, this reads as follows:

> *L. l. oxiana* (from the province of Petropolitana) differs from typical *L. lutra* in its paler colouring, being hoary on the upper side, in its white throat and neck, in its longer tail, and in its narrower skull. The guard hair of the back is of a dark smoky colour ['*fumigatofuscum*'] (of a sepia tint) but not at all tawny, and is more or less grizzled with stiff hairs which are partly whitish; the underfur is also of a dark smoky colour but is white at the base; on the underside the colour is white without any yellow tint, and the underfur of the abdomen, chest and neck is also white, but slightly tipped with a pale smoky colour; the throat, neck and lips are white, with totally white underfur without dark tips; the tail is bicoloured, the underside being whitish with dark underfur, while above it is the same colour as the back. The skull is elongated, rather broad posteriorly, with powerful teeth, molars and premolars in the upper jaw, especially in the type specimen . . .

864 Ognev comments that only a single, defective skull of *oxiana* is to be found in the Zoological Museum of the Academy of Sciences, and says:

> This makes it impossible to express an opinion on the craniology of this otter . . . The otter which ranges in the Pamirs is an inhabitant of mountainous terrain considerably different from the marshy lowlands of Seistan. Its great similarity to the Persian subspecies is thus all the more strange; this makes it even more likely that the name given by A. Birulya [*sic*] to the Pamir otter on the basis of good collections will be restored.

Ognev naturally had access to Birula's three specimens of *seistanica*, and as his description of them is somewhat more detailed than Birula's it is well worth quoting.

> General tone of back glossy light brown (close to cinnamon drab), but with marked spottiness. Head somewhat lighter than back. Flanks dirty yellowish-white (close to olive-buff in tone, changing to deep olive-buff). Belly whitish-yellow, even lighter than flanks. Paws dirty yellow (close to deep olive-buff). Tail markedly bi-color, superiorly similar to back, inferiorly dirty yellowish white. Claws yellowish white; vibrissae of same hue.

Underfur typical of Seistan otter – white at very roots, with slight cinnamon shade. Distal parts of underfur dull brownish gray (tone intermediate between drab and hair brown). Guard hairs glossy, yellowish-whitish brown, with somewhat darker tips (tone – drab). The characteristic bright coloring is imparted by the combination of underfur clearly visible through the guard hairs and the bright glossy guard hairs. Pale grayish-cinnamon root portions (tone – avellaneous and wood brown) are seen on underparts and in region of whitish-yellow fur. These darkened roots are particularly marked in groin region, but are not present on neck. Hair tips on neck usually somewhat lighter, forming an indistinct lightly colored neck patch.

All three Seistan otters are of a quite uniform type in fur coloring. Specimen no. 8364 (cotype) is somewhat browner and more rust. Some intermingling of chestnut (cinnamon-brown tone) observed in underfur. Guard hairs yellowish, interspersed with light rust. Paws also somewhat more rust and more intensive. Though the animal is more brightly colored, the general type remains similar to that characteristic of Seistan otter.

The third specimen is somewhat darker than the above. Dark grayish-brown tones intermingled in underfur. The characteristic spottiness of the type is lacking in the coloration of the back.

Meanwhile, Pohle's Palestinian forms have still to be considered. Pohle says of them: 923

The skins from Palestine which I have in front of me, and which are of adult animals ... show in their colouring so much resemblance to *seistanica* that I would like to assign them also to this subspecies. The only difference is in the fact that although the lower side of the neck is distinctly whitish, there is no clear white spot.

Pohle goes on to point out that in his view the proportionately long tail on which Birula partly relies is not a critical character; moreover, an animal from the Jordan mentioned by Birula shows almost exactly the same relative proportions of head and body to tail as does the type of *seistanica*. He adds that one of his own specimens, from Tabgha [Bethsaida], has precisely the same measurements as Birula's Jordan example. Strangely enough, he makes no mention of *oxiana*.

Ognev's comments on Pohle's conclusions are brief.   864

Pohle ... includes Palestinian otters in *L. l. seistanica*. This is hardly correct. The collection of ZMAS contains a specimen [from the Dead Sea at the mouth of the Jordan River] which is grayer than *L. l. lutra* and possesses a number of features (uniformly colored tail and browner color) which distinguish it from the Seistan subspecies.

860 This view appears to be substantiated by Novikov, who does not include Palestine in the range of *seistanica*. With regard to its general appearance he says:

General colour of back light glossy grey-brown, with distinct ripple. Tail markedly bicoloured, (above coloured as on back, underparts dirty yellowish-white).

Size: Type: head and body 41 in. (1040 mm.), tail 26 in. (660 mm.), total 67 in. (1700 mm.); another specimen, head and body 35½ in. (900 mm.), 181 tail 26½ in. (670 mm.), total 62 in. (1570 mm.). Birula, 1912.

L. l. oxiana: head and body about 35¾ in. (910 mm.), tail about 22½ in. (570 182 mm.), total about 58¼ in. (1480 mm.). Birula, 1915.

Palestinian example: head and body 34¼ in. (870 mm.), tail 20¾ in. (530 181 mm.), total 55 in. (1400 mm.). Birula, 1912.

For skull measurements see page 316.

Distribution:

181 Type locality: Helmand River, Seistan, E. Persia; range: Helmand, Hamun and Naizar rivers and reed beds. (Birula, 1912.)

182, 864 *L. l. oxiana:* type locality, neighbourhood of Lyangar, Pyandzh river basin, in Roshan, Pamirs. (Birula, 1915 and Ognev, 1931.)

840 ? Argandab, Baluchistan [A. Murray, undated]; ? mouth of River Jordan, Dead Sea [Birula, 1912]; ? Crocodile River, Caesarea; ? Nahr Rubin, s. Jaffa; ? Tabgha [Bethsaida], Tiberias; ? Tell Halaf, on the Chabur 923 [Khabur] river, a tributary of the Euphrates. (Pohle, 1920.)

860 Pamirs; eastern Iran; Afghanistan. (Novikov, 1962.)

453

927

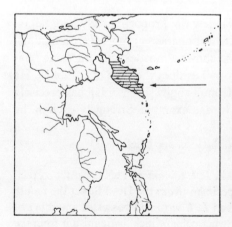

LUTRA STEJNEGERI Goldman, 1936.

Goldman based this form on a single skull in the US National Museum, although according to Poole & Schantz the type material consists of both skull and skeleton. So far as I am aware, no other example has since been recorded, and in these circumstances this species must be treated as unconfirmed and would probably best be placed in the synonymy of *L. l. lutra*. Goldman says of it:

[The skull] represents a rather young but nearly or quite full-grown individual, apparently normal in every way. In the narrowness of the upper molars and in other cranial details, however, it exhibits differential features in contrast to other Asiatic otters that seem to warrant the segregation of a new form . . .

Characters – Closely allied to the widely dispersed geographic races of the Eurasian species *Lutra lutra*, and evidently a member of the same restricted group. Skull very similar in general to that of *Lutra lutra lutra* of Sweden, but apparently smaller, with braincase more rounded and inflated; palate more concave near middle, broader behind molars, the posterior border without the small, spinous, median projection usually present in *L. l. lutra*; dentition lighter; upper carnassial [pm^4] with small anterior cusp less developed and cingulum of outer side slightly concave in outline as viewed from below (nearly straight in *L. l. lutra*); upper molar relatively much narrower, its width near middle less than crown width of upper carnassial (in *L. l. lutra* the upper molar is decidedly broader than carnassial); postero-internal lobe of upper molar less prominent, scarcely differentiated from cingulum; posterior heel of lower carnassial [m$_1$] less elevated above cingulum, less trenchant. Similar to that of *Lutra whiteleyi* of Japan [= *L. l. lutra*] in the anteriorly rounded form of the interpterygoid fossa, but apparently differing otherwise in about the same characters as from *L. l. lutra* . . .

Remarks – The comparatively close relationship of *Lutra stejnegeri* to *Lutra lutra* clearly is indicated, and the former may prove to be an isolated geographic race assignable to the latter species. It requires no close comparison with *Lutra lutra meridionalis* Ognev of the Northern Caucasus, USSR., nor with any other form known to me. Relationship to *Viverra aterrima* Pallas from the Amur River region, south of the Okhotsk Sea, may be somewhat problematical, but even the generic identity of that animal seems to be uncertain.

It may be appropriate to mention here an unusual example from Kamchatka, expressly described by Ognev. This must not, of course, be taken as implying identity with Goldman's form. Ognev writes:

The coloration of [an] otter . . . from Kamchatka . . . is extremely noteworthy. The general tone is gray, with slight brownish-straw (drab) overtones. Underparts even lighter, with glossy yellow shade. Neck whiter than belly. Paws yellowish-gray-white. Tail uniform in color, indistinguishable in tone from back (drab). This is most probably merely an aberration of the common otter . . . another specimen from Kamchatka [has] completely typical coloring.

Size: For skull measurements *see* page 316.
Distribution: Type: from near Petropavlovsk, Kamchatka. Known only from the type locality, but probably ranging wherever conditions have remained suitable on the Kamchatka Peninsula. (Goldman, 1936.)

167

468 LUTRA SUMATRANA Gray, 1865.

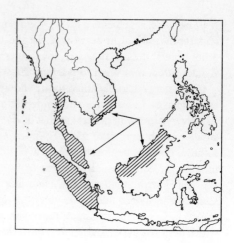

'Barang' Raffles, 1822.
'Ambrang' Raffles, 1822.
? *Lutra simung:* Schinz, 1844; Cantor, 1846.
Lutra barang: Cantor, 1846.
Lutra leptonyx: Cantor, 1846.
Barangia sumatrana Gray, 1865.
Lutra lovii Günther, 1876; Lyon, 1908; Pohle, 1920.
Lutra brunnea Pohle, 1920.
Lutra lowii Chasen, 1940.
Lutra sumatrana lovii Pocock, 1941.
Lutra sumatrana brunnea Pocock, 1941.

Essential characters: The rhinarium covered with hair (sometimes abraded in old individuals), only the narrow upper edge of the nostril bare; claws well developed; palms and soles hairless; the upper surface of the web of the hind feet covered with close hair, the lower surface naked.

Colour: Generally dark, varying from a reddish chestnut to very dark chocolate brown; the underside very little paler than the back; the white of the throat very limited in extent, but sharply contrasted with the adjacent darker areas; underfur very pale.

Size: Fairly large; head and body $27\frac{1}{2}$–$32\frac{1}{2}$ in. (700–826 mm.), tail $13\frac{3}{4}$–20 in. (350–509 mm.), total $41\frac{1}{4}$–$52\frac{1}{2}$ in. (1050–1335 mm.). For skull measurements *see* page 316.

Range: Type locality – Sumatra. Sumatra; Peninsular Siam; Malay States; North Borneo; Annam.

38 *Illustration:* Anderson, 1878, vol. II, plate X. Coloured plate. (*See* plate 9.)

468 LUTRA (LUTROGALE) Gray, 1865 – The Indian 'smooth-coated' Otter.
Lutrogale Gray, 1865; Flower, 1929; Pocock, 1941; Hayman, 1957.

LUTRA (LUTROGALE) PERSPICILLATA Geoffroy, 1826.
? *Mustela lutra:* Marsden, 1811.
Lutra perspicillata Geoffroy, 1826.
Lutra simung Lesson, 1827; Robinson & Kloss, 1919.
Lutra tarayensis Hodgson, 1839; Wroughton, 1919; Allen, 1938.
Lutra nair: ? Elliot, 1839; Cantor, 1846; Jerdon, 1874; Anderson, 1878; Blandford, 1888; Flower, 1929.

168

Lutra indica Gray, 1865.
Lutra tavayensis Gray, 1865 and 1869.
Lutra macrodus Gray, 1865 and 1869.
Lutra monticola: Anderson, 1878 [skull only]; Blanford, 1888; Thomas, 1889.
Lutra ellioti Anderson, 1878; Blanford, 1888.
Lutra taraiyensis Blanford, 1888; Pocock, 1940.
Lutra barang: Thomas, 1889.
Amblonyx cinerea perspicillata Pohle, 1920.
Lutra sumatrana: Dammerman, 1929.
Lutrogale tarayensis Flower, 1929.
Lutra barang barang Sody, 1929.
Lutrogale barang Pocock, 1941.
Lutra (Lutrogale) macrodus Pocock, 1941.
Lutrogale perspicillata Pocock, 1941; Hayman, 1957.

Essential characters:

Of the *subgenus* –
Form robust; the upper and lower borders of the naked rhinarium almost straight; the tail very markedly flattened, nearly triangular in section; pelage short, smooth; claws short, sharp; feet rather large, the third phalange of fingers and toes free of webbing; skull somewhat arched, less depressed than in *Lutra lutra,* muzzle length considerably reduced, and the eyes set lower on the face; teeth massive, particularly pm⁴ and m¹.

Of the *species* –
Colour: Variable, from blackish-brown to sandy brown; area around mouth, chin and throat whitish or yellowish; underside somewhat paler than the upper.
Size: Average, robust; total length of males up to nearly 48 in. (1210 mm.); weight 20–25 lb. (9·1–11·4 kg.).
Range: Very extensive, ? discontinuous; from Tigris marshes in the west, throughout India (in suitable habitat) from the lower Himalayas to Madras and Travancore; Burma; Assam; Malay Peninsula; ? western Yunnan; Sumatra; Java; Borneo; Indo-China; ? south-western China.

LUTRA (LUTROGALE) PERSPICILLATA PERSPICILLATA Geoffroy, 1826.   433
Lutra perspicillata Geoffroy, 1826.
Lutra (Lutrogale) barang tarayensis Pohle, 1920.
Lutrogale perspicillata perspicillata Pocock, 1941.

Essential characters: As in the subgenus.

Colour: Rather variable; dark or chestnut brown above, below generally lighter and with a reddish tint; neck and throat yellowish white.

Size: Average, but massively built; head and body 26–31¼ in. (660–790 mm.), tail 16–20 in. (406–505 mm.), total 43½–51 in. (1103–1293 mm.); weight 16–24·6 lb. (7·3–11·17 kg.). For skull measurements *see* page 316.

Range: Type locality – Sumatra. Throughout India, from the lower Himalayas; Burma; Assam; Yunnan, to 6000 ft. (1830 m.); Laos; Malay Peninsula; Sumatra; Borneo; Java; south-western China.

38 *Illustration:* Anderson, 1878 [as *L. monticola*], plate XII, figures 1–3. Views of skull. (*See also* plates 13, 15, 16.)

LUTRA (LUTROGALE) PERSPICILLATA MAXWELLI Hayman, 1957.
Lutrogale perspicillata maxwelli Hayman, 1957.

538

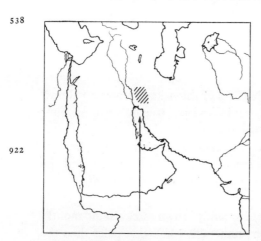

922

Hayman describes the type, an apparently adult male, as follows:

Entire animal much darker than in any other *Lutrogale*. The general colour of the head and body is a very dark chocolate brown, darker than the darkest Burmese skins referred to by Pocock (1941). In all other *perspicillata* skins seen, the throat and lower neck are a dirty cream or buffy white, the colour gradually darkening between the forelegs, and the feet are much pale than the general body colour. In *maxwelli*, on the other hand, the throat is a distinct iron-grey, and the lower neck and underparts are only a little paler than the dorsal surface. The feet are very little lighter in colour than the body . . .

Size: Type: head and body 29½ in. (749 mm.), tail 17 in. (432 mm.), total
538 46½ in. (1181 mm.). Hayman, 1957.
Adult female: head and body 24½ in. (625 mm.), tail 14¾ in. (375 mm.),
535 total 39¼ in. (1 m.). Hatt, 1959.
Distribution: Type: skin purchased at Abusakhair, about 5 miles west of the Persian frontier and about 35 miles south-east of Amara, on the Tigris,
538 Iraq. (Hayman, 1957.)
535 Tigris River, near Al Azair, Iraq. (Hatt, 1959.)
773 *Illustrations:* Maxwell, 1960, between pages 100 and 101. Twelve photographs.

Maxwell, 1961. Fourteen photographs. [774]

Maxwell, 1962. Facing page 4, colour photograph. Following page 12, 25 [775] photographs. (*See also* plate 14.)

LUTRA (LUTROGALE) PERSPICILLATA SINDICA Pocock, 1940. [921]

Lutrogale perspicillata sindica Pocock, 1940.

Essential characters: Much paler than other representatives of *L. perspicillata.*

Colour: Drabby, tawny or sandy brown above.

Size: Average; adult female, head and body 25·8 in. (655 mm.), tail 16·2–17·8 in. (412–452 mm.), total 42–43·6 in. (1067–1107 mm.); weight 16 lb. (7·3 kg.). For skull measurements *see* page 318.

Range: Type locality – Chak, in the Sukkur district of Sind. The Indus valley at least from Bahawalpur southwards to Sind; eastern Nara, Khairpur; range beyond the lower Indus unknown.

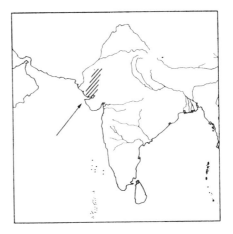

[940]

AMBLONYX Rafinesque, 1832 – The Asian 'clawless' or short-clawed Otter.

Amblonyx Rafinesque, 1832.
Aonyx: Gray, 1837; and many later authors.
Leptonyx Lesson, 1842.
Micraonyx J. A. Allen, 1922.
Micraonyx: G. M. Allen, 1938.

AMBLONYX CINEREA Illiger, 1815. [606]

Lutra cinerea Illiger, 1815; Thomas, 1889; Pocock, 1921.
Lutra perspicillata: Gray, 1843b; Thomas, 1889.
Aonyx horsfieldii: Blyth, 1863; Thomas, 1889.
Lutra (Aonyx) leptonyx Blyth, 1863; Anderson, 1878.
Lutra barang: Blyth, 1863.
Lutra indigitata: Blyth, 1863; Thomas, 1889.
Lutra leptonyx: Thomas, 1889.
Aonyx sikimensis: Thomas, 1889.

Lutra swinhoei: Thomas, 1889.
Amblonyx cinereus Pocock, 1921.
Amblonyz cinerea Pocock, 1921.
Micraonyx cinerea J.A.Allen, 1922.
Lutra cinerea Banks, 1931.
Micraonyx cinerea: G.M.Allen, 1938.
Aonyx (Amblonyx) cinerea Ellerman & Morrison-Scott, 1951.

Essential characters: Claws on fingers and toes rudimentary, more or less erect; digits webbed to proximal ends of digital pads; skull short, broad; first upper premolar generally absent; size, small.
Colour: Variable; pale ashy-brown to deep lustrous chocolate.
Range: Discontinuous; Siam; Malay Peninsula; Sumatra; Java; Borneo; Palawan; south China; ? Indo-China. In India from Kumaon in the west, through Sikkim; Bhutan; Assam; Upper Burma; Yunnan; Bengal; Arakan. Also in southern India in Coorg; Nilgiri Hills; Travancore.

AMBLONYX CINEREA CINEREA
Illiger, 1815.

606

'Grijze Otter' Wurmb, 1784.
Lutra cinerea Illiger, 1815; Gray,
   1843b, etc.; Everett, 1893.
Lutra leptonyx Horsfield, 1824;
   Fischer, 1829; Gray, 1837, etc.;
   Wagner, 1841; Lesson, 1842.
Aonyx horsfieldii Gray, 1837, etc.
Leptonyx barang Lesson, 1842;
   Gervais, 1855.
Lutra perspicillata: Lesson, 1842;
   Gray, 1843b, etc.; Cantor, 1846;
   Anderson, 1878.
Barang: Lesson, 1842.
Aonyx leptonyx Gray, 1843b, etc.
Mustela fusca: Gray, 1843b, etc.
Mustela lutra: Gray, 1843b, etc.
Lutra barang: Schinz, 1844.
Semul Gray, 1865 and 1869.
Lutra (Aonyx) horsfieldii Anderson, 1878.
Amblonyx cinerea wurmbi Sody, 1933.
Aonyx (Amblonyx) cinerea cinerea Ellerman & Morrison-Scott, 1951.

Essential characters: As for the species.

Colour: Variable, much seasonal variation; brown with a rufous cast to very dark lustrous chocolate brown above, sometimes with a few scattered white hairs.

Size: Small; head and body 16–25 in. (406–635 mm.), tail 9¾–12 in. (246–304 mm.), total 25¾–37 in. (652–939 mm.); weight usually 5·9–11·9 lb. (2·7–5·4 kg.). The females are on average only a little smaller than the males. For skull measurements *see* page 318.

Range: Type locality – Batavia, West Java. Java; Sumatra; Malay Peninsula; Siam; Annam; Laos; Karimon Island; Borneo; Palawan; southern China.

Status: Probably fairly common locally.

Illustration: Walker, 1964, vol. II, page 1218. Photograph. (*See also* plate 21.)   1180

AMBLONYX CINEREA CONCOLOR Rafinesque, 1832.   940

Lutra amblonyx Rafinesque, 1832.

Lutra concolor Rafinesque, 1832.

Lutra indigitatus Hodgson, 1839.

Lutra indigitata Hodgson, 1841; Schinz, 1844; Gray, 1846, etc.

Aonyx indigitata Gray, 1843a, etc.; Pocock, 1941.

Aonyx indigitatus Gray, 1846; Horsfield, 1851; Gerrard, 1862.

Aonyx sikimensis Horsfield, 1855; Gray, 1865 and 1869.

? *Lutra (Hydrogale) swinhoei* Gray, 1867.

Lutra (Aonyx) indigitata Anderson, 1878.

Aonyx leuconyx Inglis, 1919.

? *Amblonyx cinerea fulvus* Pohle, 1920.

Amblonyx concolor Pohle, 1920.

Amblonyx indigitata Pohle, 1920.

? *Lutra swinhoei:* Pocock, 1941.

? *Lutra (Lutrogale) swinhoei* Pocock, 1941.

Aonyx (Amblonyx) cinerea concolor Ellerman & Morrison-Scott, 1951.

Alonyx cinerea concolor Harris & Harris, 1959.

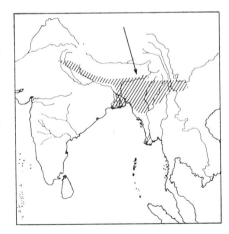

173

Essential characters: As in the species, but skull less muscularly moulded than in typical *cinerea*. The absence of anal scent glands had been noted on one occasion.

Colour: Somewhat variable; drabby, greyish, earthy or rufous brown above; the pale cheek and throat more extensive posteriorly and more sharply defined from the adjacent darker areas than in typical *cinerea*.

Size: Small; head and body 18–24 in. (457–610 mm.), tail 10½–13·2 in. (267–333 mm.), total 30–37 in. (762–940 mm.). For skull measurements *see* page 319.

Range: Type locality – Garo Hills, Assam. Assam, to 4500 ft. (1373 m.); Upper Burma and Arakan, to 6000 ft. (1830 m.); Yunnan, to 4500 ft. (1373 m.); in India, from Garhwal area and Kumaon south-eastwards and through Sikkim to Calcutta.

Illustration: See plates 22–25.

921　AMBLONYX CINEREA NIRNAI Pocock, 1940.

Lutra leptonyx: Blanford, 1888.
Lutra cinerea: Blanford, 1891.
Aonyx (Amblonyx) cinerea nirnai Ellerman & Morrison-Scott, 1951.

Essential characters: As for the species.

Colour: Generally very deep chocolate, almost blackish-brown, sometimes with a rufous tinge; paler below.

Size: Small; head and body 22–24 in. (558–610 mm.), tail 10½–13·8 in. (267–351 mm.), total 32½–37 in. (825–940 mm.); weight of adult male type 9½ lb. (4·3 kg.). For skull measurements *see* page 319.

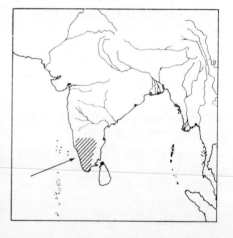

Range: Type locality – Virajpet, South Coorg. The hill ranges of southern Ind; to 5800 ft. (1770 m.).

Chapter 3

African Otters

LUTRA (HYDRICTIS) Pocock, 1921 – The African 'spotted-necked' Otter.   919
Hydrogale Gray, 1865.
Hydrictis Pocock, 1921; Schouteden, 1944–6.

LUTRA (HYDRICTIS) MACULICOLLIS Lichtenstein, 1835.   702
Lutra maculicollis Lichtenstein, 1835.
Lutra grayi Verreaux, 1857; Gray, 1865.
Lutra grayii Gerrard, 1862.
Hydrogale maculicollis Gray, 1865.
Hydrictis maculicollis Pocock, 1921; Schouteden, 1944–6.
? *Hydrictis (Maculicollis) poensis* Perret & Aellen, 1956.
Lutra (Hydrictis) maculicauda Walker, 1964.

Essential characters:
  Of the *subgenus* –
Rhinarium reduced, the upper border doubly convex; throat, neck and chest pale, irregularly spotted with brownish or reddish markings; similar markings may appear in the inguinal area; all claws well developed; soles and palms naked; the extensive webs, which reach to the distal ends of the digital pads on their inner sides, scattered below with fine short hairs; the plantar pad poorly defined; teeth rather small.
  Of the *species* –
Colour: Very variable, both of guard hair (light, chestnut, or very dark brown) and underfur (basally white or brown, apically dark brown), the paler ventral areas very variable and irregular in extent.
Size: Rather small; total length 34–42 in. (864–1070 mm.); weight does not generally exceed 20 lb. (9·1 kg.).
Range: Africa, south of lat. 10°N., approximately.

LUTRA (HYDRICTIS) MACULICOLLIS MACULICOLLIS Lichtenstein, 1835.   702
Hydrictis maculicollis maculicollis Schouteden, 1944–6.

Essential characters: As in the subgenus; pelage glossier above than below; first upper premolar between the canine and pm², not internally beside the canine as in *Aonyx*. Groups seen on the move in January, possibly partly migratory.

Colour: Very variable, especially in the extent of the asymmetrical white markings; deep chestnut or dark brown, at times with a rufescent suffusion,

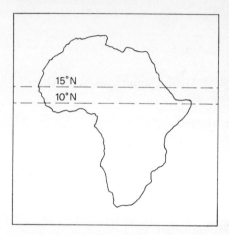

at others with an olivaceous tone; underfur narrowly tipped with dark brown apically, basally white, silvery, cream or buff; there is frequently a white spot on the knee. *Size:* Rather small; head and body 22½–26 in. (575–660 mm.), tail 13–17½ in. (330–445 mm.), total 37½–42 in. (950–1070 mm.); weight does not normally exceed 20 lb. (9·1 kg.). For skull measurements *see* page 319.

Range: Type locality – Bambusbergen, north-east Cape Colony. Liberia; Nigeria; Cameroons; Spanish Guinea; Congo; Angola; ? Abyssinia; Kenya; Tanganyika; the Rhodesias; Mozambique; Transvaal; Orange Free State; Natal; Cape province.

Status: Abundant in Northern Rhodesia (1960) and Lake Victoria (1963), less common than *Aonyx* elsewhere.

936 *Illustration:* Procter, 1963, pages 98 and 99. Four excellent photographs. (*See also* plates 26 and 27.)

970 LUTRA (HYDRICTIS) MACULICOLLIS CHOBIENSIS Roberts, 1932.

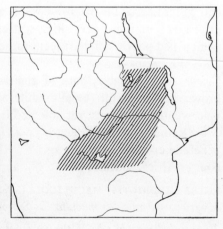

Lutra maculicollis chobiensis
Roberts, 1932.
Lutra malculicollis chobiensis
Roberts, 1932.

Essential characters: Darker than the typical form; the teeth may be smaller than in typical *maculicollis*.

Colour: 'Seal-brown' or dark brown, darkest on the dorsum; sides of face, chin and inside of forelegs near to chestnut, but remaining brown ventral parts hardly lighter than upper parts; underfur

176

grey; a corduroy effect to the fur was noticed on the belly of one female.

Size: Rather small; head and body about 24 in. (608 mm.), tail about 15 in. (380 mm.), total about 39 in. (990 mm.); weight about 10 lb. (2·2 kg.). For skull measurements *see* page 320.

Range: Type locality – Kabulabula on the Chobe River, north-east Bechuanaland. North-east Bechuanaland to Lake Bangweulu, Northern Rhodesia; Zambesi River.

LUTRA (HYDRICTIS) MACULICOLLIS KIVUANA Pohle, 1920.   923

Lutra maculicollis kivuana Pohle, 1920.

Hydrictis maculicollis kivuana Schouteden, 1944–6.

Essential characters: Skull similar to typical race, but higher at the back (more than 20 mm.), and broader facially.

Colour: Variable; as in typical *maculicollis.*

Size: Rather small; head and body 27½ in. (690 mm.), tail 13¾ in. (350 mm.), total 41 in. (1040 mm.). For skull measurements *see* page 320.

Range: Type locality – Kissenji, on the north shore of Lake Kivu. Lake Kivu and neighbouring lakes, Congo; Lake Victoria.

Illustration: Pohle, 1920, page 46, and plate III, figures 3–5. Views of skull.   923

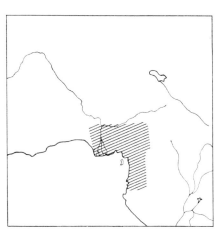

LUTRA (HYDRICTIS) MACULICOLLIS   245
MATSCHIEI Cabrera, 1903.

Lutra matschiei Cabrera, 1903.

Hydrictis maculicollis matschiei Perret & Aellen, 1956.

Essential characters: Pelage very dark; teeth relatively very large.

Colour: Guard hairs deep sepia brown or very dark coffee colour, almost black, with metallic reflections, the roots yellow on the body, whitish on the head and tail.

Size: Average; head and body 30 in. (765 mm.), tail about 16 in. (406 mm.), total about 46 in. (1171 mm.). For skull measurements *see* page 321.

Range: Type locality – Cape S. Juan, Spanish Guinea. Nigeria; Cameroons; Rio Muni.

246   *Illustration:* Cabrera, 1903–10, between pages 60 and 61, plate III. Coloured lithograph.

1148

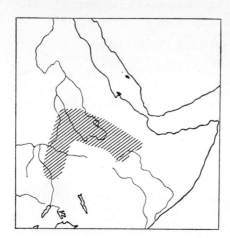

LUTRA(HYDRICTIS)MACULICOLLIS NILOTICA Thomas, 1911.

? *Lutra concolor* Neumann, 1902.

Lutra maculicollis nilotica Thomas, 1911.

Essential characters: Larger than the other subspecies; teeth comparatively large.

Colour: As in the typical race.

Size: For skull measurements *see* page 321.

Range: Type locality – Malek, just south of Bor, Upper [White] Nile.

Anglo-Egyptian Sudan; ? Abyssinia, in Lake Tsana and tributaries of the Blue Nile.

923   LUTRA (HYDRICTIS) MACULICOLLIS TENUIS Pohle, 1920.

Lutra tenuis Pohle, 1920.

Lutra maculicollis mutandae Hinton, 1921b.

Lutra maculicollis tenuis Allen, 1939.

Essential characters: Very dark in colour; teeth small; skull small and delicate, flatter than in true *maculicollis.*

Colour: Very dark, slightly paler below; the light areas very conspicuous.

Size: Rather small; head and body 24 in. (610 mm.), tail 15 in. (380 mm.), total 39 in. (990 mm.). For skull measurements *see* page 321.

Range: Type locality – Lake Mutanda, Kigesi district, Uganda. The lakes on the borders of Ruanda/Uganda/Tanganyika.

AONYX Lesson, 1827 – The African 'clawless' Otter.   695
Aonyx Lesson, 1827.
Aonix Lesson, 1842.
Anahyster Murray, 1860.
Lutra: Thomas, 1889.

AONYX CAPENSIS Schinz, 1821.   1034
Lutra capensis Schinz, 1821; G.Cuvier, 1829; Thomas, 1889.
Lutra inunguis F.Cuvier, 1823; Lesson, 1827; Schinz, 1844.
Aonyx delalandi Lesson, 1827.
? *Lutra poensis* Waterhouse, 1838.
Anahyster calabaricus Murray, 1860.
Aonyx inuguis Gerrard, 1862.
Aonyx lalandii Gray, 1865 and 1869.
Lutra gambianus Gray, 1865.
Lutra lenoiri Rochebrune, 1888.
? *Lutra capensis poensis* Thomas, 1904.
Aonyx (Aonyx) capensis Schouteden, 1944–6 and 1948.

Essential characters:
    Of the *genus* –
Claws on fingers absent, on toes rudimentary or vestigial, some often absent altogether; fingers almost unwebbed, toes webbed to terminal phalange; skull typically massive, cheek teeth large and broad; feeds mainly on crustaceans, using the hands to convey the food to the mouth; terrestrial in habit.
    Of the single *species* –
Colour: Variable; from pale coffee to deep chocolate brown; throat and chest white; a few individuals show slight frosting of the head and shoulders.
Size: Large; head and body 30–36 in. (762–913 mm.), tail 16–22½ in. (406–570 mm.), total 46–64 in. (1168–1625 mm.); weight normally 35–45 lb. (15·9–20·5 kg.), occasionally up to about 60 lb. (27·3 kg.). For skull measurements *see* page 321.
Range: Type locality – probably vicinity of Port Elizabeth (Cape). Throughout Africa, in suitable habitat, south of lat. 15°N., approximately, up to 10,000 ft. (3046 m.). (*See* map on page 176.)
Status: Fairly plentiful in South Africa (1936); generally common in Northern Rhodesia (1960).

13   179

773   *Illustration:* Maxwell, 1960, between pages 180 and 181. Many excellent photographs. *See also* plates 28–30.

AONYX CAPENSIS subspp.

30   Although no subspeciation of *A. capensis* has been fully established, five local forms have been proposed. Allen (1922) wrote of them:

> ... as these five forms appear to have been described in each case from a single specimen, without flesh measurements and in some instances from poorly prepared material, none of them can be said to rest on a very satisfactory basis. The differences in coloration indicated by the descriptions of these forms are more than covered in the present series ... of some 20 specimens from a single locality ... while the individual difference in size is more than covered by the 12 adults.

Although Allen's five are not the same as mine – one of his now being grouped with *Paraonyx*, and one of mine being published subsequent to his article – his general remarks still apply. None the less, their descriptions may be of interest and are accordingly here reproduced.

I. AONYX CAPENSIS ANGOLAE Thomas, 1908.

1147   The type specimen, an adult female, is described by Thomas as follows:

External characters much as in true *capensis*, though with rather a greater tendency to a whitening of the bases of the wool-hairs. Hairs of head and nape tipped with whitish. Ears with light edges. Hairs of chin and throat white to their bases, the brown round the angles of the mouth at a minimum. Second and third phalanges of fingers quite naked above.

563

It may be assumed that Hill & Carter's specimen (1941) belongs to the same race. They describe it as having the following characters:

General coloration, above and below, darker than Mars Brown ... grizzled by the presence of dirty whitish tips, especially on the anterior part. Cheeks, nose, throat and sides of neck, dirty whitish; a Y-shaped whitish marking from the rhinarium over the eyes; a whitish stripe along dorsal margin of the ear. A large triangular area of near Mars Brown in front of each eye.

Size: Type, adult female: head and body about 31½ in. (800 mm.), tail 18½ in. (470 mm.), total about 50 in. (1270 mm.). Thomas, 1908. For skull measurements see page 322. [1147]

Distribution:
? Uiôllo River, Gambos. (Bocage, 1890.) [191]
Type: from Coporole River, Angola. (Thomas, 1908.) [1147]
? Otjipahe, Mossamedes, Angola. (Jentink, 1887.) [627]
Lake Ngami, Bechuanaland [Noack, 1889]; Zambesi Delta [Peters, 1852]; Pietermaritzburg [Lönnberg, 1908]; south-west Transvaal; Bloemfontein; w. Ssongea. (Pohle, 1920.) [923]

2. AONYX CAPENSIS COOMBSI Roberts, 1926.

The type of *coombsi* is an old female from the Hennops River, Pretoria. Three further skulls are said to exhibit remarkably constant characters. Roberts' article reads as follows: [969]

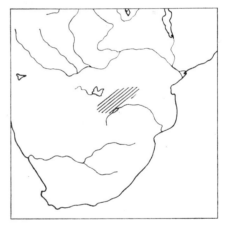

It has been customary in the past to place specimens of the Cape Otter from anywhere within the Union limits under the typical form; but comparison of specimens from the upper Limpopo River goes to prove that they are directly intermediate between the Angola and Natal forms ... Colour characters have not sufficient importance to require detailed description, and all that need be said of the type of *coombsi* is that it is dark brown above, with lighter bases to the hair, from the nose to the end of the tail and the sides and underparts only a little lighter coloured; the dull white area embraces the upper lips and moustachial bristles, cheeks and sides of neck, in a well-defined line, straight except for an extension downwards of the brown in front of the eyes, to the shoulders, and on the throat petering out backwards as a narrow point on the chest.

Size: Type, old female: head and body 28½ in. (725 mm.), tail 20½ in. (525 mm.), total 49 in. (1250 mm.). Roberts, 1926. [969]
Immature female: head and body 30 in. (760 mm.), tail 18 in. (455 mm.), total 48 in. (1215 mm.). Roberts, 1951. For skull measurement *see* page 322. [971]
Distribution: Hennops and upper Limpopo rivers, Transvaal. (Roberts, 1926.) [969]

181

3. AONYX CAPENSIS HELIOS Heller, 1913.

548   The type is described by Heller as follows:

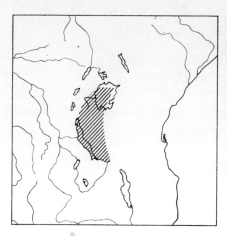

[This otter] resembles *meneleki* of Abyssinia closely in coloration, having the top of the snout as far as the inter-orbital region and the tip of the ears white as in that species, but it differs by its much smaller body size. *hindei* of the Tana River drainage differs by the absence of white on the top of the snout and the tips of the ears . . . but it resembles it closely in body size.

Coloration of the body and limbs dark seal-brown, deepest on back and palest on underparts, where it is burnt umber in colour. Top of head seal-brown like the body. Underfur on body pale drab-gray. The throat, sides of head to the level of the eyes and ears, lips and top of snout, patch above eye and tip of ear, silky white in striking contrast to the general dark brown color. The lips at angle of mouth and the sides of the snout are dusky brown in color.

734   A further brief description is provided by Maberly:

The ears are very small, and the colour ranges from dark to pale reddish-brown, with upper lips, cheeks, chin and throat white.

742   Loveridge reports finding both ticks and a flea (*Ctenocephalus felis*) on a female of *A. c. helios.*

923   It may be mentioned that Pohle considered this form to be synonymous with *A. c. hindei.*

Size and weight: 'No flesh measurements are available. The tanned skin measures' head and body $27\frac{1}{2}$ in. (700 mm.), tail $18\frac{1}{2}$ in. (470 mm.), total
548   46 in. (1170 mm.). Heller, 1913.

Head and body about 36 in. (914 mm.), tail about 24 in. (610 mm.), total about 60 in. (1524 mm.); 'weight up to about 40 lb. [18·2 kg.], but records
734   up to 63 lb. [28·6 kg.] have been killed in Natal.' Maberly, 1960.

Distribution: 'The race here described is doubtless confined to the Nile drainage and is the Uganda or Nyanza representative of the giant Abyssini-
548   an otter, *meneleki* . . .' (Heller, 1913.)

Sotik area between Kisii and Kericho, South Kavirondo district, Kenya; specimens recorded from Kingoni; Bagiro, Bunduki; Tendigo; Wanda-wewe Hills; Dongobesh; Lake Victoria; Karagwe; Lake Rukwa; upper

Lupa River; Sira River; Igali, Kantesya River, Mbozi; Lake Tanganyika; Ifume River; Kalambo River. (Swynnerton & Hayman, 1950.)

Status: Rare in Nairobi National Park, but common at Amboseli and Mara. (Maberly, 1960.)

4. AONYX CAPENSIS HINDEI Thomas, 1905.

Aonyx (Aonyx) capensis hindei Schouteden, 1944–6.

Thomas' account of the type, an old male, reads:

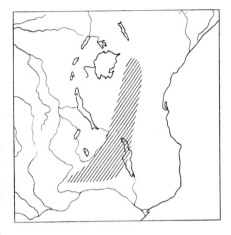

In external characters [this] otter agrees more closely with South-African specimens than with that from Abyssinia (*L. c. meneleki*) [=*A. c. meneleki*] as it has the wool hairs of the body broadly tipped with brown as in the former animal, while in the latter they are nearly wholly white. Throughout it is a dark form, the throat less white than in most members of the group, and the dark patches at the base of the whiskers unusually well marked. Ears entirely brown, without white edging.

In 1908, Lönnberg gives quite a detailed account of an otter shot by Sandberg at about 13°S. lat. on the Makondo River, a tributary of the Zambesi, which 'closely agrees' with *hindei*:

The fur . . . is dark brown and the wool-hairs as well are broadly tipped with brown. The ears are entirely brown. The dark patches in front of the eyes and above the base of the whiskers are much pronounced, as Thomas describes . . . The whiskers themselves appear to consist of a considerably smaller number of bristles than in a specimen of the true *L. capensis*, perhaps only two-thirds of the number in the latter. The single bristles are also shorter in the otter from Rhodesia . . . so that the longest do not attain a length of 5 cm. but in a specimen of the South African race the longest bristles measure 8½ cm. [3·3 inches] although stunted at the tip. This is evidently a characteristic of biological importance.

As mentioned above, Pohle held that *helios* was synonymous with *hindei*, and he considered that neither the zygomatic breadth nor the presence or absence of white edges to the ears were constant differentiating characters. He points out that the area of distribution concerned is a relatively small one for there to be two subspecies living within it, and further notes that there is considerable individual variation in markings, especially with regard to the white spots on the nose, within this geographical area.

720

Size: Dry skin: head and body about 35½ in. (900 mm.), tail about 20¾ in. (530 mm.), total about 56¼ in. (1430 mm.). Lönnberg, 1908.

1041

Head and body attains 39½ in. (1 m.), tail 19¾ in. (500 mm.), total 59 in. (1500 mm.). Schouteden, 1948. For skull measurements *see* page 323.

1146

Distribution: Type: from Fort Hall, Kenya District, B.E.A. (Thomas, 1905.)

Range: Fort Hall and Lake Naivasha, Kenya, southwards at least to the Makondo River, 13°S. lat., and perhaps as far south as Barotse, N. Rho-

720

desia. (Lönnberg, 1908.)

Umba-Ebene, near Nasi; Kingani, near Bagamoyo; Pavagga; Upogoro;

923

Ndembere River, near Gominyi. (Pohle, 1920.)

'The watershed between the Congo and the Zambese [*sic*] river systems is ... evidently also the boundary line between' *A. c. hindei* and *A. (P.) con-*

723

gica. (Lönnberg, 1919–20.)

Mkongo, Sankuru; Lualaba; Moba, Tanganyika; Lukafu, Upper Katanga.

1040

(Schouteden, 1944–6.)

'Widely and generally distributed in suitable areas of swamp and riverine

675

country' in N. Rhodesia. (Lancaster, 1953.)

720

Illustrations: Lönnberg, 1908, page 5. Photograph of occipital region of skull plate I. Photograph of palatal aspect of skull.

5. AONYX CAPENSIS MENELEKI Thomas, 1902.

1144

Thomas' account of this race is as follows:

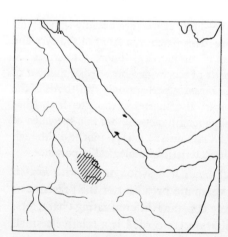

Size very large; colour very strong and dark, deep chocolate brown on the back, darkening anteriorly almost to black on the nape and crown, where it is distinctly grizzled with white. Lips, cheek, and sides of neck sharply contrasted white. Ears brown, with prominently white edges. Chin and throat dull yellowish white; belly brown, little paler than the upper surface. Limbs and tail dark brown as usual.

Underfur of body all over, and notably of back, silvery white, the extreme tips only of the hair brown.

548

From Heller's account of *helios* it may be gathered that *meneleki* has the top of the snout as far as the inter-orbital region white.

184

Pohle notes that the skull is very large, broad and massive, and that it has an appearance of being particularly flat; this is because of the contrast between its normal height and greatly increased width. The dentition is normal. 923

Size: Type: male, head and body 35½ in. (900 mm.), tail 26½ in. (670 mm.), total 62 in. (1570 mm.). Thomas, 1902. For skull measurements *see* page 323. 1144

Distribution: Type: from Zegi, Lake Tsana, Abyssinia. (Thomas, 1902.) 1144 Jambus and Tumat rivers [Heuglin, 1877]; Takasseh; Bellagas Tal, between Simehn and Woggara; Blue Nile [Heuglin & Fitzinger, 1866]. (Pohle, 1920.) 555
556
923

AONYX (PARAONYX) Hinton, 1921. 566

Paraonyx Hinton, 1921a; Pocock, 1921; G.M.Allen, 1939; Rosevear, 1939; Schouteden, 1941–2; Walker, 1964.

AONYX (PARAONYX) CONGICA Lönnberg, 1910. 721

Aonyx capensis congica Lönnberg, 1910.

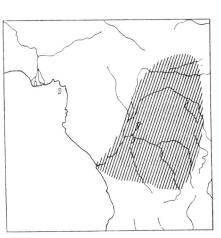

Aonyx congica Pohle, 1920.

Aonyx capensis: J.A.Allen, 1922.

Paraonyx congicus Pocock, 1921.

Paraonyx congica Hinton, 1921a; Schouteden, 1941–2; G. M. Allen, 1939.

Paraonyx capensis congica Schouteden, 1941–2.

Aonyx (Paraonyx) congica congica Schouteden, 1944–6 and 1948.

Essential characters:

Of the *subgenus* –
Fingers without nails, naked, unwebbed; toes almost naked, webbed to the base of the second phalange, only the second, third and fourth showing rudiments of claws; fur shorter and thinner than *Aonyx*; upper surface of the head and neck extensively frosted; vibrissae weakly developed, superciliary and upper genal tufts absent; teeth relatively light; terrestrial in habit.

Of the *species* –
Colour: Dorsally dark chocolate brown; the ears with a whitish margin; chin and throat white, otherwise ventral surface but little paler than dorsal; fur generally rather coarse.

Size: Large; head and body 31¼–37½ in. (796–950 mm.), tail 19¾–22 in. (500–560 mm.), total 52–59¼ in. (1320–1500 mm.); weight 30–40 lb. (13·6–18·1 kg.). For skull measurements *see* page 324.

Range: Type locality – 'Lower Congo'. Throughout the Belgian Congo.

Status: Seems to be common (1948).

30   *Illustration:* J.A.Allen, 1922, pages 91, 93, 102–105. Drawings of rhinarium, under surface of fore and hind feet, skulls and mandibles; plate X, figures 1–3. Photographs of adult and juvenile male.

923   AONYX (PARAONYX) MICRODON Pohle, 1920.

Aonyx microdon Pohle, 1920.

Paraonyx microdon Allen, 1939.

Aonyx (Aonyx) microdon Perret & Aellen, 1956.

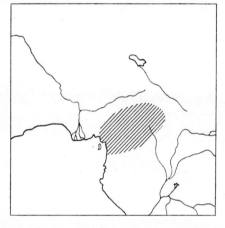

Essential characters: As in the sub-genus; teeth generally smaller; skull delicate.

Colour: As in *congica*; underfur grey on neck, grey-brown elsewhere; in the description of the type there is no mention of dorsal frosting.

Size: Large; head and body 38 in. (970 mm.), tail 16¼ in. (410 mm.), total 54¼ in. (1380 mm.). For skull measurements *see* page 325.

Range: Type locality – Bomse, Nana River, Cameroons. Nigeria; Cameroons.

Status: Not uncommon in the Ndop Plain near the Nun River, Nigeria (1939).

923   *Illustration:* Pohle, 1920, plate VIII, figures 1 and 2. Photograph of skull and mandible.

566   AONYX (PARAONYX) PHILIPPSI Hinton, 1921.

Paraonyx philippsi Hinton, 1921a; Allen, 1939.

Paraonyx phillipsi Schouteden, 1942.

Paraonyx congica philippsi Schouteden, 1942.

Aonyx (Paraonyx) congica philippsi Schouteden, 1944–6 and 1948.

Essential characters: As in the subgenus.

186

Colour: Dark chocolate brown, almost black, darker than *congica*; frosting very conspicuous; ears not white-edged; fur fine, thin.

The size of the type appears to be misprinted in the original text, the head and body length being given as 350 mm., or 13¾ in. On the basis that this is an error for 850 mm., the correct measurements would be:

Type, adult female, head and body 33½ in. (850 mm.), tail 19 in. (480 mm.), total 52½ in. (1330 mm.). For skull measurements *see* page 325.

Range: Type locality – south-west Lake Bunyonyi, Kigesi district, Uganda.

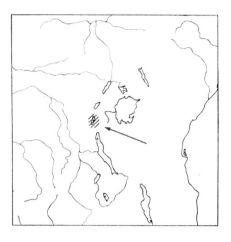

From Kivu through Ruanda to Uganda.

Chapter 4

North American Otters

1042 LUTRA CANADENSIS Schreber, 1776 – The Canadian Otter.

Mustela lutra canadensis Schreber, 1776.
Mustela hudsonica Desmarest, 1803.
Mustela canadensis Turton, 1806.
Lutra hudsonica Cuvier, 1823; and many others.
Lutra brasiliensis: Harlan, 1825; Godman, 1826.
Lutra vulgaris var. *canadensis* Wagner, 1841.
Lutra braziliensis De Kay, 1842.
Latax lataxina Gray, 1843a.
Latax canadensis Gray, 1865.
Lontra canadensis: Flower, 1929.

Essential characters: Rhinarium naked, broad, with a large ascendant central point above, a very small descendant central point below; the hind feet with four small, calloused, circular rugosities on the sole near the heel; the soles with tufts of hair beneath the toes; moustachial pads well developed; skull flattened dorsally; rostrum wider, premaxillary area shorter, than in *L. l. lutra.*
Colour: Very variable; generally darkest in northern, palest in southern subspecies; considerable seasonal variation in some forms; albinism rare.
Size: Average, variable; males from 36 to a little over 50 in. (915–1270 mm.); weight 11–30 lb. (5·0–13·7 kg.); females rather smaller and lighter.
Range: North America, below the Arctic Circle except in extreme northwest, south to lat. 25°N. approximately, in suitable habitat.

LUTRA CANADENSIS CANADENSIS Schreber, 1776.

Mustela lutra canadensis Schreber, 1776.
Lutra americana Wyman, 1847.
Lutra destructor Barnston, 1863.

In the past there has been much taxonomic dispute as to the correct original author of the name *Lutra canadensis,* and a discussion of this may be found in an article by Allen (1898). Schreber's engraving was published in 1776 and predated the accompanying text by two years. The text itself is mainly concerned with the common otter and the sea otter, but Schreber notes several differences between the European form and that of North America. He remarks that

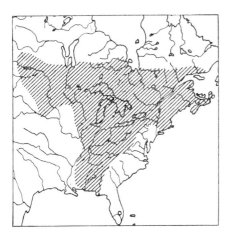

> Some of the American otters are coloured on the back like the European ones, but are yellow-brown on the stomach and have less white at the throat. Others have a much darker colour, at times almost blackish brown; they are paler on the stomach, and at the throat yellowish and greyish going over to whitish. Sometimes they are markedly grey; this is always caused by age . . .

Over and above their [larger] size, pelts from American otters are distinguished by the greater fineness of the hairs, the greater amount of the undercoat, and the colour . . .

In 1792 Kerr had described the common otter as inhabiting 'Europe, North America and Asia', and as late as 1823 Sabine is found writing that 'The Otter of America has hitherto been identified with that of Europe, from which it was considered to differ in size only', while at the same time he notes that imports in 1822 from Hudson's Bay had amounted to 7300 skins. But Sabine finds a number of differences between the American and European race, and describes the former as follows:

> The chin and throat are dusky white and all the rest of the body is a glossy brown, finer and thicker than that of the European Otter. The neck is elongated, not short, and the head narrow and long, in comparison with the short broad visage of the other animal; the ears are consequently much closer together. The tail is more pointed and shorter, being considerably *less* than one half of the length of the body, whilst the tail of the European Otter is *more* than half the length of its body . . .

Confirmation that naturalists seem not to have sought to examine imports of American skins is found in Cuvier (also 1823) who writes that the Canadian otter – as opposed to *lataxina* from South Carolina – was known to him only from its skull, and this same statement is repeated by Lesson four years

19, 1042
1043

657
1002

321

695

189

later. (It may be mentioned that Thomas examined this same skull some years later and doubted its North American origin.)

There were, of course, a great many descriptions of typical *canadensis* published during the nineteenth century, but parts of that by Baird (1857) may be selected as being more than usually detailed. His specimen came from the Potomac River, near Washington, DC. The possibility that this animal was the neighbouring subspecies *lataxina* is ruled out by the hairiness of the feet.

The naked muzzle is quite large, its posterior outline running up into the forehead, so as to be as long, or rather longer than broad; this outline is decidedly ∧-shaped, the acute angle behind; the lines are not quite straight, but slightly sigmoid. The anterior outline of the muzzle is gently semi-circular, and anteriorly sends down a narrow point, dividing the hair of the lip over about one-sixth of its length. The nostrils are large and open, their posterior line extending not beyond the centre of the naked muffle . . .

The eyes are very small, the orbits not exceeding half an inch in length. The ear is small, tapering, but rounded at the tip, rather higher than wide (a little more than half an inch). The eye is considerably in advance of the median point between the ear and tip of muzzle.

The feet are broad and webbed to a point opposite the root of the claws, the greater portion of the terminal naked pads being free. In the fore feet the palms or under surfaces are entirely hairy, excepting the central basal portion, which is naked and papillose; there is, however, a small peninsula of hair extending forward in this naked space from below the carpal joint. The pads at the ends of the toes are naked, but they are entirely cut off from the naked central portion by the hairy area . . .

The characteristics of the hind feet are much like those of the fore feet, the inside surfaces or soles are hairy over the membranes, the central basal portion being naked. The naked pads are entirely isolated from the central bare spots by the hair on the membrane. The extreme posterior portion of the heel is hairy. In the naked surface posteriorly are three small tubercles . . .

The general color of the outer fur in a Washington [DC] specimen examined is a highly lustrous dark liver brown, but little lighter on the belly. The under fur here is, however, decidedly lighter, which imparts this general character to the pelage. On the sides of the head below the eyes (including the lips), and on the chin, extending along the throat to between the legs, the color is a dirty whitish, tinged with brown. The under fur generally is of a yellowish white, like raw silk, at the base, and light liver brown at the tip, the latter color predominating on the back, the former on the belly and sides. The legs and upper surfaces of the tail are rather darker than elsewhere.

Coues' description seems likely to have been modelled at least in part on that of Baird, but he adds some useful details. He remarks that the shape of the nasal pad is somewhat reminiscent of the ace of spades, and like Baird notes the hind feet as having

three or four peculiar small circular elevated callosities arranged around the posterior border of the main bald plantar surface.

The colour is described as liver-brown, with a purplish gloss. He continues:

The claws are similar on both fore and hind feet [being] short, stout, compressed, much arched, rapidly contracted from the thick base to an acute point. Those in front are rather larger, sharper, and more arched than the hinder ones.
The Fur is of great beauty, very thick, close, short, and shining, an exaggeration . . . of that of the Mink . . . The longer hairs are stout and glistening; the very copious underfur is lanuginous and lustreless. The top of the tail is ordinarily the darkest part of the animal . . .

Coues adds that this race apparently continues to grow for several years after puberty.

There is a very considerable seasonal variation in the colour of the pelage. From my own observations (in England) the fur is at its darkest when the coat is new after the moult, being then a shining black-brown with the individual hairs very fine. This very dark stage lasts a comparatively short time, perhaps not more than a few weeks, the fur becoming longer and thicker as it reverts to its normal or seal brown colour. In time the tips of the hairs slowly fade, and at their palest may present an appearance of having been singed, with a dead, brittle appearance and curled, blunt tips.

There seems to be no wholly satisfactory explanation of this 'singeing'. Seton describes the long outer hairs as being 'curled or kinked at the end like card teeth' and adds that this condition is known as 'sun curl' by the fur buyers, who suppose it to be caused by the reflection of the sun from the ice in winter. It does appear to be a winter phenomenon, at least in America and Canada, and Rand writes of otters in Manitoba becoming 'prime' in the first half of November and 'singed' in March. [1060] [943]

In my own experience – again in England – there is a very quick and almost imperceptible moult in September, preceded by a slightly singed appearance. The spring moult, however, is a more elaborate affair, starting at the end of March with a paling of the hair tips on the head and shoulders. This is accompanied by a ravenous appetite. The first fur to be shed seems to be that along the upper centre line of the tail, the side edges of the tail shedding next. At about the same time or very shortly afterwards the area immediately behind the shoulder-blades starts, as does the face. Here it begins immediately above the eyes, in more or less circular patches, and temporarily gives the animal a very curious piebald appearance. Moult of the throat, chest and stomach soon follows. By this time the guard hairs on the body have paled almost exactly to the colour of the underfur and the patches of moult and their progress are far more easily seen if the animal is dry. Once the shedding starts it proceeds fairly rapidly, and there may be a day or two when the animal appears to have no guard hair at all, although it is dark in colour. This must be caused by the new guard hair growing through the underfur, for within a few days the new fine, dark coat is complete, this happening by the end of June or early July. In the case of the pair on which this account is based the male seems to start and finish this process about a month in advance of the female.

Apart from the colour changes caused by moult, I have observed that in some zoos where the otters have insufficient shade and are excluded from their beds by day their fur becomes bleached by the sun to a more or less reddish tint.

The Canadian otter makes a variety of noises, although on the whole it is much less vocal than either Indian forms of *Lutra*, *Aonyx* or *Amblonyx*. Its most characteristic sound, and one which I believe to be confined to this species, is a curious low grunting noise, in a very deep register, which certainly gives the appearance of being a form of conversation. This noise may best be imitated by closing the lips and uttering 'hm! hm!' in as deep a voice as possible, in rapid groups of three, four or five at a time. The effect of two otters thus conversing underwater is a very unusual one.

Size and weight:

Head and body 42 in. (1068 mm.), tail 18 in. (457 mm.), total 60 in. (1525
1002 mm.). Sabine, 1823.

Head and body 39–48 in. (990–1220 mm.), tail 14–18 in. (355–457 mm.).
340 De Kay, 1842.

'Finally attaining a length of four feet [1220 mm.] or more, some specimens, however, touching five feet [1525 mm.];' weight 20–25 lb. (9·1–
306 11·3 kg.). Coues, 1877.

960 'Total length rarely exceeding 1100 mm.' ($43\frac{1}{4}$ in.). Rhoads, 1898.

Adult male: head and body 28 in. (711 mm.), tail vertebrae 18 in. (457
1120 mm.), total 46 in. (1168 mm.). Swenk, 1920.

Total length 40–45 in. (1015–1142 mm.), tail vert. $12\frac{1}{2}$–15 in. (318–381 mm.); weight from 18 to 25 lb. (8·2–11·3 kg.), average 20 lb. (9·1 kg.).
127 Anthony, 1928.

Head and body 26–30 in. (661–762 mm.), tail 12–17 in. (305–432 mm.);
239 weight 10–20 lb. (4·5–9·1 kg.). Burt, 1952. For skull measurements *see* page 326.

Distribution and Status (from north to south):

Type locality: eastern Canada. Miller, 1911.   802

Ontario: North Bay (uncommon); Peninsula Harbor and Nepigon (numerous); Mount Forest (scarce); Milton (very rare). Miller, 1897.   799

Very rare in Wellington and Waterloo Counties; recorded every few years from the London region. (Soper, 1923.)   1082

Ghost River, Lake Abitibi Region. (Snyder, 1928.)   1079

Quetico Provincial Park ('greatly reduced in recent years'). Cahn, 1937.   258

Renfrew County ('populations appear to remain steady'). Brown & Lanning, 1954.   219

St Lawrence: Prince Edward Island (few). Young, 1900.   1231

Anticosti Island (small quantity). Newsom, 1937.   855

Cape Breton Island (nowhere abundant); Prince Edward Island (very rare); Anticosti Island (small population). Cameron, 1958.   259

Nova Scotia: 'practically unknown near Kedgemakooge . . . has been seen on Little and West rivers'. (Sheldon, 1936.)   1063

New Brunswick: Grand Manan Island (reported as occurring). Copeland & Church, 1906.   300

'Now generally rare.' (Morris, 1948.)   826

Quebec: Godbout. (Preble, 1902.)   932

Gaspé Peninsula: Cap Chat; Ste Anne (very scarce). Goodwin, 1924.   456

Maine: Mount Desert Island ('scarce, if not extinct'). Manville, 1942.   762

New Hampshire: northern part of the state ('very rarely found'). Jackson, 1922.   613

Vermont: Clarendon; Wallingford; Rutland; Essex County (rare). F. L. Osgood, 1938.   871

New York: '. . . now exceedingly scarce. In the counties of Kings, Queens, Suffolk and Richmond, it is now extirpated.' (De Kay, 1842.)   340

'. . . still found in the Hudson . . . now become extremely scarce'. (Mearns, 1898.)   783

Massachusetts: Swift River; Connecticut Valley ('surprising abundance'); Charles River ('occasionally seen'). Gordon, 1908.   460

Kingston [Rhoads, 1893]. Pohle, 1920.   923

Hampshire County ('rather rare'). Crane, 1931.   314

Amherst. (Dearden, 1954.)   338

Michigan: Drummond Island ('still taken occasionally'). Manville, 1950.   763

Wisconsin: Menominee Indian Reservation ('numerous along the rivers and creeks throughout the reservation. They are found also, though not

666 so abundantly, along the lakes in the southeastern section'). Komarek, 1932.

645 Nicolet National Forest (few). Kelker, 1943.

Minnesota: not rare in many parts of the state. (Herrick, 1892.)

Itasca County ('common throughout the county, and steadily and rapid-
257 ly increasing in numbers'). Cahn, 1921.

Northern Lake County ('may be expected to show a steady increase').
633 Johnson, 1922.

St Louis, Todd, Winona, Cook, Lake of the Woods, Pine and Sherburne Counties ('fairly common in much of the northern part of the state . . .
486 occasionally seen in some of the southern counties'). Gunderson & Beer, 1953.

140 Montana: Glacier National Park. (Bailey, 1918.)

1055 Iowa: Cambridge. (Scott, 1937.)

North Dakota: 'A few otters are still found along the principal streams . . .
142 and around some of the larger lakes.' (Bailey, 1926.)

880 South Dakota: eastern side of state. (Over & Churchill, 1945.)

143 Wyoming: Willow Park, on Obsidian Creek. (Bailey, 1930.)

Illinois: 'records indicate a sporadic occurrence in all but the north-eastern
576 part of the state'. (Hoffmeister & Mohr, 1957.)

934 Ohio: Morrow County (mentioned once, in 1880). Preble, 1942.

'Some Ohio mammalogists have long considered the river otter to be extirpated . . . [but] several recent records . . . may indicate that there is
274 some hope for [its] restoration.' (Chapman, 1956.)

514 Virginia: Shenandoah, Rockbridge and Pulaski Counties. (Handley & Patton, 1947.)

958 Tennessee: Reelfoot Lake; Open Lake ('rare but constant'). Rhoads, 1896.
Hardeman, Haywood, Monroe, Morgan, Pickett and Wayne Counties; Hatchie River; Duck River; and tributaries of the Mississippi (elsewhere
1047 practically nonexistent). Schultz, 1954.

Alabama: Ashford; Orange Beach; Bayou Labatre; Oakchia; Muscle Shoals ('generally distributed . . . but in most places occurs rather sparingly').
589, 505 Howell, 1921. (*See* Hall & Kelson, 1959, vol. II, page 947 for distribution map.)

Principal illustrations:

1042 Schreber, 1776, figure CXXVI B.

475 Griffith, 1827, facing page 315. Engraving.

340 De Kay, 1842, plate III. Coloured engraving.
plate XXXIII. Engraving of views of skull.

Coues, 1877, plate XVII. Drawings of skull. 306

Bangs, 1898b, page 226. Skull from above. 149

Rhoads, 1898, plate XXIV, figure 1. Skull from above; figure 2. Skull from below. 960

Friley, 1949, pages 103–104. Photographs of baculum. 426

Liers, 1951b, pages 320–326. Several photographs. 704

Wilmar, 1953, page 19. Photographs of tracks and slides in snow. 1208

Kirkland, 1955, frontispiece, and between pages 240 and 241. Three photographs. 661

Jex, 1960, pages 114–115. Two photographs. (*See also* plates 31–37.) 631

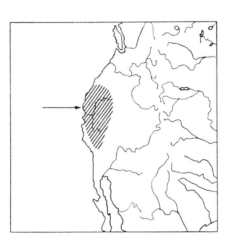

479

LUTRA CANADENSIS BREVIPILOSUS Grinnell, 1914.

Lutra canadensis pacifica: Grinnell, 1933.

Lutra hudsonica: Merriam, 1899; Grinnell, 1933.

Lutra hudsonica pacifica Grinnell, 1933.

Lutra pacifica Grinnell, 1933.

Essential characters: Skull small, with high narrow cranium; dentition light; pelage short, dorsal guard hairs grizzled.

Colour: Little seasonal variation; above bistre, grizzled; paler on sides and below; young darker than adults.

Size: Average; head and body averages $27\frac{3}{8}$ in. (695 mm.), tail $16\frac{5}{8}$ in. (422 mm.), total between 40 and 48 in. (1015–1220 mm.); weight 11–23 lb. (5·0–10·5 kg.). For skull measurements *see* pages 325–6.

Range: Type locality – Grizzly Island, Suisun Bay, Solano Co., California. Extreme south of Oregon; north-western California; extreme west of Nevada, up to 9000 ft. (2745 m.).

Status: Neither rare nor plentiful in California (1942).

Illustration: Fisher, 1942, page vi. Photographs of external aspect. Throughout the text are a number of anatomical drawings. 408

LUTRA CANADENSIS CHIMO Anderson, 1945.

This form is based on a series of 12 skulls, and there is thus no external description. Anderson quotes Low as saying that 'The skins taken in the 40

northern region have the darkest and most glossy fur'. Anderson notes that
the skulls differ from typical *canadensis*

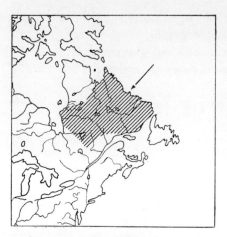

... in being longer and with zygomata heavier, more widely spreading and less arched; nasals longer; braincase broader, flatter, more triangular, and less tapering posteriorly; distance between tips of postorbital processes usually greater; rostrum broader, with greater width across base of canines; interorbital length averaging greater; palate broader and palatal length greater; basioccipital generally broader; audital bullae considerably larger and longer, and auditory meatus wider ... molariform teeth in general heavier, but last upper molar proportionately slightly lighter and shorter.

259 Cameron (1948) characterizes the skull of *chimo* as 'massive'.

Size: Average; head and body 24¾–35 in. (632–889 mm.), tail 16–18 in. (406–457 mm.), total 42–51¾ in. (1067–1312 mm.). For skull measurements

40 *see* Anderson, 1945, and page 327.

Range: Type locality – Fort Chimo, Ungava district, Quebec.
Quebec; Labrador; ? occasional specimens seen in Newfoundland.

148 LUTRA CANADENSIS DEGENER
Bangs, 1898.

Lutra degener Bangs, 1898; Allen,
1898; Rhoads, 1898.

Essential characters: Small; tail
short; skull small and weak.

Colour: Deep lustrous seal brown
to almost black, palest on cheeks;
underfur light greyish-brown at
base, deep rich brown at tip.

Size: Rather small; head and body
about 26 in. (660 mm.), tail about
14 in. (355 mm.), total 40–43½ in.

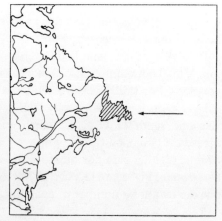

(1015–1100 mm.). For skull measurements *see* pages 327–8.

Range: Type locality – Bay St George, Newfoundland. Confined to Newfoundland.

Status: Nowhere common, but does not seem to have decreased (1948).
Illustration: Rhoads, 1898, plate XXIV, figure 5. Photograph of skull. [960]

LUTRA CANADENSIS EVEXA Goldman, 1935.

This is alphabetically the first of nine North American otters first published by Goldman in 1935. This form is based on a series of 36 skulls, all [452] from the type locality, and no description of the external appearance is available. The type specimen, an adult male from Stuart Lake, near the headwaters of the Fraser River, British Columbia, is described by Goldman as follows:

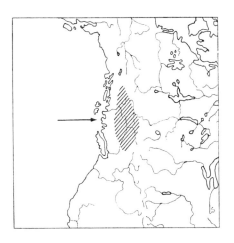

A medium-sized subspecies, with vault of cranium high and evenly rounded. Skull similar in size to that of *L. c. preblei* but braincase more highly and usually more narrowly arched; basioccipital region more bulging downward between audital bullae; mastoid processes more strongly deflected downward, more hook-like; dentition about the same. Skull closely resembling that of *L. c. pacifica* of western Washington, but decidedly smaller; braincase higher; basioccipital region more bulging downward between audital bullae; bullae much more inflated; dentition lighter.

For skull measurements *see* page 328.
Distribution: Western slope of Rocky Mountains in central British Columbia. (Goldman, 1935.) [452]
British Columbia: Bear Lake; Indianpoint Lake; n. fork of Eagle River, Kettle Valley; Chezacut. (Cowan & Guiguet, 1956.) [309]

LUTRA CANADENSIS EXTERA Goldman, 1935.

This subspecies is based on a single skull, probably male, with parts of a skeleton, from Nagai Island, Shumagin Islands, Alaska. Goldman describes [452] it as follows:

Cranium low with strongly developed sagittal crest. In general resembling that of *L. c. yukonensis,* but braincase with sides more gradually tapering to a narrower postorbital constriction; palatal shelf narrower behind molars; mastoid processes more strongly deflected downwards and inward; audital bullae

flatter, more deeply excavated along inner sides; dentition similar, but rather light. Compared with *L. c. kodiacensis* the braincase is slightly lower and flatter, with sides tapering more evenly to a narrower postorbital constriction; palatal shelf narrower behind molars; audital bullae similarly flat, but more deeply excavated along inner sides; dentition lighter ...

Close alliance to *yukonensis* is indicated, but the characters pointed out appear to be beyond the probable range of individual variation and therefore distinctive.

For skull measurements *see* page 328.

452 *Distribution:* Known only from Nagai Island. (Goldman, 1935.)

1120 LUTRA CANADENSIS INTERIOR Swenk, 1918 (1920).

Lutra canadensis sonora: Lantz, 1905.
Lutra canadensis lataxina: Hibbard, 1933.

Essential characters: Paler and larger than typical *canadensis*; hind foot shorter, about 120 mm.; inferior side of webs more densely haired.

Colour: Summer pelage – dark reddish-brown above, the neck paler and grizzled; below paler, wood brown

964 [Ridgway, 1912] overlaid with long white hairs.

Size: Average; head and body 35 in. (888 mm.), tail 18 in. (456 mm.), total 53 in. (1344 mm.). For skull measurements *see* page 328.

Range: Type locality – Lincoln Creek, west of Seward, Seward Co., Nebraska. Nebraska; Tennessee; Colorado; (Kansas); Oklahoma; Arkansas; Mississippi; Minnesota; ? North Dakota; ? South Dakota.

Status: Extinct in Kansas since

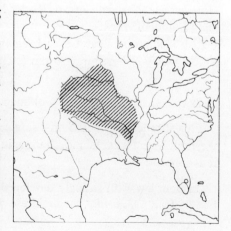

198

1904; rare except locally in Tennessee (1954); increasing locally in Arkansas (1940).

Illustration: Swenk, 1920, page 7. Photographs of skull. 1120

LUTRA CANADENSIS KODIACENSIS Goldman, 1935.

Goldman writes: 452

This insular race is based on [fifteen] skulls only picked up by various col-

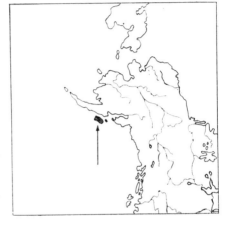

lectors at different times ... [and] more or less fragmentary material dug out of the kitchen middens of former inhabitants ... All of the skulls agree in a combination of cranial details that sets them somewhat apart from the other subspecies. A skull from the neighbouring island, Afognak, is larger with heavier dentition than any of those available from Kodiak Island, but it is provisionally referred to the same form.

The skull itself Goldman describes as

Similar to *L. c. yukonensis* and *L. c. optiva*, but skull somewhat higher and narrower than either; braincase less inflated laterally, more highly and narrowly arched; incisive foramina larger, more widely open; basioccipital region more - inflated, bulging downward between audital bullae; audital bullae rather flat, much as in *optiva*; dentition medium.

For skull measurements *see* page 329.

Distribution: Type: from Uyak Bay, Kodiak Island, Alaska; specimens (skulls only) from Lake Karluk, Kodiak Island and Afognak Island. (Goldman, 1935.) 452

'Is found in every part of the island group.' (Clark, 1958.) 281

Status: 'It appears to maintain its numbers with little difficulty.' (Clark, 1958.) 281

LUTRA CANADENSIS LATAXINA Cuvier, 1823. 321

Lutra lataxina Cuvier, 1823.
Lataxina mollis Gray, 1843b.
Lutra lataxima Lesson, 1842.
Lutra rhoadsi Cope, 1897.
Lutra rhoadsii Gidley & Gazin, 1933.

Essential characters: Usually smaller, and lighter in colour, than the typical form; soles of feet less hairy; skull small, teeth relatively massive.

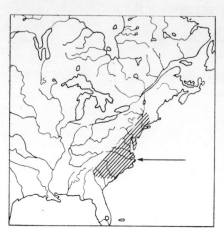

Colour: Dorsally dark brown, more reddish ventrally; sides of head and neck washed with pale yellowish. Southern specimens may be lighter than northern ones.

Size: Average; head and body 27–33 in. (686–838 mm.), tail about 17 in. (432 mm.), total 44½–50 in. (1130–1270 mm.); weight up to 23 lb. (10·4 kg.), more usually nearer 16 lb. (7·25 kg.). For skull measurements *see* page 329.

Range: Type locality – South Carolina. Connecticut; New Jersey; Pennsylvania; Maryland; Virginia; North and South Carolina.

Status: Presumably scarce in South Carolina (1937); not uncommon in parts of southern New Jersey (1953).

133   *Illustration:* Audubon & Bachman, 1854, vol. III, facing page 96. Coloured plate.

LUTRA CANADENSIS MIRA Goldman, 1935.

Lutra mira Goldman, 1935.

452
505   This form was originally proposed by Goldman as having specific rank, but as Hall & Kelson suggest, there seem no compelling grounds for this assumption. Goldman himself writes:

   L. mira differs so markedly in size from the known races of *L. canadensis* that in the absence of material indicating intergradation it seems best to treat it as a full species. Owing to the proximity of islands of the Alexander Archipelago to the mainland coast it may be expected to pass gradually into a more typical form of *canadensis.*

Goldman based his *mira* on five specimens of which the type, from

200

Kasaan Bay, was a young adult male. Only the skull exists and is described as follows:

Size largest of the *L. canadensis* group. Color of an October specimen uniform vandyke brown (Ridgway, 1912) above, and near verona brown below, thinly overlaid with grayish on under side of neck and cheeks, becoming more distinctly gray on upper lip. Skull very large, the braincase broad, relatively low and flat; audital bullae very flat. Skull similar in general to those of *L. c. preblei* and *L. c. optiva*, but contrasting strongly in much greater size. Compared with *L. [c.] periclyzomae*, of the Queen Charlotte Islands, a departure in combination of cranial characters is exhibited as follows: Size much larger, nasal region less depressed, the nasals shorter, less extended posteriorly beyond maxillae; incisive foramina narrower, less broadly oval; palate with a small, pointed posterior median projection (absent in *periclyzomae*); outer side of upper carnassial less deeply emarginate.

For skull measurements *see* page 329.

Distribution: Alexander Archipelago and probably adjacent mainland, south-eastern Alaska. Specimens procured from Prince of Wales Island and Shrubby Island. (Goldman, 1935.)

LUTRA CANADENSIS NEXA Goldman, 1935.

Lutra hudsonica: Merriam, 1891.
Lutra canadensis sonora: Barnes, 1922.

Goldman describes the type, an adult male, as follows:

A medium-sized, comparatively light-colored subspecies, with cranium broad, low, smoothly rounded and weakly developed. Color of type (winter pelage): Upper parts near mikardo brown (Ridgway, 1912) in general tone, the tips of longer hairs somewhat lighter and producing an indistinctly grizzled effect; under parts overlaid with much lighter brown, paling gradually anteriorly to silvery grayish on throat, cheeks, and lips; feet light brownish; tail above like back, somewhat paler below. Similar in general to *L. c. brevipilosus* . . . but apparently

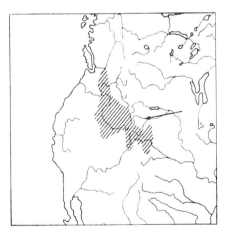

paler; skull more weakly developed, less angular; braincase usually lower and broader; postorbital processes of both frontals and jugals shorter and less

201

prominent; mastoid processes less deflected downward, less hook-like; bullae and dentition about the same. Color paler and skull decidedly smaller, less angular, than in *L. c. pacifica* . . . braincase similar in height, but skull differing otherwise in about the same details as from *brevipilosus*. Similar in size to *L. c. interior* . . . but color paler and skull less angular; zygomata more slender; post-orbital processes of frontals and jugals shorter, more weakly developed; audital bullae less inflated; dentition about the same. Resembling *L. c. sonora* . . . but skull less angular; postorbital processes shorter; lambdoid crest less developed (projecting and trenchant in *sonora*); audital bullae less inflated, less projecting below plane of basioccipital; maxillary tooth row longer; dentition, especially the upper molars, somewhat heavier.

358   Durrant says of this form that its brown colour is 'lighter than mink', and that it probably intergrades with *L. c. sonora* in the western part of the Uinta mountains.

Size: Adult female, head and body 27 in. (687 mm.), tail vert. 18¼ in. (463 mm.), total 45¼ in. (1150 mm.); weight 19 lb. (8·6 kg.). For skull measurements *see* page 329.

Range: Type locality – near Deeth, Humboldt River, Elko County, Nevada. Oregon; Idaho; Nevada; Utah; Colorado.

Status: Much reduced in Idaho (1946); rare in Utah (1955–60).

LUTRA CANADENSIS OPTIVA
Goldman, 1935.

This form is based on 16 specimens, of which the type is an adult male. It is described by Goldman as follows:

General color rather dull, near van-dyke brown (Ridgway, 1912). Similar to *L. c. preblei* . . . but skull somewhat larger, more angular; zygomata heavier; basioccipital region flatter, less bulging between audital bullae; audital bullae usually still flatter, less projecting below level of basioccipital; dentition heavier. Skull similar in general to that of *L. c. pacifica* . . . but relatively broader, less elongated; braincase less highly arched; audital bullae decidedly flatter.

Several mammals are known only from Montague Island, but the otters of the adjacent mainland agree closely with the insular animal. *L. c. optiva* requires no close cranial comparison with typical *canadensis* of eastern Canada, which is decidedly smaller with conspicuously larger, more inflated audital bullae.

452

964

For skull measurements *see* page 330.

Distribution: Montague and Hinchinbrook Islands and adjacent Kenai Peninsula. Specimens secured from Zaikof Bay, Montague Island (type locality); Cape Elizabeth, Kenai Peninsula; and Hinchinbrook Island (Goldman, 1935.)

452

Status: 'Apparently rather uncommon' in Cook Inlet [? *optiva*]. (Osgood, 1901.)

873

LUTRA CANADENSIS PACIFICA Rhoads, 1898.

960

Lutra californica: Baird, 1857.

Lutra californicus Baird, 1857.

Lutra hudsonica pacifica Rhoads, 1898.

Lutra atterima Elliot, 1901.

Lutra paranensis: Elliot, 1901.

Essential characters: Usually lighter in colour than the typical race; inferior surface of feet and webs nearly naked; rhinarium shorter than it is wide; skull very large, dentition relatively weak.

Colour: Normally ruddy seal brown, Alaskan coast specimens sometimes much darker; ventrally paler, greyish; guard hairs lightest at the apex, chestnut in colour; underfur liver brown apically, yellowish white at the base. Summer pelage lighter, more hazel.

Size: Large; head and body 27–33 in. (687–837 mm.), tail 17–19 in. (432–482 mm.), total 45–52 in. (1143–1319 mm.), sometimes larger in Alaskan examples; weight of an old female 19 lb. (8·6 kg.). For skull measurements *see* page 330.

Range: Type locality – Lake Keechelus, Kittitas County, Washington, at 3000 ft. (914 m.). South-eastern Alaska; British Columbia; Washington; Oregon; Idaho; north-eastern California.

Status: Found sparingly in Oregon (1936).

Illustration: Rhoads, 1898, plate XXV, figures 1 and 3. Superior aspect of skull.

960

LUTRA CANADENSIS PERICLYZOMAE Elliot, 1905.

Lutra periclyzomae Elliot, 1905.

This subspecies was based on three skulls, but the presumed sex of the type is not stated by Elliot. He describes the type skull, from Gawi, on the

371

west coast of Moresby Island, in the Queen Charlotte Islands group, in the following terms:

General characters: Skull: Size large; intertemporal region long and narrow, greatly restricted for its entire length; in young animals this constriction is not so apparent. Rostrum short and very broad; postorbital processes greatly elongated; braincase without crests, rounded, and widest posteriorly; bullae small and flat, barely rising above the level of the basioccipital; pterygoid fossa broad for its entire length, the sides nearly straight but widening gradually to tips of pterygoid processes where the width is greatest; upper molars very large, the cusps on exterior side very high and acute; last molar square-shaped, slightly widest on interior edge.

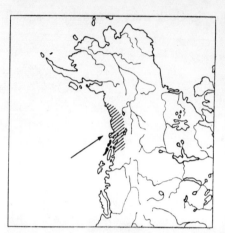

Elliot adds that 'It is evidently a large and powerful animal, possibly exceeding in size its near relative' [*L. c.*
372 *pacifica*]. Twelve years later he published the following external description:

Color: Head, entire upperparts and sides of neck dark cinnamon-brown, changing with the lights, at times brilliant with silvery reflections; lips, throat and chest warm buff; abdomen and inguinal region similar to upperparts but paler; tail, like back, the apical half with the hairs white-tipped giving this part the appearance of being frosted . . .

For skull measurements *see* page 330.

547 *Distribution:* Windfall Harbour, Admiralty Island; Savok Bay, Baranof Island (Heller, 1909.)
398 Anklin River, Yakutat Bay, Alaska. (Fisher, 1933.)
805 Known from Queen Charlotte Islands only. (Miller & Kellogg, 1955.)
505 British Columbia; Alaska; Queen Charlotte Islands. (Hall & Kelson, 1959.)
Status: 'Otters are rather rare on the Queen Charlottes, though perhaps no more so than on the mainland . . . annual receipts from the Indians have
873 seldom included more than a dozen skins . . .' (Osgood, 1901.)

LUTRA CANADENSIS PREBLEI Goldman, 1935.

452 Goldman based this form on 36 specimens of which the type, skull only, is an adult male. His original description of it is as follows:

Very similar to *Lutra canadensis canadensis* of eastern Canada, but skull larger; nasals longer, extending farther posteriorly beyond ends of maxillae (as shown by sutures visible in young); audital bullae more flattened, less inflated and projecting below level of basioccipital; dentition heavier. Compared with that of *Lutra canadensis interior* of Nebraska, the skull is very similar in size and general form, but audital bullae decidedly flatter, less rounded, less inflated and therefore less projecting below level of basioccipital; dentition lighter.

Specimens from Oxford House and other localities in Manitoba grade towards typical *canadensis*, but in size are more properly referable to the present form. Farther south *L. c. preblei* undoubtedly intergrades with *L. c. interior*, to which form examples from Elk River, Minnesota, appear to be assignable.

An early account (1861) by Ross says:

The color of the overlying hairs varies from a rich and glossy brownish black to a dark chestnut. In summer the color is a rusty brown, and the fur is shorter and thinner.

989

For skull measurements *see* page 331.

Distribution: Found throughout the Hudson Bay region; up the Churchill River; north of Churchill originally as far as lat. 62°; upper part of Hill River. (Preble, 1902.)   932

Fort Resolution, and lower Anderson River, Mackenzie. (Macfarlane, 1905.)   743
Mackenzie: Fort Simpson; Fort Rae; Lake Hardisty; MacTavish Bay, Great Bear Lake; Fort Good Hope; Lockhart River; Fort Anderson. (Preble, 1908.)   933

Napie Falls, Talston River, Great Slave Lake. (Harper, 1932.)   518

Range: Mackenzie River basin and east to Hudson Bay; south to Alberta, Saskatchewan and Manitoba. Specimens secured, from Alberta: Henry House; Slave River; Whitemud. Mackenzie: Fort Liard; MacTavish Bay, Great Bear Lake (type locality); Fort Resolution; Fort Smith. Manitoba: Cross Lake; Oxford House; Norway House. Type from near MacTavish Bay, Great Bear Lake (on canoe route from Lake Hardisty), Mackenzie. (Goldman, 1935.)   452

Mackenzie: Reliance, east end of Great Slave Lake; Baker Lake (1927); Padley (1937); Yellowknife Region (1937). (Clarke, 1940.)   282

929 Mackenzie River Delta. (Porsild, 1945.)

Alberta: headwaters of the McLeod River, south-west of Mountain Park;
1084 Wildhay River, a few miles downstream from Moberley Creek. (Soper, 1947.)

Status: Rare over most of the wooded part of the Athabasca-Mackenzie region; fairly common in the area between Fort Rae and Great Bear Lake.
933 (Preble, 1908.)

Fairly common at the west end of Great Bear Lake . . . occasionally taken
1100 at the east end. (Stefánsson, 1913.)

'Now exceedingly rare, if not entirely absent in large sections of the [Wood Buffalo] Park and adjoining territory . . . this condition is particularly applicable to the eastern section adjoining Slave River . . . The species is more numerous in the far west-central part of the Park, somewhat less common in the Northwest Territories portion, and scarcest of all in the
1083 country south of Peace River.' (Soper, 1942.)

944 Rare in the north of Alberta. (Rand, 1948.)

Appears to have been exterminated over most of the Peace River region. 'No definite information regarding its present occurrence . . . except in the region southwest of Wapiti River. The Indians asserted that a few . . . still exist on some streams in the Rocky Mountain foothills and in country to
1085 the east . . .' (Soper, 1948.)

519 'Somewhat sparingly distributed in southwestern Keewatin.' (Harper, 1956.)

'At present undoubtedly scarce, or rare, throughout its natural haunts in the Canadian Zone . . . In most of this territory it is gone beyond recall. A few pairs still inhabit the wilder and more remote sections of Prince Albert
1086 Park.' (Soper, 1961.)

960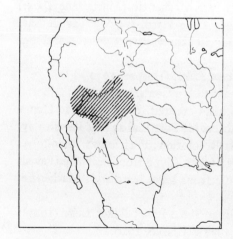

LUTRA CANADENSIS SONORA
Rhoads, 1898.

Lutra canadensis: Mearns, 1891.
Lutra hudsonica sonora Rhoads, 1898.

Essential characters: Large; light in colour; the hind foot very long.
Colour: Upperparts brown, grizzled with light tipped hairs; under parts light greyish brown shading to silvery white on the chest; underfur white shading to greyish at the tip.

206

Size: Large; head and body about 32 in. (815 mm.), tail about 20 in. (508 mm.), total up to 53 in. (1348 mm.); weight 19½–25 lb. (8·8–11·3 kg.). For skull measurements *see* page 331.

Range: Type locality – Montezuma Well, Beaver Creek, Yavapai County, Arizona. ? south-eastern Nevada; south-eastern California; southern Utah; Arizona; New Mexico.

Status: Extremely rare (1954).

Illustration: Elliot, 1901, facing page 353. Photographs of skull.   368

LUTRA CANADENSIS TEXENSIS Goldman, 1935.

Originally described by Goldman as   452

A medium-sized, rather light brown subspecies, with short pelage and moderately broad skull. Color (topotype): Upper parts near verona brown (Ridgway, 964 1912), becoming somewhat lighter on top of head and neck; under parts a mixture of lighter browns, changing to silvery gray on throat and lips, this color extending upward over cheeks; feet near mikado brown; tail above like back, somewhat paler below. Resembling *L. c. interior*, but color apparently lighter, pelage shorter; skull very similar but mastoid processes less strongly turned downward; audital bullae distinctly less fully inflated, less projecting below level of basioccipital; dentition about the same. Compared with *L. c. vaga*, pelage similarly short, but color 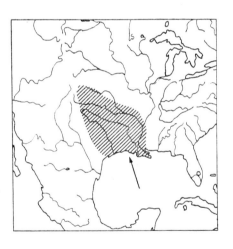 lighter brown; skull broader, braincase about equal in height, but decidedly broader, more rounded and inflated; basioccipital broader; palate broader behind molars; bullae less inflated; dentition nearly the same. Similar in size to *L. c. sonora* . . . skull more smoothly rounded, less angular; braincase more abruptly inflated behind postorbital constriction, as viewed from above; mastoid processes less strongly turned downward, less hook-like; basioccipital region more inflated, tending to bulge between bullae; bullae flatter, less projecting below level of basioccipital; maxillary tooth row longer; dentition decidedly heavier.

L. c. texensis is closely allied to *L. c. interior* of Nebraska and *L. c. vaga* of Florida, and doubtless intergrades with both. It agrees with *vaga* in shortness of pelage, but skins examined are lighter colored; cranial details shown in skulls from northern Louisiana suggest a closer approach to *interior*.

Size and weight: Head and body 31 in. (787 mm.), tail 18 in. (457 mm.),
total 49 in. (1244 mm.); weight 20 lb. (9·1 kg.). Audubon & Bachman, 1851.
For skull measurements *see* page 331.

133

Distribution: Colorado, in Texas. (Audubon & Bachman, 1851.)
133

Type: skull only of adult male, from 20 miles west of Angleton, Brazoria
County, Texas. Range: lower Mississippi River valley in Louisiana and
doubtless Mississippi, and west in the Gulf coast region at least to Bay
City, Texas. Specimens secured from Louisiana: Morgan City, Tallulah;
from Texas: Angleton, Bay City. (Goldman, 1935.)
452

Mobeetie; Texarkana; vicinity of Austin. (Bailey, 1905.)
138

Status: 'Not uncommon in the streams of eastern Texas . . .'; common in
Liberty and Hardin counties. (Bailey, 1905.)
138

'Rare throughout eastern Texas . . .' (Peterson, 1946.)
902

149

LUTRA CANADENSIS VAGA Bangs,
1898.

Lutra hudsonica vaga Bangs, 1898.

Essential characters: Dark red-
brown; underfur darker than guard
hair; pelage short; inferior surface
of webs and feet nearly naked; skull
large, teeth relatively small; tail
proportionately longer than in typical *canadensis.*

Colour: Above and below, dark rich
chestnut brown; paler area of throat
and neck very restricted; face and sides of neck grizzled with yellowish.

Size: Rather large; head and body about 31½ in. (798 mm.), tail about 19½
in. (495 mm.), total about 51 in. (1293 mm.). For skull measurements *see*
page 332.

Range: Type locality – Mico [or Micco], Brevard County, Florida. Florida;
southern Georgia.

Status: Believed to have increased by 40% between 1939 and 1942 (1946).

Illustration: (Anon.), 1956, page 63. Photograph of mother and four young.
120

LUTRA CANADENSIS VANCOUVERENSIS Goldman, 1935.

Lutra vancouverensis Goldman, 1935.

Goldman based this form on three skulls, all from the type locality. He
describes the type, an adult male, as follows:
452

Skull large, very broad, angular and massive; mastoid processes of squamosal widely extended and shelf-like. Not very unlike that of *L. c. pacifica* in general, but much broader and heavier, with broader braincase and more widely extended mastoid processes; basioccipital broader; audital bullae flatter, less extended below level of basioccipital; dentition heavier. Skull similar in length to that of *L. [c.] periclyzomae*, but much broader and more massive; nasal region less depressed, the nasals shorter, broader, less extended beyond ends of maxillae; mastoid process of squamosal forming a broad shelf extending farther laterally, but narrowing more rapidly along margin leading to lambdoid crest (as viewed from above); incisive foramina smaller, less broadly oval; audital bullae more rounded, less flattened; dentition much heavier, the outer side of upper carnassial less deeply excavated near middle. Contrasted with that of *L. c. evexa* the skull is much larger, broader, and more massive; braincase much broader and lower; audital bullae less inflated; dentition much heavier. Differing from *L. [c.] mira* notably in smaller size ...

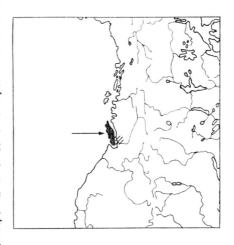

Among members of the *L. canadensis* group *L. vancouverensis* is exceeded in size only by the geographically somewhat remote *L. mira* of Prince of Wales Island, Alaska. It is treated here as a full species, but may prove to intergrade with a mainland form. The upper part of a skull apparently picked up at the head of River Inlet, on the mainland of British Columbia, agrees closely with *vancouverensis* but circumstances suggest that the locality may be erroneous.

For skull measurements *see* page 332.
Distribution: Type: from Quatsino, Vancouver Island, British Columbia; definitely known only from Vancouver Island. (Goldman, 1935.) 452
Range: Vancouver Island, and San Juan Islands of northern Puget Sound and adjacent marine waters. (Miller & Kellogg, 1955.) 805
Black Rock, San Juan County, Washington. (Dalquest, 1948.) 325

LUTRA CANADENSIS YUKONENSIS Goldman, 1935.

Lutra canadensis canadensis: Dixon, 1938.

This form was based by Goldman on 16 specimens of which the type 452 (skull only of an adult female) came from Unalakleet, Norton Sound, Alaska. Goldman describes it as having characters

Similar to *L. c. preblei* . . . but skull distinctly smaller; audital bullae more rounded and inflated. Compared with *L. c. optiva* . . . the skull is smaller; mastoid processes less deflected downward, less hook-like; audital bullae more inflated; dentition lighter. A few specimens from widely dispersed localities appear to be referable to the form here described. Specimens from the Alaska Peninsula grade toward *L. c. optiva* in cranial characters. In color, however, the two forms appear to be nearly identical.

Goldman describes *optiva* with the words: 'General color rather dull, near vandyke brown (Ridgway, 1912).'

For skull measurements *see* page 332.

Distribution: Iliamna River and Lake; Lake Clark; Swan River. (Osgood, 1904.)

Sullivan Creek, near Tanana; at the heads of the Tozi and Melozi; on the Bering Sea tundra near Bethel. (Dice, 1921.)

Bering Sea coast, Alaska Peninsula, Kuskokwim and Yukon River drainage, east to central Yukon, Canada. Specimens secured from Alaska: between Portage Bay and Becharof Lake; Becharof Lake; Frosty Peak (Alaska Peninsula); Kuskokwim River (East Fork and base of Mount Sischoo); Mission; Nushagak River; Ruby; Tanana River; Unalakleet. From Yukon: Pelly River (mouth of MacMillan River). (Goldman, 1935.)

Wonder Lake area, Mt McKinley National Park, Alaska. (Dixon, 1938.)

MacMillan River, Yukon. (Rand, 1945.)

Teslin Lake, near Yukon, British Columbia. (Anderson, 1947.)

Kanayut Lake, about 15 miles north-east of Tolugak Lake, Alaska. (Rausch, 1950.)

Alaska; Yukon; British Columbia. (Hall & Kelson, 1959.)

Status: 'Now quite rare.' (Osgood, 1900.)

'Somewhat rare in the extreme north' of British Columbia [? *yukonensis*]. (Stone, 1900.)

Quite rare throughout east central Alaska; very scarce in the Ogilvie Range, Yukon; scarce on MacMillan River, Yukon. (Osgood, 1909.)

Chapter 5

Central and South American Otters

IT must be pointed out that the so-called *annectens* 'group' is the only one amongst the Lutrinae which includes amongst its members subspecies the rhinarium of which is variable in shape. Typical *annectens*, as well as *colombiana*, *repanda* and *parilina* all have the posterior margin of the nose-pad projecting upwards in the centre (as does *canadensis*) to a greater or lesser extent, the two margins of this projection being more or less concave. It would seem that this projection is probably greatest in *parilina* and least in *colombiana*. On the other hand, this same border is flat in the case of *latidens*, and actually has a downwards central projection (that is to say, the hair from above protrudes onto the naked area) in *mesopetes*. This variation of rising, level and falling upper margins cannot be accounted for in any logical geographical way, as a glance at the distribution maps will show.

Not only is the rhinarium of *mesopetes* unique in this group; in any comparative table of cranial measurements of *annectens* and its supposed subspecies, *mesopetes* is at once seen as the 'odd man out', for every single measurement (of an adult female) which Cabrera gives is less than the corresponding one of any other form in this 'group'. Additionally, the rudimentary nature of the nails of the fore-feet should be noted in this race, this characteristic not occurring, so far as I am aware, in any other otter from the New World.

Without further material and information it is impossible to judge the correct status of *mesopetes* with certainty. The present indications, however, all point to this race meriting specific status – as Cabrera originally proposed – and to its exclusion from the *annectens* 'group' into which it has been placed by Hall & Kelson, presumably solely on geographic grounds.

For these reasons I shall here treat it as a species in its own right.

LUTRA ANNECTENS Major, 1897.

Lutra annectans Ingles, 1956.
Lutra repanda: Cabrera, 1957.

Essential characters: Upper border of contracted rhinarium with an ascendant central projection bordered by two concave lines (typical *annectens,colombiana,repanda* and *parilina*) or alternatively an almost straight line (*latidens*); skull slightly convex dorsally; muzzle shorter than in *L. canadensis*; soles of feet naked; plantar callosities absent.

Colour: Upper parts sepia brown to pale reddish-brown; under parts grey brown; throat, pectoral and inguinal regions paler; lips and inner side of forelegs dirty white.

Size: Average; total length 37–50 in. (940–1270 mm.); weight up to 32½ lb. (14·75 kg.).

Range: From approximately 27°N. lat. southwards to northern Ecuador.

754

LUTRA ANNECTENS ANNECTENS
Major, 1897.

Lutra californica: Coues, 1877.
Lutra felina: True, 1884.
Lutra brasiliensis: True, 1884.

Essential characters: Upper profile of skull not as straight as in *canadensis*, facially steeper, muzzle somewhat shorter; bullae ossae less flat; mastoid processes widely expanded; premolars very small, a diastema between pm_1 and pm_2; feet small; rhinarium with a central upward projection bordered by two concave lines.

Colour: As for the species.

Size: Average; head and body 22¾ in. (580 mm.), tail 17 in. (430 mm.), total 39¾ in. (1010 mm.); weight 32½ lb. (14·75 kg.). For skull measurements *see* page 333.

Range: Type locality – Terro Tepic, Rio de Tepic, Jalisco, Mexico. Mexico; ? Coban, Guatemala; El Salvador.

20 LUTRA ANNECTENS COLOMBIANA Allen, 1904.

Lutra colombiana Allen, 1904.
Lutra emerita Thomas, 1908.

Essential characters: Rhinarium with an ascendant central point bordered by two concave lines, the lower border straight, half as long again in width as in height; teeth relatively large, compressed; brain-case high, rounded.

Colour: Above, pale reddish-brown; below, pale greyish-brown; guard hairs with long yellowish-white or soiled white tips.

Size: Rather small; head and body about 21½ in. (546 mm.), tail about 17¾ in. (450 mm.), total about 39 in. (991 mm.), but a specimen of 49 in. (1243 mm.) is recorded, with a weight of 30 lb. (13·6 kg.). For skull measurements see page 333.

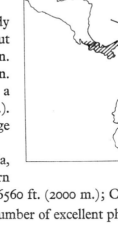

Range: Type locality – Bonda, Santa Marta, Colombia. Eastern Venezuela and Colombia, up to 6560 ft. (2000 m.); Costa Rica.

Illustration: Wisbeski, 1964. A number of excellent photographs.

1214

LUTRA ANNECTENS LATIDENS Allen, 1908.

23

Lutra latidens Allen, 1908.
? *Lutra paraensis* Gidley & Gazin, 1933.

Essential characters: Pelage short, thin; upper border of rhinarium slightly rounded or almost straight; dentition massive; skull large, broad.

Colour: Dorsally dark brown, snuff brown or warm sepia; below paler, brownish washed with buffy white; upper side of fore and hind feet very pale.

Size: Average; head and body 21⅔–31 in. (550–790 mm.), tail vert. 18⅓–19¼ in. (465–490 mm.), total 40–50¼ in. (1015–1280 mm.). For skull measurements *see* page 334.

Range: Type locality – Lavala [or Savala], Matagalpa, Nicaragua. Nicaragua; Mexico; Honduras; ? Costa Rica.

LUTRA ANNECTENS PARILINA Thomas, 1914.

1149

Lutra parilina Thomas, 1914.

Essential characters: Rhinarium with an ascendant central point above.

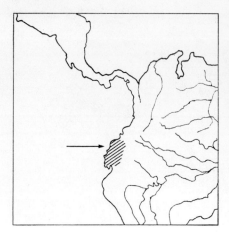

Colour: As in *L. a. colombiana.*

Size: ? above average; subadult female, head and body 22½ in. (570 mm.), tail 16½ in. (423 mm.), total 39 in. (991 mm.). For skull measurements *see* page 334.

Range: Type locality – St Juan, 15 miles west of Huigra, Ecuador. Western Ecuador; ? Colombia.

Note: This subspecies may not be validly separable from *L. a. colombiana.*

450   LUTRA ANNECTENS REPANDA Goldman, 1914.

Lutra repanda Goldman, 1914.
Lutra anectens repanda Cabrera, 1957.

Essential characters: Small; skull low, flat; upper molars and pm⁴ narrow.

964   *Colour:* Above, warm sepia or mars brown (Ridgway, 1912); beneath, greyish brown; lips and inner sides of forelegs soiled whitish, outer sides of forelegs dark brown.

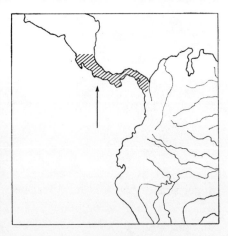

Size: Below average; head and body 23–24¾ in. (585–630 mm.), tail 18¼–19¾ in. (465–500 mm.), total 42¾–43 in. (1085–1095 mm.). For skull measurements *see* page 334.

Range: Type locality – Santa Cruz de Cana, upper Rio Tuyra, Darien, Panama, at 2000 ft. (610 m.). Panama; Costa Rica.

Status: Quite common in Darien (1916).

451   *Illustration:* Goldman, 1920, page 261, plate 35. Photographs of skull.

321   LUTRA ENUDRIS Cuvier, 1823.

Lutra enudris Cuvier, 1823.
Lutra enydris Fischer, 1829; Lesson, 1842; Schinz, 1844.
? *Lontra canadensis* Gray, 1843a.

214

Lutra enhydris Gray, 1865; Thomas, 1889; Major, 1897.
Lontra enhydris Gray, 1865.
Lutra latifrons Nehring, 1887.
? *Lutra brasiliensis:* Quelch, 1901.

Essential characters: Rhinarium with an unbroken band of hair running vertically between the nostrils; profile of head slightly arched from the occipital area to the nostrils.
Colour: Bay or chestnut brown above; lips, chin and throat yellowish or brownish white.
Size: Average; 42–52 in. (1065–1318 mm.); one male weighed 25¼ lb. (11·5 kg.).
Range: Trinidad; eastern Venezuela; the Guianas; 'Amazonia'; the west coast of Brazil.

LUTRA ENUDRIS ENUDRIS Cuvier, 1823.

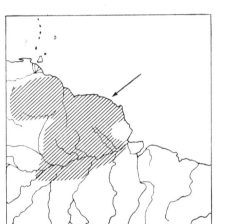

321

Lutra enudris Cuvier, 1823.
Lutra mitis: Cabrera, 1957.

Essential characters: As in the species; teeth massive.
Colour: Light bay to dark chestnut brown above; beneath much paler, greyer, almost white on the throat; tail concolorous with body, but lighter beneath than above.
Size: Average; head and body 24–29¼ in. (609–740 mm.), tail 18–22½ in. (457–570 mm.), total 42–51¾ in. (1066–1310 mm.); one male weighed 25¼ lb. (11·5 kg.), one female 8½ lb. (3·86 kg.). For skull measurements *see* page 334.
Range: Type locality – Guiana. The Guianas; ? Amazonia, Brazil.
Illustration: Pohle, 1920, page 39, figure 3 (f). Sketch of rhinarium.   923

LUTRA ENUDRIS INSULARIS Cuvier, 1823.   321

Lutra insularis Cuvier, 1823.
Lontra ? *insularis* Gray, 1865.

Essential characters: Muzzle apparently naked, its upper and lower edges straight; fur short, smooth, glossy.

Colour: Dorsally light chestnut brown, more yellowish-white ventrally;

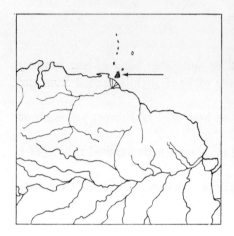

underfur whitish, tipped with brown in the darkest parts and yellowish on head, neck and chest.
Size: Average; head and body 27–28¾ in. (686–731 mm.), tail 18–19¼ in. (457–487 mm.), total 45–48 in. (1143–1218 mm.). For skull measurements *see* page 334.
Range: Type locality – Trinidad. Confined to Trinidad.
Status: Rare (1893).
Note: Some doubt must remain as to whether this race should not retain, as *L. insularis,* the specific rank sought for it by Cuvier, owing to the apparent nakedness of the muzzle as compared to typical *enudris* and *L. e. mitis.*

1147 LUTRA ENUDRIS MITIS Thomas, 1908.

Lutra mitis Thomas, 1908.

Essential characters: As in the species; teeth light and delicate; the band of hair between the nostrils narrower than in the typical form; skull small, light.
Colour: Dark generally.
Size: For skull measurements *see* page 334.
Range: Type locality – Surinam. Guiana and eastern Brazil.
923 *Illustration:* Pohle, 1920, page 39, figure 3 (e). Sketch of rhinarium.

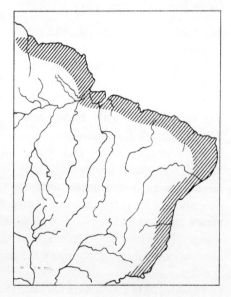

816 LUTRA FELINA Molina, 1782.

Mustela felina Molina, 1782.
M[ustela] *Lutra chilensis* Kerr, 1792.
Lutra chilensis Bennett; 1832; Waterhouse, 1838; Schinz, 1844.

216

Lutra californica Gray, 1837.
Lutra peruviensis Gervais, 1841.
Lutra brachydactyla Wagner, 1841.
Lutra californiæ Lesson, 1842.
Nutria felina Gray, 1865.
Lutra platensis: Gray, 1865 and 1869.
Lutra cinerea: Thomas, 1908.
Lutra peruensis Pohle, 1920.
? *Lutra provocax:* Mann, 1957–8.

Essential characters: Upper border of naked rhinarium almost straight, or a flattened semicircle; fur semi-erect, rather harsh, slightly grizzled; toes with blunt claws, the webs scattered with hair above, naked beneath, the ends of the toes free of webbing; tail relatively short; skull small, much flattened, short facially; teeth large, compressed; habitat almost exclusively coastal.

Colour: Generally dark, the guard hairs lighter tipped, the dorsal surface darkening progressively posteriorly; underfur brownish-grey, or with a bluish tinge; ventral surface but little paler than dorsal; chin, cheeks and throat somewhat lighter.

Size: Rather small; head and body 22½–31 in. (570–787 mm.), tail 11¾–14¼ in. (300–362 mm.), total 35⅚–45¼ in. (910–1149 mm.); one adult male weighed 9 lb. (4·1 kg.). For skull measurements *see* page 335.

Range: Western coast of South America, from (?) Ecuador in the north to the Strait of Lemaire in the south, and the coastal islands.

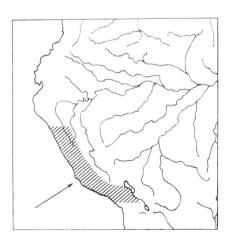

Status: Practically exterminated in the Cape Horn area (1950).

Illustration: Gay, 1847; 'Atlas', page 2. Fine coloured plate. (*See* plate 40.)

431

LUTRA INCARUM Thomas, 1908.   1147

? *Lutra montana* Tschudi, 1844.
? *Lutra fusco-rufa:* Gray, 1865.
? *Lutra fusco irrorata:* Gray, 1865.
? *Lutra subtus nigricans:* Gray, 1865.
? *Lutra supra obscura:* Gray, 1865.
Lutra incarum Thomas, 1908.
Lutra enudris incarum Pohle, 1920.

Lutra emerita Thomas, 1920.
? *Lutra incana* Colyer, 1936.

Essential characters: Upper border of rhinarium formed of two convex lines, with a small central descending projection, the lower border with a central ascending projection; skull large, massive; dentition heavy.
Colour: Rather pale.
Size: ? less than average; female, head and body 23·6–24·15 inches (600–613 mm.), tail 14¾–15½ in. (375–393 mm.), total 38·9–39·1 in. (988–993 mm.). For skull measurements *see* page 335.
Range: Type locality – Marcapata, Cuzco province, Peru. Peru, at least to 2000 ft. (610 m.); ? Bolivia.

251

LUTRA MESOPETES Cabrera, 1924.

Lontra mesopetes Cabrera, 1924.
Lutra annectens mesopotes Miller & Kellogg, 1955.
Lutra annectens mesopetes Hall & Kelson, 1959.

Essential characters: Upper border of rhinarium with a descendant central point; nails short, rudimentary on forefeet; skull small.
Colour: Prout's brown and cinnamon brown above, a little paler below.

Size: ? small. The original (and only available) figures, for the adult female type, appear to be misprinted, Cabrera giving the head and body length as 252 mm. (9·9 in.); if it is assumed that this is a misprint for 552 the measurements would then be: head and body 21¾ in. (552 mm.), tail 10½ in. (270 mm.), total 32¼ in. (822 mm.). For skull measurements *see* page 335.
Range: Type locality – Costa Rica. Limits of range unknown.

1187   LUTRA PLATENSIS Waterhouse, 1838.

Lutra longicaudis Olfers, 1818.
Lutra platensis Waterhouse, 1838b.
Lutra solitaria Wagner, 1842.
Lutra paranensis: Burmeister, 1861 and 1879; Ihering, 1911; Devincenzi, 1935.
Lutra pratensis Gerrard, 1862.

Lutra latifrons Nehring, 1887.
Mustela lutris: Larranaga, 1923.
Lontra platensis Flower, 1929.

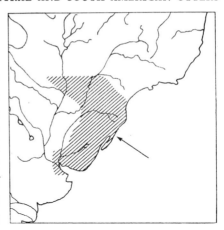

Essential characters: Upper border of small, naked rhinarium almost straight or slightly concave; the flattened tail with a fringe of hair 'against the grain' on each lateral margin; feet naked below, except for the posterior part in front of the heel; dentition of male much heavier than that of female; nocturnal in habit.

Colour: Lustrous dark brown above, paler or greyer below; chin yellowish white; cheeks and throat pale brown; underfur very pale brown, deeper externally.

Size: Average; head and body 19½–28 in. (500–710 mm.), tail 18–20½ in. (457–520 mm.), total 39¼–47¼ in. (1000–1200 mm.). For skull measurements *see* page 335.

Range: Type locality – Maldonado, Uruguay. Uruguay; Argentina; Brazil.

Status: Much hunted by the Indians and becoming progressively rarer (1955).

Illustration: D'Orbigny & Gervais, 1847. Plate 15. Fine coloured engraving. (*See* plate 41.) 354

Note: In the opinion of Hershkovitz (1959) the name *Lutra longicaudis* Olfers, 1818 is valid and antedates Waterhouse. 553
866

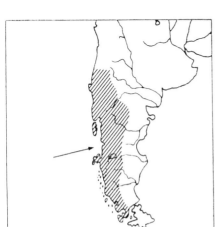

LUTRA PROVOCAX Thomas, 1908. 1147

Lutra huidobria Gay, 1847.
? *Lutra paranensis:* Thomas, 1889.

Essential characters: Upper border of rhinarium with a central ascendant projection; skull noticeably flattened.

Colour: Dorsal surface dark brown, ventral surface considerably paler in contrast.

Size: Average; head and body 24–27½ in. (610–700 mm.), tail 15¾–18

219

in. (400–460 mm.), total 39¾–45½ in. (1010–1160 mm.). For skull measurements *see* page 336.

Range: Type locality – south of Lake Nahuel Huapi, Argentina. Central and southern Chile; West Patagonia; Argentina.

Status: Commoner than *felina* on the islands around Cape Horn (1950).

462 PTERONURA Gray, 1837. – The Giant Brazilian Otter.

Saricovia Zimmermann, 1777; Lesson, 1842.
Mustela: Gmelin, 1788; Lesson, 1842.
Lutra: Shaw, 1800; and many other authors.
Pteronura Gray, 1837.
Pterura Wiegmann, 1839; Schinz, 1844.
Pteronurus Lesson, 1842.
Lontra Gray, 1843a and 1843b.
Pteroneura Sanderson, 1949.

445 PTERONURA BRASILIENSIS Gmelin, 1788.

Lutra brasiliensis Ray, 1693; Zimmermann, 1777; Bechstein, 1800; F. Cuvier, 1823; Geoffroy, 1826; Schinz, 1844; Thomas, 1889.
? *Lutra nigricans* Barrère, 1749.
Lutra atri coloris Brisson, 1762.
Mustela lutris brasiliensis Gmelin, 1788.
Lutra nitens Olfers, 1818.
? *Lutra solitaria:* Natterer, 1842.
Saricovia brasiliensis Lesson, 1842.
Mustela brasiliensis Lesson, 1842.
Lontra brasiliensis Gray, 1843b.
Pterura sambachii Schinz, 1844.
Lutra lupina: Thomas, 1889.
Lutra paraguaensis: Thomas, 1889.
? *Lutra subtus nigricans:* Gray, 1865
Pteroneura brasiliensis Sanderson, 1949.

Essential characters:

Of the *genus* –

Rhinarium haired; toes long, with strong claws; webs greatly developed; feet large, naked below; head with very short facial area; tail of distinctive shape, like a fer-de-lance, greatly flattened; dentition heavy; skull large, basal length to 150 mm., zygomatic breadth to 100 mm.

Of the *species* –

Colour: Rather variable, from fawn to reddish or darker brown; the neck and throat irregularly white or yellowish, strongly contrasted with the rest of the body, the two colours sharply separated; fur short, close, shortest on the tail.

Size: Very large, apparently up to almost 8 ft. (2·44 m.); weight of some specimens 50–70 lb. (22·7–31·8 kg.).

Range: South America, from the Guianas to Uruguay, on the major river systems.

PTERONURA BRASILIENSIS BRASILIENSIS Gmelin, 1788.   445

Mustela lutris brasiliensis Gmelin, 1788.
Lutra brasiliensis: Kerr, 1792; and many others.
Lutra brasiliana Shaw, 1800.
Lutra lupina Schinz, 1821.
Pteronura sambachii Gray, 1837.
Pterura sambachii Wiegmann, 1838.
Pteronurus sandbackii Lesson, 1842.
Lutra sandbackii Lesson, 1842.
Pterura sambachii Schinz, 1844.
Lontra brasiliensis Gray, 1842b; Cabrera, 1957.
Pteronura sanbachii Gray, 1865.
Pteronura sandbachii Gray, 1869.
Pteronura brasiliensis lupina Pohle, 1920.

It is extraordinary that so much confusion and lack of agreement should exist about an animal as distinctive as the giant Brazilian otter. Even the correct original author is debated, the rival claims of Zimmermann (1777),   1235
Gmelin (1788) and Blumenbach (1810) being argued by taxonomists.   445, 187

Probably the clearest explanation of the various muddles regarding this otter is that given by Pohle, who goes into these problems at very consider-   923
able length. To summarise briefly Pohle's conclusions, the *Pteronura* was first mentioned by Marcgrave (1648), but in his account   764

The whole animal is black in colour, excepting the head which is very dark, and there is a yellow patch on the throat . . .

together with other characteristics which accurately fit this form, he is thought to have confused the otter and the Taira, or Tayra [*Galera barbara*]. Alternatively, this confusion arose after Marcgrave's death when his papers were taken back to Europe, sorted and published. Apparently Marcgrave employed some form of private script, very difficult to decode, and it seems not improbable that the error was that of his editor, Johannes de Laët, rather than that of Marcgrave himself. It may additionally be mentioned that while Marcgrave did leave an illustration of the Taira he left none of an otter – or if he did it has not been found. The Taira illustration, however, is not specifically described by him; nor does the plate show a yellow throat as the animal is portrayed facing the observer, and the throat is hidden.

710   Pohle adds that Linnaeus (1758) amalgamated the sea otter (*Enhydra lutris*) and the giant South American otter because they were the same size.

It can confidently be assumed that very few of the early naturalists had ever seen a specimen of this giant otter. By the latter part of the eighteenth century the sea otter, on the other hand, was very well known on account 896 of the value of its fur, and Pennant's *Synopsis of Quadrupeds* (1771), in which he describes this latter animal as 'excessively black and glossy' must have been very widely read. (Had Pennant written in Latin he would surely 764 have used the very words employed by Marcgrave: '*atri est coloris*'.)

1104   Steller's long and important description of the sea otter had been published just twenty years earlier, and his phrases are frequently found applied to the *Pteronura*, often almost verbatim.

Thus throughout the early descriptions there is found this confusion between these two very different forms, one from the icy fogs of the Aleutians and the other from the steaming jungles of South America! As a rule these descriptions are such that it is virtually impossible to tell which animal the author thinks he is describing; similarly, the range is given as extending from Brazil to Kamchatka.

It is not difficult to follow the perpetuation of error as each writer, quot-949 ing his predecessor, repeats it. Ray's version of his '*Lutra* Brasiliensis' 1104 (1693) is curiously similar to part of Steller's account (1751) of the sea otter, the same words being used in the same order, although the Latin varies slightly. Steller, however, avoids the yellow throat ('*sub gutture macu-*161 *la flava*') which Ray took from Marcgrave. Barrère (1749), acknowledging 214 Marcgrave, contents himself with '*LUTRA nigricans*'. Brisson (1756) in his turn quotes Marcgrave, Barrère and Ray, although in French, but adds that he is uncertain whether the feet are webbed or not; this is peculiar, as 949 Ray distinctly says '*digiti pedum membranis connexi*' (the digits of the feet connected by a membrane).

The confusion between *Enhydra* and *Pteronura* becomes, as it were,

explicit with Zimmermann (1777) and for the first time this double identity   1235
is questioned. A free translation reads:

As we learn from Barrère, otters are also found in Brazil, which are blackish   161
['*nigricans*'] in colour and have a flat and hairless tail. Marcgrave called his ani-   764
mal the *Jiya* or *Cariguebeiu*, while Buffon used the name *Saricovienne* . . . [des-   228
cribing] this animal as completely similar to our native [otter]. But the Brazilian
otter has a well-marked golden yellow throat . . . which [characteristic] Steller
never, or at all events very rarely, observed in Kamchatka. Moreover, the tail of
Marcgrave's otter was said by him to be the same length as its foot; Steller, on the   764
other hand, states the tail of his Kamchatka [otter] to be three and a half times the
length of the toes on the foot. [Steller actually gives the length of the tail as '13 p.   1104
5 d.', which translated into modern terms would be a fraction over 16¼ inches
(411 mm.) if he were using Roman measures, or perhaps 13 inches 5 lines = 13·42
inches (341 mm.) if he was simply 'Latinising' English measurements.] Finally,
his otter [lived] in the sea close to Kamchatka and hardly ever frequented the
rivers and freshwater lakes; whereas the *Saricovia* is found not only in the rivers
of Brazil, but also in the Orinoco and La Plata rivers, where it spends its life. So
finally it may well be wondered whether [the otters] of Brazil and Kamchatka can
really be grouped together as climatic varieties; indeed, it seems difficult for them
to be the same, although there may be doubt about it . . .

Pennant's description of the Brazilian otter in his *History of Quadrupeds*   897
(1781) is by no means as accurate as were his remarks on the sea otter 10
years previously. His account is taken mainly from those authors mentioned above, with the exception of Zimmermann. He inclines to equate it   1235
with the *Guachi* of Gumilla (*Hist. de l'Orénoque*, iii, 239 – not seen by me),
perhaps because Guache is another name for the Tayra, saying:

If this is the Guachi, as probably it is, it burrows on the banks of rivers, and
lives in society: are extremely cleanly, and carry to a distance the bones and
reliques of the fish they have been eating; are very fierce, and make a strong
defense against the dogs; but if taken young are soon tamed . . .

In his *Animal Kingdom* of 1792 Kerr also shows the *Guachi* as a synonym   657
for the Brazilian otter, but his account follows that of Pennant so closely
that it must be assumed he is merely quoting.

In the same year as Zimmermann attempted to unravel the confusions of   1235
his predecessors, Erxleben is found perpetuating them, giving as synonyms   383
for his sea otter ('*Lutra marina*') both the sea otter of Pennant and the *Lutra
brasiliensis* of Ray and Klein. The otter of this latter author, both in 1743   663
and 1751, is again the familiar composite, and his accounts need not be   664
quoted.

223

228   Buffon's *Saricovienne* is described at some length in 1787, but this account is again a muddled one drawn from the usual sources; Buffon makes it apparent that he had never seen this animal.

445   The following year Gmelin's version appeared, and as he is widely canvassed as one of the possible original authors of this form it may be of interest to quote his account.

Head flattened, with very small ears, which are hairy and more or less round. The face is very blunt, with plentiful stiff whiskers. These are found above the eyebrows, to the rear of the eyes, behind the curve of the mouth, at the sides of the lower lips, and beneath the throat. There are six equal sized incisors in the upper jaw, and six below, these having two alternately placed interiorly, the two lateral ones being bilobate. There are five toes on each foot, the feet being palmate. The tail is flattened, and a little shorter than the body . . .

816   Gmelin goes on to query whether the form he is describing is the same as that of Molina (*felina*), described six years earlier. Fortunately, he does not combine the two!

1169   Turton (1806) quotes Gmelin accurately, but once more classifies this South American otter as a variant form of the sea otter, giving as its habitat both the coasts between Asia and America and the rivers of South America.

344   Desmarest, however, in his *Nouveau Dictionnaire* of 1817 clearly separates the two forms and apart from failing to stress the peculiar and characteristic shape of the tail gives a good description:

It is double the size of [the otter] of Europe, and the body is proportionately more elongated, although the feet are much shorter. A very fine specimen in the collection of the Natural History Museum in Paris . . . has very short fur, of a fawn-brown colour, lying very flat on the body and still shorter on the tail where the colour is brownish, darker at the extremity than at the base. The flanks and stomach are the same fawn-brown as the back; only the lower jaw, as well as the underside of the neck and the throat, are a dirty white, slightly yellow tinted . . .

Desmarest goes on to quote Sonnini ('*édit.* de Buffon, tom. 33, page 298') who says that they are to be feared more in April, when they have their 1184 young with them, than at any other time. (Warden writes in 1819 that 'the 345 female brings forth in the month of March'.) To quote Desmarest:

'At about this time of year,' says the traveller, 'I found myself surrounded by a multitude of *saricoviennes*, and it was a most singular and frightening spectacle. Their loud and sustained cries, and those of the men imitating them; their menacing jaws; the water being thrown at them to irritate them and make them come nearer; the constant reports of the guns; the uproar of the hunted and of the hunters; the solitude of this place – all combined to give this hunt a style of its own and to create a fantastic and picturesque situation . . .'

Desmarest adds that apart from being hunted by man these animals are also pursued by jaguars (*Felis onca*) and cougars (*Puma concolor*). According to Rengger (1830), the water snake can be added to this list of assailants, and he reports finding an otter in the stomach of one such reptile, some 18 ft. in length. Strangely enough, Santos states that these otters are not molested by alligators.   956   1012

Harlan gives a useful short account of a specimen in the Philadelphia   517
Museum; owing to its small size (see below) it must be assumed that this was a young animal.

Char. Essent. General colour reddish-brown, with the throat white or yellowish.

Head globular; neck very long; hair rather short, of a reddish-brown, lying flat to the body; more sparse upon the tail; tail brownish, darkest towards the end; body beneath of the same colour with the back; lower jaw and throat of a dirty brown, slightly tinged with yellow.

Harlan also mentions the gregariousness of this otter, as do many other authors such as Griffith. This trait is not remarked by G. Cuvier, but he does   475, 323
mention the hairiness of the rhinarium, perhaps the first author to do so.

In 1837 the name *Pteronura* appears for the first time, originated by Gray. His description of this new genus reads: 462

Head large, depressed. Muzzle hairy. Feet large; toes 5:5 distinct, very largely webbed. Tail elongate, subcylindrical, with a fin-like dilatation on each side of the hinder half. Cutting teeth $\frac{6}{6}$; the four upper middle ones larger, equal, lancet-shaped; the outer ones small, conical; canines elongate, grinders like *Lutra*? Nostrils with only a slight naked space on their upper edge. Eyes small. Ears small, round, very hairy on the inner side. Feet very large, intermediate in size between those of the otter and the fin-shaped feet of the *Enhydra*. Toes elongate with long acute claws; the hinder toes very long; two outer ones longest, and the others gradually shorter to the inner ones.

This genus is intermediate between *Lutra* and *Enhydra*.

Can this last remark be an echo of the confusions of an earlier generation?

Gray further proposes *Pteronura sambachii*, from Demerara, as a new species, saying of it:

Fur soft, liver-coloured brown; orbits paler. Lips, chin and throat yellow; the latter brown spotted . . .

Lesson treats Gray's new name as a subgenus (spelling it incorrectly   696
as *Pteronurus*) and also treats Buffon's *Saricovia* – which he lists quite separately – in the same manner.

225

468
470
In 1865 Gray further described this form but only from a badly prepared skin. As a result, he revised this account three years later, explaining that

in the preparation . . . [the tail] has been too much depressed on the sides, and the sides also are artificially extended, giving it a fin like appearance, which induced me to give it the name of *Pteronura. Craspedura*, or margin tailed, would have been a much more appropriate one. The bones have been almost entirely extracted from the skin of the feet, and they have been evidently flattened by the stuffer. The size and flatness of the feet in this specimen . . . do not exist in the unstuffed specimen . . .

[New description:] Head depressed; ears hairy, small; muzzle entirely covered with hair. Feet large and strong; toes 5 . 5, elongate, strong, widely webbed to the ends; toes on fore feet nearly equal, thumb smaller; the three outer toes of the hind feet are rather longer than the first toes, and the great toe a little smaller; claws large, compressed, acute; soles and palms bald to the heel, striated. Tail conical, tapering, rather depressed, covered with short hair and furnished with a subcylindrical ridge on each side; end more depressed, two edged, and fringed at the tip.

464
In 1843 Gray had characterized the tail as 'elongate, with a fin on each side'.

Gray then proceeds to redescribe his species *sanbachii* [*sic*], now held to be synonymous with *brasiliensis*:

Fur bright bay brown above and below; hairs all nearly of a uniform brown colour; lips and a large irregular patch on the throat and some spots on the side of the throat bright yellow.

Gray further describes what he terms 'Var.[iety] *kappleri*', as we would to-
471
day denote a subspecies. He refers to it again in 1869 in identical words, but it never reappears and must be counted as an individual variation. It came from Surinam, and remarking that 'The white hairs are better seen when the fur is examined by a hand magnifier' Gray describes it as

Bright golden brown above and below; hairs brown, with numerous white hairs intermixed; lips, chin, and an elongated streak on each side of the throat, which is dilated behind, and one branch of it extended up to the side of the chest, white.

Young duller, greyer; lips and throat spotted, white.

Despite the fact that Gray gives the total length of his *sanbachii* as 67 in.
437
(1700 mm.), Gervais speaks of it as being smaller than the European otter.
696
Like Lesson, he separates the *Pteronura* and the *Saricovia*, and gives the latter a size of at least 57 in. (1450 mm.).

It is a pity that no living specimen should have been available in Europe for zoologists to examine; had this opportunity occurred (which, so far as I can ascertain, did not happen until 1899 – see Nehring: 1900) one feels that Thomas would not have been so ready to dismiss the genus *Pteronura*, finding its characters 'clearly of specific and not generic importance'! Of the highly distinctive tail he writes: [848] [1143]

> The corded margin to the tail is only an exaggeration, suitable to so large a species, of the flattened state of that organ in other Otters . . .

and he triumphantly concludes that

> The whole of the living species of Otters, excepting of course the Sea-Otter, appear therefore to be most correctly placed in one single genus only . . . *Lutra*.

While many people may feel that the subsequent proliferation of names has been overdone, Thomas' suggestion – which seems never to have been noticed favourably – was surely going too far in the opposite direction. Thomas himself retracted this view in 1908, albeit rather grudgingly, saying: [1147]

> I am now prepared to admit, with other authors, that . . . the margined-tailed otter of Brazil (*Pteronura*) should be recognized as generically different from the ordinary otters of the genus *Lutra*.

A further brief description is provided by Fountain (1902), who gives the colour as 'dark reddish brown on the back, and a lighter shade of the same colour' below. He says of this otter that [421]

> . . . it was fond of crawling onto the broad leaves of the *Victoria regia* [water-]lily, which were well capable of supporting its weight. Frequently I have seen them asleep, or basking, on these lilies, and they resort to them to eat the fish which they have captured, as well as to play and gambol with each other . . .

Pohle's able analysis of the early history of the *Pteronura* has already been mentioned; his subspeciation, however, is open to criticism, here as elsewhere. Schinz's *Lutra lupina* (1821), equated by Pohle with Gray's *sambachii*, is now taken to be synonymous with *brasiliensis*, although it is retained by Pohle as a valid subspecies, *P. b. lupina*. In any event the name is a *nomen nudum*, being preoccupied both by Illiger (1815) and by Olfers (1818), as noticed by Hershkovitz. Of *brasiliensis* Pohle says: [923] [1034] [553] [923]

> Body and tail, both above and below, almost of the same colour, that is nut-brown according to Blumenbach, but nowadays somewhat faded. The legs are the same colour as the body, but a little darker in shade. On the head, the colour of the body is carried up approximately to the rear edge of the eyes; from there it runs as a median process approximately up to the centre of the nose. The area around the eyes, the cheeks, the upper side of the nose and the nasal septum are [187]

light brown, becoming lighter still towards the front. The lips, chin, and the whole of the throat are yellowish white, laterally about up to the height of the corners of the mouth. The light area is delimitated to the rear and at the top in an irregular but very sharp manner . . .

1034   Of '*lupina*' Pohle notes that Schinz's description is as brief as possible, saying no more than that the animal is dark brown, as large as a pointer ('*Hühnerhund*'), and comes from the Orinoco. Pohle finds himself unable to distinguish this Orinoco specimen from Gray's *sambachii*, and himself suggests that *lupina* may be synonymous with *brasiliensis*. He describes it as follows:

The body and upper side of the head are similar to *brasiliensis* Blumenbach [see above] but somewhat darker. The lips and chin are yellow. The spot on the chin runs to a point on each side on the lower part of the head, and reaches to about the distance of the rear edge of the ear. Between these points the skin has the same brown colour as the body. On the lower side of the neck there are individual spots of the same [yellow] colour which sometimes unite on one side only to form a lateral band. Thus the impression [is given] that the throat is yellow with brown spots. This yellow is most intensive on the lips, and sometimes assumes a whitish-yellow shade posteriorly.

255   Cabrera & Yepes describe this species as being

very dark brown in colour, between sepia and chocolate, appearing almost black when wet; the underside is slightly lighter, and the neck is generally spotted with golden yellow, which in adults may unite to form a half collar . . . The skull is of a very unusual shape in that the facial area is very small in proportion to the size of the cerebral area, but the number of teeth is the same [as in *Lutra*].

346   Devincenzi writes that owing to the collared effect given by the more or less contiguous yellow spots on the throat the *Pteronura* is known to hunters as the 'Lobo gargantilla' or 'Lobo corbata' (literally, necklaced or cravatted wolf). He, too, mentions that the fur appears almost black when wet, and adds that the area between the nostrils is abundantly haired. Of the tail he says:

It is flattened from the base downwards, and shows two very clear fringes on its outer edges, from which it has been compared in shape to a two-edged sword.

1012   Santos writes that although its staple diet is fish, including very large 'surubim' [*Platystoma fasciatum*], it does not disdain waterfowl, seizing them from below by the legs.

In South America the giant Brazilian otter is generally known as the 'Ariranha' as opposed to 'Lontra' which is used for the various species of *Lutra*; the latter are sometimes also referred to as 'Onça d'água'.

228

Size and weight:

Head and body about 38 in. (967 mm.), tail a little less than 18 in. (457 mm.), total about 56 in. (1424 mm.). Desmarest, 1817. [345]

'Some of the largest weigh thirty pounds' (13·6 kg.). Warden, 1819. [1184]

Head and body at least 39½ in. (1000 mm.), tail 17¾ in. (450 mm.), total 57¼ in. (1450 mm.). Gervais, 1855. [437]

Head and body 43 in. (1092 mm.), tail 24 in. (610 mm.), total 67 in. (1702 mm.). Gray, 1869. [471]

Total length of one specimen 64 in. (1625 mm.). Waterton, 1879. [1189]

Female: total length 64¾ in. (1645 mm.). Nehring, 1900. [848]

'A very fine specimen . . . measures just over six feet [1830 mm.] . . . much larger specimens are occasionally secured.' Quelch, 1901. [937]

Weight: two specimens, 70 lb. (31·8 kg.) and 75 lb. (34·2 kg.), the larger being 'over six feet' long (1830 mm.). Fountain, 1902. [421]

An old male: head and body 40 in. (1020 mm.), tail 22½ in. (575 mm.), total 62½ in. (1595 mm.); an old female: head and body 39¼ in. (1000 mm.), tail 20¾ in. (530 mm.), total 60 in. (1530 mm.). Allen, 1910. [27]

Head and body 48½ in. (1230 mm.), tail 25½ in. (650 mm.), total 74 in. (1880 mm.). Pohle, 1920. [923]

Average size of Uruguayan skins: head and body 45 in. (1140 mm.), tail 26 in. (660 mm.), total 71 in. (1800 mm.). Devincenzi, 1935. [346]

There are frequent examples with head and body 47¼ in. (1200 mm.), tail 27½ in. (700 mm.), total 74¾ in. (1900 mm.); old males have been hunted which have a head and body length of 47¼ in. (1200 mm.), tail 39¼ in. (1000 mm.), total 86½ in. (2200 mm.). Cabrera & Yepes, 1940. [255]

Head and body 55¼ in. (1400 mm.), tail about 39¼ in. (1000 mm.), total 94½ in. (2400 mm.); this skin was 35½ in. (900 mm.) in width. Santos, 1945. [1012]

Weight: 52 lb. 13 oz. (24 kg.). Sanderson, 1949–50. [1011]

Total length 78 in. (1982 mm.). Burton, 1962. [241]

'Attains . . . nearly seven feet [2130 mm.] . . . males . . . probably do not exceed about seventy pounds' (31·8 kg.). Davis, 1964. [333]

Note: Mr Gavin Maxwell has kindly shown me a letter from Mr D.R.H. Levy, of Brazil, part of which reads as follows: 'The eight living and numerous dead specimens which I have seen lead me to believe that the size of this animal has been greatly exaggerated. Furthermore, I have a book put out by the (Brazilian) Ministry of Education and Culture as recently as 1959 which states that typical measurements of the species are 120 cm. [47¼ in.] for the body and 70 cm. [27½ in.] for the tail; it adds that these measurements were 140 and 100 [55 and 39¼ in.] respectively in "the largest specimens yet hunted." ' These figures would give a total length of 94½ in. (2400 mm.), or very little short of 8 ft. For skull measurements *see* pages 336–7.

Distribution:

470   Surinam. (Gray, 1868.)

471   Demerara; Surinam; ? Ypanema, Brazil. (Gray, 1869.)

953   Minas Geraes. (Reinhardt, 1869.)

1141   Ecuador. (Thomas, 1880.)

937   Tapacooma Lake, British Guiana. (Quelch, 1901.)

421   Upper Purus River, Brazil. (Fountain, 1902.)

27   Rio Mocho, Caura, Venezuela. (Allen, 1910.)

Para; ? Bahia; Ilheos, Belmonte; Rio Itabapuana; Rio San Francisco; Borba; Marabitanos; Rio Negro; Rio Guaporé; Lagoa Santa; Iquitos,

923   Loreto, Peru; Rio Ocoa, near Villavicenzia. (Pohle, 1920 in part quoting Prinz du Wied, 1826; Pelzeln, 1883; Winge, 1895; and Bürger, 1919.)

From the Guianas to Uruguay, but predominantly in the north; in Uruguay, found especially in the Rio Uruguay, to the north of the Rio Negro,

346   and its main tributaries. (Devincenzi, 1935.)

'Though its area of distribution nearly encircles . . . [the Guiana] region, evidence of its presence in the extreme northeast (the lower reaches of the Orinoco) seems to be wanting. It appears to be one of those genera of Amazonian mammals . . . which have not completed a northward encirc-

1131   ling of the Guiana area . . .' (Tate, 1939.)

The Guianas; Brazil; 'Amazonas'; from Para as far as Bahia north of

1176   Goiaz; Matto Grosso; Minas Gerais. (Vieira, 1955.)

Brazil, ? restricted to the River São Francisco, on the borders of Alagoas.

254   (Cabrera, 1957.)

Note: It may be said that in general *Pteronura* confines its habitat to the major river systems of South America; *Lutra*, on the other hand, chiefly favours the smaller rivers or, in some cases, the coastal areas.

Status:

622   'Presumed to be rare in the wild.' Jarvis & Morris, 1962 (page 271).

Principal illustrations:

470   Gray, 1868, pages 62–63. Drawings of skull.

       plate VII. Fine coloured lithograph, but most inaccurate.

923   Pohle, 1920. Following page 247, plate VI, figures 1–3. Photographs of lower side of skull; lower jaw; side view of skull.

1233   Zeller, 1960, between pages 78 and 79, plate xxix. Excellent photograph.

Skeldon, 1961, facing page 50, plates ix and x. Photograph. (*See also* plates 1074
42 and 43.)

PTERONURA BRASILIENSIS PARANENSIS Rengger, 1830.

Mustela lutra brasiliensis: Azara, 1802.
Lutra paraguaensis Schinz, 1821; Thomas, 1889.
Lutra paranensis Rengger, 1830; Nehring, 1886 and 1887.
Lutra brasiliensis: Boitard, ? 1842;
Burmeister, 1879; ? Nehring, 1886;
  Ribiero, 1914.
Lutra paroensis Lesson, 1842.
Lutra parœnsis Gervais, 1855.
Lutra paraguensis Gray, 1865 and
  1869.
Lutra (Pteronura) paranensis Neh-
  ring, 1900.
? *Lutra paranaensis* Vieira, 1952.

956

The type specimen described by
Rengger appears to have had abnor-
mal dentition, with only four
molariform teeth on each side of
the upper jaw instead of the normal
five. (It is interesting that Nehring's female [1900] showed the same pecu-   848
liarity, pm^1 on each side being missing.) But for this, Rengger writes, he
would have regarded the Paraguayan subspecies as merely a variety of the
larger Brazilian form, for he remarks that their general appearance is very
similar. He writes:

The coat is composed of two kinds of hair, which grow thickly and almost
vertically from the skin. The hairs of the under coat are some half an inch in
length, straight and exceptionally soft to the touch. The hairs of the outer coat
differ from those of the under coat only in being about a twelfth of an inch longer,
somewhat stiff and not quite so soft to the touch, and in addition are extremely
shiny in upper half... The bridge of the nose, eyelids, and underside of the toes
and webbing are bare. [The hair on the nose was presumably rubbed off.]

The colour of the whole pelt, with the exception of the throat, is shiny dark
brown. On the throat is a large, almost rectangular light patch, the colour of
which varies according to the age of the animal. I found it to be brownish-red in
very young individuals which still had their milk teeth, turning to reddish-yellow
in those that had just lost them, whilst in fully adult specimens, several years old,
it was yellowish-white. One other feature worth noting are some brownish-red

hairs at the front of the upper lip of the cubs, which are replaced by brown ones at the first change of coat . . .

136
     The head . . . is large in proportion to the rest of the body, flattened from above, and broad. The face occupies only a quarter of the head's length. The muzzle, rounded towards the front, projects somewhat beyond the lower jaw. The nostrils are almost covered by half-moon-shaped flaps, with a convex edge facing downwards; Azara compares them to a letter C with the ends pointing upward. These flaps seal off the nostrils when the animal dives. The eye is small, round, black and shining, with the eye-socket placed well forward . . . The muscular neck is almost as broad as the head . . . The toes are joined by thick webbing, which leaves only the last joint free and on the outer toe extends in fact as far as the nail. The nails, though small, are powerful; they are laterally compressed and only slightly curved . . .

956
1038
     Rengger notes the social habits of this otter, when in the summer groups of up to 20 individuals may be seen together, and this gregarious disposition is confirmed by Schomburgk. He describes *paranensis* as being

of a light mouse-colour, rather reddish on the belly, with the white spot on the breast. In their habits, appearance, and mode of living they exactly resemble the larger species [typical *brasiliensis*] . . . but while that species is seldom found in societies, and generally only in pairs, the smaller is decidedly gregarious. Their head appears broader than in the former [larger] species.

234
     Burmeister's *Lutra paranensis* is in fact *L. platensis*, but he discusses true *paranensis* briefly under the name *L. brasiliensis*. He compares it with *platensis*, saying:

This species is very different from the other [*platensis*], having a shorter fur, the nose completely haired over the entire surface between the nostrils, very strong bristles on its upper lip, and on the cheeks and above the eyes; its tail is more distinctly flattened on the outer edges throughout its length, and it has a noticeably heavier dentition, though of the same formula.

848
     The first living specimen to reach Europe seems to have been that described by Nehring in 1900, who examined it after it had been in the Berlin Zoo for some three or four months. He writes of this young female:

The tail is oval in cross-section for the proximal third of its length, very muscular and *relatively* thickly covered with long hair. The middle and last sections are considerably flattened horizontally – [footnote:] to put this more precisely: for the second and last third of its length, the tail is quite flat on its underside, almost bare, and dark in colour, whilst the upper side is gently curved and covered with fine sparse dark-brown hair [end of footnote] – 80–90 mm. wide, and have very short hair, so that they appear almost hairless when wet; they are smooth and sharp at the sides like a two-edged sword. Looked at from above, the tip of the tail is rounded; its shape may be compared with a *truncated* Gothic arch or with a narrower version of the tail-tip of a *Castor fiber* [European beaver] . . .

The head is relatively large, the muzzle short, thick and high (not so flattened as in other otters), the eyes set well to the front. The whole muzzle, together with the bridge of the nose, is covered with short hairs. The feet are low and podgy, with very strong and broad webs. There are four teats arranged in a square on the abdomen.

The fur is short, soft and scanty, and when dry is like cut plush; the hairs of the outer coat are not much longer than those of the undercoat. The colour of the fur is a fine chocolate-brown on both the top and underparts of the body . . . On the chin and lower jaw a sharply defined yellow patch in the shape of a horseshoe can be observed. The front curve of this is on the chin, the sides following the lines of the lower jaw and extending a little beyond the corners of the mouth. The interior of the horseshoe is brown. On the lower part of the throat some thin, irregular, yellowish-white patches can be seen, disconnected from the markings on the lower jaw. The thin lower edge of the upper lip, barely visible from the front, is yellow. The remaining part of the muzzle, as far as the eye, appears light brown when dry; there is also a light brown stripe running back from the muzzle over and behind the eye on each side.

According to Pohle, the teeth of this subspecies are larger than those of 923
typical *brasiliensis*, and the breadth of the skull is also greater. Although he
states that the material in the Berlin Zoological Museum (two skins, three
skulls and a specimen in alcohol) differs somewhat externally from the
description given by Rengger (see above), there appears in fact to be very 956
little difference, judging from Pohle's own description, except that the pale
areas on the neck and throat are rather more extensive. Pohle gives no
external measurements.

Size: Four-months-old skeleton: head and body 12¾ in. (324 mm.), tail 7½
in. (191 mm.), total 20¼ in. (515 mm.); 'large male': head and body 26·2
in. (665 mm.), tail 19 in. (483 mm.), total 45·2 in. (1148 mm.). Rengger,
1830. 956
Nehring (1900) converts these same measurements, originally given in 848
inches, into millimetres as follows: 707 plus 514 = 1221 (48 in.)
Head and body about 34–35 in. (864–890 mm.), tail about 13–14 in. (330–
356 mm.), total about 48 in. (1220 mm.). Schomburgk, 1840. 1038
Head and body 28 in. (711 mm.), tail 18 in. (457 mm.), total 46 in. (1168
mm.). Burmeister, 1879. 234
Subadult female: head and body about 30¼ in. (770 mm.), tail about 19¾ in.
(500 mm.), total about 50 in. (1270 mm.). Nehring, 1900. 848
Male: head and body 45¾ in. (1160 mm.), tail 16½ in. (420 mm.), total 62¼

in. (1580 mm.); female: head and body 43 in. (1090 mm.), tail 22¾ in. (580
mm.), total 65¾ in. (1670 mm.). Vieira, 1952. [These dimensions seem more
likely to apply to the typical form than to *paranensis*.] For skull measurements *see* page 337.

Distribution: R. Parana; R. Paraguay; more rarely on their tributaries.
(Rengger, 1830.)

1175

959

Rio Paraguay [*sic*, ? R. Uruguay], Entre-Rios province, Argentina. (Burmeister, 1879.) [Not R. Uruguay in Paraguay, as stated by Pohle.]

234

Mundo Novo, Rio Grande do Sul. (Nehring, 1886.)

846

Puerto Viña, Salvador, [Argentina]; Piracicaba, [San Paulo], Brazil. (Pohle,
1920.)

923

São Domingos, Rio das Mortes, Mato Grosso. (Vieira, 1952.)

1175

Argentina; Uruguay; Brazil; São Paulo to the Rio Grande do Sul. (Vieira,
1955.)

1176

Restricted to the R. Paraná. (Cabrera, 1957.)

254

Chapter 6

The Sea Otter

It was, as I have seen it in his life, A sable silver'd.

Hamlet, i.2.242.

ENHYDRA Fleming, 1822 – The Sea Otter. 415

Mustela Linnaeus, 1758; Kerr, 1792.
? *Lutra:* Bechstein, 1800; Pallas, 1811; Schrenk, 1859.
Pusa Oken, 1816.
Enhydra Fleming, 1822.
Latax Gloger, 1827; Lesson, 1842; Merriam, 1904; Taylor, 1914; Pohle, 1920.
Enydris Lichtenstein, 1827–34; Fischer, 1829.
Lutra: Steller, 1751; Erxleben, 1777; Cuvier, 1823; Lesson, 1827 and 1842; Richardson, 1829; Gray, 1837.
Phoca Pallas, 1831.
Enchydris Lesson, 1842.
Enhydris Lesson, 1842; Schinz, 1844; Gray, 1865; and many others.
Sutra Elliot, 1874.

ENHYDRA LUTRIS Linnaeus, 1758. 710

Lutra marina Steller, 1751; Erxleben, 1777.
Mustela lutris Linnaeus, 1758.
Mustela lutra lutris Kerr, 1792.
? *Lutra gracilis* Bechstein, 1800; Shaw, 1800.
? *Lutra aterrima* Pallas, 1811; Schrenk, 1859.
Pusa orientalis Oken, 1816.
Enhydra marina Fleming, 1822.
Lutra lutris Cuvier, 1823; Lesson, 1827 and 1842.
Enhydris stelleri Lesson, 1827 and 1842.
Lutra stelleri Lesson, 1827.
Enydris marina Lichtenstein, 1827–34.

235

Figure 13.

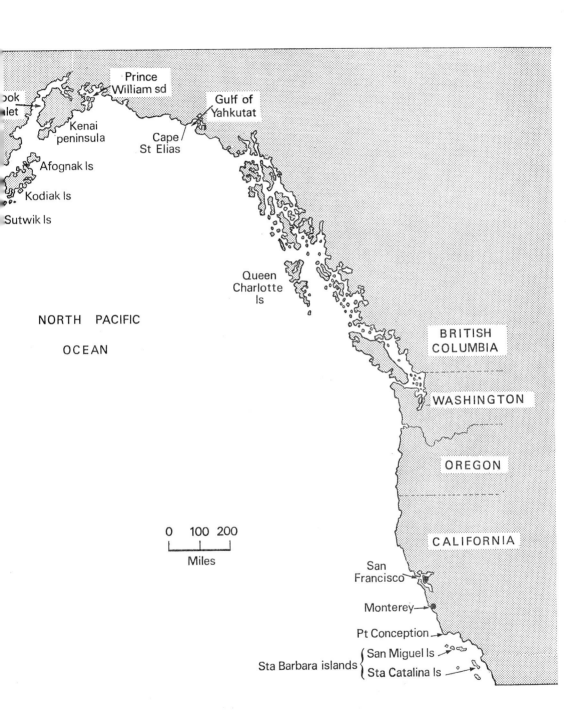

ook
let

Prince
William sd

Gulf of
Yahkutat

Kenai
peninsula

Cape
St Elias

Afognak Is

Kodiak Is

Sutwik Is

Queen
Charlotte
Is

NORTH   PACIFIC

OCEAN

BRITISH
COLUMBIA

WASHINGTON

OREGON

0   100 200

Miles

CALIFORNIA

San
Francisco

Monterey

Pt Conception

Sta Barbara islands {
San Miguel Is

Sta Catalina Is

? Enydris gracilis Fischer, 1829.
Enydris stelleri Fischer, 1829.
Lutra (Enhydra) marina Richardson, 1829.
Phoca lutris Pallas, 1831.
Lutra latrix Gray, 1827.
? Latax gracilis Lesson, 1842.
Latax marina Lesson, 1842.
Latax var. *argentata* Lesson, 1842.
Enhydris marina Schinz, 1844.
Enhydris lutris Gray, 1865 and 1869; True, 1884; Burton, 1962.
Sutra marina Elliot, 1874.
Enhydra lutris kamtschatika Dybowski, 1922.
? Viverra lutra Ognev, 1931.

Essential characters: Dental formula 3/2, 1/1, 3/3, 1/2 = 32; molars broad, flat; front feet short, compact, the fingers fused together, the palms almost without divisional lines between the individual pads; fore claws short, nearly erect, set well back from distal margin of fingers; the hind feet uniquely developed, flipper-like, the digits increasing in length from first to fifth, the sole completely covered with hair except for small digital pads; head large and blunt, neck thick and short; tail less than a quarter of total length; guard hair very sparse; anal scent glands absent; habit exclusively maritime. For cranial characters and measurements *see* pages 337–9.
Colour: Variable, from glossy black (sometimes grizzled) through dark brown to reddish; albinism very rare.
Size: Large; total length of males up to about 60 in. (1524 mm.), females to about 50 in. (1270 mm.); respective weights, up to 80 lb. (36·4 kg.) and 65 lb. (29·5 kg.).
Range: Originally Kuriles, Aleutian chain, western coast of North America, intermittently as far south as lat. 30°N., approximately; now much reduced, only local populations remaining. (*See* figure 13.)

710 ENHYDRA LUTRIS LUTRIS Linnaeus, 1758 – The Northern Sea Otter.

793 ENHYDRA LUTRIS NEREIS Merriam, 1904 – The Southern Sea Otter.

Latax lutris nereis Merriam, 1904.
Latax lutris gracilis Pohle, 1920.

The sea otter is a very different creature to its 'cousin' the land (or river) otter, different in appearance, structure, food, habits and mode of life. It is now almost exclusively maritime, hardly ever coming ashore; it eats prac-

238

tically no fish, and its teeth are quite unlike those of other otters; its strange
appearance has given it the name of The Old Man of the Sea or sometimes,
The King of Sea Beavers. Its devotion to its young has amazed naturalists
– and hunters – and won their admiration for generations, and it may be the
sea otter which lies at the back of many of the mermaid legends. The literature on the sea otter is vast, and its harrowing history is closely interwoven
with the search for the North-west Passage and the discovery and development of the North Pacific. Captain Cook, Catherine the Great and the silver
mines of Mexico all play their part in its story, the story of the sea otter's
fabulous fur, rarest and finest of all precious furs, that so nearly led to the
animal's final disappearance.

The habitat of the sea otter

is a region so gloomy, so pitilessly beaten by wind and waves, by sleet, rain and
persistent fog, that the good Bishop Veniaminov, when he first came among the
natives of the Aleutian Islands, ordered the curriculum of hell to be omitted from
the church breviary, saying, as he did so, that these people had enough of it here
on this earth!

In these words does Elliott describe the setting for 170 years of man's   375
slaughter of an immense hoard of defenceless and attractive animals, a
slaughter so unremitting, a persecution so extensive, that by the end of the
nineteenth century Pennant's 'vast abundance' of sea otters had been   896
reduced to the very brink of extermination. Nor are these mere empty
phrases. At times the hunt continued not only throughout the year but
both by day and night; Coues writes that in some areas the sea otters   306

do not have a day's rest during the whole year. Parties [of hunters] relieve each
other in succession, and a continuous warfare is maintained . . .

It is not easy to read the story of the sea otter with equanimity. Pennant   896
says of them that they

are most harmless animals; most affectionate to their young, will pine to death at
the loss of them, and die on the very spot where they have been taken from them:
before the young can swim, they carry them in their paws, lying in the water on
their back . . . are very sportive; embrace each other, and even kiss . . .

Seton quotes Steller as saying that   1060, 1104

When they sleep at sea, they fold their young in their arms just as mothers do
their babes. They throw the young ones into the water to teach them to swim, and
when tired out, they bring them to shore again, and kiss them just like human
beings . . . They embrace their young with an affection that is scarcely credible
. . . I have sometimes deprived females of their young on purpose, sparing the

239

mothers themselves, and they would weep over their affliction just like human beings. I once carried off two little ones alive, and the mothers followed me at a distance like Dogs, calling to their young with a voice like the wailing of an infant; and when the young ones heard their mothers' voice, they wailed too.

I sat down in the snow, and the mothers came close up and stood ready to take the young ones from my hand, if I should set them down in the snow. After 8 days, I returned to the same place, and found one of the females at the spot where I had taken the young, bowed down with deepest sorrow. Thus she lay, and I approached without any sign of flight on her part. Her skin hung loose, and she had grown so thin in that one week that there was nothing left but skin and bones . . .

1103   Although Stejnegger states that Steller was 'the first white man to set foot on Alaskan soil' and from this it is generally inferred that he was the first to discover the sea otter, in fact Padre Taraval had previously found them on Cedros Island, over 3000 miles away, in 1737, four years before Steller's arrival on what was to become known as Bering Island. On Bering's death, Steller effectively headed the remains of the expedition and his extensive account, published in 1751, preceded by six years that of Taraval and laid the foundations of the fur trade which so nearly placed the sea otter in the same sad category as that of the Dodo.

Steller and Bering were greeted by the sea otters as they arrived.

1060   They covered the shore in great droves . . . they would come up to our fires, and would not be driven away until, after many of them had been slain, they learned to know us and run away. Nevertheless, we killed upwards of 800 of them and if the narrow limits of the craft we constructed had permitted, we should have killed three times as many.

At first sight the castaways were in doubt as to what sort of animal this was,
1103   some thinking they were bears and others wolverines; but as Stejneger puts it:

The fearlessness of the otters and foxes at once convinced Steller that he had come to a land where the animals had not yet made the acquaintance of man . . .

The expedition was without food and suffering terribly from scurvy. As
236   Burney writes:

Of the marine animals which served as nourishment for the shipwrecked crew, they had at first only the *loutres* [otters] . . . the flesh of which, of the males, especially, was hard, and so tough, that it could scarcely be torn to pieces with the teeth, so that it was found necessary to chop it into small pieces. A *loutre* furnished 40 to 50 *lbs.* of flesh. The intestines were mostly used as food for the sick.

However, Steller says: 1060

The flesh of the young otter is most delicious; it cannot easily be distinguished from the flesh of an unweaned lamb, whether roasted or boiled, and the gravy from its preparing, in either way, is most delicious. The liver, heart, and kidneys tasted exactly like those of the calf ...

This finds confirmation in a much later account by Allan: 8

We secured six full-grown otters and a pup; the last was skinned without delay when we got on board, and made into a very appetising curry. Tender as a spring chicken, the only drawback to a delicate stomach being the remembrance of a strong and rather fetid odour exhaled by its larger relations, with the hot sun shining upon them in the boat.

Steller's party had other troubles as well as scurvy.

The sickness had scarcely subsided when a new and worse epidemic appeared,   1103
I mean the wretched gambling with cards ... at first for money, now held in low esteem, and when this was gambled away, for the fine sea-otters, which had to offer up their costly skins ... Men who had completely ruined themselves tried to recoup their losses by means of the poor sea-otters, which were slaughtered without necessity and consideration only for their skins, their meat being thrown away.

The unfortunate animals were hunted in several different ways, as Steller accurately informs us. The first method involved spearing them while they   1104
slept or swam in the water and, according to Scammon, was mostly em-   1020
ployed in calm weather.

The implement used to capture the animals is a spear of native make, composed of bone and steel, fitted to a long pole by a socket ... When within reach, the spear is launched into the unwary creature. In its efforts to escape, it draws the spear [-head] from the pole. There is a small but strong cord connecting the spear and pole, which admits them to separate a few feet, but does not free the Otter. The animal dives deeply, but with great effort, as the unwieldy pole greatly retards its progress ... When it rises upon the surface to breathe, it is beset with clubs, paddles, and perhaps another spear, and is finally dispatched, after repeated blows or thrusts.

Figure 14

A drawing of the spear-head used is given by Scammon and is reproduced above (two-thirds size), from a tracing.

375   An alternative method, as recounted by Elliott, was to pursue the animal at sea until it was exhausted.

> The whole fleet of twenty or thirty craft is launched . . . The bidarkies [Aleutian native boats] are deployed into a single long line, keeping well abreast, at intervals of a few hundred feet between. In this manner they paddle slowly and silently over the water, each man peering sharply and eagerly into the vista of tumbling water just ahead, ready to catch the faintest evidence of the presence of an otter . . . Suddenly [one] is discovered, apparently asleep, and instantly the discoverer makes a quiet signal, which is flashed along the line. [But the otter dives and] . . . the hunter brings his swift bidarka to an abrupt standstill directly upon the bubbling wake . . . He hoists his paddle high in the air, and holds it there, while the others whirl themselves over the water into a large circle around him, varying in size from $\frac{1}{4}$ to $\frac{1}{2}$ mile in diameter, according to the number of boats engaged . . . The kahlan has gone down – he must come up again soon somewhere within reach of the vision of that Aleutian circle . . . instantly as its nose appears above the surface, the native nearest it detects the movement; the yell has sent the otter down again far too quickly for a fair respiration, and that is what the hunter meant to do, as he takes up his position over the spot of the animal's last diving, elevates his paddle, and the circle is made anew . . . In this method the otter is continually made to dive and dive again without scarcely an instant to fully breathe, for a period, perhaps, of two or even three hours . . .

8   If, on such an occasion as this, the otter was a female accompanied by her pup, the hunters' work was simplified. Allan writes:

> It is very seldom that she will desert it, as she almost invariably clings to it with the truest maternal devotion to the last . . . Hampered with a charge whose plaintive cries strike deeper, deadlier than the hunter's bullet, her sole, unselfish anxiety is centred in her offspring . . . warned by the hushed plaint and catching breath, she knows that but a few more dives beneath the protecting element and the life of what she loved so well would be taken . . .

712   Littlejohn remarks that

> when the weather is foggy the only otter that can be chased with any degree of success is the mother with her baby, whose cries betray her. . . . diving at short intervals . . . she well knows that if she remains too long beneath the water the young will perish. Each time the surface is reached the little fellow utters a loud cry, and this at once attracts the attention of the hunter. To deaden the outcry the mother will often duck the head of her offspring beneath the water repeatedly.

306   Coues instances a different method:

> The young men have nearly all been supplied with rifles, with which they patrol [the beaches] . . . and whenever a sea-otter's head is seen in the surf, a

24. *Amblonyx cinerea concolor*, adult ♀.

25. *Amblonyx cinerea concolor*, adult ♀.

26. *L. (Hydrictis) maculicollis*. Photo: B. Campbell, Armand Denis
Productions/Photo Researchers.

27 (*above*). *L.* (*Hydrictis*) *maculicollis*. Photo: B. Campbell, Armand Denis Productions/Photo Researchers.

28 (*below*). *Aonyx capensis*, ♂ and ♀ cubs. Photo: Joan Wedekind.

29. *Aonyx capensis*, subadult ♀. Photo: Joan Wedekind.

30. *Aonyx capensis*, adult ♀. Photo: Gavin Maxwell.

31. *L. canadensis*, subadult ♀ and ♂.

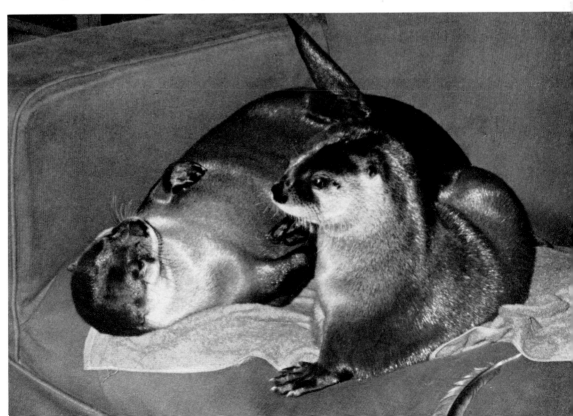

32. *L. canadensis*, adult ♂ and ♀.

33. *L. canadensis*, adult ♀.

34 (*above*). *L. canadensis*, adult ♂.

35. *L. canadensis*, adult ♀, underwater holding a pebble.

thousand yards out even, they fire, the great distance and the noise of the surf preventing the sea-otter from taking alarm until it is hit . . . the hunter waits until the surf brings his quarry in . . . This shooting is kept up now [1877] the whole year round.

An 'improvement' on this system is given by Scammon.   1020

The difficulty in shooting from the shore, when the marksman stands nearly on a level with the everchanging swell, has always been an aggravating annoy-ance; to avoid which, the hunters now use a sort of ladder . . . on which the hunter climbs in order to gain elevation. The ladders are made of light material, so that they can be easily carried at any time, should the sea be ruffled by a local wind or waves from seaward . . . It is estimated that the best shooters average at least 25 shots to every otter obtained, and that about one half of the number killed are secured by the rightful owners . . . the carcass either drifting out to sea, or to shore, possibly, with the following night tide, and the object so patiently and eagerly sought for is at last stealthily appropriated by some skulking savage.

Littlejohn also discusses how the otters were netted.   712

Many of the otters not killed with a rifle were taken in nets. These were of large mesh and about 6 fathoms long by 2 fathoms deep [10·9 by 3·6 m.]. They were anchored at one end so as to allow them to swing with the tide and with the wind . . . At night, when the animals dove for food, they were unable to see the nets and were soon enmeshed. In struggling to free themselves from this new species of sea-weed they attracted others of their kind . . . The infuriated otters would bite each other and the wooden floats on the nets and within a few hours all, or nearly all, were drowned.

According to Coues, nets were also spread out over the cave mouths and   306
surf-holes in the cliffs. He continues:

The clubbing is only done in the winter time . . . when tremendous gales [force the otters to seek shelter in the kelp beds]. The noise of the gale is greater than that made by the . . . hunters, who, armed each with a short heavy wooden club, dispatch the animals one after another . . . in this way two Aleuts were known to have slain 78 in less than $1\frac{1}{2}$ hours.

Before the otters became wary and began to spend almost all their time in the sea, clubbing was more frequently resorted to. Steller's party, newly arrived, took full advantage of this, and Steller writes: 1060

When it receives a vigorous blow upon the head, it falls upon the ground, covers its eyes with its paws, and keeps them so, no matter how many times it is struck upon the back. But if one hits it upon the tail, which is extended out as the animal runs, it turns about and faces the striker in the most absurd fashion. But more frequently it happens that they fall down at the first blow and pretend that they are dead. And then, as soon as they see that we turn our attention to others, they suddenly take to flight . . . Oftentimes, we would drive them into narrow places on purpose, without any thought of doing them any harm; we would hold our clubs ready, and they would fall down, fawning and looking in every direction. Then they would slowly shrink past us like Dogs, and as soon as they saw that they were out of danger, they would hurry with mighty leaps to the sea.

503   Littlejohn was hunting sea otters as late as 1885.

[On dark nights the natives hunted by] feeling all over the rocks until they located the otter . . . they would just feel along and find his head and hit him with a light tap for fear of waking the other ones up and then they would go along and hit another . . . there would be two or three natives so as to cover the rock in a short time . . .

Over on the Kuril Islands there was a flat rock probably two acres in extent . . . one year we went there and the rock looked like a seal rookery with otter . . . we just kind of got on three sides of the rock with our boats and kept them running back and forth . . .

We often hunted them until 9 o'clock at night and then went out again at 2 o'clock in the morning . . .

The natives, both Aleutian and Kamtchatkan, seem to have set little store
898   by the sea otters until the arrival of the fur traders. Pennant writes that the Kamtchatkans used their fur to face their garments, and also kept the skins of sables wrapped in common (river) otter skins, 'which are preserved better
1103   in Otter skins than any other way'. (Stejneger writes that 'the sable was the "golden fleece" which lured the Russian argonauts into the Siberian
403   wilds.') Fisher notes that sea otter fur mixed with sulphur was used by the Indians as tinder, the sparks from two flints struck together being allowed to fall upon it.

351   But the natives soon learned. Captain Dixon visited the Queen Charlotte Island group in July 1787, and writes thus of his arrival there:

A scene now commenced, which absolutely beggars all description, and with which we were so overjoyed, that we could scarcely believe the evidence of our senses. There were ten canoes about the ship, which contained, as nearly as I could estimate, 120 people; many of these brought most beautiful beaver cloaks; others excellent skins . . . and the rapidity with which they sold them, was a circumstance additionally pleasing; they fairly quarrelled with each other about which should sell his cloak first; and some actually threw their furs on board, if nobody was at hand to receive them . . . that thou mayest form some idea of the cloaks we purchased here, I shall just observe, that they generally contain three good sea otter skins, one of which is cut in two pieces, afterwards they are neatly sewn together, so as to form a square, and are loosely tied about the shoulders with small leather strings fastened on each side.

244

A similar scene is described by Captain Cook during his Pacific voyage in 296
1778.

> A great many canoes, filled with the natives, were about the ships all day . . .
> The articles which they offered to sale [sic] were skins of various animals . . . in
> particular, of the Sea Otters, which are found at the islands east of Kamtschat-
> ka . . .

Elliott, quoted by Coues, confirms this attitude of the natives. 306

> When the Russian traders opened up the Aleutian Islands they found the natives
> commonly wearing Sea-otter cloaks, which they parted with at first for a trifle,
> not placing any especial value on the animal . . . but the offers of the greedy
> traders soon set the natives after them.

In the early days, the main market for the sea otter furs was China and
Japan, and as Fisher remarks: 403

> Sea otter furs were used by the Japanese nobles and feudal lords for several
> hundred years before the commercial exploitation started.

To a great extent the history of the exploration of the northern Pacific is
bound up with the sea otter trade, and Russian expansion in this area, based
on Kamtchatka, was greatly stimulated by the demands of the Chinese fur
markets. Doubtless many furs also found their way to Russia itself, for
Sollars records that 1081

> Catherine the Great, always voluptuous in her tastes, was enraptured by the new
> furs. She immediately ordered a mantle [of sea otter fur] which was to sweep from
> throat to ankle.

The reader will not need reminding that during the period under discussion Alaska and the Aleutian Island chain belonged to Russia, while California was a Spanish possession. The former were purchased by the United
States in 1867, while the latter first came under American (military) gover-
norship in 1846. The Russian ownership of Alaska stemmed directly from
the eastward advance of the fur traders along the Aleutian chain to the
mainland, and it was the stories – and skins – brought back by the survivors
of Bering's party which caused this territorial expansion. It must, however,
be mentioned that the sea otter was by no means the only prize sought by
the hunters; no less important was the northern fur seal (*Callorhinus ursi-
nus*), and it was only by the ratification of the so-called Fur Seal Treaty in
1911 that the sea otter was saved from extinction for, almost by chance, it
was included in the protective measures originally designed exclusively for
the fur seal. Steller's Sea-Cow was less fortunate: for according to Cahalane 256

only 27 years sufficed for its extermination. (There is a remote possibility
617   that it still exists: the IUCN *Bulletin* for April–June 1964 lists *Hydroda-
malis stelleri* as a rare – and still extant – mammal.)

The hunt for the sea otter was carried on not only by the Russians but
also by the Japanese, Spanish, English, French and Portuguese fur traders.
403   As Fisher writes, every adult sea otter that could be found was killed, as
were all cubs over six months old. Younger cubs were sometimes killed or
more often left to sink, swim or starve. It is impossible to calculate how
many animals were killed, though a selection of figures gives some idea of
694   the immense numbers involved. Lensink writes that

a list of American ships in the fur trade for the years 1799–1802 shows that during
these four years 47,800 skins were obtained. [From another source] 1804–1807
... produced 59,364 skins and 1805 alone produced 17,445. According to a third
source, the next 5 years produced 47,962 skins.

It was estimated that British and American vessels had obtained 10/15,000
pelts annually between 1794–1803. By 1825 the maritime fur trade of the North-
west Coast as an entity had ceased, although the Russians continued to obtain
1000–2000 skins annually, mostly from Kodiak and westward to the Aleutian
Islands. In the last five years of their occupation of Alaska they got 11,137 skins.
The total number of sea otters killed by hunters of all nationalities during the 126
years of Russian occupation of Alaska probably exceeded 800,000.

Lensink relates that as early as 1821 the Russian-American Company had
tried to institute certain conservation measures, for instance by setting
'harvest quotas' for each district, and by attempting to kill only males. On
the mainland, however, as opposed to in the Aleutians, 'ungoverned
exploitation' continued, and on the purchase of Alaska and the Aleutians by
the Americans in 1867 all conservation measures were abandoned.

During the first four years after the transfer Americans took 12,208 skins.
The tempo of the slaughter increased over the next two decades. From 1871–1880
at least 40,283 were killed, and from 1881–1890 an additional 47,842 are known
to have reached the market. The next decade showed the effect of the excessive
kill, as only 6143 animals were obtained by the Alaska Commercial Company
which by then had nearly monopolised the Alaska fur trade.

The Japanese had also attempted to control the killing of sea otters, and
403   Fisher writes that all hunting in the Hokkaidô (Yezo) area was strictly
prohibited in 1884.

... on the other hand the Minister might grant to whomever he pleased special
permits to hunt in this area for any sum that he might care to charge ...

864   (As recently as 1931 Ognev comments on illicit hunting by the Japanese,

246

and Eyerdam writes in 1933:   388

> Natives of Atka who own fox farms on some of the islands told me that they always go to their islands in company and heavily armed for fear of attack by Japanese poachers . . .)

In 1823, according to Fisher, the Spaniards and Russians had agreed that   403
Russians hunting off the coasts of California were to split their catch equally
with the Spaniards.

> This system worked well for the Russians . . . for example, in 1826 one take of 63 skins was divided so that the Russian half was 44 and the Spanish half was 19 . . .

(According to Grinnell *et al.* the Spaniards had planned to collect the skins   482
from the natives through the missions and ship them to China in exchange
for the quicksilver which was greatly needed for the Mexican mines.)
Fisher writes that between 1785 and 1803 at least 74,528 sea otters were
taken, most of them by the Americans, and over 13,000 from along the
Californian coast.

Figures given by Nelson supplement to a certain extent some of those   850
already quoted.

> When the Fur Seal Islands [now the Pribilofs] were discovered these animals [sea otters] were very numerous, and two sailors killed 5000 there [at St. Paul] the first year. The next year less than 1000 were killed, and from the end of the next six years to the present day [1887] the sea otter has been unknown there. From the Aleutian Islands south to Oregon the Russians found these otters so numerous that they were obtained in numbers running from 2 to 3000 skins per year in many places, and in 1804 Baranov sailed from Alaska with a single cargo of 15,000 skins. At that time the district about Unalaska Island furnished about 1000 skins annually. In 1826 only 15 skins were taken there; in 1835 about 100 were taken, and . . . in 1867 the entire Aleutian chain, with the adjacent coast south, only yielded to the Russians from 6 to 800 skins annually. In 1873 the Americans secured nearly 4000 skins from this same region, and in 1880 and 1881 from 6 to 8000 skins are estimated to have been secured on the same ground. This great increase in the catch during the later years is entirely due to the greater vigor with which the animal has been hunted, and the introduction of fine long-range rifles . . .

Kenyon reports that   651

> the last recorded skin in the Pribilofs was taken from an otter found dead in 1892. Of this once thriving colony only scattered bones remain.

306, 374   The sad story is repeated by Coues (quoting Elliott, 1874, which I have been unable to obtain):

When Shellikov's party first visited Cook's Inlet, they secured three thousand; during the second year, two thousand; in the third only eight hundred; the following season six hundred; and finally, in 1812, less than a hundred, and since then not a tenth of that number.

The first visit made by the Russians to the Gulf of Yahkutat in 1794, two thousand sea-otters were taken, but they diminished so rapidly that in 1799 less than three hundred were taken.

222   Bryant adds that

upwards of 18,000 sea otter skins were collected for the China market in that year [1801] by the American vessels alone.

1104   In 1751 Steller had written:

Such is the beauty of the animal and especially of its skin that this otter alone is incomparable and without equal, for in the amazing beauty and softness of its fur it surpasses all other creatures of the vast ocean.

Such a temptation was not to be resisted.

It is not surprising that as the supply diminished the price rose, although at times in the past it had periodically declined. The price commanded by a sea otter skin at various dates may be found from a variety of sources. In those that follow the rouble was worth approximately 50 c., according to

406   Fisher (1941).

	1740's	80–100 roubles. (Fisher, 1941.)
1103	pre-1758	60–80 roubles to the Chinese at Kiakhta. (Stejneger, 1936.)
236	pre-1758	80–100 roubles in the same circumstances. (Burney, 1819.)
296	1778	about 20 skins sold at Canton for $800. (Cook & King, 1785.)
406	1780	80–140 roubles at the Chinese frontier. (Fisher, 1941.)
	1786	$60 in Canton. (Fisher, 1941.)
	1786	$70 and $91 in Canton. (Fisher, 1941.)
222	1799	$25 in Canton. (Bryant, 1915.)
	1800	$22 in Canton. (Bryant, 1915.)
178	1800	70–100 roubles to the Chinese. (Bewick, 1800.)
222	1801	$21 in Canton. (Bryant, 1915.)
	1802	$20 in Canton. (Bryant, 1915.)
306	1804	$65. (Coues, 1877.)
406	1808	$30–$40 in Chinese markets. (Fisher, 1941.)
	1840	$15 at the Chinese frontiers. (Fisher, 1941.)
	1847	$60 each for the last 42 in San Francisco Bay. (Fisher, 1941.)

248

1855	800–1500 French francs. (Gervais, 1855.)	437
1869	$30 at Fort Nisqually, Hudson's Bay Co. (Beidleman, 1958.)	170
1869	$20 gold; London average price 175s., about $43.75. (Fisher, 1941.)	
1873	$75. (Fisher, 1941.)	406
1874	$50. (Scammon, 1874.)	1020
1880	$475 in London for a 'superior' skin. (Fisher, 1940.)	403
1880	$100–$155. (Littlejohn, 1916.)	712
1885	about $362 each. (Griffith, 1953.)	477
1887	$100 good quality; $150 northern skin; $350 exceptionally fine. (Fisher, 1941.)	406
1888	£21 ($105) London. (Fisher, 1941.)	
1888	£21 10s. ($107.50). (Poland, 1892.)	924
1889	£33 ($165). (Poland, 1892.)	
1891	£57 ($285). (Poland, 1892.)	
1903	£88–£200 ($440–$1000). (Fisher, 1941.)	406
1903	£225 ($1125) extra rich large skins. (Fisher, 1941.)	
1910	$1703.33 (£340). (Seton, 1926 quoting Taylor, 1916.)	1060

Writing in 1916, Littlejohn speaks of prices at that time as being in the $1500–$2000 range, and Seton writes of the price that

712
1060

since then, it has steadily climbed, and $2000 and $2500 became common prices during the 1920 fur boom.

Similar figures are mentioned by East (1947). Fisher cites Evermann (1923) as giving the prices of sea otter pelts at that time as $2000 to $3000 each, but she adds that it has proved impossible to verify such figures. She writes that Bergman (1929) records that skins taken by the Japanese government are auctioned yearly, the largest and darkest bringing £500–£600 apiece, but she gives the figures realized for Alaskan skins confiscated by the US government and sold at public auction as follows:

364, 406

1924	4 skins $300; $295; $270; $155.
1925	2 skins $205; $190.
1927	2 skins $60; $30.
1929	5 skins $450; $300; 3 at $71.
1931	2 skins $370; $60.
1933	12 skins from $465 down to 2 at $12.
1934	1 skin $3 (pup).
1935	4 skins $300; $105; $50; $40.
1936	4 skins $310; $125; $85; $6.50.

> 1937 12 skins from $410, to 3 at $20, and 2 pups at $3, 2 at $1.
> 1939 1 skin $125.
> 1940 2 skins $73; $54.

Three other skins, not sold by the US government, fetched $350 (1935), $88 (1938) and $255 (1938).

The great variation in these prices can be ascribed not only to a variation in the quality of the skins but also to the fact that they vary widely in colour.

885 According to Parker (1910) sea otter, amongst the Precious Furs, is accorded the highest rank for durability, as is ordinary otter (*Lutra*) amongst the less valuable ones. Sea otter skins weigh $4\frac{1}{4}$ oz. per sq. ft. (132 gm. per

897 929 sq. cm.), and according to Pennant in 1781 each skin weighs $3\frac{1}{2}$ lb. (1587 gm.). These figures would give the average skin a total area of just over 13 sq. ft., but from the furrier's point of view Parker gives the size as

885 50 × 25 in. (1·27 m. × 0·635 m.). Parker writes:

> Unlike other aquatic animals the skin undergoes no process of unhairing [or removal of the guard hairs], the fur being of a rich dense silky wool with the softest and shortest of water hairs. The colours vary from pale grey brown to rich black, and many have even or uneven sprinkling of white or silvery-white hairs. The blacker the wool and the more regular the silver points, the more valuable the skin.

694 Lensink believes that a nucleus of not less than 500 animals still survived when hunting was ended by the provisions of the Fur Seal Treaty in 1911. In his opinion

> it seems probable that a nucleus of animals survived in each population centre, and that widespread migration to form new colonies did not occur.

(Assuming for the sake of argument that in all 1000 individuals survived in 1911, and had increased to 25,000 in 1961, on a 'compound interest' basis this would show a net annual increase of about $6\frac{2}{3}\%$; if only 500 had originally remained, the corresponding figure would be about $8\frac{1}{3}\%$.)

236 Opinions are divided as to what extent, if at all, periodic or seasonal migrations occur. As early as 1819 Burney is found writing (page 176):

> In the month of March the loutres or sea otters disappeared, whether from custom of changing their place of abode at particular seasons of the year, or that their persecution had given a general alarm to them, is doubtful . . .

1104
482 Steller observed a summer movement to the inland lakes, although he did not consider the otters as being migratory. More recently, Grinnell *et al.* discussed this question with Mr W. J. Evans in 1918, whose view of the Californian subspecies was that

the otters apparently were not migratory, and an individual, if unmolested, probably spent its life within a few miles of one spot.

Jones (1951) is more cautious, saying   637

> We have no evidence of migratory actions [but] . . . during the summer months . . . migrations may . . . take place though not apparent to the observer.

That there may be a periodic or occasional mass movement is suggested by Griffith in 1953, who notes that there was evidence of a general eastward   477
migration in about 1880, sea otters beginning to reappear in Cook's Inlet 'where formerly they had been almost exterminated'. Griffith himself found evidence of 'seasonal movement' between the various Aleutian islands, and stresses that no satisfactory explanation has been found for the fluctuation in numbers observed in the Amchitka area. He also mentions that whereas 41 otters were seen on Sutwik Island in January 1949, there were 355 there in the summer of 1951.

That there is a seasonal change of habitat is supported by Ognev,   864
although the movement of which he writes appears to be a fairly local one.

> . . . the occurrence of migrations may be noted to take place in summer. At this time the sea otters move in large companies from the northwest corner to the southern portions of Mednyi [Copper] Island. Lekh [1907] explains this motion   689
by the desire of the animals to avail themselves of the more abundant food, since the migratory sea otters take up positions some 20 miles to the south in patches of sea kale which abound in young fish at this time. If the animal is not disturbed during this time and the weather is not particularly stormy, the herds spend considerable periods in these feeding places (6 to 8 weeks). At the end of August or the beginning of September . . . they return to their permanent homes . . .

It is hardly surprising that there are a very large number of accounts describing the wonderful fur of the sea otter. Captain Cook describes a 'rather   296
young' example as being

> of a shining or glossy black colour; but many of the hairs being tipped with white, gave it a greyish cast at first sight. The face, throat, and breast were of a yellowish white, or very light brown colour, which, in many of the skins, extended the whole length of the belly.

A long and detailed article on the anatomy of the sea otter was published by Home & Menzies in 1796. Of its external appearance they say: 579

> The colour of this animal varies in different subjects, but in general the head and neck are grey, or of a silver colour; the back, sides, legs and tail, black and glossy; in some, the longest hairs are tipped with white, which gives them a beautiful greyish cast; the breast and belly also vary from a silver grey, to different shades of light brown. The long hairs shine with a brilliant gloss, but the short

fur is exceedingly fine, soft, and thick set; and its colour is either a light chesnut-brown [*sic*], or it has a silver hue, and a beautiful silky gloss. In the cub state, the hair is a long, coarse, shaggy fur, of a brown colour, destitute of any gloss; but as the animal grows up the fur becomes finer and more beautiful.

403, 864 Fisher writes that cubs attain adult pelage at six months, and Ognev partially confirms this, saying:

The first molt after birth takes place after 5 to 6 months. The sea otter acquires its true fur and characteristic underfur toward the end of the first year and the beginning of the second year; two to three-year-olds have the finest fur.

345 Desmarest describes an example in the Paris Museum collection as follows:

The pelage is very soft to the touch and composed of a most silky felt ['*feutre*'], longer than in the other species, pierced by guard hairs of shining dark brown and sprinkled with white hairs; as a result the general appearance is of a brown-black body marked with little points of white, with the exception of the head, the throat, the front feet and an area running towards the belly, where the fur is in general a dirty white, ticked with brown.

321 This is probably the same specimen as that described by Cuvier six years later whose account, as usual, is very complete and a model of observation.

The back of the neck, the shoulders, the top and sides of the body, the rump and the thighs are covered with a thick fur of woolly hairs of the greatest softness, amongst which may be noticed, although in very small quantities, guard hairs of a slightly greater length. The head, the lower part of the legs, the underside of the throat and body are, on the contrary, so covered with guard hairs as to hide the underfur, at least in part; the former are rather less numerous on the tail. The back of the neck, the shoulders, the top and sides of the body, the rump, thighs, back legs and the tail are dark chestnut brown, with all the refulgence of velvet; the woolly hairs on all these parts are pale brown at their base and dark brown towards the apex, while the guard hairs are dark brown on the hind legs and on the tail, and white tipped on the body. The head, throat, underside of the neck and body, and the lower part of the front legs are silvery grey, the muzzle having a reddish tint; on all these parts the guard hairs are a brilliant white; the underfur is brown on the body and reddish on the head, throat and beneath the neck.

Cuvier adds that this example was obtained from a furrier.

1020 It is interesting that Scammon mentions that the colour of the female changes, being quite black when 'in season' (his quotation marks) and dark brown at other times. I have not found confirmation of this suggestion elsewhere.

1060 Seton writes that the process of moulting seems to be so gradual that the pelt is nearly always prime, and the question of adult moulting is further discussed by Ognev, who states that contradictory data are found. 864

According to N. A. Grebnitskii (1902), partial molt takes place in July and August. Sea otters in summer pelage are less highly valued. The best pelts may be found in April and May . . .

As opposed to this information, S. Lekh [1907] asserts that the quality of the 689 fur has no connection with season, and adds that it is impossible to establish a definite molting period, since whenever sea otters are obtained some specimens are undergoing molt. Never was mass molting found in captured individuals. It may be added that according to Lekh more molting skins are nevertheless encountered in January and February than in other months . . .

Cahalane, however, writes that although the moult is extremely gradual the 256 largest quantities of hair are shed in May and June.

Seton notes that the sexes are alike in colour, and also that the skin may 1060 be stretched to some 6 ft. in length, although '4 or 4½ feet are considered maximum lengths for the animal itself'. The skin is exceedingly loose. Elliott remarks that when the animal is lifted up by it 'it is as slack and 374 draws up like the hide on the nape of a young dog'. As Jones puts it: 637

When the animal is picked up the abdominal contents slosh to the end that is down . . .

He adds that the intestine is some 40 ft. long, a figure confirmed by Stullken 1116 & Kirkpatrick. (Home & Menzies give this measurement as 52 ft. in one 579 individual.) The skin is so loose that according to Kirkpatrick, Stullken & 662 Jones the otter can bite a hand holding it by the scruff of the neck!

Ognev (1931) gives a detailed picture of the typical coloration. 864

Coloration of very rich and extremely soft silky fur, with its exceptionally dense long underfur, varies from different shades of dark brown to almost black. Guard hairs very sparsely distributed among underfur. Guard hair characterised by dark brown color; tips whitish-silver. Head and neck lighter than trunk and either silver-brownish gray or rust brown. Tail and paws blackish, darker than rest of trunk. Sea otters with overall rust coloring encountered relatively rarely. General tone of back and belly of young individuals a deep and warm dark brown close to bone brown. Paws and tail somewhat more intense and black. Head and neck markedly lighter, since in these regions the straw-gray shade marked on hair tips is clearly visible. Cheeks and lower part of chin particularly light. Region from eyes to nose (in form of two rather broad stripes) and vicinity of nose and chin (bordering mouth region) – intense dark brown. Light whitish-yellow vibrissae quite marked on this general dark background, forming a characteristic pattern on light head. In conclusion it may be added that the roots of the underfur (in back region) are markedly lighter than the tips. Albino forms are encountered as a great rarity.

¹⁰³¹ Scheffer & Wilke stress the degree of variation found (quoting Stevenson, *Rep. U.S. Comm. Fish and Fisheries* for 1902 (1904): 321):

> The color of the pelt varies considerably, the predominant shade being deep lustrous brown brightened with silvery overhairs. Some pelts are a deep brown or a brownish black, and are known in the trade as 'black.' Others are brown with a tendency toward bluish green or dark-plum color, and are known as 'dark.' The fur is in all cases lighter on the abdomen than on the back. The hair on the head is lighter in color, and is light brown in the brown variety, but in the black animal it is almost completely white, the effect of the large number of white overhairs. The skins from British Columbia, Washington, and Oregon are frequently of a yellowish-brown hue, and albino skins have been taken rarely.

²⁹⁶ To a certain extent the variation in coat colour is a factor dependent on the age of the individual, as was first remarked on by Captain Cook (vol. II, pages 295–296):

> These changes of colour certainly take place at the different gradations of life. The very young ones had brown hair, which was coarse, with very little fur underneath; but those of the size of the entire animal, which came into our possession ... had a considerable quantity of that substance; and both in that colour and state the sea-otters seem to remain, till they have attained their full growth. After that, they lose the black colour, and assume a deep brown or sooty colour; but have then a greater quantity of very fine fur, and scarcely any long hairs. Others, which we suspected to be older still, were of a chestnut brown; and a few skins were seen that had even acquired a perfectly yellow colour.

⁶³⁷ Jones (1951) points out that whatever the age, the head

> is of a different color than the body, with the greatest disparity in the old adult. The pup is born with his head a lighter shade than his body but not sufficiently marked to be apparent from any distance. The cub maintains this same relative coloration. When subadulthood is reached ... about 1 to 3 years old, the head assumes an olive-buff color. As the animal grows older this becomes a distinctive marking especially apparent when the fur is dry. In the older animals the head looks gray and bewhiskered, creating a striking likeness to an old man, hence the name 'Old Man of the Sea'.

⁴¹⁵ The genus *Enhydra* was proposed for the sea otter by Fleming in 1822. (The oft-encountered '*Enhydris*', is wrong; apart from any other reason, it is the name of a form of sea snake.) Before *Enhydra* appeared, a large number of synonyms were in current use and one of them, *Latax*, was incorrect⁹²³ ly revived by Pohle in 1920.

Gray suggested in 1865 that the sea otter was sufficiently distinct to be   468
placed in a 'tribe' of its own which he called Enhydrina. Ognev (1931) refers   864
to the 'numerous very distinct unique features' of the sea otter as possibly
warranting its being placed in a separate subfamily of its own, although I
find no trace of Pocock's suggesting Lataxinae as a subfamily name in 1921,   919
as stated by Ognev; in any event, Pocock's article on the sea otter dates   920
from 1928, but even there no new subfamily is proposed.

Fleming's diagnosis of his new genus was quite brief: 415

ENHYDRA. Sea Otter. Six incisors above, and four below. Tail much shorter than
the body. No anal scent bags.

This lack of musk glands had been noted previously by Home & Menzies   579
(1796).

Gray's description of his new 'tribe' Enhydrina is a little more detailed   468
than the generic diagnosis quoted above:

Marine. Head depressed. Hind feet large, elongated, rather fin-like, hairy
above and below, oblique, truncated; the outer toes longest; claws small. Tail
short, cylindrical. Muzzle bald, oblong, triangular. Soles entirely hairy, like the
upper surface of the feet; teeth 34. Premolars 3/3, 3/3. [There are, in fact, only 32
teeth.]

The hind foot is like a compressed fin, quite as much, and even more so than
in the case of the Seal. It differs from the foot of the Seal in the toes gradually increasing in length from the inner to the outer one, making the foot appear
obliquely truncated.

The somewhat superficially seal-like appearance of the sea otter's hind foot
has always proved something of a pitfall for zoologists. Fleming 'ventured   415
to remove the Otters from the Polecats, and unite them with the Seals', and
Pallas in 1831 had gone so far as to consider that the sea otter *was* a form of
seal, calling it *Phoca lutris*. Heude, too, questions the correctness of classify-   554
ing '*Enhydris marina*' as a member of the otter family.

Lydekker wrote that the hind flippers are 'doubled back' and that   728

Their mode of locomotion is by a series of short springs from the hind flipper
... [they do not] *walk* in ordinary acceptance of the term, i.e. by moving the
limbs alternately.

But the following year (1896) he revised his previous account, and ex-   730
plained that he had meant that the 'fingers' of the hind feet were doubled
under the foot when walking, being bent at the 'knuckle', a fallacy accepted
by Pohle. But as Pocock remarks in 1928:   923, 920

I think ... that there must still be some mistake connected with this point. At
all events, the dorsal surface of the hind digits ... show no trace of wearing of the

hair, and the retention of the digital pads suggests that the foot is planted on the ground in the usual manner during progression.

833 Murie confirms Pocock's supposition in these words:

> Some writers have thought that in walking the animal doubles the long webbed hind toes under and that consequently it actually walks on its 'knuckles.' Observation proved this not to be the case. The animal places its whole flipper forward, sole down.

662 This is, of course, the case and it is well described by Kirkpatrick *et al.*, who say:

> The peculiar hobbling gait of a sea otter is not unlike that of a land otter, though more clumsy. The head and hips are held higher than the shoulders, with the lumbar region arched even higher than the hips; the tail may drag, or be held at an upward angle. Ordinarily, when not moving, the otters do not stand but drop to their bellies, sides, or backs.
>
> At their usual slow gait, an otter's paws [front feet] and flippers [back feet] on opposite sides move alternately as in other fur-bearing animals. A laborious gallop is possible for short distances with both paws hitting together alternating with both flippers hitting together. When hurrying there is sometimes no co-ordination as the short front legs are moved rapidly, together or alternately, and the hind legs are moved more slowly. At a slow walk, the flippers may be placed outward about 30 degrees from the line of forward motion and at other times the toes may be directed straight forward.

333 The front feet are almost as unusual as the back ones, and are equally 'un-otterlike'. Davis remarks that the forepaws look like little more than stumps.

> Seen from above the toes seem to have been amputated, and only on the underside can indentations be found that correspond (nearly) to toe separations. One of these is actually two toes, bearing on its upper surface two inconspicuous claws, rather than one. There is, however, no webbing between the toes, nor in fact any functional separation.

920 Pocock has described the strange structure of this front foot in some detail.

> The foot is exceedingly short and compact, about as wide as long, with a convex, lobate, distal margin. The digits are tightly tied together almost to the distal edge of the digital pads, and are merely defined by marginal angular notches and by shallow grooves and the claws on the upper surface. The proportional length of the digits is normal . . . The third and fourth are more intimately fused than the rest, the first being apparently capable of greater independent movement than the others. But perhaps the most remarkable modification of the fore foot is the almost complete suppression of divisional lines between the individual pads, the

lower surface being covered by an almost continuous granularly coraceous [*sic*] cushion, showing only indistinctly the digital, plantar, and carpal elements of which it is composed. In two young specimens . . . there is a band of hair passing across the middle of the foot from the outer edge. This seems to indicate the anterior margin of the plantar pad. This band, however, is undeveloped in the adult example. In the latter the claws are nearly erect and set well behind the distal margins of the digital pads, which entirely conceal their points when the foot is viewed from the lower side.

Pocock's material was limited to one adult and four young skins, preserved in the British Museum. His information and sketches were prepared by softening the feet in water, no spirit-preserved specimens being available. On the other hand, Kirkpatrick *et al.* had the great (almost unique) advantage of observing and handling captive specimens. They write that 920 662

the fore paws are pad-like with no separation of the digits, although the terminal phalanges are movable and give great flexibility to the tips of the paws. The short and slightly curved claws are normally retracted on to the back of the paw but may be rotated forward to extend beyond the tip of the paw.

The sea otter is one of the very few tool-using mammals, perhaps as a result of, or in spite of, its peculiar front feet. A number of authors have described the way in which it will grasp a mollusc in its hands and smash the shell by hammering it on a piece of rock resting on its chest. Thus Fisher writes: 400

It is not an uncommon thing to hear a sharp clicking sound . . . made by an otter that is trying to crack open something with a very hard stonelike shell. The object is held with both paws and with full arm action from well above the head it is brought down hard on a piece of rock that rests on the otter's chest. These pieces of stone are brought to the surface at the same time as the food.

Similarly, Murie describes how 833

the otter would come up from underwater foraging and when it turned over on its back there would be a piece of rock resting on its abdomen or chest. Then with a vigorous sweep of its paws it beat a tattoo on the rock with what appeared to be some medium-sized mollusc . . . the tapping sound was audible at a considerable distance.

Hopkins gives a like account. 583

First they dove . . . a few minutes later each would reappear at the surface with a shellfish and a flat rock. The rock was placed rather fussily . . . and when it was just right, the otter would hold the shellfish in both forepaws and pound with extreme speed.

257

708 Limbaugh observes that the rocks used as feeding aids were commonly $2\frac{1}{2}$ to $3\frac{1}{2}$ in. in diameter, although sometimes flat ones as large as 6 in. in diameter were employed. Occasionally, the same rock was carried on a series of
333 successive dives. Davis writes in a similar vein:

> Diving to the bottom, an otter would return to the surface with a water-rounded stone. Some of the stones we saw were a bit smaller than hen's eggs and roughly the same shape, while others were larger and ranged from more or less spherical to rather flattened. Resting the stone on its chest, the otter would hold the mussel between its forepaws, one end in each paw, and strike it smartly a number of times against the stone until the shell cracked. After eating some of the meat the otter would often hammer what was left of the shell on the stone again before returning to its meal . . .

1022 Schaller records one animal breaking up 54 mussels in this way, striking them on a stone 2237 times, in the space of one and a half hours; and in a
506 detailed study Hall & Schaller write of tool-using sea otters:

> The same stone was frequently retained for several successive food items, and such retention would seem to imply an anticipation of use that goes beyond the immediate situation. The tendency of otters to manipulate and to pound is far from stereotyped in its application and seems to provide the basis for learning the use of tools in feeding behavior.

374 From all these accounts it appears that Elliott was in error when he suggested that the sea otter breaks sea-urchins 'by striking the shells together'.

It would seem that this habit of resting stones on the chest is by no
834 means unusual, as Murie found the pectoral hairs abraded on Alaskan
662 specimens, presumably from this cause, as did Kirkpatrick et al. Nor is
652 their use of stones invariably an adjunct of feeding. Kenyon found a captive sea otter using a rock to pound loose a bolt securing the mesh strainer over the drain-hole in her pool; although discouraged, she persisted until she was successful.

It has already been remarked that the sea otter differs greatly from the river otter in many details, and some instances of such differences have been given. While it is perhaps unnecessary to describe all these variations in too great a detail some must be recorded, especially the teeth. Owing to its specialised feeding habits, which are discussed later, the sea otter's teeth have become considerably modified. The first upper premolar on each side is missing, as are two of the lower incisors, giving a dental formula of 3/2, 1/1, 3/3, 1/2 or a total of 32 teeth, compared to all other otters (with the exception of *Amblonyx*, where the first upper premolar is similarly very frequently absent) which show 3/3, 1/1, 4/3, 1/2 or a total of 36 teeth

258

(A detailed comparison of the osteological and dental characters of *E. lutris* and *L. canadensis* may be found in Taylor: 1914.) Coues remarks that   1132, 306

All the teeth, including those of even the youngest specimens, have an appearance of being greatly worn, as is not, however the case.

According to Scheffer, the new-born sea otter pup has five teeth, all   1028
deciduous, in each half of each jaw, giving a formula of I 3/3, C 1/1, PM
1/1. I have not found confirmation of this elsewhere, and it may be noted
that if it is correct the sea otter has twelve deciduous incisors, but only ten
permanent ones. Pohle gives the milk tooth formula as 2/2, 1/0, 3/3 as com-   923
pared with that of *Lutra*: 3/3, 1/1, 3/3. Barabash-Nikiforov states that the   153
young are born with 'a complete set' of teeth, while Davis writes 'almost a
full set'.

Jones considers that   637

The teeth of the adult otter give a clue to age. In the subadult form no decay is
evident but sometime in the adult life serious erosion and decay begin, eventually
reducing the teeth to a condition of near uselessness . . . breaking the shells with
the paws appears to be an adaptation for survival.

Fisher remarks that the northern sea otters exhibit a greater number and a   407
larger size of cavities in their teeth than do their southern relatives.

A few other variations from the 'normality' of *Lutra* may be touched on
briefly. With regard to the vibrissae, Pocock found   920

no trace of the superciliary, genal, and interramal tufts . . . but Coues records the   306
presence of a few superciliary vibrissae . . .

Lydekker describes them as resembling the whiskers of a cat, but coarser,   728
while Coues writes that they are 'few, short, extremely stout and stiff,   306
directed downwards for the most part'. Baird states that the bristles are   146
arranged in three rows.

Harlan's account of 1825 (which appears to follow remarkably closely   517
that of Desmarest of 1817) speaks of the tongue as being   345

rather long, slightly notched at the extremity, covered with corneous papillae.

This confirms Home & Menzies, who describe the 4-in.-long tongue as   579
having a slight fissure in its rounded end, 'giving the tip a bifid appearance'.

But perhaps the most marked external difference to the river otter shown
by the sea otter is in the very short tail, this appendage being only some 12–
13 in. long in full grown specimens. Pennant describes it as 'flat, fullest of   896
hair in the middle; sharp pointed'. More recently, Coues characterizes it as   306
'terete, obtuse' i.e. having a cylindrical or slightly tapering form, circular in

18   259

⁵¹⁷ cross-section. Harlan terms the tail 'thick and depressed', while Lydekker
⁷²⁸ writes:

> With regard to the *tail*, it is *not* cylindrical but *flattish*, being more than twice
> as broad as it is thick. It only tapers to a very slight extent, except at the extreme
> end, where it runs off sharply to a bluntish point.

⁴⁰⁵ This is confirmed by Fisher, who states that 'the tail is most decidedly flat-
⁹²³ tened for its entire free length'. Pohle notes that there are only 18–21 caudal
vertebrae as compared with 24 in *Lutra*.

The proportional length of the tail is well shown in the following table
¹⁵³ given by Barabash-Nikiforov in 1935:

	Head and body		Tail		Weight	
	in.	mm.	in.	mm.	lb.	gm
Embryo	12·1	307	5·1	130	3·08	1400
Newborn	17·3	440	6·1	155	4·4	2000
About 5 months	23	585	7·9	200	12·3	5600
1 year	27·7	703·5	10·3	262·5	24·9	11,300
2 years	31·8	806	11·7	297	41·8	19,000
3 years	35·6	905	12·2	310	46·6	21,200
4–5 years	39·9	1015	12·4	316	52·3	23,800
5–6 years	41·5	1056·5	12·6	320	56	25,500
6–7 years	44·8	1138·8	12·7	322·3	66·5	30,200
7·8 years	47·5	1207·6	12·75	324	71·5	32,500
8 years and over	51·3	1304·9	13	330	77	35,000

⁸⁸⁹ As in other forms, there is a certain amount of individual variation in the
size of sea otters. Pearson gives figures for a foetal specimen showing a total
length of 18¼ in. (464 mm.), of which the tail was only 3·2 in. (82 mm.); the
weight is given as 3 lb. (1361 gm.). This example must have been nearly at
term as, apart from its size, its eyes were open.

¹⁰²⁸ It appears, as might be expected, that males run a little larger and heavier
than females. Scheffer gives the measurements of three 'very small' sea
otters, two females and one male, as 21·7, 22·0 and 25 in. respectively (551,
560 and 635 mm.), with a tail length of 4·8, 5·3 and 6·3 in. (123, 134 and 160
mm.); their weights were 3·6, 4·3 and 5·4 lb. (1630, 1950 and 2440 gm.).
Although there was no indication that these pups were necessarily of an age,
⁶⁵¹ Scheffer states that age for age males are larger. Kenyon states that the
⁴⁰¹ young at birth weigh from 3–5 lb. (1361–2268 gm.), while Fisher writes
that the smallest pups are some 15 in. (381 mm.) in length.

Barabash-Nikiforov gives the average normal measurements for sea 153 otters in the Commander Islands group as being somewhat over 39¼ in. (1 m.) for the head and body, with a tail length of about 12½ in. (320 mm.); the weight of such an animal would be around 66¼ lb. (37 kg.).

Scheffer & Wilke write in 1950 that 'the largest Aleutian sea otter on 1031 record' had a length of 58 in. (1473 mm.), but larger examples have in fact been recorded. A year later Scheffer writes of one of 58¼ in. (1478 mm.) 1028 which weighed 76 lb. (34·5 kg.), and in the same year Jones, remarking that 637 the average adult weighs around 50 lb. (22·7 kg.), mentions that the largest animal measured was 61½ in. (1562 mm.), while the heaviest weighed 79 lb. (35·9 kg.). Another animal of 61½ in. is recorded by Brandt. Kenyon (1957) 211, 651 states that females will reach 65 lb. (29·5 kg.) and males will go up to 85 lb. (38·6 kg.), while Murie records an old male of 80 lb. (36·4 kg.). 834

A separate subspecies for the Californian, or southern, sea otter was pro- posed by Merriam in 1904 with the name of *Enhydra lutris nereis*, the type 793 locality being San Miguel Island, Santa Barbara Islands, California. Its variation from the typical northern form consisted solely in the cranial characters, described by Merriam as follows:

Skull large, broad, and high, with long and high saggital crest and swollen braincase. Compared with *lutris* the following differences appear: Skull as a whole less flattened, braincase more swollen and rounded, the sides (viewed from above) more convex and swollen, especially behind the constriction; anterior part of zy- gomata more broadly and squarely expanded; basioccipital forming an angle with basisphenoid; coronoid processes sloping strongly backward; saggital crest much higher and more decurved posteriorly; inner cusp of large upper premolar (pm 3) elongated along anterior part of the inner lobe (instead of conical) and showing a tendency to subdivide into two parts; 1st lower molar broader and more broadly truncate posteriorly. The specimen in the flesh measured 6 feet in length.

Although the type specimen was an adult male the length of 6 ft. cannot be accepted.

The validity of *nereis* was strongly attacked by Scheffer & Wilke in 1950, 1031 who considered from an examination of 56 adult skulls that those of the southern race were no higher than northern ones, with the solitary excep- tion of Merriam's type skull. They add:

The height measurement is a difficult one to take and is unsatisfactory because of irregularities on the skull . . .

Other cranial differences between the northern and southern forms are dis- counted one by one. They find some evidence of a colour difference between the two races, but question its validity throughout the seasons of the year. These authors conclude:

793

> Some of the features described by Merriam in 1904 as diagnostic of the subspecies *nereis* are applicable to the type specimen alone, while others are applicable to northern as well as southern individuals. Though there may be a north–south gradient in certain features, we suspect that it is a smooth and uninterrupted one. Were we handed a skull from an unknown source we could not, with confidence, assign it to its proper locale. Neither on the basis of demonstrable variation nor on the grounds of geographical isolation is there support for a southern subspecies of the sea otter.

805, 505

Although I have seen no express vindication of Merriam's race published subsequent to this attack, both Miller & Kellogg (1955) and Hall & Kelson (1959) treat the southern form as distinct, and I shall accordingly do the same.

923

167

406

It is to be regretted that Pohle should have sought to equate *nereis* with Bechstein's *Lutra gracilis* (1800), and solely on the grounds that Bechstein's (rather inadequate) description seemed to him to fit that of a Berlin example of the sea otter from San Francisco Bay. If Fisher is right that the last sea otter was taken from San Francisco Bay in 1847 Pohle's specimen must have been at least 70 years old and – to judge by the single adult example in the British Museum – had probably 'aged' somewhat. Bechstein's place of origin, 'Statenland', Pohle assumes to be either an island near Fireland (*'Feuerland'*) or the Staten Island off New York. In any event Pohle states that sea otters are found in neither place and that Pennant (the skin of whose animal Bechstein was describing) must have got the place of origin wrong.

578

Hollister, in reviewing Pohle's monograph of 1921 writes that Stejneger had called his attention to the fact that

> the Statenland of Pennant is without doubt the most southern island of the Kurile group, north of Japan; so named by its discoverer, de Vries, a Dutch navigator, in 1643.

254

805

553

This island is now called Etorofu but Cabrera may be correct when he assigns Statenland to the neighbouring island, Kunashiri. Cabrera discounts the suggestion of Miller & Kellogg that the locality intended is the Isla do los Estados, close to Tierra del Fuego, and the consequent identification of *gracilis* with *felina*. Hershkovitz (1959) does likewise, but assigns to Kunashiri the *gracilis* of Shaw, also published in 1800.

167

It seems unlikely that it will ever be known with certainty what Bechstein (or Pennant) meant by Statenland, and the point is perhaps a little academic. From the measurements given by Bechstein (head and body 4 ft.

4 in., tail 1 ft. 1 in.) it can be assumed with some confidence that he was describing a sea otter, but at the same time Pohle's assumption that this example was a member of the southern race seems inadequately established. [923]

Merriam's type description does not mention the external characters, but the southern sea otter has been described at length and in detail by Lichtenstein, whose account Pohle quotes. Lichtenstein writes of two skins from San Francisco Bay, one fully grown and the other half grown. [793] [701] [923]

The entire body is covered by an extremely fine, thick, silky underfur. This is of a brownish grey colour, and when slightly magnified is found to be in the shape of wide spirals, of unequal thickness in younger animals but regular in older ones, like the best sheepskin though not so long and curly. In its natural curl the hair is 18 mm. long, stretched out straight barely 25 mm. When one blows on the hair the star thus formed has throughout the same depth and size, and the actual skin itself is invisible, even if the hair is separated with tweezers. Amongst the underfur guard hairs protrude which are even in distribution and length, the tips of these projecting beyond the underfur by a few millimetres and giving the whole pelage that beautiful, shining, dark brown colour for which it is so much admired. When still only a year old the animal has many of these guard hairs tipped with white, and their number increases with age; so that eventually the whole fur appears to be covered with a hoar-frost. The white-tipped hairs exceed the length of the other hairs by just the length of the tip, which can thus be seen in its entirety. The beauty thus given to the fur owes much to the regular spacing of these white-tipped hairs, so that one can count 8 to 10 shorter hairs between each two longer white guard hairs, and if the hair is completely smooth they are found to be placed alternately in adjoining rows. But what must most please the expert of such skins is the regularity and fineness of design almost throughout the body. The back, sides, chest and stomach are everywhere covered with equally fine, long dark hairs, and on every part of these areas the number and thickness of the white-tipped hairs is the same. Only the head, the nape of the neck and the feet prove an exception to this; the two former because their basic colour is lighter, and the latter because the hairs have no white tips. On the nape of the neck the paler colouring is due to a thinning of the dark guard hairs which allows the lighter underfur to show through. This colour sometimes extends to the back of the neck, gradually disappearing between the shoulders. On the head the lighter colour is given by the guard hair itself, especially on the sides from the corners of the mouth up to the eyes and ears, where the colour is a lustrous reddish grey. Above the eye of the younger specimen there is a narrow curve of this same colour, delimitated by the dark colour of the forehead and crown; in the older example the entire head has a dirty reddish-grey tint, and where this colour extends the shining, smooth guard hairs are absent. This hair appears rather loose and stiff, as in foxes and cats.

On both sides of the blunt, bare, black muzzle there are three rows of strong white bristles two to four centimetres long. They are not round, but flattened in a crooked curve, but without twisting. A single bristle of the same structure is found on each side between the wing of the nose and the eye, and another, half as long, is placed close above each eye.

The hair on the feet is shorter than that on the body, and lacks white tips. Apart from that, it is similar to the body hair, but is a little darker, almost blackish brown. The thickest and finest fur is that of the tail.

According to Anthony, *nereis* is 'browner, less black', than typical *lutris* and has fewer white-tipped hairs, and it seems probable that the skin described above by Lichtenstein was an exceptionally fine one. Fisher examined a subadult male in 1939, and writes:

> The color of this animal is very dark or blackish brown with very few white hairs sprinkled on the body. The head proper is quite light, and there is a light spot on the chest between the two paws or arms. The underside of the tail contains many white hairs and the upper side practically none . . .

Pearson found the fur on an unborn female pup to be longer than that of the mother.

> The fur over the head and shoulders is Hair Brown (Ridgway, 1886) while over the rest of the body, except for the pale chin, it is darker (Clove Brown), not golden brown or straw-colored as has been reported for nursing young sea otters. The feet are black.

He adds that the mother was a white-headed individual.

Despite the coldness of the waters in which the sea otter lives – around 38°–47°F. (3·3°–8·3°C.) at Amchitka (see Kirkpatrick *et al.*, 1955) – it appears normally to have little or no subcutaneous fat. This is reported by Jones (1951) and Vincenzi (1961), though the latter may be quoting the former. It is also borne out by Rausch (1953) who says they 'apparently have little or no subcutaneous or intra-abdominal fat deposit'. On the other hand, Stullken & Kirkpatrick (1955) carried out necropsies on seven normal animals which

> appeared to be in good physical condition as indicated by the presence of considerable amounts of subcutaneous and visceral fat.

Similarly, a dead female in a state of advanced pregnancy was examined by Pearson (1952) who found 'much subcutaneous and mesenteric fat'; this may, however, have been due to its gravid condition.

Sea otters appear to have no special season for giving birth to their young, at least according to Elliott, amongst others, who writes that they are born at all seasons of the year and that 'the natives get young pups every month'.

Later research, however, would seem to show at least a peak of reproduction in the spring. Scheffer points out that his three very young specimens from western Alaska (mentioned above) were all collected in April or May, and the pregnant female from Monterey examined by Pearson was found at the end of May. Jones writes that the bulk of the young are born in late spring and early summer, and Kenyon & Scheffer observed newly born pups in the Aleutians in early March. However, the same authors note cases of very young pups being seen in California and in the Shumagin Islands off Alaska in late August. They state that off California mating activities 'were observed continuously from mid-April to early September'. Ognev writes in a similar vein:

889

637

655

864

> The period of oestrus is not limited to any definite season, but there are numerous individual variations. Impelled by rut, herds begin to collect toward March and remain together for some 3 to 4 months. The weather probably plays a major part in the beginning of the oestrus. Copulation was observed by Lekh (1907) to occur only in the water. Mating never occurs ashore or on the rocks, although courting first begins on the shore alone. At this time the male rubs his head against the female's muzzle, strokes her with his paw and attempts to edge her into the water by various means. Great tenderness is observed in all their movements, and not the violent sexual desire seen among fur seals . . . 'The female lies on her back during the act of copulation, the waves serving as a bed.' – Lekh.

689

This account may be compared with a fuller and more recent one, that of Fisher in 1939, who agrees with Ognev that 'rough water seems to act as a stimulus to the reproductive instinct'. Fisher writes:

400

Courtship is the seeking out of an individual of the opposite sex that responds positively . . . many times an otter was observed to rise up and give a too inquisitive animal a slap with the full force of the whole arm. The intruder usually departed forthwith . . . [When mating] the male grasps the female somewhere on the head with his teeth and then holds on tightly. He appears to have hold of her nose or chin, certainly not the skin of the back of her head and neck [as in the case of the river otter] . . . If he can maneuver so that the two bodies are parallel he then grasps her with his arms around her neck or chest . . . finally the male gets such a hold on the female that her back rests against his ventral side and then with turning he manages to hold her uppermost and mostly out of the water. In this position the male is completely submerged and the head of the female is held under water. Usually the chest and abdomen of the female are bowed up high out of the water.

Sea otters are slow breeders, and Barabash-Nikiforov believes the annual increase to be only 7%. More recently, Griffith suggests in 1953 that it may be as high as 10%, quoting as his authority Katsumi Miyataki, an aquatic

153

477

834   biologist of the Japanese Bureau of Fisheries. It is this latter's opinion also that females only bear young once every two or three years. (Murie reports in 1959 that the Japanese are said to be managing sea otters commercially in the Kurile Islands.)

153,864   Barabash-Nikiforov gives the sex ratio as 6:4 in favour of males. Ognev records Grebnitskii (1902) as saying that on Mednyi Island females out-
1117   number males, but he notes that Suvorov (1912) holds the opposite view, saying that males are more abundant than females in the ratio of 57:43.

While there appear to be no conclusive data, all authorities unite in agree-ing that the gestation period is of the order of eight to nine months. The
825   only authors I have found to commit themselves more exactly are Morris &
241   Jarvis (1959) who give 255 days as an approximation, and Burton (1962) who gives 240–270 days; the latter may be 'quoting' the former.

Some early accounts of the sea otter's affection for and behaviour with its young have already been given. All observers agree that they are very
401   devoted mothers, and Fisher gives a good picture of their life together.

> While [the mother] hunted the pup was left to float on the surface in a tiny pool in the midst of the big tubular kelp . . . he floated on his back with his head, arms, feet and tail up. Every time the mother returned to the surface she always went to him.
>
> The mother comes to the surface . . . and with her paws rolls the pup on to her chest. The mother paddles along on her back, frequently turning her head to choose her course.
>
> The pup sleeps with his head on his chest and his tiny paws folded across his chest; his short tail and long webbed feet are turned up and rest on his abdomen. The mother uses her paws to hold him in place until he is sound asleep, then slowly and quietly she sinks into the water leaving the pup floating on the surface.

651   Kenyon writes:

> Once I watched a pup working its way round the rocks until it was hidden from its mother's view. Suddenly it missed her and uttered a harsh, frightened cry. Confused by the echo of the sound, the mother screamed in distress and swam frantically about. Both animals appeared almost hysterical by the time the mother discovered her wandering offspring.

708   Limbaugh describes how the young

> appeared to derive great enjoyment from sneaking up behind an old male and pulling him underwater while he fed or slept. Playing consisted of ducking or wrestling. If a youngster was getting the worst of the play, he would emit a cry similar to that of a seagull. At this sound the mother otter grasped him by the shoulders and carried him away from the play area.

An interesting suggestion is made by Murie: 834

> When startled, the mother puts an arm around the little one and dives with it. On some occasions, the mother seemed to pat the little one on the head first, as if by this patting or pushing motion she were warning it of the impending immersion. This was never clearly seen, however, and it needs to be verified . . .

It is generally agreed that the female has only two mammae and that it is most unusual for more than a single pup to be born at a time. Seton, however, quotes Snow as saying that he had taken two foetuses from the womb of a sea otter he had killed, and Ognev records a dead female being found with two young in the uterus.   1060 1078 864

It seems likely that before sea otters were persecuted the young were normally born on the mainland or on rocks close to the shore. Certainly Steller says as much, and is so quoted by Pennant. Littlejohn was of the opinion that latterly they give birth at sea. This is confirmed by Allan, who records   898, 503 8

> . . . shooting them with newly-born pups, many miles from either shore or kelp beds, the placenta not having yet been voided.

Kenyon & Scheffer note that the reports are 'conflicting', and write that the young are born 'on the floating kelp beds and on rocks near the sea'. Murie affirms that   655 834

> it is known that the young are born on the kelp beds, but in Alaskan waters, where kelp beds disappear during the winter, the procedure is uncertain.

He quotes Herendeen as saying that the young are born at sea.   550

Both Kerr and Pennant thought the young to have been suckled for 12 months, and this is repeated by Desmarest. No modern confirmation of this information has been seen by me but Elliott (1875), as quoted by Coues, states that 'the pup sucks a year at least, and longer if its mother has no other'. It is certain, however, that the young otter generally remains with its mother at least up to and often beyond the time that the next season's pup is born, a mother with two cubs, one a yearling and the other quite small, not being an uncommon sight.   657, 897 345 374 306

There is a similar lack of precise information with regard to the age at which the sea otter is sexually mature. Steller wrote that they first mate in their second year, but both Snow (as quoted by Lydekker) and Jones (1951) consider it more probable that they attain maturity in their third year.   1104 728, 637

Limbaugh observes that young otters spend a considerable amount of time in cleaning and preening their fur, and that one adult was seen to be   708

1104 cleaning himself with a piece of seaweed. Steller, whose observations were remarkably complete, writes that

> they shake off all the water before they lie down to sleep [on land]; then, with their paws, they wash their faces, just as Cats do, smooth out their bodies, straighten out their fur, turn their head from one side to the other as they look themselves over, and seem to be greatly pleased with their personal appearance.

193 More recent observers confirm this. Thus Bolin writes:

> They spend a great deal of time scratching themselves . . . the front paws massage the head, which is brought forwards within reach, the operation looking very like vigorous washing.

779 May has an account of a captive sea otter which, having finished eating

> carefully brushed the remnants of the meal off its chest; then, dipping its hands in the water, the animal rubbed them together just as a person does when washing with soap and water. This finished, the creature proceeded to wash its face carefully, even going behind its ears like any human being. Finally, to complete the toilet, the whiskers were brushed off sideways.

662 Kirkpatrick *et al.* also observed captive otters preening themselves.

> Preening was carried out in any position. A supine animal might raise its head, thrust its nose into the fur of the chest or abdomen, and rub it rapidly from side to side, snorting and blowing. Simultaneously the paws rubbed sides, haunches, face, ears, or neck with rapid rotary, and to and fro motions. Folds of the lose [*sic*] body skin were repeatedly gathered and scrubbed vigorously between the paws . . . [One otter] was adept at rubbing her right elbow with her left paw while rubbing her face with the back of her right paw. With arms folded before the chest, the otter rubbed opposite forelegs or shoulders with both paws simultaneously or the backs of the opposite paws alternately . . . There seemed to be no part of the body the fore paws could not reach and rub. There was much snake-like wriggling on the straw accompanied by pushing of the flippers against the floor and ear rubbing while the otters were on their backs, sides, or bellies. In the cage the wire was used as a rubbing surface for head, neck, and sides. When the fur was wet, the head and neck were shaken vigorously, in many positions, occasionally accompanied by a flipper scratching the shoulder region. Vigorous shaking in a half-reclining position swung the paws away from the body centrifugally, and even rotated the whole body to some extent . . . When reclining, the otters occasionally drew bunches of loose grass over themselves, rubbing the grass between the paws and against the body . . .

400 Fisher has described how an otter's ticklishness may upset its sleeping routine.

Before going to sleep [in the water] many of them will roll over and over in such a way as to wrap several strands of kelp around them. This habit of wrapping up prevents the otter from drifting away. Sometimes an otter will be settled for the night carefully wrapped up in kelp and then several parasites will start biting. In its strenuous efforts to scratch all the places the otter is soon completely out of its kelp wrappings and has to wrap up again.

Similarly, Hopkins writes: 583

Twenty otters were sound asleep ... many held a piece of sea weed firmly under one fat forearm, sometimes with it streaming across their stomachs.

Fisher also records that they often 'place their paws over their eyes so that 400 they can sleep during the daylight'.

Barabash-Nikiforov describes sea otters sleeping on shore or on isolated 153 rocks in the Commander Islands.

They generally choose a spot not more than 10 metres from the water's edge. Their trails in the snow are very characteristic, in the shape of an arch or horse-shoe, the ends of which run into the sea. The broad top of the arch is formed by the bed (marked by heaps of excrement), the sides are formed by the tracks made when the animal goes to and leaves the bed. Judging by exit tracks, which are almost always a direct continuation of the entrance tracks, it appears that the sea otter passes the entire night without changing its position. By preference the bed is located in the shelter of some spur or projecting rock, and the direction of the exit tracks seems to indicate that the animal lies with its head pointing up the wind. The sense of smell is the most highly developed, and those of sight and hearing are much less acute.

This last remark is confirmed by other authors although Newcombe, excep- 853 tionally, quotes a Mr Lohbrunner as finding them extremely keen-sighted. If Elliott's account, as quoted by Coues, be taken literally the sea otter's 306 sense of smell must be almost supernatural:

The natives [hunting otters] do not live upon the Island [Saanach], because the making of fires and scattering of food-refuse alarms the otters, driving them off to sea ... and fires are never built unless the wind is from the southward, for no sea-otters are ever to be found north of the Island ...
The quick hearing and acute smell ... are not equalled by any other creatures in the Territory. They will take alarm and leave from the effects of a small fire, four or five miles to windward of them; and the footstep of man must be washed by many tides before its trace ceases to alarm the animal and drive it from landing there should it approach for that purpose.

Limbaugh noticed that they could 'hear and locate' an operating motion- 708 picture camera from a distance of 100 yeards.

269

153
400
The degree of social organisation amongst the sea otter herds has been little studied. Barabash-Nikiforov remarks on their 'peaceable and equable disposition', no fighting being observed among them, and sees no social indications 'such as a recognized leader or the like'. On the other hand, Fisher writes of the southern form:

> There seem to be some otters that are domineering over others, and one of these appears to be master of the entire herd.

193
She comments that food stealing from each other is quite common but rarely leads to fighting as 'the original owner gives up the food without a protest'. Bolin considers that outlying otters, separate from the main herd, may be acting as sentinels.

662
Kirkpatrick *et al.* found captive otters to derive 'moral support' from each others' presence and to be depressed by isolation; and they quote Mal'kovitch's example of intraspecific cooperation, when one otter, being afraid of man, tried to protect its companion by dragging him into the water when a man approached.

685
Kenyon & Scheffer describe the noises made by the sea otter as varying

> from the harsh kitten-like mewing of the pup to the grunts, growls, and high pitched shrieks of the adults.

153
400
Barabash-Nikiforov mentions a loud squeak, resembling a whistle when heard at a distance, which is not an alarm note; while Fisher ascribes quite an extensive vocabulary to the sea otter and notes that the voice is loud enough to be heard at least two to three hundred feet away. She describes these noises as:

> Er-er-r-r-r, a deep sound repeated at different lengths. It appeared to be like a growl.
> Ar-wak! Ar-wak!, these sounds are uttered when one otter has a too painful hold on another.
> Meo-ak!, seems to be associated with a painful bite from another otter.
> E-e-e-e-eh!, a long drawn out sound that is like a squeak seemed to be caused by a nip from a passing otter.

662
This last noise is also mentioned by Kirkpatrick *et al.*, who describe it as

> a multi-syllabled shriek, variable among individuals, phonetically rendered as *eeee-eeee-eh*, or *eeee-eh*, or *eeee-er*. The first syllables were always high in pitch, given either with a quaver or as a clear, shrill shriek. The last syllable was short and grunt-like, in a much lower tone, and was inaudible at a distance of a few feet.

270

Captive otters in great distress, particularly moribund animals, uttered combinations of these sounds in high-pitched, ear-piercing screams. One young pup of $4\frac{1}{2}$ pounds cried continuously, giving utterance about every two seconds with a two-syllabled *eee-ee*, which at a distance resembled the mewing of a kitten . . .

A series of low, soft grunts, *uh-uh-uh-uh*, were uttered by otters feeding together. Grunts of objection have been described as well as vigorous hawking in attempts to clear the throat . . .

Even before the intrusion of man the sea otter was not wholly without natural enemies. A number of authors have listed seals and sea lions amongst their predators (probably harking back to Steller), and Seton [1060] writes:

Many a Sea-otter, a large percentage of all Sea-otters, indeed, find their last rest in the Sea-lion's capacious maw.

But this does not seem to be borne out by more recent observers. Barabash- [153] Nikiforov writes that he was unable to detect any fear of seals; similarly, Jones writes of seals, sea lions and sea otters all occupying the same waters [637] with no form of predation occurring, while Davis watched Steller's sea [333] lions (*Eumetopias jubata*) swimming within a few feet of otters, some of which had cubs with them, and 'no more than the most casual attention' was paid. In the same way, Rausch found sea otters, Steller's sea lions and [946] harbour seals (*Phoca vitulina*) all sharing the same hauling grounds.

The killer whale (*Grampus rectipinna*) is another matter. Littlejohn [712] writes that the sea otter

makes off instantly from this enemy, but if he finds that he has not evaded his pursuer he knows that flight is useless; he then doubles up as if dead and remains motionless. The whale does not eat carrion, and thinking this to be such, he passes on to locate the living otter that has seemingly escaped . . .

Barabash-Nikiforov considers that the killer whale 'may be considered an [153] active enemy', although Murie found little opportunity of verifying this. [834] Bolin, however, reports an attack on a herd of sea otters by a small school of [193] killer whales.

Sharks may also be reckoned as occasional predators. Allan records an in- [8] stance where an otter had been chased almost to its last gasp but suddenly vanished, and 'instead there rose from the spot where it disappeared the back fin of a shark'. More conclusive evidence is given by Orr (1959), who [869] examined three dead sea otters found at Pebble Beach, Monterey County, California.

A series of gashes, arranged in the form of a semicircle, was present on the back of the female just behind the shoulders. In one of these wounds a portion of shark tooth was found. The larger of the two males had wounds on each side of the thoracic area, on the right side of the neck and on the back. The smaller male had a wound behind the left shoulder that extended into the thoracic cavity . . .

The tooth was identified as coming from a maneating shark, *Carcharadon carcharias*, not uncommon in Californian waters and usually about 9 ft. in length.

832   In 1940, Murie had reports from natives that eagles killed young sea otters, but on investigation remained unconvinced, finding no trace of sea otter in 28 eagle nests or pellets. Sea otter fur was, however, found in a few

834   blue fox (*Alopex*) droppings. In 1959 Murie referred again to the suspicion that the northern bald eagle (*Haliaeetus leucocephalus alascanus*) preyed on young sea otters, but although he failed to find any contributary evidence he adds 'it is possible that this may occur on rare occasions'. In 1953, how-

672   ever, Krog had found (and illustrated) direct evidence of such predation at Amchitka Island.

One of the nests . . . had, when found on June 10, one young about $1\frac{1}{2}$–2 weeks old. Piled up in the nest was a large amount of food and, among other things, three young sea otters. One of the young sea otters weighed 1137 grams [$2\frac{1}{2}$ lb.]. The carcass, lacking head, was in good condition; its length was 24 cms. [9·45 in.]. Of the other two otters only the skins were left. The skin had been removed in one piece from the abdominal side, the legs turned inside out and the tarsal bone cut to loosen the meat from the skin in a very 'professional' manner. The possibility that the sea otters were found dead on the beach by the eagles seems very unlikely, as no animals were found which had died recently even after considerable time was spent looking for carcasses for other reasons. An autopsy performed . . . on the freshly killed sea otter revealed no immediately visible pathological changes, and the freshness of the blood and meat support the assumption that the animal was a healthy one, captured and killed by the eagle the morning it was found. All three sea otters found in the nest were decapitated, and no fragments of skulls were present, a fact which suggests that decapitation occurs before the captured animals are brought to the nest . . .

There is . . . the possibility that one member of this pair of eagles had 'specialised' in preying on sea otter . . . Specialisation of that sort is known to occur among birds. Hair of sea otter was recovered by Schiller from the stomach of the adult eagle that was killed . . .

With regard to the food of the sea otter itself a fair amount of systematic research has now been carried out, most of this relatively recently.

153   Barabash-Nikiforov (1935) analysed some 500 spraints and found the composition to be:

Sea urchins	59%	*Strongylocentrotus polyacanthus* and *S. droebachiensis*
Molluscs	23·3%	*Mya, Spisula,* and more rarely *Mytilus*
Crabs	10%	*Telmessus cheiragonus* and *Chionoectes opilio,* more rarely *Hyas* sp. and some others
Fish	6·7%	Most of the local species from smallest (*Ammodytes* and *Mallotus*) to large cod (*Gadus*) are eaten
Seaweeds and accidentals	1%	
	100·0%	

The author comments that although remains of octopus (*Polypus*) are rarely found,

This fact does not correctly indicate the importance of this animal as a source of food, as evidently they eat only the bodies and reject the heads. Remains of *Natica* are occasionally found, those of *Volutopsis* very seldom ... the winter food consists chiefly of sea urchins and molluscs, while the summer food is considerably enriched by fish and crabs.

Further spraint analyses were carried out by Williams (1938), in this instance 70 samples being collected. His results may be tabulated as follows: [1205]

Sea urchins	78%	*Strongylocentrotus droebachiensis*
Molluscs:		
Gastropods	4%	Snails and limpets (*Acmaea* spp.)
Amphineura	3%	Chitons of several kinds
Pelecypods	6%	*Mytilus edulis, Musculus vernicosus, Pecten islandica*
Crabs	4%	*Dermaturus mandtii, Pagurus gilli, P. hirsutiusculus, Cancer oregonensis*
Coral rock	2%	
Fishes	3%	More than half roe, thought to be mostly herring; fish found included *Ammodytes alascanus* and *Gymnocanthus pistilleger*
	100%	

Other items included bits of hydroids (*Abietinaria* sp. and *Thuaria robustus*), algae, geophilid fragments, a ground beetle (*Eurystellus californicus*), larvae of *Scatophaga* sp., remains of a bird's egg, some grass (*Poa* sp.), and a few sea-otter hairs. The author remarks that these items were either taken incidentally or without particular desire for them as food.

An analysis of 198 spraints was undertaken by Murie in 1940, who found the food in order of frequency of occurrence to be: [833]

Sea urchin (*Strongylocentrotus droebachiensis*).
Mussel (*Mytilus, Modiolus* and *Musculus*).

Chiton (chiefly *Tonicella ruber* and a few *Schizoplax brandtii*).
Crab, limpet, snail, fish and fish roe.
Rock oyster (*Pododesmus macroschisma*).
Other bivalves.
Traces of pecten (*Pecten beringianus*).
Octopus, unidentified crustacea, sea otter hair, pebbles, coral barnacle, seaweed, bryozoa and black dirt.

[834] In 1959 he makes the following comments on the sea otter's eating habits:

It is a well known fact that dead sea otters occasionally are washed up on the beach . . . [and] in the postwar years a higher mortality rate has become evident . . . The cause is not yet known . . . [but] one cannot refrain from speculating whether the specialization in food, which involves hard and sharp mollusk shells, tests and spines of sea urchins, barnacles and similar materials . . . are causing the sea otter some difficulty. Do some individuals succumb through injuries caused by such materials ? . . . even the byssus of the mussel, often with pieces of stone or coral attached, is swallowed. In one instance, pebbles made up 21·8% of the contents of one scat.

[402] Murie additionally notes that Fisher (1940) had reported gastric perforations in the sea otter.

A further report on the sea otter's food was prepared from a small sample by R.T.Mitchell at Amchitka in 1949, the findings being published by [637] Jones in 1951. They compare very closely with those quoted above, showing sea urchins 45%, molluscs 40%, isopods (from one sample) 10%, and hydroids and accidentals 2%. Jones remarks:

Thus the importance of the sea urchin in the diet is clear. In the Aleutian Islands the commonest, hence most utilized form is *Strongylocentrotus droebachiensis*. The common blue mussel is second in importance, with miscellaneous crabs third and fish fourth . . . Flounder and sculpin are the only fish commonly taken at Amchitka . . .

[1204] Of further interest is the study by Wilke (1957), as it is the only one based on the examination of stomach contents as opposed to spraint analyses. Five sea otters from Amchitka Island were examined, with the results as set out below.

Item	% by volume	Frequency
Starfish (*Asteroidea*)	trace	1
Green sea urchin (*S. droebachiensis*)	86	3
Hermit crab (Paguridae)	trace	2
Limpet (Acmeidae)	trace	1
Horse mussel (*Volsella modiola*)	3	1
Mussel (*Modiolaria vernicosa*)	5	1
Fringed greenling (*Hexagrammus superciliosus*)	6	1

36. *L. canadensis*, adult ♀ collecting nest material.

37. *L. canadensis*, ♀ with her five cubs, two-and-a-half months old.

39. *L. enudris mitis*, adult ♀. Photo: Art Doering.

38 (*opposite*). *L. annectens colombiana*, adult ♂. Photo: Art Doering.

40. *L. felina*. Gay, *Historia Fisica y Politica de Chile* (Atlas), 1854.

41. *L. platensis*. D'Orbigny & Gervais, *Voyage dans l'Amérique Méridionale*, 1847.

42. *Pteronura b. brasiliensis*, adult ♀. New York Zoological Society Photo.

43. *Pteronura b. brasiliensis*, adult ♀.

44. Sea Otter and Pup. Steller, *De Bestiis Marinis*, 1751.

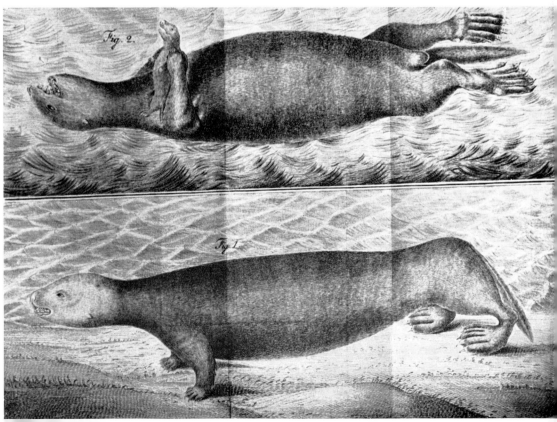

45. Sea Otter. Gray, *Proc. zool. Soc. Lond.*, 1865.
(Noted by Gray in 1869 as being drawn from life.)

46. Sea Otter, adult ♀, breaking a clam on a rock resting on her chest. Photo: S. B. Hertz. Woodland Park Zoo, Seattle, Wash.

47. Sea Otter mother with young pup, at Amchitka Island, Alaska. Photo: K. W. Kenyon, U. S. Fish & Wildlife Service.

48. European Otter tracks, or 'seals'. Photo: Ernest Neal/ Photo Researchers.

49. Canadian Otter slide-marks in the snow.

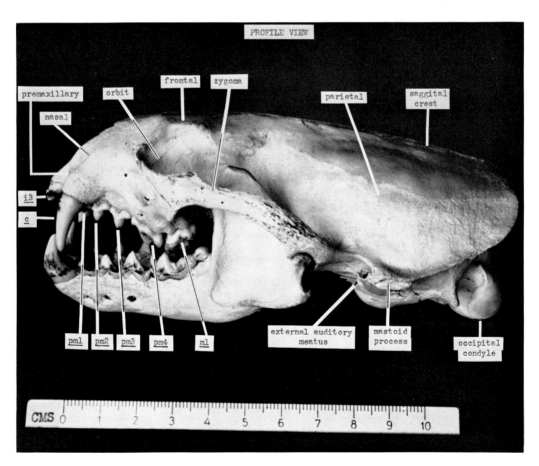

50. Skull of adult ♂ *Lutra lutra*, from Norfolk, England. Profile view.

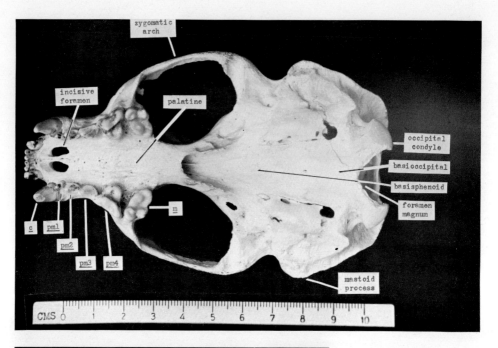

51. Skull of adult ♂ *Lutra lutra*, from Norfolk, England. Palatal view.

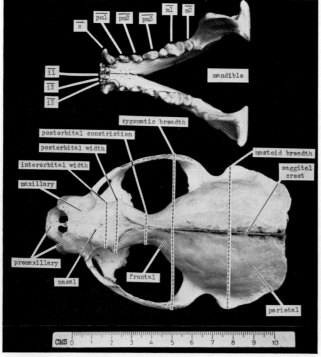

52. Skull of adult ♂ *Lutra lutra*, from Norfolk, England. Dorsal view.

As the author points out, neither spraint analysis nor stomach content analysis can necessarily provide an accurate index of the relative importance of the various foods.

For example, the shell of the rock oyster, *Pododesmus macroschisma*, is usually discarded, and the soft parts of limpets are also extracted from their shells. By contrast, small sea urchins and mussels are simply crunched, shell and all, and swallowed.

Despite these reservations, however, a reasonably full and consistent picture emerges of the wild sea otter's diet. The only apparent deviation from the normal order of preference is shown by the southern form, a large part of whose diet is made up of the red abalone, *Haliotis rufescens*, stated by Fisher to be the mollusc most commonly eaten. Limbaugh, indeed, gives [400, 708] the abalone pride of place over the sea urchin in his list of the dietary items of the Californian sea otter, writing that the animals observed by him fed on

Red abalone (*H. rufescens*).
Sea urchin (*Strongylocentrotus franciscanus*).
Purple-hinged scallops (*Hinnites gigantea*).
California mussel (*Mytilus californianus*).

as well as snails, and possibly the giant chiton *Cryptochiton stelleri*. Davis (1964), however, who observed sea otters at Point Lobos, some 80 miles [333] south of San Francisco, states that

the otters eat relatively few abalone, but when they do they leave telltale evidence behind in the form of a characteristic missing piece from each shell that lies on the ocean floor. Mussels and sea urchins form the bulk of the otter's diet . . .

Sea otters normally forage in relatively shallow waters, although it seems that if need be, or the mood takes them, they can swim to considerable depths. Thus Taylor (1914) quotes Snow as asserting that their ordinary [1132, 078] depth of dive is some 10–25 fathoms and Littlejohn was of the opinion that [712] they are 'unable to reach the bottom when the water is much over 60 fathoms'. Seton writes of the otter diving to '100 feet or more', staying sub- [1060] merged for four or five minutes, and quotes Sheldon (1912) as saying that

they range for feeding about 60 miles. They have special feeding-grounds in shallow water, on 'banks', or near the shore, and feed at night.

Grinnell *et al.* also speak of them as foraging in waters of 10–25 fathoms, [482] while Anthony states that they are capable of diving to 300 ft. or more. [127]

Hall quotes Littlejohn (verbatim) as saying he knew of a regular feeding [503] place 'about 50 fathoms deep where they go to the depth of the water to

562
651 feed', while Hill writes of a typical feeding-ground as being at a depth of 60 to 150 ft., in line with several of the authorities already quoted. Kenyon favours a shallower area, having found them feeding usually in water from 5 to 50 ft. in depth.

898
579
1060
728
637 Certainly, at times, the sea otter will venture considerable distances from land. Pennant writes in his *Arctic Zoology* of them being found 100 leagues out to sea, and this same figure is repeated (? 'quoted') by Home & Menzies. Seton quotes Sheldon as saying that they go 30 miles or more off shore to sleep, while Lydekker writes of them being seen 10 to 15 miles from land. Feeding excursions are presumably more limited in distance and Jones considers that these probably do not exceed a mile or two, at any rate dur-712 ing the winter. It was Littlejohn's opinion that when far from land, and hence unable to feed from the bottom, the sea otter eats squid.

759, 760 The earliest attempts at maintaining the sea otter in captivity are probably those reported by Malkovitch in 1937 and 1938. He writes that Barabash-Nikiforov first started experimenting on these lines on Mednyi (Copper) Island in 1932, but only with two animals and these both died. In 1934, Malkovitch himself began a systematic programme on Copper Island, housing the otters in a large iron cage part of which was flooded by the tide, but having in addition a constant flow of fresh water. Apparently the otters soon felt quite at home in these conditions and could be hand fed after four or five days.

One otter, kept alone, became bored and lost its appetite. As soon as a second animal was placed in the enclosure, however, it recovered its previous friskiness. The new arrival, more timid than the original occupant, would always try to protect its companion by dragging it into the water as soon as any human being appeared. In 1935 a wholly fresh-water environment was tried, but it was found that the supply had to be constant to be successful.

In Malkovitch's experience it was not possible to rear pups younger than three months old unless their mothers were present with them. But much younger pups accompanied by the mother caused no anxiety and one such, captured with its mother when only a fortnight old, gained 28 lb. (12·8 kg.) in five months.

The heavy food requirements of captive sea otters is stressed, an animal of some 70 lb. (32 kg.) eating $12\frac{1}{2}$ lb. (5·7 kg.) of food a day. This compares 313 fairly closely with Crandall's findings, mentioned below. Malkovitch records an otter dying of starvation after being fed between $6\frac{1}{2}$ and $7\frac{3}{4}$ lb. (3·0 and 3·5 kg.) of food daily. Food fed to captive otters in these experiments included both sea- and fresh-water fish, sea urchins and molluscs, and the adaptability of these animals is shown by the fact that they readily accepted filleted or gutted fish as well as fish that had been frozen.

Malkovitch persuaded a pair of captive sea otters to mate, but only after the female's pup had been removed from her. It appears that her fondness for her pup over-ruled the sex instinct while it remained with her. Although it is recorded that the male proved to be polygamous it is not stated whether this mating proved fruitful.

Late in 1937 it was decided to try and transplant sea otters from Copper Island to the Kola Peninsula in Murmansk. Catching was effected with large nets spread in the water surrounding the rocks on which the otters spent the night. Very gentle handling was necessary, and the problem of transporting them proved considerable. Wooden baths on the deck were continuously supplied with fresh sea-water by the ship's pumps, but by the time Vladivostok was reached seven out of nine animals had died. The remaining pair, both males, were then put into a special railway carriage with a galvanized water tank of 20 tons capacity, this being replenished from time to time from the fountains on railway stations. The 'land' area of the carriage was spread with special mattresses to minimise jolting as it was found that this seriously exhausted the animals. Both freshly frozen fish – plaice, ruff, bullhead and cod – was provided and also salted cod; that latter was much preferred. Fresh beef was also taken freely, and the surviving pair apparently settled down happily in their new home on the Yarnyshnyi inlet after a journey of 27 days. It would be interesting to know for how long these Russian experiments continued and to what degree they were successful.

That the sea otter is moderately adaptable in its diet has been shown by behaviour in captivity, although at the same time it must be admitted that the successful maintenance of captive sea otters is still fraught with difficulty. May (1942) writes of a sea otter at the Russian Sea Otter Experimental Station at Gladskuvskaya happily eating fish thrown to it by one of the scientists, but unfortunately no further mention is made of what the animals are fed on. Stullken & Kirkpatrick also fed their sea otters with fish, an item which hardly figures at all in their natural diet, as has been shown. This fish was [779] [1116]

usually chopped into small chunks. Occasionally marine invertebrates, primarily blue mussels, limpets, hermit crabs, and octopus, were given in small amounts to supplement the fish diet. Every other day about 10 grams of a dehydrated milk-like product, Terralac (Pfizer) was sprinkled on the food of each otter . . .

A not dissimilar diet was provided by Kirkpatrick *et al.* who fed fringed [662] greenling (*Lebius superciliosus*) as the main dietary item, supplementing this with limpets, blue mussels, sea urchins, periwinkles, hermit crabs, starfish and an occasional octopus; small quantities of 'Terralac' were added to the diet periodically. The authors note that food was masticated very thoroughly. With regard to molluscs, they write:

Small limpets, blue mussels, and snails were chewed up entire with loud crunching noises, and then swallowed. Larger limpets were usually extracted from the shells by holding the molluscs' flesh against the lower canines and pulling downward on the shell with the paws. If this was not successful, the shell was held with the paws at the side of the mouth and cracked by the molars; the pieces were then cleaned in the same manner as the whole mollusc. Otters habitually cleaning shells in this way would wear the anterior surfaces of the lower canines and incisors, as noted by Hildebrand (1954).

561

Steller had noted the sea otter as being fond of meat – in his case the meat being the skinned carcase of another sea otter! – and it is therefore perhaps not surprising that Kirkpatrick *et al.* report that their otters, if hungry, would accept both goose and seal flesh, though they became more particular in a very short time. It is suggested, however, that much of the otter's fussiness over food may disappear in time, and the authors persuaded their otters to take (thawed) frozen flounder fillets which they came to prefer to the fresh greenling. Later, at Adak, large quantities of live shrimp were fed, as well as chitons, sea urchins, and crabs, all more numerous there than at Amchitka. These three otters, 'held in a dry environment', consumed between them about a gallon of fresh water daily.

662

651

Kenyon found that many wild sea otters

are very tractable and will quietly take food from our hands within a few minutes of capture. On the other hand, a yearling female which we caught in September 1955 was so shy that nearly a week passed before she could be induced to take food that we held out to her. When first captured she leaned against the back of her cage in a half sitting position watching our movements wide-eyed, as if in astonishment. When we brought her sea urchins and fish she placed her forepaws on her cheeks and hissed in a very cat-like way, or pushed the proffered food away with her paws. After she had become accustomed to us she readily took food from our hands, never offering to bite . . . When rocks and clams were placed in our captive's pool, she gathered them from the bottom and holding the clams between her forepaws, banged them against the rock resting on her chest until the shells broke.

This animal was subsequently transferred to the Woodland Park Zoo in Seattle, where she lived for a further 6 years, 17 days (see Crandall, 1964).

313

The habit of breaking clams on a stone on her chest persisted, and is further described by Vincenzi in 1961. With regard to her diet Vincenzi writes: 1177

Our otter's diet consisted of a variety of sea foods; primarily clams, codfish, rockfish, red snapper, octopus and squid (which she greatly relished). If available, sea urchins and shellfish would be preferred and greatly beneficial foods. We fed Susie three times per day, giving her a daily total of approximately 10 to 12 lb. of fillet fish, about 3 lb. of clams in the shell, plus such other delicacies as might be available. We found that she was inclined to be wasteful by selecting only the choicest parts of the food.

Three other sea otters previously kept at the same zoo while awaiting transfer to the National Zoological Park, are reported by Crandall to have been   313 fed mainly on

... fish of several kinds, including smelts, various cods, herring, and whiting, all of which were taken well. Flat fishes were taken less readily. Fresh land crabs, clams, and frozen squids were accepted eagerly.

Crandall comments:

... it is somewhat surprising to find that fish can so readily be substituted for what appear to be the normal food sources.

It has now been established that captive sea otters need a food intake of 25–35% of their body weight per day, 'preferably given in four meals at six-hour intervals', according to Crandall. Early failures with captive sea otters were undoubtedly caused, amongst other things, by seriously under-estimating their food requirements. Stullken & Kirkpatrick found that 'the   1116 shells of molluscs included in the food ... appeared in the feces from 2 hrs. 45 m. to 3 hrs. 15 m. after ingestion'. All food is masticated extremely thoroughly, and 'most bones and pieces of skin are completely ground before swallowing'. The passage of food was similarly timed, with identical results, by Kirkpatrick *et al.*   662

Kenyon has stressed the importance of their fur being kept clean, and   651 hence waterproof, a point also made by Vincenzi. This problem is not made any easier by the otter's habit of lying on its back in the water, using its chest as a 'table'.

Early in 1964 a young southern sea otter, washed up on the beach near Monterey, was taken to the Steinhart Aquarium where efforts were made by Jenne to hand-rear it. Considerable trouble was taken in this instance to   625 keep the fur clean and free of snarls, the animal being bathed, towelled, and thoroughly brushed twice a day. On arrival this female pup was estimated to be six weeks old, having a total length of 21 in. (53.3 cm.) and a weight of 6 lb. 14 oz. (3156 gm.). In this instance it would seem that failure was caused more by incorrect feeding than by chilling due to the soiling of the fur; it appears, however, that no post-mortem was carried out and so the precise cause of death remains unknown.

This animal lived a little over a week, being fed throughout on solid food composed mainly of a mixture of strips of mackerel and chopped clams, the latter being dipped in cod-liver oil, with two drops of 'Avitron' added to the cod-liver oil. A number of the permanent teeth were erupting at this period and seemed to cause her considerable discomfort. It was found that a temperature of 70°F. (21·1°C.) for both air and water produced the best results.

241   Her temperature on the morning of the day she died was 101·1°F. (38·38°C.). Burton (1962) gives 101·2°F. as normal for the sea otter.

At no time was any attempt made at bottle-feeding. During its brief life ashore, the animal was subjected to television cameras, force-feeding, constant handling and involuntary hot and cold baths; at times she was dampened, at others dried. While it is only fair to record that she appeared to

1116   enjoy being 'fondled', Stullken & Kirkpatrick write in 1955:

> Excessive handling, abrupt temperature changes, change of diet, isolation, and unusual stimulations should all be considered potential neurological stress-provoking stimuli capable of directly or indirectly precipitation [sic] captivity mortality.

946   Rausch, too, stresses the importance of gentle handling.

> Their abdominal muscles are relatively flaccid, and the visceral organs are not firmly supported. As a result, it would seem that the rather rough handling to which they are usually subjected during capture might have a detrimental effect upon otter having numerous visceral adhesions.

625   As Jenne points out, at least one major problem remains to be solved:

> Sea otters must be kept in water so that the fur will not snarl; however, so far all the young otters kept in water in captivity have died of chilling and resultant enteritis.

The maintenance and health of the sea otter in captivity are subjects of more than merely academic interest. Apart from the general desirability of measures directed towards the conservation of this unique animal, there remains also the possibility of some form of 'fur-farming' which could be of considerable economic importance. The restoration of sea otters to some of the localities from which they have been exterminated was suggested as

879   long ago as 1914 by Osgood, Preble & Parker, although in their opinion the

280

project of repopulating the Pribilofs in this way was a 'doubtful' one. Nothing very positive seems to have been done in this direction for some years, but according to Novikov: 860

Experiments in keeping and breeding sea-otters in captivity began in 1932, and in 1937 acclimatization began on the Murmansk Coast of the Kola Peninsula, which has shown that cage breeding of sea-otters is feasible.

It appears that the Russians subsequently established at least one further experimental station, for Osborn writes in 1944 of such a one on Copper 870 (Mednyi) Island, and May's reference to that at Gladskuvskaya has already 779 been mentioned.

Here, with the assistance of a few Aleuts, a Russian biologist is studying these interesting animals and also breeding them in captivity for the first time in history ... large pens have been erected on a salt-water lake in which the tide rises and falls. In these pens the sea otters are kept segregated. In order to determine whether the sea otter can live indefinitely in fresh water, one pen has been built in a fresh-water lake near by. Over a century ago Russian fur hunters reported seeing sea otters in inland lakes of the Aleutians, but it is not known whether this was their natural habitat or whether they were visiting there. The animals we saw in the fresh-water pen appeared to be every bit as active and healthy as those in the salt-water pens ... A short time before we arrived one sea otter was having great difficulty in giving birth to her pup ... In order to save the life of this mother sea otter, the biologist had to operate. He was successful in saving the life of the mother, but he was chagrined to lose the pup ...

The fresh-water experiment is an interesting one. Steller found sea otters 1104 visiting inland lakes and wrote:

In summer they enter the rivers, and swim up as far as the freshwater lakes which please them greatly, and on hot days they seek the secluded valleys and shady parts of the mountains, where they play like monkeys.

The female kept at Woodland Park Zoo, already referred to, was kept there throughout her time in fresh water, but as Vincenzi notes: 1177

The post mortem examination ... showed that Susie had never attained normal development, and [it was felt] that her fresh water environment might have been a contributing factor.

The first American efforts with captive sea otters appear to have taken place in 1951 (see Griffith: 1953 and Stullken & Kirkpatrick: 1955), when an 477, 1116 attempt was made to transplant 35 sea otters from Amchitka to various other localities which they had previously colonized. This was a dismal

281

failure, the average survival period being only three to four days. Subsequent efforts were equally unsuccessful, and in February and March of 1954 research was undertaken at Amchitka Island, as reported by Stullken & Kirkpatrick, with the main object of developing techniques and knowledge to avoid future captivity mortality.

1116

This is a somewhat technical report, but a number of the author's findings have already been mentioned. Very briefly, however, it was found that the two main causes for previous failures had been inadequate feeding and environmental stress. The authors' general comments on the sea otter are worth quoting:

> ... it is difficult, if not impossible, to understand clearly its requirements and stage of adaptation between a terrestrial and aquatic existence. This adaptation may not be complete and the evolutionary changes which are in progress appear to have left the animal with a very narrow range of environmental tolerance. This might explain the slow recovery of the species from near annihilation even with complete protection for over 40 years, and the difficulties encountered in working with individuals in captivity.

297

Coolidge writes of an attempt in 1955 to establish 16 animals on Otter Island, in the Pribilof group, but the success or otherwise of this venture is unknown to me.

To what extent has the sea otter population recovered during its period of protection, and what is its present status? The southern form, *E. l. nereis*, has recently (April–June, 1964) been placed on the Rare Mammal List of the International Union for the Conservation of Nature and Natural Resources – see Jarvis: 1963, page 328 n. – and its position must still be considered precarious. Anthony (1925–6) writes that in 1887

617
125

> they were generally considered as extinct. There were, however, a few of the old-time hunters who assured me that in the region of certain kelp beds south of Ensenada there were a few to be found. This, I learned, was true, and a small colony was established that by now might have been of large commercial importance had it neen protected. Unfortunately, it was discovered by certain 'beach combers' in 1897, and to the best of my information some 50 were killed. There is a report of 28 being killed 8 or 9 years later at the same point, but I am unable to authenticate it. That a few still exist, as far south as Cedros, there can be little doubt, as one was killed by a fisherman in 1919, at San Benito Island 15 miles west of Cedros.

1060

Seton, writing in 1926, speaks of 'odd ones' being reported throughout the previous range, and occasional sightings had occurred from time to time in previous years. Thus Farnsworth records 31 sea otters, two of which were

390

282

young, being seen to the south of Catalina Island in March 1916, and two
were reported off Delmonte in October of the same year by Oyer. Seton [881, 1060]
quotes Taylor as suggesting in 1916 that they were 'increasing slightly' off
the Monterey coast.

Then suddenly, in 1938, Bolin writes of a herd of 'several hundred' [193]
reported in March of that year off the coast of Monterey County. This
estimate seems to have been something of an exaggeration, for the following
year Fisher, referring to this same herd, writes that: [400]

At no time has the count exceeded 94 . . . the usual number to be seen together
at one time is generally 60 to 80.

None the less, the rediscovery of the southern sea otter seems to have
caused something of a furore, and in 1941 Scofield writes: [1053]

The reader will recall the fanfare of newspaper misinformation of a year or two
ago, heralding the phenomenal reappearance of the sea otter along the coast of
Monterey County, California, after an alleged complete absence of many decades . . .

There was no disappearance and magical reappearance of the sea otter. The
State Division of Fish and Game well knew the species survived along the little
frequented Monterey–San Luis Obispo County coast . . . then came the building
of the Carmel–San Simeon highway with inevitable discovery by the general
public.

This southern form has been found at least as far north as the Straits of
S. Juan de Fuca (see Taylor & Shaw, 1929), while the southerly limit is [1134]
given by Scammon (1874) as Sebastian Vizcaino Bay, Lower California. [1020]

In 1940 Murie estimated their density as being 10 sea otters per mile of [833]
coast. While in 1951 Bonnot pointed out that it was 'a felony even to possess [200]
a skin', by 1956 Hopkins is writing of an estimate of their numbers at 500 as [583]
being conservative. This was confirmed by Boolootian in 1961, who used a [202]
helicopter to photograph each individual herd off the Californian coast. He
found that

the number of individuals in each herd varied considerably, the largest herd being
found at Carmel Bay and the smallest at Point Conception. In all, 638 animals
were counted in 14 different herds, the largest of which contained 144
individuals . . .

He adds that

Although the distribution of the otter populations seems to be in discrete col-
onies, individuals have been recorded between herds . . . Thus, it is reasonable
to conclude that their distribution is actually continuous.

No census appears to have been made of the populations off the coasts
of Oregon and Washington, although the fact that they do still exist in these

892   areas is evidenced by Pedersen & Stout (1963). Their numbers in these regions must, however, be presumed to be very small, and it seems likely that of the original 'vast abundance' less than a thousand now remain.

    So far as the northern animal is concerned the picture is rather happier. That the Queen Charlotte Islands population was not completely extermin-

887   ated is shown by Patch (1922), who was told by a Haida indian that one had been shot at near North Island in 1918.

864   In 1931 Ognev gives the population of Mednyi Island as being between 300 and 500 sea otters, and suggests that in the view of Arsen'ev (1923) their numbers were gradually increasing. (This was encouraging, for previous years had shown an apparent diminution on Mednyi, Ognev giving the following figures for the years shown: 1917, 31 plus one young one;

153   1918, 31; 1919, 27; 1920, 17; 1921, 10.) In 1935 Barabash-Nikiforov estimated the total for the Commander Islands group, including Mednyi, as 600–

477   700, and in the same year, according to Griffith, coastguard personnel counted 600 sea otters on Amchitka.

388   Two years before, Eyerdam confirms their presence both on Sitkin Island, in the Andreanof group, where there were 'upwards of forty', and also on Sanakh Island, where they 'are also seen again quite frequently'.

637   Little is then heard until 1951, when Jones gives a fairly comprehensive report:

> The principal populations of sea otter occur today in the Delarof and the Rat Islands, two groups comprising a portion of the Aleutian Archipelago . . . This region has come to be known as the sea otter belt. The belt extends from Tanaga on the east to Kiska on the west and apparently includes all the islands between, a straight-line distance of about 160 miles. We have no reliable reports of otter west of Kiska in American waters though they are known to exist in the Commander Islands and in the Kuriles. To the east we find a pod at Amlia Island, a few animals around Unimak Island, and a substantial (though undetermined) group in the Sanak Islands.
>
> Of these populations, comprising the known range in the Aleutians, those at Amchitka Island are by far the largest . . . in August 1949 . . . we counted 1321 animals around the two islands [Amchitka and Rat.]
>
> East of the Aleutians there are otter in unknown numbers in the Sandman Reefs, the Shumagin Islands (particularly Simeonof) and at Sutwik Island. Still further east there are otter off Shuyak Island in the Kodiak-Afognak group, St. Augustine Island in lower Cook's Inlet and in Prince William Sound . . .

672
946   Amchitka Island seems as populous as any. Krog writes that in the summer of 1952 an 'unofficial estimate' of the sea otters there was 1500, and Rausch (1953) considers that 'An estimate of 3–4000 sea otter on Amchitka may not

be unreasonable'. Rausch, indeed, goes so far as to suggest that this local population may 'have exceeded the carrying capacity of the habitat'.

Since then there seems to have been a further general increase, for Coolidge states in 1957 (1959) that 'today's estimate of Sea otter populations run as high as 20,000'. 297

A few are presumably killed by the Alaskan natives who have certain legal privileges, and in 1951 Scott writes that 1054a

they may take sea otter and fur seals at any time by aboriginal means, outside of refuge areas . . . In addition, natives and whites alike come under the provisions of a clause in the Alaska Game Law which permits taking of fish and game (except migratory birds) at any time when in need of food and other food is not available . . .

The most extensive recent survey of the status of the sea otter is that published by Lensink in 1960, whose summary is as follows: 694

Cape St Elias to the Kenai Peninsula	1,000– 2,000
Kodiak Archipelago	800– 1,500
Alaska Peninsula	3,900– 5,000
Fox Islands to Islands of Four Mountains	1,100– 1,500
Andreanof Islands	7,200–13,000
Delarof Islands	3,000– 4,000
Rat Islands	10,000–20,000
	27,000–47,000

Kenyon counted 2260 otters at Adak in 1962, and estimated the Amchitka population in 1963 at 2000–3000. In line with Lensink, above, he considers the world population to lie between 25,000 and 40,000. 653

Thus the northern sea otter has been saved, and it is to be hoped that a salutary lesson has been learnt.

It is not for the zoologist to moralize, but I do not think it idle to suggest that such accounts as this – and there are many of them – of man arriving for the first time in a new and untouched region of the earth where the animals are trusting and unsuspicious, ought to move the reader to remorse. Is there no shame to be found in the fact that there is no wild animal, which having made the acquaintance of man, has not quickly learned to fear him?

This was perhaps more strongly appreciated in the Middle Ages than it is today, for the *hortus conclusus* was not merely a garden, but also partly a zoological garden, if we may judge from the illustrations that survive of this imaginary vision of 'what might have been' in a world more ideal and less materialistic.

In the last 100 years alone some 100 species have disappeared from the face of the earth, species representing the outcome of countless thousands of years of evolution. The effect of their removal, by man's agency, is unknowable; possibly to most of those who read this it will prove unimportant. But we are ourselves the result of an unthinkably complex ecology stretching back over millenniums of time and the tiny links in this long chain, though individually small, have been all-important to us. It is only during a minute period that man has been able to influence the world around him – and being able, has not hesitated to do so, often without knowledge or thought of the consequences.

Can such a headlong course be justified? The sea otter may have been saved, and no one can know what results this may have. But other destructive and irreversible processes still continue and none can know their long-term results. This is, or should be, a cautionary thought.

Principal illustrations:

1104   Steller, 1751, plate XVI, figure 1. Sea otter on land.
         figure 2. Mother and pup in water. (*See* plate 44.)

897   Pennant, 1781, frontispiece.

475   Griffith, 1827, facing page 316. 'The Sea Otter. White headed var.'

701   Lichtenstein, 1827–34, plate XLIX. Fine coloured lithograph.
         plate [L]. Litho: views of skull.

437   Gervais, 1855, facing page 119. Engraving of three sea otters.

468   Gray, 1865, plate VII. Coloured engraving. (*See* plate 45.)

306   Coues, 1877, plates XIX and XX. Drawings of skull.

368   Elliot, 1901, facing page 354. Photographs of skull.

369   Elliot, 1904, facing page 537. Excellent photograph of skull.

1132   Taylor, 1914, page 468. Drawing of skeleton of *E. l. nereis*.
         page 487. Drawing of pelves of river and sea otters.
         page 490. Skeletal drawing of posterior limbs.

923   Pohle, 1920, plate VIII, figures 4 and 5. Photographs of skull.

919   Pocock, 1928, page 984. Drawings of ear and nose.
         pages 986–988. Drawings of feet.
         page 990. Drawing of foot.

833   Murie, 1940, page 129. Photographs of fore and hind feet.

116   (Anon.), 1950, page 367. A number of photographs.

505   Hall & Kelson, 1959, page 949. Drawing of skull of *E. l. nereis*.

1180   Walker, 1964, page 1189. Photograph of skull and lower jaw.
         page 1222. Three photographs: A, mounted specimen; B, with clam on chest; C, mother and pup. (*See also* plates 46 and 47.)

Appendices
and
References

Alphabetical Synonymy of the Genera, Species and Subspecies of Recent Otters

ABBREVIATIONS

Gen.	Generic name (of)
hab.	*Habitus*
mis.	Misprint for or mis-spelling of
nom. nud.	Nomen nudum, a name zoologically invalid
obs.	Obsolete
Sp.	Species
subgen.	Subgenus
subsp.	Subspecies
sup.	Superseded or replaced by
syn.	Synonymous with

Ariz.	Arizona	Nebr.	Nebraska
Ark.	Arkansas	Nev.	Nevada
Cal.	California	Okla.	Oklahoma
Colo.	Colorado	Oreg.	Oregon
Conn.	Connecticut	Penn.	Pennsylvania
Fla.	Florida	S.C.	South Carolina
Ga.	Georgia	S. Dak.	South Dakota
La.	Louisiana	Tenn.	Tennessee
Mass.	Massachusetts	Tex.	Texas
Miss.	Mississippi	Va.	Virginia
Mont.	Montana.	Wyo.	Wyoming

For reasons of space the geographical range of the various races is not given in full detail.

Note. A colon placed before the name of an author signifies either that the author is not the originator of the Latin name in question or that he is using it in a sense different to its original one.

Amblonyx Rafinesque, 1832 Gen. Asiatic 'clawless' otter.

Amblonyx cinerea Illiger, 1815 Sp. *hab.* Kumaon to Upper Burma and Yunnan, hill ranges of S. India, Malay Peninsula, Sumatra, Java, Borneo.

Amblonyx cinerea cinerea Illiger, 1815 subsp. *hab.* Siam, Malay Peninsula, Sumatra, Java, Borneo, Palawan, S. China, ? Indo-China.

Amblonyx cinerea concolor Rafinesque, 1832 subsp. *hab.* Kumaon, Sikkim, Bhutan, Assam, Upper Burma, Yunnan, Bengal, Arakan.

Amblonyx cinerea fulvus Pohle, 1920 ? syn. *Amblonyx cinerea concolor.*

Amblonyx cinerea nirnai Pocock, 1940 subsp. *hab.* hill ranges of S. India.

Amblonyx cinerea perspicillata Pohle, 1920 syn. *Lutra (Lutrogale) perspicillata.*

Amblonyx cinerea wurmbi Sody, 1933 syn. *Amblonyx cinerea cinerea.*

Amblonyx cinereus Pocock, 1921 mis. *Amblonyx cinerea.*

Amblonyx concolor Pohle, 1920 syn. *Amblonyx cinerea concolor.*

Amblonyx indigitata Pohle, 1920 syn. *Amblonyx cinerea concolor.*

Amblyonyx cinerea fulvus Hollister, 1921 mis. *Amblonyx cinerea fulvus* (q.v.).

Amblonyz cinerea Pocock, 1921 mis. *Amblonyx cinerea.*

'Ambrang' Raffles, 1822 obs. syn. 'Barang' Raffles, 1822 (q.v.).

Anahyster Murray, 1860 obs. syn. *Aonyx* Lesson, 1827.

Anahyster calabaricus Murray, 1860 obs. syn. *Aonyx capensis.*

Aonix Lesson, 1842 mis. *Aonyx* Lesson, 1827.

Aonyx: Gray, 1837 and many other authors obs. sup. *Amblonyx.*

Aonyx Lesson, 1827 Gen. African 'clawless' otter.

Aonyx (Aonyx) capensis hindei Schouteden, 1944–6 syn. *Aonyx capensis hindei.*

Aonyx (Aonyx) microdon Perret & Aellen, 1956 syn. *Aonyx (Paraonyx) microdon.*

Aonyx aurobrunnea Gray, 1843a obs. syn. *Lutra lutra aurobrunnea.*

Aonyx capensis Schinz, 1821 Sp. *hab.* African south of lat. 15°N.

Aonyx capensis angolae Thomas, 1908 ? subsp. *hab.* Angola.

Aonyx capensis capensis Schinz, 1821 typical subsp. *hab.* Cape Colony.

Aonyx capensis congica Lönnberg, 1910 syn. *Aonyx (Paraonyx) congica.*

Aonyx capensis coombsi Roberts, 1926 ? subsp. *hab.* Transvaal.

Aonyx capensis helios Heller, 1913 ? subsp. *hab.* Kenya.

Aonyx capensis hindei Thomas, 1905 ? subsp. *hab.* Kenya.

Aonyx capensis meneleki Thomas, 1902 ? subsp. *hab.* Abyssinia.

Aonyx cinerea Ellerman & Morrison-Scott, 1951 obs. sup. *Amblonyx cinerea.*

Aonyx cinerea cinerea Davis, 1962 obs. sup. *Amblonyx cinerea cinerea.*

Aonyx cinerea cinerea Ellerman & Morrison-Scott, 1951 obs. sup. *Amblonyx cinerea cinerea.*

Aonyx cinerea concolor Ellerman & Morrison-Scott, 1951 obs. sup. *Amblonyx cinerea concolor.*

Aonyx cinerea nirnai Ellerman & Morrison-Scott, 1951 obs. sup. *Amblonyx cinerea nirnai.*

Aonyx congica Pohle, 1920 syn. *Aonyx (Paraonyx) congica.*

Aonyx delalandi Lesson, 1827 syn. *Aonyx capensis.*

Aonyx delalandii Anderson, 1867 mis. *Aonyx delalandi* (q.v.).

Aonyx horsfieldii Gray, 1837 etc. obs. syn. *Amblonyx cinerea cinerea.*

Aonyx indigitata Gray, 1843a, etc. obs. syn. *Amblonyx cinerea concolor.*

Aonyx indigitatus: Gerrard, 1862 obs. syn. *Amblonyx cinerea concolor.*

Aonyx indigitatus Horsfield, 1851 obs. syn. *Amblonyx cinerea concolor.*

Aonyx inunguis Gerrard, 1862 syn. *Aonyx capensis.*

Aonyx lalandei Pohle, 1920 mis. *Aonyx delalandi* (q.v.).

Aonyx lalandii Gray, 1865 and 1869 mis. *Aonyx delalandi* (q.v.).

Aonyx leptonyx Gray, 1843b, etc., obs. sup. *Amblonyx cinerea cinerea.*

Aonyx microdon Pohle, 1920 syn. *Aonyx (Paraonyx) microdon.*

Aonyx (Paraonyx) congica Lönnberg, 1910 Sp. *hab.* 'Lower Congo'.

Aonyx (Paraonyx) congica congica Schouteden, 1948 syn. *Aonyx (Paraonyx) congica.*

Aonyx (Paraonyx) congica philippsi Schouteden, 1948 syn. *Aonyx (Paraonyx) philippsi.*

Aonyx (Paraonyx) microdon Pohle, 1920 Sp. *hab.* Cameroons.

Aonyx (Paraonyx) philippsi Hinton, 1921 Sp. *hab.* British Ruanda.

Aonyx (Paraonyx) poensis Perret & Aellen, 1956 ? syn. *Lutra (Hydrictis) maculicollis.*

Aonyx poensis Pohle, 1920 ? syn. *Lutra (Hydrictis) maculicollis.*

Aonyx sikimensis Horsfield, 1855 and 1856 obs. syn. *Amblonyx cinerea concolor.*

'Barang' Raffles, 1822 obs. syn. *Lutra sumatrana* Gray, 1865.

'Barang' Lesson, 1842 obs. syn. *Amblonyx cinerea cinerea.*

Barangia Gray, 1865 obs. sup. *Lutra* Brisson, 1762.

Barangia nepalensis Gray, 1865 obs. syn. *Lutra lutra aurobrunnea.*

Barangia nipalensis Jerdon, 1874 mis. *Barangia nepalensis* (q.v.).

Barangia sumatrana Gray, 1865 obs. sup. *Lutra sumatrana* Gray, 1865.

Enchydris Lesson, 1842 obs. sup. *Enhydra* Fleming, 1822.

Enhydra Fleming, 1822 Gen. sea otter.

Enhydra lutris Linnaeus, 1758 Sp. *hab.* N-W. and N. American coasts, S. Kamchatka, Commander Islands, Kurile Islands.

Enhydra lutris kamtschatica Dybowski, 1922 syn. *Enhydra lutris lutris.*

Enhydra lutris lutris Linnaeus, 1758 subsp. *hab.* as Sp.

Enhydra lutris nereis Merriam, 1904 subsp. *hab.* coast of Washington and California.

Enhydra marina Fleming, 1822 syn. *Enhydra lutris.*

Enhydrina Gray, 1825 obs. sup. Lutrinae.

Enhydrinae Gill, 1872 obs. sup. Lutrinae.

Enhydris lutris: Burton, 1962 syn. *Enhydra lutris.*

Enhydris lutris Gray, 1865 and 1869 syn. *Enhydra lutris.*

Enhydris lutris: True, 1884 syn. *Enhydra lutris.*

Enhydris marina Schinz, 1844 syn. *Enhydra lutris.*

Enhydris stelleri Lesson, 1827 and 1842 syn. *Enhydra lutris.*

Enydris: Fischer, 1829 obs. sup. *Enhydra.*

Enydris gracilis Fischer, 1829 ? syn. *Enhydra lutris.*

Enydris marina Lichtenstein, 1827–34 syn. *Enhydra lutris.*

Enydris stelleri Fischer, 1829 syn. *Enhydra lutris.*

Hydrictis Pocock, 1921 subgen. African 'spotted-necked' otter.

Hydrictis maculicollis kivuana Schouteden 1944–6 syn. *Lutra (Hydrictis) maculicollis kivuana.*

Hydrictis maculicollis matschiei Perret & Aellen, 1956 syn. *Lutra (Hydrictis) maculicollis matschiei.*

Hydrictis maculicollis poensis Krumbiegel, 1942 ? syn. *Lutra (Hydrictis) maculicollis.*

Hydrictis (Maculicollis) poensis Cabrera, 1929 ? syn. *Lutra (Hydrictis) maculicollis.*

Hydrogale Gray, 1865 obs. sup. *Hydrictis.*

Hydrogale maculicollis Gray, 1865 obs. syn. *Lutra (Hydrictis) maculicollis.*

Hygrogale maculicollis: Pocock, 1921 obs. syn. *Lutra (Hydrictis) maculicollis.*

Latax Gloger, 1827 obs. sup. *Enhydra.*

Latax: Gray, 1843a, etc., obs. syn. *Lutra* Brisson, 1762.

Latax var. *Argentata* Lesson, 1842 syn. *Enhydra lutris.*

Latax canadensis Gray, 1865 syn. *Lutra canadensis* Schreber, 1776.

Latax gracilis Lesson, 1842 ? syn. *Enhydra lutris.*

Lataxia Gervais, 1855 obs. syn. *Lutra* Brisson, 1762.

Lataxina Gray, 1843b obs. syn. *Lutra* Brisson, 1762.

Lataxina mollis Gray, 1843b syn. *Lutra canadensis lataxina* Cuvier, 1823.

Lataxinae Burmeister, 1850 obs. sup. Lutrinae.

Latax lataxina Gray, 1843a syn. *Lutra canadensis* Schreber, 1776.

Latax lutris nereis Merriam, 1904 syn. *Enhydra lutris nereis.*

Latax marina Lesson, 1842 obs. syn. *Enhydra lutris.*

Leptonyx Lesson, 1842 obs. sup. *Amblonyx.*

Leptonyx barang: Gervais, 1855 syn. *Amblonyx cinerea cinerea.*

Leptonyx barang Lesson, 1842 syn. *Amblonyx cinerea cinerea.*

Leutronectes Gray, 1869 mis. *Lutronectes* Gray, 1867 (q.v.).

Leutronectes whiteleyi Gray, 1869 mis. *Lutronectes whiteleyi* (q.v.).

Lontra: Cabrera, 1924 syn. *Lutra* Brisson, 1762.

Lontra: Flower, 1929 syn. *Lutra* Brisson, 1762.

Lontra Gray, 1843a and 1843b [*see* note 1, page 305].

Lontra brasiliensis Gray, 1843b obs. sup. *Pteronura brasiliensis.*

Lontra canadensis: Flower, 1929 obs. syn. *Lutra canadensis* Schreber, 1776.

Lontra canadensis Gray, 1843a ? syn. *Lutra enudris.*

Lontra enhydris Gray, 1865 syn. *Lutra enudris.*

Lontra ? insularis Gray, 1865 syn. *Lutra enudris insularis.*

Lontra mesopetes Cabrera, 1924 obs. sup. *Lutra mesopetes.*

Lontra platensis Flower, 1929 obs. syn. *Lutra platensis* Waterhouse, 1838.

Loutra Gervais, 1855 mis. *Lutra* Brisson, 1762.

Lustra vulgaris Erxleben, 1777 mis. *Lutra vulgaris* Brisson, 1762 (q.v.).

Lutra Brisson, 1762 Gen. river otter.

Lutra: Shaw, 1800 obs. sup. *Pteronura.*

Lutra: Thomas, 1889 [*see* note 2, page 305].

Lutra amblonyx Rafinesque, 1832 syn. *Amblonyx cinerea concolor.*

Lutra americana Wyman, 1847 syn. *Lutra canadensis canadensis* Schreber, 1776.

Lutra anectens repanda Cabrera, 1957 mis. *Lutra annectens repanda.*

Lutra angustifrons Lataste, 1885 ? syn. *Lutra lutra lutra.*

Lutra annectens Major, 1897 Sp. *hab.* S. Mexico to N. Ecuador.

Lutra annectens annectens Major, 1897 subsp. *hab.* Mexico, Guatemala.

Lutra annectens colombiana Allen, 1904 subsp. *hab.* Venezuela, Colombia, Costa Rica.

Lutra annectens latidens Allen, 1908 subsp. *hab.* Mexico, Nicaragua.

Lutra annectens mesopetes Hall & Kelson, 1959 syn. *Lutra mesopetes.*

Lutra annectens mesopotes Miller & Kellogg, 1955 mis. *Lutra annectens mesopetes* (q.v.).

Lutra annectens parilina Thomas, 1914 subsp. *hab.* Ecuador, ? Colombia.

Lutra annectens repanda Goldman, 1914 subsp. *hab.* Panama, Costa Rica.

Lutra (Aonyx) horsfieldii Anderson, 1878 obs. syn. *Amblonyx cinerea.*

Lutra (Aonyx) indigitata Anderson, 1878 obs. syn. *Amblonyx cinerea concolor.*

Lutra (aonyx) inunguis Fischer, 1829 obs. syn. *Aonyx capensis.*

Lutra (Aonyx) leptonyx: Anderson, 1878 obs. syn. *Amblonyx cinerea.*

Lutra (Aonyx) leptonyx Blyth, 1863 obs. syn. *Amblonyx cinerea.*
Lutra aterrima Pallas, 1811 ? syn. *Enhydra lutris.*
Lutra ? aterrima Schrenk, 1859 ? syn. *Enhydra lutris.*
Lutra atri coloris Brisson, 1762 obs. syn. *Pteronura brasiliensis.*
Lutra atterima Elliot, 1901 syn. *Lutra canadensis pacifica* Rhoads, 1898.
Lutra aureobrunnea Blanford, 1888 mis. *Lutra aurobrunnea* (q.v.).
Lutra aureobrunnea: Fulton, 1903 mis. *Lutra aurobrunnea* (q.v.).
Lutra auriventer Blyth, 1863 ? syn. *Lutra aurobrunnea* (q.v.).
Lutra aurobrunnea Hodgson, 1941 sup. *Lutra lutra aurobrunnea.*
Lutra auro-brunneus Hodgson, 1839 syn. *Lutra lutra aurobrunnea.*
Lutra aurobruunea Anderson, 1878 mis. *Lutra aurobrunnea* (q.v.).
Lutra barang Cuvier, 1823 sup. *Lutra lutra barang.*
Lutra barang: Cantor, 1846 syn. *Lutra sumatrana* Gray, 1865.
Lutra barang: Flower, 1929 syn. *Lutra (Lutrogale) perspicillata.*
Lutra barang: Schinz, 1844 syn. *Amblonyx cinerea cinerea.*
Lutra barang: Thomas, 1889 syn. *Lutra (Lutrogale) perspicillata.*
Lutra barang barang Sody, 1929 syn. *Lutra (Lutrogale) perspicillata.*
Lutra brachydactyla Wagner, 1841 syn. *Lutra felina* Molina, 1782.
Lutra brasiliana Shaw, 1800 obs. syn. *Pteronura brasiliensis brasiliensis.*
Lutra brasiliensis: Bechstein, 1800 obs. syn. *Pteronura brasiliensis.*
Lutra brasiliensis: Boitard, 1842 obs. syn. *Pteronura brasiliensis paranensis.*
Lutra brasiliensis: Cuvier, 1823 obs. syn. *Pteronura brasiliensis.*
Lutra brasiliensis: Godman, 1826 syn. *Lutra canadensis* Schreber, 1776.
Lutra brasiliensis: Harlan, 1825 syn. *Lutra canadensis* Schreber, 1776.
Lutra brasiliensis: Quelch, 1901 ? syn. *Lutra enudris.*
Lutra brasiliensis: Nehring, 1886 ? syn. *Pteronura brasiliensis paranensis.*
Lutra brasiliensis Ray, 1693 obs. syn. *Pteronura brasiliensis.*
Lutra brasiliensis: Ribeiro, 1914 obs. syn. *Pteronura brasiliensis paranensis.*
Lutra brasiliensis: True, 1884 syn. *Lutra annectens annectens.*
Lutra brasiliensis: Wagner, 1842 ? syn. *Pteronura brasiliensis paranensis.*
Lutra brasiliensis: Zimmerman, 1777 obs. syn. *Pteronura brasiliensis brasili-*
ensis.
Lutra brasiliiensis Gray, 1865 mis. *Lutra brasiliensis* Ray, 1693 (q.v.).
Lutra braziliensis De Kay, 1842 mis. *Lutra brasiliensis:* Harlan, 1825 (q.v.).
Lutra brunnea Pohle, 1920 syn. *Lutra sumatrana* Gray, 1865.
Lutra californiæ Lesson, 1842 mis. *Lutra californica* Gray, 1837 (q.v.).
Lutra californica: Baird, 1857 syn. *Lutra canadensis pacifica* Rhoads, 1898.
Lutra californica: Coues, 1877 syn. *Lutra annectens annectens.*
Lutra californica Gray, 1837 syn. *Lutra felina* Molina, 1782.
Lutra californicus Baird, 1857 mis. *Lutra californica:* Baird, 1857 (q.v.).

Lutra canadensis: Mearns, 1891 syn. *Lutra canadensis sonora* Rhoads, 1898.

Lutra canadensis Schreber, 1887 Sp. *hab.* North America.

Lutra canadensis brevipilosus Grinnell, 1914 subsp. *hab.* Cal., Oreg.

Lutra canadensis canadensis: Dixon, 1938 syn. *Lutra canadensis yukonensis.*

Lutra canadensis canadensis Schreber, 1776 subsp. *hab.* Canada, Mass., Va., S. Dak., Mont., Wyo, etc.

Lutra canadensis chimo Anderson, 1945 subsp. *hab.* Quebec, Labrador.

Lutra canadensis degener Bangs, 1898 subsp. *hab.* Newfoundland.

Lutra canadensis evexa Goldman, 1935 subsp. *hab.* British Columbia.

Lutra canadensis extera Goldman, 1935 subsp. *hab.* Nagai Island (Alaska).

Lutra canadensis interior Swenk, 1920 subsp. *hab.* Nebr., Tenn., Ark., Miss., Okla., Colo.

Lutra canadensis kodiacensis Goldman, 1935 subsp. *hab.* Alaska, Kodiak Island.

Lutra canadensis lataxina Cuvier, 1823 subsp. *hab.* Conn., S.C., Va., Penn.

Lutra canadensis lataxina: Hibbard, 1933 syn. *Lutra canadensis interior.*

Lutra canadensis mira Goldman, 1935 subsp. *hab.* Alexander Archipelago.

Lutra canadensis nexa Goldman, 1935 subsp. *hab.* Nev., Colo., Utah, Oreg., Idaho.

Lutra canadensis optiva Goldman, 1935 subsp. *hab.* Alaska.

Lutra canadensis pacifica: Grinnell, 1933 syn. *Lutra canadensis brevipilosus.*

Lutra canadensis pacifica Rhoads, 1898 subsp. *hab.* Wash., Alaska, B. Columbia, Oreg.

Lutra canadensis periclyzomae Elliot, 1905 subsp. *hab.* B. Columbia, Alaska, Queen Charlotte Islands.

Lutra canadensis preblei Goldman, 1935 subsp. *hab.* Mackenzie, Manitoba, Alberta.

Lutra canadensis sonora: Barnes, 1922 syn. *Lutra canadensis nexa.*

Lutra canadensis sonora: Lantz, 1905 syn. *Lutra canadensis interior.*

Lutra canadensis sonora Rhoads, 1898 subsp. *hab.* Ariz., Colo., N. Mexico, Cal., Nev., Utah.

Lutra canadensis texensis Goldman, 1935 subsp. *hab.* Tex., La.

Lutra canadensis vaga Bangs, 1898 subsp. *hab.* Fla., Ga.

Lutra canadensis vancouverensis Goldman, 1935 subsp. *hab.* Vancouver, B. Columbia.

Lutra canadensis yukonensis Goldman, 1935 subsp. *hab.* Yukon, B. Columbia.

Lutra capensis Schinz, 1821 sup. *Aonyx capensis.*

Lutra capensis poensis Thomas, 1904 ? syn. *Lutra (Hydrictis) maculicollis.*

Lutra chilensis Bennett, 1832 syn. *Lutra felina* Molina, 1782.

Lutra chilensis: Schinz, 1844 syn. *Lutra felina* Molina, 1782.

Lutra chilensis: Waterhouse, 1838 syn. *Lutra felina* Molina, 1782.

Lutra chinensis Gray, 1837 sup. *Lutra lutra chinensis.*

Lutra cinera Banks, 1931 mis. *Lutra cinerea* Illiger, 1815 (q.v.).

Lutra cinerea: Blanford, 1891 syn. *Amblonyx cinerea nirnai.*

Lutra cinerea Illiger, 1815 obs. sup. *Amblonyx cinerea cinerea.*

Lutra cinerea: Pocock, 1921 syn. *Amblonyx cinerea* Illiger, 1815.

Lutra cinerea: Thomas, 1908 syn. *Lutra felina* Molina, 1782.

Lutra colombiana Allen, 1904 sup. *Lutra annectens colombiana.*

Lutra concolor: Neumann, 1902 ? syn. *Lutra (Hydrictis) maculicollis nilotica.*

Lutra concolor Rafinesque, 1832 obs. sup. *Amblonyx cinerea concolor.*

Lutra degener: Allen, 1898 syn. *Lutra canadensis degener.*

Lutra degener Bangs, 1898 sup. *Lutra canadensis degener.*

Lutra degener: Rhoads, 1898 syn. *Lutra canadensis degener.*

Lutra destructor Barnston, 1863 syn. *Lutra canadensis canadensis.*

Lutra ellioti Anderson, 1878 syn. *Lutra (Lutrogale) perspicillata.*

Lutra ellioti: Blanford, 1888 syn. *Lutra (Lutrogale) perspicillata.*

Lutra ellioti: Thomas, 1889 syn. *Lutra (Lutrogale) perspicillata.*

Lutra emerita Thomas, 1908 syn. *Lutra annectens colombiana.*

Lutra emerita: Thomas, 1920 syn. *Lutra incarum.*

Lutra (Enhydra) marina Richardson, 1829 obs. syn. *Enhydra lutris.*

Lutra enhydris Gray, 1865 syn. *Lutra enudris.*

Lutra enhydris: Major, 1897 syn. *Lutra enudris.*

Lutra enudris Cuvier, 1823 Sp. *hab.* Trinidad, Venezuela, the Guianas, Brazil.

Lutra enudris enudris Cuvier, 1823 subsp. *hab.* Venezuela, the Guianas, Brazil.

Lutra enudris incarum Pohle, 1920 syn. *Lutra incarum.*

Lutra enudris insularis Cuvier, 1823 subsp. *hab.* Trinidad.

Lutra enudris mitis Thomas, 1908 subsp. *hab.* the Guianas, Brazil.

Lutra enydris Fischer, 1829 syn. *Lutra enudris.*

Lutra enydris: Lesson, 1842 syn. *Lutra enudris.*

Lutra enydris: Schinz, 1844 syn. *Lutra enudris.*

Lutra felina: Alston, 1879–82 [see note 3, page 305].

Lutra felina Molina, 1782 Sp. *hab.* coasts of Ecuador, Peru, Chile.

Lutra felina: True, 1884 syn. *Lutra annectens annectens.*

Lutra flavicans Illiger, 1815 nom. nud.

Lutra fluviatilis Leach, ? 1816 syn. *Lutra lutra lutra.*

Lutra fusco-rufa: Gray, 1865 ? syn. *Lutra incarum.*

Lutra fusco irrorata: Gray, 1865 ? syn. *Lutra incarum.*

Lutra gambianus Gray, 1869 syn. *Aonyx capensis.*

Lutra gracilis Bechstein, 1800 ? syn. *Enhydra lutris.*

Lutra gracilis: Shaw, 1800 ? syn. *Enhydra lutris.*

Lutra grayi Verreaux, 1857 syn. *Lutra (Hydrictis) maculicollis.*

Lutra grayii Gerrard, 1862 syn. *Lutra (Hydrictis) maculicollis.*

Lutra hanensis Matschie, 1907 syn. *Lutra lutra chinensis.*

Lutra hudsonica Cuvier, 1823 and other authors syn. *Lutra canadensis* Schreber, 1776.

Lutra hudsonica: Grinnell, 1933 syn. *Lutra canadensis brevipilosus.*

Lutra hudsonica: Merriam, 1891 syn. *Lutra canadensis nexa.*

Lutra hudsonica: Merriam, 1899 syn. *Lutra canadensis brevipilosus.*

Lutra hudsonica pacifica: Grinnell, 1933 syn. *Lutra canadensis brevipilosus.*

Lutra hudsonica pacifica Rhoads, 1898 sup. *Lutra canadensis pacifica* Rhoads, 1898.

Lutra hudsonica sonora Rhoads, 1898 sup. *Lutra canadensis sonora* Rhoads, 1898.

Lutra hudsonica typica Bangs, 1898 syn. *Lutra canadensis canadensis* Schreber, 1776.

Lutra hudsonica vaga Bangs, 1898 sup. *Lutra canadensis vaga.*

Lutra huidobria Gay, 1847 syn. *Lutra provocax.*

Lutra (Hydrictis) maculicollis Lichtenstein, 1835 Sp. *hab.* Africa south of lat. 10°N.

Lutra (Hydrictis) maculicollis chobiensis Roberts, 1932 subsp. *hab.* Bechuanaland, N. Rhodesia.

Lutra (Hydrictis) maculicollis kivuana Pohle, 1920 subsp. *hab.* Tanganyika.

Lutra (Hydrictis) maculicollis maculicollis Lichtenstein, 1835 subsp. *hab.* S. Africa.

Lutra (Hydrictis) maculicollis matschiei Cabrera, 1903 subsp. *hab.* Gaboon.

Lutra (Hydrictis) maculicollis nilotica Thomas, 1911 subsp. *hab.* Sudan.

Lutra (Hydrictis) maculicollis tenuis Pohle, 1920 subsp. *hab.* Congo.

Lutra (Hydrogale) swinhoei Gray, 1867 obs. ? syn. *Amblonyx cinerea concolor.*

Lutra incana Colyer, 1936 ? mis. *Lutra incarum.*

Lutra incarum Thomas, 1908 Sp. *hab.* Peru, ? Bolivia.

Lutra indica Gray, 1837 syn. *Lutra lutra nair* Cuvier, 1823.

Lutra indica: Gray, 1843b syn. *Lutra lutra chinensis.*

Lutra indica: Gray, 1865 syn. *Lutra (Lutrogale) perspicillata.*

Lutra indigitata Hodgson, 1841 syn. *Lutra indigitatus* (q.v.).

Lutra indigitatus Hodgson, 1839 obs. syn. *Amblonyx cinerea concolor.*

Lutra insularis Cuvier, 1823 sup. *Lutra enudris insularis.*

Lutra intermedia Pohle, 1920 syn. *Lutra lutra barang.*

Lutra inunguis Cuvier, 1823 syn. *Aonyx capensis.*

Lutra inunguis: Lesson, 1827 syn. *Aonyx capensis.*

Lutra inunguis: Schinz, 1844 syn. *Aonyx capensis.*

Lutra katab Gray, 1865 mis. *Lutra kutab* (q.v.).

Lutra kutab Schinz, 1844 sup. *Lutra lutra kutab.*

Lutra lataxima Lesson, 1842 mis. *Lutra lataxina* (q.v.).

Lutra lataxina Cuvier, 1823 sup. *Lutra canadensis lataxina* Cuvier, 1823.

Lutra latidens Allen, 1908 sup. *Lutra annectens latidens.*

Lutra latifrons Nehring, 1887 [*see* note 4, page 305].

Lutra latrix Gray, 1837 obs. syn. *Enhydra lutris.*

Lutra lenoiri Rochebrune, 1888 syn. *Aonyx capensis.*

Lutra leptonix Lesson, 1842 mis. *Lutra leptonyx* Horsfield, 1824 (q.v.).

Lutra leptonyx: Blanford, 1888 obs. syn. *Amblonyx cinerea nirnai.*

Lutra leptonyx: Cantor, 1846 syn. *Lutra sumatrana* Gray, 1865.

Lutra leptonyx Horsfield, 1824 obs. syn. *Amblonyx cinerea cinerea.*

Lutra longicaudis Olfers, 1818 syn. *Lutra platensis* Waterhouse, 1838.

Lutra lovii Günther, 1876 syn. *Lutra sumatrana* Gray, 1865.

Lutra lovii: Lyon, 1911 syn. *Lutra sumatrana* Gray, 1865.

Lutra lowii Chasen, 1940 mis. *Lutra lovii* (q.v.).

Lutra lupina Illiger, 1815 nom. nud.

Lutra lupina: Schinz, 1821 syn. *Pteronura brasiliensis brasiliensis.*

Lutra lupina: Thomas, 1889 syn. *Pteronura brasiliensis.*

Lutra lutra Linnaeus, 1758 Sp. *hab.* Palaearctic and Oriental regions.

Lutra lutra angustifrons Lataste, 1885 ? syn. *Lutra lutra lutra.*

Lutra lutra aurobrunnea Hodgson, 1839 subsp. *hab.* Nepal, Garhwal.

Lutra lutra barang Cuvier, 1823 subsp. *hab.* Annam, Siam, Sumatra, ? Java.

Lutra lutra ceylonica Pohle, 1920 syn. *Lutra lutra nair* Cuvier, 1823.

Lutra lutra chinensis Gray, 1837 subsp. *hab.* China, Hainan, Formosa.

Lutra lutra japonensis Jarvis & Morris, 1962 syn. *Lutra lutra lutra.*

Lutra lutra var. *japonica* Nehring, 1887 syn. *Lutra lutra lutra.*

Lutra lutra kutab Schinz, 1844 subsp. *hab.* Kashmir, Tibet.

Lutra lutra lutra Linnaeus, 1758 subsp. *hab.* throughout Europe, parts of Asia and N. Africa.

Lutra lutra meridionalis Ognev, 1931 subsp. *hab.* Transcaucasus, Iran.

Lutra lutra monticola Hodgson, 1839 subsp. *hab.* Punjab, Kumaon, Nepal, Sikkim, Assam.

Lutra lutra nair Cuvier, 1823 subsp. *hab.* S. India, Ceylon.

Lutra lutra nair: Pohle, 1920 syn. *Lutra lutra monticola.*

Lutra lutra nair: Ward, 1929 ? syn. *Lutra lutra kutab.*

Lutra lutra oxiana Birula, 1915 syn. *Lutra lutra seistanica.*

Lutra lutra roensis Ogilby, 1834 ? syn. *Lutra lutra lutra.*

Lutra lutra seistanica Birula, 1912 subsp. *hab.* Pamir Mts, Iran, ? Palestine.

Lutra lutra splendida Cabrera, 1906 syn. *Lutra lutra angustifrons* (q.v.).

Lutra lutra whiteleyi Ognev, 1931 syn. *Lutra lutra lutra.*

Lutra lutris Cuvier, 1823 obs. syn. *Enhydra lutris.*

Lutra lutris: Lesson, 1827 and 1842 obs. syn. *Enhydra lutris.*

Lutra (Lutrogale) macrodus Pocock, 1941 syn. *Lutra (Lutrogale) perspicillata.*

Lutra (Lutrogale) perspicillata Geoffroy, 1826 Sp. *hab.* Iraq, Himalayas and Sind to Madras, Indo-China, Travancore, Burma, Malay, Sumatra, Java, Borneo, ? W. Yunnan.

Lutra (Lutrogale) perspicillata maxwelli Hayman, 1957 subsp. *hab.* marshes north of Basra.

Lutra (Lutrogale) perspicillata perspicillata Geoffroy, 1826 subsp. *hab.* as Sp. but not Sind or Iraq.

Lutra (Lutrogale) perspicillata sindica Pocock, 1940 subsp. *hab.* Sind.

Lutra (Lutrogale) swinhoei Pocock, 1941 syn. *Amblonyx cinerea concolor.*

Lutra macrodus Gray, 1865 syn. *Lutra (Lutrogale) perspicillata.*

Lutra maculicauda Walker, 1964 mis. *Lutra (Hydrictis) maculicollis.*

Lutra maculicollis Lichtenstein, 1835 sup. *Lutra (Hydrictis) maculicollis.*

Lutra maculicollis chobiensis Roberts 1932 sup. *Lutra (Hydrictis) maculicollis chobiensis.*

Lutra maculicollis kivuana Pohle, 1920 sup. *Lutra (Hydrictis) maculicollis kivuana.*

Lutra maculicollis maculicollis Lichtenstein, 1835 sup. *Lutra (Hydrictis) maculicollis maculicollis.*

Lutra maculicollis matschiei Cabrera, 1903 sup. *Lutra (Hydrictis) maculicollis matschiei.*

Lutra maculicollis mutandae Hinton, 1921b syn. *Lutra (Hydrictis) maculicollis tenuis.*

Lutra maculicollis nilotica Thomas, 1911 sup. *Lutra (Hydrictis) maculicollis nilotica.*

Lutra maculicollis tenuis Allen, 1939 syn. *Lutra (Hydrictis) maculicollis tenuis.*

Lutra malculicollis chobiensis Roberts, 1932 mis. *Lutra maculicollis chobiensis.*

Lutra marina: Erxleben, 1777 obs. syn. *Enhydra lutris.*

Lutra marina Steller, 1751 obs. syn. *Enhydra lutris.*

Lutra matschiei Cabrera, 1903 sup. *Lutra (Hydrictis) maculicollis matschiei.*

Lutra mesopetes Cabrera, 1924 Sp. *hab.* Costa Rica.

Lutra mira Goldman, 1935 sup. *Lutra canadensis mira.*

Lutra mitis Thomas, 1908 sup. *Lutra enudris mitis.*

Lutra montana Tschudi, 1844 ? syn. *Lutra incarum* [see note 5, page 305].

Lutra monticola: Anderson, 1878 syn. *Lutra (Lutrogale) perspicillata* [skull only].

Lutra monticola: Blanford, 1888 syn. *Lutra (Lutrogale) perspicillata.*

Lutra monticola Hodgson, 1841 sup. *Lutra lutra monticola.*

Lutra monticola: Thomas, 1889 syn. *Lutra (Lutrogale) perspicillata.*

Lutra monticolus Hodgson, 1839 syn. *Lutra monticola* Hodgson, 1841 (q.v.).

Lutra nair: Anderson, 1878 syn. *Lutra (Lutrogale) perspicillata.*

Lutra nair: Blanford, 1888 syn. *Lutra (Lutrogale) perspicillata.*

Lutra nair: Blyth, 1863 ? syn. *Lutra (Lutrogale) perspicillata.*

Lutra nair: Cantor, 1846 syn. *Lutra (Lutrogale) perspicillata.*

Lutra nair Cuvier, 1823 sup. *Lutra lutra nair* Cuvier, 1823.

Lutra nair: Elliot, 1839 ? syn. *Lutra (Lutrogale) perspicillata.*

Lutra nair: Flower, 1929 syn. *Lutra (Lutrogale) perspicillata.*

Lutra nair: Jerdon, 1874 syn. *Lutra (Lutrogale) perspicillata.*

Lutra nair: Swinhoe, 1861 and 1862 syn. *Lutra lutra chinensis.*

Lutra nais Gerrard, 1862 mis. *Lutra nair* Cuvier, 1823 (q.v.).

Lutra nepalensis Thomas, 1889 syn. *Lutra lutra aurobrunnea.*

Lutra nigricans Barrère, 1749 ? syn. *Pteronura brasiliensis.*

Lutra nitens Olfers, 1818 syn. *Pteronura brasiliensis.*

Lutra nudipes Melchior, 1834 syn. *Lutra lutra lutra.*

Lutra pacifica Grinnell, 1933 syn. *Lutra canadensis brevipilosus.*

Lutra paraensis Gidley & Gazin, 1933 ? syn. *Lutra annectens latidens.*

Lutra paraguaensis Rengger, 1830 ? syn. *Pteronura brasiliensis brasiliensis.*

Lutra paraguaensis: Thomas, 1889 syn. *Pteronura brasiliensis.*

Lutra paraguensis: Cabrera, 1957 syn. *Pteronura brasiliensis paranensis.*

Lutra paraguensis Schinz, 1821 syn. *Pteronura brasiliensis paranensis.*

Lutra paranaensis Vieira, 1952 ? mis. *Lutra paranensis* Rengger, 1830 (q.v.).

Lutra paranensis: Burmeister, 1854 syn. *Pteronura brasiliensis.*

Lutra paranensis: Devincenzi, 1935 syn. *Lutra platensis* Waterhouse, 1838.

Lutra paranensis: Elliot, 1901 syn. *Lutra canadensis pacifica* Rhoads, 1898.

Lutra paranensis: Elliot, 1901 syn. *Lutra canadensis pacifica* Rhoads, 1898.

Lutra paranensis: Ihering, 1911 syn. *Lutra platensis* Waterhouse, 1838.

Lutra paranensis: Nehring, 1886 ? syn. *Lutra platensis* Waterhouse, 1838.

Lutra paranensis Rengger, 1830 syn. *Pteronura brasiliensis paranensis.*

Lutra paranensis: Thomas, 1889 ? syn. *Lutra provocax.*

Lutra parilina Thomas, 1914 sup. *Lutra annectens parilina.*

Lutra paroensis Lesson, 1842 syn. *Pteronura brasiliensis paranensis.*

Lutra parœnsis Gervais, 1855 mis. *Lutra paroensis* (q.v.).

Lutra periclyzomae Elliot, 1905 sup. *Lutra canadensis periclyzomae.*

Lutra perspicillata: Cantor, 1946 obs. syn. *Amblonyx cinerea.*

Lutra perspicillata Geoffroy, 1826 sup. *Lutra (Lutrogale) perspicillata.*

Lutra perspicillata: Gray, 1843b and 1869 obs. syn. *Amblonyx cinerea.*

Lutra perspicillata: Lesson, 1842 obs. syn. *Amblonyx cinerea.*

Lutra perspicillata perspicillata Geoffroy, 1826 sup. *Lutra (Lutrogale) perspicillata perspicillata.*

Lutra perspicillata sindica Pocock, 1940 sup. *Lutra (Lutrogale) perspicillata sindica.*

Lutra peruensis Pohle, 1920 syn. *Lutra felina* Molina, 1782.

Lutra peruviensis Gervais, 1841 syn. *Lutra felina* Molina, 1782.

Lutra platensis: Gray, 1865 and 1869 syn. *Lutra felina* Molina, 1782.

Lutra platensis Waterhouse, 1838 Sp. *hab.* Brazil, Paraguay, Argentina, Uruguay.

Lutra poensis Waterhouse, 1838 ? syn. *Lutra (Hydrictis) maculicollis* [*see* note 6, page 305].

Lutra pratensis Gerrard, 1862 mis. *Lutra platensis* Waterhouse, 1838.

Lutra provocax: Mann, 1957 ? syn. *Lutra felina* Molina, 1782.

Lutra provocax Thomas, 1908 Sp. *hab.* Chile, Argentina.

Lutra (Pteronura) paranensis Nehring, 1900 syn. *Pteronura brasiliensis paranensis.*

Lutra repanda Goldman, 1914 sup. *Lutra annectens repanda.*

Lutra rhoadsi Cope, 1897 syn. *Lutra canadensis lataxina* Cuvier, 1823.

Lutra rhoadsii Gidley & Gazin, 1933 mis. *Lutra rhoadsi* (q.v.).

Lutra roensis Ogilby, 1834 ? syn. *Lutra lutra lutra.*

Lutra simul Gray, 1869 ? syn. *Lutra lutra monticola.*

Lutra simung: Cantor, 1846 syn. *Lutra sumatrana* Gray, 1865.

Lutra simung: Horsfield, 1851 syn. *Lutra lutra barang.*

Lutra simung Lesson, 1827 syn. *Lutra (Lutrogale) perspicillata.*

Lutra simung: Robinson & Kloss, 1919 syn. *Lutra (Lutrogale) perspicillata.*

Lutra simung: Schinz, 1844 syn. *Lutra sumatrana* Gray, 1865.

Lutra sinensis Hodgson, 1855 ? syn. *Lutra lutra chinensis.*

Lutra sinensis: Trouessart, 1897 syn. *Lutra lutra chinensis.*

Lutra solitaria Natterer, 1842 ? syn. *Pteronura brasiliensis.*

Lutra solitaria Wagner, 1842 syn. *Lutra platensis* Waterhouse, 1838.

Lutra stelleri Lesson, 1827 obs. syn. *Enhydra lutris.*

Lutra stejnegeri Goldman, 1936 ? syn. *Lutra lutra lutra.*

Lutra subtus nigricans: Gray, 1865 ? syn. *Lutra nigricans* (q.v.).

Lutra sumatrana: Dammerman, 1929 syn. *Lutra (Lutrogale) perspicillata.*

Lutra sumatrana Gray, 1865 Sp. *hab.* Borneo, Banka, Sumatra, Malay States n. to Annam.

Lutra sumatrana brunnea Pocock, 1941 syn. *Lutra sumatrana* Gray, 1865.

Lutra sumatrana lovii Pocock, 1941 syn. *Lutra sumatrana* Gray, 1865.

Lutra supra obscura: Gray, 1865 ? syn. *Lutra incarum.*

Lutra swinhoei Swinhoe, 1870a ? syn. *Amblonyx cinerea concolor.*

Lutra taraiyensis Blanford, 1888 mis. *Lutra tarayensis* (q.v.).

Lutra taraiyensis: Pocock, 1940 mis. *Lutra tarayensis* (q.v.).

Lutra tarayensis Hodgson, 1839 syn. *Lutra (Lutrogale) perspicillata.*

Lutra tavayensis Gray, 1865 and 1869 mis. *Lutra tarayensis* (q.v.).

Lutra tenuis Pohle, 1920 sup. *Lutra (Hydrictis) maculicollis tenuis.*

Lutra vancouverensis Goldman, 1935 sup. *Lutra canadensis vancouverensis.*

Lutra var. *variegata* Lesson, 1842 syn. *Lutra lutra lutra.*

Lutra vittata Traill,   sup. *Grison vittatus,* a Sp. of Grison.

Lutra vulgaris: Anderson, 1878 syn. *Lutra lutra monticola.*

Lutra vulgaris: Blanford, 1888 syn. *Lutra lutra nair* Cuvier, 1823 [in part.].

Lutra vulgaris: Blanford, 1888 syn. *Lutra lutra monticola* [in part.].

Lutra vulgaris: Blanford, 1891 syn. *Lutra lutra aurobrunnea.*

Lutra vulgaris Brisson, 1762 syn. *Lutra lutra lutra.*

Lutra vulgaris: Buechner, 1892 syn. *Lutra lutra chinensis.*

Lutra vulgaris: Sclater, 1891 [*see* note 7, page 305].

Lutra vulgaris: Scully, 1881 syn. *Lutra lutra kutab.*

Lutra vulgaris: Thomas, 1889 syn. *Lutra lutra aurobrunnea* [in part.].

Lutra vulgaris: Thomas, 1889 syn. *Lutra lutra monticola* [in part.].

Lutra vulgaris barang Robinson & Kloss, 1918 syn. *Lutra lutra barang.*

Lutra vulgaris var. *amurensis* Dybowski, 1922 nom. nud.

Lutra vulgaris var. *canadensis* Wagner, 1841 syn. *Lutra canadensis* Schreber, 1776.

Lutra vulgaris var. *kamtschatica* Dybowski, 1922 nom. nud.

Lutra vulgaris var. *marinus* Billberg, 1827 syn. *Lutra lutra lutra.*

Lutra whiteleyi Goldman, 1936 syn. *Lutra lutra lutra.*

Lutra whiteleyi: Pocock, 1941 syn. *Lutra lutra lutra.*

Lutridae De Kay, 1842 obs. syn. Lutrinae.

Lutrina Bonaparte, 1838 obs. syn. Lutrinae.

Lutrinae Baird, 1857 subfamily of the Mustelidae comprising the Otters.

Lutris Duméril, 1806 sup. *Lutra* Brisson, 1762.

Lutrix Rafinesque, 1815 sup. *Lutra* Brisson, 1762.

Lutrogale Gray, 1865 subgen. Indian 'smooth-coated' otter.

Lutrogale barang: Pocock, 1921 syn. *Lutra (Lutrogale) perspicillata.*

Lutrogale barang Pohle, 1920 syn. *Lutra (Lutrogale) perspicillata.*

Lutrogale barang aurobrunnea Pohle, 1920 ? syn. *Lutra lutra aurobrunnea.*

Lutrogale perspicillata Pocock, 1941 syn. *Lutra (Lutrogale) perspicillata.*

Lutrogale perspicillata maxwelli Hayman, 1957 syn. *Lutra (Lutrogale) perspicillata maxwelli.*

Lutrogale perspicillata sindica Pocock, 1940 syn. *Lutra (Lutrogale) perspicillata sindica.*

Lutrogale tarayensis Flower 1929 obs. syn. *Lutra (Lutrogale) perspicillata.*

Lutronectes Gray, 1867 sup. *Lutra* Brisson, 1762.

Lutronectes whiteleyi Gray, 1867 syn. *Lutra lutra lutra.*

Micraonyx J.A. Allen, 1922 sup. *Amblonyx.*

Micraonyx cinerea J.A. Allen, 1922 syn. *Amblonyx cinerea.*

Micraonyx cinerea: G.M. Allen, 1938 syn. *Amblonyx cinerea.*

Micraonyx cinerus Allen & Coolidge, 1940 syn. *Amblonyx cinerea cinerea.*

Mustela: Gmelin, 1788 sup. *Pteronura.*

Mustela brasiliensis Lesson, 1842 obs. syn. *Pteronura brasiliensis.*

Mustela canadensis Turton, 1806 obs. syn. *Lutra canadensis* Schreber, 1776.

Mustela felina Molina, 1782 sup. *Lutra felina* Molina, 1782.

Mustela flavicans Olfers, 1818 nom. nud.

Mustela fusca: Gray, 1843b. obs. syn. *Amblonyx cinerea.*

Mustela hudsonica Desmarest, 1803 sup. *Lutra canadensis* Schreber, 1776.

Mustela lutra: Gray, 1843b obs. syn. *Amblonyx cinerea.*

Mustela lutra Linnaeus, 1758 sup. *Lutra lutra.*

Mustela lutra: Marsden, 1811 ? syn. *Lutra (Lutrogale) perspicillata.*

Mustela lutra brasiliensis Gmelin, 1788 obs. syn. *Pteronura brasiliensis.*

Mustela lutra brasiliensis: Azara, 1802 syn. *Pteronura brasiliensis paranensis*

Mustela lutra canadensis Schreber, 1776 obs. sup. *Lutra canadensis.*

Mustela (Lutra) chilensis Kerr, 1792 syn. *Lutra felina* Molina, 1782.

Mustela lutra lutris Kerr, 1792 obs. syn. *Enhydra lutris.*

Mustela lutra piscatoria Kerr, 1792 obs. syn. *Lutra lutra lutra.*

Mustela lutris: Larranaga, 1923 syn. *Lutra platensis* Waterhouse, 1838.

Mustela lutris Linnaeus, 1758 sup. *Enhydra lutris.*

Mustelidae Swainson, 1835 the family of Mustelids.

Mustelini Fischer, 1817 obs. syn. Mustelidae.

Mustelladae Gray, 1821 obs. syn. Mustelidae.

Nutria Gray, 1865 sup. *Lutra* Brisson, 1762.

Nutria felina Gray, 1865 obs. syn. *Lutra felina* Molina, 1782.

Paraonyx Hinton, 1921 subgen. African 'clawless' otter.

Paraonyx capensis congica Schouteden, 1942 syn. *Aonyx (Paraonyx) congica.*

Paraonyx congica: G. M. Allen, 1939 syn. *Aonyx (Paraonyx) congica.*

Paraonyx congica Hinton, 1921a syn. *Aonyx (Paraonyx) congica.*

Paraonyx congicus Pocock, 1921 mis. *Paraonyx congica* (q.v.).

Paraonyx microdon G. M. Allen, 1939 syn. *Aonyx (Paraonyx) microdon.*

Paraonyx philippsi Hinton, 1921a syn. *Aonyx (Paraonyx) philippsi.*

Paraonyx phillipsi Schouteden, 1942 mis. *Paraonyx philippsi* (q.v.).

Phoca lutris Pallas, 1831 obs. syn. *Enhydra lutris.*

Pteroneura Sanderson, 1949 mis. *Pteronura.*

Pteroneura brasiliensis Sanderson, 1949 mis. *Pteronura brasiliensis.*

Pteronura Gray, 1837 Gen. giant Brazilian otter.

Pteronura brasiliensis Gmelin, 1788 Sp. *hab.* S. America from Guianas to
Uruguay.

Pteronura brasiliensis brasiliensis Gmelin, 1788 subsp. *hab.* the Guianas,
Venezuela, 'Amazonia', Uruguay, Peru, ? Ecuador, on the major river
systems.

Pteronura brasiliensis lupina Pohle, 1920 syn. *Pteronura brasiliensis brasiliensis.*

Pteronura brasiliensis paranensis Rengger, 1830 subsp. *hab.* S. Brazil, Paraguay, Argentina, Uruguay.

Pteronura sambachii Gray, 1837 syn. *Pteronura brasiliensis brasiliensis.*

Pteronura sanbachii Gray, 1865 mis. *Pteronura sambachii* (q.v.).

Pteronura sandbachii Gray, 1868 and 1869 mis. *Pteronura sambachii* (q.v.).

Pteronurus Lesson, 1842 mis. *Pteronura.*

Pteronurus sandbackii Lesson, 1842 mis. *Pteronura sambachii* (q.v.).

Pterura: Schinz, 1844 obs. syn. *Pteronura.*

Pterura Wiegmann, 1838 obs. syn. *Pteronura.*

Pterura sanbachii Wiegmann, 1838 obs. syn. *Pteronura brasiliensis brasiliensis.*

Pusa Oken, 1816 sup. *Enhydra.*

Pusa orientalis Oken, 1816 obs. syn. *Enhydra lutris.*

Saricovia Lesson, 1842 sup. *Pteronura.*

Saricovia brasiliensis Lesson, 1842 obs. syn. *Pteronura brasiliensis.*

'Semul' Gray, 1865 and 1869 obs. syn. *Amblonyx cinerea cinerea.*

'Simung' Raffles, 1822 obs. syn. *Lutra lutra barang.*

Suricoria Gray, 1865 syn. *Lontra* Gray, 1843 (q.v.).

Sutra marina Elliot, 1874 mis. *Lutra marina* Steller, 1751 (q.v.).

Viverra lutra Ognev, 1931 ? syn. *Enhydra lutris.*

NOTES:

1. *Lontra* Gray, 1843a and 1843b.   464, 465

Under this generic name, now suppressed, Gray includes both *Lutra brasiliensis* Ray [1693] = *Pteronura brasiliensis* and also '*L. canadensis*', pre-   949
sumably of Schreber, although the rhinarium is typified as hairy.

2. *Lutra:* Thomas, 1889.   1143

In this ill-considered article Thomas concludes that *Aonyx* (including *Amblonyx* in this case) and *Pteronura* should be abandoned in favour of *Lutra*. He retracted this view in 1908.   1147

3. *Lutra felina:* Alston, 1879–82.   34

Under this name Alston groups various species from as far apart as the Pacific slopes of North America southwards to Chile. His *felina* is in fact a composite, and it is now impossible to determine what it was he thought he was describing.

4. *Lutra latifrons* Nehring, 1887.   847

Nehring attempted to group all previously described forms from South America under this one name, and thus employs it as a synonym of all of them.

5. *Lutra montana* Tschudi, 1844.   1166

There is considerable doubt whether this animal is an otter at all; accord-ing to Pohle it has never been rediscovered. Tschudi's diagnosis reads as follows (*fide* Pohle):   923

. . . The tip of the nose is very small and bare, rounded off above, and black. The lower lip is covered with hair. The entire upper body is blackish brown with red-dish brown shades in it. The stomach is blackish. The face, throat and lips are brown. The feet are black, with the front two-thirds bare and black. The tail is more rounded off than in the *L. chilensis* [=*felina*]. The underfur is shining black, the guard hair blackish brown with reddish brown tips and it is thicker than in the preceding species [*felina*].

Length of body 1′ 6″, of the tail 10″ . . .

6. *Lutra poensis* Waterhouse, 1838.   1186

The majority of taxonomists place this skin from Fernando Po in the synonymy of *Aonyx*. Owing to the fact that there is no accompanying skull and that the skin itself is defective, the feet being absent, it is impossible to be dogmatic. But the assignment to *Aonyx* was first seriously questioned by Lönnberg in 1911–13 and Carbrera (1929) supported his view. Having   721, 252
examined the relevant literature I am strongly inclined to agree with them.

7. *Lutra vulgaris:* Sclater, 1891.   1051

Amongst the many synonyms to this name listed by Sclater are *nair*, *chinensis*, *monticola*, *kutab*, etc.

The New Zealand 'Otter'

AS is well known, New Zealand has no indigenous mammals, and never has had any. Such mammals as there are, or were, have all been introduced either by the Maoris (for instance dogs), by visiting ships (cats and rats), or have flown – or been blown – from Australia (bats). The case for an indigenous otter in New Zealand does not, therefore, need to be argued; accordingly, the majority of enquirers have wrongly assumed that reports of an otter-like animal at large in New Zealand cannot be substantiated.

It is, however, a fact that the Maoris refer to some hitherto unexplained creature which they call the 'waitoreke', although opinions differ as to what extent this animal is mythical or real, or a combination of the two. This question is examined at some length by Heuvelmans in *On the Track of Unknown Animals* (London, 1958), who finds the evidence in favour of the waitoreke having a basis in fact to be moderately convincing.

In 1960 J. S. Watson contributed to the *Records of the Canterbury Museum* a paper entitled 'The New Zealand "Otter"' in which he claimed to bring together 'all the available information'. He discusses this at some length and finally concludes that

there is very little ground for any belief in the animal's [i.e. the otter's] existence; nevertheless a shadow of doubt remains and it would be unwise altogether to ignore the possibility however remote it may be.

A new champion for the New Zealand Otter appears in 1964 with a privately circulated paper by G. A. Pollock of Cambridge, New Zealand. Mr Gavin Maxwell has kindly made available to me a copy sent to him by the author, and I in turn have had a copy made and placed in the Library of the Zoological Society of London.

Pollock brings together considerably more evidence than that amassed by Watson, in particular quoting from what he refers to as The Henderson Papers (unpublished), which appears to be a file of newspaper reports, personal statements, and eye-witness accounts relating or thought to relate to the infrequent sightings of the otter, or to accounts of otherwise inexplicable

557

1191

925

306

tracks and occurrences of an otter-like nature. It must at once be conceded that a number of these accounts do read very convincingly; certainly they go far towards convincing any reader unfamiliar with the fauna of New Zealand that for many years some unexplained animal has been at large, and an aquatic animal at that. It may be noted that all accounts arise from the South Island, and from a limited area – albeit rather a large one – from Lake Ellesmere on the east coast across country to the Sounds just north of the south-west tip of the island, a straight-line distance of some 300 miles.

Up to this point Pollock makes a persuasive case, but his attempt to account for the introduction of otters to New Zealand will not stand up to scrutiny. According to Pollock there are a number of reasons for thinking that Tamils from India may at some point in the past have reached New Zealand, and he adds:

… I see nothing improbable in a Tamil vessel, setting out on a long adventure, carrying fishing otters on board; they would be a highly sensible insurance against hunger on the seas … Had such a Tamil vessel come to grief, say on the Canterbury coast, the otter's presence would be explained.

Pollock finds support for this theory on etymological grounds.

This name [waitoreke], commonly used by South Island Maoris for the otter-like animal they described, is not the least of the mysteries with which it has been surrounded, for even Sir Peter Buck declared it quite ungrammatical, and inferentially meaningless. In face of such authority, it needs some boldness to suggest a possible derivation; yet I find not one, but two.

Consider first the rather common practice, in South Island Maori dialect, of rendering 'ng' as 'k' – for instance, Waitangi – Waitaki; (Wh)angaroa – Akaroa. On this basis, the classical Maori equivalent of 'waitoreke' could be 'waitorengi', meaning 'disappearing in the water' logical, surely, even if perhaps a little too pat. It is more likely, I think, that the word is a Maoricised version of the name which accompanied the animal to New Zealand. Disregarding 'wai', which would be a later Maori addition of obvious [?] significance, can we find, in the animal's presumed original home, a reasonable equivalent for 'toreke'?

Sanscrit gives the answer, for one meaning of 'tiryang/tiryak' is 'an amphibious animal', and S. E. Asian tongues, notably Malayalam, the Tamil dialect spoken at Cochin, are full of Sanscrit borrowings. Though I have been unable to obtain a Tamil dictionary, the fact that one Malayan name for the Smooth Otter [L. perspicillata] is 'Lutra Tarayensis' shows that 'tiryang' does have derivations specifically connoting the otter race. Compare the Gypsy name 'Tarka' and the Old English 'tek', which could well be cognate.

It is worth noting that the Lake Ellesmere Spit, near the spot which all the evidence pinpoints as the otter's first New Zealand home, was called by the Maoris

'Kaitorete' – 'the place where parakeets were eaten'. This may be so, but that bleak, bare shingle bank seems a most inappropriate habitat for a forest bird like the parakeet, nor would it be a likely diet amid such abundance of more substantial fare. If however the name were really 'Kaitoreke', that would be much more logical – it would commemorate the place where some old Maori ate an otter, and possibly found it notably distasteful!

It seems strange that Pollock is so ready to abandon the attractive idea of equating 'waitoreke' with 'waitorengi' if this latter word really does mean 'disappearing in the water', especially as his alternative, the proposed Tamil root for 'toreke', cannot be accepted on the basis he provides. For Hodgson named his otter *Lutra tarayensis* not because this was the native name for the animal but because it came from the Tarai area of Nepal, that is to say the strip of level, cultivated and forest land lying along the southern border. In fact, the Tamil name for this otter is 'Niru-kuka' (see Pocock: 1941). Whether or not the words 'toreke' and 'tiryang/tiryak' are related may best be argued by philologists.

572

922

What, then, are we to make of the New Zealand Otter? Pollock's hypothesis, although unconvincing as set forth by him, might still be correct; the possibility of a ship from southern India having one or more otters on board is not all that remote. But I have no knowledge of the tenability or otherwise of the theory that travellers from Asiatic regions had reached New Zealand before the advent of Captain Cook in 1779. Certainly Tasman visited the South Island in 1642, but he did not land. Perhaps he brought an otter with him from Java?

On balance, with such evidence as is at present available, I find myself unable to accept as likely that there are otters in New Zealand living in a wild state. Admittedly, the uninitiated may live amongst otters for many years and fail to realise it – a point much stressed by Pollock – but anyone who knows what to look for can tell very quickly whether there are otters present on any particular stretch of water, or even if they have been there at all recently. It is not necessary to see the animal to assert its presence; indeed, one is most unlikely to do so. But the very characteristic footprints ('seals') and the even more easily distinguished spraints – which remain intact for a remarkably long time – must by now have been found by at least one competent naturalist if they have been searched for properly, and if the otter were there to leave them.

Cranial Measurements

LUTRA LUTRA LUTRA (L.)

Ognev notes that the variation in size between male and female skulls is [864] very marked. The skull of the female is not only smaller but also differs in the following respects:

(a) There is an almost complete absence of saggital crests, even in adults.
(b) The nasal aperture is smaller.
(c) The infraorbital foramina are relatively smaller.
(d) The mesopterygoid fossa is somewhat shorter and narrower.
(e) The skull is narrower in section over the canines.

In young individuals the skull is less angular than in adults. The occipital region is markedly elevated, and is much higher than the rostrum; the elevation of the rostrum increases with age. The postorbital interstice is wider than in adults, and whereas in adults the postorbital processes protrude laterally to a considerable degree in the young they are but slightly marked.

Ognev gives the *normal range* as follows:

	Males	Females
Overall length of skull	111·1–122·6	102·3–110·8
Condylobasal length	113·0–125·6	103·0–113·6
Zygomatic width	67·3– 82·0	61·0– 70·2
Maximum width of braincase	61·0– 71·3	57·5– 63·0
Height in region of osseous bullae	35·1– 42·5	36·3– 40·1

Amongst others, the following individual measurements (in mm.) are given:

	Estonia m.	Nr. Kiev m. (sen.)	B.-Litovsk f.	L. Baikal f.	Kamchatka m.	Sakhalin I. m.	Kamchatka f.
(a)	122·6	113·8	110·8	105·0	122·0	119·1	108·3
(b)	113·5	105·0	102·1	95·2	113·0	110·3	98·9
(c)	125·6	116·1	113·6	107·0	125·2	120·5	109·9

	Estonia m.	Nr. Kiev m. (sen.)	B.-Litovsk f.	L. Baikal f.	Kamchatka m.	Sakhalin I. m.	Kamchatka f.
(d)	80·3	73·0	68·3	68·8	82·0	76·5	70·2
(e)	23·2	21·1	19·5	19·2	22·2	–	21·1
(f)	71·3	64·9	61·9	63·0	69·1	69·1	63·0
(g)	54·6	49·9	47·2	45·2	52·3	–	46·0
(h)	39·9	35·9	35·3	34·3	38·5	35·5	34·0
(i)	47·0	42·2	41·2	40·1	46·3	44·1	40·0
(j)	18·3	14·9	13·9	12·1	15·5	18·0	13·6
(k)	42·0	41·6	38·1	38·7	42·3	40·3	36·9

Key: (a) overall length of skull; (b) basal length: (c) condylobasal length; (d) zygomatic width; (e) interorbital width; (f) maximum width between mastoid processes; (g) length of palate; (h) length of upper toothrow; (i) length of lower toothrow; (j) length of interorbital space; (k) height in region of osseous bullae.

The following measurements of western European *L. l. lutra* are given by Miller:

803

	A	B	C	D	E	F	G
(1)	122·0	115·0±	109·2	104·6	107·0±	120·2	114·0
(2)	75·0	70·2	66·8	66·6	64·6	71·6	70·4
(3)	67·6	64·8	59·6	56·8	61·0	68·0	65·6
(4)	14·2	–	–	–	–	13·8	13·8
(5)	21·0	19·2	19·4	17·2	18·4	21·8	19·6
(6)	28·2	27·0	24·8	25·0	25·0	27·8	27·2
(7)	38·3	36·4	34·8	33·0	–	35·6	34·0
(8)	26·0	23·6	22·2	22·2	23·0	26·2	24·6
(9)	78·0	73·4	68·6	67·2	66·4	77·2	71·2
(10)	38·2	34·2	34·2	33·0	32·4	36·8	35·2
(11)	46·0	42·0	41·0	40·4	39·0	45·8	43·2

	H	I	J	K	L	M	N
(1)	115·2	105·0	–	124·0	107·0	117·4	122·6
(2)	69·6	64·8	–	76·4	67·2	71·2	73·2
(3)	65·4	57·6	58·2	–	63·0	66·8	68·6
(4)	14·4	14·0	14·6	12·2	–	18·0	13·8
(5)	21·0	19·2	17·0	21·8	21·0	20·4	22·8
(6)	26·8	24·6	24·8	30·2	26·6	27·2	28·2
(7)	35·8	32·0	–	37·0	34·6	38·2	38·4
(8)	24·2	23·0	23·0	26·8	25·0	25·0	27·6
(9)	72·2	65·4	66·6	79·6	68·0	73·4	78·0
(10)	34·6	33·2	31·0	38·8	34·6	35·2	35·0
(11)	42·8	40·6	39·6	46·6	41·0	43·8	44·0

	O	P	Q	R	S	T	U
(1)	–	107·4	111·6	–	115·0	121·0	118·0
(2)	–	64·6	64·8	–	71·0	75·6	78·0
(3)	–	59·4	60·2	–	65·4	67·4	69·8
(4)	–	13·2	11·2	13·0	14·4	13·4	13·8
(5)	19·0	19·0	18·6	–	20·8	20·0	21·2
(6)	25·2	26·0	26·2	26·4	29·6	26·6	28·2
(7)	–	33·8	32·6	–	–	38·0	36·6
(8)	23·2	22·0	22·6	22·6	27·2	26·6	27·8
(9)	68·8	66·0	71·2	69·2	75·0	77·8	79·2
(10)	32·2	34·0	35·6	32·2	35·6	33·2	33·6
(11)	40·0	40·4	42·0	39·8	43·2	45·4	43·2

Key: (1) condylobasal length; (2) zygomatic breadth; (3) mastoid breadth; (4) postorbital constriction; (5) interorbital constriction; (6) rostral breadth over canine; (7) occipital depth; (8) palatal depth between tooth rows; (9) length of mandible; (10) length of maxillary toothrow; (11) length of mandibular toothrow.
A, Sweden, ? m.; B, Sweden, ? m.; C, Sweden, f!; D, Sweden, ? f.; E, Sweden, ? f.; F, Norway, ? m.; G, Norway, ? m.; H, Norway, ? m.; I, Norway, ? f.; J, Ireland, type of *roensis*; K, England, m!; L, France, f!; M, France, m!; N, Germany, m!; O, Czechoslovakia (Bohemia), ? f.; P, Hungary, f.; Q, Italy, ? f.; R, Spain, f!; S, Spain, ? m.; T, Spain, ? m.; U, Spain, ? m.

The measurements given above under J. for the type of *roensis* differ slightly from those given by Hinton (1920) for the same skull, which he contrasts with that of three known female Irish otters:

	roensis	f1	f2	f3
Condylobasal length	–	–	108·3	–
Zygomatic breadth	–	64·7	65·8	65·3
Mastoid breadth	58·4	60·0	61·2	60·4
Postorbital constriction	14·5	14·2	–	13·8
Interorbital constriction	16·9	18·0	19·4	18·7
Occipital depth	–	–	34·7	–
Maxillary toothrow (c–m)	33·1	33·7	33·2	32·8
Mandible	66·6	68·0	68·2	68·0
Breadth of rostrum over canines	25·2	24·7	24·7	24·7

Pohle gives the cranial measurements of no less than 73 *L. l. lutra*, from which the following figures are selected. The ones chosen are all those shown as fully adult (all sutures closed, skull surface smooth, all crests developed) of which the sex is known.

	A	B	C	D	E	F	G
(1)	109·5	20·9	24·1	13·3	53·8	65·0	73·5
(2)	104·2	20·7	24·3	13·8	54·7	64·4	69·9
(3)	114·4	22·3	26·1	26·6[sic]	58·5	70·7	75·2
(4)	116·3	20·7	23·8	–	57·5	70·1	75·2
(5)	102·0	19·2	21·7	13·7	53·8	60·8	–
(6)	108·6	19·5	21·3	13·5	55·9	66·1	72·5
(7)	–	21·3	24·4	15·2	57·2	68·4	75·8
(8)	113·1	21·7	23·5	14·4	56·1	67·9	76·2
(9)	115·5	22·6	24·9	13·2	57·0	69·3	73·5
(10)	98·5	18·8	20·0	14·8	51·6	57·8	63·2
(11)	99·9	18·2	21·4	12·0	49·9	60·1	66·9
(12)	101·1	19·0	22·2	13·2	49·8	58·7	65·7
(13)	–	20·1	21·0	11·2	55·2	66·4	75·3

Key: A, basal length; B, interorbital breadth; C, postorbital width; D, intertemporal breadth; E, breadth of braincase; F, mastoid breadth; G, zygomatic breadth. (1) West Prussia, m.; (2) Poland, f.; (3) Silesia, m.; (4) Silesia, m.; (5) Silesia, f.; (6) Silesia, m.; (7) Silesia, m.; (8) Germany, m.; (9) Germany, m.; (10), (11) and (12) France, all f.; (13) Russia, m.

Pohle also gives the following figures for '*L. l. angustifrons*' which may be of interest in comparison with those of *L. l. lutra*:

	A	B	C	D	E	F	G
(1)	110·0	20·0	22·0	11·0	–	–	69·0
(2)	103·3	19·6	22·0	17·5	54·4	60·3	66·3
(3)	–	18·6	20·6	13·6	50·1	58·7	65·7
(4)	–	17·5	18·8	16·0	52·5	57·2	64·3
(5)	–	20·6	22·3	14·5	53·6	63·6	69·9
(6)	101·2	19·5?	22·–?	13·1	–	–	70·9
(7)	115·1	23·4	25·8	15·3	55·3	70·4	76·9
(8)	–	17·7	18·7	12·2	–	–	66·0
(9)	102·3	19·0	19·3	16·7	53·6	57·7	64·3
(10)	97·1	19·5	20·5	14·8	53·6	59·4	64·2
(11)	109·4	19·5	21·7	13·2	55·5	66·0	69·6

Key: letters A–G as in the preceding table. (1) Morocco, m.; (2) Morocco, milk teeth shed, basilar suture still open; (3) Morocco, adult; (4) Morocco, basilar suture closed, skull still rough; (5) Algeria, adult f.; (6) Algeria, adult f.; (7) Algeria, adult m.; (8) Algeria, adult m.; (9) Algeria, milk teeth shed, basilar suture still open, m.; (10) as no. 9, but f.; (11) Tunisia, basilar suture closed, skull still rough, f.

Finally, Pohle gives the measurements of a number of examples of '*L. l. whiteleyi*' from Japan of which the following are the fully adult specimens, sex not stated:

A	B	C	D	E	F	G
–	19·7	21·8	14·9	–	–	71·4
101·8	23·7	28·3	13·0	56·5	66·3	76·4
114·0	25·3	29·5	14·1	58·5	69·4	–
–	20·6	21·6	14·0	54·8	62·0	70·4
112·7	21·6	23·2	12·5	55·9	65·8	–
100·1	20·7	21·9	13·9	54·5	60·5	67·5

Key: letters A–G as in the preceding table.

LUTRA LUTRA AUROBRUNNEA

Pocock (1941) gives the following measurements: 922

	Adult m.	Adult ? f.
Total length of skull	109	–
Condylobasal length	107	–
Zygomatic width	62	61
Postorbital width	11	–
Interorbital width	17	17
Maxillary width	23	23

The first of these animals came from Garhwal; the second originated from Nepal and is the type of *Barangia nepalensis* Gray.

LUTRA LUTRA BARANG

The following measurements are given by Pocock (1941). 922

	A	B	C	D	E	F
(1)	111·0	106·0	66·0	13·0	21·0	25·0
(2)	104·0	106·0	60·5	14·0	19·0	–
(3)	103·0	102·0	63·0	13·0	16·0	22·0
(4)	101·0	97·0	59·0	15·0	17·0	21·0
(5)	100·0	97·0	60·0	13·0	17 –	21·0
(6)	–	100·0	68·8	–	–	–

Key: Numbers (1)–(3) are adult males from Sumatra; (4) adult male, Annam; (5) and (6) adult females, Annam.
A, total length of skull; B, condylobasal length; C, zygomatic width; D, postorbital width; E, interorbital width; F, maxillary width.

LUTRA LUTRA CHINENSIS

Pocock (1941) gives the following figures: 922

	A	B	C	D	E	F
(1)	112 plus	112·0	68·0	13·5	19·0	25·0
(2)	105·0	108·0	61·0	13·0	17·0	24·0

	A	B	C	D	E	F
(3)	–	108·0	63·0	15·0	–	–
(4)	110·0	107·0	69·0	13·0	19·0	24·0
(5)	–	109·0	57·0	14·0	–	–
(6)	–	96·5	54·5	16·0	–	–

Key: (1) Adult m., Amoy; (2) adult m?, Foochow; (3) adult m., Fokien; (4) adult f., Formosa; (5) adult f., Hainan; (6) adult f., Szechwan. Letters A–F as in the preceding table.

G. M. Allen (1938) remarks that 'the skull of the Eastern Chinese Otter is smaller than that of the European or Indian race, with apparently smaller teeth and shorter tooth rows. The frontal region between the orbits is very narrow, and practically parallel sided, except for the slight projection caused by the blunt postorbital processes . . .'

He gives the following measurements:

	A	B	C	D	E	F
m.	108·0	99·5	49·5	63·0	57·0	15·0
f.	100·0	93·0	45·0	57·0	51·5	14·0
–	96·5	88·4	43·6	54·4	49·7	16·0
? m.	112·0	104·5	49·7	67·2	60·2	–
? f.	107·5	100·0	45·8	60·6	56·3	–

Key: A, condylobasal length; B, basal length; C, palatal length; D, zygomatic width; E, mastoid width; F, postorbital constriction.

Pohle lists only one adult example of *chinensis*, for which he gives the following measurements:
Basal length 102·5; interorbital breadth 20·7; postorbital width 22·9; intertemporal breadth 14·0; breadth of braincase 53·7; zygomatic breadth 69·0.

LUTRA LUTRA KUTAB

Pocock (1941) gives the following figures for two adult males, the first from Gilgit and the second from Kashmir:

Total length of skull	124·0	115·0
Condylobasal length	121·0	114·0
Zygomatic width	75·0	72·0
Postorbital width	11·0	13·0
Interorbital width	20·0	19·0
Maxillary width	30·0	30·0

314

LUTRA LUTRA MERIDIONALIS

The following measurements are given by Ognev (1931): 864

	m.	f.	f.	m.
Overall length of skull	115·9	106·1	106·1	106·1
Basal length	107·7	98·7	97·1	98·9
Condylobasal length	119·2	108·4	107·6	108·1
Zygomatic width	70·2	67·9	69·0	59·0
Interorbital width	20·3	19·3	19·0	19·2
Maximum width between mastoid processes	64·6	59·1	61·2	54·7
Length of palate	50·0	45·9	44·2	48·3
Length of upper toothrow	36·2	34·2	35·6	34·2
Length of lower toothrow	44·8	42·0	42·9	41·3
Length of interorbital space	14·1	12·8	13·0	11·9
Height in region of osseous bullae	40·6	36·3	38·8	39·0

LUTRA LUTRA MONTICOLA

Pocock (1941) gives the measurements of four skulls. The first two 922 originate from the Himalayas, the third from Nepal (these all being ex Hodgson), and the last from Kumaun.

	ad. ? m.	ad. ? f.	yg/ad. ? f.	ad. ? f.
Total length of skull	129·0	114·0	110·0	–
Condylobasal length	123·0	113·0	112·0	–
Zygomatic width	77·0	72·0	64·0	68·0
Postorbital width	15·0	13·0	14 –	15·0
Interorbital width	22·5	19·0	21·0	19·0
Maxillary width	30·0	27·0	24·0	27·0

LUTRA LUTRA NAIR

Pocock (1941) gives the measurements of nine individuals. 922

	A	B	C	D	E	F
(1)	110·0	110·0	65·0	–	19·0	25·0
(2)	111·0	–	67·0	12·0	–	21·0
(3)	109·0	106·0	66·0	14·0	20·0	24·0
(4)	102·0	102·0	–	14·0	16·0	21·5
(5)	107·0	104·0	67·0	13·0	18·0	23·5
(6)	103·0	101·0	63·0	14·0	18·5	23·0
(7)	100·0	97·0	61·0	16·0	17·5	23·0
(8)	111·0	109·0	61·0	14·0	17·0	23·0
(9)	107·0	–	65·0	15·0	18·0	24·0

Key: (1) Adult m., Madras (the type of indica Gray, 1837); (2) adult m., Coorg; (3) adult m., Coorg; (4) adult f., Coorg; (5)–(7) adult m., Ceylon; (8) and (9) adult f., Ceylon.
A, Total length of skull; B, condylobasal length; C, zygomatic width; D, postorbital width; E, interorbital width; F, maxillary width.

LUTRA LUTRA SEISTANICA

864   Ognev (1931) gives the following measurements of a male specimen. Overall length of skull ± 120·0; zygomatic width 72·0; interorbital width 20·1; maximum width between mastoid processes 59·9; length of palate 52·0; length of upper toothrow 37·3; length of lower toothrow 43·3; length of interorbital space 17·6.

LUTRA STEJNEGERI

453   The dimensions of the skull of the type are given by Goldman (1936) as follows:

Condylobasilar length 111·4; zygomatic breadth 64·7; height of braincase (over audital bullae) 39·5; breadth of braincase (across mastoid processes) 64·7; interorbital breadth 19·2; postorbital constriction 15·3; palatal constriction (behind molars) 13·8; maxillary toothrow (alveoli) 32·7.

LUTRA SUMATRANA

731   Lyon (1908) notes two adult females of which the greatest length of skull is 101·0 and 100·2, and the basal length 94·3 and 91·4 respectively.

922   Pocock (1941) lists six examples.

	A	B	C	D	E	F
(1)	–	(119±)	73·0	12·0	18·0	26·0
(2)	–	(115±)	70·0	12·0	17·0	27·0
(3)	–	(110±)	63·0	10·5	16·0	25·0
(4)	100·0	100·0	55·0	15·0	15·0	21·0
(5)	–	–	62·0	13·0	16·0	24·0
(6)	–	–	60·0	19·0	18·0	24·0

Key: (1) and (2) adult m., Malacca; (3) adult f., Singapore; (4) young f., Sumatra (the type of *sumatrana* Gray); (5) young f., Borneo; (6) young m., Borneo (the type of *lovii* Günther).
A, Total length of skull; B, condylobasal length; C, zygomatic width; D, postorbital width; E, interorbital width; F, maxillary width.

LUTRA (L.) P. PERSPICILLATA

11   G.M.Allen (1938) quotes Anderson's figures (1878) for the latter's *monticola* under the name of *tarayensis* [= *perspicillata*].

316

Greatest length of skull 126·5; basal length 106·0; palatal length 60·8; zygomatic width 79·5; mastoid width 66·8.

Pocock (1941) gives a number of examples:

922

	A	B	C	D	E	F
(1)	128·0	125·0	80·0	22·0	22 +	29 −
(2)	126·0	–	75·0	18·5	21·0	26·0
(3)	122·0	122·0	72·0	19·0	22·0	25·0
(4)	120·0	117·0	78·0	23·0	22·0	26·5
(5)	121·0	117·0	72·0	22·0	22·0	25·0
(6)	123·0	120·0	76·0	18·0	22·0	27·0
(7)	126·0	122·0	74·0	18·0	23·0	27·0
(8)	120·0	115·0	71·0	18·0	19·0	26·0
(9)	128·0	128·0	80·0	20·0	27·0	28·0
(10)	122·0	118·0	74·0	18·0	21·0	26·0
(11)	130·0	125·0	82·0	20·0	25·0	27·0
(12)	127·0	123·0	76·0	17·0	22·0	27·0
(13)	126·0	122·0	81·0	20·0	22·0	29·0
(14)	122·0	118·0	75·0	18·0	22·0	26·0
(15)	118·0	116·0	72·0	17·0	20·5	25·0
(16)	111·0	107·0	62·0	18·0	18·0	26·0

Key: (1) Adult m., Kindat; (2) adult m., Kindat; (3)–(5) adult m., Toungoo; (6) adult m., Sadyia; (7) adult m., Himalayas (ex Hodgson); (8) adult m., Nepal (the type of *tarayensis* Hodgson); (9) adult ? m., Bengal; (10) adult m., Nerbudda; (11) adult m., Ankulam Lagoon; (12) adult f., Dikhu River; (13) adult f., Chibi River; (14) adult f., Ghazipur; (15) adult f., Ghazipur; (16) adult f., Goona. Letters A–F as in the preceding table.

The following figures are taken from van Bemmel (1949).

173

	m.	m.	m.	m.	? f.
Greatest length of skull	129·2	131·7	131·0	128·0	120·0
Palatal length	61·5	64·0	62·8	62·0	57·8
Zygomatic width	83·6	81·8	83·4	80·1	76·9
Mastoid width	71·9	72·0	72·7	69·8	66·0
Interorbital constriction	23·3	22·8	23·7	24·0	19·6
Upper cheek teeth	37·5	38·8	39·1	37·4	36·3
Lower cheek teeth	43·0	45·1	45·0	43·2	38·0

The origin of the first three males is W. Java, the fourth is from South-west Sumatra, and the ? female is from N.E. Borneo.

LUTRA (L.) PERSPICILLATA SINDICA

922   Pocock (1941) gives the following figures.

	yg. ad. f.	yg. ad. f.	yg. ad. m.
Total length of skull	123·0	122·0	121·0
Condylobasal length	119·0	116·0	115·0
Zygomatic width	73·0	71·0	68·0
Postorbital width	25·0	21·0	21·0
Interorbital width	22·0	22·0	21·0
Maxillary width	26·0	27·0	27·0

AMBLONYX CINEREA CINEREA

30   The following measurements are taken from J. A. Allen, 1922.

	? m.	m.	f.	f.	f.	m.
Condylobasal length	–	91·4	88·7	90·3	84·6	90·8
Zygomatic breadth	63·6	61·2	61·7	62·1	58·6	62·8
Interorbital breadth	17·5	19·7	17·0	18·0	17·2	18·4
Postorbital constriction	13·4	13·6	14·4	15·8	16·4	–
Breadth of braincase	–	48·8	48·0	48·3	43·7	48·8
Mastoid breadth	–	54·4	54·9	53·4	52·0	54·7
Postorbital process	20·0	29·0	25·6	24·4	24·1	25·1
Breadth at base of in- cisors	20·1	24·3	21·7	21·4	20·8	22·8
Breadth at base of canines	33·4	37·1	32·0	33·4	34·5	34·8

These examples came from Palawan, Karimon Island, W. Sumatra, N.E. Borneo, S.E. Borneo, and E. Java, respectively.

277   The following figures are given by Chasen & Kloss (1931):

	Basal length	Condylobasal length	Palatal length	Zygomatic breadth
Male	78·4	84·6	40·6	60·0
Male	77·0	84·5	38·2	58·6
Male	77·5	84·0	40·6	56·0
Male	75·1	82·0	40·0	55·0
Male	75·5	82·0	39·0	57·0
Male	74·5	80·5	38·5	54·2
Female	75·5	82·9	38·5	57·2

These seven examples were all adult.

318

AMBLONYX CINEREA CONCOLOR

The following figures are taken from Pocock (1941).   922

	A	B	C	D	E	F
(1)	86·0	80·0	54·0	18·0	14·0	18·0
(2)	88·0	(82)	56·0	17 −	15 +	19·0
(3)	88·0	82·0	58·0	18·0	18·0	20·0
(4)	84·0	80·0	56·0	21·0	17 −	19·0
(5)	92·0	87·0	57·0	15·0	16 −	19·0
(6)	88·0	85·0	58·0	19·0	17·0	20·0
(7)	89·0	84·0	58·0	18 −	16·5	19·0
(8)	86·0	82·0	55·0	18·0	15 −	19 −

Key: (1) Adult f., Upper Burma; (2) adult m., Dikhu River; (3) adult m., Gola-ghat; (4) adult f., Dabadubhi River; (5) adult f., Garwhal; (6) and (7) adult, Garwhal; (8) adult, Kumaun. Letters A–F as before.

AMBLONYX CINEREA NIRNAI

Pocock (1941) publishes the following.   922

	ad. m. (type)	adult	yg. ad.
Total length of skull	94·0	87·0	84·0
Condylobasal length	90·0	82·0	79·0
Zygomatic width	60·0	57·0	54 −
Postorbital width	21·0	15·0	21·0
Interorbital width	18·0	17·0	16·0
Maxillary width	21·0	19·0	19 −

LUTRA (HYDRICTIS) MACULICOLLIS

J. A. Allen, 1922 gives the following measurements of four adult skulls.   30
The first three come from Niapu, and the fourth from Faradje, in the
Congo.

	m.	m.	f	f.
Condylobasal length	105·7	105·0	97·2	102·5
Palatal length	46·4	44·7	42·0	44·1
Zygomatic breadth	62·2	65·0	−	55·9
Interorbital breadth	15·1	18·7	18·4	13·8
Breadth of braincase	52·2	52·1	47·7	43·8
Breadth at P⁴	32·0	34·0	29·0	28·9
Breadth at C	24·0	23·3	20·2	20·2
Incisive breadth	12·2	12·8	10·7	11·4
Upper toothrow C–M¹	33·7	32·3	29·2	31·0

319

563 Hill & Carter (1941) quote the following measurements for two specimens.

Greatest length of skull	110·0	96·0
Basal length	100·0	88·0
Palatal length	45·0	42·0
Zygomatic breadth	61·0	52·0
Mastoid breadth	53·0	50·0
Temporal constriction	14·0	15·0

971 The following figures for the typical form are taken from Roberts (1951).

	m.	? m.	f.
Greatest length of skull	105·0	109·0	97·5
Basilar length	95·5	97·0	87·5
Zygomatic width	63·0	63·5	59·5
Mastoid width	56·0	58·4	53·0
Interorbital constriction	16·0	18·5	14·5
Length of mandible	63·0	64·7	56·0

LUTRA (HYDRICTIS) MACULICOLLIS CHOBIENSIS

971 Roberts (1951) gives the following dimensions:

	m.	f.	m.
Greatest length of skull	108·0	94·2	108·5
Basilar length	96·2	84·0	99·0
Zygomatic width	63·5	52·0	65·0
Mastoid width	52·0	48·4	55·0
Interorbital constriction	16·5	12·5	18·0
Length of mandible	62·0	52·6	62·0

LUTRA (HYDRICTIS) MACULICOLLIS KIVUANA

923 Pohle gives the measurements of three adults, the first two from Kissenji and the third from Bukoba.

Basal length	96·3	–	–
Interorbital breadth	16·3	17·6	17·4
Width across postorbital processes	17·1	18·5	19·7
Intertemporal breadth	15·8	15·2	16·5
Intertemporal length	10·0	10·0	11·0
Mastoid breadth	52·1	51·9	55·5
Zygomatic width	58·1	61·0	63·3
Palatal length	45·3	43·7	45·8

LUTRA (HYDRICTIS) MACULICOLLIS MATSCHIEI

Pohle gives the following measurements for an adult from Bipindi: [923]
Basal length 99·5; interorbital breadth 17·9; width across postorbital processes 18·8; intertemporal breadth 21·7; intertemporal length 16·0; mastoid breadth 57·0; zygomatic width 68·6; palatal length 49·0.

LUTRA (HYDRICTIS) MACULICOLLIS NILOTICA

Pohle quotes the following figures for an adult male and female from [923]
Malek.

	m.	f.
Basal length	103·5	96·8
Interorbital breadth	20·5	18·5
Mastoid breadth	59·0	54·0
Zygomatic width	69·0	63·0

LUTRA (HYDRICTIS) MACULICOLLIS TENUIS

Pohle gives these dimensions for two adults from Lake Mohasi. [923]

Basal length	87·1	86·5
Interorbital breadth	11·6	10·7
Width across postorbital processes	14·0	14·4
Intertemporal breadth	13·4	14·1
Intertemporal length	10·0	10·0
Mastoid breadth	–	46·0
Zygomatic width	54·7	52·0
Palatal length	–	40·2

AONYX CAPENSIS CAPENSIS

Lönnberg (1908) gives the following figures for a specimen from Natal. [720]
Basal length 128·0; zygomatic width 104·5; mastoid breadth 102·5; interorbital breadth 36·0; width across interorbital processes 46·0; intertemporal breadth 31·0; palate length exclusive of median spine 64·0; length of lower jaw measured from middle of condyle 94·5.

Pohle gives the following figures for an adult from the Cape. [923]
Basal length 118·5; interorbital breadth 31·0; width across postorbital processes 36·0; intertemporal breadth 26·8; intertemporal length 19·0; mastoid breadth 90·0; zygomatic width 94· ?; palatal length 63·8.

971 Roberts (1951) gives the measurements of two males and a female.

	m.	m.	f.
Greatest length of skull	136·0	131·5	125·0
Basilar length	122·0	118·0	112·0
Zygomatic width	99·5	95·5	91·0
Mastoid width	98·0	92·5	86·0
Interorbital constriction	32·3	31·7	28·5
Intertemporal constriction	28·5	27·0	28·0
Length of mandible	–	84·0	–

AONYX CAPENSIS ANGOLAE

923 Pohle gives the measurement of two adults, the first from South-west Transvaal and the second from Ssongea.

Basal length	127·0	123·0
Interorbital breadth	32·0	26·0
Width across postorbital processes	38·?	36·7
Intertemporal breadth	30·8	27·0
Intertemporal length	25·0	21·0
Mastoid breadth	–	–
Zygomatic width	101·?	93·?
Palatal length	65·4	65·3

969 Roberts (1924–6) quotes Thomas' figures for his adult female.
Basal length 128·0; zygomatic width 91·5; mastoid width 92·5; interorbital constriction 27·0; width at postorbital processes 30·5.

563 Hill & Carter (1941) give the following measurements in 'The Mammals of Angola'.
Greatest length of skull 130·0; basilar length 115·5; palatilar length 59·4; zygomatic width 90·6; interorbital breadth 27·4; mastoid breadth 89·6; breadth of rostrum behind canine 32·5; temporal constriction 26·4.

AONYX CAPENSIS COOMBSI

969 Roberts (1924–6) gives the dimensions of the type, an old female, as follows:
Basal length 130·0; zygomatic width 98·0; mastoid width 93·5; interorbital constriction 30·5; width at postorbital processes 36·5.

971 In 1951 Roberts shows the zygomatic width of this same specimen as being 96·0. He also gives the measurements of another female and a male.

322

	m.	f.
Greatest length of skull	133·0	133·8
Basilar length	121·0	121·0
Zygomatic width	101·5	91·2
Mastoid width	99·7	92·2
Interorbital constriction	34·8	29·0
Intertemporal constriction	30·0	26·5

AONYX CAPENSIS HELIOS

Pohle quotes Heller's figures (under the name *A. c. hindei*) for the adult [923] female type.
Basal length 117·0; interorbital breadth 30·0; width across postorbital processes 38·5; intertemporal breadth 27·0; mastoid breadth 84·0; zygomatic width 91·0; palatal length 57·0.

AONYX CAPENSIS HINDEI

Lönnberg (1908) gives the measurements both of Thomas' type, an old [720] male, and of another specimen, from Rhodesia.

	Type	Rhodesia
Basal length	118·0	116·0
Zygomatic breadth	94·0	94·0
Mastoid breadth	80·0	90·5
Interorbital breadth	29·5	28·5
Width of interorbital processes	34·5	35·0
Intertemporal breadth	26·5	28·0*
Palate length exclusive of median spine	62·5	60·5

* Measured at the greatest constriction just in front of the braincase; in front of this constriction the breadth is 29·0 mm.

Pohle gives the following figures for an adult from Upogoro: [923]
Basal length 115·9; interorbital breadth 26·8; width across postorbital processes 31·?; intertemporal breadth 27·0; intertemporal length 15·0; mastoid breadth 86·4; zygomatic width 90·2; palatal length 60·3.

AONYX CAPENSIS MENELEKI

The only available figures appear to be those of Thomas (1902). [1144]
Basal length 131·0; zygomatic width 106·0; mastoid breadth 102·0; interorbital breadth 35·0; width across interorbital processes 51·0; intertemporal breadth 28·5; palate length exclusive of median spine 66·5.

AONYX (PARAONYX) CONGICA

Lönnberg (1911–13) remarks that the skull of the type specimen is very badly crushed and mutilated, but gives the following measurements.

Distance from *crista occipitalis* to anterior end of nasals 126·5; distance from *crista occipitalis* mesially to tip of postorbital process 99·0; distance from tip of postorbital process to tip of nasals mesially 35·5; breadth of braincase exclusive of mastoid flange 80·0; distance from tip to tip of post-orbital processes 42·0; interorbital breadth 36·0.

As previously explained, it is assumed that the following figures as given by J.A.Allen, 1922 under the heading of *Aonyx capensis* are in fact to be attributed to *Aonyx (Paraonyx)*. All these examples come from Faradje except no. 11, which comes from Niapu.

	(1)	(2)	(3)	(4)	(5)	(6)
A	121·0	130·4	124·4	125·0	125·7	116·8
B	58·0	58·4	58·3	62·0	60·0	54·0
C	82·7	98·0	99·7	89·5	94·0	88·3
D	28·4	28·4	33·3	29·7	28·4	30·5
E	37·0	32·2	34·4	33·4	32·6	37·8
F	73·0	70·7	70·6	72·6	70·8	69·9
G	82·2	94·0	87·5	91·5	84·0	86·8
H	38·7	38·8	41·0	39·3	40·2	37·9
I	33·1	33·6	33·7	33·4	33·5	31·3
J	39·7	39·5	37·9	38·8	39·2	36·7

	(7)	(8)	(9)	(10)	(11)	(12)
A	120·0	136·7	110·0	108·5	–	129·7
B	54·5	63·2	53·6	54·0	–	62·2
C	84·6	93·1	81·2	75·9	89·5	95·8
D	27·0	30·5	29·4	26·7	–	33·5
E	–	33·5	34·4	–	–	36·4
F	70·3	73·8	69·3	70·6	71·2	69·5
G	86·9	92·6	82·7	76·5	90·8	90·0
H	39·2	–	39·6	37·7	–	40·2
I	32·9	35·3	31·3	30·3	32·3	32·2
J	38·8	40·2	36·3	37·0	38·4	38·8

Key: A, Condylobasal length; B, palatal length; C, zygomatic breadth; D, inter-orbital breadth; E, postorbital constriction; F, breadth of braincase; G, mastoid breadth; H, breadth P^4–P^4; I, upper toothrow P^1–M^1; J, upper toothrow C–M^1. (1) young adult male; (2) and (3) old adult males; (4) young adult male; (5) old adult female; (6)–(8) adult females; (9) and (10) young adult females; (11) and (12) old adult females.

AONYX (PARAONYX) MICRODON

Pohle gives the following figures for four adults. The first is the type 923 from Bomse, the second comes from Dume, the third from Bipindi and the last from Bukoba.

Basal length	112·5	110·2	117·2	–
Interorbital breadth	28·6	30·3	30·1	27·3
Width acoss postorbital processes	37·1	39·2	37·2	35·8
Interorbital breadth	28·0	31·5	30·5	28·?
Interorbital length	20·0	20·0	22·0	21·0
Mastoid breadth	87·0	87·?	93·8	–
Zygomatic width	87·1	85·0	96·9	–
Palatal length	57·1	53·7	58·2	57·4

AONYX (PARAONYX) PHILIPPSI

Hinton gives the following figures for the female type and an old female, 566 respectively.

Condylobasal length 121, 116·5; zygomatic breadth —, 84·7; interorbital breadth 28·7, 26·2; cranial breadth 69·3, 72·1; mastoid breadth 86·7, 83·5.

LUTRA CANADENSIS BREVIPILOSUS

Fisher (1942) gives the following figures, taken from a total of 22 speci- 408 mens.

	Averages			Males		Females	
	m.	f.	all	min.	max.	min.	max.
(1)	111·2	108·0	110·1	105·0	115·1	104·7	110·0
(2)	108·0	104·8	106·9	102·1	112·0	101·4	106·5
(3)	99·5	96·5	98·4	94·3	103·5	92·9	98·3
(4)	49·9	48·0	49·1	47·2	54·0	46·7	50·4
(5)	71·6	69·5	71·2	66·4	76·3	67·8	71·3
(6)	65·9	63·6	65·2	63·1	68·4	61·3	65·4
(7)	34·0	33·5	33·9	29·8	37·2	30·1	35·5
(8)	23·9	23·8	23·9	22·1	26·2	22·1	25·2
(9)	26·8	25·4	24·1	24·8	28·0	24·3	26·5
(10)	40·9	40·2	40·5	39·1	41·9	37·1	41·5
(11)	36·3	35·3	35·8	34·3	38·3	33·8	36·6
(12)	20·7	20·8	20·8	18·8	22·6	18·7	22·4

Key: (1) Greatest length of skull; (2) condylobasal length; (3) basilar length of Hensel; (4) palatine length; (5) zygomatic width; (6) mastoid width; (7) postorbital width; (8) interorbital width; (9) width of rostrum; (10) skull height at bullae; (11) height from basioccipital to supraoccipital; (12) least width of frontals.

482   The following figures are taken from Grinnell, Dixon & Linsdale (1937).

Seven males

								Average
A	108·9	111·5	107·7	108·3	111·2	112·2	108·6	109·7
B	108·7	111·8	109·1	108·9	112·7	112·9	110·4	110·6
C	97·5	99·9	98·3	97·4	101·1	102·5	99·8	99·5
D	48·1	49·2	48·7	48·7	49·4	51·6	50·2	49·4
E	73·7	75·4	72·2	72·5	71·9	73·9	68·3	72·5
F	66·5	67·3	66·3	66·9	65·3	68·1	64·1	66·3
G	32·7	34·3	36·0	37·7	33·7	35·1	34·8	34·9
H	22·6	24·9	22·8	26·3	24·3	23·6	23·8	24·0
I	25·9	26·8	26·1	26·5	26·3	26·0	26·2	26·2
J	41·7	41·5	41·8	41·2	39·8	42·1	40·3	41·2

Six females

							Average
A	108·6	106·9	107·9	105·1	104·6	105·1	106·3
B	108·8	108·3	109·3	106·4	104·2	106·5	107·2
C	98·5	97·5	98·4	95·6	93·1	95·7	96·5
D	49·4	48·0	48·4	47·3	47·0	46·5	47·8
E	70·3	69·4	71·7	68·2	71·4	69·4	70·1
F	64·4	65·6	65·0	61·8	61·1	64·1	63·7
G	35·8	35·9	33·0	32·9	34·9	30·3	33·8
H	23·4	24·3	25·2	23·2	23·8	22·3	23·7
I	24·4	25·5	25·9	24·3	24·7	24·4	24·8
J	41·4	41·3	41·6	39·7	42·0	40·5	41·1

Key: A, Greatest length of skull; B, condylobasal length; C, basilar length; D, palatilar length; E, zygomatic breadth; F, mastoid breadth; G, breadth across postorbital processes; H, interorbital width; I, width of rostrum; J, height of braincase at bullae.

1120   The following dimensions are given by Swenk, 1918 (1920).
Total length of skull 109·5; greatest zygomatic width 75·3; mastoid width 67·1; least interorbital width 24·9; width across postorbital constriction 20·0. These are the figures for the type, an adult female.

LUTRA CANADENSIS CANADENSIS

505   Hall & Kelson characterize the skull of *L. canadensis* as follows:
'Skull strongly flattened; muzzle short; braincase broad, long, arched; interorbital breadth less than width of muzzle; infraorbital foramen as

large as, or larger than, alveolus of canine; orbit open, postorbital processes varying from large to rudimentary; alisphenoid canal absent; opening of external auditory meatus large; parioccipital process not in contact with bulla.'

The measurements of the skulls of two adult males, from Maine and Massachusetts, are quoted by Pohle: [923]

Condylobasal length	109·0	112·0
Interorbital length	25·5	26·0
Width across postorbital processes	37·0	38·0
Intertemporal breadth	21·5	22·0
Intertemporal length	14·0	15·0
Mastoid breadth	66·0	69·0
Zygomatic width	73·5	76·0

LUTRA CANADENSIS CHIMO

Pohle gives the following figures for six adults from Labrador: [923]

A	–	c. 105·0	99·0	110·3	103·5	92·9
B	23·0	20·8	22·2	25·3	25·0	21·7
C	35·0	29·0	36·0	33·0	36·6	31·4
D	19·0	20·0	18·3	20·0	20·4	20·4
E	67·0	65·0	63·9	63·4	68·1	60·7
F	74·5	72·5	72·7	73·6	76·4	66·3

Key: A, Basal length; B, interorbital length; C, width across postorbital processes; D, intertemporal breadth; E, mastoid breadth; F, zygomatic width. Note: c. indicates condylobasal length.

LUTRA CANADENSIS DEGENER

Bangs (1898a) gives the following measurements of (a) a young adult male and (b) an old adult female: [148]

	(a)	(b)
Basal length	94·6	95·4
Zygomatic breadth	66·8	70·0
Mastoid breadth	60·0	63·0
Interorbital constriction	22·2	22·8
Greatest constriction behind postorbital process	18·8	19·4
Distance across postorbital processes	32·4	33·6
Greatest length of single half of mandible	63·2	65·8

OTTERS

1120   Swenk, 1918 (1920) gives the cranial dimensions of the type, a young adult male, as follows:

Total length of skull	101·0
Zygomatic width	66·0
Mastoid width	60·0
Least interorbital width	22·0
Width across postorbital processes	32·5
Postorbital constriction	19·5

LUTRA CANADENSIS EVEXA

452   The following are Goldman's figures for the type and for an adult female topotype.

	ad. m.	ad. f.
Condylobasal length	113·4	107·8
Zygomatic breadth	78·0	74·9
Breadth of braincase across mastoid processes	69·5	63·9
Height of braincase over audital bullae	44·5	40·4
Interorbital breadth	25·4	22·8
Postorbital constriction	22·9	21·1
Palatal constriction	14·6	13·9

LUTRA CANADENSIS EXTERA

452   The dimensions of the type skull, that of an adult, probably male, are given by Goldman as follows:
Condylobasal length 112·3; zygomatic width 74·7; breadth of braincase across mastoid processes 67·6; height of braincase over audital bullae 40·3; interorbital breadth 24·3; postorbital constriction 19·4; palatal constriction 13·7.

LUTRA CANADENSIS INTERIOR

1120   Swenk, 1918 (1920) gives the following as the measurements of the skull of the type, an old male:
Total length of skull 112·0; greatest zygomatic width 74·5; mastoid width 66·5; least interorbital width 24·0; width across postorbital processes 35·7; postorbital constriction 21·5.

284   The following figures are given by Cockrum (1952).

	m.	f.
Basilar length (Hensel)	103·0	–
Interorbital constriction	–	43·0
Mastoid breadth	66·5	62·8
Zygomatic breadth	74·5	70·8

328

LUTRA CANADENSIS KODIACENSIS

Goldman gives the following dimensions for (a) the type, and (b) another [452] adult, probably male.

	(a)	(b)
Condylobasal length	111·5	116·0
Zygomatic breadth	72·7	74·4
Breadth of braincase across mastoid processes	65·9	66·5
Height of braincase over audital bullae	40·6	40·5
Interorbital breadth	24·3	24·2
Postorbital constriction	21·3	21·0
Palatal constriction	14·5	15·3

LUTRA CANADENSIS LATAXINA

Elliot (1901) gives the following: [368]
Occiput to anterior end of maxilla 100·0; zygomatic width 69·5; mastoid width 65·0; interorbital constriction 22·8; postorbital constriction 20·0.

Swenk 1918 (1920) gives these measurements: [1120]
Total length of skull 104·0; greatest zygomatic width 71·0; mastoid width 62·0; least interorbital width 22·0; width across postorbital processes 33·0; postorbital constriction 22·0.

LUTRA CANADENSIS MIRA

Goldman gives the following figures for (a) the type, a young adult male, [452] and (b) a young female topotype.

	(a)	(b)
Condylobasal length	127·7	114·9
Zygomatic breadth	84·8	71·2
Breadth of braincase across mastoid processes	80·1	71·1
Height of braincase over audital bullae	42·2	49·9
Interorbital breadth	31·5	26·7
Postorbital constriction	19·6	23·4
Palatal constriction	16·1	16·0

LUTRA CANADENSIS NEXA

Goldman gives the following figures for (a) the type, an adult male, and [452] (b) an adult female.

	(a)	(b)
Condylobasal length	113·7	111·4
Zygomatic breadth	75·0	70·7
Breadth of braincase across mastoid processes	71·2	69·0
Height of braincase over audital bullae	42·6	40·6
Interorbital breadth	–	23·6
Postorbital constriction	20·6	21·4
Palatal constriction	15·2	14·4

LUTRA CANADENSIS OPTIVA

452   Goldman gives the following figures for (a) the type, an adult male, and (b) an adult female.

	(a)	(b)
Condylobasal length	116·0	111·7
Zygomatic breadth	79·7	75·3
Breadth of braincase across mastoid processes	72·6	67·8
Height of braincase over audital bullae	40·0	38·0
Interorbital breadth	27·8	25·9
Postorbital constriction	20·1	18·6
Palatal constriction .	15·0	13·6

LUTRA CANADENSIS PACIFICA

1120   Swenk, 1918 (1920) gives the dimensions of the skull of the type, a young adult male, as follows:

Total length of skull	115·5
Greatest zygomatic width	72·5
Mastoid width	69·0
Least interorbital width	25·0
Width across postorbital processes	36·5
Postorbital constriction	20·0

923   Pohle quotes the following figures for four adult females.

Condylobasal length	110·5	113·5	119·0	110·0
Interorbital length	29·0	27·3	34·0	27·0
Width across postorbital processes	43·0	41·0	49·0	41·5
Intertemporal breadth	21·5	24·0	25·0	18·0
Mastoid breadth	70·0	70·4	76·0	73·0
Zygomatic width	77·0	74·5	83·0	78·0

LUTRA CANADENSIS PERICLYZOMAE

371   The dimensions of the skull of the type, sex unstated, are given by Elliot, 1905 (1906) as follows:

Total length of skull	122·0
Hensel	107·0
Zygomatic width	81·0
Intertemporal constriction	20·0
Width of postorbital processes	40·0
Width of rostrum at canines	30·5
Palatal length	55·0
Total length of mandible	76·0
Length of upper toothrow	40·0

LUTRA CANADENSIS PREBLEI

Goldman gives the following dimensions for (a) the type, an adult male, and (b) an adult female.

452

	(a)	(b)
Condylobasal length	116·7	111·1
Zygomatic breadth	79·2	71·8
Breadth of braincase across mastoid processes	69·0	67·0
Height of braincase over audital bullae	39·9	38·5
Interorbital breadth	25·6	26·5
Postorbital constriction	19·0	22·0
Palatal constriction	14·3	14·0

LUTRA CANADENSIS SONORA

Grinnell, Dixon & Linsdale give these measurements for a male and female, both from San Bernadino County, Cal.

482

	m.	f.
Greatest length of skull	129·9	118·5
Basilar length	117·4	106·1
Palatilar length	57·4	51·9
Zygomatic breadth	82·3	74·3
Mastoid breadth	75·5	71·9
Breadth across postorbital processes	41·2	36·9
Interorbital width	29·9	26·3
Width of rostrum	31·8	28·3
Height of braincase at bullae	44·8	42·8

A few further measurements are given by Elliot (1904):

369

Occipito-nasal length	88·6
Greatest zygomatic width	73·2
Basal length of Hensel	96·0
Palatal length	48·0

Goodwin gives the following as the dimensions of the type, an adult ? female [see original text].
Greatest length of skull 114·0; zygomatic breadth 75·0; length of maxillary toothrow 36·2.

459

LUTRA CANADENSIS TEXENSIS

Goldman gives the following measurements of (a) the type, an adult male, and (b) an adult female topotype.

452

	(a)	(b)
Condylobasal length	112·3	109·8
Zygomatic breadth	73·8	69·4
Breadth of braincase across mastoid processes	69·1	66·3
Height of braincase over audital bullae	42·2	39·7
Interorbital breadth	24·6	24·1
Postorbital constriction	19·5	17·9
Palatal constriction	15·8	14·2

LUTRA CANADENSIS VAGA

368   Elliot (1901) gives the dimensions of the type, a young adult male, as follows:

Basal length 106·6; zygomatic breadth 71·0; mastoid breadth 71·2; interorbital constriction 24·0; greatest constriction 18·6; width across postorbital processes 35·0; length of single half of mandible 74·4.

1120   Swenk gives these measurements, presumably relating to a male:
Total length of skull 116·0; greatest zygomatic width 79·0; mastoid width 76·5; least interorbital width 27·0; width across postorbital processes 39·5; postorbital constriction 20·5.

923   Pohle gives the following for an adult female:
Basal length 99·0; interorbital length 21·4; width across postorbital processes 30·0; intertemporal breadth 17·8; mastoid breadth 67·0; zygomatic width 72·0.

LUTRA CANADENSIS VANCOUVERENSIS

452   Goldman gives the measurements of the type, an adult male, as follows.
Condylobasal length 120·0; zygomatic breadth 89·8; breadth of braincase across mastoid processes 77·9; height of braincase over audital bullae 41·1; interorbital breadth 29·1; postorbital constriction 20·6; palatal constriction 15·7.

LUTRA CANADENSIS YUKONENSIS

452   Goldman gives the measurements of the type, an adult female, as follows:
Condylobasal length 105·3; zygomatic breadth 73·8; breadth of braincase across mastoid processes 65·3; height of braincase over audital bullae 39·5; interorbital breadth 24·9; postorbital constriction 21·1; palatal constriction 15·0.

332

LUTRA ANNECTENS ANNECTENS

Although Major (1897b) gives a number of cranial measurements these [755] are of little direct use owing to his unusual treatment of them. Being concerned as he was to compare *canadensis* and *enudris* with *annectens*, he first averaged the measurements of the skulls available to him and then reduced these results to a common base for the sake of comparison. From the figures he gives it does not appear possible to 'reconstruct' the original dimensions.

He does, however, give the true measurements of the male type of *annectens*, as follows:
Basal length 106·2; greatest breadth 79·8; cranial breadth over audital bullae 63·5; breadth between upper canines 30·0; interorbital breadth 26·0; greatest posterior breadth 77·2; palatal length 48·7.

Elliot (1904) notes of one example: [369]
Basal length 97·8; greatest breadth 75·1; palatal length 45·9–46·5.

J.A.Allen (1904) gives the following figures: [20]
Occipito-nasal length 118·0; basal length 112·0; zygomatic breadth 83·0; interorbital breadth 25·5; postorbital breadth 18·0; mastoid breadth 76·0; length of palatal floor 48·0.

Thomas (1908) gives for a male skull: [1147]
Condylobasal length 117·0; zygomatic breadth 80·0; mastoid breadth 78·0.

J.A.Allen (1910b) gives the following figures for an adult male: [26]
Condylobasal length 113·0; palatal length 45·0; zygomatic breadth 68·0; interorbital breadth 21·0; postorbital breadth 18·5; width across postorbital processes 32·0; mastoid breadth 65·0; length of lower jaw 62·5.

Pohle shows the following for an adult male from Durango: [923]
Basal length 113·0; interorbital breadth 27·8; width across postorbital processes 35·0?; intertemporal breadth 21·0; mastoid breadth 83·7; zygomatic breadth 85·0.

LUTRA ANNECTENS COLOMBIANA

J.A.Allen (1904) gives the measurements of four examples. Of these the [20] first and third are females, the sex of the other two being unknown. The first is the type specimen.

Occipito-nasal length	107·0	103·0	98·0	103·5
Basal length	101·0	98·0	94·0	92·6
Zygomatic breadth	67·0	–	66·0	64·0
Interorbital breadth	22·0	22·3	21·6	19·0
Postorbital breadth	15·0	15·0	16·3	18·5
Mastoid breadth	64·6	64·0	61·0	–
Length of palatal floor	43·5	43·0	41·0	42·0

LUTRA ANNECTENS LATIDENS

26   J.A.Allen (1910b) gives the following figures for an adult male:
Condylobasal length 117·0; palatal length 52·0; zygomatic width 76·5;
interorbital breadth 25·0; postorbital breadth 19·0; width of postorbital
processes 36·0; mastoid breadth 75·0; length of lower jaw 72·0.

458   Goodwin (1946) gives the length of the maxillary toothrow (c–m^1) in an
459   adult male from Honduras as 38·5, and the same author (1953) gives for the
type, a young adult male:
Greatest length of skull 107·0; zygomatic breadth 67·0; length of maxillary
toothrow 34·5.

LUTRA ANNECTENS PARILINA

923   Pohle quotes the following figures for the subadult female type:
Condylobasal length 112·0; interorbital breadth 19·7; width across postorbital processes 23·5; mastoid breadth 63·0; zygomatic breadth 64·0.

LUTRA ANNECTENS REPANDA

372   Elliot (1917) gives the following dimensions:
Greatest length of skull 117·2; occipito-nasal length 95·6; Hensel 95·6;
zygomatic width 72·0; intertemporal breadth 23·1; mastoid width 69·9;
palatal length 49·8.

LUTRA ENUDRIS ENUDRIS

1147   According to Thomas (1908) the type skull has a 'length' of 112·0 and
a 'breadth' of 80·0 mm.

923   Pohle gives the following figures for an adult male from Surinam:
Basal length 111·3; intertemporal breadth 25·7; width across postorbital
processes 37·2; intertemporal breadth 25·7; mastoid breadth 78·8; zygomatic width 85·?.

LUTRA ENUDRIS INSULARIS

20   J.A.Allen (1904) gives figures for this race as follows:
Occipito-nasal length 107·0; basal length 104·5; zygomatic breadth 70·5;
interorbital breadth 22·0; postorbital breadth 18·5; mastoid breadth 76·5;
length of palatal floor 45·0.

LUTRA ENUDRIS MITIS

1147   Thomas (1908) gives the following measurements for the type, an adult
male.

334

Condylobasal length 103·5; basal length 94·5; zygomatic breadth 68·0; mastoid breadth 65·0; interorbital breadth 20·0; height of braincase 37·0; length of palate 47·0.

LUTRA FELINA

Pohle gives the measurements of two skulls, both adult. 923

Basal length	90·?	87·5
Interorbital breadth	24·0	22·3
Width across postorbital processes	31·0	27·7
Intertemporal breadth	65·8	58·8
Zygomatic width	–	64·5

LUTRA INCARUM

Thomas gives the following figures relating to an old male. 1147
Condylobasal length 118·0; mastoid breadth 72·0; zygomatic breadth 77·5; interorbital breadth 24·8; length of palate 54·0.

The following figures from Sanborn relate to two females, the first from 1006
the Marcapata River and the other from Huajyumbe.

Greatest length of skull	105·8	112·6
Condylobasal length	103·4	112·4
Palatal length	44·6	44·9
Interorbital width	20·6	20·8
Intertemporal width	15·1	18·3
Zygomatic width	67·3	68·4
Mastoid width	61·3	61·6
Width of braincase	56·0	56·3

LUTRA MESOPETES

Cabrera (1924) gives the following figures for the adult female type. 251
Condylobasal length 86·0; palatal length 41·5; zygomatic breadth 56·4; interorbital breadth 17·0; postorbital constriction 14·0; breadth of braincase 45·0; mastoid breadth 51·4.

LUTRA PLATENSIS

From amongst the numerous examples of this form listed by Pohle the 923
following are selected on the basis that they are all fully adult and of a determinate sex, the first six being male and the remainder female.

	A	B	C	D	E	F
(1)	105·0	23·5	35·0	16·3	75·0	75·6
(2)	107·1	23·3	36·7	18·7	76·8	79·5
(3)	104·8	22·8	32·5	15·4	76·6	78·5
(4)	111·5	24·8	38·3	16·0	80·5	83·3
(5)	110·3	26·0	32·5	21·9	77·9	84·3
(6)	104·7	24·8	38·?	14·9	75·3	79·9
(7)	94·3	19·3	29·3	16·0	64·2	66·7
(8)	90·7	20·8	32·8	18·0	63·5	67·0
(9)	93·0	19·7	30·6	15·2	67·2	68·0
(10)	97·5	21·6	32·8	15·3	64·6	69·3
(11)	89·1	22·0	22·2	15·3	60·0	66·1
(12)	96·0	20·3	27·7	15·2	–	63·2

Key: A, Basal length; B, interorbital breadth; C, width across postorbital processes; D, intertemporal breadth; E, mastoid breadth; F, zygomatic breadth.
(1)–(3) Rio Grande do Sul; (4) and (5) Mundo Novo; (6) Jaragua; (7)–(9) Rio Grande do Sul; (10) Ararangua; (11) Ypanema; (12) Piracicaba.

LUTRA PROVOCAX

1147

Thomas (1908) gives the following figures for an old male example. Condylobasal length 115·0; basal length 106·0; zygomatic breadth 78·5; mastoid breadth 74·0; interorbital breadth 25·0; palatal length 56·0.

923

Pohle lists three additional adult specimens, all from Puerto Montt:

	A	B	C	D	E	F
(1)	108·7	25·9	33·9	16·6	77·8	81·5
(2)	102·6	22·2	30·4	17·6	75·3	78 – ?
(3)	–	24·5	30·8	18·8	–	–

Key: Letters A–F as in the preceding table.

PTERONURA BRASILIENSIS

As is not uncommonly found when dealing with this genus, there is some confusion as to which is the typical form *brasiliensis* and which is *paranensis*. In many cases the only certain method of deciding this seems to be on geographic grounds. Pohle's division appears to be correct, apart from the unnecessary intrusion of '*lupina*'. But Nehring's figures of 1886 ostensibly relating to *paranensis* seem to me almost certainly to apply not to *Pteronura* at all but to *L. platensis*, while his measurements of *brasiliensis* are to be applied – geographically – to *paranensis*. It is to be noted that Nehring's specimens came from Mundo Novo, Rio Grande do Sul, and not Mundo Novo, Bahia.

923
846

336

PTERONURA BRASILIENSIS BRASILIENSIS

Pohle gives full measurements for two adults, one from Para and the other from ? Bahia.

923

Condylobasal length	147·1	147·5
Basal length	136·5	135·?
Interorbital breadth	18·6	16·2
Width across postorbital processes	23·8	19·2
Intertemporal length	32·0	27·0
Mastoid breadth	75·3	77·3
Zygomatic width	93·7	92·1

PTERONURA BRASILIENSIS PARANENSIS

The following are Pohle's figures for two adult females:

923

Condylobasal length	148·0	154·0
Basal length	135·0	142·0
Width across postorbital processes	31·0	24·6
Interorbital breadth	19·3	18·4
Intertemporal length	37·0	34·0
Mastoid breadth	97·7	85·2
Zygomatic width	97·4	97·9

Nehring (1886) gives for an adult male:

846

Basilar length of skull 142·0; total length of skull 157·0; greatest zygomatic width 99·0; width of mastoid processes 88·0; height of forehead of skull (including lower jaw) 74·0.

Vieira gives the following figures for a male and female respectively:

1175

Condylobasal length	149·0	164·0
Total length	150·0	165·0
Zygomatic breadth	98·0	98·0
Length of mandible	105·0	105·0

ENHYDRA LUTRIS

Ognev (1931) remarks that compared to the male the female skull is markedly smaller. In addition, the female crests are weaker; the zygomatic arches are less massive; the palate is narrower; and the teeth are much smaller.

864

He adds:

In very young sea otters in which canines and incisors are beginning to emerge, and with skulls having a maximum length of only approximately 78 mm., the entire occipital part of the skull is extremely well developed, while the rostrum is very slightly developed . . . thus the length of the brain case in a young otter constitutes 83% of the total skull length, while the length of the nasal region is 24% that of the brain case. In adults markedly different ratios are observed, the first . . . being approximately 55% and the second 45%. In addition, the occipital section is very expanded, height [being up to] 54% of total skull length. In adults this figure is approximately 44% . . .

The following changes take place with age: development of orbits; elongation of facial portion; appearance of slightly marked and bluntly rounded supraorbital processes, and slightly marked postorbital constriction, its width in a skull 120 mm. long [being] not less than [the] interorbital distance.

505   Hall & Kelson characterize the skull of *Enhydra* as

High, inflated, flattened dorsally; facial region broad and flat; orbits relatively large; postorbital processes small; auditory bullae small; palate extending posterior to plane of M1 only a short distance.

864   Ognev gives the following measurements:

	A	B	C	D	E	F	G	H
(1)	140·6	128·5	134·2	125·2	134·7	139·9	127·0	137·0
(2)	122·0	112·6	118·9	107·8	117·9	117·3	112·8	118·1
(3)	139·0	128·2	133·0	123·1	137·2	136·0	126·1	137·0
(4)	106·8	96·1	108·3	93·2	106·7	105·0	91·3	110·1
(5)	42·8	38·1	46·0	40·0	44·9	41·1	37·0	46·5
(6)	99·5	94·2	97·3	88·0	104·0	98·3	89·0	108·0
(7)	60·0	57·3	60·0	48·1	59·2	58·0	53·5	60·2
(8)	48·1	48·6	47·1	46·0	47·0	48·0	46·0	50·0
(9)	54·0	51·0	54·1	50·0	51·3	53·2	49·0	53·3
(10)	21·7	17·2	15·0	15·3	21·8	22·0	14·0	20·6
(11)	62·1	56·7	61·1	62·0	65·3	61·0	60·2	65·0

Key: (1) Overall length of skull; (2) basal length; (3) condylobasal length; (4) zygomatic width; (5) interorbital width; (6) maximum width of mastoid processes; (7) length of palate; (8) length of upper toothrow; (9) length of lower toothrow; (10) length of interorbital space, from end of postorbital process to maximum interorbital compression; (11) height in region of osseous bullae.
A, Mednyi Island, m. sen.; B, Mednyi Island, f. sen.; C, Bering Island, m. sen.; D, Bering Island, f. ad.; E, Aleutian Islands, m. sen.; F, Commander Islands, m. sen.; G, Commander Islands, f. ad.; H, Kamchatka, m. sen.

864   In his general diagnosis Ognev gives the following range:

	males	females
Overall length of skull	130·0–143·2	121·0–128·5
Condylobasal length	130·5–144·0	120·2–128·2
Width between mastoid processes	93·9–108·0	88·0– 95·3
Height in region of osseous bullae	56·2– 67·1	–
Length of upper toothrow	46·2– 51·4	44·3– 48·6

338

369   Elliot (1904) gives these measurements:

Occipito-nasal length 111·0; Hensel length 109·0; zygomatic width 98·0; width of postorbital processes 48·0; interorbital constriction 28·0; mastoid breadth 96·0; palatal length 56·0; length of braincase 62·0.

923   Pohle gives the cranial dimensions of three adults, these originating from (a) the Bering Straits, (b) Sanak, (c) unknown.

	(a)	(b)	(c)
Basal length	118·9	115·9	116·0
Interorbital breadth	40·3	–	41·0
Width across postorbital process	44·6	–	43·9
Intertemporal breadth	29·8	32·3	30·5
Intertemporal length	21·0	15·0	17·0
Mastoid breadth	100·4	94·2	96·3
Zygomatic width	103·1	97·7	99·0
Palatal length	61·8	60·7	58·0

All the preceding measurements are given in millimetres.

Glossary

Adpressed: pressed close to; lying flat (of fur).

Aliform: wing-shaped.

Altricial: requiring care or nursing after birth.

Apical: of, or belonging to, an apex or tip.

Apophysis: a natural protuberance or process arising from, and forming a continuous part of, a bone.

Canescent: hoary; dull white or greyish.

Canthus: the outer or inner corner of the eye, where the lids meet.

Carnassial: (sectorial) in carnivores, in the upper jaw, the most posterior of the teeth which have predecessors, i.e. PM⁴; in the lower jaw, the most anterior of the teeth without predecessors in the milk dentition, i.e. M₁.

Carpus: that part of the skeleton uniting the hand to the forearm, i.e. the 'wrist'; adj. *carpal*.

Cheek teeth: molars and premolars.

Coriaceous: resembling leather in texture or appearance.

Cotype: one of that group of zoological specimens on which a new nominal species is jointly based.

Diastema: a space between two teeth.

Dilatation: the action or process of dilating.

Distal: situated further from the main part; terminal; the opposite of *proximal*.

Follicle: a simple lymphatic gland in the form of a sac.

Fulvous: reddish-yellow; tawny; dull yellowish-brown.

Genal: relating to the cheek.

Hallucal: of or belonging to the innermost of the digits of the hind foot, i.e. the 'big toe'.

Inguinal: belonging to, or situated in, the groin.

Interramal: situated between the rami or branches of the lower jaw.

Kahlan or *Kalan:* native name for the sea otter.

Mesial: median; in the middle; adj. *mesially*, centrally.

Metacarpus: that part of the hand between the wrist and the fingers, i.e. the 'palm'.

Nearctic (region): temperate and arctic North America, with Greenland.

Neotropical (region): that part of the American continent south of, and including, Mexico.

Palaearctic (region): Europe to the Azores and Iceland, temperate Asia from the high Himalaya and west to the Indus, with Japan, and China from Ningpo and to the north of the watershed of the Yang-tse-kiang; also North Africa and Arabia, to about the line of the tropic of Cancer.

Papilla: any minute nipple-like protuberance, e.g. the *papillae* of the tongue.

Phalange: a bone of the finger or toe.

Plantar: pertaining to the sole of the foot.

Pollical: relating to the innermost digit of the forefoot, i.e. the 'thumb'.

Porrect: stretched out; extended.

Proximal: situated nearer to the main part; opposite of *distal*.

Recent: in geology, that time division which embraces the youngest of all the formations; holocene; post-glacial.

Rhinarium: the nose, especially in animals that part naked of hair.

Rugosity: a wrinkle or corrugation; a protuberant roughness.

Sectorial: see *carnassial*.

Septum: the partition between the nostrils.

Sigmoid: crescent-shaped; semicircular.

Spraint: the excrement of an otter.

Superciliary: of or pertaining to the eyebrow.

Suture: the junction of two bones forming an immovable articulation, especially those of the cranium.

Tarsus: the flat part of the foot between the toes and the heel, i.e. the 'sole'.

Terete: having a cylindrical or slightly tapering form, circular in cross-section.

Topotype: a zoological specimen of the same species and from the same place as the *type*.

Tragus: the prominence at the entrance to the external ear, in front of and partly closing the orifice.

Type: that specimen selected by the original author on which to base a new nominal species.

Vibrissae: stiff or bristly hairs, especially those growing from the face; whiskers.

For an explanation of cranial terms see plates 50–52.

A few words are included in the above list on the grounds that although they do not appear in the text they occur fairly frequently in the literature.

Biblography and List of References

AELLEN, V., *see* Perret, J-L. & Aellen, V.

1 AGACINO, E.M.(1933) Datos y observaciones sobres algunos mamíferos marroquíes. *Boln Soc. esp. hist. nat.* **33**: 262

2 AGACINO, E.M.(1945) Algunos datos sobre ciento mamíferos del Sáhara occidental. *Boln Soc. esp. hist. nat.* **43**: 201–203

3 AITKEN, E.H.(1886) [Editor] Catalogue of the mammalia in the collection of the Society. *J. Bombay nat. hist. Soc.* **1**: 9

4 ALDERMAN, C.W.(1884) An otter on board a yacht. *Field* **63**: 560

5 ALDRICH, J.W. & BOLE, B.P. (1937) The birds and mammals ... of the Azuero Peninsula (Republic of Panama). *Scient. Publs Cleveland Mus. nat. hist.* **7**: 158–159

6 ALDROVANDI, U.(1645) *De quadruped' digitatis oviparis.* **2**: 292–295. Bologna

7 ALIX, M.E.(1879) Sur une tête de loutre marine ... *Bull. Soc. zool. Fr.* **4**: 119–123

8 ALLAN, A.(1910) *Hunting the sea otter.* 188 pp. London: Horace Cox

9 ALLANSON, A.I.(1955) Sea otters on San Miguel. *Pacif. Disc.* **8**(3): 24–25

10 ALLEN, G.M.(1929) Mustelids from the Asiatic expeditions. *Am. Mus. Novit.* No. 358: 1–12

11 ALLEN, G.M.(1938) *The mammals of China and Mongolia.* **1**: 402–417. New York: Amer. Mus. nat. Hist.

12 ALLEN, G.M. (1939) A checklist of African mammals. *Bull. Mus. comp. Zool. Harv.* **83**: 186–188

13 ALLEN, G.M. & COOLIDGE, J.H.Jr. (1940) Mammal and bird collections of the Asiatic primate expedition. *Bull. Mus. comp. Zool. Harv.* **87**(3): 150

14 ALLEN, J.A.(1869a) Notes on the mammals of Iowa. *Proc. Boston Soc. nat. Hist.* **12**: 183

15 ALLEN, J.A.(1869b) Catalogue of the mammals of Massachusetts. *Bull. Mus. comp. Zool. Harv.* **1**: 178

16 ALLEN, J.A.(1876) Geographical variation among North American mammals. *Bull. U.S. geol. geog. Surv. Terr.* **2**(4): 331

17 ALLEN, J.A.(1895) On the names of mammals given by Kerr ... *Bull. Am. Mus. nat. Hist.* **7**: 188

18 ALLEN, J.A.(1898a) Sea otter. *Am. nat.* **32**: 356–358

19 ALLEN, J.A.(1898b) Nomenclatorial notes on certain North American mammals. *Bull. Am. Mus. nat. Hist.* **10**: 459–460

20 ALLEN, J.A.(1904). Report on mammals from ... Santa Marta, Colombia. *Bull. Am. Mus. nat. Hist.* **20**: 452

342

21 ALLEN, J.A. (1906a) Mammals from . . . Sinaloa and Jalisco. *Bull. Am. Mus. nat. Hist.* **22**: 235

22 ALLEN, J.A. (1906b) Mammals from the island of Hainan, China. *Bull. Am. Mus. nat. Hist.* **22**: 479–480

23 ALLEN, J.A. (1908) Mammals from Nicaragua. *Bull. Am. Mus. nat. Hist.* **24**: 660–661

24 ALLEN, J.A. (1909) Mammals from Shen-si province, China. *Bull. Am. Mus. nat. Hist.* **26**: 430

25 ALLEN, J.A. (1910a) Mammals from Palawan Island, Philippine Islands. *Bull. Am. Mus. nat. Hist.* **28**: 17

26 ALLEN, J.A. (1910b) Additional mammals from Nicaragua. *Bull. Am. Mus. nat. Hist.* **28**: 104–105

27 ALLEN, J.A. (1910c) Mammals from the Caura district of Venezuela. *Bull. Am. Mus. nat. Hist.* **28**: 146

28 ALLEN, J.A. (1919) Preliminary notes on African carnivora. *J. Mammal.* **1**: 23–25

29 ALLEN, J.A. (1920) [Footnote to] Thomas, O. (1920). (Q.V.): 225

30 ALLEN, J.A. (1922) Carnivora collected by the American Museum Congo expedition. *Bull. Am. Mus. nat. Hist.* **47**: 84–108

31 ALLEN, J.A. & CHAPMAN, F.M. (1893) On a collection of mammals from the island of Trinidad. *Bull. Am. Mus. nat. Hist.* **5**: 208–209

32 ALSTON, E.R. (1866) Notes on the quadrupeds of Lanarkshire. *Zoologist* (2) **1**: 10

33 ALSTON, E.R. (1872) The otter. *Field* **39**: 184

34 ALSTON, E.R. (1881) Mammalia. *Biologia Centrali-Americana* **6**: 86–87

35 AMES, A.E. (1874) Mammalia of Minnesota. *Bull. Minn. Acad. nat. Sci.* **1**: 69

36 AMUNDSON, R. (1950) Carolina otter. *Iowa Cons.* **9**(9): 65, 69

37 ANDERSON, F.H. (1933) An otter loses his dinner to an osprey. *Yellowstone Nat. Notes* **10**: 7

38 ANDERSON, J. (1878) *Anatomical and zoological researches . . .* **1**: 200–213. London: Bernard Quaritch

39 ANDERSON, J. (1883) *Guide to the Calcutta Zoological Gardens:* 105–106. Calcutta: Honorary Committee of Management

40 ANDERSON, R.M. (1945) Three mammals . . . added to the Quebec list. *Rep. Provancher Soc. nat. Hist. Can.* **1944**: 56–61

41 ANDERSON, R.M. (1947) Catalogue of Canadian recent mammals. *Bull. natn. Mus. Can.* No. 102: 69–72

42 ANDREWS, C.L. (1937) Decline of the sea otter. *Nature Mag.* **29**: 107–108

43 ANDREWS, C.L. (1938) Children of the sea. *Alaska Sportsm.* **4**(7): 8–9, 27–28, 31–32

44 ANNANDALE, N. (1915) Fauna of the Chilka lake. *Mem. Indian Mus.* **5**: 165–166

45 ANNANDALE, N. & ROBINSON, H.C. (1903) *Fasciculi Malayenses.* **1**: 11. London: Universities of Edinburgh and Liverpool

46 ANONYMOUS (1855) The otter. *Field* **5**: 168–169

47 ANONYMOUS (1857) On the Canadian otter . . . *Can. Nat.* **1**: 228–232

48 ANONYMOUS (1858) Otters. *Field* **11**: 263
49 ANONYMOUS (1860) Salmon poaching, otters, coracles. *Field* **15**: 413
50 ANONYMOUS (1861a) Otter-hunting and its influence on fisheries. *Field* **16**: 82
51 ANONYMOUS (1861b) Influence of otter-hunting on fisheries. *Field* **16**: 145
52 ANONYMOUS (1861c) A few words for the otter. *Field* **16**: 169
53 ANONYMOUS (1861d) Spotted otter. *Field* **16**: 438
54 ANONYMOUS (1861e) The otter a poacher. *Field* **17**: 284
55 ANONYMOUS (1862a) Reminiscences of otter-hunting. *Field* **19**: 435
56 ANONYMOUS (1862b) Deeside, Aberdeenshire – the otter. *Field* **19**: 485
57 ANONYMOUS (1862c) Albino, spotted, cream and zebra otters. *Field* **20**: 275
58 ANONYMOUS (1862d) Otters. *Field* **20**: 473
59 ANONYMOUS (1863) The otter. *Field* **22**: 15
60 ANONYMOUS (1864) Tame otter. *Field* **24**: 166
61 ANONYMOUS (1865) Otters caught in eel-nets. *Field* **25**: 301
62 ANONYMOUS (1866a) An otter attacking a man. *Field* **27**: 130
63 ANONYMOUS (1866b) Otters, part 2. *Land Wat.* **1**: 422
64 ANONYMOUS (1867a) [untitled] *Field* **29**: 335
65 ANONYMOUS (1867b) Otters in Cape Colony. *Field* **30**: 31
66 ANONYMOUS (1868a) Otters in the Shannon. *Field* **31**: 482
67 ANONYMOUS (1868b) Curious death of an otter. *Field* **32**: 415
68 ANONYMOUS (1869a) Otter seizing a hooked fish. *Field* **33**: 430
69 ANONYMOUS (1869b) Carlisle otter hounds – an extraordinary hunt. *Field* **34**: 35
70 ANONYMOUS (1870) Large otter. *Field* **35**: 273
71 ANONYMOUS (1871) Large otter. *Field* **37**: 21
72 ANONYMOUS (1873a) The destruction of otters. *Field* **41**: 545
73 ANONYMOUS (1873b) Otters and Wildfowl. *Field* **41**: 545
74 ANONYMOUS (1873c) *Natural history of North China*: 36. Shanghai
75 ANONYMOUS (1876) Otters sinking when shot. *Field* **47**: 678
76 ANONYMOUS (1878) Capture of an otter with a bait for salmon. *Field* **51**: 554
77 ANONYMOUS (1881a) Food of the otter. *Field* **57**: 255
78 ANONYMOUS (1881b) Remarkable capture of otters. *Field* **58**: 275
79 ANONYMOUS (1884a) Otter trapping. *Field* **63**: 406
80 ANONYMOUS (1884b) Otter taking young lambs. *Field* **63**: 447
81 ANONYMOUS (1884c) Otters in Shropshire. *Field* **63**: 488
82 ANONYMOUS (1884d) [A drowned otter.] *Field* **63**: 549
83 ANONYMOUS (1886) Otter in the Menai Straits. *Field* **67**: 172
84 ANONYMOUS (1887) Otters in the Thames. *Field* **69**: 315
85 ANONYMOUS (1888a) Otters attacking a dog. *Field* **71**: 193
86 ANONYMOUS (1888b) Otters and their food. *Field* **71**: 458
87 ANONYMOUS (1888c) Otters and otter hunting. *Field* **71**: 594
88 ANONYMOUS (1888d) The haunt of the otter in Bedfordshire. *Field* **71**: 632
89 ANONYMOUS (1891) Notes. *Fishg Gaz., Lond.* **22**: 213
90 ANONYMOUS (1894) [Notices of new books] *Zoologist* (3) **18**: 74
91 ANONYMOUS (1897) A tame otter. *Field* **89**: 454
92 ANONYMOUS (1898a) Otter killing wild ducks. *Field* **91**: 93

93 ANONYMOUS (1898b) Otter attacking dog in defence of young. *Field* **91**: 242

94 ANONYMOUS (1898c) Otters and otter hunting. *Field* **91**: 488

95 ANONYMOUS (1899a) Country notes. *Ctry Life* **5**: 260

96 ANONYMOUS (1899b) Tame otter. *Ctry Life* **5**: 416

97 ANONYMOUS (1903) The otter hounds of Henry VIII. *Field* **101**: 394

98 ANONYMOUS (1904a) A large dog otter. *Field* **103**: 4

99 ANONYMOUS (1904b) Young otters reared by a cat. *Field* **104**: 327

100 ANONYMOUS (1904c) The preservation of otters. *Field* **104**: 414

101 ANONYMOUS (1904d) The food of otters. *Field* **104**: 955

102 ANONYMOUS (1917) Otter capturing pike. *Field* **130**: 464

103 ANONYMOUS (1922a) Otter in eel trap. *Field* **139**: 692

104 ANONYMOUS (1922b) The otter in Essex. *Field* **140**: 539

105 ANONYMOUS (1938a) Return of the sea otters. *Westways, Beverly Hills* **30**(9): 14–15

106 ANONYMOUS (1938b) The 'extinct' sea otter swims back to life. *Life* **4**(25): 30

107 ANONYMOUS (1938c) Reappearance of the sea otter off the coast of California. *J. Soc. Preserv. Fauna Emp.* N.S. pt. 35: 39–43

108 ANONYMOUS (1941a) Otter breeding. *Am. Fur Breeder* **14**(6): 36

109 ANONYMOUS (1941b) Michigan otter still a puzzle. *Mich. Conserv.* **10**(5): 5

110 ANONYMOUS (1943) Sea otter on exhibit. *Acad. Newsl. Calif. Acad. Sci.* **37**: 3–4

111 ANONYMOUS (1944) Mr. Otter, nature's playboy . . . *Iowa Conserv.* **3**(3): 1, 21

112 ANONYMOUS (1945a) Little is known about breeding otters. *Fur of Canada* **10**(1): 18

113 ANONYMOUS (1945b) Orphan otter found on DeKalb stream. *Outdoor Georgia* **5**(30): 7

114 ANONYMOUS (1949) Otter trapped in Chesterfield County, Virginia. *Va Wildl.* **10**(4): 25

115 ANONYMOUS (1950a) Otters in the stream. *Field* **196**: 255

116 ANONYMOUS (1950b) [untitled] *Ill. Lond. News* **217**: 367

117 ANONYMOUS (1950c) Sea otters to be transplanted along Alaska coast. *Natn. Wildl. Conserv. Dig.* **1**(4): 35–39

118 ANONYMOUS (1950d) 'Old men of the sea' are ready to spread . . . *Nat. Humane Rev., Albany* **38**(5): 9–10

119 ANONYMOUS (1950e) Sea otters to be transplanted along Alaska coast. *Am. Nat. Fur Market J.* **28**(9): 5–6, 17

120 ANONYMOUS (1956) Behind the scenes. *Anim. Kingd.* **59**: 63

121 ANONYMOUS (1963) Hunting the otter. *The Times* July 6

122 ANSELL, W.F.H.(1947) Notes on some Burmese mammals. *J. Bombay nat. hist. Soc.* **48**: 379–383

123 ANSELL, W.F.H.(1960) *Mammals of Northern Rhodesia*: 35. Lusaka: Government Printer

124 ANSELL, W.F.H.(1963) Additional breeding data on Northern Rhodesian mammals. *Puku* **1**: 14–15

125 ANTHONY, A. W.(1925–26) Expedition to Guadalupe Island, Mexico. *Proc. Calif. Acad. Sci.* (4)**14**: 303–304

126 ANTHONY, H.E.(1916) Panama mammals collected in 1914–1915. *Bull. Am. Mus. nat. hist.* **35**: 372–373

127 ANTHONY, H.E.(1928) *Field book of North American mammals*: 114–119. New York: G. P. Putnam

128 APLIN, O.V.(1894) Field notes on the mammals of Uruguay. *Proc. zool. Soc. Lond.* **1894**: 300–301

129 APSTEIN, C.(1915) Nomina conservanda. *Sber. Ges. naturf. Freunde Berl.* **1915**: 198–202

ARISTOTLE, *see* Thompson, D'A.W.

130 AROCA, J.(1944) Los rios de Zamora (Datos y notas). *Publcoës Fed. Esp. Pesca* **1**: 1–30

131 ASHBROOK, F.G.(1948) *Fur farming for profit*: 237–242. New York: Grange Judd Publishing Co.

132 ASHBROOK, F.G. & McMULLEN, H.J.(1928) Fur-bearing animals of the United States (otter). *Fur J.* **2**: 26–27

133 AUDUBON, J.J. & BACHMAN, J.(1851) *Quadrupeds of North America* **2**: 1–12. New York: V.G.Audubon

134 AUDUBON, M.R. & COUES, E.(1898) *Audubon and his Journals.* **1**: various pp. London

135 AYER, M.Y.(1938) What do you know about the sea otter? *Frontiers, Philad.* **3**: 24–26

136 AZARA, F.DE (1802) *Apuntamientos para la Historia natural de los Quadrúpedos del Paragüay.* 304–309. Madrid: La Viuda de Ibarra

BACHMAN, J., *see* Audubon, J.J. & Bachman, J.

137 BAILEY, J.W.(1946) *The mammals of Virginia.* 146–148. Richmond, Va.

138 BAILEY, V.(1905) Biological survey of Texas. *N. Am. Fauna* **25**: 195–196

139 BAILEY, V.(1909) Otter as a fur bearer. *Am. Breed. Mag.* **5**: 313–320

140 BAILEY, V.(1918) *Wild animals of Glacier National Park*: 85. Washington: Dept. Int. Natl Pk Service

141 BAILEY, V.(1924) The otter. *Nature Mag.* **4**: 237–238

142 BAILEY, V.(1926) A biological survey of North Dakota. *N. Am. Fauna* **49**: 179–181

143 BAILEY, V.(1930) *Animal life of Yellowstone National Park*: 142. Springfield, Ill.

144 BAILEY, V.(1932) Mammals of New Mexico. *N. Am. Fauna* **53**: 323–324

145 BAILEY, V.(1936) The mammals and life zones of Oregon. *N. Am. Fauna* **55**: 56, 301–302

146 BAIRD, S.F.(1857) *Mammals. General Report upon the Zoology of the several Pacific Railroad Routes*: 184–190. Washington, D.C.

147 BALSTON, R.J.(1873) Otter and wildfowl. *Field* **41**: 463

148 BANGS, O.(1898a) Descriptions of the Newfoundland Otter … *Proc. biol. Soc. Wash.* **12**: 35–36

149 BANGS, O.(1898b) The land mammals of peninsular Florida and the coast region of Georgia. *Proc. Boston Soc. nat. Hist.* **28**: 224–227

150 BANHAM, P.R.(1965) Otter (*Lutra lutra*). *Norfolk Bird Mammal Rep.* **20**: 245–246

151 BANKO, W.E.(1960) The trumpeter swan. *N. Am. Fauna* **63**: 132

152 BANKS, E.(1931) A popular account of the mammals of Borneo. *J. Malay. Brch R. Asiat. Soc.* **9**(2): 60–61

153 BARABASH-NIKIFOROV, I.(1935). The sea otters of the Commander Islands. *J. Mammal.* **16**: 255–261

154 BARABASH-NIKIFOROV, I.(1938a) [The sea otter and the stages in its study] *Priroda, Mosk.* **1938**(2): 51–61

155 BARABASH-NIKIFOROV, I.(1938b) Mammals of the Commander Islands . . . *J. Mammal.* **19**: 426

156 BARABASH-NIKIFOROV, I.(1958) [Conservation of *Enhydra lutris*] *Zool. Zh.* **37**: 1104–1105

157 BARABASH-NIKIFOROV, I.(1963) *Der Seeotter oder Kalan* . . . Wittenberg Lutherstadt: A. Ziemsen. 92 pp.

158 BARGER, N.R.(1950) Otter. *Wisc. Conserv. Bull.* **15**: 33

159 BARNES, C.T.(1927) Utah mammals. *Bull. Univ. Utah* **17** (12): 47

160 BARNSTON, G.(1863) Remarks on the genus *Lutra* . . . *Can. Nat. Geol.* (1) 8. **12**: 147–188

161 BARRÈRE, P.(1749) *Essai sur l'histoire naturelle de la France equinoxiale*: **155**. Paris: Piget

162 BARRETT-HAMILTON, G.E.H.(1912) Biological survey of Clare Island. Pt 17. Mammalia *Proc. R. Ir. Acad.* **31**

163 BARTELS, M.Jr.(1937) Zur Kenntnis der verbreitung und der lebensweise javanischer Säugetiere. *Treubia* **16**: 161–163

164 BASILIO, R.P.A.(1952) *La vida animal en la Guinea española*. Madrid: Marca la Ley. 149 pp.

165 BATTEN, H.M.(1930) Otters Trail . . . *Field* **155**: 692

166 BAYLIS, H.A.(1923) New ascarid from an otter. *Ann. Mag. nat. Hist.* (9)**11**: 459–463

167 BECHSTEIN, J.M.(1800) *Thomas Pennant's allgemeine übersicht der vierfüssigen Thiere.* **2**: 401–408. Weimar

168 BEECHEY, F.W.(1831) *Narrative of a voyage to the Pacific* . . . London: Colburn & Bentley

BEER, J.R., *see* Gunderson, H.L. & Beer, J.R.

169 BEESLEY, T.(1857) List of the larger wild animals. In *Geology of Cape May*: 137. Cook, G.H. ed. New Jersey: Geol. Survey of New Jersey

170 BEIDLEMAN, R.G.(1958) Early fur returns from the Pacific northwest. *J. Mamm.* **39**: 146–147

171 BELL, T.(1837a) *A history of British quadrupeds*: 129–140. London

172 BELL, T. (1837b) Observations on the genus *Galictis* . . . *Proc. zool. Soc. Lond.* **1837**: 45–46

173 BEMMELL, A.C.V.van (1949) Notes on Indo-Australian mammals. *Treubia* **20**: 375–380

174 BENKOVSKI, L.M.(1958) [On the biology of the otter in South Russia] *Zool. Zh.* **37**: 1105

175 BENNETT, E.T.(1832) Characters of a new species of *otter* ... *Proc. zool. Soc. Lond.* **1832**: 1–2

176 BENTLEY, W.W.(1959) Sea otter along the California coast. *J. Mammal.* **40**: 147

177 BEST, A.(1962) The Canadian otter, *Lutra canadensis*, in captivity. *Int. Zoo Yb.* **4**: 42–44

178 BEWICK, T.(1800) *A general history of quadrupeds*: 487–492. 4th Ed. New-castle: Hodgson, Beilby & Bewick

179 BIEMILLER, C.L.(1951) Torpedo in fur. *Holiday, Philad.* **9**(1): 13–14, 16

180 BILLBERG, G.J.(1827) *Synopsis fauna Scandinavia*: 28. Holmiae

181 BIRULA, A.(1912) Contributions à la classification ... des mammifères. *Ezheg. zool. Mus.* **17**: 274–277

182 BIRULA, A.(1914) Notice sur la loutre du Pamir, *Lutra lutra oxiana*, n. subsp. *Ezheg. zool. Mus.* **19**: xxi

183 BISCHOFF, Th.(1865) Ueber einen beutel der Fischotter – placenta. *Sber. bayer. Akad. Wiss.* **1**: 213–224

BLACK, J.D., *see* Dellinger, S.C. & Black, J.D.

BLAKE, J., *see* Hamerstrom, F.N. & Blake, J.

BLANCHARD, R., *see* Regnard, P. & Blanchard, R.

184 BLANFORD, W.T.(1877) On an apparently new hare, and some other mammalia from Gilgit. *J. Asiatic Soc. Beng.* **46**: 324

185 BLANFORD, W.T.(1888) *The fauna of British India.* Mammalia. **1**: 182–188. Appendix (1891) 601–602. London: Taylor & Francis

186 BLASIUS, J.H.(1857) *Naturgeschichte der Säugetiere Deutschlands* ...: 236–241. Brunswick: F. Viewey & Sons

187 BLUMENBACH, J.F.(1810) *Abbildungen naturhistorischer Gegenstände.* Nr 93 Grottingen

188 BLYTH, E. (1842) Proceedings: Mammalia. *J. Asiatic Soc. Beng.* **11**: 99

189 BLYTH, E.(1863) *Catalogue of the Mammalia in the Museum of the Asiatic Society of Bengal*: 71–74 Calcutta

190 BLYTH, E. (1875) *Catalogue of the mammals and birds of Burma.* Hertford

191 BOCAGE, J.V.B.DU (1890) Mammifères d'Angola et du Congo. *Jorn. Sci. math. phys. nat.* (2)**1**: 185

192 BOITARD, P.(1842) *Jardin des Plantes*: 147–150. Paris

BOLE, B.P., *see* Aldrich, J.W. & Bole, B.P.

193 BOLIN, R.L.(1938) Reappearance of the southern sea otter. *J. Mammal.* **19**: 301–303

194 BONAPARTE, C.L.PRINCE (1838a) Synopsis vertebratorum systematis. *N. Ann. Sci. Nat.* Anno I. II: 111

195 BONAPARTE, C.L.PRINCE (1838b) La nouvelle classification des animaux vertébrés. Mammifères. *Revue Zool.* **1**: 213

196 BONAPARTE, C.L.PRINCE (1839) *Iconografia Fauna Italica.* **1**. [pp. unnumbered]

197 BONAPARTE, C.L.PRINCE (1858) *Catalogue des Mammifères et des Oiseaux observés en Algerie par le Capitaine Loche*: 10 Paris.

198 BONHOTE, J.L.(1900) On the mammals collected during the 'Skeat Expedition ...' *Proc. zool. Soc. Lond.* **1900**: 874

199 BONHOTE, J.L.(1903) Zoology. In *Fasciculi Malayenses*. 1: 11. Annandale, N. & Robinson, H.C.(Eds). London: Universities of Edinburgh and Liverpool

200 BONNOT, P.(1951) The sea lions, seals and sea otter of the California coast. *Calif. Fish Game* **37**: 371–389

201 BOOLOOTIAN, R.A.(1958) *The playful sea otter*. Outdoor California, Dept. of Fish & Game, August. 2 pp.

202 BOOLOOTIAN, R.A.(1961) The distribution of the California sea otter. *Calif. Fish Game* **47**: 287–292

203 BOOTH, H.B.(1928) Precocious young otter. *Naturalist, Lond.* No. 862: 324

204 BOURLIÈRE, F.(1955) *The natural history of mammals*. 23–26, 190. [trans. Parshley, H.M.] London

205 BOUTAN, L.(1906) Mammifères No. 5. *Decades Zoologiques Mission Scientifique permanente d'exploration Indo-Chine*. Hanoi

206 BOWDEN, J.(1869) *Naturalist in Norway*: 71. London

207 BOYLE, H.(1919) River otter plays on moonlight nights. *Calif. Fish Game* **5**:98

208 BRADT, G.W.(1945) What about the otter? *Mich. Conserv.* **14**(2): 4, 10

209 BRADT, G.W.(1946) Otter – playboy of streams and lakes. *Mich. Conserv.* **15**: 6–7

210 BRANDER, J.D.B.(1885) The enemies of salmon and trout. *Field* **66**: 654

211 BRANDT, J.F.(1880–83) Beobachtungen über die verschiedenen kleider der Seeotter. *Mél. Biol.* **11**: 1–12

212 BRASS, E.(1911) *Aus dem Reiche der Pelze*. Berlin

213 BRAUNS, D.(1884) Bemerkungen über die Musteliden Japans ... *Jena. Z. Nat.* **17**: 458–464.

214 BRISSON, M.J.(1756) *Le Règne Animal*: 277–279. Paris: J.B.Bouche

215 BROUWER, G.A.(1940) De uitroeing van den vischotter (*Lutra lutra* L.) in Nederlande aanstaande. *Levende nat.* **45**: 1–31

216 BROUWER, G.A.(1945a) De vischotter in den winter van 1940/41. Part 1. *Levende Nat.* **46**: 170–174

217 BROUWER, G.A.(1945b) De vischotter in den winter van 1940/41. Part 2. *Levende Nat.* **46**: 183–187

218 BROWN, C.E.(1936) Rearing wild animals in captivity, and gestation periods. *J. Mammal.* **17**: 12

219 BROWN, N.R. & LANNING, R.G.(1954) The mammals of Renfrew County, Ontario. *Can. Fld Nat.* **63**: 176

220 BROWNE, T.(1902) *Notes and letters on the natural history of Norfolk*: 56. [edited by Southwell, T.] London: Jarrold

221 BRUCE, J.(1881) Otter caught in a sewer. *Field* **57**: 797

222 BRYANT, H.C.(1915) California's fur-bearing mammals. *Calif. Fish Game* **1**: 96–102

223 BRYANT, J.(1950) Value of otters. *Field* **196**: 833

224 BRYDEN, H.A.(1936). *Wild life in South Africa*: 155–160. London: G.G. Harrap

225 BUCHANAN, A.(1920) *Wild life in Canada*: 218. London: Murray

226 BUCKLAND, F.(1887) *Notes and jottings from animal life*: 96–112. London: Smith, Elder & Co.

BUCKLEY, T.E., *see* Harvie-Brown, J.A. & Buckley, T.E.

227 BUFFON, G.L.L.(1758) *Histoire naturelle*. 7: 134–160. Paris

228 BUFFON, G.L.L.(1787) *Histoire naturelle*. 6: 175–202. (New Edition.) Paris

229 BULLEN, J.B.S.(1899) An otter's freak. *Field* 94: 8

230 BÜRGER, O.(1919) *Reisen eines Naturforschers im tropischen Südamerika*. 2 Aufl. 214. Leipzig

231 BURGESS, T.W.(1924) Sliding otter. *J. Mammal.* 5: 76

232 BURMEISTER, H.(1854) *Systematische Uebersicht der Thiere Brasiliens*. No. 1: 114. Berlin: Georg Reimer

233 BURMEISTER, H.(1861) *Reise durch die La Plata-Staaten*. 2: 410–411. Hallé

234 BURMEISTER, H.(1879) *Description Physique de la République Argentine*. 3: 165–168. Buenos Aires: Paul-Emile Cori

235 BURNE, R.H.(1899) On the bile ducts of the common otter. *Proc. Anat. Soc. Lond.* 20 and *J. Anat.* 33 (n.s. 13) xx–xxi

236 BURNEY, J.(1819) *A chronological history of north-eastern voyages of discovery*. London

237 BURNS, E.(1953) *The sex life of wild animals*: 29, 95, 106, 163–164, 189. New York

238 BURT, W.H.(1946) *The mammals of Michigan*: 145–148. Ann Arbor: Univ. Mich. Press

239 BURT, W.H.(1952) *A field guide to the mammals*: 40, 42, 47. Cambridge, Mass: Houghton Miflin Co.

240 BURT, W.H. & STIRTON, R.A.(1961) The mammals of El Salvador. *Misc. Publs Mus. Zool. Univ. Mich.* No. 117: 47–48

241 BURTON, M.(1962) *Systematic dictionary of mammals of the world*: 167–169. London: Museum Press

242 BUXTON, A.(1935–38) Travellers of the dusk. *Trans. Norfolk Norwich Nat. Soc.* 14: 220

243 BUXTON, A.(1940) The frost of January–February, 1940. *Trans. Norfolk Norwich Nat. Soc.* 15: 102–105

244 BUXTON, A.(1946) *A fisherman naturalist*: 117–121. London: Collins

245 CABRERA, A.(1903) Nota sobre una nutria de la costa de Guinea. *Boln Soc. esp. Hist. nat.* 3: 181–182

246 CABRERA, A.(1903–10) Mamíferos de la Guinea Espanola. *Mems R. Soc. esp. Hist. nat.* 1: 30

247 CABRERA, A.(1906) Mamíferos de Magador. *Boln Soc. esp. Hist. nat.* 6: 360

248 CABRERA, A.(1908) Lista de los mamíferos de las posesiones españolas del Golfo de Guinea. *Mems R. Soc. esp. Hist. nat.* 1: 446

249 CABRERA, A.(1912) Catálogo metódica de las colecciones de mamíferos del museo de ciencias naturales de Madrid. *Trab. Mus. Cienc. nat. Madr.* Serie zool. No. 11: 78

250 CABRERA, A.(1914) *Fauna Ibérica*: Mamíferos: 177–178. Madrid: Mus. nac. cienc. nat. Madrid

251 CABRERA, A.(1924) Una nueva nutria de la America Central. *Boln Soc. esp. Hist. nat.* 24: 52–53

252 CABRERA, A.(1929) Catálogo descriptivo de las mamíferos de la Guinea española. *Mems R. Soc. esp. Hist. nat.* 16: 31–32

253 CABRERA, A.(1932) Los mamíferos de Marruecos. *Trab. Mus. nac. cienc. nat. Madr.* Serie zool. **57**: 147

254 CABRERA, A.(1957) Catálogo de los mamíferos de America del Sur. *Revta Mus. argent. Cienc. nat. Bernardino Rivadavia* **4**: 271–275

255 CABRERA, A. & YEPES, J.(1940) *Historia natural ediar*: 154–157. Buenos Aires: Nagel & Co.

256 CAHALANE, V.H.(1961) *Mammals of North America*: 198–209. 4th Ed. New York: Macmillan

257 CAHN, A.R.(1921) The mammals of Itasca County, Minnesota. *J. Mammal.* **2**: 71

258 CAHN, A.R.(1937) The mammals of the Quetico Provincial Park of Ontario. *J. Mammal.* **18**: 24

259 CAMERON, A.W.(1958) Mammals of the islands in the Gulf on St. Lawrence. *Bull. natn. Mus. Can.* No. 154. various pp.

260 CANTOR, T.(1846) Catalogue of mammalia inhabiting the Malayan Peninsula and islands. *J. Asiatic Soc. Beng.* **15**: 195–196

261 CANTUEL, P.(1949) *Faune des Vertébrés du Massif Central de la France*: 99. Paris: Paul Lechevalier

262 CARPENTER, G.D.H.(1925) *A naturalist in East Africa*: 54. Oxford: Clarendon Press

263 CARPENTER, W.B.(1857) *Zoology* **1**: 224. New edition revised by Dallas, W.S. London: Henry G. Bohn

264 CARTER, J.(1872) Otters and pheasant eggs. *Field* **39**: 398

265 CARTER, J.(1875) Curious death of an otter and a kingfisher. *Field* **46**: 148

266 CARTER, J.(1894) Habits of the otter. *Zoologist* (3) **18**: 457–458

267 CARTER, J.(1897) Otter hooked by an angler. *Field* **90**: 552

CARTER, J., *see* Hill, J.E. & Carter, J.

268 CARTER, T.D., HILL, J.E. & TATE, G.H.H.(1945) *Mammals of the Pacific world*: 84. New York: McMillan

269 CARY, M.(1911) A biological survey of Colorado. *N. Am. Fauna* **33**: 182

270 CERVA, F.A.(1930) Beobachtungen bei der Zähmung des Fischotters. *Zool. Gart., Lpz.* **3**: 319–323

271 CHAIGNEAU, A.(1938) Notes sur la loutre. *Mammalia* **2**: 99–102

272 CHAINE, J.(1929) Fracture consolidée d'un os pénièn. *P.-v. Soc. linn. Bordeaux* **8**: 92

273 CHAPMAN, A.C.(1894) Habits of the otter. *Zoologist* (3) **12**: 108

274 CHAPMAN, F.B.(1956) The river otter in Ohio. *J. Mammal.* **37**: 284

CHAPMAN, F.M., *see* Allen, J.A. & Chapman, F.M.

CHAPMAN, L., *see* Chapman, W. & Chapman, L.

275 CHAPMAN, W. & CHAPMAN, L.(1937) Pet otters. *Nature Mag.* **29**: 140–143

276 CHASEN, F.N. (1940) A handlist of Malaysian mammals. *Bull. Raffles Mus.* No. 15: 92–93

277 CHASEN, F.N. & KLOSS, C.B. (1931) Mammals from the lowlands & islands of north Borneo. *Bull. Raffles Mus.* No. 6: 15, 52

278 CHRISTIAN, J. & RATCLIFFE, H.L.(1952) Shock disease in captive wild mammals. *Am. J. Path.* **23**: 725–737

CHURCH, M.L., *see* Copeland, M. & Church, M.L.

279 CHURCHER, C.S.(1965) Mammals at Fort Albany circa 1700 A.D. *J. Mammal.* **46**: 354–355

CHURCHILL, E.P., *see* Over, W.H. & Churchill, E.P.

280 CLAPHAM, R.(1922) *The book of the otter.* 158 pp. London: Heath Cranton, Ltd.

281 CLARK, W.K.(1958) The land mammals of the Kodiak islands. *J. Mammal.* **39**: 576

282 CLARKE, C.H.D.(1940) A biological investigation of the Thelon Game Sanctuary. *Bull. natn. Mus. Can.* **96**: 35

283 CLARK-KENNEDY, A.(1869) Otters in Suffolk. *Zoologist* (2) **4**: 1557–1558

284 COCKRUM, E.L.(1952) Mammals of Kansas. *Univ. Kans. Publs Mus. nat. Hist.* **7**(1): 260–261, 267

285 COCKRUM, E.L.(1962) *Introduction to mammalogy*: 90. New York: Ronald Press

286 COCKRUM, E.L.(1964) Southern river otter, *Lutra annectens*, from Sonora, Mexico. *J. Mammal.* **45**: 634–635

287 COCKS, A.H.(1877) On the breeding of the otter. *Zoologist* (3) **1**: 100–101

288 COCKS, A.H.(1881) Note on the breeding of the otter. *Proc. zool. Soc. Lond.* **1881**: 249–250

289 COCKS, A.H.(1882) On the breeding of the otter. *Zoologist* (3) **6**: 201

290 COCKS, A.H.(1890) Destruction of otters in the Thames. *Zoologist* (3) **14**: 308

291 COLLIER, W.P.(1908) Notes on the otter (*Lutra vulgaris*). *Zoologist* (4) **12**: 92–96

292 COLYER, F.(1936) *Variations and diseases of the teeth of animals*: 99, 355–356. London: John Bale, Sons & Danielsson, Ltd.

293 CONISBEE, L.R.(1953) *Index Generum Mammalium*: 38, 50, 66. London: Trustees of the British Museum

294 CONNOR, P.F.(1953) Notes on the mammals of a New Jersey Pine Barrens Area. *J. Mammal.* **34**: 231

295 COOK, D.B.(1940) An otter takes a ride. *J. Mammal.* **21**: 216

296 COOK, J.& KING, J.(1785) *A voyage to the Pacific Ocean.* **2**: 270, 295–296. **3**: 346, 369, 429. 2nd Ed. London: G. Nichol

297 COOLIDGE, H.J.(1957) [1959] Notes on progress in wildlife conservation ... *Proc. 9th Pacif. Sci. Congr.* **7**: 39

298 COOTE, A.P.(1922) An otter and her cubs. *Field* **140**: 714

299 COPE, E.D.(1896) New and little known mammalia from the Port Kennedy bone deposit. *Proc. Acad. nat. Sci. Philad.* **1896**: 391–392

300 COPELAND, M. & CHURCH, M.L.(1906) [1907] Notes on the mammals of Grand Manan, N.B. .... *Proc. biol. Soc. Wash.* **19**: 1251

301 COPLEY, H.(1950) *Small mammals of Kenya*: 42–43. London: Longmans

302 COPPINGER, R.W.(1883) *Cruise of the 'Alert'*: 58. London

303 CORBIN, G.B.(1872) Otter. *Zoologist* (2) **7**: 3304

304 CORBIN, G.B.(1873) Large otter. *Zoologist* (2) **8**: 3487

305 CORNELI, R.(1884) [1885] Der Fischotter, dessen Naturgeschichte, Jagd, und Fang ... Berlin. 148 pp., *see Zoological Record* **21** Mammals: 41

306 COUES, E. (1877) *Fur-bearing animals.* 294–348. Washington: Government Printing Office. *See* Audubon, M.R. & Coues, E.

307 COUES, E. & YARROW, H.C.(1875) *Zoological Exploration west of* 100 *Meridian.* **5**: 63

308 COVENTRY, G.M.(1870) Otters in Hampshire. *Land Wat.* **9**: 259

309 COWAN, I.McT. & GUIGUET, C.J.(1956) The Mammals of British Columbia. *Hdbk Br. Columb. prov. Mus.* **11**: 331

310 COWARD, T.A. & OLDHAM, C.(1895) The mammalian fauna of Cheshire *Zoologist* (3) **19**: 220–221

311 COWARD, T.A. & OLDHAM, C.(1910) *The vertebrate fauna of Cheshire and Liverpool Bay* **1**: 33. London: Witherby & Co.

312 COX, L.C.(1947) Otters in the sea. *Field* **190**: 638
CRAM, W.E., *see* Stone, W. & Cram, W.E.

313 CRANDALL, L.S.(1964) *Management of wild mammals in captivity.* 337–348. Chicago: Univ. Chicago Press

314 CRANE, J.(1931) Mammals of Hampshire County, Massachusetts. *J. Mammal.* **12**: 268

315 CRESAP, F.(1937) Otter trapping. *Trapper* **1**(2): 10

316 CROGGON, C.C.(1948) An otter problem. *Cntry Life* **103**: 535–536

317 CUNNINGHAM, D.D.(1903) *Some Indian friends and acquaintances:* 282–283. London: John Murray

318 CURTIS, L.(1962) Aquarium-type outdoor otter exhibit. *Int. Zoo Yb.* **4**: 42–44

319 CUSHING, J.E.jr.(1939) Sea otters and abalones. *J. Mammal.* **20**: 371

320 CUSHNY, F.(1897) Otters killing sparrows. *Field* **89**: 203

321 CUVIER, F.(1823) *Dictionnaire des sciences naturelles.* **27**: 237–250. Paris

322 CUVIER, G.L.(1817) *Le Règne Animal.* **1**: 151. Paris

323 CUVIER, G.L.(1829) *Le Règne Animal.* **1**: 147–148. (New Edition.) Paris

324 CUVIER, G.L.(1831) *Das Thierreich geordnet nach seiner Organisation.* Leipzig

325 DALQUEST, W.W.(1948) Mammals of Washington. *Univ. Kans. Publs Mus. nat. Hist.* No. 2: 110

326 DAMMERMAN, K.W.(1929) On the zoology of Java, Appendix 1. A list of the mammals known from Java. *Treubia* **11**: 35

327 DANIEL, W.B.(1812) *Rural sports.* **1**: 619–633. London: B. & R.Crosby

328 DANIEL, W.B.(1813) *Supplement to the rural sports:* 53–56. London: B. & R. Crosby

329 DARLING, F.F.(1947) *Natural history in the Highlands and Islands:* 211. London: Collins

330 DAUNT, A.(1876) Otters sinking when shot. *Field* **47**: 677–678

331 DAVIS, D.D.(1958) Mammals of the Kelabit Plateau, northern Sarawak. *Fieldiana: Zool.* **39**: 138–139

332 DAVIS, D.D.(1962) Mammals of the lowland rain-forest of North Borneo. *Bull. natn. Mus. St. Singapore* No. 31: 98

333 DAVIS, J.A.,Jr. (1964). The sea otters of Point Lobos. *Anim. Kingd.* **67**: 146–151

334 DAVIS, W.B.(1939) *The recent mammals of Idaho:* 140. Caldwell, Idaho: Caxton Printers

335 DAVIS, W.B. & LUKENS, P.W.(1958) Mammals of the Mexican state of Guerrero. *J. Mammal.* **39**: 358–359

336 DAY, F.(1873) On some new or little-known fishes of India. *Proc. zool. Soc. Lond.* **1873**: 709–710

337 DEARBORN, N.(1932) Foods of some predatory fur-bearing animals in Michigan. *Bull. Sch. For. Conserv. Univ. Mich.* **1**: 52 pp.

338 DEARDEN, L.C.(1954) Extra premolars in the river otter. *J. Mammal.* **35**: 125–126

339 DE BALSAC, H.H.(1936) Biogéographie des Mammifères . . . de l'Afrique du Nord. *Bull. biol. Fr. Belg.* (Sup. num.) **21**: 43

340 DE KAY, J.E.(1842) *Natural history of New York.* Zoology **1**: 39–40. Albany: C.van Benthuysen & Sons

341 DE KOCK, L.L.(1960) Distribution of carotid body tissue in an otter. *Acta anat.* **39**: 259–264

342 DELLINGER, S.C. & BLACK, J.D.(1940) Notes on Arkansas mammals. *J. Mammal.* **21**: 188

343 DENWOOD, J.R.(1894) Dimensions of otter. *Zoologist* (3) **18**: 423

344 DESMAREST, A.G.(1817) *Nouveau Dictionnaire d'histoire Naturelle.* **18**: 208–219

345 DESMAREST, A.G.(1820). *Mammalogie.* **1**. Paris

346 DEVINCENZI, G.J.(1935) Mammiferos del Uruguay. *An. Mus. Hist. nat. Montevideo* **4**: 10, 52–53

347 DEVOE, A.(1944a) Amikuk, the Sea Otter. *Frontiers, Lanc.* **8**: 138, 158–159

348 DEVOE, A.(1944b) Winning ways of the Sea Otter. *Reader's Dig.* **44** (226): 29–31

349 DICE, L.R.(1921) Notes on the mammals of interior Alaska. *J. Mammal.* **2**: 23

350 DICKESON, F.(1887) A tame otter. *Field* **69**: 765

351 DIXON, G.(1789) *A voyage round the world . . . :* 201. 2nd Ed. London: G. Goulding

352 DIXON, J.S.(1938) *Birds and mammals of Mount McKinley National Park, Alaska*: 156. Washington: Fauna Nat. Pks. U.S. series

353 DODERLEIN, P.(1872) *Alcune generalità intorno la Fauna Sicula . . . :* 4. Modena

354 D'ORBIGNY, A. & GERVAIS, P.(1847) *Voyage dans l'Amérique Méridionale*: 20. Paris: Pitois-Levrault

355 DOUGLAS, W.O.(1928) Natural history notes from Baker Lake, N.W.T. *Can. Fld Nat.* **42**: 106

356 DOVETON, F.B.(1875) A very bold otter. *Field* **46**: 419

357 DUNSCOMBE, R.(1881) Otters seizing prey while hunted. *Field* **57**: 153

358 DURRANT, S.D.(1952) Mammals of Utah, taxonomy and distribution. *Univ. Kans. Publs Mus. nat. Hist.* **6**: 434–437, 478

359 DURRANT, S.D., LEE, M.R. & HANSEN, R.M.(1955–60) Additional records and extensions of known ranges of mammals from Utah. *Univ. Kans. Publs Mus. nat. Hist.* **9**: 78

360 DYBOWSKI, B.N.(1922) *Archiwm Tow. nauk. Lwow* **1**: 350

361 DYK, V.(1962) Ausserodentliche Grösse eines Fischotters. *Sborn. Krajsk. Vlast. Muz. Přirod. věd.* **3**: 186–187

362 DYMOND, J.R.(1928) The mammals of the Lake Nipigon region. *Trans. R. Can. Inst.* **16**: 241

EADIE, W.R., *see* Hamilton, W.J.Jr. & Eadie, W.R.

363 EAST, B.(1944) Sea otter hunt. *Fld Stream* **49** (4): 34–36, 63–65

364 EAST, B.(1947) The sea beaver is coming back. *Anim. Kingd.* **50**: 124–129

365 ECKSTEIN, K.(1930) Aus dem jugendleben des Fischotters. *Z. Saugetierk.* **5**: 40–47

366 ELLERMAN, J.R.& MORRISON-SCOTT, T.C.S.(1951) *Checklist of palaearctic and Indian mammals*: 275–279. London: Trustees of the British Museum

367 ELLERMAN, J.R., MORRISON-SCOTT, T.C.S. & HAYMAN, R.W.(1953). *Southern African Mammals:* 115–117. London: Trustees of the British Museum

368 ELLIOT, D.G.(1901) A synopsis of the mammals of North America ... *Publs Field Mus. nat. Hist.* Zool. **2**: 352–354

369 ELLIOT, D.G.(1904) The land and sea mammals of middle America and the West Indies. *Publs Field Mus. nat. Hist.* Zool. **4**(2): 534–537

370 ELLIOT, D.G.(1905) Checklist of mammals of the North American Continent. *Publs Field Mus. nat. Hist.* Zool. **6**: 433–436

371 ELLIOT, D.G.(1905) [1906] Descriptions of three apparently new species of mammals. *Proc. biol. Soc. Wash.* **18**: 80–81

372 ELLIOT, D.G.(1917) *A check-list of mammals of the North American continent – Supplement.* 142–143. New York: Am. Mus. Nat. Hist.

373 ELLIOT, W.(1839) A catalogue of the species of mammalia found in the southern Mahratta country ... *Madras J.* **10**: 100

374 ELLIOTT, H.W.(1874) *Report on the condition of affairs in the Territory of Alaska.* 54–62. Washington: Govt. Publs.

375 ELLIOTT, H.W.(1886) *An arctic province*: 127. London: Sampson Low, Marston, Searle & Rivington

376 ELLIOTT, H.W.(1887). The sea-otter fishery. *Fisheries and Fishery Ind. U.S.* sect. 5. **2**: 483–491

377 ELLISON, N.F.(1954–56) Otter in North Wirral, Cheshire. *NW Nat.* (n.s.) **2**: 138

378 ELMHIRST, R.(1938) Food of the otter in the marine littoral zone. *Scott. Nat.* **1938**: 99–102

379 EMMONS, E.(1838) *Report on the quadrupeds of Massachusetts*: 25. Boston: Commissioners of the Zoological Survey of the State

380 EMMONS, E.(1840) *Report on the quadrupeds of Massachusetts*: 46. Boston: Commissioners of the Zoological Survey of the State

ENDERS, R.K., *see* Pearson, O.P. & Enders, R.K.

381 ERLINGE, S.(1963) Uttern och arstiderna. *Skanes Nat.* **50**: 133–146

382 ERRINGTON, P.L.(1962) Wilderness islands of the north. *Nat. Hist., N.Y.* **71** (5): 8–17

383 ERXLEBEN, J.C.P.(1777) *Systema Regni Animalis.* Mammalia: 445–451. Lipsiae: Weygand

384 ESCHWEGE, W.L.(1818) *Journal von Brasilien* ...: 233. Wiemar

385 ESTANOVE, J.(1952) La loutre et sa disparition. *Mammalia* **16**: 256–257

386 EVERETT, A.H.(1889) Remarks on the zoo-geographical relationships of the island of Palawan. *Proc. zool. Soc. Lond.* **1889**: 223

387 EVERETT, A.H.(1893) A nominal list of the mammals inhabiting the Bornean group of islands. *Proc. zool. Soc. Lond.* **1893**: 495

388 EYERDAM, W.J.(1933) Sea otters in the Aleutian islands. *J. Mammal.* **14**: 70–71

389 EYRE, M.(1963) *Otter in our parlour.* 109 pp. Cape Town: Tafelberg-Uitgewers

390 FARNSWORTH, G.(1917) Sea otters near Catalina Island. *Calif. Fish Game* **3**: 90

391 FATIO, V.(1869) *Faune des Vertébrés de la Suisse.* **1**. Mammifères: 341–342. Geneva: H.Georg

392 FERRANT, V.[undated] *Faune du Grand-Duché de Luxembourg.* Mammifères. 59

393 FEUER, R.C.(1958) Mammals collected in the Karluk Lake Region, Kodiak Island, Alaska. *Murrelet* **39**: 37–39

394 FIGUEIRA, J.H.(1894) Contribucion al conocimiento de la fauna Uruguaya. *An. Mus. nac. Montevideo* **2**: 189–217

FILCHNER, W., *see* Matschie, P.(1907)

395 FISCHER, J.B.(1829) *Synopsis Mammalium*: 224–229. Stuttgart: J.G.Cottae

396 FISHER, A.H.(1940) Expert diver (*Lutra*). *Nature Mag.* **33**: 23

397 FISHER, A.H.(1947) Nature's expert fisherman. *Fld Stream* **52**: 52

398 FISHER, E.M.(1933) A fractured femur of the Alaskan river otter. *J. Mammal.* **14**: 362–365

399 FISHER, E.M.(1935) An anomalous muscle in the California river otter. *Science, N.Y.* **82**: 172–173

400 FISHER, E.M.(1939) Habits of the southern sea otter. *J. Mammal.* **20**: 21–36

401 FISHER, E.M.(1940a) Early life of a sea otter pup. *J. Mammal.* **21**: 132–137

402 FISHER, E.M.(1940b) A sea otter with gastric perforations. *J. Mammal.* **21**: 357–359

403 FISHER, E.M.(1940c) The sea otter past and present. *Proc. 6th Pacif. Sci. Congr.* **3**: 223–236

404 FISHER, E.M.(1940d) Sea otter in California. *Proc. 6th Pacif. Sci. Congr.* **4**: 231–240

405 FISHER, E.M.(1940e) Death comes to a sea otter. *Calif. Fish Game* **26**: 278–281

406 FISHER, E.M.(1941a) Prices of sea otter pelts. *Calif. Fish Game* **27**: 261–265

407 FISHER, E.M.(1941b) Notes on the teeth of the sea otter. *J. Mammal.* **22**: 428–433

408 FISHER, E.M.(1942) *The osteology and myology of the California River Otter.* 66 pp. Stanford, Calif.: Stanford Univ. Press

FISHER, W.R., *see* Gurney, J.H. & Fisher, W.R.

409 FITTER, R.S.R.(1945) *London's natural history*: 160, 195–196. London: Collins

410 FITTER, R.S.R.(1949) A check-list of the mammals ... of the London area, 1900–1949. *Lond. Nat.* **28**: 104

411 FITTER, R.S.R.(1953) The otter investigation. *Oryx* **2**: 188

412 FITTER, R.S.R.(1964a) Irish otters and deer in danger. *Wld Wildl. News* **22**: 5

413 FITTER, R.S.R.(1964b) In danger of extinction in France. *Wld Wildl. News* **24**: 5

414 FITZINGER, L.J.(1860) *Bilder-Atlas Naturgeschichte der Säugetiere*. Fig. 71. Vienna: K.K.Hof-Staatsdruckerei

FITZINGER, L.J., *see* Heuglin, M.T. & Fitzinger, L.J.

415 FLEMING, J.(1822) *The philosophy of zoology*. **2**: 187–188. Edinburgh: Archibald Constable

416 FLETCHER, J.M.(1956) A white otter. *Scott. Nat.* **68**: 59–60

417 FLOWER, S.S.(1900) On the mammalia of Siam and the Malay Peninsula. *Proc. zool Soc. Lond.* **1900**: 334–335

418 FLOWER, S.S.(1929) *List of the vertebrated animals exhibited in the . . . Zoological Society of London*, 1828–1927. **1**: Mammals: 128–129. London: Zoological Society of London

419 FLOWER, S.S.(1931) Contributions to our knowledge of the duration of life in vertebrate animals. V. Mammals. *Proc. zool. Soc. Lond.* **1931**: 175

420 FLOWER, W.H.(1910–11) Otter. *Encyc. Br.* **20**: 371. 11th ed. Cambridge: Univ. Press

FOMITCHEVA, N.I., *see* Rukovsky, N.N. & Fomitcheva, N.I.

421 FOUNTAIN, P.(1902) *The great mountains and forests of South America*: 117. New York: Longmans, Green & Co.

422 FRANCIS, F.(1865) Man attacked by otter. *Field* **25**: 397

423 FRANKE, D.(1959) Een nest met jonge visotters in de Oude Verren. *Levende Nat.* **62**: 169–172

FRANKLIN, J., *see* Sabine, J. & Franklin, J.

424 FRANTZIUS, A.VON (1869) Die Säugethiere Costa Ricas. *Wiegm. Arch. Naturg.* **1869**: 289

425 FREEMAN, G.E. & SALVIN, F.H.(1859) *Falconry* . . .: 350–352. London: Longmans, Green, Longman & Roberts

426 FRILEY, C.E.Jr.(1949) Age determination, by use of the baculum, in the river otter. *J. Mammal.* **30**: 102–110

427 FROHAWK, F.W.(1922) The otter in Essex. *Field* **140**: 386

FRY, T.B., *see* Hinton, M.A.C. & Fry, T.B.

428 FULTON, H.(1903) Rough notes on the mammalia of Chitral. *J. Bombay nat. Hist. Soc.* **14**: 759

429 GAPPER,(1830) Observations on the quadrupeds of Upper Canada. *Zool. J.* **5**: 201–207

GARNETT, R.[translator], *see* Heuvelmans, B.

430 GATES, G.A.(1898) Otter attacking rabbit. *Field* **91**: 61

431 GAY, C.(1847) *Historia fisica y politica de Chile*. **1**: 44–48. (*Atlas*, 1854, pl. 2). Paris

432 GAZIN, C.L.(1934) Upper pliocene mustelids from the Snake River basin of Ohio. *J. Mammal.* **15**: 143–149

GAZIN, C.L., *see* Gidley, J.W. & Gazin, C.L.

433 GEOFFROY, S-H.I.(1826) Le Simung. *Dict. Class. d'Hist. Nat.* **9**: 519

434 GERRARD, E.(1862) *Catalogue of the bones of Mammalia* . . .: 100–101. London: British Museum (Nat. Hist.)

435 GERVAIS, P.(1841) *Voyage autour du Monde . . . sur la corvette 'La Bonite'*: 15–17. Paris

436 GERVAIS, P.(1848) Sur les animaux vertébrés de l'Algérie. *Ann. Sci. Nat.* (3) **10**: 206

437 GERVAIS, P.(1855) *Histoire naturelle des Mammifères.* **2**: 116–120. Paris: L. Curmer

GERVAIS, P., *see* D'Orbigny, A. & Gervais, P.

438 GESNER, C.(1551) *Medici Tigurni. Historiae Animalium.* **1.** de Quadrupedibus viviparis: 775–777. Tiguri: Christ. Frosehoverum

GIDLEY, J.W., *see* Matthew, W.D. & Gidley, J.W.

439 GIDLEY, J.W. & GAZIN, C.L.(1933) New mammalia in the pleistocene fauna. *J. Mammal.* **14**: 349

440 GIEBEL, C.G.(1855) *Die Säugethiere*: 789. Leipzig: A. Abel

441 GIEBEL, C.G.(1878) [*Pterura sambachi* – skull and dentition] *Z. ges. Naturw.* **51**: 373–377

442 GILL, T.(1872) [1874] Arrangement of the families of mammals. *Smithson. misc. Collns* **11** (230): 65–66

443 GILMORE, R.(1956) *Our endangered wildlife*: 7–8. Sea otter. Nat. Wildl. Fed.

444 GLOGER, C.W.L. & GRAVENHORST, J.L.C.(1827) Bemerkungen über ein Paar Schlesische Säugethierarten . . . *Nova acta Acad. Caesar Leop. Carol.* **13**: 511

445 GMELIN, J.F.(ed) (1788) *Linné, C. Systema Naturae* **1**: 93.C. (13th edition). Bruxelles: Lemairé

446 GODMAN, J.D.(1826) *American natural history.* **1**: 225–226. Philadelphia: Carey & Lee

447 GOELDI, E.A.(1893) *Os mammiferos do Brazil*: 71–72. Rio de Janeiro

448 GOIN, O.B.(1947) The otter is a gentleman. *Fauna* **9**: 39–41

449 GOLDER, F.A.(1925) *Bering's voyages* **2**: 222–224

450 GOLDMAN, E.A.(1914) Descriptions of five new mammals from Panama. *Smithson. misc. Collns* **63** (5): 3–4

451 GOLDMAN, E.A.(1920) Mammals of Panama. *Smithson. misc. Collns* **69** (5): 165–166

452 GOLDMAN, E.A.(1935) New American mustelids of the genera *Martes, Gulo* and *Lutra. Proc. biol. Soc. Wash.* **48**: 178–186

453 GOLDMAN, E.A.(1936) A new otter from Kamchatka. *J. Mammal.* **17**: 164

454 GOLDSMITH, O.(1811) *A history of the earth and animated nature*: **2**: 335–340. New ed. Liverpool: Blackie & Sons

455 GOODPASTER, W.W. & HOFFMEISTER, D.F.(1952) Notes on the mammals of western Tennessee. *J. Mammal.* **33**: 366

456 GOODWIN, G.G.(1924) Mammals of the Gaspé Peninsula, Quebec. *J. Mammal.* **5**: 254

457 GOODWIN, G.G.(1942) Mammals of Honduras. *Bull. Am. Mus. nat. Hist.* **79**: 179

458 GOODWIN, G.G.(1946) Mammals of Costa Rica. *Bull. Am. Mus. nat. Hist.* **87**: 432–434

459 GOODWIN, G.G.(1953) Catalogue of the type specimens of recent mammals in the American Museum of Natural History. *Bull. Am. Mus. nat. Hist.* **102**:361

460 GORDON, C.E.(1908) The otter in Massachusetts. *Science, N.Y.* (n.s.) **28**:774
461 GORDON, E.B.(1950) Otter cub indoors. *Field* **196**: 1138
GRAVENHORST, J.L.C., *see* Gloger, C.W.L. & Gravenhorst, J.L.C.
462 GRAY, J.E.(1837) Description of some new or little known mammals . . .
Mag. zool. Bot. **1**: 580
463 GRAY, J.E.(1839) On some new or little known Mammalia. *Ann. Mag. nat.
Hist.* **2**: 286
464 GRAY, J.E.(1843a) Descriptions of some new genera and species of mammalia . . . *Ann. Mag. nat. Hist.* **11**: 118–119
465 GRAY, J.E.(1843b) *List of the specimens of Mammalia in the collection of the
British Museum*: 70–72. London: British Museum
466 GRAY, J.E.(1846) *Catalogue of the specimens and drawings . . . presented by
B.H.Hodgson, Esq. to the British Museum*: 14. London: British Museum
467 GRAY, J.E.(1863) *Catalogue of the specimens and drawings . . . presented by
B.H.Hodgson, Esq. to the British Museum.* 2nd Ed.: 7. London: British
Museum
468 GRAY, J.E.(1865) Revision of the genera and species of Mustelidae in the
British Museum. *Proc. zool. Soc. Lond.* **1865**: 100–154
469 GRAY, J.E.(1867) Notice of *Lutronectes whiteleyi,* an otter from Japan. *Proc.
zool. Soc. Lond.* **1867**: 180–182
470 GRAY, J.E.(1868) Observations on the margin-tailed otter, *Pteronura sandbachii. Proc. zool. Soc. Lond.* **1868**: 61–66
471 GRAY, J.E.(1869) *Catalogue of carnivorous . . . Mammalia in the British Museum*: 80–81, 100–119. London: British Museum
472 GREEN, H.U.(1932) Observations of the occurrence of the otter in Manitoba
in relation to beaver life. *Can. Fld Nat.* **46**: 204–206
473 GREER, K.R.(1955) Yearly food habits of the river otter . . . in Montana . . .
Am. Midl. Nat. **54**: 299–313
474 GREVÉ, C.(1894) Die geographische verbreitung der jetzt lebenden Roubthiere. *Nova Acta Acad. Caesar Leop. Carol.* **63** (1)
475 GRIFFITH, E.(1827) *The Animal Kingdom . . . [of] Baron Cuvier*: 312–317.
London
476 GRIFFITH, H.A.C.(1927) Otters in County Down. *Ir. Nat. J.* **1**: 275
477 GRIFFITH, R.E.(1953) What is the future of the sea otter? *Trans. N. Am.
Wildl. Conf.* **18**: 472–478
478 GRIMM, O.(1883) *Fishing and hunting in Russian waters.* pt. 10. St Petersburg
479 GRINNELL, J.(1914) Distribution of river otters in California. *Univ. Calif.
Publs Zool.* **12**: 305–311
480 GRINNELL, J.(1923) A systematic list of the mammals of California. *Univ.
Calif. Publs Zool.* **21**: 316
481 GRINNELL, J.(1933–35) Review of the recent mammal fauna of California.
Univ. Calif. Publs Zool. **40**: 104
482 GRINNELL, J., DIXON, J.S. & LINSDALE, J.M.(1937) *Fur bearing mammals
of California.* **1**: 271–292. Berkeley: Univ. Calif. Press
483 GRUVEL, M.(1789) *Essai sur l'Histoire Naturelle du Chili par M. l'Abbé
Molina*: 265–268. Paris
484 GUDGER, E.W.(1927). Fishing with the otter. *Am. Nat.* **61**: 193–225

485 GUIGUET, C.J., River otter. *Victoria Nat.* **18**: 53
   GUIGUET, C.J., *see* Cowan, I. McT. & Guiguet, C.J

486 GUNDERSON, H.L.& BEER, J.R.(1953) The mammals of Minnesota. *Occ. pap. Minnesota Mus. Nat. Hist.* No. 6:150–151

487 GUNN, T.E.(1866) Otter feeding in gardens. *Zoologist* (2) **1**: 152

488 GUNN, T.E.(1869) Notes on the mammalia of Norfolk. *Zoologist* (2) **4**: 1926

489 GÜNTHER, A.(1876) Report on some of the additions to the collection of mammalia in the British Museum. *Proc. zool. Soc. Lond.* **1876**: 736

490 GURNEY, J.H.(1868) Superstitions concerning the liver of the otter. *Zoologist* (2) **3**: 1217

491 GURNEY, J.H.(1869–70) Stray notes on Norfolk and Suffolk mammalia. *Trans. Norfolk Norwich Nat. Soc.* **1**: 24–25

492 GURNEY, J.H.(1881) Voracity of the otter. *Field* **57**: 275

493 GURNEY, J.H. & FISHER, W.R.(1848) Ornithological and other observations in Norfolk. *Zoologist* **6**: 2185

494 GUYON, G.(1867) Diseased otter. *Zoologist* (2) **2**: 553

495 GYLDENSTOLPE, N.(1914) Mammals collected, or observed by the Swedish Zoological Expedition to Siam, 1911–1912. *Ark. Zool.* **8** (23): 27

496 GYLDENSTOLPE, N.(1917) On birds and mammals from the Malay Peninsula. *Ark. Zool.* **10** (26): 25–26

497 GYLDENSTOLPE, N.(1919) A list of the mammals at present known to inhabit Siam. *J. nat. Hist. Soc. Siam* **3**: 3, 145–146

498 HAAGNER, A.(1920) *South African mammals:* 39–40. London: H.F. & G. Witherby

499 HACKETT, W.A.(1873) Otter in a lobster pot. *Field* **42**: 138

500 HADFIELD, H.(1874) Large otter in the Isle of Wight. *Zoologist* (2) **9**: 3952

501 HAINARD, R.(1948) *Les Mammifères Sauvages d'Europe.* **1**: 205–215. Neuchâtel: Delachaux & Niestlé

502 HALL, D.B.(1898) Otter attacking dog in defence of young. *Field* **91**: 180

503 HALL, E.R.(1945) Chase Littlejohn, 1854–1943. Observations by Littlejohn on hunting sea otters. *J. Mammal.* **26**: 89–91

504 HALL, E.R.(1946) *Mammals of Nevada:* 198–199. Berkeley: Univ. Calif. Press

505 HALL, E.R. & KELSON, K.R.(1959) *The mammals of North America* **2**: 943–950. New York: Ronald Press

506 HALL, K.R.L. & SCHALLER, G.B.(1964) Tool-using behavior of the California Sea otter. *J. Mammal.* **45**: 287–298

507 HAMERSTROM, F.N.& BLAKE, J.(1939) A fur study technique. *J. Wildl. Mgmt* **3**: 57–58

508 HAMILTON, E.(1890) *The river-side naturalist:* 5–10. London: Sampson Lowe

509 HAMILTON, W.J.Jr.(1939) *American mammals:* 392, 395. London: McGraw-Hill Publ. Co.

510 HAMILTON, W.J.Jr.(1943) *The mammals of eastern United States:* 151–156. New York: Comstock Publ. Co.

511 HAMILTON, W.J.Jr.(1961) Late fall, winter and early spring foods of 141 otters from New York. *N.Y. Fish Game J.* **8**: 106–109

512 HAMILTON, W.J.Jr. & EADIE, W.R.(1964) Reproduction in the otter, *Lutra canadensis. J. Mammal.* **45**: 242–252

513 HAMLETT, G.W.D.(1935) Delayed implantation and discontinuous development in mammals. *Q. Rev. Biol.* **10**: 432–447

514 HANDLEY, C.O.Jr. & PATTON, C.P.(1947) *Wild animals of Virginia*: 133. Richmond, Va.: Commission Crane Island Fisheries

HANSEN, R.M., *see* Durrant, S.D., Lee, M.R. & Hansen, R.M.

515 HARDING, A.R.(1909) *Fur farming*: 203–208. Columbus, Ohio

516 HARDY, M.(1911) The otter. *For. & Stream* March 4, March 11

517 HARLAN, R.(1825) *Fauna Americana*: 70–74. Philadelphia: A.Finley

518 HARPER, F.(1932) Mammals of the Athabasca and Great Slave Lakes region. *J. Mammal.* **13**: 24

519 HARPER, F.(1956) The mammals of Keewatin. *Univ. Kans. Misc. Publs Mus. nat. Hist.* **12**: 72–73

520 HARPER, R.J.(1865) An otter attacking a man. *Field* **25**: 377

521 HARRIS, A. & HARRIS, C.J.(1959) An otter about the house. *Ctry Life* **126**: 1010–1011

522 HARRIS, C.J.(1962) [Contribution to] International survey of hand-rearing techniques. *Int. Zoo Yb.* **4**: 314

HARRIS, C.J., *see* Harris, A. & Harris, C.J.

523 HARRISON, R.J.(1955) Adaptations in diving mammals. *Sci. News Harmondsworth* **35**: 80–81, 85

524 HARTING, J.E.(1864) Occurrence of the otter at Kingsbury Reservoir. *Zoologist* (1) **22**: 9155

525 HARTING, J.E.(1865) Otters in Middlesex. *Zoologist* (1) **23**: 9429

526 HARTING, J.E. (1875a) *Rambles in search of shells*: 38. London: J. van Voorst.

527 HARTING, J.E. (1875b) *The fauna of the Prybilov Islands*: 13–14. London

528 HARTING, J.E. (1877) Autumnal breeding of the otter. *Zoologist* (3) **1**: 17–18

529 HARTING, J.E.(1883) *Essays on sport and natural history*: 235–238, 428–429. London: Horace Cox

530 HARTING, J.E.(1886) White chamois, white otter and white fox in Germany. *Zoologist* (3) **10**: 104

531 HARTING, J.E.(1894) The otter, *Lutra vulgaris. Zoologist* (3) **18**: 1–10, 41–47, 379–385

532 HARVEY, J.W.(1953) Lambs & otters. *Field* **201**: 1129

533 HARVIE-BROWN, J.A.(1906) *A fauna of the Tay Basin and Strathmore*: 366–368. Edinburgh: David Douglas

534 HARVIE-BROWN, J.A. & BUCKLEY, T.E.(1892) *A vertebrate fauna of Argyll and the Inner Hebrides*: 16–18. Edinburgh: David Douglas

535 HATT, R.T.(1959) The mammals of Iraq. *Misc. Publs Mus. Zool. Univ. Mich.* **106**: 44

536 HAUGHTON, S.(1867) Notes on animal mechanics. *Proc. R. Ir. Acad.* **9**: 511–515

537 HAVNØ, E.J.(1929) Tam oter. *Naturen* **1929**: 156–159

538 HAYMAN, R.W.(1957) A new race of the Indian smooth-coated otter from Iraq. *Ann. Mag. nat. Hist.* (12) **9**: 710–712

HAYMAN, R.W., *see* Ellerman, J.R., Morrison-Scott, T.C.S. & Hayman, R.W.

HAYMAN, R.W., *see* Moreau, R.E. & Hayman, R.W.

HAYMAN, R.W., *see* Swynnerton, G.H. & Hayman, R.W.

539 HEARNE, S.(1795) *Journey from Prince of Wales's Fort in Hudson's Bay to the Northern Ocean*: London

540 HEARNS, P.(1862) An otter-fight with two salmon. *Field* **20**: 459

541 HEBER, R.(1829) *Indian journal* **3**: 157–162. 4th Ed. London

542 HECHT, K.(1940) Fischotter beim wintersport. *Dte Jagd, Berlin* Nos. 15–16: 142–143

543 HEDGEPETH, J.W.(1943) Sea otter and the course of empire. *Frontiers, Philad.* **7**(3): 69–72

544 HEINEMAN, A.(1904) The food of otters. *Field* **104**: 1074

545 HEINEMAN, A.(1922) Weight of otters. *Field* **140**: 624

546 HELDREICH, Th.de (1878) *La Faune de Grèce*: 9. Athens: La Philocalie

547 HELLER, E.(1909) [Mammals section of] Birds and mammals of the 1907 Alexander expedition . . . *Univ. Calif. Publs Zool.* **5**: 262

548 HELLER, E.(1913) New races of carnivores. *Smithson. misc. Collns* **61** (19): 1–2

549 HENDRICKSON, J.R.(1956–57) Young otters in captivity. *Malay. Nat. J.* **11**: 127–130

550 HERENDEEN, E.P.(1892) Habits of sea otter. *For. & Stream* **1892**: June

551 HERRICK, C.L.(1892) The mammals of Minnesota. *Bull. geol. nat. Hist. Surv. Minn.* **7**: 128–135

552 HERSHKOVITZ, P.(1951) Mammals from British Honduras . . . *Fieldiana Zool.* **31**: 561

553 HERSHKOVITZ, P.(1959) Nomenclature and taxonomy of the neotropical mammals described by Olfers, 1818. *J. Mammal.* **40**: 342

554 HEUDE, P.M.(1898) Questions sur l'Enhydris . . . *Mém. Hist. nat. Emp. chin.* **4**: 24–31

555 HEUGLIN, M.T.v (1877) *Reise in Nordost-Afrika*: 39. Braunsweig

556 HEUGLIN, M.T.v & FITZINGER, J.L.(1866) Systematische Uebersicht der Säugethiere Nordost-Africa . . . *Sber. Akad. Wiss. Wien* **54**: 564

557 HEUVELMANS, B.(1958) *On the track of unknown animals*: 246–250, 271–275. [trans. Garnett, R.] London: Rupert Hart-Davis

558 HEWITT, C.G.(1921) *The conservation of the wildlife of Canada*: 232. New York

559 HEWITT, J.(1918) *Guide to the fauna of the Albany district*. Part 1. Grahamstown: Albany Museum

560 HEWITT, J.(1931) *Guide to the vertebrate fauna of South Cape Province*. Part 1. Grahamstown: Albany Museum

561 HILDEBRAND, M.(1954) Incisor tooth wear in the sea otter. *J. Mammal.* **35**: 595

562 HILL, J.E.(1947) Sea otter. *Nat. Hist., N.Y.* **56**: 285

563 HILL, J.E.& CARTER, T.D.(1941) The mammals of Angola, Africa. *Bull. Am. Mus. nat. Hist.* **78**: 139, 205

HILL, J.E., *see* Carter, T.D., Hill, J.E. & Tate, G.H.H.

564 HILL, W.C.O.(1939) A revised checklist of the mammals of Ceylon. *Ceylon J. Sci.* (B) **21**: 158

565 HINTON, M.A.C.(1920) The Irish otter. *Ann. Mag. nat. Hist.* (9) **5**: 464

566 HINTON, M.A.C.(1921a) *Paraonyx* – A new genus of clawless otter . . . *Ann. Mag. nat. Hist.* (9) **7**: 194–200

567 HINTON, M.A.C.(1921b) Some new African mammals. *Ann. Mag. nat. Hist.* (9) **7**: 368

568 HINTON, M.A.C.& FRY, T.B.(1923) . . . Mammal survey of India . . . no. 37. Nepal. *J. Bombay nat. Hist. Soc.* **29**: 415–417

569 HODGSON, B.H.[n.d.] [MS. in the possession of the Zoological Society of London]

570 HODGSON, B.H.(1832) On the mammalia of Nepal. *J. Asiatic Soc. Beng.* **1**: 341–342

571 HODGSON, B.H.(1834) On the mammalia of Nepal. *Proc. zool. Soc. Lond.* **1834**: 97

572 HODGSON, B.H.(1839) Summary description of four new species of otter. *J. Asiatic Soc. Beng.* **8**: 320

573 HODGSON, B.H.(1841) Classified catalogue of mammals of Nepal. *J. Asiatic Soc. Beng.* **10**: 909

574 HODGSON, B.H.(1844) Classified catalogue of mammals of Nepal. *Calcutta J. nat. Hist.* **4**: 287

575 HODGSON, B.H.(1855) On the geographical distribution of the mammals and birds of the Himalaya. *Proc. zool. Soc. Lond.* **1855**: 126

HOFFMEISTER, D.F., *see* Goodpaster, W.W. & Hoffmeister, D.F.

576 HOFFMEISTER, D.F. & MOHR, C.O.(1957) *Fieldbook of Illinois mammals*: 104–106. Urbana, Ill: Natural History Survey Division

577 HOLLISTER, N.(1912) A list of mammals of the Philippine Islands. *Philipp. J. Sci.* **7** (D): 21

578 HOLLISTER, N.(1921) [Recent literature: Pohle, Hermann] *J. Mammal.* **2**: 177–178

579 HOME, E. & MENZIES, A.(1796) A description of the anatomy of the sea otter. *Phil. Trans. R. Soc.* **86**: 385. (Reprint: London, 1809. **18**: 34–38)

580 HOOKER, J.D.(1855) *Himalayan journals* **2**: 339. New edition. London

581 HOOPER, C.L.(1897) *Report on the sea otter banks of Alaska.* U.S. Treasury Dept. doc. no. 1977. 35 pp.

582 HOOPER, E.T. & OSTENSON, B.T.(1949) Age groups in Michigan otter. *Occ. pap. Mus. Zool. Univ. Mich.* No. 518: 1–22

HOPKINS, G.H.E., *see* Moreau, R.E. & Hopkins, G.H.E.

583 HOPKINS, J.W.(1956) Sea otter watching. *Mus. Talk S Barbara Mus. nat. Hist.* **31**(2): 17–23

584 HORSFIELD, T.(1824) *Zoological researches in Java.* London: Kingsbury, Parbury & Allen. (pp. unnumbered]

585 HORSFIELD, T.(1851) *A catalogue of the mammalia in the museum of the Hon. East-India Company*: 115–120. London: J. & H.Cox

586 HORSFIELD, T.(1855) Brief notices of several new or little known species of mammalia. *Ann. Mag. nat. Hist.* (2) **16**: 109–110

587 HORSFIELD, T.(1856) Catalogue of a collection of mammalia from Nepal, Sikkim and Tibet ... *Proc. zool. Soc. Lond.* **1856**: 399

588 HOSE, C.(1893) *A descriptive account of the mammals of Borneo*: 27. London

589 HOWELL, A.H.(1921) A biological survey of Alabama. *N. Am. Fauna* No. 45: 40–41

590 HOWSON, C.(1938) Otters and crocodiles. *J. Bombay nat. Hist. Soc.* **40**: 557–558

591 HRDLICKA, A.(1945) *The Aleutian and Commander Islands* ...: 396. Philadelphia

592 HÜGEL, C.A.A.v. (1842) *Kaschmir und das Reich der Siek. Reise.* **2**: 571. Stuttgart

593 HUGHES, M.D.(1949) Otter at Teddington, *Field* **193**: 358

594 HUMBOLDT, A.v (1860) *Reise Aequinoctial-Gegenden neuen Kontinents.* Stuttgart

595 HUME, A.C.(1872) Contribution to the ornithology of India. *Stray Feathers* **1**: 110

596 HUNT, J.(1847) Note on the breeding of the otter in confinement. *Proc. zool. Soc. Lond.* **1847**: 27–28

597 HUNTER, W.P.(1838) *The natural history of the quadrupeds of Paraguay* ... **1**: 326–330, Edinburgh [translation of Azara, 1802]

598 HURLEY, S.J.(1885) Tame otters. *Field* **66**: 776

599 HURLEY, S.J.(1898) White otters. *Field* **91**: 142

600 HURRELL, E.(1963) *Watch for the Otter.* pl. 41, facing p. 81. London: Country Life

601 HUTCHINSON, A.S.(1885) Otters in Derbyshire. *Field* **66**: 742

602 HUTTON, T.(1845) Rough notes on the zoology of Candahar. *J. Asiatic Soc. Beng.* **14**: 351

603 HYSING-DAHL, C.(1959) The Norwegian otter *Lutra lutra* (L.), a craniometric investigation. *Årb. Univ. Bergen* (Nat. rek.) No. 5: 1–44

604 IHERING, H.v. (1911) Os mammiferos do Brazil meridional. 1. Contribuiçao, Carnivora. *Revta Mus. paul.* **8**: 259–265

605 ILLIGER, J.K.W.(1811) *Prodromus Systematis Mammalium* ...: **137**. Berolini

606 ILLIGER, J.K.W.(1804–11) [1815] Ueberblick der Säugethiere nach ihrer Vertheilung über die Welttheile. *Abh. preuss. akad. Wiss.* **1815**: 99

607 INGLES, L.G.(1956) Notas acerca de los mamíferos mexicanos. *An. Inst. Biol. Univ. Méx.* **27**: 405–406

608 INGLIS, C.M.*et al.* (1919) A tentative list of the vertebrates of the Jalpaiguri district, Bengal. *J. Bombay nat. Hist. Soc.* **26**: 823

609 IRVING, L.(1939) Respiration in diving animals. *Physiol. Rev.* **19**: 112–134

610 IRVING, L.(1942) The action of the heart and circulation during diving. *Trans. N.Y. Acad. Sci.* (2) **5**: 11–16

611 ISHUNIN, G.I.(1961) [The otter in Uzbekistan] *Zool. Zh.* **40**: 1745–1746

612 ISRAELS, J.(1942) Fetch, Otties! *Saturday Evening Post* **214**(33): 16–17, 74–76

613 JACKSON, C.F.(1922) Notes on New Hampshire mammals. *J. Mammal.* **3**: 15

614 JACKSON, H.H.T.(1931) Otter, playfellow of the wild. *Home geog. Month.* **1** (9): 44–48

615 JACOBI, A.(1938) Der Seeotter. *Kleint. Pelzt., Lpz.* **1938** (8). 93 pp.

616 JARDINE, J.(1866) Otters in the Itchen. *Field* **27**: 464

617 JARVIS, C.[Editor] (1963) Mammals bred in captivity. *Int. Zoo Yb.* **5**: 338

JARVIS, C., *see* Morris, D. & Jarvis, C.

618 JARVIS, C. & MORRIS, D.[Editors] (1960a) Dimensions of moats and ditches at Detroit Zoo. *Int. Zoo Yb.* **2**: 66–67

619 JARVIS, C. & MORRIS, D.[Editors] (1960b) Mammalian longevity survey. *Int. Zoo Yb.* **2**: 296

620 JARVIS, C. & MORRIS, D.[Editors] (1961) Breeding seasons of mammals in captivity. *Int. Zoo Yb.* **3**: 294

621 JARVIS, C. & MORRIS, D.[Editors] (1962a) Mammals bred in captivity. *Int. Zoo Yb.* **4**: 229

622 JARVIS, C. & MORRIS, D.[Editors] (1962b). Census of rare animals. *Int. Zoo Yb.* **4**: 271

623 JEFFERY, W.(1868) Food of the otter. *Zoologist* (2) **3**: 1253–1254

624 JENKINS, D.H.(1951) What we otter know. *Mich. Conserv.* **20** (2): 9–10, 23–24

625 JENNE, F.(1964) [February report of] *Steinhart Aquarium.* Calif. Acad. Sci. (mimeo.)

626 JENNISON, G.(1928) *Noah's cargo*: 218–224. London: A. & C. Black

627 JENTINK, F.A.(1887) On mammals from Mossamedes. *Notes Leyden Mus.* **9**: 172

628 JENTINK, F.A.(1898) Zoological results of the Dutch Scientific Expedition to central Borneo. *Notes Leyden Mus.* **20**: 121–123

629 JENYNS, L.(1835) *A manual of British vertebrate animals*: 13. Cambridge

630 JERDON, T.C.(1874) *Mammals of India*: 86–89. London

631 JEX, H.S.(1960) Lutra, the elusive. *Audubon Mag.* **62**: 114–115, 135, 148

632 JOBELL, W.(1904) Otters eaten in Monmouthshire. *Field* **104**: 460

633 JOHNSON, C.E.(1922) Notes on the mammals of Northern Lake County, Minnesota. *J. Mammal.* **3**: 38–39

634 JOHNSON, T.B.(1851) *The gamekeeper's directory*: 111–112. London

635 JOHNSTON, H.(1903) *British mammals*: 5, 138–140. London: Hutchinson & Son

636 JOLEAUD, L.(1934) *La science au Maroc . . .*: 255. Casablanca: Assoc. Franç. pour l'Avanc. des Scienc.

637 JONES, R.D.(1951) Present status of the sea otter in Alaska. *Trans. N. Am. Wildl. Conf.* **16**: 376–383

638 JONES, R.D.(1951) [1953] A report of sea otter investigations conducted during 1951. *Proc. 2nd Alaskan Sci. Conf*: 351–355

639 JONES, R.D.(1965) Sea otters in the Near Islands, Alaska. *J. Mammal.* **46**: 702

JONES, R.D., *see* Kirkpatrick, C.M., Stullken, D.E. & Jones, R.D.

640 JONES, W.H.S.[Translator] (1963) *Pliny. Natural History.* **3**: 79; **8**: 553. London

641 KAPLIN, A.A.(1959) [On sea otters] *Priroda* **9**: 107–109

642 KAUKL, M.O.(1950) Game farm otter. *Wisc. Conserv. Bull.* **15** (12): 21–22

643 KEITH, E.F.(1944) Facts about otters. *Outdoorsmen, Chicago* **86**: 26–28

644 KELAART, E.F.(1852) *Prodromus Faunae Zeylanicae*: 34–35. Ceylon

645 KELKER, G.H.(1943) A winter wildlife census in northeastern Wisconsin. *J. Wildl. Mgmt* **7**: 133

646 KELLOGG, R.(1939) Annotated list of Tennessee mammals. *Proc. U.S. natn. Mus.* **86**: 263

KELLOGG, R., *see* Miller, G.S. & Kellogg, R.

647 KELSALL, H.J.(1894) A journey on the Sebrong River: list of mammals. *J. Straits Bch R. Asiat. Soc.* **26**: 16

KELSON, K.R., *see* Hall, E.R. & Kelson, K.R.

648 KELWAY, P.(1940) Otter. *Game Gun and Angl. Mon.* **17** (174): 122–125

649 KELWAY, P.(1944) *The Otter book.* 144 pp. London: Collins

650 KENNICOTT, R.(1859) *Quadrupeds of Illinois*: 247

651 KENYON, K.W.(1957) The sea otter. *Oryx* **4**: 153–158

652 KENYON, K.W.(1959) The sea otter. *Rep. Smithson. Inst.* **1958**: 399–407

653 KENYON, K.W.(1963) Recovery of a fur bearer. *Nat. Hist., N.Y.* **72** (9): 12–21

654 KENYON, K.W. & SCHEFFER, V.B.(1953) The seals, sea-lions and sea otter of the Pacific coast. *Leafl. U.S. Fish Wildl. Serv.* No. 344: 1–28

655 KENYON, K.W. & SCHEFFER, V.B.(1955) The seals, sea-lions and sea otter of the Pacific coast. *Circ. Fish Wildl. Serv., Wash.* **32**: 3–5

656 KERR, J.G.(1892) Remarks on the late Captain John Page's expedition ... *Proc. zool. Soc. Lond.* **1892**: 175

657 KERR, R.(1792) *The animal kingdom or zoological system* ...: 171–174. London: J.Murray

KING, J., *see* Cook, J. & King, J.

658 KIPLING, J.L.(1891) *Beast and man in India*: 327–328. London: MacMillan

KIRIS, I.B., *see* Pavlov, M.P. & Kiris, I.B.

659 KIRK, C.(1903) Cream-coloured otter. *Ann. Scot. nat. Hist.* **12**: 117

660 KIRK, J.(1864) List of mammalia met with in Zambesia ... *Proc. zool. Soc. Lond.* **1864**: 652

661 KIRKLAND, W.(1955) *Adventures of a cameraman*: 241–244. London: MacMillan

KIRKPATRICK, C.M., *see* Stullken, D.E. & Kirkpatrick, C.M.

662 KIRKPATRICK, C.M., STULLKEN, D.E. & JONES, R.D.(1955) Notes on captive sea otters. *Arctic* **8** (1): 46–59

663 KLEIN, J.T.(1743) *Circa classes Quadrupedum et Amphibiorum*: 16. Lipsiae

664 KLEIN, J.T.(1751) *Quadrupedum Dispositio*: 91. Lipsiae

KLOSS, C.B., *see* Chasen, F.N. & Kloss, C.B.

KLOSS, C.B., *see* Robinson, H.C. & Kloss, C.B.

665 KLUMOV, S.K.(1957) [*Enhydra lutris* in the Kurile islands] *Dokl. Akad. Nauk SSSR* **117**: 153–156

KOCK, L.L.de, *see* de Kock, L.L.

666 KOMAREK, E.V.(1932) Notes on mammals of Menominee Indian Reservation, Wisconsin. *J. Mammal.* **13**: 205

667 KOZHANTSCHIKOV, L.(1924) Die Gewerbe-Jagd und Fischerei im Urwalde des Minussinsk Bezirks. *Ezheg. gosud. Muz. N.M. Mart'yonova* **2** (2): 79–183

668 KRAGLIEVICH, L.(1917) La perforacion astragaliana en *Conepatus, Lutra* y *Sarcophilus. Physis, Buenos Aires* 3: 416

669 KRAUSS (1886) Varietät einer Fischotter. *Jh. Ver. vaterl. Naturk. Wurtt.* 42: 344–345

670 KREBSER, W.(1959) Die Bestandsaufnature des Fischotters (*Lutra l. lutra*) in der Schweiz, 1951–53. *Säugetierk. Mitt.* 7: 67–75

671 KRISHNA GOWDA, C.D.(1962) [Contribution to] International survey of handrearing techniques. *Int. Zoo Yb.* 4: 314–315

672 KROG, J.(1953) Notes on the birds of Amchitka Island, Alaska. *Condor* 55: 301–304

673 KRUMBIEGEL, I.(1942) Zur Kenntnis der Säugetierfauna von Fernando Po. *Arch. Naturgesch.* N.F. 11: 343

674 LAGLER, K.F. & OSTENSON, B.T.(1942) Early spring food of the otter in Michigan. *J. Wildl. Mgmt* 6: 244–254

675 LANCASTER, D.G.(1953) *A check list of the mammals of Northern Rhodesia*: 23. Lusaka: Northern Rhodesia Government

676 LANCUM, F.H.(1951) Wild mammals and the land. *Bull. Minist. Agric. Fish. Fd, Lond.* No. 150: 14–16

677 LANG, H.(1924) Position of limbs in the sliding otter. *J. Mammal.* 5: 216–217

678 LANGKAVEL, B.(1900) Gewicht und lange des Fischotters. *Zool. Gart., Frankf.* 41: 244–245

LANNING, R.G., *see* Brown, N.R. & Lanning, R.G.

679 LANTZ, D.E.(1905) A list of Kansas mammals. *Trans. Kans. Acad. Sci.* 19: 171–178

680 LARKEN, E.P.(1889) Badgers and otters in Surrey. *Zoologist* (3) 13: 23–24

681 LARRANAGA (1923) *Escritos* 2: 345

682 LATASTE, F.(1885) Étude de la faune des vertébrés de Barbarie . . . *Act. Soc. linn. Bordeaux* (4) 39 (9): 168, 237–238

683 LATASTE, F.(1887) *Exploration Scientifique de la Tunisie.* Zoologie – Mammifères: 18–19. Paris

684 LAUGHLIN, J.(1955) River otter noted east of Sierran crest. *Calif. Fish Game* 41: 189

685 LAUT, A.(1921) Sea otter and land otter. *For. & Stream* 91: 8–9

686 LAW, J.P.(1921) Rearing an otter cub. *Field* 138: 672

687 LAWSON, D.A.(1919) Measurements and weights of otters. *Field* 134: 134

688 LAYARD, E.L.(1861) *Catalogue of specimens in the South Africa Museum.* 1. Mammals: 28–29. Capetown

689 LECH, S.(1907) [Notes on the sea otter] *Zap. Obšhčh. zučh. amursk. Kraya* 10: 1–37

690 LECHE, W.(1915) Zur Frage nach der stammesgeschichtlicher Bedeutung des Milchgebisses bei den Säugetieren. *Zool. Jb.* (Syst.) 38: 339–343

LEE, M.R., *see* Durrant, S.D. & Lee, M.R.

691 LEE, R.B.(1885) Young otters and fish. *Field* 66: 689

692 LEE, R.B.(1904) The breeding time of otters. *Field* 103: 189

693 LEGGE, J.(1898) White otters. *Field* 91: 124

LEKHE, S., *see* Lech, S.

694 LENSINK, C.J. (1960) Status and distribution of sea otters in Alaska. *J. Mammal.* **41**: 172–182

695 LESSON, R.P. (1827) *Manuel de Mammalogie*: 153–157. Paris

696 LESSON, R.P. (1842) *Nouveau Tableau du Règne Animal*. Mammifères: 71–73. Paris

697 LETT, W.P. (1884) The Canadian otter. *Trans. Ottawa Fld Nat. Cl.* **2** (2): 177–188

698 LEVITRE, J. (1929) *La Loutre – Piègeage à Chasse*. Paris

699 LEWIS, J.B. (1940) Mammals of Amelia County, Virginia. *J. Mammal.* **21**: 425

700 LICHTENSTEIN, K.M.H. (1815) Die werke von Marcgrave. *Abh. preuss. Akad. Wiss.* **1815**: 220

701 LICHTENSTEIN, K.M.H. (1827–34) *Darstellung ... Säugethiere*. pls. XLIX; [L]. Berlin

702 LICHTENSTEIN. K.M.H. (1835) Ueber *Lutra maculicollis* Lichtenst. aus dem Kafferlande. *Arch. Nat. Berl.* **1**: 89–92

703 LIERS, E.E. (1951a) Notes on the river otter (*Lutra canadensis*). *J. Mammal.* **32**: 1–9

704 LIERS, E.E. (1951b) My friends the land otters. *Nat. Hist., N.Y.* **60**: 320–326

705 LIERS, E.E. (1953) *An otter's story*. 191 pp. New York: Viking Press

706 LIERS, E.E. (1958) Early breeding in the river otter. *J. Mammal.* **39**: 438–439

707 LIERS, E.E. (1960) Notes on breeding the Canadian otter. *Int. Zoo Yb.* **2**: 84–85

708 LIMBAUGH, C. (1961) Observations on the California sea otter. *J. Mammal.* **42**: 271–272

709 LINCOLN, F.C. (1957–58) Saving North America's endangered species. *Oryx* **4**: 365–366

710 LINNAEUS, C. (1758) *Systema Naturae*. Bk. I: 45. 10th Ed. Stockholm
LINSDALE, J.M., *see* Grinnell, J., Dixon, J.S. & Linsdale, J.M.

711 LINSLEY, J.H. (1842) A catalogue of the mammalia of Connecticut. *Silliman's J.* **43**: 345–354

712 LITTLEJOHN, C. (1916) Habits and hunting of the sea otter. *Calif. Fish Game* **2** (2): 79–82

713 LLOYD, J.I. (1951a) When do otters breed? *Field* **197**: 1035

714 LLOYD, J.I. (1951b) Secrets of an otter. *Field* **198**: 645

715 LLOYD, J.I. (1962) Where are the otters? *Gamekpr & Countryside* **65**: 299–300

716 LLOYD, P. (1878) Curious capture of an otter. *Field* **54**: 854

717 LLOYD-EDWARDES, T. (1886) Otters caught in nets at sea. *Field* **68**: 331

718 LOCHE, V. (1867) *Exploration Scientifique de l'Algérie ...* 1840–42. Mammifères: 49–51. Paris
LOCKER, B., *see* Rausch, R. & Locker, B.

719 LOGAN, W. (1943) Otter taking hooked trout. *Ir. Nat. J.* **8** (3): 78

720 LÖNNBERG, E. (1908) On the clawless otter of central Africa (*Lutra capensis hindei* Thomas) ... *Ark. Zool.* **4** (12): 1–11

721 LÖNNBERG, E. (1911–13) A new subspecies of clawless otter (*Aonyx capensis congica*) from Lower Congo. *Ark. Zool.* **7** (9): 1–8

722 LÖNNBERG, E.(1913–14) Notes on new and rare mammals from Congo. *Revue zool. Afr.* **3**: 275–276

723 LÖNNBERG, E.(1919–20) Remarks on some Congo mammals. *Revue zool. Afr.* **7**: 243

724 LOVERIDGE, A.(1923) Notes on East African mammals, collected 1920–23. *Proc. zool. Soc. Lond.* **1923**: 713

725 LOW, J.(1752) *Publ. Swedish Acad.* **13**: 139–149
LUKENS, P.W., *see* Davis, W.B. & Lukens, P.W.

726 LUTHE, W.(1924) Ueber die Fusswurzelknochen der Fischottern. *Arch. Naturgesch.* **110** A.4: 59–141

727 LYDEKKER, R.(1880) Notes on some Ladák mammals. *J. Asiatic Soc. Beng.* **49** (2): 6

728 LYDEKKER, R.(1895a) Note on the structure and habits of the sea otter. *Proc. zool. Soc. Lond.* **1895**: 421–423

729 LYDEKKER, R.(1895b) *A handbook of British mammalia*: 134–140. London

730 LYDEKKER, R.(1896) Additional note on the sea otter. *Proc. zool. Soc. Lond.* **1895**: 235–236

731 LYON, M.W.Jr.(1908) Mammals collected in western Borneo by Dr W.L. Abbott. *Proc. U.S. natn. Mus.* **33**: 560–561

732 LYON, M.W.Jr.(1909) Additional notes on mammals of the Rhio-Linga Archipelago. *Proc. U.S. natn. Mus.* **36**: 485–486; pl. 39

733 LYON, M.W.Jr.(1911) Mammals collected by Dr W.L.Abbott in Borneo . . . *Proc. U.S. natn. Mus.* **40**: 118–119

734 MABERLY, C.T.A.(1960) *Animals of East Africa*: 161. Cape Town: Howard Timmins

735 MACALISTER, A.(1873) On the anatomy of *Aonyx. Proc. R. Ir. Acad. Science.* (2) **1**: 539–547

736 McCANN, C.(1923) Some notes on the common Indian otter. *J. Bombay nat. Hist. Soc.* **29**: 275–276

737 McCLELLAN, J.(1954) An otter catch on the Gila River in southwestern New Mexico. *J. Mammal.* **35**: 443

738 McCRACKEN, H.(1920) When the sea otter flourished. *For. & Stream* **90**: 298, 332–333

739 McCRACKEN, H.(1927) Mysterious sea otter. *Nature Mag.* **5**: 169–172

740 McCRACKEN, H.(1942) *Last of the sea otters.* 99 pp. Philadelphia: F.A. Stokes Co.

741 MACDIARMID, J.(1830) *Sketches from nature.* Edinburgh

742 MACDONALD, A.S.(1938) *Pacific pelts* . . . 12 pp. [priv. printed] Oakland, Calif.

743 MACFARLANE, R.(1905) Notes on mammals collected and observed in the northern Mackenzie River district. *Proc. U.S. natn. Mus.* **23**: 716–717

744 MACGILLIVRAY, W.(1838) *A history of British quadrupeds*: 174–181. Edinburgh

745 McINTOSH, A.(1939) *Diplostomum fosteri* n. sp. from a Panama otter, *Lutra repanda* Goldman. *J. Parasit.* **25** suppl: 25

746 Mc'INTOSH, J.(1849) Frequent occurrence of the badger, otter and polecat in Dorsetshire. *Zoologist* (1) **7**: 2407

747 MACINTYRE, D.(1950) Habits of the otter. *Field* **196**: 546

748 MACKENZIE, G.A.(1950) Value of otters. *Field* **196**: 738

MACLATCHY, A., *see* Malbrant, R. & Maclatchy, A.

749 MACLAY, D.J.(1937) Case of the otter. *N. Region News* **1937**: 34

750 McLEAN, D.D.(1938) Southern sea otter on Pacific coast. *Ass. Sportsm.* **5** (5): 6–7

751 MACLOUGHLIN, J.H.(1950) An otter in Belfast. *Ir. Nat. J.* **10** (2): 42

752 McMASTER, A.C.(1870) *Notes on Jerdon's Mammals of India.* 18–22, 176–177. Madras

McMULLEN, H.J., *see* Ashbrook, F.G. & McMullen, H.J.

753 MACPHERSON, H.A.(1892) *A vertebrate fauna of Lakeland*: 37. Edinburgh

754 MAJOR, C.J.F.(1897a) Der centralamerikanische Fischotter und seine nächsten Verwandten. *Zool. Anz.* **20**: 136–142,

755 MAJOR, C.J.F.(1897b) The otter of Central America. *Ann. Mag. nat. Hist.* (6) **19**: 618–620

756 MALBRANT, R. & MACLATCHY, A.(1949) *Faune de l'Équateur Africain Français.* **2**: Mammifères. Paris: Lechevalier

757 MALDZHYUNÄITE, S.A.(1960) [Distribution and feeding of otter in Lithuania] *Liet. TSR Mokslu Akad. biol. Inst. Darb.* C 3 (23): 181–189

758 MALDZHYUNÄITE, S.A.(1962) [Occurrence of otter in the delta of the River Nyamunas] *2nd Zool. Conf. Lith. S.S.R. Summ. Rep.*: 69–72

759 MALKOVITCH, T.A.(1937) [The sea otter in captivity] *Priroda, Mosc.* **3**: 81–87

760 MALKOVITCH, T.A.(1938) [Acclimatizing the sea otter in the Murmansk Region] *Priroda, Mosc.* **7** & **8**: 194–197

761 MANN, F.G.(1957–58) Clave de determinacion para les especies de mamíferos silvestres de Chile. *Investnes zool. chile* **4**: 123

762 MANVILLE, R.H.(1942) Notes on the mammals of Mount Desert Island, Maine. *J. Mammal.* **23**: 394

763 MANVILLE, R.H.(1950) The mammals of Drummond Island, Michigan. *J. Mammal.* **31**: 358–359

764 MARCGRAVE, G.(1648) *Historia Rerum Naturalium Brasiliae*: 234. Amsterdam

765 MARGOLIS, L.(1954) List of the parasites recorded from sea mammals caught off the west coast of North America. *J. Fish. Res. Bd Can.* **11**: 267–283

766 MARR, P.(1950) Emil Liers, the otter man. *Nature Mag.* **43** (3): 127–129

767 MARSDEN, W.(1811) *The history of Sumatra*: pl. XI. London

768 MARTIN, W.(1836) Description of the osteology of the sea otter ... *Proc. zool. Soc. Lond.* **1836**: 59–62

769 MATSCHIE, P.(1895) *Die Säugetiere Deutsch-Ost-Afrikas*: 86. Berlin

770 MATSCHIE, P.(1907) Über chinesische Säugetiere ... [in Filchner, W. *Zoologisch-Botanische Ergebnisse der Expedition China-Tibet*: 150–151]

771 MATTHEW, W.D. & GIDLEY, J.W.(1904) New or little known mammals ... of South Dakota. *Bull. Am. Mus. nat. Hist.* **20**: 256

772 MATTHEWS, L.H.(1952) *British mammals.* Various pp. London: Collins

773 MAXWELL, G.(1960) *Ring of bright water.* 211 pp. London: Longmans, Green

774 MAXWELL, G.(1961) The life and times of Mij & Edal. *Nat. Hist., N.Y.* **70** (3): 50–61

775 MAXWELL, G.(1962) *The otter's tale.* 43 pp. London: Longmans, Green

776 MAXWELL, G.(1963a) The misunderstood otter. *Animals* 19 February 1963: 27

777 MAXWELL, G.(1963b) *The rocks remain.* 186 pp. London: Longmans, Green

778 MAXWELL, H.(1929) Fate of two otters. *Scott. Nat.* **1929** (175): 7

779 MAY, A.G.(1942) The northern sea otter. *Nat. Hist., N.Y.* **52**: 22–23

780 MAYNARD, C.J.(1883) The mammals of Florida. *Q. Jl Boston zool. Soc.* **2**: 1, 5–6

781 MAYNARD, L.A.(1947) *Animal nutrition*: 409. New York: McGraw-Hill

782 MEARNS, E.A.(1890–91) Notes on the otter (*L. canadensis*) of Arizona. *Bull. Am. Mus. nat. Hist.* **3**: 252–256

783 MEARNS, E.A.(1898) A study of the vertebrate fauna of the Hudson Highlands. *Bull. Am. Mus. nat. Hist.* **10**: 347

784 MEARNS, E.A.(1899) Notes on the mammals of the Catskill Mountains ... *Proc. U.S. natn. Mus.* **1899**: 360

785 MEDWAY, LORD (1965) *Mammals of Borneo*: 143–144. Singapore: Malaysian Branch Royal Asiatic Soc.

786 MELCHIOR, H.B.(1834) *Den danske Stats og Norges Pattedyr*: 50, & pl. V. Kjöbenhaven

787 MENNELL, H.T. & PERKINS, V.R.(1863–4) Catalogue of the mammalia of Northumberland and Durham. *Trans. Tyneside Nat. Fld Club* **6**: 126–134

788 MENZEL, C.(1660) *Theatri Rerum Naturalium Brasiliae.* **3** (2): 75

MENZIES, A., *see* Home, E. & Menzies, A.

789 MERRIAM, C.H.(1882) The vertebrates of the Adirondacks Region. *Trans. Linn. Soc. N.Y.* **1**: 87–91

790 MERRIAM, C.H.(1890) Results of a biological survey of the San Francisco mountain region ... *N. Am. Fauna* **3**: 85

791 MERRIAM, C.H.(1891) Results of a biological reconnoissance of south-central Idaho. *N. Am. Fauna* **5**: 82–83

792 MERRIAM, C.H.(1899) Results of a biological survey of Mount Shasta, California. *N. Am. Fauna* **16**: 106

793 MERRIAM, C.H.(1904) A new sea otter from southern California. *Proc. biol. Soc. Wash.* **17**: 159–160

794 MERTENS, R.(1935) Aus dem Leben des Seeotters. *Natur Volk* **65**: 401–407

795 MERTZ, O.(1931) Weitere Erfahrungen in der heutigen Nerzranz. *Deutsche Pelztierzüchter* **11**: 303–304

796 MEYERRIECKS, A.J.(1963) Florida otter preys on common gallinule. *J. Mammal.* **44**: 425–426

797 MIDDENDORF, A.T.v (1858) *Reise in den aussersten Norden und Bater Siberiens.* **2**: 70. St Petersburg

798 MILLAIS, J.G.(1905) *The mammals of Great Britain and Ireland.* **2**: 1–36. London: Longmans, Green

799 MILLER, G.S.Jr.(1897) Notes on the mammals of Ontario. *Proc. Boston Soc. nat. Hist.* **28**: 41

800 MILLER, G. S. Jr. (1899) Preliminary list of the mammals of New York. *Bull. N.Y. St. Mus.* **6** (29): 271–390

801 MILLER, G. S. Jr. (1907) The mammals collected by Dr W. L. Abbott in the Rhio-Linga Archipelago. *Proc. U.S. natn. Mus.* **31**: 270

802 MILLER, G. S. Jr. (1912a) List of North American land mammals in the United States National Museum, 1911. *Bull. U.S. natn. Mus.* **79**: 113–115

803 MILLER, G. S. Jr. (1912b) *Catalogue of the mammals of western Europe*: 354–364. London: Trustees of the British Museum

804 MILLER, G. S. Jr. (1923) List of North American recent mammals. *Bull. U.S. natn. Mus.* **128**: 129–131

805 MILLER, G. S. Jr. & KELLOGG, R. (1955) List of North American recent mammals. *Bull. U.S. natn. Mus.* **205**: 762–767

MILLER, J. E., *see* Miller, W. & Miller, J. E.

806 MILLER, W. & MILLER, J. E. (1899) *U.S. Fur Seals Investigation.* pt. 3: 179–218

807 MILLER-BEN-SHAUL, D. (1962) The composition of the milk of wild animals. *Int. Zoo Yb.* **4**: 337

808 MILLS, J. P. (1923) . . . Mammal survey of India, Burma and Ceylon. Rep. no. 36. Naga Hills. *J. Bombay nat. Hist.* **29**: 225

809 MILNE-EDWARDS, A. (1891) *Mission Scientifique du Cap Horn.* **6**: A14–A15. Paris

810 MISONNE, X. (1959) Analyse zoogéographique des mammifères de l'Iran. *Mém. Inst. Sci. nat. Belg.* (2) No. 59: 32

811 MITCHELL, F. B. (1951) When do otters breed? *Field* **198**: 189

812 MITCHELL, P. C. (1911a) On longevity and relative viability in mammals . . . *Proc. zool. Soc. Lond.* **1911**: 441

813 MITCHELL, P. C. (1911b) *The childhood of animals:* 42. London: Heinemann

814 MOFFAT, C. B. (1927) The otter. *Ir. Nat. J.* **1**: 209–212

MOHR, C. O., *see* Hoffmeister, D. F. & Mohr, C. O.

815 MOLINA, G. I. (1776) *Compendio della Storia Geographica, Naturale, e Civile . . . del Chile*: 80–81. Bologna: Aquino

816 MOLINA, G. I. (1782) *Saggio sulla Storia naturale del Chili*: 284–287. Bologna: Aquino

817 MONARD, A. (1935) Mission scientifique Suisse dans l'Angola: Mammifères. *Bull. Soc. neuchatel. Sci. nat.* **57**: 64–66

818 MONARD, A. (1951) Résultats de la Mission zoologique Suisse du Cameroun. *Mém. Inst. fr. Afr. noire* ser. Sci. Nat. **1**: 13

819 MONAT, M. E. (1915) Otter (*Lutra vulgaris*) at Barrahead Lighthouse. *Scott. Nat.* **37**: 333

820 MÖNNIG, H. O. (1934) *Veterinary helminthology and entomology*: 50, 247, 387. London: Ballière, Tindall & Cox

821 MOORE, J. C. (1946) Mammals from Welaka, Putnam County, Florida. *J. Mammal.* **27**: 54

822 MOORE-WILSON, M. (1898) Florida otter pets. *For. Stream* **1898**: – July 30: 84

823 MOREAU, R. E., HOPKINS, G. H. E. & HAYMAN, R. W. (1945–6) The type localities of some African mammals. *Proc. zool. Soc. Lond.* **115**: 408

824 MOREAU-SAINT-MÉRY, L.E.(1801) *Essais sur l'Histoire Naturelle des Quadrupédes de la Province du Paraguay*: 348–354. Paris [a translation of Azara, 1802 (*sic*)]

MORRIS, D., *see* Jarvis, C. & Morris, D.

825 MORRIS, D. & JARVIS, C.[Editors] (1959) Mammalian gestation periods. *Int. Zoo Yb.* **1**: 159

826 MORRIS, R.F.(1948) The land mammals of New Brunswick. *J. Mammal.* **29**: 169

MORRISON-SCOTT, T.C.S., *see* Ellerman, J.R. & Morrison-Scott, T.C.S.

MORRISON-SCOTT, T.C.S., *see* Ellerman, J.R., Morrison-Scott, T.C.S. & Hayman, R.W.

827 MORTIMER, M.A.E.(1963) Notes on the biology and behaviour of the spotted-necked otter ... *Puku* **1**: 192–206

828 MOSELEY, H.N.(1892) *Notes by a naturalist on the 'Challenger'*: 132–133. New & rev. ed. London

829 MULLER, G.F.(1758) *Sammlung Ruszischer Geschichte* **3**: 529

830 MULLER, G.W.(1922) Otters catching eels. *Field* **139**: 778

831 MÜLLER, S.(1839–44) *Over de Zoogdieren van den Indischen Archipel.* **2**: 27, 51

832 MURIE, O.J.(1940a) Food habits of the northern bald eagle ... *Condor* **42**: 202

833 MURIE, O.J.(1940b) Notes on the sea otter. *J. Mammal.* **21**: 119–131

834 MURIE, O.J.(1959) Fauna of the Aleutian Islands and Alaska Peninsula. *N. Am. Fauna.* **61**: 278–287

835 MURPHY, M.F.(1939) Sea otter – past and present. *Nature Mag.* **32**: 425–428

836 MURPHY, R.C.(1937) Hunting we will go! ... *Nat. Hist., N.Y.* **39**: 231–236

837 MURR, E.(1929) Zur erklärung der verlängerten tragdauer bei säugetieren. *Zool. Anz.* **85** (5–8): 113–129

838 MURRAY, A.(1859–62a) Contributions to the natural history of the Hudson's Bay Company territories. *Proc. R. phys. Soc. Edinb.* **2**: 26

839 MURRAY, A.(1859–62b) Contributions to the fauna of Old Calabar – Mammals. *Proc. R. phys. Soc. Edinb.* **2**: 157–158

840 MURRAY, A.(n.d.) *Zoology of Beloochistan*: 34. Bombay

841 MUSY, M.(1918) La destruction de la loutre en Suisse. *Bull. Soc. Sci. nat. Fribourg* **24**: 163–171

842 MYER, K.G.(1947) Betty the otter. *Zoo Life* **2**: 125–126

843 NAIR, R.K.(1962) [Contribution to] International survey of hand-rearing techniques. *Int. Zoo Yb.* **4**: 315

844 NEAL, E.G.(1961) *Topsy and Turvy, my two otters.* 69 pp. London: Heinemann

845 NEAL, E.G.(1962) *Animals of Britain. No. 8. Otters.* 25 pp. London: *Sunday Times*

846 NEHRING, A.(1886) Über *Lutra brasiliensis, L. paranensis* ... *Sber. Ges. naturf. Freunde Berl.* **1886**: 144–150

847 NEHRING, A.(1887) Über die Gray'schen Fischotter-gattungen *Lutronectes, Lontra* und *Pteronura. Sber. Ges. naturf. Freunde Berl.* **1899**: 21–25

373

848 NEHRING, A.(1899) [1900] Über *Lutra (Pteronura) paranensis* . . . *Sber. Ges. naturf. Freunde Berl.* **1899**: 221–228

849 NEHRING, A.(1901) Einige Notizen ueber die *Lutra (Pteronura) paranensis* des niesigen zoologischen Gartens. *Sber. Ges. naturf. Freunde Berl.* **1901**: 133–135

850 NELSON, E.W.(1887) *Report upon natural history collections made in Alaska.* Washington. No. 3: 250–251

851 NEUMANN, O.(1902) Über neue nordost- und ostafrikanische Säugetiere. *Sber. Ges. naturf. Freunde Berl.* **1902**: 55–56

852 NEUSEL, A.(n.d.) *La Loutre.* Lausanne

853 NEWCOMBE, W.A.(1928) [1929] The sea-otter. *Rep. prov. Mus. nat. Hist. Anthrop. Br. Columb.* **1928**: F12–F14

854 NEWMAN, G.C.(1953) An otter's toll. *Field* **201**: 1088

855 NEWSOM, W.M.(1937) Mammals on Anticosti Island. *J. Mammal.* **18**: 438

856 NIETHAMMER, J.(1962) Die Säugetiere von Korfu. *Bonner zool. Beitr.* **13**: 26

857 NILSSON, S.(1847) *Skandinavisk Fauna.* I. Däggdjuren: 174–182. Lund

858 NOACK, T.(1889) Beiträge zur Kenntnis der Säugetierefauna von süd- und süd-west Afrika. *Zool. Jb.* (Syst.)4: 168

859 NOPSCSA, F.(1905) Remarks on the supposed clavicle of . . . *Diplodocus. Proc. zool. Soc. Lond.* **1905 2**: 292

860 NOVIKOV, G.A.(1956) *Carnivorous mammals of the fauna of the U.S.S.R.*: 216–218 [trans. 1962]. Jerusalem

861 OAKLEY, E.F.(1903) Weight of otter. *Field* **101**: 1091

862 OGDEN, A.(1941) The California sea otter trade, 1784–1848. *Univ. Calif. Publs Hist.* **36**: 1–25

863 OGILBY, W.(1834) Notice of a new species of otter from the north of Ireland. *Proc. zool. Soc. Lond.* **1834**: 110–111

864 OGNEV, S.I.(1931) *Mammals of Eastern Europe and Northern Asia*: 2: 374–410 [trans. 1962]. Jerusalem

865 OKEN, L.(1816) *Lehrbuch der Naturgeschichte*: 985–991. Jena
OLDHAM, C., *see* Coward, T.A. & Oldham, C.

866 OLFERS, I.V.(1818) Chapter 10. In *Journal von Brasilien.* Eschwege, W.L. (ed.) (q.v.)

867 OLROG, C.C.(1950) Notas sobre mamíferos y aves del archipielago de Cabo de Hornos. *Acta zool. lilloana* **9**: 509–510

868 OLSTAD, O.(1945) *Jaktzoologi.* [Game animals of Norway] Oslo

869 ORR, R.T.(1959) Sharks as enemies of sea otters. *J. Mammal.* **40**: 617

870 OSBORN, F.(1944) *The Pacific World*: 186–187. New York: W.W.Norton & Co.

871 OSGOOD, F.L.(1938) The mammals of Vermont. *J. Mammal.* **19**: 437

872 OSGOOD, W.H.(1900) Results of a biological reconnaissance of the Yukon River region. *N. Am. Fauna.* **19**: 41

873 OSGOOD, W.H.(1901) Natural history of Q. Charlotte Islands, B.C., and of the Cook Inlet region, Alaska. *N. Am. Fauna* **21**: 32, 69

874 OSGOOD, W.H.(1904) A biological reconnaissance of the base of the Alaska Peninsula. *N. Am. Fauna* **24**: 45

875 OSGOOD, W.H.(1909) Biological investigations in Alaska and Yukon Territory. *N. Am. Fauna* **30**: 29, 57, 82

876 OSGOOD, W.H.(1912) Mammals from western Venezuela and eastern Colombia. *Publs Field Mus. nat. Hist.* Zool. **10**: 60

877 OSGOOD, W.H.(1932) Mammals of the Kelly-Roosevelt and Delacour Asiatic expeditions. *Publs Field Mus. nat. Hist.* Zool. **18**: 262

878 OSGOOD, W.H.(1943) The mammals of Chile. *Publs Field Mus. nat. Hist.*
Zool. **30**: 88–91

879 OSGOOD, W.H., PREBLE, E.A. & PARKER, G.H. (1914) The fur seals and
other life of the Pribilof Islands, Alaska, in 1914. *Bull. U.S. Fish. Commn* **34**:
130–131

OSTENSON, B.T., *see* Lagler, K.F. & Ostenson, B.T.

OSTENSON, B.T., *see* Hooper, E.T. & Ostenson, B.T.

880 OVER, W.H. & CHURCHILL, E.P.(1945). *Mammals of South Dakota*: 17.
Vermilion: Univ. S. Dakota

881 OYER, P.H.(1917) Sea otters seen near Monterey. *Calif. Fish Game.* **3**: 88

882 PALLAS, P.S.(1811) *Zoographia Rosso-Asiatica* **1**: 100. St Petersburg

883 PALMER, T.S.(1904) Index Generum Mammalium. *N. Am. Fauna* **23**:
various pp.

884 PANOUSE, J.B.(1957) Les mammifères du Maroc. *Trav. Inst. scient. cherif.*
(Zool.) No. 5: 81–85; pl. 5

PARKER, G.H., *see* Osgood, W.H., Preble, E.A. & Parker, G.H.

885 PARKER, W.S.(1910–11) Fur. *Encyc. Britt.* **11**: 346–357. 11th ed.

886 PAROVSHCHIKOV, V.J.(1960) [On the biology . . . of the otter] *Zool. Zh.* **39**:
1111

PARSHLEY, H.M.[translator], *see* Boulière, F.

887 PATCH, C.A.(1922) A biological reconnaisance on Graham Island of the
Queen Charlotte group. *Can. Fld Nat.* **36**: 103

PATTON, C.P., *see* Handley, C.O.Jr. & Patton, C.P.

888 PAVLOV, M.P.& KIRIS, I.B.(1960) [Feeding habits of the otter] *Zool. Zh.* **39**:
600–607

889 PEARSON, O.P.(1952) Notes on a pregnant sea otter. *J. Mammal.* **33**: 387

890 PEARSON, O.P. & ENDERS, R.K.(1944) Duration of pregnancy in certain
Mustelids. *J. exp. Zool.* **95**: 21–35

891 PEATTIE, D.C.(1961) Return of the sea otter. *Readers' Dig.* **1961** August:
105–109

892 PEDERSEN, R.J. & STOUT, J.(1963) Oregon sea otter sighting. *J. Mammal.* **44**:
415

893 PELT, W.G.(1956) Trix, het visottertje. *Artis* **1** (6): 126–129

894 PELZELN, A.v(1883) Brasilianisches Saugetiere. *Verh. zool.-bot. Ges. Wien* **33**:
53

895 PENNANT, T.(1768) *The British zoology*: 67–70. 2nd ed. London

896 PENNANT, T.(1771) *Synopsis of quadrupeds*: 238–239. Chester

897 PENNANT, T.(1781) *History of quadrupeds.* **2**: 351–357. London

898 PENNANT, T.(1784) *Arctic zoology.* **1**: 86–91. London

899 PENNEY, J.T.(1950) Distribution and bibliography of the mammals of
South Carolina. *J. Mammal.* **31**: 85

PERKINS, V.R., *see* Mennell, H.T. & Perkins, V.R.

900 PERRET, J-L. & AELLEN, V.(1956) Mammifères du Cameroun. *Revue suisse Zool.* **63**: 397–400

901 PETERLE, T.J.(1954) An observation on otter feeding. *J. Wildl. Mgmt* **18**: 141–142

902 PETERSON, R.L.(1946) Recent and pleistocene mammalian fauna of Brazos County, Texas. *J. Mammal.* **27**: 166

903 PHILLIPS, W.W.A.(1935) *Manual of the mammals of Ceylon*: 199–202. Ceylon

904 PICHOT, P-A.(1915) Animaux à fourrure; la loutre de mer. *Bull. Soc. natn. Acclim. Fr.* **66**: 13

905 PIGUET, P.(1961) Capture peu banale d'une loutre sur le rivage algérois. *Bull. Soc. Hist. Nat. Afr. N.* **51**: 137–138

906 PIKE, O.G.(1949) Scenes in the life of an otter. *Ill. Lond. News* **215** (5764): 554

907 PIKE, O.G.(1950) *Wild animals in Britain*: 87–99. London: MacMillan & Co.

908 PIKE, O.G.(1952) The hunted otter. *Beds Mag.* **3** (23): 289–293

909 PINART, A.L.(1875) *Voyages à la côte nordouest de l'Amérique.* **1**: 43–48. Paris

910 PITMAN, C.R.S.(1922) Notes on Mesopotamian mammals. *J. Bombay nat. Hist. Soc.* **28**: 476

911 PITMAN, C.R.S.(1931) *A game warden among his charges*: 140–142. London: Nisbet & Co.

912 PITMAN, C.R.S.(1942) *A game warden takes stock*: 237–238. London: Nisbet & Co.

913 PITT, F.(1925) *Waterside creatures:* 39–83. London: B.T.Batsford

914 PITT, F.(1927) *Animal mind*: various pp. London: B.T.Batsford

915 PITT, F.(1934a) *British animal life*: 28–70. London: B.T.Batsford

916 PITT, F.(1934b) To those who would keep an otter. A story – and a warning. *Field* **163** (4228): 21

917 PITT, F.(1938) *Wild animals in Britain*: 18–22. London: B.T.Batsford

918 PITT, F.(1952) The enigmatic otter. *Ctry Life* **112**: 922–923

Pliny, *see* Jones, W.H.S.

919 POCOCK, R.I.(1921) On the external characters of some species of Lutrinae (Otters). *Proc. zool. Soc. Lond.* **1921**: 535–546

920 POCOCK, R.I.(1928) Some external characters of the sea otter . . . *Proc. zool. Soc. Lond.* **1928**: 983–991

921 POCOCK, R.I.(1940) Notes on some British Indian otters . . . *J. Bombay nat. Hist. Soc.* **41**: 514–517

922 POCOCK, R.I.(1941) *The fauna of British India.* Mammalia **2**: 267–317. London: Taylor & Francis

923 POHLE, H.(1919) [1920] Die Unterfamilie der Lutrinae. *Arch. Naturgesch.* **85** Ab. H.Heft 9: 1–247

924 POLAND, H.(1892) *Fur-bearing animals in nature and commerce*: 142–151. London: Gurney & Jackson

925 POLLOCK, G.A.(1964) *An otter of our own?* Priv. Circ. 16 pp. [The New Zealand 'Otter']

926 PONTOPPIDAN, E.(1755) *The natural history of Norway* **2**: 27–28. London

927 POOLE, A.J. & SCHANTZ, V.S.(1942) Catalog of the type specimens of mammals ... *Bull. U.S. natn. Mus.* No. 178: 61, 63–66

928 POOLE, E.L.(1954) Otter – Pennsylvania's rarest furbearer. *Penn. Game News* **25** (3): 4–9

929 PORSILD, A.E.(1945) Mammals of the Mackenzie delta. *Can. Fld. Nat.* **57**: 11

930 POURNELLE, G.H.(1959) Otter nonsense. *Zoonooz* **32**: 3–5

931 PRATT, A.E.(1892) *To the snows of Tibet through China*: 24. London: Longmans, Green & Co.

932 PREBLE, E.A.(1902) A biological investigation of the Hudson Bay region. *N. Am. Fauna* **22**: 65

933 PREBLE, E.A.(1908) A biological investigation of the Athabasca-Mackenzie region. *N. Am. Fauna* **27**: 228
PREBLE, E.A., *see* Osgood, W.H., Preble, E.A. & Parker, G.H.

934 PREBLE, N.A.(1942) Notes on the mammals of Morrow County, Ohio. *J. Mammal.* **23**: 84

935 PROCTOR, C.F.(1928) Otters near Hull. *Naturalist, Lond.* **1928** (855): 105

936 PROCTOR, J.(1963) A contribution to the natural history of the spotted-necked otter ... in Tanganyika. *E. Afr. Wildl. J.* **1**: 93–102

937 QUELCH, J.J.(1901) *Animal life in British Guiana*: 48–50. Georgetown

938 RADDE, G.(1862) *Reisen im Süden von Ost-Sibirien* ... **1**. Die Säugetierfauna: 54–55. St Petersburg

939 RAFFLES, T.S.(1822) Descriptive catalogue of a zoological collection ... *Trans. Linn. Soc. Lond.* **13**: 254

940 RAFINESQUE, C.S.(1832) Description of a new otter, *Lutra concolor*, from Assam in Asia. *Atlant. J.* **1**: 62

941 RAND, A.L.(1943) Animals using tools. *Can. Fld Nat.* **57** (3–4): 94

942 RAND, A.L.(1945) Mammals of Yukon. *Bull. natn. Mus. Can.* **100**: 31

943 RAND, A.L.(1948a) ... Manitoba mammals of the Herb Lake – Flin Flon area. *Can. Fld Nat.* **62**: 143–144

944 RAND, A.L.(1948b) Mammals of the eastern Rockies and western plains of Canada. *Bull. natn. Mus. Can.* **108**: 96–97
RATCLIFFE, H.L., *see* Christian, J. & Ratcliffe, H.L.

945 RAUSCH, R.(1950) Notes on the distribution of some arctic mammals. *J. Mammal.* **31**: 466

946 RAUSCH, R.(1953) Studies on the helminth fauna of Alaska ... *Ecology* **34**: 584–604

947 RAUSCH, R. & LOCKER, B.(1950) On some helminths parasitic in the sea otter, *Enhydra lutris* (L.). *Proc. helminth. Soc. Wash.* **18**: 77–81

948 RAVEN, H.C.(1935) Wallace's Line and the distribution of Indo-Australian mammals. *Bull. Am. Mus. nat. Hist.* **68**: 258

949 RAY, J.(1693) *Synopsis Methodica Animalium Quadrupedum* ...: 189. London

950 REEKS, H.(1870) Notes on the zoology of Newfoundland. *Zoologist* (2) **5**: 2037–2038

951 REES, A.H.(1862) Contest between a pike and an otter. *Field* **19**: 460

952 REGNARD, P. & BLANCHARD, R.(1883). Étude sur la capacité respiratoire du sang des animaux plongeurs. *Bull. Soc. zool. Fr.* **8**: 136–138

953 REINHARDT, J.(1869) [letter from] *Proc. zool. Soc. Lond.* **1869**: 57–58

954 REINWALDT, E.(1960) Über einen weiteren Fall von Fraktur des Baculums beim Fischotter ... *Ark. Zool.* (2) **13**: 307–310

955 RENGGER, J.R.(1826) *Lehrbuch der Naturgeschichte.* Th. 3. Zool-Abth. 990

956 RENGGER, J.R.(1830) *Naturgeschichte der Säugetiere von Paraguay*: 128–138. Basle: Schweighausersche

957 RHOADS, S.N.(1894) New Jersey otters. *Friend* **1894**: 244–245

958 RHOADS, S.N.(1896) Contributions to the zoology of Tennessee. No. 3. Mammals. *Proc. Acad. nat. Sci. Philad.* **1896**: 197

959 RHOADS, S.N.(1897) A contribution to the mammalogy of northern New Jersey. *Proc. Acad. nat. Sci. Philad.* **1897**: 23

960 RHOADS, S.N.(1898) Contributions to a revision of the North American beavers, otters and fishers. *Trans. Am. phil. Soc.* (2) **19**: 423–439

961 RHOADS, S.N.(1903) *The mammals of Pennsylvania and New Jersey*: 157. Philadelphia

962 RICHARDSON, J. (1829) *Fauna Boreali-Americana.* **1**: 57–58. London: John Murray

963 RIDGWAY, R.(1886) *A nomenclature of colors for naturalists* ... Boston: Little, Brown & Co.

964 RIDGWAY, R.(1912) *Color standards and color nomenclature.* Washington

965 RIDLEY, H.N.(1894) List of mammals recorded from Pahang. *J. Straits Brch R. Asiat. Soc.* **25**: 58

966 RIDLEY, H.N.(1895) The mammals of the Malay Peninsula. *Nat. Sci., Skodsborg* **6**: 94

967 RITCHIE, J.(1920) *The influence of man on animal life in Scotland*: 168–169. Cambridge: Univ. Press

968 RIVIERE, B.B.(1941) Two otter cubs. *Trans. Norfolk Norwich Nat. Soc.* **15**: 160–162

969 ROBERTS, A.(1924–26) Some new S. African mammals. *Ann. Transv. Mus.* **11**: 246–247

970 ROBERTS, A.(1932) Preliminary description of fifty-seven new forms of South African mammals. *Ann. Transv. Mus.* **15**: 7

971 ROBERTS, A.(1951) *The mammals of South Africa*: 210–211, 566. Johannesburg: Trustees of the 'Mammals of South Africa' book fund
ROBINSON, H.C., *see* Annandale, N. & Robinson, H.C.

972 ROBINSON, H.C. & KLOSS, C.B.(1918) Mammals of Korinchi. *J. fed. Malay St. Mus.* **8** (2): 13–14

973 ROBINSON, H.C. & KLOSS, C.B.(1919) On mammals, chiefly from the Ophir district, west Sumatra. *J. fed. Malay St. Mus.* **7**: 306–307

974 ROBINSON, H.W.(1909a) The weight and length of otters. *Ann. Scot. nat. Hist.* **18**: 134–139

975 ROBINSON, H.W.(1909b) [Weight and length of otters] *Field* **113**: 1126

976 ROBINSON, H.W.(1917) Unusual weight of bitch otter. *Field* **130**: 429

977 ROBINSON, H.W.(1927) Large dog otter. *Scott. Nat.* **1927** (165): 95

978 ROBINSON, H.W.(1928) Size of otters. *Field* **151**: 614

979 ROBINSON, T.H.(1904) Otter bolted by ferret. *Field* **103**: 34

980 ROCHEBRUNE, A-T. DE (1883) *Faune de la Sénégambie*: 96. Paris

981 ROCHEBRUNE, A-T.de (1888) *Arbeit. Vert. Nov. Afr. Occ.* (3) 9. [Priv. circ.]

982 ROCHON-DUVIGNEAUD, A.(1943) *Yeux et Vision Vertébrés*: 668–670. Paris

983 RODD, E.H.(1877) Autumnal breeding of the otter. *Zoologist* **17** (3): 1

984 RODD, F.R.(1873) Otters and wildfowl. *Field* **41**: 532

985 ROEBUCK, W.D.(1896) Otters feeding on freshwater mussels. *Naturalist, Lond.* **21**: 90

986 ROSEVEAR, D.R.(1936) The weasels and otters of Nigeria. *Niger. Fld* **5**: 113

987 ROSEVEAR, D.R.(1939) Note on a new otter. *Niger. Fld* **8**: 47

988 ROSEVEAR, D.R.(1953) *Checklist and atlas of Nigerian mammals*: 112, and maps 175a, 176, 177. Lagos: Government Printer

989 ROSS, B.R.(1861) A popular treatise on the fur-bearing animals of the Mackenzie River district. *Can. Nat. Geol.* **6**: 35

990 ROSS, D.(1927) Large dog otter. *Scott. Nat.* **1927** (164): 44

991 ROSSIKOV, K.N.(1887) [Sketch of the Mammalia in the valley of the River Malka] *Mem. Acad. Sci. St. Petersburg* **54**: 1–97

992 ROTH, V.(1941) *Animal life in British Guiana*: 92–96. Georgetown

993 RUDNEV, F.F.(1961) [Dispersal of the otter . . . in the basin of the river Bystraya Sosna] *Zool. Zh.* **40**: 468

994 RUKOVSKY, N.N. & FOMITCHEVA, N.I.(1960) [On the relationship between the river beaver and the otter] *Byull. mosk. Obshch. Ispȳt. Prir.* (Biol.) **65** (5): 102–105

995 RUPPMANN, E.(1931) Von der Nerzranz. *Dte Pelztierzüchter* **7**: 180

996 RUSCONI, C.(1932) La presencia del género 'Lontra' en la fauna ensenadense de Buenos Aires. *An. Soc. cient. argent.* **114** (3): 149–151

997 RUSSELL, C.P.(1928) New mammal for Yosemite. *Yosemite Nat. Notes* **7**: 78

998 RUSSELL, H.(1910) Notes on the mammals of Islay. *Zoologist* (4) **14**: 114

999 RUST, H.J.(1946) Mammals of northern Idaho. *J. Mammal.* **27**:315

1000 RUTLEDGE, A.(1920) The otter: playboy of nature. *Ctry Life* **38** (6): 106, 110, 112, 114

1001 RYDER, R.A.(1955) Fish predation by the otter in Michigan. *J. Wildl. Mgmt* **19**: 497–498

1002 SABINE, J.(1823) *Zoological appendix to Capt. John Franklin's narrative of a Journey to the shores of the Polar Sea . . .*: 653–654. London

1003 ST. QUINTIN, W.H. & WELCH, F.D.(1923) Otters eating birds. *Naturalist, Lond.* **48**: 296

1004 SALTER, G.F.(1897) A large otter. *Field* **89**: 194

1005 SALVIN, F.H.(1866) A domesticated otter. *Land Wat.* **1**: 199

1006 SANBORN, C.C.(1951) Mammals from Marcapata, southeastern Peru. *Publcoes Mus. Hist. nat., Lima* No. 6(A): 25

1007 SANDBERG, A.(1908) The fauna of the Barotse valley. *Proc. Trans. Rhod. scient. Ass.* **7** (2): 33

1008 SANDEN, W.v (1956) *Ingo.* 109 pp. [trans. Vesey, D.I.] London: Museum Pr.

1009 SANDEN-GUJA, W.v. (1956) Der geheimnisvolle Fischotter. *Beitr. Naturk. niedersachs.* **1956** Suppl: 85–88

1010 SANDERSON, G.C.(1954) Recent records of the otter in Iowa. *Iowa Conserv.* **13** (7): 52, 55

1011 SANDERSON, I.T.(1949) A brief review of the mammals of Suriname. *Proc. zool. Soc. Lond.* **119**: 773–774

1012 SANTOS, E.(1945) *Entre o Gambá e o Macaco*: 184–188. Rio de Janeiro: F. Brigúiet & Cie.

1013 SÁNYÁL, R.B.(1892) *A handbook of the management of animals in captivity in Lower Bengal*: 90–93. Calcutta: Zoological Gardens

1014 SARTON, G.(1944) Fishing with otters. *Isis* **35**: 178

1015 SAUNDERS, G.B. *et al* (1950) A fish and wildlife survey of Guatemala. *Spec. scient. Rep. U.S. Fish Wildl. Serv.* No. 5: 1–162

1016 SAWAYA, P.(1934) Annotoções craneologicas [*L. paranensis*]. *Ann. Fac. Med. S. Paulo* **10**: 197–219

1017 SAWYER, F.E.(1950) The otter's prey. *Fish. Gaz., Lond.* **132** (3830): 696

1018 SAXBY, H.L.(1864) The otter in salt water. *Zoologist* (1) **22**: 8872

1019 SCAMMON, C.M.(1870) The sea otters. *Am. Nat.* **4** (2): 65–74

1020 SCAMMON, C.M.(1874) *The marine mammals of the north-western coast of North America*: 168–175. San Francisco

1021 SCHACHT, H.(1892) Die Raubsäugethiere des Teutoburger Walder: VIII. Der Fischotter. *Zool. Gart., Frankf.* **33**: 41–48

1022 SCHALLER, G.B.(1965) *The year of the gorilla*: 244. London: Collins
SCHALLER, G.B., *see* Hall, K.R.L. & Schaller, G.B.
SCHANTZ, V.S., *see* Poole, A.J. & Schantz, V.S.

1023 SCHARFF, R.F.(1909) On the occurrence of a speckled otter in Ireland. *Ir. Nat.* **18**: 141

1024 SCHARFF, R.F.(1915) The speckled otter. *Ir. Nat.* **24**: 76

1025 SCHEFFER, V.B.(1939) The os clitoris of the Pacific Otter. *Murrelet* **20**: 20–21

1026 SCHEFFER, V.B.(1940) Sea otter on the Washington coast. *Pacif. NW Q.* **31**: 370–388

1027 SCHEFFER, V.B.(1950) Reflections on the skull of a sea otter. *Nature Mag.* **43** (3): 151–152

1028 SCHEFFER, V.B.(1951) Measurements of sea otters from western Alaska. *J. Mammal.* **32**: 10–14

1929 SCHEFFER, V.B.(1953) Otters diving to a depth of sixty feet. *J. Mammal.* **34**: 255

1030 SCHEFFER, V.B.(1958) Long life of a river otter. *J. Mammal.* **39**: 591

1031 SCHEFFER, V.B. & WILKE, F.(1950) Validity of the subspecies *Enhydra lutris nereis*, the southern sea otter. *J. Wash. Acad. Sci.* **40**: 269–272
SCHEFFER, V.B., *see* Kenyon, K.W. & Scheffer, V.B.

1032 SCHELLING, C.(1928) Otter taking a heron. *Field* **152**: 368

1033 SCHILLER, E.L.(1934) Notes on the intermediate stages of some helminth parasites of the sea otter. *Biol. Bull. mar. biol. Lab., Wood's Hole* **106**: 107–121

1034 SCHINZ, H.R.(1821) *Das Tierreich . . . von dem Herrn. Ritter von Cuvier*: **1**: 211–214, 879. Stuttgart

1035 SCHINZ, H.R.(1844) *Synopsis Mammalium*. **1**: 348–358. Solothurn

1036 SCHMIDT, M.(1880) On the duration of life of the animals in the zoological gardens at Frankfort-on-the-Main. *Proc. zool. Soc. Lond.* **1830**: 304

1037 SCHNEIDER, C.A.(1936) Ficha craneometrica del Güillin (*Lutra felina*). *Comun. Mus. Concepción* **1** (8): 142–144

1038 SCHOMBURGK, R.(1840) Information respecting botanical and zoological travellers. *Ann. nat. Hist.* **5**: 282–288

1039 SCHOUTEDEN, H.(1941–2) Les lutrides du Congo Belge. *Revue zool. Bot. afr.* **35**: 412–416

1040 SCHOUTEDEN, H.(1944–6) De zoogdieren van Belgisch Congo en van Ruanda-Urundi. *Annls Mus. r. Congo belge Ser. 4to. C. Zool.* (2) **3**: 236–240

1041 SCHOUTEDEN, H.(1948) Fauné du Congo Belge et du Ruanda Urundi. *Annls Mus. Congo Belge Ser. 8vo.* **1**: Mammifères: 161–162

1042 SCHREBER, J.C.D.v (1776) *Die Säugetiere.* plates CXXVIA, CXXVIB, CXVIII, CXVIII$_x$. Erlangen

1043 SCHREBER, J.C.D.v (1778) *Die Säugetiere* **3**: 455–470. Erlangen

1044 SCHREITMUELLER, W.(1953) Einiges neber zahme Fischottern. *Z. Säugetierk.* **17** (3): 172–173

1045 SCHRENK, L.v (1859) *Reisen und Forschungen im Amur-Lande.* **1**: 43. St Petersburg

1046 SCHRODER, H.H.(1947) Otter adventures. *Nat. Mag.* **40** (3): 134–136

1047 SCHULTZ, V.(1954) Statuts of the beaver and otter in Tennessee. *J. Tennessee Acad. Sci.* **29**: 73–81

1048 SCHUZ, E.(1962) Fischotter einst am oberen Schlossgartensee in Stuttgart. *Jh. Ver. vaterl. Naturk. Wurtt.* **116**: 299–300

1049 SCHWARZ, E.(1912) Die indischen viverriden. *Arch. Naturgesch.* **78A**: 12

1050 SCLATER, P.L.(1897) Note on the Irish otter. *Proc. zool. Soc. Lond.* **1897**: 311

1051 SCLATER, W.L.(1891) *Catalogue of mammalia in the Indian Museum, Calcutta.* **2**: 291–298. Calcutta: Trustees of the Indian Museum

1052 SCLATER, W.L.(1900) *The mammals of South Africa.* **1**: 106–109. London

1053 SCOFIELD, W.L.(1941) The sea otters of California did not reappear. *Calif. Fish Game* **27**: 35–38

1054 SCOTT, H.H.(1927) Double malignant tumour of thyroid and parathyroid. *Proc. zool. Soc. Lond.* **1927**: 859–864

1055 SCOTT, T.G.(1937) Mammals of Iowa. *Iowa St. J. Sci.* **12**: 61

1056 SCOTT, W.E.(1939) Swimming power of the Canadian otter. *J. Mammal.* **20**: 371

1057 SCULLY, J.(1881) On the mammals of Gilgit. *Proc. zool. Soc. Lond.* **1881**: 203

1058 SETH-SMITH, D.(1935). Exhibition of a mounted specimen of an albino otter. *Proc. zool. Soc. Lond.* **1935**: 947

1059 SETON, E.T.(1910) *Life histories of northern animals.* **2**: 817–839. London: Constable & Co.

1060 SETON, E.T.(1926) *Lives of game animals.* **2**: 642–709. New York: Doubleday, Doran & Co.

1061 SEVERINGHAUS, C.W.& TANCK, J.E.(1948) Speed and gait of an otter. *J. Mammal.* **29**: 71

1062 SHAKESPEARE, W.(? 1597–8) *Henry IV. Part 1.* Act 3, Scene 3, Line 143. Globe ed. London

SHAW, W.T., *see* Taylor, W.P. & Shaw, W.T.

1063 SHELDON, C.(1936) The mammals of Lake Kedgemakooge and vicinity, Nova Scotia. *J. Mammal.* **17**: 211

1064 SHELDON, W.G. & TOLL, W.G.(1964) Feeding habits of the river otter in a reservoir in central Massachusetts. *J. Mammal.* **45**: 449–455

1065 SHEPHEARD, S. & TOWNSHEND, E.O.(1937) The otters of Norfolk. *Trans. Norfolk Norwich Nat. Soc.* **14**: 138–142

1066 SHEPPARD, R.W.(1951) An otter at Niagara Falls. *Can. Fld Nat.* **65**: 82–83

1067 SHERMAN, F.(1937) Some mammals of western South Carolina. *J. Mammal.* **18**: 512

1068 SHERMAN, H.B.(1936) [1937] A list of the recent wild land mammals of Florida. *Proc. Fla Acad. Sci.* **1**: 111

1069 SHIMIZU, E.(1959) [On the skull of the Japanese otter] *J. mammal. Soc. Japan* **1**: 137–138

1070 SHOMON, J.J.(1949) Lute, the otter. *Va Wildl.* **10** (12): 16–17, 23

1071 SHORTRIDGE, G.C.(1934) *The mammals of South West Africa.* **1**: 187–192. London: Heinemann

1072 SIMON, E.S.(1943) Life span of some wild animals in captivity. *J. Bombay nat. Hist. Soc.* **44**: 117–118

1073 SIMPSON, G.G.(1945) The principles of classification . . . *Bull. Am. Mus. nat. Hist.* **85**: 1–350

1074 SKELDON, P.C.(1961) Brazilian giant otters (*Pteronura brasiliensis*) at Toledo zoo [Ohio]. *Int. Zoo Ybk* **3**: 30–31, pls. IX and X

1075 SMITH, G.(1951) Vegetarian otter? *Field* **198**: 224

1076 SMITH, L.H.(1939) Notes on an otter fishing. *J. Mammal.* **20**: 370–371

1077 SMUTS, J.(1832) *Enumerationem Mammalium Capensium*: 13. Leyden

1078 SNOW, H.J.(1910) *In forbidden seas*: 278–280, 481

1079 SNYDER, L.L.(1928) The mammals of the Lake Abitibi region. *Univ. Toronto Stud.* (Biol. ser.) **32**: 9

1080 SODY, H.J.V.(1933) Ten new mammals from the Dutch East Indies. *Ann. Mag. nat. Hist.* (10) **12**: 441–442

1081 SOLLARS, K.(1945) The sea otter comes back. *Fauna* **7**: 11–13

1082 SOPER, J.D.(1923) The mammals of Wellington and Waterloo counties, Ontario. *J. Mammal.* **4**: 251

1083 SOPER, J.D.(1942) Mammals of Wood Buffalo Park, northern Alberta and District of Mackenzie. *J. Mammal.* **23**: 129

1084 SOPER, J.D.(1947) Observations on mammals and birds in the Rocky Mountains of Alberta. *Can. Fld Nat.* **61**: 149

1085 SOPER, J.D.(1948) Mammal notes from the Grande Prairie . . . Alberta. *J. Mammal.* **29**: 56

1086 SOPER, J.D.(1961a) Field data on the mammals of southern Saskatchewan. *Can. Fld Nat.* **75**: 39

1087 SOPER, J.D.(1961b) The mammals of Manitoba. *Can. Fld Nat.* **75**: 208–209

1088 SOUTHERN, H.N.[Editor] (1964) *The handbook of British mammals*: 54, 56, 349, 381–385. Oxford: Blackwell

1089 SOUTHWELL, T.(1871) Mammalia and reptilia of Norfolk. *Zoologist* (2) **6**: 2754

1090 SOUTHWELL, T.(1872-3) The otter. *Trans. Norfolk Norwich Nat. Soc.* **1872-73**: 79–90

1091 SOUTHWELL, T.(1873) Large otter. *Zoologist* (2) **8**: 3407

1092 SOUTHWELL, T. (1877) On the breeding of the otter. *Zoologist* (3) **1**: 172–174
1093 SOUTHWELL, T. (1879) Young otter in December. *Zoologist* (3) **3**: 122
1094 SOUTHWELL, T. (1882) Otters taken in a bow-net. *Zoologist* (3) **6**: 391
1095 SOUTHWELL, T. (1895) Large otters. *Field* **86**: 1053
1096 SOUTHWELL, T. (1903) British mammals. *Field* **102**: 1943
SOUTHWELL, T., *see* Browne, T. (1902)
1097 SOWERBY, A. DE C. [Editor] (1924) Otter near Quinsan. *China J. Sci. Arts* **2**: 161
1098 SOWERBY, A. DE C. (1932) Fishing with the otter in west China. *China J. Sci. Arts* **17**: 315
1099 STANFORD, J. K. (1954) The diet of the otter. *Field* **204**: 707
1100 STEFÁNSSON, V. (1913) *My life with the Eskimo*: 523. London: MacMillan
1101 STEJNEGER, L. (1883). Contributions to the history of the Commander Islands. *Proc. U.S. natn. Mus.* **6**: 87
1102 STEJNEGER, L. (1896–7) [1898] *Report of the Fur Seal investigation*. Part 4: 29–30
1103 STEJNEGER, L. (1936) *Georg Wilhelm Steller*: various pp. Cambridge, Mass.: Harvard Univ. Press
1104 STELLER, G. W. (1751) *De Bestiis Marinis*. **2**: 367–398, pl. xvi. Petropoli
1105 STEPHENS, F. (1906) *Californian mammals*: 233. San Diego
1106 STEPHENS, M. N. (1953) Otters. *Zoo Life* **8**: 9–11, 39
1107 STEPHENS, M. N. (1953–4) Otter research. *Oryx* **2**: 320–324
1108 STEPHENS, M. N. [1957] *The Otter Report*. 88 pp. London: UFAW
1109 STERNDALE, R. A. (1884) *Natural history of the Mammalia of India and Ceylon*: 153–156. Calcutta
1110 STEVENSON, C. H. (1904) Utilization of the skins of aquatic animals. *Rep. U.S. Commnr Fish* **1902**: 321
1111 STEVENSON-HAMILTON, J. (1950) *Wild life in South Africa*: 241. 2nd Ed., London
STIRTON, R. A., *see* Burt, W. H. & Stirton, R. A.
1112 STOLL, N. R. *et al.* [Editors] (1961) *International code of zoological nomenclature*. 176 pp. London: International Commission Zoological Nomenclature
1113 STONE, A. J. (1900) Some results of a natural history journey to northern British Columbia. *Bull. Am. Mus. nat. Hist.* **13**: 59
1114 STONE, W. & CRAM, W. E. (1903) *American animals*: 222. London: Rowland Ward
1115 STOPHLETT, J. J. (1947) Florida otters eat large terrapin. *J. Mammal.* **28**: 183
STOUT, J., *see* Pedersen, R. J. & Stout, J.
STRUGNELL, W. B., *see* Witchell, C. A. & Strugnell, W. B.
STULLKEN, D. E., *see* Kirkpatrick, C. M. & Stullken, D. E.
1116 STULLKEN, D. E. & KIRKPATRICK, C. M. (1955) Physiological investigation of captivity mortality in the sea otter . . . *Trans. N. Am. Wildl. Conf.* **20**: 476–494
1117 SUVOROV, E. K. (1912) [*The Commander Islands and their fur trade*] 34 pp. St Petersburg
1118 SWAINSON, W. (1835) *On the natural history and classification of quadrupeds*. (Lardner's Cyclop). London

1119 SWEENEY, R.C.H.(1959) *A preliminary annotated check list of the mammals of Nyasaland*: 19–20. Blantyre: Nyasaland Soc.

1120 SWENK, M.H.(1918) On a new subspecies of otter from Nebraska. *Univ. Stud. Univ. Neb.* **18**: 1–6

1121 SWINHOE, R.(1861) [Extracts from a letter relating to specimens sent from China] *Proc. zool. Soc. Lond.* **1861**: 390

1122 SWINHOE, R.(1862) On the mammals of the island of Formosa (China). *Proc. zool. Soc. Lond.* **1862**: 348

1123 SWINHOE, R.(1864) [Extract from letter of 10 August] *Proc. zool. Soc. Lond.* **1864**: 381

1124 SWINHOE, R.(1870a) On the mammals of Hainan. *Proc. zool. Soc. Lond.* **1870**: 229–230

1125 SWINHOE, R.(1870b) Catalogue of the mammals of China (south of the River Yangtsze) and of the island of Formosa. *Proc. zool. Soc. Lond.* **1870**: 624–625

1126 SWYNNERTON, G.H.(1955) *Rep. Game Dep. Tanganyika* **1954**: 24

1127 SWYNNERTON, G.H.(1957) *Rep. Game Dep. Tanganyika* **1955–56**: 24

1128 SWYNNERTON, G.H. & HAYMAN, R.W.(1950) A checklist of the land mammals of the Tanganyika Territory and the Zanzibar Protectorate. *Jl E. Africa nat. Hist. Soc.* **20**: 326–327

1129 SYKES, W.H.(1831) Catalogue of the *mammalia* of the Dukhun (Deccan) . . . *Proc. zool. Soc. Lond.* **1831**: 100

TANCK, J.E., *see* Severinghaus, C.W. & Tanck, J.E.

1130 TATE, G.H.H.(1931) Random observations on habits of South American mammals. *J. Mammal.* **12**: 253

1131 TATE, G.H.H.(1939) The mammals of the Guiana region. *Bull. Am. Mus. nat. Hist.* **76**: 203–204

TATE, G.H.H., *see* Carter, T.D., Hill, J.E. & Tate, G.H.H.

1132 TAYLOR, W.P.(1914) The problem of aquatic adaptation in the Carnivora as illustrated in the osteology of evolution of the sea otter. *Univ. Calif. Publs Geol.* **7** (25): 465–495

1133 TAYLOR, W.P.(1916) The conservation of the native fauna. *Scient. Mon., N.Y.* **1916**: 402

1134 TAYLOR, W.P. & SHAW, W.T.(1929) Provisional list of land mammals of . . . Washington. *Occ. Pap. Charles R. Connor Mus.* **2**: 12

1135 TAYLOR-PAGE, F.J.[Editor] (1963) Otter (*Lutra lutra*). *Norfolk Bird Mammal Rep.* **20**: 185

1136 TCHENG, K.T. & SHIH, P.C.(1958) [Structure of kidney of *L. l. chinensis*] *Acta zool. sin.* **10**: 125–129

1137 TEMMINCK, C.J.(1847) *Fauna Japonica*: 35–36. Leyden

1138 TEPLOV, V.P.(1953) [Otter in the region of the Pecheroilychskiy Nature Reserve] *Bull. Mosc. Soc. Nat. (Biol. Sect.) N.S.* **58** (6): 7–16

1139 TETLEY, H.(1945) Colour variation in Scottish seagoing otters. *Proc. zool. Soc. Lond.* **115**: 188–193

1140 THOMAS, E.M.(1952) Furbearing mammals of Wyoming. Part 9. Otter. *Wyo. Wildl.* **16** (11): 30–34

1141 THOMAS, O.(1880) On mammals from Ecuador. *Proc. zool. Soc. Lond.* **1880**: 396

1142 THOMAS, O.(1881) Account of the zoological collections made during the survey of H.M.S. *Alert* . . . 1. Mammalia. *Proc. zool. Soc. Lond.* **1881**: 3

1143 THOMAS, O.(1889) Preliminary notes on the characters and synonymy of the different species of otter. *Proc. zool. Soc. Lond.* **1889**: 190–200

1144 THOMAS, O.(1902) On a collection of mammals from Abyssinia. *Proc. zool. Soc. Lond.* **1902** 2: 309–310

1145 THOMAS, O.(1904) On mammals from the island of Fernando Po. *Proc. zool. Soc. Lond.* **1904** 2: 185

1146 THOMAS, O.(1905) New African mammals . . . *Ann. Mag. nat. Hist.* (7) **15**: 77–83

1147 THOMAS, O.(1908) On certain African and South American otters. *Ann. Mag. nat. Hist.* (8) **1**: 387–395

1148 THOMAS, O.(1911) Four new African carnivores. *Ann. Mag. nat. Hist.* (8) **8**: 726

1149 THOMAS, O.(1914) New *Nasua*, *Lutra* and *Proechimys* from South America. *Ann. Mag. nat. Hist.* (8) **14**: 59

1150 THOMAS, O.(1920) Mammalia collected in Peru by Heller. *Proc. U.S. natn. Mus.* **58**: 225

1151 THOMAS, O.(1922) On mammals from the Yunnan highlands. *Ann. Mag. nat. Hist.* (9) **10**: 396

1152 THOMAS, O.(1928) The Delacour exploration of French Indo-China. Mammals. *Proc. zool. Soc. Lond.* **1928**: 147

1153 THOMPSON, D'A.W.(1910) *Aristotle's Historia Animalium*: 594b30–595a4. Oxford: Univ. Press

1154 THOMPSON, W.(1856) *The natural history of Ireland*. **4**: 5–6. London: H.G. Bohn

1155 THORBURN, A.(1920) *British mammals*: **1**: 65–67, and pl. 17. London: Longmans

TOLL, W.G., *see* Sheldon, W.G. & Toll, W.G.

1156 TOMES, R.F.(1861) Report of a collection of mammals made . . . at Dueñas, Guatemala . . . *Proc. zool. Soc. Lond.* **1861**: 279–280

1157 TOPSEL, E.(1658) *The history of four-footed beasts and serpents*: 444–446. London

1158 TOWNSEND, C.H.(1915) Hope for the sea otter. *Bull. N.Y. zool. Soc.* **18**: 1286

1159 TOWNSHEND, E.O.(1935-8) Travellers of the dusk. *Trans. Norfolk Norwich Nat. Soc.* **14**: 217–219

TOWNSHEND, E.O., *see* Shepheard, S. & Townshend, E.O.

1160 TRAUTMAN, M.B.(1936) Analysis of . . . otter scats . . . from Michigan. *Inst. Fisheries Res. Rep.* no. 367

1161 TREGARTHEN, J.C.(1906) The survival of the otter. *Mon. Rev., Lond.* **69**: 81–93

1162 TREGARTHEN, J.C.(1909) *The life story of an otter*. 186 pp. London: John Murray

1163 TREGARTHEN, J.C.(1929) The otter and its occurrence in Cornwall. *Jl R. Instn Cornwall* **23** (1): 38–47

1164 TROUESSART, E-L.(1910) *Faune des Mammifères d'Europe*: 86. Berlin: R. Friedlander

1165 TRUE, F.W.(1884) [1885] A provisional list of the mammals of North and Central America ... *Proc. U.S. natn. Mus.* 7: 609

1166 TSCHUDI, J.J. v (1844–6) *Untersuchungen über die Fauna Peruana*: 118–120. St Gallen

1167 TUCHOFF, W.N.(1906) [*L. lutra* in Kamchatka] *Zap. russk. Balneol. Gbshch. Pyatigorski* 37 (2): 1

1168 TURK, F.A.(1959) The otter in Cornwall ... *Lizard* (N.S.) 3: 17–20

1169 TURTON, W.(1806) *A general system of nature.* 1: 57. London

1170 UTZON, H.(1934) Mein freund – der Fischotter. *Dte Pelztierzüchter* 9 (22): 431–435

1171 VELICH, R.(1961) Notes on mammals from Nebraska and southwestern Iowa. *J. Mammal.* 42: 93–94

1172 VERNER, W.(1864) An otter bolted by a ferret. *Field* 13: 211
VESEY, D.I.[translator], *see* Sanden, W. v. & Vesey, D.I.

1173 VESEY-FITZGERALD, B.(1946) *British game*: 207. London: Collins

1174 VESEY-FITZGERALD, B.(1964) Odd about the otter. *Sphere* 1964: 25 January. 133

1175 VIEIRA, C.O.DA C.(1952) Notas sobre os mamíferos obtidos pela expedicão do instituto Butantã ao Rio das Mortes e Serra do Roncador. *Papeis Dept. Zool. S. Paulo* 10: 117

1176 VIEIRA, C.O.DA C.(1955) Lista remissiva dos mamíferos do Brasil. *Archos Zool. Est. S. Paulo* 8: 451

1177 VINCENZI, F.(1961) The sea otter (*Enhydra lutris*) at Woodland Park Zoo. *Int. Zoo Yb.* 3: 27–29, pls. ix, x

1178 WAGNER, J.A.(1841) *Die Säugetiere von Schreber.* Supp. II: 249–276. Erlangen

1179 WAGNER, J.A.(1842) Diagnosen neuer arten brasilianischer säugetiere. *Arch. Naturgesch.* 8: 358

1180 WALKER, E.P.(1964) *Mammals of the world.* 1: 562–563; 2: 1215–1223; **Bibliog**: 391–394. Baltimore: Johns Hopkins Press

1181 WALTON, I.(1653) *The compleat angler.* London: J.F. & C.Rivington

1182 WARD, A.E.(1929) The mammals and birds of Kashmir ... *J. Bombay nat. Hist. Soc.* 33: 68–70

1183 WARD, F.(1919) *Animal life under water*: 44–83. London: Cassell

1184 WARDEN, D.B.(1819) *A statistical, political and historical account of the United States of North America*: 206–207. Edinburgh

1185 WARREN, E.R.(1942) *The mammals of Colorado*: 72. Univ. Okla. Press

1186 WATERHOUSE, G.R.(1838) On some new species of mammalia from Fernando Po. *Proc. zool. Soc. Lond.* 1838: 60

1187 WATERHOUSE, G.R.(1838) [1839] *The zoology of the voyage of HMS Beagle*: pt. 2. Mammalia: 21–22. London

1188 WATERS, A.H.(1907) The mammals of south Cambridgeshire. *Zoologist* (4) 11: 246

1189 WATERTON, C.(1879) *Wanderings in South America*: 442–444. London

1190 WATSON, A.[Editor] (1956). A white otter. *Scott. Nat.* 68: 60

1191 WATSON, J.S.(1960) The New Zealand 'otter'. *Rec. Canterbury Mus.* 7: 175–183

1192 WATT, H.B.(1901) *Fauna and flora of the Clyde Area*: Mammalia. Br. Ass. Handbk on Nat. Hist. of Glasgow, etc.: 155–158

1193 WEBB, G.C.(1957) *A guide to West African mammals*: 22. Ibadan: Univ. Press

1194 WEBER, M.(1890–1) Mammalia from the Malay Archipelago. *Zool. Ergeb. Niederland. Ost-Ind.* **1**: 110

1195 WEBER, M.(1902) *Der indo-australische Archipel und die Geschichte seiner Tierwelt.* Jena

1196 WEBER, M.(1904) *Die Säugetiere.* **2**: 335. Jena: Gustav Fischer
WELCH, F.D., *see* St Quintin, W.H. & Welch, F.D.

1197 WELDON, E.F.(1881) Food of the otter. *Field* **57**: 217

1198 WHEELER, T.(1887) Large otter. *Field* **50**: 545

1199 WHITLOCK, R.(1953) *Wild life on the farm*: 34–35. London

1200 WHITNEY, G.(1939) California river otter in Yosemite national park. *Yosemite Nat. Notes.* **18** (2): 9–10

1201 WIED, M.PRINCE (1826) *Beiträge zur Naturgeschichte von Brasilien*: 319–329. Weimar

1202 WIEGMANN, A.F.A.(1838) Bestrachtungen über das Gebiss der Raubtiere. *Arch. Naturgesch.* **4**: 284–286

1203 WILHELM, J.H.(1933) *J. S.W. Africa Scient. Soc.* **6**: 51–74

1204 WILKE, F.(1957) Food of sea otters and harbor seals at Amchitka Island. *J. Wildl. Mgmt* **21**: 241–242
WILKE, F., *see* Scheffer, V.B. & Wilke, F.

1205 WILLIAMS, C.S.(1938) Notes on food of the sea otter. *J. Mammal.* **19**: 105–107

1206 WILLIAMSON, H.(1928) *Tarka the otter.* (1940 reprint: 192 pp.) Harmondsworth: Penguin Books

1207 WILLINK, T.(1905) Mammalia vorkommende in Nederlandsch Indië. *Natuurk. Tijdschr. Ned. Indië* **65**: 222–223, 324

1208 WILMAR, H.(1953) Nature's footprints in the snow. *Nat. Hist., N.Y.* **62**: 18–23

1209 WILSON, K.A.(1954) The role of mink and otter as muskrat predators in northeastern North Carolina. *J. Wildl. Mgmt* **18**: 199–207

1210 WILSON, K.A.(1959) The otter in North Carolina. *Proc. Ann. Conf. S.E. Ass. Game Fish Commn* **13**: 267–277 [Mimeo]

1211 WINDLE, B.C.A.(1897) On the myology of the terrestrial Carnivora. Pt. 1. *Proc. zool. Soc. Lond.* **1897**: 374, 384

1212 WINDLE, B.C.A.(1898) On the myology of the terrestrial Carnivora. Pt. 2. *Proc. zool. Soc. Lond.* **1898**: 174

1213 WINGE, H.(1895) [1896] Jordfunde og nulevende rovdyr fra Lagoa Santa, Miñas Geraes, Brasilien. *E. Mus. Lund.* 2B: 42

1214 WISBESKI, D.(1965) *An otter in the house.* 238 pp. London: Methuen

1215 WITCHELL, C.A. & STRUGNELL, W.B.(1892) *The fauna and flora of Gloucestershire*: 15–19. Stroud

1216 WOLLEY, E.(1853) Occurrence of the otter in various localities. *Zoologist* (2) **11**: 3843

1217 WOOD, I.(1929) Tame otters. *Field* **153**: 73

1218 WOODS, E.G.(1928) Otters killing swans. *Field* **151**: 806

WOODWARD, J.D.S., *see* Woodward, R.B. & Woodward, J.D.S.

1219 WOODWARD, R.B. & WOODWARD, J.D.S. (1875) Notes on the natural history of South Africa. *Zoologist* (2) **10**: 4389

1220 WORTHING, A.O.(1870) Strange capture of an otter in the Trent. *Field* **36**: 458

1221 WOSCHINSKI, E.(1956) Ist die Kreuzotter ein Feind der Bodenbrüter? *Beitr. Naturk. Niedersachs.* **9**: 25–26

1222 WRIGHT, G.M.(1934) The primitive persists in birdlife of Yellowstone Park. *Condor* **36**: 151

1223 WRIGHT, W.(1904) The wanton destruction of otters. *Field* **103**: 321–322

1224 WROUGHTON, R.C.(1916) Bombay Natural History Society's mammal survey. Report No. 24, Sind. *J. Bombay nat. Hist. Soc.* **24**: 755

1225 WROUGHTON, R.C.(1919) Summary of the results of the Indian mammal survey ... Pt. 3. *J. Bombay nat. Hist. Soc.* **26**: 348–349

1226 WURMB, F. v (1784) *Verh. batav. Genoot. Kunst. Wet.* **2**: 456

1227 WYMAN, J.(1847) [On *Lutra americana*] *Proc. Boston Soc. nat. Hist.* **2**: 249–250

1228 WYNNE-EDWARDS, V.C.(1962) *Animal dispersion in relation to social behaviour*: 104. Edinburgh: Oliver & Boyd

YARROW, H.C., *see* Coues, E. & Yarrow, H.C.

1229 YATES, W.C.(1880) In the haunts of the otter. *Field* **55**: 748

1230 YEAGER, L.E.(1938) Otters of the delta hardwood region of Mississippi. *J. Mammal.* **19**: 195–201

YEPES, J., *see* Cabrera, A. & Yepes, J.

1231 YOUNG, R.T.(1900) Notes on the mammals of Prince Edward Island. *Am. Nat.* **34**: 486

1232 YOUNG, S.P.(1945) Bullets beyond the breakers. *Am. Rifleman* **93** (6): 8–9, 27

1233 ZELLER, F.(1960) Notes on the giant otter *Pteronura brasiliensis* at Cologne zoo. *Int. Zoo Yb.* **2**: 81

1234 ZELLER, F.(1961) 'Schnurzel', ein Reisenotter. *Kosmos* **57**: 457–461

1235 ZIMMERMANN, E.A.G.(1777) *Specimen Zoologiae Geographicae, Quadrupedum*: 303–304, 485. Leyden

1236 ZIMMERMANN, E.A.G.(1780) *Geographische Geschichte des Menschen und der vierfüssigen Tiere.* **2**: 316. Leipzig.

1237 ZUCKERMAN, S.(1953) The breeding seasons of mammals in captivity. *Proc. zool. Soc. Lond.* **122**: 848

Addenda:

74a ANONYMOUS (1874) Curious breeding place of an otter. *Field* **43**: 444

88a ANONYMOUS (1890) Durata della gestazione nei mammiferi. *Monit. zool. ital.* **1**: 580

92a ANONYMOUS (1898aa) White otters. *Field* **91**: 141–142

98a ANONYMOUS (1904aa) Otters bolted by ferrets and attacking dogs. *Field* **103**: 50

175a BENSON, R.B.(1888) Otters away from water. *Field* **72**: 656

277a CHRISTIAN, G.(1963) *While some trees stand:* 32–43. London: Newnes

378a EMERSON, P.H.(1895) *Birds, beasts and fishes of the Norfolk Broadland:* 339–343. London. David Nutt

413a FITTER, R.S.R.(1964c) Otters, the angler's friends. *Wld Wildl. News* **26**: 3

588a HOWELL, A.B.(1930) *Aquatic mammals:* 13, 30, 31, 192, 194–195, 246, 285–287, 299–300; figs. 42, b, c, e, f; 43, d–g; 46. Springfield: Charles C. Thomas

707a LIERS, E.E.(1966) Notes on breeding the Canadian otter ... *Int. Zoo Yb.* **6**: 171–172

761a MANSFIELD, K.(1949) An Asiatic Tarka. *Zoo Life* **4**: 85–86

1054a SCOTT, R.F.(1951) Wildlife in the economy of Alaska natives. *Trans. N. Am. Wildl. Conf.* **16**: 511

1183a WARD, S.(1775) *A modern system of natural history.* **3**: 100–106. London

Index

Figures in bold print indicate the main treatment of the entry

26—o.